FAMILIES AND INTIMATE RELATIONSHIPS

Families
and
Intimate
Relationships

GLORIA BIRD   KEITH MELVILLE

Virginia Polytechnic Institute and State University   *Public Agenda Foundation and The Fielding Institute*

McGraw-Hill, Inc.

New York   St. Louis   San Francisco   Auckland   Bogotá   Caracas
Lisbon   London   Madrid   Mexico City   Milan   Montreal   New Delhi
San Juan   Singapore   Sydney   Tokyo   Toronto

FAMILIES AND INTIMATE RELATIONSHIPS

This book is printed on acid-free paper.

2 3 4 5 6 7 8 9 0   DOW   DOW   9 0 9 8 7 6 5 4

ISBN 0-07-041701-6

This book was set in Palatino by Ruttle, Shaw & Wetherill, Inc.
The editors were Jill Gordon and Curt Berkowitz;
the designer was Joan Greenfield;
the production supervisor was Leroy A. Young.
The photo editor was Elyse Rieder.
R. R. Donnelley & Sons Company was printer and binder.

Library of Congress Cataloging-in-Publication Data

Bird, Gloria W.
    Families and intimate relationships / Gloria Bird, Keith
Melville.
        p.   cm.
    Based on Marriage and family today, by Keith Melville.
    Includes bibliographical references and index.
    ISBN 0-07-041701-6
    1. Family—United States.   2. Man-woman relation-
ships—United States.   3. Marriage—United States.
4. Mate selection—United States.   I. Melville, Keith.
II. Melville, Keith.   Marriage and family today.   III. Title.
HQ536.B517   1994
306.8'0973—dc20   93-43169

About the Authors

GLORIA BIRD teaches family studies courses and pursues her research interests at Virginia Polytechnic Institute and State University (Virginia Tech). She took bachelor's and master's degrees from Kansas State University and a Ph.D. from Oklahoma State University. Gloria has authored numerous articles in professional journals such as *Family Relations, Journal of Marriage and the Family, Journal of Social and Personal Relationships,* and *Journal of Early Adolescence.* Her teaching and research interests include dual-career families, marital conflict and negotiation, marital communication, stress and coping, and dating violence. She recently completed a study of 300 city managers and their marital partners and continues to gather follow-up information from participants in a longitudinal study of dual-career couples she initiated in 1986.

KEITH MELVILLE completed the Ph.D. in sociology at Columbia University. Formerly a professor at the City University of New York, he has been Vice President of the Public Agenda Foundation in New York City since 1982. He is a member of the graduate faculty at the Fielding Institute, which is based in Santa Barbara, California. He is the author of four books and numerous articles. As senior writer for the National Issues Forums, he has written more than 30 magazine-length publications on issues ranging from health care and poverty to immigration, the public debt, and economic policy.

Gloria Dedicates This Book to Her Family:
Jerry, Martyn, Margie and Vincent, Bert and Dorothy, Diana and Larry,
Sherryl and Cindy, and Nancy Wolfe Ritchie Farris.

Contents

Preface

Because of the substantial alterations and additions to what started out as the fifth edition of *Marriage and Family Today,* including the introduction of coauthor Gloria Bird, we felt compelled to offer this book, appropriately, as something new. In keeping with its fresh perspective, a different title seemed in order. We chose *Families and Intimate Relationships* because it very clearly represents the underlying themes of the expanded and updated text.

Major efforts have been made to undergird this edition with research-based information. From that strong foundation, we feel confident that students will be motivated to think carefully and systematically about contemporary issues that affect families, as well as make practical applications to their own intimate relationships.

We have continued the book's emphasis on social analysis and remain staunch advocates for encouraging students to think of families and other close relationships as surrounded and influenced by the broader social context. Other major themes that appear regularly throughout the text are the effects of changing demographic trends on family form and function, the relevance of cultural and structural diversity to understanding individual and family behavior, the impact of gender on interaction in romantic and marital relationships, and the significance of understanding the *process* as well as the outcomes of family behavior.

CHANGES SINCE THE FOURTH EDITION OF *MARRIAGE AND FAMILY TODAY*

We approached this writing task with three purposes in mind—to make some organizational changes, to include new scholarship, and to expand coverage of emerging issues and perspectives on family life and other intimate relationships. To that effect, we merged the two chapters on sexuality into one, "Sexuality: Patterns and Attitudes" (Chapter 6), and moved the chapter on gender roles, "Gender Roles and Changing Relationships" (Chapter 2), to follow the discussion of "American Marriages and Families: A Changing Society" (Chapter 1). We also combined information from the chapters on the marital agreement and the marital life cycle into one, "Marriage over the Life Course" (Chapter 7). Additionally, we incorporated details from two former chapters on mate selection and dating into one, "Dating, Courtship, and Marital Choice" (Chapter 4).

New Chapters, Extended Coverage

Four chapters were added to the text: "Love and Intimacy" (Chapter 3), "Power and Violence" (Chapter 12), "Stress: Individual and Family Perspectives" (Chapter 13), and "Single-Parent Families" (Chapter 15). Although a comprehensive listing of changes in the organization, structure, and content of each chapter would be too extensive to fully explore, some of the new or extended topics include:

- historical development of families
- family theory
- research methods
- gender in families
- feminization of love
- contemporary love styles
- relationship development
- theories of marital choice
- dating violence
- singlehood
- cohabiting lifestyles

- gay and lesbian relationships
- AIDS and sexuality
- sexual harassment
- adult development
- unmarrieds with children
- family and work roles
- family policy
- kinship ties
- friendship patterns
- communication processes
- gendered patterns of communication
- power bases and strategies
- violence in families
- stress theory
- strategies and styles of coping
- marital support
- causes and consequences of divorce
- divorce mediation
- children's adjustment to divorce and remarriage
- single parenting after divorce
- stepparenting
- characteristics of second marriages

Throughout the text we have continued to incorporate information on family diversity with particular attention to ethnicity, class, and structural uniqueness.

New Features

Several new features appear in this edition. Summary Points, Key Terms, and Review Questions are now included at the end of each chapter. Five types of boxes inform the text material:

- *Point of View* boxes focus either on the personal viewpoints of family scientists, social analysts, or people in the midst of dealing with a particular family concern or relational issue.
- *Diversity* boxes highlight racial, ethnic, or cultural uniqueness.
- *Dilemmas and Decisions* boxes contain material designed to make students aware of common difficulties in their personal lives, families, or intimate relationships. Sometimes specific problem-solving techniques or intervention strategies are suggested.

- *Changing Lifestyles* boxes provide a glimpse of some of the developing trends in families and intimate relationships.
- *Snapshots* boxes are brief snippets of information designed to provoke heightened awareness, thoughtful reflection, and insightful class discussion relative to a particular social, relational, or family concern.

Concluding each box are "Explorations," asking students to examine their reactions to the material presented. We have also included additional figures and tables in each chapter to provide expanded visual demonstrations of key text matter.

Updated Instructor's Manual, New Assessment Manual

The *Instructor's Manual* was prepared by Thomas B. Holman of Brigham Young University. It contains a brief overview of each chapter, supplemental material for instructors to use in lectures, suggestions for experiential learning in the classroom, suggestions for papers and other outside-of-class projects, and recent media. It also contains a test bank of approximately 25 multiple-choice questions, 15 true/false questions, and several essay questions for each chapter.

The *Assessment Manual,* also drafted by Thomas Holman, is another unique feature of this text. It contains the PREParation for Marriage (PREP-M) Questionnaire, which is a highly reliable and valid tool for assessing premaritally a couple's consensus and readiness for marriage. Besides PREP-M, the *Assessment Manual* includes one or two other assessment instruments for each text chapter. Each instrument is "real" in the sense that it is taken from published research reports and most likely was used to generate the findings reported in the book chapters. Assessment materials are useful for application of the chapter content to students' personal lives. Instruments can be completed outside the classroom, used in class to generate discussion, or used to collect data for a student paper.

Appendix

A goal of ours was to maintain the quality of coverage without making the text so lengthy that the cost would be prohibitive for the typical student budget. Some cuts had to be made as the length of the book became an issue. For example, extraneous material was removed from the Appendix, leaving only the chapter on "Managing Personal and Family Finances," and information from the Afterword was moved to other chapters.

ACKNOWLEDGMENTS

All writers, but most especially textbook writers, are indebted to a great many other writers and researchers whose work provides the building blocks out of which a text is constructed. Textbook writers are by definition intellectual pack rats, taking information from a great many sources and, in turn, leaving something behind. Our hope is that the leavings do justice to the takings. We are especially indebted to Rosalind Barnett, Grace Baruch, Jessie Bernard, Arlene Skolnick, Linda Thompson, Deborah Tannen, Francesca Cancian, John Scanzoni, Catherine Surra, Sally Lloyd, and Leonard Pearlin for demonstrating to us through their published work that it is possible to write with intelligence and insight about marriages, families, and intimate relationships.

We received helpful criticisms and suggestions from a great many people, including the instructors who used the fourth edition. The text reviewers are owed a special note of thanks for their thoughtful and challenging comments. The revision was significantly improved by their informed reviews. Special thanks go to

Paul Aschenbrenner, Hartnell College

Clifton E. Barber, Colorado State University, Fort Collins

Michael G. Breci, St. Cloud State University

Susan S. Coady, The Ohio State University

Saul Feinman, University of Wyoming

Elizabeth Grauerholz, Purdue University

Delbert J. Hayden, Western Kentucky University

Peter Heller, Middle Tennessee State University

Karen J. Hossfeld, San Francisco State University

Christa Reiser, East Carolina State University

Cherylon Robinson, The University of Texas, San Antonio

Roger H. Rubin, University of Maryland at College Park

Margaret P. Stafford, Cazenovia College

Stuart A. Wright, Lamar University

Additional accolades are due acquisitions editor Sylvia Shepard for her insightful suggestions and intelligent, encouraging words. The skillful editorial comments of Marilyn Miller also benefited this project. And we should not leave out Curt Berkowitz, who provided much practical advice and was particularly supportive in the production phase of the text. Working with photo manager Kathy Bendo was an additional pleasure.

Gloria Wanager Bird is especially appreciative of the substantive emotional support and practical help provided by Gerald Bird, who wrote the Appendix chapter on "Managing Personal and Family Finances" despite an already heavy work schedule that included finishing a college text of his own, *Personal Financial Planning*. Martyn Wanager Bird also deserves recognition for his caring attitude and the persuasive tactics he sometimes employed to convince us of the healthful, rejuvenating effects of adult play. He also made numerous emergency treks to the library to sleuth out that really essential book or article we just could not do without. Special thanks are extended to Paula DuPrey, Cosby Steele Rogers, and Sandi Stith—friends who offered encouraging words and encompassing hugs along the way.

Gloria Bird
Keith Melville

FAMILIES AND INTIMATE RELATIONSHIPS

PART I

Understanding Marriage, Family, and Relationships Today

1

Bill Barrett, *SF59, cast bronze maquette*, 1992

American Marriages and Families: A Changing Society

It is hardly news that families are not what they used to be.
—ANDREW HACKER

During the last 150 years, there have been times when it seemed to some observers that the American *family*—the traditional nuclear household of male breadwinner, full-time homemaker wife, and their 2.1 dependent children—was in decline. This observation, accurate or not, was generally greeted with dismay, as the *nuclear family* was—and to a great extent, still is—held up as the ideal family form in our society. Marriage and family, after all, are universal and core institutions of all societies, so circumstances that appear to threaten them make people uncomfortable.

Recent debate over whether family values have eroded reflects to some degree the anxiety Americans feel about the alternative forms of family life that now constitute the majority of American households. Some critics contend that such diversity—families headed by separated or divorced individuals, single (never-married) parents, childless couples, stepfamilies, and families in which both fathers and mothers work away from home—is a sign of the family's decline. Others argue that they are modern adaptions to other changes in our culture and constitute proof of the family's enduring vitality. Some label the current discussion as misguided because it is suffused with moral and ethical overtones and relies on the stereotypical white, middle-class family of the 1950s as the role model of what today's families ought to be.

If, instead, we view marriage and family life across a historical continuum, a pattern of gradual evolution of family structure and function emerges. Like families of the past, women and men today are actively creating families that are far from the idealized relationships depicted in television classics like "Ozzie and Harriet," "The Brady Bunch," "Father Knows Best," "The Waltons," or "Leave It to Beaver." Drawing on resources never imagined in previous generations, families are revising existing strategies and devising new ones for managing the more complex lifestyles of the 1990s. Each family is, in effect, forever in process—always changing, never the same from year to year or decade to decade. Just as individual family members develop physically and emotionally, interact, age, and otherwise change over the life course, so does the family as a unit. Just as economic conditions, cultural values and beliefs, demographic trends, and government policies change, so does the family.

Not only are marriage and family relationships buffeted by the stresses and strains of the larger society—for example, drug use, AIDS, and the decline of high-wage, blue-collar jobs—but changes in these two institutions alter profoundly that society as well. For example, the economic needs that propelled many American women into the work force after the 1950s affected, among other things, the domestic power structure between husbands and wives, as women gained more economic independence. One result has been a redefinition of traditional gender roles. Moreover, the lives of many children were also changed as increasing numbers of parents divorced. And governmental policy continues to be affected, as the recent debates over family leave and health insurance reflect. Marriage and families have not disappeared, dissolved, or disintegrated so much as they have changed in definition and composition.

In this book we explore these changes in all their complex diversity, not only in marriage and family life but also in other forms of intimate relationships. We begin by identifying critical markers of change that have occurred in marriage and family arrangements throughout American history and how our expectations of these most familiar institutions have altered. We discuss, in this context, the increasing diversity of family forms and households and the pervasive influence of new attitudes about men's and women's roles in family life and the work force. And we see that family arrangements have become matters of increasingly public controversy. A question we raise is why there is a need to study marriage and family behavior when we already know so much about it from personal experience. We include a discussion of family theory and identify scientific methods for investigating marriage, family, and other intimate relationships.

Although our main concern is with what is happening *today*, we believe it is valuable to look closely at historical change as a way of understanding contemporary arrangements and alternatives. The problem

with this perspective is that many of the historical writings about family life rely on accounts of the lives of mostly middle-class white Americans; therefore, written and oral histories of American families sometimes ignore ethnic, race, and class differences. Some scholars like Arlene Skolnick, author of *Embattled Paradise: The American Family in an Age of Uncertainty* (1991), contend that historical accounts are nevertheless valuable because the middle-class family has consistently defined the norms, expectations, values, and dreams for most other types of families.

In this chapter we describe the history of both mainstream middle-class families and other family types—Native Americans and black Americans, in particular. In addition, we detail the experiences of various immigrant families—Europeans, Hispanics, and Asian-Americans. When possible, we include an explanation of how experiences differed by social class. Even though historical examinations of these diverse populations are sparse, we attempt to include them as often as we can. We start with an exploration of the first families and move forward in time to the 1990s.

MARRIAGE AND FAMILIES IN COLONIAL AMERICA

Native Americans

Depending on which account you read, between 1 and 12 million Native Americans lived within what is now the United States when the Spanish established the first permanent European settlement in 1565 at St. Augustine, Florida. There were at least 240 Native American *tribes*, as the Europeans called them, "each with its own political structure, language, economy, and pattern of family and kinship" (Mintz & Kellogg, 1988, p. 26). Although the various Native American nations did not practice the same religion, religion permeated all aspects of Native American life (Michaelson, 1983). While most nations were *patrilineal*, that is, rights and property descended from the father, many were *matrilineal*, with rights and property descended from the mother.

For most Native American families, women, men, and children worked together to provide food and shelter for the tribe. Women often enjoyed high status and considerable power, especially in matrilineal tribes. The life of the Native American family in colonial America was probably not much different from that of the colonists. The women were in charge of the home, including making clothes, cooking, and caring for the children, while the men were responsible for hunting, tending the crops, and defense. Women tended to spend most of their time with other women and children, even in mixed gatherings.

However, the Native American woman enjoyed a much greater degree of independence and security than the colonial woman. Because of the extensive kinship networks that characterized tribal societies, the care and feeding of the family was often the obligation of the entire tribe. A colonial woman, on the other hand, tended to be dependent on one man, and if she were widowed, she was forced to accept charity. This was considered a demeaning and embarrassing situation (Niethammer, 1977).

Kinship was greatly valued and ancestral connections formed the basis of each Native American nation's religious, economic, and leadership systems. The "Diversity" box on the Hopi provides one example of a Native American kinship system. Marriages were public events that generally served to cement ties between kinship groups or nations. Some nations left mate selection to the young man and woman, but usually the kinship group chose. Girls married between the ages of 12 and 15, boys between 15 and 20. Most Native American nations practiced *monogamy*—having a sexually exclusive relationship. The birth and naming of children were celebrated with ceremonies and rituals, as were critical markers in a child's life—first step, acts of courage, coming of age, and so forth. The death of many children at birth and during infancy kept most families small. To socialize children, parents tended to use praise and rewards rather than physical discipline. Misbehavior met with shame and disapproval.

The arrival of the colonists forever altered the lives of Native Americans. The colonists were often shocked that Native American behaviors and customs did not correspond to their own, and rather than accept diversity, they tried to introduce their "superior" civilization to the "savages." Although Native Americans were not enslaved, as black Africans later were, they endured forced relocation, segregation, and the dismantling and outlawing of valued cultural practices (Brown, 1970). The colonists also introduced diseases such as chicken pox, measles, and influenza, against which the Native Americans had no natural immunities. By 1700, these diseases and various battles be-

tween the colonists and Native Americans had wiped out over 85 percent of the Native American population on the eastern coast (Thornton, 1987).

Colonial Americans

Probably the most striking difference between colonial families and families today was their emphasis on community. Personal life was not private as it is today; families fell under the almost constant scrutiny of community members. The expectation was that family members would operate within the fairly rigid role structure ordained by the community and the church. Deviations from the expected norms were promptly dealt with. A child, for example, who the community decided was being improperly socialized, was removed from the home and placed with another family. A married woman who left her family would be found, punished, and forced to return home. Not only was each community self-sufficient, but each household was, according to sociologist William Goode (1963), a "little commonwealth" functioning as business, school, job-training institute, church, maternity ward and hospital, as well as social services agency. The architecture of the home encouraged a specific kind of intimacy, not necessarily emotional:

> Intimacy in the colonial period mainly referred to physical proximity, and in that sense intimacy was an inevitable consequence of the architecture of daily life. Within households, people were almost always within monitoring range of one another. Families were large and houses small; of the few rooms there were, most were multipurpose. Even if a person were alone in a room, almost any of his/her activities could be overheard . . . beds were typically shared and benches more common than single chairs. (Gadlin, 1977, pp. 35–36)

In colonial America, death and the ensuing disruption and reorganization of families was a given. Many mothers and infants died during or after childbirth. Only half of the children who survived lived to adulthood. Of these, 50 percent died by age 50. The high mortality rates compressed the family life cycle so orphans and remarriage were common; only about one-third of marriages lasted more than 10 years. Death, not divorce, caused remarriage (Wells, 1982).

In choosing a mate, romantic love was frowned on; parents frequently arranged their children's marriages. Love, then, was the consequence of, not the reason for

The Hopi Kinship System

Among the Hopi, it has been traditional that larger social groups within the culture, rather than the family, are the focus of life. The Hopi have been present in the mesas of the southwest for at least 12,000 years. There, they spoke several languages with shared features of a common language, the Uto-Aztecan. For centuries the Hopi culture remained basically intact, undisturbed, and unaltered mainly because of the isolation and privacy provided by the geography of the southwest. As Puebloan Indians, the Hopis resided in villages extending across three mesas in the states of Colorado, Arizona, and New Mexico. Each Hopi village was independent from the others but shared a distinctive social structure (Rushforth & Upham, 1992).

At the bottom of the social structure was the household, or extended family unit, composed of matrilineal kin—women, their daughters and granddaughters, and the men they married. They lived as a group, worked together, and shared resources. However, their ties were primarily social, rather than economic, political, or religious, and consequently, so unimportant in the eyes of the larger community that there is no word in the Hopi language to symbolize or represent this family group. The next layer in the social structure was the lineage, or larger kinship group, including descendents of female relatives from other households and other villages. Lineages then formed the larger, more powerful clans. Hopi clans controlled ceremonial and religious offices, appointed priests, and owned agricultural lands, religious objects, and communal clan houses where clan leaders resided and tended the clan's sacred religious symbols (Whiteley, 1988). Village priests were also community political leaders, and religious ceremonies and rituals dominated political decision making. At the top of the Hopi social structure was the phratry, made up of groups of clans. Clans belonging to the same phratry shared some religious rituals and ceremonial items and treated each other as extended family. Membership in a religious society was expected, and societies were controlled by priests appointed by particular clans, but members represented a cross section of all clans of a village. Marriage and membership in religious societies created loyalties and alliances among households, lineages, clans, and phratries.

Between 1900 and 1992, as greater numbers of the American population moved into the desert and the federal government instituted Indian reservations, the Hopi culture began to change. Today, fewer than one-third of the Hopi population live on the reservation. With reservation life came a shift in the economic base of the Hopi, with most giving up agricultural work for industrial and service-oriented jobs off the reservation. These changes then led to other modifications in the social structure of the villages. Reservation towns, built around essential tribal services—missions, schools, trading posts, federal agencies—have replaced the villages as centers of social discourse and action. As the Hopi became more westernized, ancestral religious societies have declined in importance. Most ceremonies and rituals are no longer practiced. "Associated with the loss of traditional religious institutions, knowledge, and power, and of the authority of traditional religious leaders is the decline of religiously based ethical standards that were fundamental to the organization of Hopi life" (Rushforth & Upham, 1992, p. 170). The nuclear family, however, has taken on greater importance as the reliance on lineages, clans, and phratries has decreased.

EXPLORATIONS   *The Hopi experience illustrates how a decision made by one group in a society—in this case, the federal government mandated reservation living for Native Americans—can change the basic social structure and functioning of another group. Can you recall other instances in which the institution of a societal change resulted in similar consequences?*

marriage. By love, the colonists meant respect and care. To love one's marital partner was both a duty and an obligation. Authority, not affection, formed the basis of marital and family life. "The father was head of the family, just as the king was head of the state" (Skol-nick, 1991, p. 24). To New England Puritans, spousal love signified obedience to God. Such love held families together, and families were the lifeblood of the community. According to historian John Demos, "The family and the wider community were joined in a re-

In contrast to today's emphasis on family privacy, Puritan families, even when on seeming private expeditions, usually were not far from the watchful eyes of members of their community.

lation of profound reciprocity; one might say they were continuous with one another'' (1986, p. 28).

Despite being subordinate to men by custom and law, women's labor was essential within the home. Women washed, cooked, made clothes, gardened, and so forth. Mothers were the primary caretakers of infants and children. But fathers had much greater responsibility for a child's socialization into appropriate cultural norms and beliefs. As sociologist Joseph Pleck (1987) explains:

> This emphasis on the paternal role was rooted in this period's conception of the differences between the sexes and the nature of children. Men were thought to have superior reason, which made them less likely than women to be misled by the ''passions'' and ''affections'' to which both sexes were subjected. Children were viewed as inherently sinful, ruled by powerful impulses as yet ungoverned by intellect. . . . Mothers were less able to provide these needed influences because of their own tendency to ''indulge'' or be excessively ''fond'' of their children. (p. 85)

In rare cases of marital separation, the father won child custody. Fathers took their parental role very seriously,

as the diary of New England Puritan Cotton Mather illustrates:

> I took my daughter Katy into my study and there I told my child that I am to die shortly, and she must, when I am dead, remember everything that I said unto her. I set before her the sinful and woeful condition of her nature, and I charged her to pray in secret places every day without ceasing . . . I gave her to understand that when I am taken from her she must look to meet with more humbling afflictions than she does now [when] she has a careful and tender father to provide for her. (in Demos, 1982, p. 426)

Fathers could offer such close leadership and attention to a child because their work was not only located at home, but children were actively enlisted in that labor at fairly young ages. ''Fathers were a visible presence, year after year, day after day'' (Demos, 1982, p. 429).

Black Americans

The majority of early slaves were male, so to write about slave families in the colonies during the seventeenth century is almost impossible. But by the 1700s, the situation began to change. As the size of farms, businesses, and households grew, so did the need for more slaves, and increasing numbers of black African women were imported. Their influx made it possible to start families, which many partners did, despite the legal prohibitions against slave marriages. The majority of slaves on southern plantations raised their children in two-parent families. Yet, since every slave and his or her descendants were the property of their owners, children were not considered to be members of a particular family. Thus, owners had the right to break up a slave family by selling a husband, wife, or child.

Family life was amazingly close and stable given the extraordinary strains families faced, including the use of communal nurseries, removal of children even in preadolescence, the little time parents could spend away from work, and the inability of parents to protect their offspring—or themselves (Gutman, 1975; Malson, Mudimbe-Boyi, O'Barr, & Wyer, 1990).

What facilitated the cohesiveness of the slave family? For one thing, the slave culture encouraged monogamy and marital stability. To establish family continuity, parents named their children after themselves or relatives, sometimes even assuming their owner's surname (Berry & Blassingame, 1982). In addition, plantation slaves fashioned elaborate and enduring bonds of kinship, or family relationships, by treating each other as relatives. Such kinship networks provided a vehicle to socialize children, giving them an identity distinct from that assigned by their owners. For example, black children addressed black adults outside of the nuclear family as "aunt" or "uncle" and other black children who were not relatives as "brother" and "sister." This kinship network functioned from one generation to the next.

A further sense of communality and kinship was transmitted through the teaching of Afro-American crafts and story telling, which served to pass down a sense of culture through folklore and oral history. Along with slave religion—a combination of Christianity and elements of African religion—the kinship network made slaves feel they were not simply oppressed and alone but members of a larger community. Indeed, it may be said that to some extent, all the slaves on a plantation belonged to a single, extended family, whose members could depend on each other in time of trouble (Berry & Blassingame, 1982; Malson et al., 1990).

MARRIAGE AND FAMILIES IN THE NINETEENTH CENTURY

Marriage, Family, Community: Altered Relationships

During the nineteenth century, the ties between the family and the community loosened. Greater prosperity lessened the need for community members to work together to ensure social stability. Because most families now had enough to eat and a safe place to live, they could accumulate the skills, abilities, and tools needed to function with more efficiency and with less danger to themselves in their new environment. Access to free land also encouraged family mobility. Inheritance no longer constituted the primary path to owning property or learning a job skill. Married couples were to some degree released from the direct control not only of the community, but also of church and kin. Family life became more private and less public, explain Dizard and Gadlin (1990):

Parental power traditionally embraced a wide range of claims on couples . . . throughout married life. Involved were such economic considerations as who would help work the land or manage the herd, who

would remain at or near the parents' home to assist them should they grow infirm, and so on. Moreover, parental claims also represented ties that bound the couple to a network of kinfolk who were, typically, economically as well as emotionally interdependent. This elaborate web of claims greatly circumscribed the couple, implicating them in numerous reciprocal obligations. The net effect was an emphasis on the bonds between the couple and others in the network of kin that diminished the importance of the bonds between husband and wife. (p. 10)

In the nineteenth century, industrialization and the growth of towns and cities undercut the importance of the family as the unit of economic production as work gradually became separate from home. Increasing numbers of people worked in shops, factories, and offices six days a week. Except in rural areas, work stopped being defined as something both women and men did to sustain their families and the larger community. Instead, work became redefined as something that men did to earn money to support the family. The unpaid labor women performed at home was of lower status than the wage-earning work that men did outside the home, thus women's work was no longer considered equivalent to men's work. This economic and social distinction between breadwinner and homemaker changed the relationship between women and men. As Gadlin observes:

When work is moved outside the home and the people with whom one works are no longer the people with whom one lives, there develop two fundamentally separate types of relationships. . . . A conflict arises between the styles of relationships required by the workplace and home life. . . . These separate spheres of existence require different and often incompatible feelings, expectations, attitudes, interests, and behavior. (1977, p. 46)

Work was, for the most part, characterized by unkindness, selfishness, and distrust, while family and home were defined collectively as the center of warmth, unselfish giving, and life satisfaction—a spiritual and emotional retreat (Boydston, 1991).

If the breadwinner/father was head of the family, the homemaker/mother was the nurturer and caregiver.

Entrusted with the family's virtue, she was the religious beacon and emotional helmsman. Her engagement in the public sphere was ideally limited to religious activities. . . . Women came to be regarded as the force that cooled the passions awakened by the rapidly expanding stimulations of public life. . . . Self-control was an issue of considerable concern, and many looked to the home, particularly the wife, for this control. (Dizard & Gadlin, 1990, p. 20)

Marriage still meant a lifetime commitment, but one which now typically began with falling in love and subsequently developed into a deeper attachment. Intimacy and sexual relations between marital partners were not viewed as a vital part of marriage. Both partners, but especially women, retained their commitments to friends and kin. Some scholars contend that, in fact, the most intimate of relationships occurred not between marital partners, but between women friends (Cancian, 1986), which we will discuss in greater depth in Chapter 3.

Duty and obligation remained the cornerstones of marital life. Bringing up children as moral, respectable citizens was a mother's primary role. The central family relationship was not between marital partners, but between mother and child. So idealized did the mothering role become that most societal inadequacies—delinquency, crime, poverty, and mental illness—were blamed on poor mothering.

Of course, men's roles also changed dramatically. A husband was now responsible for supporting his entire family. Success at work as shown by job status and earning power came to define manhood. And, as the husband was increasingly at work, and therefore, absent from the home, his parenting role and domestic power decreased (Demos, 1982). The new assignment of roles perhaps explains why, in cases of marital separation, the mother, rather than the father, now gained custody of the children.

During the nineteenth century, the role of the child also shifted. Fewer children were born per family as women delayed the birth of their first child and stopped having children at an earlier age than their mothers. Having fewer children made parents value children more, leading to closer affectional ties and greater intimacy between parents and children. Historian Mary Stovall describes the increased concern for children that developed during this era as the "cult of the child":

. . . children were viewed as innocent and possessed of sensitive and impressionable natures more responsive to example and persuasion than to corporal pun-

ishment. Parents were enjoined by the veritable explosion in the numbers of childrearing books to mold the child's will through love and reason so that the child would early develop a proper sense of self that made further correction unnecessary. Proper punishments were shaming the child, arousing guilt, or depriving the child of company or food so that he or she could meditate on the enormity of the deed and resolve not to repeat the sin. (1989, p. 140)

Black Families

In 1860 there were more than 4 million black slaves, and approximately 500,000 free African-Americans. Many of the free blacks were former slaves or the children of slaves. But we know far more about slave families than we do about the families of free blacks.

Although it was impossible for slave husbands and fathers to have the same power and authority as free heads of families, they were able to "provide" for their families by hunting, fishing, or taking what they needed from plantation supplies. Like their husbands, women worked during the day in the fields or in the owner's household. At night, wives and mothers prepared the families' meals and performed other domestic chores. Within the family, husbands and wives exerted roughly equal authority.

After their emancipation in 1863, large numbers of black men and women wandered throughout the south mainly in search of family members from whom they had been forcibly separated, sometimes for years, through sale or the disorganization and movement of families during the Civil War (Gutman, 1983).

The Civil War inflicted severe hardship on the slave family. Even before the outbreak of war, restrictions prevented many slave husbands from regularly visiting their wives and children. More were separated as growing numbers of slave men were impressed into the Confederate cause, serving as bakers, blacksmiths, boatmen, butchers, iron makers, machinists, nurses, shoemakers, and teamsters. (Mintz & Kellogg, 1988, p. 76)

In the aftermath of the Civil War the two-parent black family still predominated. Southern black families commonly turned to sharecropping to make a living. Planters, under this system, divided their estates into plots, each to be farmed by a single black family. Profits from the sale of crops were usually divided in equal shares between the family, the landowner, and the merchant who sold seed, farm equipment, groceries, and other products necessary to farming life. Sharecropping was difficult, but it provided black families some freedom to organize their lives according to their own values and beliefs.

Immigrant Families

New Sources of Diversity

Between 1820 and 1920, more than 38 million people, mostly Europeans, poured into America in great waves. Before the 1880s, immigrants came mainly from northern and western Europe: Germany, Ireland, Great Britain, and the Scandinavian countries. They arrived in northern seaboard cities such as Boston and New York. At about the same time, Chinese immigrated in large numbers to the west coast. Then, from the 1880s through the start of World War I in 1914, the source of European immigration shifted to southern and eastern countries: Italy, Russia, Poland, Greece, and Austro-Hungary. During the same period, Hawaiians and Japanese immigrated to the west coast.

Immigration was not the only way that many ethnic groups and minorities became part of the American experience. In 1845 the United States annexed Texas, and three years later, as a result of the Mexican war gained the present states of California, Utah, New Mexico, most of Arizona, and parts of Colorado and Wyoming. More than 80,000 people of mixed Spanish and Indian origin living in this vast region were now Americans. After its loss in the Spanish-American War (1898), Spain ceded Puerto Rico and the Pacific island of Guam to the United States and agreed to the American annexation of the Philippines. The populations of these new territories came under American control. With the annexation of Hawaii (1900), the United States also incorporated the ethnic groups living there—Hawaiians, Japanese, and Chinese.

Immigrant Life

Both the old and the new immigrants were mostly poor and uneducated. The cities they crowded into, besides New York and Boston, including Philadelphia, Chicago, and San Francisco, developed many ethnic neighborhoods, which consisted of enclaves of kin and neighbors from the same or nearby towns and villages (Mintz & Kellogg, 1988). Here recent arrivals could speak their own language and practice familiar customs.

Most immigrant families followed the typical American pattern. There were two parents and their children. Immigrants married later than natives and usually had more children. Most husbands worked in factories. Wives managed the household and the children. Many mothers and children also had to work in factories to supplement the low wages most fathers earned. To survive economically, immigrant families often moved in with other families or took in boarders.

Despite these similarities, there was considerable diversity in the ways ethnic groups adapted to American culture.

> Jewish families tended to rent larger apartments and share their residences with lodgers. Italian families, in contrast, resided in smaller and cheaper single-family apartments. . . . Irish and Slavs were willing to forgo their children's education rather than send married women into the workforce . . . Jews and blacks tended to keep their children in school despite the lost earnings. Italian families, more than almost any other ethnic group, discouraged women from working. (Mintz & Kellogg, 1988, p. 93)

One of the largest groups to emigrate was the Irish. Between 1840 and 1860, political repression combined with the great potato famine caused the emigration of approximately 1.5 million Irish. Most Irish immigrants found work in factories along the east coast and settled in cities there. They were discriminated against because of their willingness to work for low wages and their Catholicism. Social scientists Susan Swap and Jean Krasnow (1992) note that children of poor immigrant families, like the Irish, were considered second-class citizens and could gain only limited access to educational institutions and skilled occupations. Despite these prejudices, two values taught in the Irish-American family led to academic and economic achievement: the values of hard work and educational attainment.

At about the same time as the Irish emigration, a Chinese emigration was also in process. Beginning in the mid-1850s, thousands of Chinese flooded California to work in the gold fields. The vast majority of these immigrants (90 percent) were male. After failing to gain riches during the gold rush, most Chinese stayed on to help build the Central Pacific Railroad. In response to job shortages in the west, immigration of Chinese laborers and miners was banned from 1882 to 1904 (Worsnop, 1991). Despite the earlier tide of immigration, few Chinese-American families existed during this period because immigration law prohibited Chinese men from bringing their wives to America (Chen, 1980; Tsai 1986).

Poverty forced many immigrant families into crowded city tenements.

Like the Irish and the Chinese, all immigrant ethnic groups have their own histories concerning why and how they came to the United States and what they experienced once they arrived. It is common for ethnic families to struggle to maintain some of their valued homeland traditions as they adopt more Americanized ways of thinking and behaving.

THE TWENTIETH CENTURY: THE COMPANIONATE FAMILY

The Beginning of the Modern Family: 1900–1920

Although immigration remained a constant in American life, with 24 million people entering the country between 1877 and 1914, the great waves of immigration ended in the 1920s with the passage of restrictive

laws (Daniels, 1990). As they had in the 1800s, immigrants in the 1900s relied on complex networks of relationships with kin, friends, and neighbors for assistance in locating housing, supplies, child care, jobs, and loans.

Throughout the twentieth century, immigrant families continued to actively create cultural, political, economic, religious, and recreational organizations designed to soften the sometimes difficult transition to American life; a transition further complicated by the ambivalent ways Americans responded to them. During hard social and economic times, for example, civic leaders would frequently blame the influx of low-wage immigrants for making matters worse, calling for such families to become "100 percent American" by speaking only English and discarding all "old country" customs and values. In better times, the pendulum would swing back toward acknowledgment of the important contributions made by various ethnic groups and encouragement of *cultural pluralism*—an appreciation for the basic right of ethnic groups to be different from the mainstream (Ponzetta, 1991).

Black families, like immigrant families, continued to operate from a strong cultural ethic that placed family well-being above individual success. The changing century and the altering of the nation's job base did not result in significant economic gains for black families. As in earlier times, economic survival rested on forming a closely connected family unit in which members pooled their resources. Discriminatory hiring and management practices meant that blacks, even more than immigrants, faced oppressive economic conditions. Blacks generally had to settle for menial agricultural jobs, seasonal work, or full-time work as domestics—maids, cooks, housekeepers, babysitters—in the homes of the white middle class. It was during this century that black women and men began to openly voice discontent with racial prejudice and advocate for social justice through better jobs, housing, schools, and community services. This was a theme that black families would bring forward to the larger American society again and again throughout the twentieth century (Jones, 1985).

Most family historians view the early 1900s as the beginning of the modern era of the family. The United States, industrialized, had become more urbanized (Ware, 1989). Middle-class family members no longer relied on each other as much for basic survival needs. Grocery stores, dress and millinery shops, hospitals, schools, and public agencies were beginning to take on traditional family functions. The growth of mass media—radio, movies, and advertising—made it much more likely that Americans would share common experiences, or at least an awareness of them. These transformations in the American way of life led to the rise of the *companionate family,* defined by emotional and sexual intimacy and shared roles. The ideal of the companionate family did not become the immediate norm of American families, but was gradually adopted, with some backsliding, as the century unfolded.

The New Focus on Emotional Needs: 1920–1950

Women got the vote and the first sexual revolution really began as women's roles expanded. Now instead of crusading for social progress, women focused on individual self-expression. "Women were photographed and depicted in advertisements . . . with bobbed hair and powdered noses, with fringed skirts just above the knees and hose rolled below, with a cigarette in one hand and a man in the other" (Filene, 1986, p. 134). Many women, of course, did not fit this image, but there was a definite move by young single women to gain more independence, and the new psychology of Sigmund Freud, with its emphasis on sex, encouraged many to become sexually emancipated. With the progress of the birth control movement, sex became identified as something separate from reproduction, an experience to be enjoyed for its own sake. Other restrictions seemed to be breaking down as well. High schools opened to both women and men, and couples began to date without chaperons. The new permissiveness led to a big jump in the divorce rate, which was also helped by the liberalized divorce laws in most states. Moreover, women began seeking employment in ever-increasing numbers. By the end of the twenties, over 10.6 million had found jobs, com-

One of the factors contributing to the new sexual freedom of women was that, because of the birth control movement, sex was now seen for the first time as separate from reproduction.

pared to 8.4 million in 1920. But most of these jobs were menial and poorly paid.

Despite the so-called emergence of the new woman, traditional gender roles remained in place. The goal of most women—to marry and have children—was unchanged. Marriage was still the only socially approved option for women (Banner, 1983). But the family itself changed in some important ways. Parenthood became less of a focus as the relationship between partners grew more significant. Increasingly, both partners were supposed to have intimacy needs for affection, care, and understanding. People expected romantic attraction to occur before marriage and love to continue to grow throughout it (Dizard & Gadlin, 1990).

With the increasing use of birth control, sexual pleasure gradually became a goal for both spouses. Nevertheless, wives were still economically dependent and submissive to their husbands. The success of a marriage remained the woman's responsibility, as was child rearing, with husbands maintaining little direct contact with their children (Cancian, 1986). As one respondent in R. S. Lynd and Helen Lynd's (1929) classic sociological analysis of families in Middletown (Muncie, Indiana) proclaimed: "It is much more important for children to have a good mother than it is for them to have a good father." The Lynds found very few differences in father involvement between blue-collar and white-collar families. In fact, one middle-class father said: "I'm a rotten dad. If our children amount to anything it's their mother who'll get the credit."

The Great Depression of 1929 reinforced this traditional thinking. Jobs became difficult to find and women were admonished not to compete against men for them. A poll conducted by the Gallup organization in 1937 found that 82 percent of those surveyed believed that wives whose husbands were employed should not be in the work force (Degler, 1980). A wife's domestic role changed when her husband lost his job. For example, women often substituted their own labor and resourcefulness for goods and labor-saving devices that they previously had been able to purchase.

Although large numbers of women joined the work force during World War II, the worlds of work and family remained very separate. For married women, love still meant personal obligation and service to others. Women employed during the war years worked for family and country. They heard regular reminders of the temporary nature of their new jobs and injunctions to retain their femininity while performing "men's work" (Hartmann, 1982). When the war ended women were admonished to give up their positions and return home. Many did, but some retained their jobs, if they could, or sought new ones. Most postwar jobs available to women, however, were not in the skilled occupations they had occupied during the war, but in traditionally female, low-paying fields (Stovall, 1989). A man's primary and equally traditional goal was to earn a decent income to support his family. Women and men believed that self-sacrifice and compromise were necessary in marital life.

The Ascendance of Domesticity: The 1950s

Arlene Skolnick describes the 1950s as a return to the Victorian *cult of domesticity*, in that the home was once again viewed as a retreat from the world, with the wife/mother at its center. And, in the words of essayist Elizabeth Hardwick:

> The 1950s seem to have taken place on a sunny afternoon that asked nothing of you except a drifting belief in the moment and its power to satisfy: a handsome young couple with two or three children, a station wagon, a large dog, a house and a summer house, a great deal of picnicking and camping together. For the middle class, the 1950s passed in a dream. . . . The treasured children would do well in school, and the psychiatrist could be summoned for the troubled. The suburbs offered the space and grass that would bless family existence. (1978, p. 3)

If this passage disregards those millions of Americans who were less fortunate, it reflects the tenor of the times, for the existence of widespread poverty was not yet generally recognized. Even social scientists who studied marriage and family life largely ignored the influence of race, ethnicity, and social class.

In such popular television programs as "Ozzie and Harriet" and "Father Knows Best," the new mass medium portrayed an idealized form of family life that mirrored the mood of the decade. Yet, in contrast to the television families of the 1950s, whose "happy problems" were resolved at the end of each half-hour segment, the real families did not so easily overcome theirs. But the customs and habits that regulated the relations between spouses and their relationship to their children seemed satisfactory enough. The relatively low divorce rate confirmed the widespread impression that the institutions of marriage and family were in good shape. Much of contemporary writing about marriage and family life supported this notion: With a little bit of personal effort, the authors promised, *every* family might attain the domestic contentment displayed in the popular sitcoms.

America in the 1950s was, to an unusual extent, a family-oriented society. In 1946, GIs returning from World War II enthusiastically embraced family life, marrying young and launching the phenomenon known as the baby boom. This trend peaked in the late fifties when women were having an average of three to four babies. The median age of first marriage, which had been rising for decades, fell to a historic low in 1956—22.5 years for men and 20.1 for women. In the same decade, the level of living even for the poorest of families rose so that 60 percent of American families earned a middle-class wage (Chafe, 1986). An ever-expanding middle class mass-produced and purchased cars, appliances, homes, furniture, and clothing. The flourishing economy propelled the movement to the suburbs where it seemed that look-alike families lived in look-alike houses.

Prosperity also gave many blue- and white-collar families the luxury of having a wife and mother who worked only at home. Indeed, there *was* a certain similarity among millions of households. Fully three-fifths conformed to the male breadwinner/full-time homemaker ideal. It was an era that placed a premium on conformity; nonconformists kept a very low profile. The separation of work from family interests led to the return to traditional rigidly defined gender roles. At the same time, the view of fatherhood changed slightly to incorporate the belief that fathers should spend more time with their children. Fathers, however, were advised not to become mothers. As one author explained the thinking of the 1950s:

> The mother had a primarily expressive relationship with both boys and girls; in contrast, the father rewarded his male and female children differently, encouraging instrumental behavior in his son and expressive behavior in his daughter. The father was supposed to be the principal transmitter of culturally based conceptions of masculinity and femininity. (Biller, 1971, p. 107)

What went unnoticed in the euphoria of the time was the fact that the 1950s marked an unusual phase in American marriage and family life—a deviation from long-term trends. During the immediate postwar period, a higher percentage of people were marrying than ever before in American history, or since. The divorce rate, which had been gradually rising for years, declined slightly. Most of all, the unusual prosperity of the postwar years made single-wage-earner families possible for more people, while causing home ownership to become a reality for unprecedented millions of Americans.

The New Questions: 1960–1980

While the 1950s satisfied Americans' desire for material possessions, the 1960s shifted the emphasis to the nonmaterial—inner peace and satisfaction, leisure pursuits, self-improvement, and self-knowledge. These changes were accompanied by a gradual erosion of the self-sacrifice ethic. If the 1950s were unusually congenial to the two institutions of marriage and the family, the 1960s were less so. The age of first marriage rose once again, the fertility rate dropped, and the divorce rate continued the upward climb that the fifties temporarily interrupted. Moreover, the second sexual revolution began.

Sharply in contrast with the promarriage climate of the 1950s, by the late 1960s hundreds of books and articles appeared with titles such as "The Crisis of the Nuclear Family," "Is Marriage Necessary?" and "Is Monogamy Outdated?" Many people began to question not just traditional roles but the family itself. Such widely publicized trends as cohabitation, experiments with communal living, and the redefinition of traditional sex codes indicated a certain defiance of traditional norms.

During the sixties and seventies, four developments convinced many people that the institutions of marriage and family were, indeed, falling apart.

Breaking Old Taboos

In the 1960s, increasing attention began to be paid to the differences between popular beliefs about the way people ought to act and their *actual* behavior. Journalists and social scientists thus began to investigate such previously taboo behaviors as abortion, child abuse, and incest. For the first time, such topics were considered appropriate subject matter for daytime soap operas as well as prime-time specials. Increasingly, families were forced to face the fact that conflict played an integral part in most family relationships and that serious problems sometimes arose even in average middle-class families.

Family Pluralism

Intimate arrangements, which had long been practiced but not publicized, also began to have vocal advocates. In the permissive climate of the 1960s, with its strong emphasis on the rights of all minorities, alternatives to the traditional family—such as cohabitation and gay and lesbian unions—became far more visible. Instead of arguing that such arrangements should be tolerated because some people are unable to conform to the norms, their advocates argued that the norms (as well as the laws) should be broadened to recognize them as legitimate alternatives.

By the early 1970s, considerable attention was devoted to alternatives to traditional marriage and family arrangements. Some of those alternatives—such as the suggestion that couples draw up a custom-designed marriage contract—were intended to help couples clarify and define roles according to personal preferences and abilities, not traditional assumptions about male and female roles. Other alternatives—such as Nena and George O'Neill's proposal for "open marriage" (1972)—were designed to reduce some of the strains of marriage by encouraging spouses to make a greater investment in other intimate relationships. A third set of alternatives—represented by "family clusters," communes, and group marriages—were aimed at creating new types of extended families.

This new emphasis on family pluralism was a development of considerable importance. It made the public aware of alternatives to prevailing middle-class patterns and provoked social science researchers to pose different questions from those that had been characteristic of family studies in the 1950s.

Redefinition of Gender Roles

It is impossible to say for sure whether the changes that have taken place in women's perceptions of their roles can be attributed to the effects of the women's movement. But we do know that the outlook of many American women has converged with that of the movement's leaders. In 1963, Betty Friedan's *The Feminine Mystique* was published, ushering in the new women's liberation movement. Friedan described the discontent of middle-class, educated women, tracing their rising dissatisfaction at being trapped in roles such as housekeeping and child rearing that no longer fit with the expectations of modern life.

Three years later, Friedan and a group of friends and colleagues founded the National Organization for Women (NOW) (Evans, 1989). NOW demanded equal pay and equal employment opportunities for women, publicly supported day-care centers, and advocated an Equal Rights Amendment to the Constitution. Feminists questioned all aspects of the traditional view of women. They asked, "To what extent is gender destiny? If gender doesn't define destiny, what does it

Funds from Betty Friedan's The Feminine Mystique *helped to create NOW, the first feminist organization since the founding of the National Women's Party more than half a century earlier.*

mean, then, to be a woman? To be a man? And how can men and women relate to each other without the security of carefully delimited roles?" (Stovall, 1989, p. 145).

By the 1970s, feminist beliefs held by only a small minority of women a few years before began to attract millions of adherents. Women's changing beliefs about gender roles were not confined to a single region of the United States, to the college-educated, or to the middle class. One survey, which focused on changing attitudes among working-class women in northern industrial cities, found that by 1974 almost half of these women no longer supported the traditional gender-based division of labor in the family. By a large majority, the women surveyed endorsed the idea that husbands should share housework with their wives and that women should have the same right to jobs, promotions, and pay that men had. By the mid-1970s, the authors of another study observed that more than half of the working women in Detroit expressed attitudes very much like those espoused by the women's movement (Brown, 1976).

Self-Expression and Self-Fulfillment

Another change—more subtle, but fundamentally important in shaping expectations about marriage and family life—surfaced during the 1970s: people began to have rising expectations about the role of intimacy in satisfying personal needs. Contemporary social surveys showed a significant trend in American values toward an emphasis on personal growth and interpersonal sensitivity, even at work. Public-opinion analyst Daniel Yankelovich summarizes the changes:

> In the 1960s, work was rejected in favor of leisure because work was seen as representing the life of the father—nose to the grindstone, a suppression of self. Self-fulfillment was found in communing with nature, friendship, artistic expression—anything but work. . . . In the 1970s, however, baby boomers made a largely unnoticed discovery, which was that you could get a lot of self-actualizing through work. Work could satisfy expressive needs by offering challenges, new skills, new roles as well as meeting the needs of making a living. Success at work became the focus of energy for many baby boomers; it met both their practical and expressive goals. ("An Interview with . . . ," 1992, p. 13)

By the mid-1970s, as the authors of a study conducted by the Institute for Social Research (ISR) at the University of Michigan explain, the "new investment in self-expression and self-fulfillment," which had begun in the 1960s, was firmly entrenched in American life (Veroff, Douvan, & Kulka, 1981). These attitudes appeared most prominently among college graduates, but were hardly limited to them.

Increasingly, Americans regarded marriage and family life not as a package of predefined roles (such as the mother as homemaker, or the husband as provider) but an arrangement to satisfy the need for intimacy. Asked in ISR surveys what they considered "the nicest things about marriage," 56 percent of the respondents in 1978 as compared to 42 percent in 1957 emphasized the emotional support it offers (Veroff, Douvan, & Kulka, 1981).

The husband's position as head of the family was giving way to a new companionate ideal. The companionate father was more available to his children and a

more attentive partner to his wife. Sexual intimacy and emotional expressiveness in marriage became essential to marital satisfaction. Although the relationship between mother and children was tremendously important, women were cautioned not to let it weaken their relationship with their husbands or to smother their children with too much attention (Cancian, 1986).

Instead, women were encouraged to develop and express their own interests and desires and to have an egalitarian relationship with their husbands (Cancian, 1986). The meaning of marital love changed to include self-expression and individuality. If women were supposed to have goals and interests independent of the family, men had to learn to express their feelings and communicate. Family roles and gender roles were up for negotiation and renegotiation. Successful marital partners had "good" communication and confronted problems. Constructive conflict led to happier relationships. Although gender roles became more flexible, women still assumed the main responsibility for relationship success. In her study of blue-collar families, marriage counselor and researcher Lillian Rubin found "new dreams stirring. . . . Intimacy, companionship, sharing—these are the words working-class women speak to their men, words that turn *both* their worlds upside down" (Rubin, 1976, p. 120). This emphasis on interdependence and companionship continues today.

The New Diversity: 1980–the Present

In the 1980s and 1990s unprecedented numbers of individuals are diverging from the 1950s norm of two parents, three to four kids, mother as homemaker, father as breadwinner. While there have always been many families with different lifestyles, American society has been unwilling to acknowledge the validity of these various families. Today, however, it is impossible to ignore the trends that show more and more individuals choosing a life course that differs significantly from past generations. The key trends that are contributing to this new mosaic of American families are a changing family structure and an increasing appreciation for preserving the unique ethnic heritage of American families.

The Changing Structure of American Families

Later Marriages. There are fewer married couples under the age of 25 today than there were 10 years ago (U.S. Bureau of the Census, 1992). Reasons for this decline include a shrinking population in this age group, a growing number of people under age 25 living with parents, and postponement of marriage (Exter, 1990).

Because American couples are more reluctant to wed in early adulthood, the median age at first marriage for men has increased to age 26 and for women to age 24. Age at first marriage is expected to increase for both women and men throughout the 1990s. The decision to postpone marriage impacts on other decisions about family life. Women and men who marry later typically have fewer children and invest more time and money in educational attainment and job preparation. For women, a higher level of education increases the attractiveness of alternatives to the wife role and raises the financial costs of marriage (Teachman, Polonko, & Scanzoni, 1987). As a group, educated women of the 1990s prefer a more egalitarian division of household work and child care and enjoy more challenging job responsibilities, while earning higher incomes than the average employed woman.

Marital postponement for women is also linked to higher employment rates. In 1992, 65 percent of married women were employed. If we look at the proportion of employed women between the ages of 25 and 44, 75 percent are employed. The largest increases in employment have been among married women with young children (U.S. Bureau of Labor Statistics, 1992). Families much more often than in the past rely on the incomes of both parents.

Declining Number of Young Children. The number of married couples with children under age 18 has also declined. In the 1990s, women are postponing childbearing until later in their lives and are having fewer children (see Figure 1-1). Fertility rates have declined sharply from the peak of the baby boom in 1957, when the average American woman had 3.8 children.

Rise in the Divorce Rate. Though it has reached something of a plateau over the past few years, the United States divorce rate remains the highest in American history. For one-half to two-thirds of all couples who marry today, their union will not last until death do them part (see Chapter 14).

Rise in Single-Parent Families. The number of *single-parent families* has risen dramatically since 1980. Today, 21 percent of all families with children are single-parent families headed by women; 4 percent are headed by men. These figures represent a 36 percent increase since 1980. Based on patterns of the last dec-

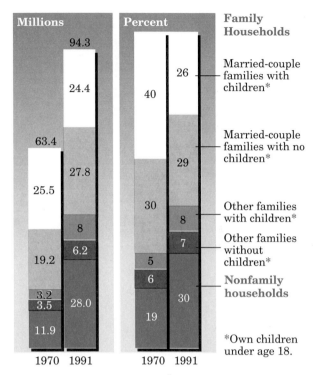

FIGURE 1-1
Household Composition: 1970 and 1991

Source: *Current Population Reports,* Special Studies, P-23, No. 177, February 1992.

ade, it is predicted that 6 out of 10 of today's children will live for some length of time with a single parent (Demo & Acock, 1991; U.S. Bureau of the Census, 1991). (Chapters 8 and 15 have additional information on single-parent families.)

Increase in Births to Unwed Mothers. Out-of-wedlock births are a major source of new families in the 1990s, with such births on the rise. Children in single-parent families are much more likely than children in two-parent families to be poor. Already 20 percent of all American children live in poverty. Studies indicate that such children are at higher risk of low educational achievement and high adult unemployment. (Chapter 8 contains further details.) (See Figure 1-2.)

Rise in Nonfamily Households. The average size of the American household has been shrinking for decades. There are currently 2.6 persons per household, compared to 2.8 persons in 1980. Because of widowhood, divorce, and the inclination of young people to stay single for several years before marriage, the num-

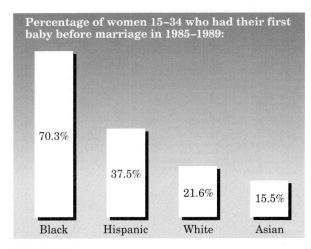

Percentage of women 15–34 who had their first baby before marriage in 1985–1989:

- Black: 70.3%
- Hispanic: 37.5%
- White: 21.6%
- Asian: 15.5%

FIGURE 1-2
Unwed Mothers by Race/Ethnic Group

Source: National Center for Health Statistics, U.S. Bureau of the Census, 1991.

ber of nonfamily households has grown to 29 million—24 percent of the total population. This figure represents a 29 percent increase since 1980 (Exter, 1990). People living by themselves make up 80 percent of nonfamily households. Most are women age 55 or older.

Obviously, the American family is no longer cut from a single template. Families of the 1990s exist in many different styles and forms, such as two-paycheck or *dual-earner families*, single-parent families, remarried or *stepfamilies* with children, and traditional families in which the husband is the provider and the wife the household manager. Most Americans are happy to live in a society that permits a wide range of options for marriage and family life. Some, however, worry about the changes that they see around them. They are unsure of how to interpret family change. Is it positive or negative? Will it benefit their children? Is it harmful to their communities? How will the school system respond?

A recent poll reflected this ambivalence. When asked whether the American family is better or worse off than it was 10 years ago, about 4 in 10 respondents replied that it is better off now, while 5 in 10 respondents were convinced that it is worse off (*Newsweek*, 1989). And, in the book, *Brave New Families*, Judith Stacey (1990) notes the "burdens of freedom . . . [where] parenting arrangements, sexuality, and the distribution of work, responsibility, and resources are all negotiable and constantly renegotiable" (p. 258).

Such freedom, Stacey contends, causes considerable conflict and insecurity.

For centuries family change has been greeted with uneasiness and worry, but the institution has survived with most functions intact. Whether the family is single-parent, dual-earner, cohabiting, or remarried, it typically provides for the basic needs of its members—food, shelter, clothing, and other economic necessities. The family still functions as a place where children are nurtured and socialized to be productive members of society who will work, support their communities, and produce future generations. Moreover, today's families continue to provide a rich heritage of racial, ethnic, and class perspectives on marriage and family living. And, finally, the family is still the place where members fulfill emotional and psychological needs through close intimate connections with others. Even the media seem reluctant to question basic family values. (See the "Changing Lifestyles" box.)

Much of what we believe about contemporary American families is based on the stereotypical middle-class family of the 1950s. Politicians, employers, and others who deal with families on a daily basis must learn to depend less on values and ideologies that contradict the practical reality of the lives of today's families. There are growing demands from the American public for policies and programs that attend to real family issues.

Parents with preschool children need reliable and affordable child care, while parents with school-aged children want well-managed after-school programs. Families in urban areas have different needs than families in suburbia or families in rural areas. The needs of a divorced parent with young children are not the same as those of a recently retired couple with grown children. A key cause of the current confusion about family needs is that:

> people grew up with one set of norms and values and now they are living another. . . . People believe in the family quite firmly, but they do not want, or they are not able, to go back to the old patterns of family life. (Suro, 1992, p. E1)

Ethnic Diversity

The current population of the United States is 250 million—a 10 percent increase since 1980. Of that population, 12 percent are black and 8 percent are Hispanic. By the year 2010, the Hispanic population is expected to become the largest minority ethnic group. Asian-Americans and other ethnic groups make up

CHANGING LIFESTYLES

TV Families: Attacking or Boosting Family Values?

In the following article, Richard Zoglin suggests that despite the widespread fear of the erosion of family values, and the appearance that television is contributing to this erosion, a survey of TV families reveals surprisingly strong support of traditional family values.

The huge success of *The Cosby Show*, which debuted in 1984, rejuvenated TV's interest in the traditional two-parent family. Today relatively stable, two-parent families make up the overwhelming majority on TV: nostalgic ones (*The Wonder Years, Brooklyn Bridge*), contemporary ones (*Home Improvement, Major Dad*), farcically expanded ones (*Step by Step*) and lovingly close-knit ones (*Life Goes On*). Even hip, teen-dominated shows like *The Fresh Prince of Bel-Air* and *Beverly Hills, 90210* have, at their center, strong families. The comparatively few single parents on TV nearly always have other caring adults around the house—a trio of fathers in *Full House,* a compassionate black housekeeper in *I'll Fly Away*—to reinforce the pro-family message.

Yet the past few years have also seen the emergence of a new sort of TV family: the grungy, dysfunctional clans of *Married . . . with Children, The Simpsons* and (to a lesser degree) *Roseanne*. All have, at one time or another, been attacked by the family-values police. *Married . . . with Children* was the chief target of Michigan housewife Terry Rakolta's 1989 campaign to clean up television. Roseanne Arnold has drawn fire for her crude behavior both on and off camera. President Bush told a group of religious broadcasters in January, "We need a nation closer to *The Waltons* than *The Simpsons*."

But what are these shows really attacking—the family, or simply TV's sentimentalized portrayal of it? For all the Bundys' biting sarcasm and Roseanne's mordant wisecracks, the one thing that is never questioned is the sanctity of the family. Roseanne's rebellious kids have something most of their real-life counterparts do not: two wise, empathetic, firmly in-control parents. Even the crass Bundys—TV's broadest caricature of a "bad" family—have a stubborn, low-down sense of togetherness.

The Simpsons too, despite its "eat my shorts" irrev-

erence, presents a cohesive family that could almost be a role model, even if its constituent parts are not. Homer may be an incompetent father and breadwinner (stuck home alone to take care of baby Maggie, he manages to lose the kid), but his heart is in the right place (he feels terrible about it). When Homer loses his job at the nuclear power plant, Marge tells the kids they will have to pitch in to help save money. Bart volunteers to skip baths and read his comic books in the store rather than buy them. Talk about family spirit.

Nor has TV embraced such perceived threats to traditional family values as teenage sex and homosexuality. Doogie Howser lost his virginity last fall, but only after so much sensitive deliberating that it seemed virtually a religious act. Brenda slept with her boyfriend Dylan on *Beverly Hills, 90210* but regretted it almost immediately. Roseanne's boss at the restaurant is gay, and C. J. (Amanda Donohoe) on *L.A. Law* is bisexual. But homosexual couples are kept almost entirely out of sight on series TV.

So are unwed mothers, though *Murphy Brown* had at least one important precursor. Molly Dodd, the neurotic single New Yorker played by Blair Brown in *The Days and Nights of Molly Dodd,* found herself pregnant two years ago, and the suspense revolved around which boyfriend was the father: the white bookstore owner or the black policeman (the law carried the day). Yet the revelation caused little stir: the show was tucked away on cable, and went off the air shortly thereafter. . . .

EXPLORATIONS *What is your impression of the way families are portrayed on television? Do you agree with Zoglin? Why or why not? What about contemporary movies?*

SOURCE: Excerpted from R. Zoglin (1992).

only 3 percent of the overall population; however, Asian-Americans are the fastest growing ethnic group in America (Allen & Turner, 1990) (see Figure 1-3). Not far into the twenty-first century, a third of the American population will consist of ethnic minorities.

Minority group families face special problems because of prejudice and discrimination, but each also identifies and uses its resources in ways that provide it with some resiliency. Some strengths of minority group families have been identified, including reliance on extended family members, openness to new ideas and situations, and maintenance of a number of strong ancestral cultural beliefs (Beck & Beck, 1989; Wilson, 1989). As a group, ethnic minority parents tend to socialize their children to be cooperative and interdependent with others rather than individualistic. Collectivism and group loyalty are emphasized (Chan, 1986; Green, Sack, & Pamburn, 1981). As Harrison and colleagues suggest: The rín in Spagein ütu

> Individuals are instructed to view themselves as an integral part of the totality of their family and the larger social structure and experience a social/psychological dependence on others. Cooperation, obligation, sharing, and reciprocity are essential elements of social interaction. These values sharply contrast with West-

FIGURE 1-3
Asian-Americans: Fastest Growing Ethnic Group
Source: W. O'Hare (1990a).

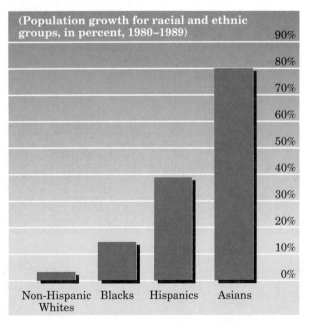

ern ideals of competition, autonomy, and self-reliance. (1990, p. 355)

Black Families. There are 31 million black Americans in the U.S. population, 96 percent of whom are descendants of slaves. The 1960s Civil Rights movement resulted in voting rights, new job opportunities, and an end to segregation laws but not to racial discrimination or the economic isolation of most black families. Some were able, however, to move upward and gain solid middle-class status (Coner-Edwards & Edwards, 1988).

Approximately 13 percent of black families have incomes of $50,000 and above, an increase of 5 percent since 1980. Another 12 percent earn $5,000 or less annually. In 1990, 60 percent of black families were dual-earners, while more than a third had a yearly income of between $25,000 and $50,000. Today's blacks represent fewer than 30 percent of poor Americans; 40 percent in highly urbanized areas (Waldrop, 1990). In the suburbs, the majority of black families (80 percent) have incomes above the poverty line. Like other families, black families stress educational attainment, the importance of religious values, cultural pride, and family togetherness (Granger, 1989; London & Devore, 1988). In a national study of three-generation black families, Bowman and Howard (1985) found the manner in which parents socialize their children is a critical factor in motivation for success. Largely due to parental modeling, children who achieve greater success are proud of their ethnicity, believe in self-development, are aware of racial discrimination, and exhibit fewer stereotypical beliefs about the characteristics and abilities of men and women.

Kinship networks, which sustained slave families, continue to provide support today (Staples, 1988). Studies show that black families frequently live in close proximity and expect and accept support from each other in times of need. Within the family, members interchange jobs, roles, and family functions (Hines & Boyd-Franklin, 1982). The tradition of helpful kin, however, is less strong in large cities than in smaller cities and rural areas (London & Devore, 1988). Divorced, widowed, and never-married individuals are more likely than married couples to rely on non-kin friends and neighbors.

During slavery, religion helped blacks survive their oppressive existence. Today, religion—in the form of the black church—remains a major source of comfort and socialization for the family. In times of need, ministers and parishioners are, in fact, more often sought

In black families kin have traditionally played strongly supportive roles, such as helping out with child-rearing tasks.

out than are mental health professionals (Hampson, Beavers, & Hulgus, 1990). Church members more often than social service and health care agencies assist in helping black families cope with health problems and discrimination-related stress (Dressler, 1985).

Because married women have historically shared joint responsibility with their husbands—and sometimes other kin—for providing economic support, black families are more egalitarian in their decision making than nonblack families (Taylor, Chatters, Tucker, & Lewis, 1990). Among black Americans, married people report higher well-being than do those without marital partners. But there has been an overall reduction in the expectation that all black women should marry and have children within a traditional family unit (Taylor et al., 1990).

Hispanic Families. Between 1980 and 1990, the Hispanic population increased by 34 percent, mainly because of new immigrants from Mexico and South America. Hispanics are a diverse group, composed of several Spanish-speaking ethnic populations, such as Mexicans, Puerto-Ricans, Cubans, and South Americans. These groups differ not only in their immigration histories—where they came from, when they arrived,

and the kind of reception they received—but in their reasons for immigrating and their social class backgrounds (Bean & Tienda, 1987).

Before the twentieth century, the small Hispanic population came from Mexico and other Latin-American countries. Then, between 1945 and 1965, hundreds of thousands of Hispanics—fueled by the needs, on the one hand, of American factories and agriculture for workers, and, on the other hand, by the poverty, civil wars, and political repression at home—flowed into the United States. Currently, most Hispanics live in Florida, Texas, New York, and California (Vega, 1990). Approximately 25 percent are poor. Although the media often portray Hispanics as impoverished, new arrivals, many have attained affluence since 1970, with upscale Hispanic households one of the nation's fastest growing groups (O'Hare, 1990b).

Largely because of their cultural heritage, including the tradition of male authority, Hispanic women are less likely to be employed, more likely to bear children at an early age and to have a greater number of children over their lifetimes than are other American women (Golding, 1990). Still, the demographic trends that have affected all American families have not bypassed the Hispanic population. The last few years have witnessed more employed women, fewer children born per family, a decrease in husband-wife families, and a rise in female-headed families and nonfamily households in the Hispanic population (Bean & Tienda, 1987). Despite the decrease in number of children per family, they are still a major focus of domestic life.

Typical working-class Hispanic families have a strong and extended kinship network. Kin form actively supportive bonds with each other and promote cooperation and family loyalty. The family protects its members, while requesting loyalty in return; thus, autonomy is less important to family members than is *dignidad* (dignity) (Hampson et al., 1990). Hispanic families usually value cooperativeness over competitiveness as a means of maintaining close family ties. This philosophy affects other family behavior like the greater tendency of Hispanics to discourage aggressive or disruptive behavior in their children (Delgado-Gaitan, 1987). Family values are supported and reinforced by the Catholic religion practiced by a majority of Hispanics.

Asian-American Families. Although we tend to think of Asian-Americans as one homogeneous population, they are actually 28 different ethnic and national groups: Japanese, Chinese, Laotians, Taiwanese, Vietnamese, Cambodians, Koreans, and so forth. Of these, each of nine groups contributes over 100,000 members to the Asian-American community (Worsnop, 1991). The preferred religions of Asian-Americans also represent diversity: Buddhism, Christianity, Hinduism, Shintoism, and Islam, to name a few. And each people has its own individual alphabet and language.

Chinese immigrants account for the largest percentage of the Asian-American population, followed by Filipinos and then Japanese. About 58 percent of Asian-Americans live in California, followed by New York, and then Hawaii. Because newly arrived Asian immigrants—like those of other nationalities—prefer to live near family, friends, and kin, they tend to cluster in particular areas within the United States (Coughlin, 1991).

Because the prevailing stereotype of Asian-Americans is one of educational excellence, prosperity, and economic success, they are increasingly viewed by other Americans as the "model minority." Yet many Asian immigrants earn low incomes and are hampered greatly by not speaking English when they first arrive in America. The primary reason for the prevalence of the "model minority" stereotype is the consistent reports that Asian-Americans excel in school and, as a group, have higher incomes than many other Americans. In addition, people are aware that the traditional Asian-American value system includes a belief that hard work, persistence, and educational achievement will eventually result in a better life. Prominent values also include a willingness to sacrifice immediate rewards in favor of long-term gains and a flexible attitude stressing change in order to survive in new situations (Worsnop, 1991).

Family support is often credited with being the key to the success of Asian-American children. Parents do encourage their children to study hard, but United States immigration policies attract some of the best and brightest Asians. The children of these well-educated new immigrants generally perform well academically. In addition, thousands of outstanding Asian students study at American universities; many of them remaining after graduation (Worsnop, 1991).

Asian-Americans themselves dislike being labeled the "model minority" (Kitano & Daniels, 1988). Although basically positive, they feel this distinction is used to set them apart from other Americans. As prominent educator, Chang-lin Tien, observes:

> Certain Asian Americans have done very well. But the stereotype of the model minority disadvantages some groups very deeply. The [newly arrived] immigrant groups, especially, have many problems. They have incredible family pressure to do well; they have language problems; they suffer from major cultural differences; they have to work to help out financially. But the feeling is that because Asians in general are doing so well, they don't need extra help. (in Worsnop, 1991, p. 954)

The Asian-American experience suggests that even a positive stereotype can be discriminatory if it is used to deny needed help, counsel students toward certain careers deemed suitable instead of other more personally appropriate careers, or avoid hiring people for jobs requiring creativity because of the inaccurate belief they possess only math and science skills.

Native Americans. The largest tribes, or nations, as Native Americans prefer to call them, are Cherokee, Navajo, Sioux, Chippewa/Aleut, and Eskimo. Most Native Americans live in the northwest and western United States. Native American life has been disrupted by government policy far more than any other population group. Beginning with the forced relocation of the Cherokee nation—the Trail of Tears—and continuing throughout the 1900s, Native Americans were moved from one parcel of land or reservation to another as the American west expanded and land was needed for settlers, mining, logging, or cattle grazing (Ortiz, 1984).

Once Native Americans were confined to reservations, the U.S. government created public schools which hastened the transmission of mainstream American values and norms to Native American children. Students were not allowed to speak their native languages in these schools, and the textbooks that were used up until recently included significant distortion and stereotyping of Native Americans (Schaefer, 1990). Some children were sent to federally funded boarding schools, further disrupting kinship ties.

The federal control of Native American education has also resulted in a system that is at odds with the socialization of children by their families. One study of the Sioux in South Dakota found that Sioux children were taught by their families to be independent and not to embarrass their peers. The school, on the other hand, looked for conformity and a nonquestioning attitude, and expected children to correct each other (Schaefer, 1990).

The Employment Assistance Program, instituted in 1962, lured almost one-quarter of the Native American population off the reservation and into big cities. Today, however, Native Americans are rediscovering their cultural heritage and some are returning to reservations, where many families still try to maintain some of the traditional practices. The "Diversity" box on the Snowbird Cherokee describes how one tribe strives to preserve their unique cultural identity.

PRIVATE LIVES, PUBLIC ISSUES

Besides the new appreciation for family diversity, another striking development in recent years is that the American family has become a source of intense political controversy. The question of which relationships should be considered a family even became an issue in the 1992 presidential campaign. The resolution of that question is not simply a matter of politics, for it ultimately affects eligibility for certain public family "benefits." With increasing frequency, the courts have begun to deal with questions that previously were considered private family matters.

Thus, in July, 1989, the court of appeals, New York State's highest court, agreed to a broader definition than the Census Bureau definition of a family: two or more persons related by birth, marriage, or adoption who reside in the same household. In a widely noted decision, the court held that the surviving member of a gay relationship retains the legal right to an apartment the couple had long shared in the same way that a surviving husband or wife would.

By declaring that a gay couple should be considered a family under New York City's rent control regulations, the appeals court took a critical step in redefining the family. Looking at the total relationship, it defined four standards for a family: (1) the exclusivity and longevity of the partner relationship; (2) the partner's level of emotional and financial commitment; (3) how the couple conduct their everyday lives and present themselves to kin, friends, colleagues, and the larger society; and (4) the extent to which the partners rely on each other for daily services.

To those arguing for a broader definition of marriage and family which does not favor male authority, heterosexuality, the traditional division of labor, or any specific parenting arrangement such as wife and husband, the decision represented a significant political victory. The court was acknowledging changes in social norms and practices. Explained Virginia Apuzzo, Governor Mario Cuomo's liaison to the gay community, "The nuclear family—the Ozzie and Harriet type—has changed dramatically, and people's minds are beginning to catch up to the reality" (*The New York Times*, July, 1989). Opponents and supporters of the decision predicted that increasing pressure to redefine social rules would add social legitimacy to nontraditional alternatives to marriage and the family.

The debate over the legal definition of the family illustrates the fundamentally different premises that people bring to discussions about public policy regarding marriage and family life. Behind the debate is this question: What is a proper balance between the claims of individuals to live as they choose and seek self-fulfillment and the claims of social or moral responsibility?

Those recognizing the diversity of family types—as New York's court of appeals did in its 1989 ruling—argue that public policy should not discriminate against nontraditional families and that individuals have a right to choose their living arrangements. But conservatives put their emphasis elsewhere. By insisting that the definition of marriage and family is a moral matter, conservatives stress social claims over individual preferences.

In the 1980s and the 1990s, conservatives have more

The Snowbird Cherokee: Preserving Family Traditions

The nuclear family form is now prevalent among Native Americans. However, strong ties based on traditional kin relationships provide support networks that help contemporary Native Americans deal with the high rates of poverty, teenage pregnancy, and alcoholism that plague reservation life. The Snowbird Cherokee is one tribe that has been particularly successful in retaining cultural traditions.

For at least 4,000 years, the Cherokee Indian nation has existed in the southern Appalachian mountains. The Snowbird Cherokee are a band of the larger nation which has its roots in North Carolina near the Great Smoky Mountains National Park. Unlike the more familiar Qualla Cherokee, who live near the park on one large reservation and have access to tourist dollars, the Snowbird are spread out over more than 10 tracts of reservation land, separated by white-owned lands and towns. Despite this geographic barrier, they are considered one of the most traditional Cherokee tribes, having

In striving to pass down to their children a sense of their tribal identity, Snowbird Cherokee adults continue to practice traditional craft skills.

in their population more full-blood Cherokee than other tribes (Neely, 1991).

Historically, the Snowbird Cherokee was a matrilineal society—rights and property descended from the mother. Today, women continue to have important roles both within the family and in the larger community. And the population strives to preserve its identity as a "real Indian" community by practicing important rituals like speaking the Cherokee language, participating in the yearly Trail of Tears singing, and always striving to reinforce their special identity as Native Americans within the surrounding white community. Other ways of asserting their heritage include passing down ancestral craft skills to the younger generation, having annual celebrations in which Cherokee dress is worn and native foods are prepared, and using native herbal medicinal cures.

Within families, as well as in the community, the Snowbird Cherokee teach a traditional value system, the "harmony ethic"—a communal, Native American identity based on being nonaggressive and noncompetitive. Individual success, the young are taught, is secondary to family and community success. When conflict arises in either of these two domains, it is typical to ask neutral third parties to intervene so that face-to-face hostility does not erupt. Communication and decisions based on a need to control others is especially frowned on. Generosity is a key component of the "harmony ethic," even when there are few resources to share (Neely, 1991).

It is important to emphasize the incredible diversity among Native American families based on their tribal heritage and their location on or off reservations. It is also important to note that the research on contemporary Native American families is very sparse. Despite the diversity, it is critical that family scholars examine Native American family patterns today as anthropologists have explored their kinship systems in the past.

EXPLORATIONS *Why do you suppose there has been a resurgence of interest among Native Americans, as well as other Americans, in exploring their family heritage? How does knowledge of historical events, rituals, and crafts contribute to our present quality of life?* ✳

actively defended traditional family values and established a political base for those values. In doing so, they bring a perspective to public debates that differs markedly from the liberal emphasis that tended to dominate discussions about marriage and the family in the 1960s and 1970s. Liberals typically stress freedom of choice and social equity. These values, conservatives believe, have encouraged casual attitudes toward marriage, divorce, and sexual behavior, and they also believe that recent court decisions have undermined the family's moral authority.

In the past, such disputes either did not arise or were settled within the home. Since the 1960s, family law—or "domestic relations" law, as it is sometimes called—has, in fact, expanded its jurisdiction beyond its traditional concerns with divorce and child custody. Judges are now often asked to rule in cases that involve such value-laden questions as whether a husband is "head" of the household, whether parents must be notified by the physician before their daughter can have an abortion, whether grandparents have custodial rights over grandchildren, and whether children can "divorce" their parents. Courts have overturned a number of religiously based laws—such as laws against abortion, sodomy, and cohabitation—and sanctioned many individual choices as valid decisions that deserve constitutional protection.

In the chapters that follow, we examine some contentious public issues that have risen around marriage and family arrangements and explore the different explanations for why certain behaviors are more common today. We also examine divergent suggestions about what should be done. Because research is often used by opposing sides to bolster various political positions relative to family life, we conclude this chapter with an examination of research methods.

RESEARCH ON MARRIAGE AND FAMILIES

Most of us were raised in families and have spent a good deal of time in and around different marriages and families. "In no other area," notes Arlene Skolnick (1973), "is there such a temptation to use one's own experience as the basis for wide-ranging generalizations" (p. 2). Yet, commonsense observation about marriage and family life is frequently distorted by our hopes and fears, and our ideas about the way things ought to be. Our memories of how our own family operated are, therefore, often inaccurate and selective.

One reason to study marriage and family life is to gain more reliable knowledge of how *most* people actually behave. Investigators of human behavior such as Murray Straus and Suzanne Steinmetz—pioneer researchers who conducted the first systematic studies of marital violence—have sometimes been questioned about their intrusion into private areas that, some critics believe, cannot be studied with any reliability. When investigations like those of Straus and Steinmetz produce evidence indicating that family behavior does not correspond closely to accepted ideas about what ought to be, such critics either deny the accuracy of the research findings or despair over declining moral standards.

The knowledge gained by careful studies of marital and family behavior serves various purposes—among them, satisfying our curiosity about how most people actually behave, rather than how we expect them to behave because of our own experience or cultural expectations. Other studies help to illuminate the ways in which marriage and family life have changed and the different forms these institutions take in today's society. Sometimes the results of family studies bring issues to public attention. For example, family research has revealed that sexual abuse can occur not only within lower-class families, but in all families regardless of their socioeconomic position.

Most research begins with an idea or hunch, gained from a researcher's reading of the literature, personal observations, and/or past research efforts. In most cases, researchers use theory to guide their work. A theory is an overall perspective or perceptual lens from which a researcher explains individual, couple, and family behavior.

Theory as a Foundation for Research

Theory has two distinct purposes. It guides the development of research questions and it provides a framework for explaining research results. Of the numerous theoretical frameworks used by marriage and family researchers, the most influential are (1) symbolic interaction theory, (2) social exchange theory, (3) general systems theory, and (4) gender theory. Any of the four could be used, for example, as a perspective from which to study why violence occurs in some dating relationships.

A researcher using *symbolic interaction theory* would assume that violence happens as a result of the interaction between dating partners. The way the couple communicates, disagrees, or shows care and intimacy must be at fault. The actual words used during conflict as well as the *process* of the couple's interaction, the sequence of behavior that leads to violence—what each partner says or does before and after an abusive episode—is very important. A symbolic interactionist might ask: Are there triggering events, discussions, or behaviors that seem to result in violent behavior? Does each partner participate equally in the verbal and physical abuse, or does one partner typically pursue while the other defends? When each partner gives his or her account of how the violence happens, are there discrepancies in the meanings attached to the actions and words of each? Do the partners define love and commitment differently? Do they define abuse and violence differently?

Another researcher may believe that continued involvement in a violent dating relationship is better explained by *social exchange theory*. This theory is based on the notion that individuals bring tangible (social status, educational achievement, income, physical attractiveness) and intangible (love, power, emotional expressiveness, charm) resources to relationships. These resources are then used to enhance the rewarding or satisfying aspects of the relationship and avoid its harmful or costly aspects.

In order to better understand dating violence, a social exchange theorist might ask: Is violence more likely to occur in relationships in which one partner has significantly more resources than the other? Does the more advantaged partner feel entitled to control most aspects of the relationship and, thus, use violence as a means of regaining and retaining power? Are individuals with greater psychological resources—self-esteem, sense of autonomy—less likely to continue dating a partner who displays violent tendencies? Do violent partners lack the negotiation skills required to ask for what they need in a nonthreatening manner? Do individuals with fewer coping skills resort to violence to reduce stress? These questions and others like them reflect an interest in how personal resources affect interaction patterns that lead to violence.

A third way to frame the research problem is from the perspective of *general systems theory*. This theory proposes that a couple, family, or even the larger society, construct a complex system of agreed-upon beliefs and patterns of behavior that organize and maintain it. A couple or family develop norms, beliefs, rules, and roles that organize daily interaction, providing a comforting balance or routine. The problem is that, because of the system's tendency to protect these established routines, change can be difficult. A systems

theorist would view dating violence as an act that is produced by couple interaction—the patterned way in which partners behave toward each other. Over time, violence has likely become a habitual way of resolving conflict. Because habits are difficult to break, alternative nonviolent ways of resolving conflict may threaten the balance of the relationship (the system).

Questions a systems theorist might ask include: How often does violence occur in the relationship and is there a discernable pattern of when and where it happens? Can the partners describe the conditions under which violence is more likely to occur and how a violent episode unfolds from beginning to end? After incidents of violence, is the responsible partner forgiven (thus reinforcing the likelihood that future violence will occur)? Does the couple have rules about the use of violence in the relationship; for example, violence is appropriate if certain relationship rules are violated—not being ready for a date when the partner arrives, being seen talking to another person in a seemingly intimate way, questioning the partner's decisions, failing to show appropriate concern or respect for the partner's feelings? Has the battered partner ever tried to stop the violence or leave the relationship? What happened?

Finally, if a researcher is convinced that it is the structure of society itself that perpetuates dating violence, she or he might choose *gender theory* to frame the research. Gender theory assumes that societal norms promote gender inequity by socializing members to believe that men should have greater power and authority in all social interactions than women. In relationships, then, the male would have the right to make decisions and in most ways dominate the interaction. Because violence is considered a male prerogative, in cases where a man's right to authority is challenged, family members, the police, and social service agencies would be slow to respond to requests for help. These traditional avenues of support might, in fact, be closed off and society members would tend to blame the battered partner for her predicament, even suggesting that what occurs within the privacy of a relationship is not the business of society.

The following questions could be used to explore dating violence from the framework of gender theory. Was physical abuse considered normal behavior in the families of the dating partners? Did either partner ever witness his or her father use violence against his or her mother? Did the father or mother ever attempt to explain the violence as something that was deserved, as a disciplinary action, or as a husband's right? In their own relationship, does either partner believe that the man is the rightful leader and decision maker? Do the roles the partners take in the relationship reflect the belief that the man should be dominant and the woman submissive? Are there certain roles or relationship rules that, if violated, justify violence?

These four theories, along with *developmental theory,* which assumes that the needs and goals of individuals and families change across the life cycle (see Chapter 7 for a thorough discussion), are regularly engaged by family researchers. All four theoretical frameworks have been used for decades to explain individual and family behavior, and each has enthusiastic proponents and large bodies of research attesting to their credibility and validity. Nevertheless, there are disadvantages to each. Symbolic interaction theory is criticized for giving too much credit to individuals, couples, and families for constructing their own norms and belief systems while ignoring how the larger social structure—economic, political, and educational institutions—influences these seemingly personal choices. Social exchange theory is derided for assuming that people can rationally assess the costs and benefits of their behavior and calculate how best to use personal resources to gain certain advantages or avoid particular costs. The criticism of general systems theory is that, because it was developed and used first by counselors and therapists, it explains dysfunctional relationships better than successful, satisfying relationships. And, finally, gender theory is denounced for concentrating too much on issues of power and dominance while ignoring the caring, loving, and cooperative aspects of interaction between relational partners.

In sum, theory directs the development of research ideas or hunches into research questions which, then, lead to the selection of research methods.

Methods of Implementing Research

The purpose of the research cited in this book is to provide accurate descriptive and explanatory accounts of what romantic, marital, and family relationships are like. Family researchers confine their investigations to matters that can be tested by self-report, observation, or experimentation. To overcome the obstacles to seeing social reality objectively and hence understanding it better, family scientists use various research methods, or systematic strategies for conducting research and generating data. The most common methods are (1) surveys, (2) qualitative research, (3) secondary analysis, and (4) triangulation.

Survey Research

Most research reported in major journals read by family studies professionals is *survey research.* In survey research, individuals from a carefully selected sample are typically asked to respond to a series of questions in which the wording and sequencing of questions are exactly alike for each respondent. Surveys may consist of questionnaires mailed to the homes or offices of respondents, structured interviews, or telephone interviews. Mailed surveys are completed by the respondent, who usually reads the questions and then either writes in or circles numbers that represent his or her responses. Telephone and structured interviews follow the same format as the mailed questionnaire, in that the survey has a formal format. In most cases, the interviewer reads the question to the research participant and then writes in or circles the responses on a carefully constructed questionnaire. Follow-up questions may be asked, but these questions, too, are very precisely worded so that they are the same for each respondent. The validity of survey research rests on the mathematically provable proposition that we can make accurate generalizations and draw valid conclusions about an entire population by sampling only a portion of it. Surveys are most often used when researchers want answers to specific questions, especially about behavior or attitudes that are difficult or costly to observe directly.

Surveys can be used in explanatory research where the researcher's purpose is to describe the correlation or causal connection between two or more variables (a *variable* is something whose value varies from case to case). The researcher might want to know, for example, if there is a correlation between being in an abusive dating relationship and having grown up in a family in which violence regularly occurred. Or, the researcher might want to know if several variables collectively explain violent dating behavior—childhood experiences of family violence, level of self-esteem, need for control, acceptance of violence as normal dating behavior, and so forth. Surveys are also used in descriptive research, where the researcher wants to identify people's attitudes, beliefs, or behavior, or ask respondents to recall what they have done under certain circumstances.

After identifying the problem to be investigated, the next steps in designing a survey are to define the population to be studied, and to select a representative sample of its members. Besides the advantage of their uniformity, surveys gather large chunks of data relatively easily and efficiently, but they have several limitations. The basic assumption that each question will be understood in the same way by each respondent may not be completely accurate. People also may hide from others or deny even to themselves painful information such as their own drug addiction or alcoholism. And it's not uncommon for survey researchers to use samples that are not randomly selected and then to treat the data as if they were. They run statistics that rely on random selection, draw conclusions, and generalize to the larger population. A major concern with mailed questionnaires is *response rate*—the percent of people receiving the survey who actually complete and return it. To get a high response rate for a survey it's necessary to send reminder letters or make reminder phone calls, design the survey so that it is simple to answer and easy to return (provide postage), and convince potential respondents that their responses are needed and valued.

Qualitative Research

When researchers want to understand the actual dynamics of human relationships—how people interact with each other in certain life situations, such as when they fall in love, argue, or break up—surveys are less useful than is *qualitative research*—unstructured interviews, case studies, or participant observation studies. Qualitative research is a method of data collection and analysis that relies on getting to know research participants by becoming actively involved in their lives and discovering their values, rituals, beliefs, and emotions.

In *unstructured interviews* respondents (sometimes called informants) are asked questions to elicit certain types of information; but the exact questions, their sequence, and sometimes even their wording may vary from person to person. The idea is for the interviewer to become aware of each informant's unique ways of speaking about and perceiving his or her life circumstances. These perceptions are then identified by the researcher and incorporated into the study findings. Interviewers can probe for in-depth information and raise and follow new leads as they appear during the interview.

The primary drawback of unstructured interviews is that interviewers must be highly skilled, aware especially of how their words and actions may interfere with obtaining valid and reliable information. For example, interviewers may have unconscious prejudices or misconceptions that may bias their choice of questions or interpretations of responses. The credibility of

qualitative research, like that of survey research, depends on how carefully research procedures are carried out. High standards of data collection and analysis must be incorporated into the study design. Data collected in this manner are useful for exploratory and explanatory research that do not rely on formal hypothesis testing as a basis for making generalizations about larger populations.

Clinical case studies are in-depth examinations of persons with specific problems who seek advice from psychologists, psychiatrists, social workers, marriage counselors, family therapists, or other helping professionals. In most cases, people are interviewed individually. Family therapists, however, may observe entire families—sometimes including relatives and other household members—as a unit, which permits them to observe how members interact with each other. The advantage of case studies is their in-depth revelation of marital and family life.

The main shortcoming is that individuals who seek professional help are nonrepresentative of the larger population, so it is impossible to generalize. For example, they may have more emotional and marital problems or be under greater stress. For this reason, conclusions based on clinical case studies need to be carefully qualified.

In *participant observation* studies the researcher observes people in their own surroundings. The researcher might actually live in a particular community under study or with a family or small group of families for several weeks, months, or even years. During this time, the investigator usually makes audiotapes or videotapes of some family interactions, arranges lengthy interviews with family members, and writes extensive field notes while observing the family group in various surroundings. From these tapes and notes, the researcher then attempts to construct hypotheses or make generalizations about typical family behavior in that particular setting.

The major problem with participant observation is that it is impossible for the observer to avoid being subjective, and this subjectivity may cause one researcher to see certain family behavioral patterns, while another sees entirely different aspects. In addition, it is often difficult to persuade families to participate in such an in-depth study. The question is sometimes asked: Are families who agree to such close scrutiny different from families who refuse? Furthermore, observational research is very time-consuming, and thus can be prohibitively expensive without a grant or other funding.

Experimental Research

When it involves experiments, the work of social scientists most closely resembles that of natural scientists, but few studies in marriage and the family rely on this research method. *Experimental research* is explanatory in that it shows how two or more variables affect other variables. It seeks, in other words, a cause-and-effect relationship among variables. Generally, experimental research begins with a specific hypothesis, or hunch (based on extensive reading of other studies in the field), about the connection between certain variables. The researcher's purpose is to determine whether his or her hypothesis is accurate.

Because experimental research requires maintaining a tight control over the variables under study, experiments are normally conducted in a setting that can be carefully monitored—a room with a one-way mirror, a child development laboratory—rather than in the field. Like other research methods, experimental research has its disadvantages. For example, in a laboratory, there is always the danger that participants in the study will modify their behavior because they are under observation or because they are being asked to respond in unfamiliar surroundings rather than in the comfort and security of their own homes. In some instances the researcher may request, for example, that a marital couple role play a situation—a disagreement over how the family income should be spent. If the situation unintentionally differs from the way the couple conducts their real-life conflicts over this issue, the study results may be contaminated.

Secondary Analysis

Researchers who study marriage and family life often rely on *secondary analysis* of data already collected by others. The most frequently used primary, or original, data of this sort are generated by government agencies, such as the U.S. Bureau of the Census, the National Office of Vital Statistics, and the Justice Department.

The chief advantage of relying on such data is that it frees the researcher from the arduous task and tremendous expense of collecting such information from thousands or millions of individuals. Thus, studies relying on secondary data make possible certain kinds of research that would otherwise be impossible. Moreover, since reports from the Bureau of the Census and other government sources are usually comprehensive and reliable, they tend to offer the best and most readily available data on broad developments in marriage and family life.

One problem with secondary analysis is that the researcher is at the mercy of the agency that collected the data. If the data were gathered systematically, thereby encouraging unbiased responses, and if no errors contaminated the data, they constitute an invaluable resource. But sometimes official data are incomplete, or unacknowledged biases appear in the responses. For example, while the Bureau of the Census gathers a wide range of data on divorce, not every state reports complete information to the federal government about the number and characteristics of divorces granted. Researchers who use those data have to take this shortcoming into account.

Triangulation

Some studies employ a *triangulation* of research methods, drawing upon several different research techniques to study the same problem using the same sample. For example, Judith Stacey's study (1990) of working-class families in Silicon Valley combined several different methods. It began as a qualitative study based on intensive, unstructured interviews with 150 electronics production workers and their spouses or intimate partners. The interviews were supplemented by *oral histories*—a person's own account or story of past experiences or particular life situations she or he has lived through—from older citizens who had lived in the area since the 1950s. Then, her research evolved into a case study focusing on several family networks. Most important to Stacey at this stage were key informants whom she interviewed in depth. Stacey supple-

Much of the data researchers rely on to describe the American family is gathered by the U.S. Bureau of the Census.

mented their detailed accounts of family interaction patterns with the information derived by observing informants and their coworkers in their work settings.

Today, there is active interest in studying marriage and family. Besides the studies conducted by family scientists, sociologists, and psychologists, using the various methods described, historians, family therapists, and legal experts are examining these institutions with new interest. In the chapters that follow, we draw on a wide range of studies that offer a basically accurate view of marriage and family life at the end of the twentieth century.

SUMMARY POINTS

■ Five hundred years ago, each of the more than 240 Native American nations operated within its own political structure, providing a unique language and culture for its children. Most tribes were patrilineal and monogamous. Children were socialized by rewards and praise. Rituals were critical markers in their lives.

■ Probably the best description of colonial American families is that each was a self-sufficient "little commonwealth." Family members took care of their own family needs and those of the larger community. People married, formed families more out of a sense of moral obligation and duty than because of romantic love or the need for intimacy. All members of the family, including children, worked at home.

■ In the nineteenth century, industrialization and the growth of towns and cities created work separate from the home, with men becoming the wage-earners and women becoming homemakers. Although marriage was based on love, intimacy and sexual satisfaction were not viewed as essential to marital happiness. The mother-child bond was idealized as the most important family relationship.

■ Despite the hardships of slavery, blacks from the 1700s to the present managed to marry, have children, raise children in two-parent families that valued monogamy and stability, create kinship networks, and pass down African-American culture by various means, such as teaching ancestral crafts, developing strong religious ties, and keeping an oral history of the family.

■ Despite the limitations slavery placed on their power and autonomy, black fathers provided for their families in whatever ways they could. Husbands and wives worked in the fields or in their owner's household. Wives and husbands shared a rough domestic equality. After their emancipation, many slaves wandered through the south, looking for family members they had been forcibly separated from during slavery.

■ Between 1820 and 1920, 38 million immigrants poured into the United States, mostly from Europe. Immigrant families relied on kin and friend networks for support during resettlement and taught their children to value family and kin connections above individual success.

■ The early 1900s marked the beginning of the modern era of the family. Transformations in the American way of life led to the rise of the companionate marriage, defined by emotional and sexual intimacy and shared roles.

■ Despite the so-called emergence of the new woman in the 1920s, traditional gender roles remained in place, but as sex became more significant, the marital relationship began to replace the mother-child relationship as the most important familial bond, with men as breadwinners and women as homemakers. Both marital partners were expected to have intimacy needs, but gender roles remained sharply divided, even in the aftermath of World War II.

■ During the 1950s, family life deviated from long-term trends such as rising divorce rates and lower fertility patterns. Sixty percent of American families earned middle-class wages and many took pride in having a single wage-earner, the husband. Many families also moved to the suburbs.

■ The 1960s saw a return to the pre-1950s family demographic trends and a search for the "self" through education and self-improvement. New family forms like cohabitation, communal living, dual-earner families, and single-parent families were seen by some as evidence that the family could be "falling apart." Increasing attention was focused on the harsher realities of family life, once considered "family secrets"—abortion, child abuse, incest. The second sexual revolution made women question their traditional roles in marriage, family, and society.

■ During the 1970s, increasing numbers of women sought greater educational and employment opportunities. The movement away from traditional gender roles and toward equal opportunity in all facets of work and family life was in full swing. Within the institutions of marriage and the family, there was a growing emphasis on personal growth and interpersonal intimacy.

■ Throughout the 1980s and into the 1990s there is evidence that the family trends that began in the 1970s seem to have continued—postponement of marriage, smaller family size, more single-parent families, larger numbers of employed women, increased pressure for changes in gender roles, and concern for acknowledging the diversity of family life. The tougher economic times of the 1990s and the growing number of American children living in poverty have also led to a focus on how to implement policies that will help families.

■ Contemporary American families have diverse forms, including two-parent families, single-parent families, and gay and lesbian families.

■ Black, Hispanic, Asian-American, and Native American families each have their own unique histories of discrimination and tactics of survival.

■ As the family is now more often the subject of public debate and political controversy, the courts are increasingly being asked to resolve family issues.

■ Family researchers rely on (1) surveys, (2) qualitative research, (3) experiments, (4) secondary analysis, and (5) triangulation. Surveys gather data from small, but representative samples of the population and generalize from them to the larger population. Mail questionnaires, structured interviews, and telephone interviews are examples of surveys. Qualitative research relies on getting to know research participants well by becoming actively involved in their lives and discovering their values, rituals, beliefs, and emotions. Clinical case studies and participant observations are ex-

amples of qualitative research. Experimental studies attempt to show how two or more variables affect each other. Experiments are usually conducted in a carefully monitored setting. Secondary analysis refers to research based on data that have been collected by others. Triangulation refers to use of several different research methods to study a particular problem.

KEY TERMS

Family	General systems theory
Nuclear family	Gender theory
Tribe	Developmental theory
Patrilineal	Survey research
Matrilineal	Variable
Monogamy	Response rate
Cultural pluralism	Qualitative research
Companionate family	Unstructured interviews
Cult of domesticity	Clinical case study
Single-parent family	Participant observation
Dual-earner family	Experimental research
Stepfamily	Secondary analysis
Symbolic interaction theory	Triangulation
Social exchange theory	Oral histories

REVIEW QUESTIONS

1. Describe colonial American family life.

2. How have mainstream perceptions of marriage and family life changed since the colonial era?

3. Compare and contrast the Americanization experiences of blacks, Hispanics, and Asians.

4. What changes do you think will occur in romantic relationships and in marriage and family life by the year 2010?

5. What public policy issues will be important in the next decade? Why?

6. If you were planning a research project on some facet of intimate relationships, marriage, or family life what method of research would you probably rely on? Why?

2

Illustration by Sandra Filippucci

Gender Roles and Changing Relationships

How many times have you been asked to "Check one: _____Male; _____Female"? In our society, as in most others, it is assumed that your answer to this question says a lot about who you are and how you behave. And it is assumed that there are obvious distinctions between males and females based upon anatomical, chromosomal, hormonal, and reproductive features. The closer we look at this seemingly simple biological division of the sexes, however, the more complicated it becomes.

Just how do females and males differ, and what is the social significance of those differences? These are age-old questions with a peculiarly contemporary significance. For nothing has influenced more changes in relationships and family life than redefined assumptions about the meaning of gender and the division of roles and responsibilities between the sexes. This chapter will examine these questions. But first let us define what gender is and how it differs from one's sex.

DEFINING GENDER

Though the terms sex and gender are sometimes used interchangeably, most scholars now distinguish between the two by explaining that *sex* refers to the biological or physiological characteristics—hormonal and anatomical—unique to being either male or female. Sex is initially decided on the basis of chromosomes. XX individuals are female, XY are male. In rare cases where the chromosomal evidence is neither clearly XX nor XY, a variety of medical methods are used to ensure appropriate classification. All individuals produce both "male" (androgenic) and "female" (estrogenic) hormones. Mature males usually produce more androgens than estrogens, while mature females produce more estrogens than androgens. But both hor-

33

monal types strongly influence bodily functions in all people, regardless of sex (Singleton, 1986).

Gender describes the psychological, sociological, and cultural aspects of being male or female. Constructing a *gender identity* allows us to interpret the meaning of our sex—what it signifies to be female or male in our particular society. All kinds of objects and behaviors take on gendered meanings, from hair barrettes (girls only) to toy trucks (boys only) to colors (pink is for girls; blue is for boys).

Barbara Lloyd (1989), author of *Sex and Gender* and *Gender Identities and Education*, provides an example of the construction of gender identity in process at the age of 4:

> Jonathan selects a pink-orange nylon nightie from the dressing-up rack and succeeds, after considerable difficulty, in getting it on. He then struggles to put a small white satin tutu on top of it. Neither of the other children nor the teacher pay attention. Eventually a girl in the class comes up and says: "It's not for you, Jonathan." Jonathan looks bemused but carries on trying to squeeze himself into the tutu. After concerted effort and failure, he takes the tutu to the teacher and asks her to help him. She exclaims: "Jonathan, this is the smallest dress we have, you won't fit into it. Let's go and look for something else." Jonathan chooses a skirt and the teacher helps him put it on. While saying "that's nice," she encourages him to put on a waistcoat from a man's three-piece suit. (p. 61)

Each person in Lloyd's story has a set of expectations about the construction of a male gender identity. To the girl, Jonathan's behavior violates a rule of gender identity establishing some types of clothing as appropriate for females only. The teacher is less restrictive in her views. She allows Jonathan to wear female clothing but urges him to put on the waistcoat because she thinks it is more appropriate to his sex. "This brief episode is silent on Jonathan's beliefs about his gender identity. He may be unaware of the gender marking of the nightie and tutu, but this is unlikely given his bemused air when tackled by a classmate. He may knowingly be violating a rule against cross dressing" (p. 61). Learning to behave in accordance with one's gender identity is a lifelong process (Bleier, 1988).

Traditional Gender Roles

Gender roles are what is said or done to indicate to others, and to oneself, one's maleness or femaleness.

They are the outward expression of one's gender identity. Gender roles are learned and consist of feminine or masculine behaviors that members of a society are encouraged to act out, such as husband and wife, father or mother. Such roles structure our choices and guide our behavior in ways that are considered appropriate for our gender. For example, mothers and fathers have socially defined sets of expectations or norms for what is permissible and usual parental behavior for their sex. Traditionally, mothers have changed diapers, bathed and fed babies, and acted as children's primary caregivers and nurturers, while fathers have provided economically for children. Fathers occasionally held babies, but were expected to be more comfortable engaging in robust and playful activities with their children (Franklin, 1988).

Gender roles are normally so much a taken-for-granted feature of our culture that many people hardly notice them. One way of calling attention to conventional assumptions about masculinity and femininity is to do a role reversal, and to notice how bizarre the result is. Imagine a society, for example, in which all the traits commonly attributed to men are assigned to women, and vice versa. Feature articles in men's magazines in this society offer diet, exercise, and beauty tips for anxious men who are told that if they don't stay fit and attractive they may lose their partners. The same magazines offer hints to help the devoted husband use his "masculine touch" to transform the house into a home; his "male intuition" to guide him toward a better understanding of relationship issues; and his "paternal instinct" to facilitate the rearing of his children. The "good" husband is expected to take care of the details of household management and child care so that his wife is free to concentrate on more important things, like her career.

Powerful women executives sit around conference tables making business decisions and joking about their gossiping, overly emotional husbands whose favorite pastime is shopping. Women hardhats and fighter pilots laugh at men's attempts to enter these traditionally female occupations. As everyone knows, men break down under stress, and they are not dependable. Aside from that, the presence of men on the job would cramp the style of the females who commonly utter a stream of obscenities and tell jokes to "let off steam," and their favorite on-the-job entertainment is "hitting on" attractive males who walk past. Even if the men who are the object of that attention are a little embarrassed and sometimes get upset, no harm is done, because—as all the women know—men are basically vain and enjoy the attention.

If such a scenario seems both improbable and unnatural, it is because we are so accustomed to a script that assigns certain traits to males and others to females. It has often been assumed that "it's only natural" for men to be aggressive and women submissive. It is commonly believed by both sexes that women fulfill their "maternal instincts" by caring for children. And many men still believe that they must protect the "weaker sex" and that women's place is in the home. Meanwhile, it has been traditional for men to take societal positions of power and privilege and enter into marriages in which women are the junior partners. Thus, gender role differences typically result in greater power and authority for men both inside and outside the family.

Changing Gender Roles

Expectations about proper gender role behavior, however, are not fixed. Gender role expectations have been observed to change across time within a culture and also to vary across societies. Each society creates its own distinctive rules or norms and through the process of socialization attempts to ensure that these preferred ways of behaving continue across generations (Peplau, 1983).

In modern society it is more difficult than in the past to define certain roles as clearly feminine or masculine. Unlike biological sex, which is either male or female, gender is defined by characteristics and behaviors that often overlap—blur into each other. Today, people are more likely to view a wider range of behaviors as proper, to some extent, for *most* individuals regardless of their biological sex. This is especially true of middle-class families and for individuals living in urban rather than rural areas of the country (Weitzman, 1984).

Sandra Bem (1975) was one of the first scholars to challenge the cultural belief that most females are generally submissive, dependent, and nurturant—behaviors traditionally associated with being feminine—while most males are generally dominant, independent, and ambitious—behaviors traditionally associated with being masculine. Bem and other researchers coined the word *androgynous* to describe individuals who assumed less rigid gender roles.

Some studies have found that androgynous males and females are more flexible in their role behavior—that they are better able to change their behavior and consequently are better prepared to cope with the ups and downs of daily life in our changing society (Harnett & Bradley, 1986; Lindsey, 1990). Sociologist Susan Losh-Hesselbart (1987) contends that in today's society, adults with adaptable, flexible gender roles experience better mental health. She maintains that having a rigid gender role orientation can be mentally and physically burdensome to oneself as well as to one's family. Gender role flexibility is often the key to the successful negotiation of family and work responsibilities and, therefore, to the greater marital satisfaction of both partners.

Gender Role Stereotypes

Widely shared societal beliefs about how males and females should behave, *gender role stereotypes*, are

1992 Cathy Guisewite. Reprinted with permission of Universal Press Syndicate. All rights reserved.

based on observations of the way people interact in everyday life. When people repeatedly observe women and men enacting different roles, they are likely to believe that these different roles are typical. Furthermore, they may assume that women and men are characterized by the personality traits associated with those roles. For example, regardless of gender, a homemaker is generally seen to possess personality characteristics of a typical female, while a bank officer is seen to possess characteristics of a typical male. Table 2-1 lists male and female stereotypes. Stereotypes are very powerful in that no area of life seems untouched by them. Their influence is felt by most people regardless of gender, race, social class, education level, or marital status.

According to Gallup pollsters Linda DeStefano and Diane Colasanto (1990) the stereotypes shown in Table 2-1 are still relevant today, though there is evidence of some change. When women and men were read a list of 31 personality traits and asked to identify which characteristics they thought were more generally true of men and which were more generally true of women, they responded along the lines of traditional gender role stereotypes. Thus, both sexes more often characterized women as emotional, talkative, sensitive, and affectionate and men as aggressive, strong, proud, and disorganized. The personality traits male and female

TABLE 2-1
Masculine and Feminine Stereotypes

Psychologist Ellen Piel Cook (1985) contends that the following stereotypes are characteristically associated with being masculine or feminine:

> Men (masculinity)—aggressive, independent, unemotional, objective, dominant, competitive, logical/rational, adventurous, decisive, self-confident, ambitious, wordly, act as a leader, assertive, analytical, strong, sexual, knowledgeable, physical, successful, good in mathematics and science, and the reverse of the feminine characteristics listed below.
>
> Women (feminine)—emotional, sensitive, expressive, aware of others' feelings, tactful, gentle, security-oriented, quiet, nurturing, tender, cooperative, interested in pleasing others, interdependent, sympathetic, helpful, warm, interested in personal appearance and beauty in general, intuitive, focused on home and family, sensual, good in art and literature, and the reverse of the masculine characteristics above. (p. 4)

SOURCE: E. P. Cook (1985).

respondents were least willing to ascribe to either sex were smart, honest, happy, and responsible. Both women and men used more positive characteristics such as confident to describe themselves and attributed the more negative characteristics such as moody to the other sex. Among other things, the women and men polled disagreed with each other as to which sex was more patient, creative, levelheaded, logical, funny, and strong. Women more often than men used the words demanding and manipulating to describe male characteristics. Men (49 percent), more than women (40 percent), strongly believed that differences in personality characteristics were due to the biological differences between women and men. Women (44 percent) were more likely than men (35 percent) to say that socialization was more responsible for these characteristic differences (DeStefano & Colasanto, 1990).

Other research shows that race is another factor in gender stereotyping. Black families tend to be less gender role stereotypical than other American families. In general, white males and females are more likely than are blacks to view women as passive, emotional, and overly concerned with physical appearance. Whites are also more disposed than are black Americans to stereotype men as emotionally inexpressive, competitive, independent, and status conscious. In addition, gender stereotypes held by black females and males are more similar to each other in terms of expressiveness and competence than are gender stereotypes held by white females and males (Cazenave, 1984; Del Boca & Ashmore, 1980; Lewis & Deaux, 1983). The greater similarity in gender stereotypes between women and men most likely stems from the more *egalitarian* marital relationships that black partners forge in order to better provide for their families.

The ideal of the husband/father being the sole provider for the family has not been attainable by most blacks and Hispanics. Racial and ethnic discrimination has prevented many of the men in such families from earning a family wage and forced their marital partners into the work force (Zinn, 1993). Though black, Hispanic, and Asian-American men may lose some power in the family as women gain financial independence, the trade-off is that the extra wages mean a significant gain in their level of living.

Stereotypes are said to be negative if they are generally untrue and are harmful to others. Sociologist Linda Lindsey gives an example of a negative gender role stereotype in her book, *Gender Roles.* Says Lindsey (1990), "If we stereotype women as passive, an individual woman may be passed over for a job requiring leadership ability. Her own individual ability in terms of job leadership may not even be considered due to the stereotype given to her gender as a whole" (p. 37). In contrast, Lindsey contends that men who request custody of their children during divorce proceedings often find their petitions denied because of the pervasive gender role stereotype that women are instinctively better qualified to parent children.

Other negative gender role stereotypes characterize Hispanic families as *patriarchal* (ruled by the father), while characterizing black families as *matriarchal* (ruled by the mother). These supposedly opposite family arrangements are frequently labeled dysfunctional or pathological and "blamed for the failure of [certain ethnic groups] to rise to a higher socioeconomic level. In other words, black and Chicano families have been blamed for the effect of racial discrimination" (Bridenthal, 1981, p. 85). These and other data lead sociologist Susan Losh-Hesselbart (1987) to conclude that both women and men, regardless of race or class, find negative gender role stereotypes stressful and damaging to their emotional and physical health. See the "Diversity" box for an example of a cross-cultural negative stereotype.

Gender Role Attitudes and Conflicts

The term *gender role attitude* describes the degree to which a person agrees with or accepts the current societal expectations that some individual characteristics and gender role behaviors are exclusively masculine and others exclusively feminine. For instance, how much a person agrees with such norms as mothers' parenting styles are superior to fathers', men are more rational decision makers than women, or women are by nature passive and dependent while men are naturally ambitious and competitive.

When an individual's internal values and beliefs about gender roles and their external behaviors are inconsistent with current societal expectations, then that individual usually feels *gender role conflict*. The conflict is a result of going against current societal beliefs and feeling the pressure against nonconformity. Pressure may range from harsh actions such as "ostracism and shunning, to the subtle disapproval of a raised eyebrow, a warning of 'what people might say,' and the training and education (socialization) of individuals to believe in the norms of their society and identify with them" (Epstein, 1988, p. 101).

Black males are said to experience gender role conflict to the extent that they accept cultural gender roles based on the assumption that the major family responsibility for men centers on their employment and provider status (Cazenave, 1984). Among black men unemployment rates are high and the gap between their earnings and those of white men has continued to increase since the early 1970s, causing increased gender role conflict (Cordes, 1985). Employed women experience gender role conflict when they have active careers but still try to maintain the household according to the same standards as those of most full-time female homemakers. Additionally, men married to women who earn more than they do often struggle with their expectations that husbands should earn more than their wives. And finally, childless couples must live with the notion that all families should have children.

When situations arise where societal and personal ways of believing and behaving clash, individuals usually attempt to bring their own views in line with societal expectations, try to ignore the differences, or attempt to negotiate change within their own family, work, or community environment so that their views are accommodated or at least tolerated (Chusmir & Koberg, 1990). Regardless of how a person tries to cope with or resolve gender role conflict, he or she will generally feel some degree of anxiety and stress. It is not unusual for someone experiencing role conflict to feel tired, run down, worried, frustrated, tense, and unhappy.

GENDER: BIOLOGICAL DESTINY OR SOCIALIZATION?

Biological Destiny

Are the differences between women and men innate, biologically determined? Is male dominance inevitable? Does anatomy determine one's destiny? One way of answering these questions is to look at the cross-cultural evidence to determine if men in *all* cultures are aggressive and authoritarian, in contrast to women who are submissive and nurturing. If the evidence suggests otherwise, it would seem to support the argument that socialization patterns—and not biology—determine masculinity and femininity.

It is for this reason that a book published in 1935

The Right Year for Girls?

All countries have certain myths that seem to engage most of the population. Some are told and retold in a humorous way as a form of entertainment. Others, like this one from Korea, promote negative gender stereotyping that, if acted upon, can actually influence the structure of society by changing the sex ratio of the population for decades to come. In Korea, government policies and laws have even been affected.

For generations Koreans have believed the superstition about women born in the Year of the Horse, the 12th year of the Chinese lunar cycle. Women born in these years are said to be smart and argumentive—in other words, bad wives. Years ago mothers tried to ensure they would have boys by eating special herbs. In 1990, again the Year of the Horse, some Koreans fear that tradition and modern medicine will cause an alarming rise in abortions of female fetuses.

Prenatal tests that can tell the sex of a fetus were introduced to the country in the early 1980s. Many Koreans worried then if women would use the technology to have boys, who are considered more valuable in Korea's patriarchal culture. In 1988, 113 South Korean boys were born for every 100 girls; the worldwide average is 102.5 boys for every 100 girls. Public concern over the issue forced the government to ban doctors from revealing fetal gender. Some doctors still tell—for up to $1,500. Abortion is illegal, but easily available. It is estimated that there are more than a million abortions a year.

To prevent that number from soaring higher this year, the government has cracked down on doctors who perform genetic tests. Eight physicians have had their licenses suspended in the last few months. Korean women can take hope from another recent development. In December the National Assembly passed legislation that made women legally equal to men. Korean feminists say the country still has a way to go, but attributes such as intelligence and assertiveness are becoming assets in modern Korea. Someday, Korean parents may be proud to give birth to a girl in the Year of the Horse.

EXPLORATIONS *Can you think of any other myths that promote stereotypes and ultimately affect the lives of women and men in our country? In another country?*

SOURCE: Excerpted from "Bad Year for Girls?" (1990).

by Margaret Mead, *Sex and Temperament in Three Primitive Societies,* has been so influential and so widely quoted. When she left for New Guinea in 1931, Mead said she "shared the general belief in our society that there was a natural sex temperament which at most could be distorted or diverted from normal expression" (1935, p. xvi). But after living among three neighboring tribes—the Arapesh, the Mundugumor, and the Tchambuli—she changed her mind.

Each culture, she found, makes a different assumption about the connection between sex and temperament. Among members of the first tribe, the Arapesh, it is assumed that there are no temperamental differences between men and women. Both males and females have what we normally think of as feminine traits. Both are gentle and passive, and share the tasks of child rearing. In contrast, both males and females of the second tribe, the Mundugumors, have what we commonly think of as masculine traits; both sexes are aggressive and combative. The members of the third tribe, the Tchambuli, believe that the sexes are different in temperament, but rather than following the role prescription of western culture, they reverse it. The Tchambuli women, who have shaven, unadorned heads, are described as solid, practical, and powerful. In contrast, it is the Tchambuli men who seem to be the outsiders. They devote their lives to self-adornment, they bicker and pout, and they exhibit the emotional ups and downs more commonly attributed to women in our culture.

How can these temperamental differences be explained? Mead attributed most of them to socialization practices. But an anthropologist who visited the Tchambuli many years after Mead stressed a different set of factors. The main "cash crop" among the Tchambuli is the plaited mosquito bag, made exclusively by women, which is traded to other tribes. Because women control the main industry, they have a source of wealth that enables them to gain status and power. It may be that women's temperament—as well as men's—is as much a product of economic arrangements as it is of socialization practices (Gewertz, 1976).

In any case, the implications of Mead's study of these tribes are highly significant. She concluded that the characteristics that we assign to one sex or the other are "mere variations of human temperament to which members of either or both sexes may, with more or less success in the case of individuals, be educated to approximate" (1949, p. xvi).

When anthropologist William Stephens compared the roles of men and women in more than 100 primitive societies, he came to the conclusion that "there is much less intercultural variation than one might expect" (1963, p. 281). Work around the house—such as cooking, cleaning, and child care—is almost everywhere the responsibility of the wife. Tasks such as hunting, herding, and handicraft with metals or stone are almost always done by men. In other words, if we look at the division of labor by sex in a variety of cultures, for many tasks a virtual consensus exists about what is woman's work and what is man's.

The anthropological evidence suggests that while there is nothing inevitable about the connection between sex and temperament, there are significant cross-cultural consistencies, especially in the division of labor. Some of these can be explained on the basis of physiological differences, but not all of them. The cross-cultural evidence indicates that biological factors are not solely or inevitably responsible for certain temperamental traits in males and females. But, at the same time, it does not rule out the influence of biology in shaping gender behavior.

Masculinity and femininity represent cultural exaggerations of the biological facts of maleness and femaleness. It is no longer possible to defend the position that either nature or nurture is entirely responsible for the differences between the sexes. Gender identity results from the interweaving of both biological and sociological factors. The general consensus among researchers is that women and men actually differ less than most people believe they do and that most differences are related to culture rather than biology (Deaux, 1984; Epstein, 1988; Hyde, 1986; Maccoby & Jacklin, 1974; Nicholson, 1984; Singleton, 1986).

Theories of Socialization

There are two primary explanations for how gender roles are acquired: social learning theory and cognitive development theory.

Social Learning Theory

Social learning theorists propose that there are two major means of facilitating the learning of gender roles. One way is through *direct training*. Parents, teachers, peers, and other significant people guide a child's attitudes, beliefs, and behaviors into appropriate channels. Through clothing, toys, and everyday conversation, a child is taught to think, feel, and behave in ways that correspond to his or her sex. The teaching is deliberate and *reinforced* through rewards and punishments.

Reinforcing behaviors include giving praise and rewards such as approving smiles and hugs. For example, a boy may come home from a game of soccer with dirty, torn jeans and a bruised and bleeding elbow. Upon entering the house he may tell of his gaming adventures and receive admiring looks and congratulations for "giving his all." A girl of similar appearance coming home from the game, in contrast, might be challenged for playing so roughly and dangerously and told to go get changed and do something about her hair. Family ears may be nonreceptive to the story of her afternoon of soccer.

Children also learn gender roles through *imitation and modeling*. A child observes the behavior of many different people and chooses to imitate or model certain ones based on several considerations, including how rewarding the experience of imitating one person is compared to imitating others, or how powerful it feels to enact certain behaviors compared to others, or how nurturant or pleasing a particular model is when imitated. Besides imitating parents, friends, and teachers, children also model behaviors of familiar television and movie characters.

Cognitive Development Theory

Cognition refers to an individual's ability to understand his or her world. Unlike social learning theory,

Even though most parents today claim that they treat different-sexed children in the same way, they frequently tend to reinforce traditional gender roles without being aware of it.

which relies more on the belief that others manipulate a child's environment to produce gender identity, cognitive development theory is based on the belief that children actively participate in their own learning (Kohlberg, 1966).

Cognitive ability develops slowly and is directly related to age. By age 2 the child identifies by sex, "I'm a girl" or "I'm a boy." By age 3, the child extends this identification to others—"Janet is a girl"; "Diego is a boy"—and then to adults—"Mommy is a girl"; "Daddy is a boy." Next, the child begins to show a preference for objects that are associated with their own sex, "I like blue; it's better than pink." By age 4, more rigid gender expectations are explored, "Boys like cereal for breakfast"; "Girls like toast." Or, "Mommies buy groceries"; "Daddies buy tools." Or, "Mommies come home from work before Daddies do." A 4-year-old girl in one study insisted that mothers could be nurses but not doctors—even though her own mother was a doctor (Maccoby & Jacklin, 1974).

By age 5, the child displays more rigid gender role behavior, "I'll mow the lawn because I'm a boy"; "You put on the necklace because you're a girl." Following

this, the child usually begins to identify with their same-sex parent, "I want to be like Daddy"; "Mommies are best, I'm like her." Then at about age 13 and continuing through adolescence, children begin to relax the use of gender role stereotypes and look at the world from a more flexible perspective, "Men can be nurses, teachers, and librarians; they can change diapers, cook, and do laundry." "Women can be physicians, business owners, and senators." "Men can be affectionate and show emotions." "Women can be leaders" (Doyle, 1985). According to cognitive development theory, in the process of learning gender roles, children seem to go through a stage in their cognitive development that relies on believing in set gender role behaviors. With age, they are able to move beyond this inflexible notion toward an acceptance of differences and diversity in male and female behavior (see Figure 2-1).

The two theories presented here, social learning theory and cognitive development theory, have been criticized for portraying gender roles as being made up of expected behavior that seems "clear, consistent, and uniform" across the population, regardless of the sit-

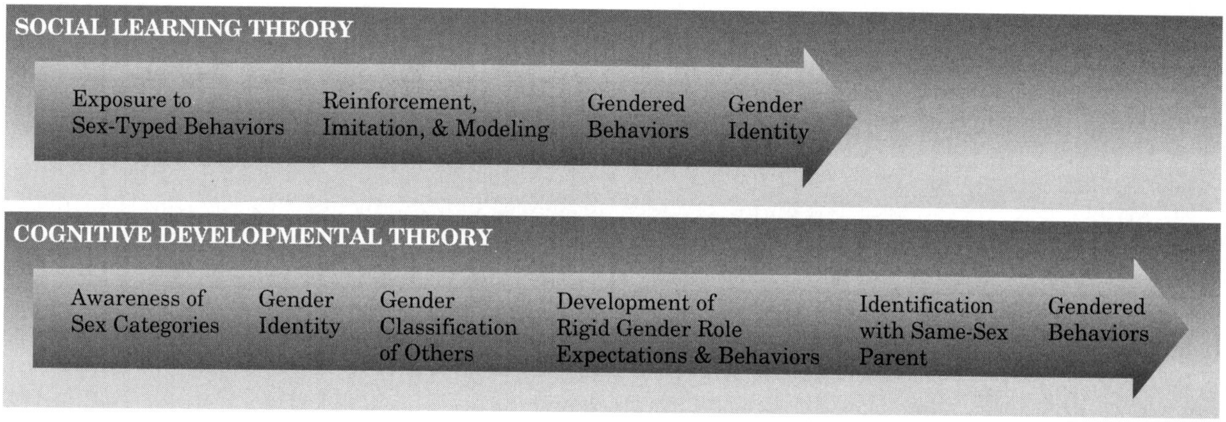

SOCIAL LEARNING THEORY

| Exposure to Sex-Typed Behaviors | Reinforcement, Imitation, & Modeling | Gendered Behaviors | Gender Identity |

COGNITIVE DEVELOPMENTAL THEORY

| Awareness of Sex Categories | Gender Identity | Gender Classification of Others | Development of Rigid Gender Role Expectations & Behaviors | Identification with Same-Sex Parent | Gendered Behaviors |

FIGURE 2-1
Theories of Gender Socialization
SOURCE: Adapted from S. Baslow (1986).

uation or setting (Ferree, 1991, p. 104). Sociologist Linda Lindsey (1990) writes about social learning theory, "Certainly imitation and rewards are important, but . . . it is far from being consistent. A girl may be rewarded for a masculine activity, such as excelling in sports, but she retains other aspects of her feminine role" (p. 40). Lindsey also finds fault with cognitive development theory because the age-related stages upon which the theory is based were developed from observations and interviews of male children. The theory also fails to explain in sufficient detail exactly how cognition works—for example, are there life events or developmental markers besides age that influence a child to move from one stage of gender socialization to the next?

One of the most enduring complaints about theories of socialization is that they ignore adulthood. It is as if individuals learn about appropriate gender behavior throughout childhood and adolescence, then socialization stops. The person is, in effect, frozen by time into an unchangeable, uniform constellation of traits and behaviors. Not true, argue a growing number of theorists (Deaux & Kite, 1987; Ferree, 1991; Thompson & Walker, 1991). Many adults change their gender attitudes and behaviors across time because of interactions with others—family members, lovers, friends, colleagues—and because of the circumstances of their lives (West & Zimmerman, 1987). We discuss adult socialization more fully later in this chapter.

Despite the complaints, social learning theory and cognitive development theory have helped us better

understand how gender awareness develops and then influences thought patterns, feelings, and behaviors. And each has been supported by a number of studies over the years.

Childhood Socialization

Learning gender roles is a longer and more complex process than most people realize, and learned behavior has enormous importance in determining all human activity. Compared to other species, we have a longer period of dependency before adulthood. A correspondingly greater part of who we are is what we are taught to be. As we have seen, this applies to a great extent to gender identity. The gender identity of an infant is "unfinished" at birth; and whatever hormonal predispositions do exist apply to only a few behavior patterns. And even in these areas the predispositions of males and females overlap. It is the parents, the teachers, the child's peers, and the communications media that act as a "finishing school."

Parents as Socializers

Although most parents believe they are treating their children in a gender-neutral way, observation disproves this perception. For example, a mother describes how she treated each of her twins—one of whom was a boy, the other a girl:

I started dressing her in little pink slacks and frilly blouses. . . . She likes for me to wipe her face, and yet my son is quite different. I can't wash his face. . . . She seems to be daintier. Maybe it's because I encourage it. I've never seen a little girl so neat and tidy. She is very proud of herself when she puts on a new dress. . . . The boy once went and took a leak in the garden. He was quite happy with himself. And I just didn't say anything. . . . The girl once took off her panties and threw them over the fence. I gave her a little swat on the rear, and I told her that nice little girls don't do that. (Money & Ehrhardt, 1974, pp. 124–128)

At home, children are given very explicit gender messages. According to Virginia Sapiro (1986), political science professor, children are told things like "Go and help your mother in the kitchen so when you grow up you'll be a good mommy, too." "You don't want that toy—that's for girls!" "Don't sit like that—it's not lady-like!" (p. 91). Children also learn from less direct messages. For example, if both parents can drive but the father always drives when the family goes out, children will get the message that the father is the preferred or more competent driver. Brothers and sisters also assist in socialization.

Teachers and Schools as Socializers

Once children begin attending school, other people besides parents and household members start to share in their socialization. Teachers have been found to expect girls to be better behaved, quieter, neater, more cooperative, and easier to control than boys (Fagot, Hagan, Leinbach, & Kronsberg, 1985; Stanworth, 1983). Boys, however, have been found to consistently and clearly dominate classroom interaction at all grade levels (Fagot, 1984; Sadker & Sadker, 1985). A report compiled by the Wellesley College Center for Research on Women from a review of more than 1,300 studies concludes that although girls and boys enter school roughly equal in measured ability, 12 years later, girls have fallen behind in math and science courses (*The AAUW Report*, 1992). Teachers call on boys more often and praise and encourage boys more frequently than they do girls.

Science teachers choose boys to assist with demonstrations before the class 80 percent of the time, and girls are far less likely than boys to have actually handled microscopes or electricity meters. Girls who learn to watch, rather than do, soon lose confidence and interest, and the gender gap in science achievement continues to grow. (Schuster, 1992, p. A9)

As researcher and educator Barbara Lloyd (1989) points out, teachers have a genuine interest in providing unbiased educational opportunities, but such bias is often unconscious and unrecognized. However, once this bias is uncovered, it may be possible to help teachers stop reinforcing traditional gender roles. For example, Lloyd provides the following illustration from a workshop she gave for a group of teachers. In a discussion about girls' and boys' use of construction toys "the head teacher suggested that it was natural for boys to be more active, stronger and hence to require more [play] space" (p. 64). Lloyd then used as a learning tool for the teachers an example from one of her own research projects in which "the same six-month-old infant was encouraged by mothers to be active when presented as a boy, but soothed and contained when presented as a girl" (p. 64). According to Lloyd, the teachers in the workshop reacted with surprise but also with pleasure. The pleasure, she noted, probably related to the realization that their own assumptions about gender roles did indeed influence their attitudes toward, and expectations for, the children and that more attention needed to be paid to this important connection.

Childrens' textbooks, like many teachers, have unconsciously reinforced traditional gender roles. Many of these books still portray women as nurturers, and men as active, assertive, and seeking recognition for their achievements. In addition, it has been argued that the educational testing process, curricular offerings, and guidance counseling in schools at times promote gender role stereotyping (*The AAUW Report*, 1992).

Peers as Socializers

Peers are another significant gender role socializer. Much of this socializing reinforces traditional gender roles:

Boys still beat up other boys for being "sissies" or for being too studious. Girls still make fun of other girls who act too smart or who don't wear the right clothes or are not interested enough in boys. . . . A boy quickly finds out that it is easier to get dates if he is the captain of the football team rather than the head of the physics club. Even in the latter case, however, he will have an easier time than will a girl who is head of the physics club, especially if he is at least good looking; a girl who is labeled the "class brain" will often have trouble finding dates, even if she is physically attractive. Being athletic is no longer the problem it once was for girls who want dates (depending on the sport), but it is still unacceptable for a girl to be able to match or beat a boy at "his" own game. (Sapiro, 1986, p. 92)

A survey of 3,000 grade school children in 1990 revealed that, beginning in adolescence, girls' self-esteem is significantly lower than boys'. Interviews by the researchers made it clear that peer pressure had a significant effect on girls' self-esteem. One girl said, "I'm afraid, when I get something wrong, the boys in the classroom might make fun of me because they usually laugh at some people if they get something wrong" (Ostling, 1992, p. 62). Being laughed at and made fun of serve to reinforce the notion that girls are to be seen but not heard.

It is important to note that peers can also serve as positive role models and active supporters of each other. "Sleeping over" is one way children have of making time for each other. Joining after-school clubs and attending sporting events is another. Moreover, some schools now have peer counseling and support groups for children to build esteem and counteract the feelings of discomfort and distress associated with various school- and family-related events—divorce, the death of a classmate, and so forth.

Media as Socializers

Media images of "masculine" men—whether they are tough guys like Arnold Schwarzenegger and Sylvester Stallone, smooth manipulators of women like the *Playboy* ideal, or sensitive husbands and family men like Bill Cosby and Phil Donahue—are confusing and contradictory. The on-screen Schwarzenegger and Stallone feel uncomfortable around women. These male characters do like women, sometimes. But at the right time and in the right place—which they choose. And always with their minds on business. As for the ideal male portrayed in *Playboy*, he seems to devote more attention to women than Schwarzenegger or Stallone, but this attention is not directed toward a female equal. *Playboy* depicts women as accessories, as decorative and useful as the "right" car or stereo. Cosby and Donahue more closely approximate the 1990s contemporary marital partner, but young men are not completely comfortable with this image either because they notice that some "women praise the sensitive man who can admit his vulnerability, yet admire the toughness of the man who refuses to bend in the face of overwhelming odds" (Lindsey, 1990, p. 159). The movie *Thelma and Louise* went against the prevailing

stereotypes of women in the movies and was criticized by some (see the "Snapshots" box).

Television programming is a particularly important agent in gender training for children, not just because children spend so many hours watching television, but also because they are not yet exposed to many alternative sources of information. Despite a greater diversity of female roles in the media than formerly, analyses of the portrayal of women on television indicate that its programming continues to reinforce traditional gender role stereotypes. Men appear on television more than two times as often as women do (Durkin, 1985). Most women on television are depicted as younger and less mature than their male counterparts. In addition, a much higher proportion of the male roles are serious ones. Starring roles in which actors achieve economic, political, or physical dominance over others more often go to men (Butler & Paisley, 1980). Men in television roles are identified more frequently by their occupational roles, and women by their family roles. Women tend to appear in supportive roles, in which their beauty and sexuality enhance the prestige of male authority figures (Durkin, 1985). And while males on television commit more acts of violence, females are the most frequent victims (Reinhold, 1983).

Robert and Linda Lichter, co-directors of the Center for Media and Public Affairs, and Stanley Rothman, a professor of government, studied the personality traits, social background, and distribution of over 2,000 women actors in television programming. They found that only 8 percent of doctors, 18 percent of business executives, and 25 percent of lawyers were female roles. On television, concluded the authors, "Women are more likely than men to act out of a desire for sex, romance or marriage. . . . Men are more likely to be motivated by political concerns or ideological principles" (1986, p. 17).

But these researchers also found that many of the more recent scripts promoted women's changing life roles, while portraying characters who put women down as losers. We are reminded by Lichter, Lichter, and Rothman that "television's view of women is influenced partly by what its creators think the audience wants, partly by what they think it needs, and partly by the stereotypes and assumptions they inadvertently impose upon their creations" (p. 19).

Women are also shortchanged in the newspaper. Social commentator and columnist Ellen Goodman writes:

SNAPSHOTS

Thelma and Louise

"Pathetic stereotypes of testosterone-crazed behavior."—RICHARD JOHNSON, New York Daily News. *"Is it feminist . . . for [a] woman with a gun to rob a grocery store?"*—SUZANNE FIELDS, syndicated columnist.

Thelma and Louise, the 1991 movie provoking these heated comments, is about a waitress and a housewife whose weekend vacation turns into a tragic-comic chase after the two women respond to an attempted rape with murderous rage.

Are Thelma and Louise appropriate role models? According to some critics, two women on a crime spree are terrible role models. But others disagree, saying that compared to the prostitute played by Julia Roberts in the box-office hit, *Pretty Woman*, they are great role models. In this view, the two friends are modeling power instead of lingerie. And as the film progresses, they only become stronger and tougher.

EXPLORATIONS   *Do you think that if Thelma and Louise were male characters instead of female characters this movie would be so controversial? Why?*

Susan Sarandon (left) and Geena Davis (right) star as two best friends whose weekend together becomes a voyage in gender-role redefinition.

Two-thirds of the bylines on front pages are male and three-quarters of the opinions on op-ed pages are by men . . . less than a third of the photographs on front pages feature women. . . . 52 percent of the population show up just 13 percent of the time in the prime news spots. (1992, A9)

So, children do not see women and men represented equally in the media sources most likely to be in the family home—on television programs and in the newspaper.

Race and Class as Socializers

Race, ethnicity, and class are additional influences on child socialization. For instance, black parents tend to socialize their daughters to be more independent than do white parents. The female stereotype predominant in black families is the capable and competent woman involved in both employment and homemaking (Gump, 1980; Malson, 1983). Black scholar and activist Angela Davis argues that black women's past experiences with slavery influenced the black community to construct an alternative definition of women's roles that included a tradition of "hard work, perseverance, self-reliance, a legacy of tenacity, resistance and insistence on sexual equality" (1981, p. 29). In contrast, Hispanic parents tend to emphasize the more traditional wife/mother roles for women and provider roles for men (Anderson, 1988). There is diversity in Hispanic families, however.

> It is very common in the contemporary literature . . . to find descriptions of the Hispanic family that contain references to continuity in traditional cultural expectations as well as evidence of female role transitions that openly challenge male dominance or a notion of a culturally ordained division of labor. For example, in a historical review . . . [one researcher] found that availability of employment was the most important determinant of whether Mexican-American women worked or not. Similar findings have been reported for Puerto Rican women. . . . (Vega, 1991, p. 298)

Class is another strong influence on gender socialization. Child socialization patterns are based on the parents' perceptions of what their children's adult roles are expected to be. Because blue-collar parents are subject to unexplained rules and authority on the job and in other aspects of their lives, they are generally less flexible about family rules and authority as-

they rear their children (Hoffman, 1984). They usually stereotype males and females more sharply than do middle-class families, with a tendency to be particularly restrictive toward females (Canter & Ageton, 1984; Cazenave, 1984). Middle-class parents allow their children more flexibility in following family rules and are less concerned with issues of authority and respect. They are more tolerant of androgynous gender roles—praising and rewarding their female children for achieving in school and preparing for a career (Langman, 1987).

Adolescent and Young Adulthood Socialization

Becoming a Man

Margaret Mead once commented that "the worry that boys will not grow up to be men is much more widespread than that girls will not grow up to be women" (1949, p. 195). She was speaking specifically about the South Sea Islands, but her comment applies to almost all cultures. In most preliterate societies, there are rites of passage for males, but not for females. There are ceremonial dramas, supervised by the men, which ease the difficult transition from boyhood to manhood. But why is so much more attention paid to the male adolescent than to the female? This difference in emphasis might be interpreted as one manifestation of the status and prestige of being a man versus a woman in most cultures. The older men lavish attention upon the younger boys because males are assumed to be more important than females.

Is "something extra" required to make a boy into a man? There is no society where the transition from the status of child into that of adult is entirely smooth. But it appears in certain respects, at least, that the contradictions between the two roles are greater for boys than for girls. In many societies, first menstruation is considered a natural sign that a girl is coming of age. But, whereas attaining womanhood is seen in terms of a biological process for girls, becoming a man is a cultural process for boys: the rites of passage are "man"-made ceremonies (see the "Changing Lifestyles" box).

Some psychologists like Nancy Chodorow (1978) suggest that, indeed, something extra is demanded of boys; their gender identity may be more fragile. The transition from infancy to adulthood for males is full of contradictions. All infants are "feminine" in their orientation to the world, as our culture usually defines

CHANGING LIFESTYLES

A Place for Men in the Heart

In 1990 poet Robert Bly appeared on the PBS special, "A Gathering of Men," and the show, along with Bly's best-selling book, Iron John *(1990), a cross-cultural analysis of male initiation rites, is said by many to have launched the men's movement. The following* Newsweek *excerpt describes what this movement is and is not.*

. . . What the movement doesn't have, at least not yet, is a serious political or social agenda. There are groups working to make divorce and custody laws more favorable to men, but it would be a mistake to think of the men's movement as merely a political response to feminism. White men cannot plausibly claim to be underrepresented in the upper echelons of American society. Nor is the movement concerned with the quotidian lives of men in relation to their lovers and families. It is not about taking paternity leave, taking out the garbage or letting one's partner come first. The movement looks inward. It seeks to resolve the spiritual crisis of the American man, a sex that paradoxically dominates the prison population as overwhelmingly as it does the United States Senate. "The women's movement has made tremendous strides in providing a place for women in the world," says Eric McCollum, who teaches family therapy at Purdue. "The men's movement is going to provide a place for men in the heart."

Take Larry Lima, who made a fairly typical middle-class mess out of his life after a promising start, earning more than $100,000 a year in his late 20s as a medical-devices product manager in Boulder Creek, Calif. In short order Lima's father died, he had major surgery on his back, he lost his job, his wife lost her job, they divorced and Lima realized he was an alcoholic. Sober and back in his hometown of Summit, N.J., with two young children, he signed up for a men's weekend at a lodge in the Adirondack Mountains. In the atavistic silliness of dancing and drumming by firelight, in the third-degree agony of squatting alongside red-glowing rocks in the stifling darkness, he felt himself cleansed and reborn into a new, more serious and responsible life. Talking with the other men that weekend, he realized the importance of men learning from one another, because—and who should know this better?—"alone, we don't know what the hell we're doing."

Lima was a fairly representative men's movement man: white, white-collar, in his 30s and divorced. He had few male friends with whom he shared anything deeper than a beer. He was not that much-ridiculed figure, a "sensitive" man. The men's movement makes a point of not propagating "sensitivity" of the wispy, flaccid, moonstruck variety. It does, however, promote "communication." Elaborate rituals have been devised to help men overcome the cultural taboo against revealing emotions. Men's groups typically set aside a special time for members to talk about their feelings. Many have found it necessary to outlaw diversionary topics such as sports, politics and cars. At the men's retreats run by psychotherapist Wilbur Courter in Kalamazoo, Mich., he forbids participants even to mention their jobs, leaving most of them "almost speechless." Courter says his work "is directed toward helping us become better human beings instead of better human doings." . . .

EXPLORATIONS *According to this brief description of the men's movement, what is the "spiritual crisis" of the American man? Do you believe that there is such a crisis?*

SOURCE: Excerpted from J. Adler et al. (1991).

femininity. Thus, babies are dependent and passive. Small children cry and cling to their mothers. But for males, the transition from child to adult is sharper.

The socialization of boys, according to Chodorow, is further complicated by the tendency of children to identify more closely with their mothers. Even as adults, both men and women are more like their mothers than their fathers in characteristics that are not sex-typed. Boys, though, are expected to shift their identification from their mothers to their fathers. This process of change is made more complicated because the father's main role—his work—takes place away from the home. Unlike his sister, the young boy cannot learn what the same-sex adult does by watching and imitating. Boys learn the masculine role by responding to many negative sanctions. They are often told what *not* to do to be a man: "Don't act like a girl!" "Don't be a sissy!" "Men don't cry!"

Sooner than girls, boys are pushed to be independent and cautioned not to be too emotionally expressive. Many boys are taught that the expression of normal human feelings like pain, inadequacy, love, and affection is "unmanly." Chodorow argues that because boys have to reject their early attachment to their mothers, they tend to suppress their emotions. Because boys need to actively shift their early identification with their mothers, their primary orientation is one of "doing," while girls, who do not need to make this shift, have an orientation of "being." Chodorow further contends that boys discover during childhood that the masculine role is of high status and value.

Socialization efforts for males in early adulthood is focused clearly and consistently on preparing boys for the male roles of family provider and achiever in the workplace. Steve Ioanilli, student and second-place winner of the North American Essay Contest (1990), reflects on one of his experiences with being a man:

> A few years ago, I was more of a man. My best friend Paul was diagnosed as having a brain tumor and scheduled for surgery. In the typical stoic male fashion, I kept my emotions hidden. Inside I was dying. . . . Having lost my father to a brain tumor, I knew that Paul had his work cut out for him. I wanted nothing more than to give him a hug and say three words to him: "I love you." It sounds easy, but I had years of training working against me. If it had been a female friend, I would have had no problem sharing my feelings with her; but since Paul was male, I felt years of

> conditioning telling me that it wasn't okay to express feelings of affection to another man. . . . True to my masculinity, I instead found myself giving Paul a punch on the shoulder and mumbling some ridiculous command to get well. Fortunately, Paul recovered fully and I had the chance to tell him that I loved him—which I later did. But I had to grow a lot before I was able to do it. (p. 21)

While Chodorow's ideas about socialization are interesting, they ignore the current realities of family life where single-parent families are 25 percent of the total population and fathers in two-parent families are more actively involved in child rearing. Chodorow's ideas also place maximum importance on early childhood experiences with parents, to the exclusion of other important socializing agents like siblings, kin, peers, teachers, and the media. Also ignored is the fact that compared to girls, boys may receive more pressure against behaving in ways inappropriate for their gender (Feinman, 1981, 1984); but, at the same time they receive more encouragement and praise from parents and teachers and generally receive more supportive attention than do girls (*The AAUW Report*, 1992).

There are at least two negative implications for marriage in this pattern of male gender role socialization. First, boys who are told implicitly or explicitly that it is bad to act like girls may grow up convinced that everything they associate with feminine is bad. Such attitudes may translate into an emotional uneasiness about dating and marital relationships where expression of feelings is both valued and expected. Second, these attitudes can also affect men's styles of parenting. Exhibiting higher anxiousness than mothers about the gender identity of their children, especially their sons, fathers more strongly reinforce stereotypical gender role attitudes and behaviors (Hoffman, 1987).

Becoming a Woman

Before reaching adolescence, girls are not as rigid in their gender role attitudes as are boys. Girls are not as determined to do only "girl" things and parents are more accepting of their cross-gender behavior. Nevertheless, sociologists Diane Bush and Roberta Simmons (1987), who have done extensive research on gender differences in early adolescence, suggest that adolescence is more stressful for girls than boys. "For boys, becoming an adolescent means moving closer to a set of valued adult roles; for girls the change is ambivalent and discontinuous . . . 'becoming a woman' is not necessarily positive. . . . Expectations regarding careers and socioemotional and intimate relationships are much less consistent for girls" (p. 198).

Adolescence is the period when girls, perhaps for the first time, face the contradictory nature of their intended societal roles. "Just as they are expected to become concerned with boys . . . girls discover that boys expect them to act dependent and not to compete. . . . At the same time, girls realize that these 'feminine' behaviors are devalued, not only in their public world of school but in the adult public world as well" (p. 200). So, in effect, girls are getting a strong double message which is at least sometimes confusing to them. In an attempt to resolve the confusion, conclude Bush and Simmons, girls may begin to choose popularity over competence and independence. This typically leads to lower self-esteem and academic performance—signs of distress. Compounding this problem is the fact that girls more than boys rely on other people's opinions of their competence, achievement, ability, morality, and the appropriateness of their future life goals. Girls also tend to blame their personal failures on their lack of ability, while attributing any successes they might have to luck or the easiness of the task.

Much of a girl's socialization is centered on her future roles as supportive marital partner and homemaker which, say Bush and Simmons, "results in expressive, other-oriented attributes, capacities and cognitions" (p. 208). There are several negative implications for women in these socialization scripts. In marriage, women often become frustrated and anxious because they feel torn between caring for themselves and caring for others. They sometimes label themselves as failures to be "good" women if important responsibilities like work interfere with caring for husbands and children (Lyons, 1988). Cultural scripts encourage women to self-sacrifice in order to be "good." But, psychologist Carol Gilligan (1988) maintains that "women who cast employment decisions in terms derived from cultural scripts, whether for good mothers or for superwomen, often show signs of depression, suggesting that cultural scripts at present are detrimental to women" (p. xxxiii).

Marital relationships in the 1990s rely more on mutuality and interdependence than on self-sacrifice and dependence, yet cultural scripts persist in emphasizing separate spheres and separate traits for women and

Working women often feel guilty leaving young children at home in the care of others, as it is hard to shake the cultural script that women should be the primary caregivers in the family.

men. As the family and work responsibilities of marital partners become more equal in the 1990s, couples will continue to seek ways of incorporating the best of both worlds, masculine and feminine, into a dynamic and more satisfying partnership.

Gender in College

Do expectations for gender roles change much between adolescence and young adulthood? To help answer this question, social scientist Anne Machung (1989) interviewed equal numbers of male and female, white, Asian-American, Chicano, and black seniors at the University of California about their future marriage and work plans. Her research confirms what other researchers have found—that college students, like younger adolescents, tend to be stereotypical in their role expectations (Losh-Hesselbart, 1987). Men, Machung found, were much clearer than women about their future career goals. In addition, men were far more knowledgeable about the types of jobs available for their chosen majors, beginning salaries, and projected future earnings. Male students expected to be continuously employed and reported that their careers would be more important than their wives' careers to family well-being. Most men envisioned themselves as the sole providers for their families, although their wives "could work if they wanted to."

What Machung found most surprising was that the majority of both women and men in the study thought that the husband's job was essential to family well-being, but viewed the wife's job as optional—"a luxury they can choose to add on or take off at will" (p. 43). The students had no expectations that they might need two incomes to maintain the middle-class standards of living they envisioned. Regardless of sex or race, respondents assumed that they would marry and stay happily married for life.

The undergraduate men in the study stated that they would "help out" at home—but not with chores like laundry and cooking. But the undergraduate women said that they expected their future husbands to share *all* the chores. "I'll be damned if I do double shift," remarked one woman. When asked what he would do if his future partner asked him to do half of the household tasks and child care, one young man replied, "I could always hire someone" (p. 46). Another said, "It depends on the work situation, who's making more money, and how important money is to the relationship. I'd probably complain . . . but it depends on how much I like her and how she asks. She'd have to make her point clear and explain things to me" (p. 47).

What about taking care of the children? Both women and men felt it was the wife's job. According to Machung: "Men see women as wanting children more, as having the instinctual capabilities to care for them better, and therefore as having to make career sacrifices for them. Women see men as not wanting children as much, as lacking parental capabilities (especially when children are small), and therefore as exempt from career sacrifices" (p. 50). The majority of the women interviewed assumed that they would marry men with high incomes and thus would have

the option of working or not. These young women expected to pursue careers until they were in their late twenties and then take extended time off to have and rear two or three children. Employers would be supportive, the women believed, of their family and work plans, giving them whatever amount of leave they needed—months or years. They expected to resume their careers later without any problems.

Many of the assumptions held by this group of soon-to-be graduates, Machung points out, directly contradict the realities of current family life. Unlike jobs, careers take a great amount of effort and commitment to sustain. Despite recent articles promoting the "mommy track" (which is covered in depth in Chapter 9) career paths don't usually allow for extended time off and certainly don't remain on hold for indefinite periods of time without some economic or personal cost.

The expectations uncovered by this study raise some important questions. After investing so much time, energy, and money into a career and considering the economic realities of family life in the 1990s, will women be able to give up the earnings, not to mention the personal fulfillment and life satisfaction that a career affords, in order to spend several years bearing and rearing children? Will women who prepare for occupations that pay slightly less, or as much or more than those of their husbands be comfortable with a marital arrangement where the husband "helps out" rather than shares the household work and child care? With husband and father becoming increasingly significant and acceptable male gender roles, will men continue to believe that only women want children and that providing economically constitutes their major contribution to family life?

These are intriguing questions with which women and men will increasingly struggle in the future. They represent areas of conflict and ambivalence for individuals caught between the desire to pattern their lives according to the traditional gender role stereotypes modeled by their parents and significant others and the blended and extended expectations of contemporary life brought about by changing social and economic circumstances. The students she interviewed, Machung suggests, will probably base their future decisions on needing two incomes to adequately provide for their families, resisting becoming another statistic in the already high divorce rates, and confronting the assumption that women and men can simultaneously combine marriage, career, and parenthood without economic and social costs.

Gender in Adulthood

Although we generally think of socialization as a process that occurs during childhood and adolescence, gender learning and the development and construction of a gender identity continue throughout adulthood (Losh-Hesselbart, 1987). As adults move through their lives, most marry and hold a series of jobs; many divorce, remarry, have children, retire, and so forth. So it is within the context of the passage of time and the assumption and termination of various life roles that adult learning takes place.

Gender training—as it relates to jobs, marriage, and parenthood—during childhood, adolescence, or even college can hardly be expected to serve adults well for their entire lives. Economic and political conditions change, new assumptions arise about how roles should be enacted, and additional knowledge is gained about people and their interactions. Adults' capacities to think and reason are more sophisticated than those of children. The quality of adult relationships with family and friends and the extent of knowledge that adults have about themselves—how they think, what they feel, who they are—differ significantly from those of childhood and adolescence (Giele, 1988).

People often make dramatic changes in their lives during adulthood. For example, many adult women and men who in their younger years believed that motherhood was a full-time job and women's exclusive responsibility are now employed parents who use day care and petition their employers for flexible work hours and their government representatives for family policies that help parents. Furthermore, some adult men and women who earlier believed that only men could be leaders and supervisors at work are now employed by female bosses and have adjusted their attitudes and behavior accordingly. And some men who had strong early beliefs that only women desire and can rear children are now involved fathers.

Even in adulthood, then, gender roles are not fixed. Sometimes adults actively seek to change their own gender role attitudes and behavior. At other times life events like marriage, divorce, or parenthood push them toward new patterns of behavior. Does this mean that adults are less stereotypical in their behavior than

younger people? Not necessarily. In fact, many adults continue to live their lives in very gendered ways, as we see in this next section.

GENDER IN FAMILIES

Does Family Life Match Traditional Perspectives?

As we learned in Chapter 1 and earlier in this chapter, the traditional division of responsibilities within the family emphasizes separate spheres—men's roles as wage earners outside the family and women's roles as partners and caregivers within the family. This separation of women and men serves to obscure the fact that most women work both inside and outside the home and that most men rank family ahead of work as a source of life satisfaction and make efforts to attend to husband and father roles.

Historically, expectations for who does what in the family have been based on a male/female dichotomy—some things are best left for men and other things are better accomplished by women. Although sociologists, psychologists, and anthropologists have documented that families are not the same across cultures and that even in our own society there are many types of families and many different ways to divide family responsibilities, this notion of an "ideal" family type with "ideal" roles still persists (Epstein, 1988). How do these "ideal" notions of gender roles fare in today's families?

In the Household

In families, just as in the workplace and in other societal institutions, expectations and behaviors differ by gender and are reinforced by cultural beliefs that affect how family members carry out their daily activities. Women are still responsible for most family work, while men "help out." Men more often get to choose the household chores they will do, and consistently pick tasks that are less time-intensive or require less daily attention—like emptying the garbage, painting the living room, mowing the lawn. Women are left with the more tiresome and repetitive family work like cooking meals, doing the laundry, or cleaning the house (Berk, 1985). When men care for their young children, they more often do fun things like read sto-

Many blue-collar and ethnic women are not working to earn "pin money," but because their economic contribution is necessary to keep the family afloat.

ries, play in the yard or park, or supervise toy pickup time. Women dress, feed, and bathe children, and see to it that children stay on schedule (eat, dress, go to bed at appropriate times) and follow the family rules. For every hour that fathers spend actively engaged with their children, mothers spend three to five hours (Lamb, 1987). In the household, then, family work is defined as a gendered activity, something women do. Women are the planners, schedulers, organizers, and delegators of daily tasks.

In the Workplace

Men are considered the family earners even though most women have jobs and, when employed full time, earn 40 percent of the family income. Women and men both resist the notion of women being coproviders of the family income, probably because women are seen as having a choice about whether or not they work, and usually choose work schedules that conform to family needs. These are, of course, false assumptions for many blue-collar and ethnic women who commonly work more hours per week and sometimes take on two or more jobs out of economic necessity.

After interviewing full-time employed working-class women for her book *Bitter Choices: Blue-Collar Women in and out of Work,* social scientist Ellen Rosen (1987) concludes that most work out of necessity. Their checks provide 45 percent of the family earnings. The sampled women noted that they really have no choice but to work and little choice over job hours. Most voice anxiety about losing their jobs or their husbands, either of which would result in family poverty. The accounts of these women closely resemble remarks of women interviewed for another study by Zavella (1987), in her book *Women's Work and Chicano Families.* And in black families, married partners confess similar anxieties and fears about loss of jobs. The results of racial discrimination in the job market make the wages of both spouses in black, Hispanic, and Asian-American families very important, if not essential to family economic survival.

Many working-class women, however, continue to downplay the importance of their wages to family well-being. They do so to protect husbands. By defining their wages as secondary to family survival and denying their importance, women can portray themselves as "helping out" rather than coproviding, and thereby help husbands save face.

> Many working-class wives realize that their husbands' pride, authority, and manhood are founded on bread-winning and willingly do whatever they can to preserve the image of their husbands as primary providers. Blue-collar women often see that, by placing ultimate responsibility and recognition for provision on their husbands, they bolster their husbands' willingness to perform that obligation. In turn, blue-collar men believe that their wives and families keep them committed to their jobs. (Thompson & Walker, 1991, p. 84)

When jobs and earnings are considered, paid work, like household or family work, is defined as a gendered activity—something men do. Men are viewed as the primary family providers regardless of the significance of women's earnings to family well-being.

In Marriage

As sociologist Jessie Bernard (1982) points out in her book, *The Future of Marriage,* every marriage really consists of two marriages—the wife's marriage and the husband's marriage. Gender role norms infuse marriage as they do household work and paid work. Women are considered the "keepers of the relationship." They are in charge of making sure that communication flows, support is given, and intimacy is shared (Markman, 1984). Their mental health is closely tied to how the marriage is faring (Williams, 1988).

The expectation that today's marriages are partnerships that encompass the expression of emotional intimacy and the development of partner interdependence in thought and action seems to imply that men are equally responsible for relationship success, but in reality women are still the monitors and nurturers of marital happiness. In marriage, women are more expressive than men. They, more than men, prize displays of emotion and caring. Words like "I love you" and expressions of intimate thoughts and feelings are very important to women. In contrast, men evaluate instrumental acts more highly. They like physical demonstrations of intimacy and caring—the sex act is demonstrated love; a home-cooked meal a symbol of caring (Cancian, 1986; Rubin, 1984).

Although men and women are traditionally divided into camps according to expressive versus instrumental stereotypes, the truth is that marital partners seem to please each other more and have less conflict if they

act *against* traditional gender role socialization. If men are more expressive and women more instrumental, marital love seems more likely to flourish in contemporary relationships.

Women Look for Change, Men Look for Cover?

Women and men continue to struggle to redefine who they are and how they should behave in families. Is this struggle a battle of the sexes, with women believing that men and families are holding them back and men believing that women are unreasonable, unfair, and inaccurate in their complaints? Not really. Women still value family life and many say that the men in their lives are supportive of their achievements (Epstein, 1987; Gilbert, 1985).

In the past two decades, women have consistently reaffirmed that their three essential roles are wife, mother, and wage-earner. Well over 90 percent of women will marry; women's commitment to a family life with at least two children is as strong as in 1975; and they regard communication, love, and monogamy as important for a good marriage. A majority of women, however, no longer express a preference for the traditional marital ideal of breadwinner/husband and homemaker/wife (Virginia Slims Opinion Poll, 1990). Most married women today are employed and, regardless of their occupation, most gain satisfaction from their work. In addition, fundamental changes have occurred in how women think their roles should be enacted, with two of the most pressing issues being how household work is divided and their husbands' lack of supportiveness.

Do these complaints by women receive support from men in families? A Virginia Slims Opinion Poll conducted by Bickley Townsend and Kathleen O'Neil of the Roper Organization (1990) shows that despite indications of marital tension, women and men agree on many key issues related to women's changing roles. Men voice approval of women's improved status in society and regard discrimination against women in the workplace as a significant problem that needs resolution. Moreover, men believe that husbands must assume more household responsibilities in order to show that they are supportive of wives who have jobs.

With both women and men agreeing about these fundamental work and family issues, one might suppose family well-being to be high and marital partners free of role conflict. That would be a misstatement. In the same poll, women "agree that most men are selfish . . . too absorbed in their outside lives to pay attention to things going on at home. . . . And while two-thirds of women in 1970 believed that men are basically kind, gentle and thoughtful, barely half (51 percent) now agree" with that statement (Townsend & O'Neil, 1990, p. 32). Men's unwillingness to take on a larger share of the family responsibilities at home, the women in the 1990 survey indicated, is the source of much of the stress in their lives. Thus, "Token help with the dishes or the children no longer inspires women's gratitude; instead, as women contribute more to the family income, they expect in return a more equal division of the household responsibilities" (p. 28). For the 1990s man, being supportive means more than giving the standard 1980s verbally soothing messages. Today's men are expected to spend more time doing the shopping, vacuuming, and child rearing.

Do these increased expectations dismay men and result in a flight from commitment? Despite their popular depiction as marriage shy, well over 90 percent of men do marry and studies reveal that they derive satisfaction from being part of a family (Cath, Gurwitt, & Gunsberg, 1989; Lewis & Salt, 1986). Being married is actually more beneficial for men than for women. It enhances their physical and mental health (Barnett & Baruch, 1987; Cleary & Mechanic, 1983). In fact, sociologist Joseph Pleck (1987), who has studied changes in male roles for more than 20 years, maintains that men's family roles are more important to their psychological well-being than are their employment roles.

Sociologist Robert Weiss (1985) adds that men describe their three main roles—worker, husband, father—in very similar ways. Through his interviews with men, Weiss has discovered that they define work and family roles as mutually supportive. Having a job means that men are meeting their primary traditional family roles as husband/father by providing income for family shelter, clothing, food, and so forth; having a family means that men's work is meaningful. But expectations for how men perform their family roles are changing. The new image of the husband/father for the 1990s is that of a man who is understanding and supportive of women's changing roles at work and at home (DeStefano & Colasanto, 1990).

According to Franklin (1988): "Fathers are increasingly expected to assume a father's role that is both active and nurturant . . . participating in child-related

Increasingly, American husbands are pitching in around the house. In many households this has had a ripple effect, with children of such families also expected to perform more domestic chores.

housework, which helps prevent mothers from experiencing role overload and simultaneously provides children with positive role models . . . playing, teaching, and caregiving" (pp. 197–198). Joseph Pleck (1987) cites studies to show that during the last two decades men have increased their share of the family chores and child care "and to more than a trivial degree" (p. 17). A recent study by Gloria Bird and Bonita Ratcliff (1990) emphasizes the importance of fathers to the daily activities of the household. Fathers in this study who shared more of the household chores not only also expected their children to do more around the house, but were available during chore time to see that their children did their share of the work. Bird and

Ratcliff conclude that increased sharing of household tasks by fathers and children may eventually reduce women's family work load.

Some scholars, however, remain skeptical. For example, sociologist Ralph La Rossa (1988) comments: "Whatever changes have taken place in the behavior of fathers . . . seem to be minimal at best . . . and have largely occurred within a single group—the middle class" (p. 456). And, family studies scholars Linda Thompson and Alexis Walker (1991) note, "abiding, attentive, active, hands-on parenting is seen as imperative for mothers but optional for fathers" (p. 91). These statements added to those of the women in the Virginia Slims Opinion Poll (1990), discussed earlier, illustrate the current struggle going on in many American families where attitudinal changes are occurring at a faster pace than behavioral changes.

Barriers to Change

What barriers exist to make gender role changes more difficult? There are many, but the most prominent are family myth and sentimental ideology, history and social structure, and individual and marital expectations.

Family Myth and Sentimental Ideology

One barrier to change in gender roles is idealization of the past. An example of this tendency was the once-popular television series, "The Waltons." Unlike most of the problems that real families face, the Waltons' problems came from the outside. Week after week, some wounded person, outcast, or misguided stranger would arrive on the mountain and bring in enough of the outside world's tensions to provide drama for an hour. No matter how great the tension, the Waltons would call upon their reserves of love and understanding and somehow set things right.

If we could, many of us would probably choose to grow up in a family like the Waltons. Three loving generations in one big house. A rural existence, insulated from industrial development and urban blight. John Walton, the father, was honest, patient, hardworking, uncompromised. Olivia Walton, the wife and mother, was a woman deeply satisfied with her role. She had dignity and pride. It was all quite satisfying. From looking at the Waltons, we imagine that things must have been better when times were simpler, poverty was somehow a noble thing, rural life offered

more satisfactions than life in the city, large families worked better than small ones, and—once upon a time—both men and women must have been deeply contented in their roles. The show probably came close enough to our ideals about how things must have been in the past to convince us, by comparison, that contemporary family life is not nearly so satisfying.

One informed student of family patterns, William J. Goode, refers to the image created in such misleading portraits as "the classical family of Western nostalgia."

> It is a pretty picture of life down on Grandma's farm. There are lots of happy children, and many kinfolk live together in a large rambling house. . . . Life is difficult, but harmonious because everyone knows his task.
>
> Like most stereotypes, that of the classical family of Western nostalgia leads us astray. When we penetrate the confusing mists of recent history, we find few examples of the "classical" family. Grandma's farm was not economically self-sufficient. Few families stayed together as large aggregations of kinfolk. Most houses were small, not large. We now see more large old houses than small ones; they survived because they were likely to have been better constructed. The one-room cabins rotted away. True enough, divorce was rare, but we have no evidence that families were generally happy. Indeed, we find, as in so many other pictures of the glowing past, that each generation of people writes of a period *still* more remote, *their* grandparents' generation, when things really were much better. (1963, p. 6)

In other words, memory serves us poorly when we try to recall what family life used to be. Perhaps it is comforting to imagine a fictional past when things were better. But such recollections, particularly when they recall family life in the past, are often inaccurate. Such myths and stereotypes of how things were and how things ought to be are formidable barriers to change.

History and Social Structure

Not only are families influenced by hundreds of years of history, but their close ties to other social institutions support their reliance on a traditional definition of gender roles. Social institutions shape our experiences and reinforce the gender role dichotomy by providing greater rewards to certain groups of people based on their sex. An examination of the workplace makes this connection clearer.

In past generations, industrial jobs were filled almost solely by men. Across the economy, men were hired for the highest paying jobs and received the highest wages. Laws, union policies, and hiring practices reflected the separation of women and men, with men always benefiting more from the division. After all, men were considered the primary family providers and norms and public policy reflected that. Currently in American families, changes in beliefs about appropriate gender roles are being hurried along rather than held back by economic and industrial change. As the economy changes its base from manufacturing jobs to service and high-technology jobs, women are finding that they sometimes have a hiring advantage over men. This is a significant change.

Will alterations in the economy affect gender role behavior and result in changes in marriage patterns and the husband/wife relationship? They already have. Women are increasingly delaying marriage and childbearing, divorcing, and living alone or in single-parent families. Each of these changes has been linked to the economy. Better jobs and higher earnings are giving women more independence and power at work and at home. Sociologist Maxine Baca Zinn (1993) points out that the economy has long been a key to the changing family structure among ethnic families. She writes:

> The high level of female-headed families among blacks and Hispanics is the outgrowth of changes in the larger economy. The long-term decline in employment opportunities for men is the force most responsible for the growth of racial ethnic families headed by women. . . . The shortage of black men with the ability to support a family makes it necessary for many black women to leave a marriage or forgo a marriage altogether. Adaptation to structural conditions leaves black women disproportionately separated, divorced, and solely responsible for their children. . . . With respect to single-parent families, teenage childbirth, working mothers, and a host of other behaviors, black families serve as barometers of social change and as forerunners of adaptive patterns that will be progressively felt by the more privileged sectors of American society. . . . Alternatives that appear new to middle-class white Americans are actually variant family patterns that have been traditional within black and other minority communities for many generations. (pp. 416–417)

In sum, the economy has tended to act as a barrier to changes in gender roles in middle-class families until relatively recently. In the 1990s, the economy may actually be more of a facilitator of change, but which changes do we want to adopt and which do we want to delay? These are issues with which families in the 1990s will continue to struggle.

Individual and Marital Expectations

Individual and marital barriers to gender role change also exist. Partners usually work out between them an understanding about the nature of their relationship. Traditionally, husbands have been expected to have more power than wives in marriage. This traditional expectation is buttressed by the tendency of women to marry men who are taller, older, more educated, and who have greater earnings and status than themselves. The cultural norm has been for men's interests to take precedence over women's. Gender roles within the family are divided in keeping with that norm. The resulting hierarchy within marriage creates a kind of domestic bottleneck for change.

As women have increased their educational attainment and sought jobs outside the home, their sense of autonomy and power has increased. More often than ever before they are negotiating for a redefinition of roles within the family. In families where change is resisted, women must accept an overload of work and family responsibilities and, as a result, risk energy depletion, physical illness, and psychological distress. Change requires a redistribution of household work, which requires a woman to negotiate with a husband who typically has more power. For men, taking on more of the household and child-care responsibilities means having less time to devote to job and leisure pursuits and a questioning of the self—"If I do this, am I still a man?"

Although intellectually there may be agreement between partners that role changes are needed, the psychological work may take longer. Activities traditionally done for other family members—preparing a meal, putting oil in the car, sewing on a button, repairing a broken clothes dryer, or pressing a crease in a faded pair of jeans—often take on enormous symbolic significance. It takes time for individuals and couples to work through these psychologically touchy issues.

SUMMARY POINTS

■ Sex refers to the biological and physiological characteristics of being either male or female, while gender describes the psychological, sociological, and cultural aspects of being male or female.

■ Gender identity—the basic sense that an individual develops of being female or male—results from both biological and sociological factors.

■ Gender roles are learned. They represent what we do and say to indicate to others that we are female or male. Each culture creates its own distinctive gender role norms and through the process of socialization passes them down from generation to generation.

■ Parents, peers, siblings, teachers, and the media all contribute to children's socialization. Children also influence their own socialization by what they choose to actively imitate and incorporate into their gender identities.

■ Androgynous individuals behave in ways that are less stereotypically female or male. By being more flexible in their gender role behavior, people may be better able to cope with everyday life problems in our changing society.

■ When our personal values and beliefs about gender behavior clash with current societal norms, we feel gender role conflict.

■ Fathers are more conscious than mothers of gender role norms and more often reinforce gendered behavior in their children.

■ Negative stereotypes are usually untrue and consequently harm the mental and physical health of those so stereotyped.

■ Black parents, compared to other parents, generally socialize their daughters to be more independent, capable, and competent.

■ Blue-collar parents rear their children to be more conscious of family rules and authority than do middle-class parents.

■ Boys' socialization is accompanied by many negative sanctions; in order to be manly, boys are encouraged to suppress emotional expressiveness and adopt characteristics that will serve them well in the workplace.

■ Girls typically find adolescence a stressful time—ambivalence and confusion result from attempting to conform to two contradictory sets of norms. One set emphasizes autonomy and competence; the other more traditional set of norms focuses on dependency and choosing popularity over performance.

■ Socialization does not end with adolescence but continues throughout adulthood. People can and do change gender role attitudes and behaviors throughout the life course, but gender roles are as stereotyped for adults as they are for children and adolescents.

■ A recent poll indicates that men today are verbally supportive of women's changing gender roles. Men believe that husbands should take on more of the household responsibilities to show support for their wives.

■ But change is slow. Women say that much of the stress in their lives is the result of taking on more role responsibilities (a job) and not receiving enough instrumental support at home from their husbands.

■ Gender role changes are made more difficult by certain barriers, including family myth and sentimental ideology, history and social structure, and individual and marital expectations.

KEY TERMS

Sex	*Matriarchal*
Gender	*Gender role attitude*
Gender identity	*Gender role conflict*
Gender roles	*Social learning theory*
Androgynous	*Direct training*
Gender role stereotype	*Reinforcement*
Egalitarian	*Imitation and modeling*
Patriarchal	*Cognitive development theory*

REVIEW QUESTIONS

1. Describe the two most prominent theories of socialization.

2. Can you remember any of your role models from childhood or adolescence? Do you recall what it was about them that you liked? Did you ever pick up certain behaviors from your friends that your family

found objectionable? What were they? How did your family go about encouraging you to adopt more acceptable behavior?

3. Which sources of socialization (parents, peers, teachers, the media) do you think most influenced your development during childhood, adolescence, and young adulthood? Explain your answers.

4. Explain why socialization can create confusion and distress for both girls and boys as they move from childhood to adolescence.

5. What do you think are the advantages and disadvantages of adopting more androgynous gender roles?

6. Do you think that the men's movement as promoted by Robert Bly will spread to encompass most of the male population? Why or why not?

7. Think of someone you know who has successfully navigated the barriers to gender role change. What barriers did they encounter? Why do you think they were successful?

PART II

Establishing Intimate Relationships

3

Illustration by John H. Howard

Love and Intimacy

Love and intimacy are matters of endless speculation and fascination. *Bartlett's Familiar Quotations* contains more quotations, a total of 769, about the topic "love" than about any other topic except "man." Love—finding it, losing it, and regaining it—is the staple of the lyrics of contemporary songwriters and talk show hosts alike. Newsstands brim with magazine titles like *Screen Romance*, *Young Love*, and *Heart Throb*.

Why is it so important to understand love and intimacy? One reason is that depression, anxiety, and other symptoms of distress seem to be strongly related to being without intimate and loving relationships. Feelings of love and of being intimately connected with a romantic partner influence how satisfied we are with our relationships, while their absence is often given as an explanation for relationship dissolution.

An intimate relationship is a major source of personal well-being and a means of escape from the loneliness and impersonality that characterize modern society. In this context it is not surprising that since the late 1970s we have increasingly emphasized relationships as sources of life satisfaction and mental health (Montgomery, 1988). We know, for example, that having a close confidant makes a significant difference in how we handle everyday stressors like an overly critical boss or a traffic jam which makes us late for class, or an unexpected crisis such as the illness or death of a parent, or a bureaucratic mixup that costs us our health-care coverage. A supportive romantic or marital partner acts as a kind of buffer or barrier between us and the problems of life.

But, love and intimacy are also sources of insecurity, conflict, and confusion especially in American culture, with its deeply ingrained individualism. As the recent rash of articles, books, and talk shows about "codependency" and "addictive love" indicates, emotional interdependence can all too easily lead to unhealthy attachment. And even for those of us who are not overly dependent, the unraveling of the bonds of intimacy can be a source of extreme emotional distress.

In this chapter we draw on the work of social scientists who have, in recent years, focused great attention on the nature of love and intimacy. We answer the questions: When someone says "I love you," what do they mean? How does love develop? What are the characteristics of love and intimacy? What makes love last? What happens when love relationships start to unravel? We begin by looking at how love and intimacy are defined and then explore cultural influences on how we express love.

DEFINING LOVE AND INTIMACY

Suppose you ask your best friend to define love. You will probably get a puzzled look, followed by a silent reflection. When social scientists record how people describe love, these words are most common: adoration, fondness, affection, lust, and desire (Shaver, Schwartz, Kirson, & O'Connor, 1987). Caring, friendship, attraction, and passion are other words we often use (Clark & Reis, 1988). Actually, it is likely that there are as many definitions of love as there are scientists studying love, but all seem to agree with Elaine Hatfield and William Walster (1978) in identifying at least two kinds—passionate and companionate—both of which may or may not be present in any one love relationship. What apparently happens in many relationships is that the fragile emotion of passionate love gradually gives way to companionate love, a sturdier if less erotic attachment.

Kinds of Love: Passionate and Companionate

Passionate Love

In their research and writing, Hatfield and Walster (1978, 1988) distinguish between passionate love and companionate love. *Passionate love* is physical and non-rational. It can flare up in a very brief time between relative strangers. When passionate love is reciprocated, we feel fulfillment and ecstasy. When it is unreturned, emptiness, anxiety, or despair are typical reactions.

Passionate love is most often described as an individual feeling or emotion that can happen all at once—like being engulfed by "love at first sight." It doesn't necessarily require a close interaction with the love object or any interaction at all. Passionate love is characterized by fantasies and daydreams about what life would be like with the beloved. Flaws are overlooked in favor of an idealized image. Adolescents, for example, often fall madly in love with movie and rock stars. Such passion is usually obsessive (the person thinks of virtually nothing else) and unstable.

Although being attracted to someone can be perfectly sensible and partly understood by our inclination to choose as partners people who offer affection, beauty, or material rewards, passionate love is not so easily explained. Under the right circumstances even unpleasant, but arousing, emotions such as rejection, frustration, and fear seem to enhance passionate love. For example, both common sense and folklore tell us that an obstacle coming between potential lovers is an important stimulant to their attraction. The barrier can take almost any form; the young woman who plays hard to get is a classic example. In this case the obstacle for her pursuer is the possibility of reluctance or outright rejection. Social psychologists explain the appeal of the hard-to-get lover by pointing out that we are most rewarded when we win the approval of people who were initially neutral or rejecting toward us. It is then that we feel the gratification of converting a nonbeliever into a believer.

Although "love at first sight" can happen at any age, it is especially characteristic of young people.

Storytellers have generally preferred more elaborate obstacles, such as social class barriers (the handsome prince in love with the beautiful peasant girl; the wealthy socialite who falls for her bodyguard) or parental interference (Romeo and Juliet, separated by their families' feud). The common thread in these scenarios is that the presence of some obstacle serves to arouse greater passion.

When we encounter a dangerous situation, struggle to overcome an obstacle, or actually overcome the obstacle, we often experience fear, anxiety, or other exhilarating and physically arousing emotions. If, in this aroused state, we encounter another person, we may mislabel the general physiological arousal as sexual arousal. One of the first studies that suggested the possibility of such mislabeling was by Donald Dutton and Arthur Aron (1974). These researchers asked one group of men to cross a suspension bridge that, due to its construction, swayed and wobbled over a 230-foot gorge. Looking down, the men saw protruding rocks and rushing water. During their crossing, they discovered that the only available handrails were made of wire cable and attached low to the floor of the bridge, making it impossible to gain a sturdy, comfortable grip. Meanwhile, a control group of men crossed a solid wooden structure only 10 feet above a slower moving, more shallow part of the river.

As each man finished crossing his bridge, he was met by a female researcher who asked him to fill out a questionnaire and make up a story about a photograph she gave him. After completing the survey, he received the woman's name and phone number in case he wanted additional information about the research. On reading the participants' stories and answers to the questionnaire, the researchers discovered that the men who crossed the wobbly suspension bridge showed more emotional and sexual arousal. Indeed, half of these men phoned the female researcher and after briefly inquiring about the study, asked her out—only 13 percent of the men who crossed the safer wooden bridge did so. The men who crossed the more dangerous bridge, Dutton and Aron concluded, mislabeled the fear and anxiety aroused in them (shaky hands, difficulty breathing, rapid heartbeat) as indicators of attraction and romantic interest.

In another study, with similar findings, Gregory White (1981) asked a group of men to do one of three things to increase their heart rate and intensify their physical arousal; run or jog, listen to a very humorous tape, or listen to a dramatic and graphic taped account of a missionary set upon and killed by an angry crowd. Afterward, each participant, along with a control group of men who experienced no intentional emotional or physical arousal, was asked to view a video of a woman discussing her family background and previous educational experiences. The men who had been exposed to prior arousing tapes or who had jogged, much more often credited the woman with being attractive, sexy, and exciting than did the nonaroused men.

Other researchers like psychologist Michael Liebowitz (1983) argue that love is not as fickle or difficult to identify as these arousal studies suggest. Indeed, it can be distinguished from other strong emotions. The intensity of our passion for someone, Liebowitz proposes, can be biologically monitored by tracking the brain's release of the chemical *phenylethylamine*, a near cousin to the better-known amphetamines.

Liebowitz's research reveals that when we are in love, phenylethylamine is released, activating the brain's pleasure center (see the "Diversity" box). Thus, in the throes of passionate love, we actually become high (exhilarated, giddy, euphoric) from these and other similar chemicals controlled by the brain. In fact, when we go through low points in our love relationships or break up with someone we love, reduction in the flow of phenylethylamine may cause us to crave chocolate, which also seems to stimulate our pleasure center. Fortunately, chocolate is something in abundant supply.

Passionate love, as you can see, is hardly a stable, trustworthy, secure feeling. While it is difficult to identify the factors that trigger the emotions associated with passionate love, there is clearly a physiological component. In fact, "love at first sight" may be inspired more by the context of the first meeting than by the individuals involved. The next time you ask yourself, "How could I ever have been attracted to him or her?," try to remember the situation in which you felt the initial attraction. You may discover that fear or anxiety was mistaken for sexual arousal.

Companionate Love

Companionate love is the "affection we feel for those with whom our lives are deeply entwined" (Hatfield & Walster, 1978, p. 9). It is characterized by friendship, trust, reliability, and a less intense, although not necessarily less frequent, sexual component. Companion-

DIVERSITY

New Sightings of Romeo and Juliet

If, as Stendhal said, "Love is like a fever," then that fever infects all peoples, anthropologists say.

Some influential Western social historians have argued that romance was a product of European medieval culture that spread only recently to other cultures. They dismissed romantic tales from other cultures as representing the behavior of just the elites. Under the sway of this view, Western anthropologists did not even look for romantic love among the peoples they studied. But they are now beginning to think that romantic love is universal and is a rogue legacy of humanity's shared evolutionary past.

The fact that it does not loom large in anthropology, they say, reflects the efforts most societies have made to quash the unruly inclination. In many countries, they suspect, what appears to be romance newly in bloom is rather the flowering of instincts that were always there, but held in check by tradition and custom.

Romantic ardor has long been at odds with social institutions that knit peoples together in an orderly fashion: romantic choices rarely match the "proper" mates a family would select. In that light, falling in love has been seen by many peoples throughout the world as a dangerous and subversive—though undeniably alluring—act, one warned against in folk tale and legend.

"For decades anthropologists and other scholars have assumed romantic love was unique to the modern West," said Dr. Leonard Plotnicav, an anthropologist at the University of Pittsburgh, and editor of the journal Ethnology. "Anthropologists came across it in their field work, but they rarely mentioned it because it wasn't supposed to happen."

Anthropologists distinguish between romantic passion and plain lust, as well as other kinds of love, like that between companions or parents and children. By "romantic love," anthropologists mean an intense attraction and longing to be with the loved one.

"Why has something so central to our culture been so ignored by anthropology?" asked Dr. William Jankowiak, an anthropologist at the University of Nevada. . . .

The reason, in the view of Dr. Jankowiak and others, is a scholarly bias throughout the social sciences that viewed romantic love as a luxury in human life, one that could be indulged only by people in Westernized cultures or among the educated elites of other societies. For example it was assumed in societies where life is hard that romantic love has less chance to blossom, because higher economic standards and more leisure time create more opportunity for dalliance. That also contributed to the belief that romance was for the ruling class, not the peasants.

But, said Dr. Jankowiak, "There is romantic love in cultures around the world." Last year Dr. Jankowiak, with Dr. Edward Fischer, an anthropologist at Tulane University, published in Ethnology the first cross-cultural study, systematically comparing romantic love in many cultures.

In the survey of ethnographies from 166 cultures, they found what they considered clear evidence that romantic love was known in 147 of them—89 percent. And in the other 19 cultures, Dr. Jankowiak said, the absence of conclusive evidence seemed due more to anthropologists' oversight than to a lack of romance.

WHAT'S THE EVIDENCE?

Some of the evidence came from tales about lovers, or folklore that offered love potions or other advice on making someone fall in love.

ate love is based on sharing thoughts, feelings, and experiences. It grows more slowly than passionate love—although it can develop from the embers of romance—and requires greater commitment to a relationship.

What most of us think of as love is what researchers call passionate love; the kind of love that scholars refer to as companionate love, most of us simply call intimacy. Unlike passionate love, which often feels irra-

tional and beyond our control, intimacy is the rational consequence of a long-term effort to negotiate the terms of a relationship. While the passion of love may wane as a healthy relationship matures, intimacy tends to grow, often providing a more fulfilling alternative to the emotional roller coaster that often characterizes relationships in their early stages.

Psychologist Robert Sternberg (1986) proposes that love can best be conceptualized as a triangle. One side

Another source was accounts by informants to anthropologists. For example, Nisa, a Kung woman among the Bushmen of the Kalahari, made a clear distinction between the affection she felt for her husband, and that she felt for her lovers, which was "passionate and exciting," though fleeting. . . .

Much of the evidence for romantic love came from cautionary tales. For example, a famous story in China during the Song Dynasty (960–1279) was that of The Jade Goddess. Similar in its description of romantic love to the European tale of Tristan and Isolde, it recounts how a young man falls in love with a woman who has been committed by her family to marry someone else, but who returns his love. The couple elope, but end in desperate straits and finally return home, in disgrace.

A QUESTION OF CHEMISTRY

Indeed, from the Kama Sutra to the poems of Sappho, tales of romance are found in ancient literatures throughout the world, though largely ignored by anthropologists and Western social historians. This is one clue that romance is a universal human trait, Dr. Helen Fisher, an anthropologist at the American Museum of Natural History, contends in "Anatomy of Love," published this month by W.W. Norton.

"The brain chemistry for romantic love evolved along with pair bonding four or five million years ago, when our species started to forage, stand on two legs, and carry food back to a safe place to eat," said Dr. Fisher. "Mothers could not do all that and carry an infant in their arms without help from a partner. That led to a major change in reproductive strategy—infatuation and attachment, the ingredients of romantic love."

Dr. Fisher added, "With the evolution of pair bonding came body chemistry that initiates and sustains bonding." She proposes that because there is a biochemical system that regulates romantic feelings, the capacity for romance is universal.

Still, given cultures may channel romantic feelings in different ways. Romantic love, Dr. Jankowiak said, may be muted or repressed by cultural mores such as marriages arranged by families while the betrothed are still children. . . .

"What's new in many cultures is the idea that romantic love should be the reason to marry someone," said Dr. Jankowiak. "Some cultures see being in love as a state to be pitied. One tribe in the mountains of Iran ridicules people who marry for love."

FIRST MARRIAGE, THEN LOVE

But that has begun to change, Dr. Narayan is finding, under the influence of popular songs and movies. "In these villages the elders are worried that the younger men and women are getting a different idea of romantic love, one where you choose a partner yourself," said Dr. Narayan. "There are starting to be elopements, which are absolutely scandalous."

The same trend toward love matches, rather than arranged marriages, is being noted by anthropologists in many other cultures. . . .

That deep fear of romance, said Dr. Jankowiak, explains the near-universality of Romeo-and-Juliet-type tales, where couples who fall in love despite the objections of their families end tragically, rather than happily ever after.

"The moral of these cautionary tales is that romantic love is the enemy of the extended family and social stability," said Dr. Jankowiak. "But as romantic marriage becomes more common in a given culture, the old, traditional bonds weaken, though they may emerge in new forms to accommodate the change.

EXPLORATIONS *Do you think romantic love results from an alteration in brain chemistry, socialization into prevailing cultural stereotypes, or some combination of both? Besides increased access to television and films, what other social factors may be influencing the spread of romantic love?*

SOURCE: Excerpted from D. Goleman (1992).

is made up of passionate love which involves physical attraction and desire for sex. Companionate love forms the other two sides of the triangle and consists of two elements—intimacy and decision/commitment. *Intimacy*, the emotional component of companionate love, consists of feelings of closeness, connectedness, and bondedness to a partner. There is also a cognitive component, which is the decision to make a commitment to the development and maintenance of the relationship over time.

In most marriages, the initial passion diminishes after a time, but intimacy and commitment keep the relationship vital and satisfying. There are some couples who manage to combine passion, intimacy, and commitment. This kind of "consummate love" is what everyone strives for and not many attain. Sternberg proposes that the type of love a person experiences toward another determines the shape of their *love tri-*

angle (see Figure 3-1). While most relationships do not attain the balance represented by the equilateral triangle, the more similar each partner's triangle is to the other's, the greater the probability of each feeling happiness in the relationship.

CULTURAL INFLUENCES ON CONCEPTIONS OF LOVE

Although we tend to focus more on personal, internal reasons for how people behave when they love each other, cultural beliefs also influence our behavior. How individuals define love not only depends on their own past experiences in love relationships, and the very private and personal interactions between themselves and their current love partners, but on the cultural stereotypes they most strongly believe in. An exploration of the prevailing cultural scenarios of a few historical time periods, beginning with the ancient Greeks and ending with the 1990s in America, allows us to sample the diversity of views.

Historical Views of Love

Love in Ancient Greece and Rome

Love has a strange and fascinating history. In ancient Greece, the philosopher Plato believed that love was a vital element in human society because it inspired virtue. He distinguished two types of love: common and heavenly. Common love, as Plato defined it, was concerned primarily with physical satisfaction. The more lofty or heavenly type of love involved spiritual pleasure, the love of the soul. Although it might be heterosexual, the preferred form as expressed in some of Plato's *Dialogues* was homosexual.

In the first century A.D., the Roman poet Ovid defined love as an essential element in the pursuit of pleasure—sensual not spiritual pleasure. Love was neither romantic nor an affair of the soul. It was not even expected to last very long. At bottom it was "a game of mutual deceit" in which each person tried to win the attention and the physical pleasures provided by the other (Reiss, 1971). Unlike Plato, Ovid was interested only in heterosexual love, but he agreed that love had very little to do with marriage.

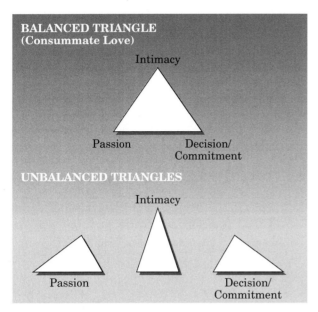

BALANCED TRIANGLE
(Consummate Love)

Intimacy

Passion   Decision/
Commitment

UNBALANCED TRIANGLES

Intimacy

Passion   Decision/
Commitment

FIGURE 3-1
Sternberg's Triangle of Love
*According to Sternberg, most love relationships have three
components: passion, intimacy, and decision/commitment,
each of which vary in intensity in each relationship. The elon-
gated point in each of the triangles indicates the area of greatest intensity. If you are in a love relationship, try to draw a
triangle representing your love. Ask your partner to do the
same. Then compare your triangles to determine your compatibility.*

SOURCE: R. J. Sternberg (1986).

Love in the Twelfth Century

By the twelfth century, love was still disconnected
from marriage and still a privilege of the upper classes.
Commoners were assumed to be incapable of it. But if
its circumstances were the same, its substance was different. The sensual game of love that Ovid had described was forgotten, replaced by the courtly lover of
the Middle Ages, who practiced an elaborate etiquette
designed to heighten his longing for the beloved. The
etiquette expressed jealousy, obsession, admiration,
and affection, thus setting courtly love apart from marriage, a relationship that, according to the medieval
view, allowed for little tenderness.

Unlike the Roman concept of love, courtly love was
a tradition defined mainly by women—the noble-
women of the feudal manors and their lady friends.
Men invented the chastity belt to discourage these
ladies from misusing their leisure while their husbands
were away fighting in the Crusades. The domestic situation for the upper classes was complicated by the

abundance of young bachelor knights around many
feudal households. In this society that severely limited
opportunities for sexual intercourse, one of the favorite
activities in the manors was the discussion of romantic
attraction.

In ancient Greece, love had been regarded as rather
undesirable, an intoxication, a divine punishment. By
the twelfth century, the troubadours, or wandering
minstrels, turned this notion around: love is suffering,
they agreed, but a sweet suffering, something to be
cultivated. Wandering from manor to manor they sang
about love as sweet longing, not sensual abandon.
Their poetry described four stages of courtship. In
stage one, the lover sees his lady from afar and falls
helplessly in love with her. In stage two, the lover
gathers the courage to talk to his lady about his
dreams, hopes, and ambitions. If she acknowledges
him as a suitor, he is permitted to advance to stage
three. In stage three, he composes love poems and
songs expressing his longing for her. Most relationships ended at this stage.

Only through extraordinary passion and extreme
courage could a lover advance to stage four—physical
contact. Pure love had previously permitted no touching, for this would compromise the reputation of the
lady (she was either single and a virgin or a married
woman). To have sexual relations without advancing
through the first three stages, therefore, was considered dishonorable and socially unacceptable (Haas &
Haas, 1990). Then, as now, love was easily the most
fascinating of topics. The troubadours, like the songwriters of today, concentrated on romantic longing
and ignored marriage.

It became quite fashionable in the twelfth century
to argue the merits of love, to discuss its true characteristics. Long debates raged among noble ladies about
the rules of love. Formal decrees were issued defining
a code of conduct appropriate in a relationship between a married woman and a knight. Some of these
decrees appeared in a book written late in the century
by Andreas Capellanus, chaplain to Countess Marie of
Champagne. Andreas informs his readers that "when
a lover suddenly catches sight of his beloved, his heart
palpitates." Later he describes love as a very unpleasant state indeed, an obsessive state with a variety of
unfortunate symptoms: "A man in love is always apprehensive. He whom the thought of love vexes eats
and sleeps very little" (1959, p. 184). There is an element of exaggeration here; yet these symptoms are still
recognizable as the side effects of the emotions stirred
by passionate love and are the foundation for much of

In the twelfth century, the new ideal of courtly love, characterized by sweetly painful yearning for the beloved lady, was spread by the songs of troubadours, or wandering minstrels.

our contemporary views of love. Even today, to see if love exists, we look for telltale signs: distraction, euphoria, and even obsession.

Love in America: 1700–1800

During the 1700s and into the 1800s in America, women relied on each other for the emotional support, affection, caring, and understanding we currently associate with romantically attached or married couples. Most middle-class women lived within communities in which home, church, and the institution of visiting— the social networks of responsibility and obligation that women created through their regular visits with each other—defined their lives. A woman's world was inhabited by children and other women. "Women helped each other with domestic chores and in times of sickness, sorrow, or trouble" (Smith-Rosenberg, 1989, p. 233). Ties between women kin and friends lasted throughout their lives and provided for women's intimacy needs. Women's diaries and letters to

each other from those times are especially poignant. "An undeniably romantic and even sensual note frequently marked females' relationships" (Smith-Rosenberg, p. 241). This does not mean that the love between women was physical, but it did involve greater emotional intimacy than love between women and men.

Romantic love began to gain recognition during the mid-1800s as the basis for marital relationships at the time industrialization was bringing about the separation of men and women into two very different worlds. Men increasingly worked outside the home and their main rewards were seen as coming from their work roles. Women's sphere was the home and they were to gain their main life satisfaction from attending to family needs. Historian Carol Smith-Rosenberg's (1989) research on women of the 1800s indicates that this rigid division of gender roles, typical of American society until recently (see Chapter 2), led to the emotional separation of men and women. The nonphysical part of a relationship between a man and a woman tended to involve a sharing of experience but often did not include the sharing of thoughts and feelings. Even the physical aspects of love were conceived of differently. Touching, for example, was not culturally approved and occurred only in the bedroom.

Men were basically excluded from this women's world of love and intimacy. The closeness, self-disclosure, and uninhibited physical contact allowed among women was not expected in male-female relationships. Indeed, courtship and marriage were set within a framework of formality that excluded most emotional and physical intimacy between women and men. This formality grew out of the cultural separation of women and men and their socialization into different roles. "With marriage," Smith-Rosenberg explains, "both women and men had to adjust to life with a person who was, in essence, a member of an alien group" (1989, p. 242).

That passionate or romantic love should be the basis of enduring marital ties is a relatively modern belief that has only existed in western societies in the last few centuries. Love is no longer an emotion present solely in extramarital liaisons or among women friends. It is a mutual sentimental bond between a couple that is expected to last a lifetime.

The Social Construction of Contemporary Love Styles

In the 1990s there are still consistent cultural beliefs in American society about love: everyone should fall in love, love makes life worthwhile, love always over-comes hardship and indifference, love can solve any problem, and love is ultimately fulfilled in marriage. Such ideals color our expectations about romantic relationships. We carry these notions with us from the very beginning of our romantic relationships into the early stages of marriage (Huston, McHale & Crouter, 1986). Not only are our beliefs about love influenced by our culture, sociologist John Lee contends that the experience of love itself is, in part, socially constructed.

Our personal experiences with love, Lee argues, are influenced by the particular preferred cultural stereotypes or scenarios of love that we believe in. Lee identifies six basic stereotypes that represent contemporary *styles of loving,* which are presented in Table 3-1.

Sometimes a person combines more than one style of loving; for example, a woman can be *Eros-Ludus* or *Pragma-Storge.* As Lee (1988) explains, "Love styles are not like signs of the zodiac. You are not born with a particular preference, and you can have more than one preference in a lifetime. In fact, you can have two different preferences at the same time, each fulfilled by a different partner" (p. 41).

These scenarios are used, more or less, to justify our feelings and the behaviors we exhibit while "in love." We build these scenarios by observing other people who say they are in love. We listen to couples talking about when they fell in love and how they know they are in love; we read magazines, novels, and watch actors on television and in the movies portraying what love feels like. Using all of these sources, plus various others, we compare our own feelings and behaviors to what we have observed and if the fit between them is good, we feel more confident in labeling our own reactions as love.

People have been found to change their outlooks on love as they age. This is partially due to experience and maturity, but it may also be attributable to a desire to conform to the stereotype of mature love. For example, as a young adult, a person typically experiences love relationships based on passionate physical attraction. Such relationships generally progress quickly from brief acquaintanceship to sexual intimacy and just as quickly fade as another attractive alternative appears. This is predictable and acceptable behavior for a young adult but might be considered immature and indulgent in a 40-year-old. Later in adulthood this same person could be in a relationship that grows slowly over a lengthy period of time through friendship, togetherness, and the intimate disclosures that

TABLE 3-1
John Lee's Styles of Loving

EROS
Eros lovers are attracted to others primarily because of their physical beauty. They search for a person whose physical appearance matches their ideal physical type. They are passionate, intense, somewhat idealistic about sexuality, willing to disclose to a lover and moderately eliciting of disclosure from others, and generally interested in seeking sensation for its own sake.

LUDUS
Playful love is the style of the Ludus lover. Ludus lovers do not get committed to a single relationship, but prefer to play the field. Within the relationship, they are oriented to casual, permissive, and sometimes manipulative sexuality. Ludus partners are generally nondisclosing (or eliciting of disclosure) and are uninhibited and easily bored. No single relationship is likely to meet their need for novelty and excitement.

PRAGMA
Pragmatic lovers are concerned with vital statistics in searching for the right person. They look for someone who has the right personality, education, religion, job, and so on. The Pragma lover is somewhat instrumental about sex (and about love) and modestly eliciting of disclosure.

AGAPE
(Pronounced a-*gay*-pay) Agape lovers show altruistic love. They give without expectation of getting anything in return and are gentle, caring, and dutiful. Agape lovers are similar to Eros lovers in some ways (idealistic about sex, disclosing to a lover) but unique in their altruism. Agapic partners are actively negative about permissive, instrumental sexuality, perceive themselves as good listeners, and are unlikely to become bored with a relationship.

MANIA
Intense romantic love is the style of manic lovers. They are jealous, think intensely and excessively about their beloved, and need repeated reassurance that they are loved in return. Manic lovers show some similarities to Eros, with moderately idealistic beliefs about sexuality, a willingness to disclose to both the beloved and friends (females only) and an interest in eliciting disclosure. When any problem erupts in their relationships, their possessivity, dependency, and low self-confidence soon appear.

STORGE
(Pronounced *stor*-gay) Storge lovers love someone as a result of a slowly developing attachment to that person. They move slowly, carefully, without great passion, to a lasting commitment. Storge lovers are moderately idealistic about sexuality, eliciting of disclosure from others and not easily bored.

characterize a mature relationship and correspond to the cultural stereotype of love in late adulthood.

While conformity to social stereotypes is one way that love is socially constructed, styles of loving are also the result of social interaction and negotiation with a partner. Clearly there are many factors affecting the way love is felt and expressed, not the least of which is the social context of love. A full understanding of this phenomenon, which seems so personal and individual, must include a knowledge of the social, emotional, and physiological factors that contribute to this uniquely human experience.

GENDER AND LOVE

Love and Power: The Intimate Connection

Do women and men love differently? Of all the factors that influence how we love someone, gender is probably one of the most powerful. One theory is that gendered beliefs about love are shaped by how we as a culture define the roles of women and men. Because, compared to women, middle- and upper-class men have historically had greater access to valued resources—an education, social status, a vocation, money—women were encouraged to depend on men for their economic survival (Rubin, Peplau, & Hill, 1981). Even in cases where women have careers, status, and considerable earnings, it is typical for them to be with partners of even greater status and power. This power differential between men and women influences how they communicate affection and caring to one another.

Men continue to associate talking about their feelings with vulnerability, despite the fact that it is within their love relationships that they are most self-disclosing. Even today, many men attempt to reduce vulnerability by withdrawing from or avoiding talk about their thoughts and feelings on intimate matters. Women are the "social-emotional specialists" in most relationships (Frazier & Esterly, 1990, p. 333). In contrast, men are less aware of their partner's needs and less sensitive to the emotional aspects of relationships that women find so important. Men are more attuned to the sexual side of intimacy.

When a man reluctantly participates in intimate conversation and discloses little personal information about his feelings, he is, in effect, controlling the topics of discussion and the level of closeness in that relationship. Women often respond by redoubling their efforts to get their partners to self-disclose. Such maneuvering imposes additional "emotional work" on the woman (Sattel, 1989). This kind of power conflict between partners—he withdraws, she pursues—reflects poorly on the relationship and is one reason some relationships break up.

Feminization of Love

This division of love by gender has led some scholars to conclude that love has become "feminized." Sociologist Francesca Cancian, in her 1987 book, *Love in America,* explains that Americans tend to identify love with emotional expression and talk about feelings, aspects of love women prefer and tend to be better at than men. In an earlier article, she concludes, "we often ignore the instrumental and physical aspects of love that men prefer, such as providing help, sharing activities, and sex" (1986, p. 692). Viewing love from this perspective, she suggests, leads us to think that women, compared to men, are more capable of loving—that men must love more like women for relationships to be successful.

Cancian provides examples of men's complaints about their wives not understanding their ways of loving: "What does she want? Proof? She's got it, hasn't she? Would I be knocking myself out to get things for her—like to keep up this house—if I didn't love her? Why does a man do things like that if not because he loves his wife and kids? I swear, I can't figure what she wants." For women, love means something entirely different. One wife explains, "It is not enough that he supports us and takes care of us. I appreciate that, but I want him to share things with me. I need for him to tell me his feelings" (1986, p. 702).

According to Cancian, working-class women are less likely to feminize love and more likely to understand men's reasoning—that the instrumental tasks a man does at work and at home are expressions of love. Working-class women's greater understanding of men's position probably comes from their long history of having to take jobs to help support their families. Love for family was their primary motivation for employment. For generations working-class women have worked in and out of the home caring for children, husbands, the elderly, and other needy extended family members out of an ethic of obligation—putting their needs second to those of the family (Allen, 1989). Thus, when working-class husbands say that the things they do at work and at home represent love, working-class women more often empathize. And when their husbands fail to share feelings as often as they might like, these women more frequently justify it as being because their husbands are tired or emotionally numb from their job responsibilities. In addition, they also more readily accept their husbands' reasoning that their sexual desires are symbols of love.

Women in middle-class marriages, because of their greater resources, are further removed from the reality of the instrumental nature of family obligation and necessity. Their lives involve more choice and control and their expectations for marriage include a stronger desire for emotional interdependence between romantic and marital partners. Therefore, middle-class women almost never accept a definition of men's love that relies on instrumental support, nor are they as willing to accept their husband's sexual advances as symbols of love. The sexual act, for such women, must be within a context of shared emotions. Without the "emotional foreplay," the sex act is not as meaningful or fulfilling.

The prevailing cultural definition of love that focuses on emotional expression, according to Cancian, puts women at a disadvantage by failing to give them credit for all the instrumental tasks they perform for their families out of love—doing laundry, preparing meals, cleaning bathrooms, and caring for children and aged family members. Defining love as only expressive devalues men's and women's provider roles in the family as well as women's competence at family caregiving. It encourages men to view love as feminine behavior, something that women should be responsible for, as it threatens male status. This view encourages men to become overinvolved in their work roles and women to specialize in caring for others.

Moving Toward an Androgynous Love

Cancian believes that contemporary American couples are attempting to incorporate both male and female views of love—instrumental and expressive—into a more androgynous framework. In the past 20 years, gender roles have become more similar as women have gained access to greater societal resources through education and employment (see Chapter 2). Though power remains unequal and love is still feminized, love for one's partner is more often idealized as occurring within an interdependent and equal re-

lationship. Men are increasingly expected to take greater responsibility for relationship development and maintenance. More than ever before they are being encouraged to express their feelings. Simultaneously, women are being encouraged to explore their sexuality.

In their book, *Habits of the Heart,* social scientists Robert Bellah and his colleagues (1985) claim that

> Americans are now torn between love as an expression of inner freedom, a deeply personal, but necessarily somewhat arbitrary choice, and the image of love as a firmly planted, permanent commitment, embodying obligations that transcend the immediate feelings, or wishes of either partner. (p. 93)

Francesca Cancian argues that we have mostly resolved the individual versus the relationship conflict that was so debated throughout the 1970s and 1980s. In the 1990s, self-fulfillment and personal autonomy are recognized as important, and both are considered possible within a loving and committed relationship that emphasizes the mutual development of both partners. As she reminds us, the definition of this 1990s kind of love is:

> . . . when two adults express affection, acceptance, and other positive feelings to each other, provide each other with care and practical assistance . . . it also includes commitment—an intention to maintain the affection and the assistance for a long time, despite difficulties, and specialness—giving the loved person priority over others . . . sexual intimacy and physical affection, as well as cooperation in the routine tasks of daily living . . . promoting each other's self-development, and communicating and understanding each other's personal feelings and experiences (1987, p. 70).

In sum, the American view of love has changed over the centuries and is closely tied to gender role expectations. As our cultural beliefs about appropriate gender role behavior have grown more androgynous, we have come to believe that love should not be the sole responsibility of women and that previous definitions of love may have been too narrow. Nevertheless, we still consider passionate or romantic love to be a prerequisite for an enduring marital relationship. We expect couples to meet and fall in love. We believe that passion, when accompanied by self-disclosure, trust, caring, and negotiation develops into intimacy.

DEVELOPING A LOVE RELATIONSHIP

The American view of romantic love is *individual centered* and considers emotional attachment as necessary for an enduring marital relationship. Some other cultures take a different view of love. They assume that if the parents make a proper choice, a satisfying kind of marital love can grow between partners. In these societies, romantic attraction and passionate love are considered disruptive—certainly no foundation for an institution as practical as marriage. Chinese and Indian beliefs, for example, are based on a *situation-centered* concept of love that does not include "matters of the heart." In these cultures, traditions rest on individuals having a shared social network and family structure (see the "Diversity" box). The Chinese, psychological anthropologist Francis Hsu (1981) argues, more strongly emphasize the individual's dependency on others. "An American asks," explains Hsu, "How does my heart feel?" A Chinese asks, "What will my family say?"

Does the American emphasis on individual-centered love make it difficult to develop intimate relationships with others and, as some suggest, contribute to a high rate of divorce (Bellah et al., 1985)? Or do most Americans value close committed relationships that extend across time and include displays of affection, trust, and interdependence?

It is a well-established finding that most relationships move from a period of self-centered individual orientation to a couple orientation as they develop and intimacy grows. As the research of George Levinger (1983) and other social psychologists, anthropologists, and sociologists suggests, individual-centered love describes only the beginning phases of most relationships. Most enduring relationships progress to a "couple-centered" and eventually a "family-centered" orientation over time.

How do couples move from passion, romantic attraction, or a special friendship to intimacy? Scholars who study love relationships tell us that intimacy is relational; it emerges from the interaction of partners. As a love relationship builds, communication usually occurs more often and penetrates deeper into the feelings, motivations, and goals of each partner. Progress toward intimacy, however, may not be constant—it usually ebbs and flows. It's more like a series of "gradual changes punctuated by occasional turning points," suggests Levinger (1983, p. 327). "Couples differ

widely in their speed of buildup . . . some pairs go from superficial acquaintance to marriage with hardly a thought, whereas others go through a very prolonged and vacillating course of involvement" (p. 329).

Intimacy is also influenced by current societal expectations. Couples test their interdependence in various ways as they negotiate the culturally approved roles, rules, and parameters of their relationship. People consider long and hard whether or not they can live with certain of their partner's attitudes and behaviors over time. Many relationships break up precisely because they cannot. Social psychologist Sharon Brehm (1985) recounts a classic story about a relationship breaking up

> . . . because the man couldn't stand the way his partner squeezed the toothpaste tube in the middle instead of, like him, rolling it up from the bottom. This sounds ridiculous, but in the context of the present discussion maybe there is a great deal of wisdom about human behavior in the story. Every day the man had to think about facing that squashed toothpaste tube for every coming morning of his life. And, standing in the bathroom, only half-awake, he may have thought, "First, the toothpaste . . . then what?" (p. 194)

For many, this process of getting to know each other is very difficult. In some cases, psychological barriers to intimacy, conflicting goals, or outside influences impede the development of the relationship to such an extent that commitment is impossible. But if couples survive the struggle to resolve conflicts and solve problems, their relationship is strengthened.

It is not enough for couples to show caring and affection for one another. For a love relationship to eventually emerge as intimate, several things must occur simultaneously between the couple and be judged by them as positive and successful. Couples with the most successful and satisfying relationships disclose personal facts and feelings to each other; they display behavior that is deemed fair and equitable toward each other; and they make a commitment to remain together long term.

Self-Disclosure

Self-disclosure, or self-revelation, is the sharing of intimate personal feelings and experiences about ourselves. We typically reveal ourselves slowly and cautiously when we expect a relationship to last for some time. In love relationships people commonly share all facets of themselves—their hopes, fears, and

DIVERSITY

Love in India

In India, love is not considered a stable enough factor to support a marital relationship. Love and romance are secondary to family obligation. Love, Indian-style, comes *after* marriage, not before. In their view, American reliance on love rituals encourages humiliating practices. For example, men and women have to call attention to themselves to attract a partner and compete with each other for dates, something that Indians don't have to do. To many Indians, their way seems superior.

In selecting mates for their children, Indian parents and kinship groups frequently enlist the aid of modern media by placing ads in the matrimonial columns of newspapers. These ads, which in America are inserted by the parties themselves, perform the same function in India as in the United States—they expand the number of possible partners. Indian ads follow a typical form. For example, one upper-middle-class family in New Delhi seeking a husband for their daughter paid for the following personal ad in the widely respected national newspaper, the *Hindustan Times*:

> Well-placed match desired for accomplished, smart, homely Brahmin girl, 26 years. B.A. Ed., brother doctor, well-to-do family. Early decent marriage. Caste no bar.

This ad indicates the socially defined qualities many Indian families look for, as well as those deemed less important in choosing a marital partner for their offspring. Unlike American personal ads, which almost never mention the person's family background, this ad emphasizes its significance. The phrase "well-to-do family" is a polite way of indicating the desirability of the family assets—wealth and prestige. The ad also shows that a high level of education and intelligence are seen as assets, while age and appearance are significant factors that must at least be mentioned in order to attract an appropriate mate. In this instance, the family specifies that the young woman is "homely," probably so as to not raise false hopes in potential partners or their families. In addition, the ad tells us that social

status, as defined in India by caste position, is far less powerful than it once was.

Suppose the ad is answered by a seemingly suitable candidate's family. Only after the socially defined requirements articulated in the ad have been satisfied do the families proceed to the next stage: assessing the personal qualities of the prospective partners (Weinraub, 1973; Augustine, 1982).

They do this by initiating inquiries into the background, character, and personality of each of the young people. Professional marriage brokers and go-betweens are usually employed for this purpose. Each family progresses very carefully, trying to enhance its own status while simultaneously trying to provide a good match for their son or daughter. The entire painstaking procedure once again shows how love is situation-centered rather than a matter of the heart. This is made fully apparent by the absence of any input by the prospective bride or groom throughout most of the selection process.

In recent years, modernization and increased geographic mobility have encouraged a change in attitudes among many college-educated Indians about love and marriage. Although only a very small minority desire as much freedom of choice as most Americans take for granted—namely the ultimate power over the selection of a mate—an overwhelming majority of educated Indians want some voice in the process (Augustine, 1982). Whether this modest gain will suffice or whether there will be further evolution toward individual-centered love American-style will certainly be answered in the next century.

EXPLORATIONS *What does the mate selection process in India reveal about the society's views toward romantic love? Do family members in America have any say about who their children choose to love? If they disapprove of an adult child's romantic partner, how do parents typically behave? Under what conditions does parental approval carry more weight with their child?*

dreams—and feel they are understood and accepted for who and what they are, for their "true self," rather than for the image they project (Miller & Read, 1987). It is this element of self-disclosure that protects people in intimate relationships from loneliness. People who

are not in an intimate relationship may have lots of friends and go out all the time. Yet, a rather common complaint of theirs is of being lonely. This is not surprising as loneliness is not due to lack of contact with others, but results from feeling misunderstood (Stokes,

One of the key factors that determines whether a love relationship becomes intimate is the willingness of couples to mutually self-disclose, or bare their deepest self to one another.

1987). If a relationship is working, both partners believe they are understood.

Self-disclosure is typically reciprocal—I tell you something about me, then you tell me something about you ("I'm really very shy"; "I'm just the opposite, kind of super extroverted"). Disclosing enables partners to make their intentions clear to one another and to explain the meaning of their behavior so that what they do to and for each other is not misinterpreted ("Sometimes I withdraw into myself but it's not because I'm angry at you") (Derlega, 1984).

Risks of Disclosure

Although self-disclosure generally plays a positive role in relationship development, social psychologists advise us that there are certain risks to it. Besides revealing our anxieties and fears, true self-disclosure

means that we let another see our least likeable characteristics and behaviors ("Winning means everything to me"; "I get jealous easily"). Elaine Hatfield (1984), psychologist and family therapist, maintains that some people are hesitant to disclose things to others that may be shameful or embarrassing or may reveal an inner self that is unattractive to their partner.

Hatfield cautions that such fears may not be unrealistic. "One of my favorite graduate students," explains Hatfield, "was a beautiful Swedish woman. At one time, three sociologists at the university were in love with her. Her problem? She pretended to be totally self-confident, bright, charming. In intimate affairs, each time she tried to admit how uncertain she was, to be herself, the men lost interest. They wanted to be in love with a *Star*, not a mere mortal" (p. 210).

A second reason for avoiding self-disclosure is fear that our confidant might reveal what we say to others. Hatfield recounts another story of an older, powerful businessman who was afraid to share with his girlfriend the concern that he was not as capable as his younger competitors, for fear that she should tell someone else and that this information would get back to the competition. Sometimes, too, people are afraid to disclose powerful negative feelings like anger because they believe expressing these would be too destructive for the relationship. In fact, anger can be destructive, but most people can learn to express their feelings in a controlled manner and thus come to realize that their emotions aren't as overpowering as they may fear.

Finally, Hatfield relates that people sometimes are afraid that if they reveal too much they will completely disappear into the other person and have nothing left of themselves. As an example she describes the Watson family. The parents seemingly wanted their daughters to be independent—to leave home, find employment, marry, and have families. However, each time the daughters (now age 50) displayed any autonomy, the parents were quick to complain that they were making incorrect, disastrous decisions. When any sign of independence was detected, the parents became angry, interfered, nagged, and complained. As a result, the daughters typically avoided any type of close relationships with people outside the family. They equated such closeness with the smothering type of control displayed by their parents.

Other risks to self-disclosure include fear of discovering that the person we are attracted to does not want to have a closer relationship with us or that our partner uses information we have revealed to try to gain control or power over us. For example, suppose you tell your partner about your deep fear of being rejected or abandoned because your father died when you were a young child and then she or he tries to gain the upper hand in a subsequent argument by threatening to leave the relationship. It is also possible to discover that our partner cannot be trusted to keep secrets, or to feel hurt or resentful because, when we reveal intimate personal information, our partner always resists reciprocating.

Despite the risks of self-disclosure, it is key to the growth of intimacy. In couples where partners mutually disclose, feelings of liking and loving are stronger. Sprecher (1987) found that couples she studied who remained together over a 4-year period disclosed more information to their partners than did couples who broke up.

Trust and Disclosure

Trust—the belief that others are reliable—is integral to self-disclosure. In an intimate relationship, trust influences the nature of the information disclosed (Rogers & Miller, 1988). Although trust develops differently in each relationship—sometimes rapidly, sometimes slowly, sometimes deeply, sometimes narrowly and self-consciously—the usual pattern is one of slow and gradual growth as partners assess each other's motivations and character. Trust also depends on mutual feelings of warmth and caring and the belief that both partners will express their own needs and be responsive to the other's needs (Chelune, Robinson, & Kommor, 1988).

The ultimate goal of each partner is to have confidence that the other is attached to the relationship. At the beginning of a relationship, passion or attraction for the partner generally obscures any concerns about trust. As the relationship develops and partners feel freer to openly communicate with each other, they become more vulnerable to exploitation and rejection. For the relationship to deepen, both persons must believe that the other will not take advantage of their vulnerability, be deliberately hurtful, or lie to them.

When partners have known each other for awhile and are at the point of making an exclusive commitment, they typically take a more evaluative look at the relationship itself—take off the rose-colored glasses. They become increasingly observant and concerned with each other's behavior, attitudes, and motives, as inevitable conflicts arise over personal preferences and styles of interaction (Holmes & Rempel, 1989). The college female may ask: "Can I trust Bill to communicate with me in an open and honest way?" "Does he keep his promises?" "Can I trust him to look out for *both* of us, not just himself?" "Will he compromise on something that means a lot to me, like being willing to share work and family responsibilities after we marry?"

Couples in love relationships watch over each other and look out for each other's needs. It is this sense of giving attention and being ready to respond to the personal needs of the other that causes both partners in an intimate relationship to feel cared for and loved (Noddings, 1984; Thompson, 1989).

Equity: A Sense of Fairness between Partners

The development of a love relationship is also based on the expectation that both partners will jointly work to make the relationship satisfying for each person. Feeling like part of a team is important to believing that the relationship is satisfactory and enjoyable. Part of this satisfaction comes from believing that the relationship is fair to both partners.

When partners believe that their relationship is fair or equitable, they are more likely to remain in it and move toward increased intimacy. What is fair? In an equitable or fair relationship, "partners have an equal opportunity to present their own views and needs, their differences are respected, and everyone's welfare is considered equally worthy," explains family scientist Linda Thompson (1989, p. 15).

Equity Theory

According to *equity theory*, which is often used to explain fairness in relationships, a person is most satisfied with a relationship when there is a balance of giving and receiving between the partners (Brehm, 1992). If one partner is consistently receiving more than the other, that partner is said to be *overbenefitted* in the relationship. The partner who is consistently receiving less than the other is said to be *underbenefitted*. Overbenefitted partners generally feel guilty while underbenefitted partners feel angry and depressed.

$$\frac{\text{What you get out of the relationship}}{\text{What you put into the relationship}} = \frac{\text{What your partner gets out of the relationship}}{\text{What your partner puts into the relationship}}$$

Couples in inequitable relationships typically make efforts to restore the balance of give and take in their relationships. For example, the underbenefitted partner might negotiate for change ("I need you to be more affectionate"; "I want you to treat me with more respect in front of your relatives"; I feel we have to spend more time together"). The overbenefitted partner may listen and try to make changes or choose to ignore or devalue the request. If the request is ignored, the slighted partner has two choices—she or he can look for reasons to remain in the relationship despite the costs, or can end it.

For example, Karen may want to keep her boyfriend Jim, despite being underbenefitted. So she focuses on how "special" Jim is and, therefore, deserves to be overbenefitted in their relationship ("Jim works so hard"; He's under a lot of stress in law school"; "His parents spoiled him"). Or Karen might look at other couples she knows and try to convince herself that, compared with them, she is really better off ("Julio's such a jerk"; "Jim is 10 times more exciting than Thomas"). Or Karen may think about the relationship as extending over a long period of time and evaluate whether the current unfairness is temporary and unlike the usual pattern of interaction between Jim and herself—or she may look to the future and become convinced that change will occur in a few months or years when circumstances change ("First-year law school is always the worst"; "My friends say he'll be a different man if he survives it").

These strategies are unconscious efforts to establish a kind of false equity, which is the result of a change in the underbenefitted partner's perception of the relationship, not the actual situation or behavior of the overbenefitted partner. This false equity is called *psychological equity* and can be viewed as a mechanism that is usually ineffective for coping with inequity in a relationship. Studies show that inequitable relationships are more often unsatisfying and can lead to unhappiness and divorce (Brehm, 1992). People who stay in such relationships usually feel that they have no other alternatives—nowhere else to go; no one else they can depend on.

Arlie Hochschild describes one couple's middle-class struggle for equity in her 1989 book *Second Shift*. Seth reflects on his wife's attempts to restore a sense of fairness to their relationship:

Jessica has been very disappointed about my inability to do more in terms of the childrearing, and about my not sharing things fifty-fifty. She says I've left the child-rearing to her. Her career has suffered. She says she's cut twice as much time from her career as I've cut from mine. She complains that I'm not like some imaginary other men, or men she knows, who take time with their children because they want to and know how important it is. On the other hand, she understands the spot I'm in. So she holds it in until she gets good and pissed off, and then she lets me have it. (p. 116)

In the end, because Seth failed to respond to Jessica's needs as the underbenefitted partner, Jessica unconsciously established psychological equity to save the marriage. She accepts her husband's long work hours by more wholeheartedly colluding in the idea that he is the helpless prisoner of his profession and his personality. "But as she does this, she makes another emotional move—away from the marriage and family. . . . She will accommodate his strategy on the surface but limit her emotional offerings underneath—give some nurturance to the children, very little to Seth, and save the rest for herself" (p. 120).

Hochschild describes another woman's struggle to restore actual equity to her marriage; on failing that, Ann attempts psychological equity. Failing that, she gives up her career to support her husband in his career:

I honestly feel Robert can contribute more than I can. He's better educated. He's just plain smarter. He's genuinely gifted, and when he's able to apply himself, he can really accomplish something, can make a name for himself. I care about him having time to think. One of the contributions I can make is allowing him to make a valuable contribution before I'm burned out. I tell him, "I want to take the pressure off of you." (p. 104)

Obviously, Ann values her marriage and wants it to work out. But it is equally obvious that Robert's position has remained unmovable, and it has been up to her to change. It is likely that Ann's struggle for equity may not be over and that she will eventually raise the issue of fairness again and attempt to renegotiate the terms of her relationship with Robert.

Couples should hardly expect that they will be able to work out fair terms on all issues at the beginning of their relationship and then never have to discuss the issue or renegotiate equity again. Relationships change. Situations change. Over time ideas of what is fair will also change. Couples who stay together long term remain flexible in their expectations and are responsive to each other's needs. Psychological equity is usually only a band-aid approach to resolving chronic relationship problems.

Commitment: I Promise to Be There for You

Commitment describes partners' avowed willingness to stay together long term, because they view what they have as viable and worthwhile. They, in effect, make a promise to ''be there'' for each other. Commitment acts as a bond between partners. Committed partners resist attempts by others to devalue or otherwise break up their relationship. They act as each other's supporters and consistently remind themselves and others of their good fortune in being together. Committed partners are loyal to each other and defend each other's beliefs and opinions.

Commitment occurs gradually over time as intimates become convinced that they want to be together exclusively. In a developing love relationship, partners typically like being together, enjoy each other's company, take pleasure in specific joint activities. But, as the relationship deepens, they begin to discover negative aspects of each other's personalities, beliefs, or general outlooks on life. These discoveries either drive the couple apart or are integrated into a more global positive perspective of each other and the relationship. We know our partner's flaws but love him or her anyway. Yes, Jason's stubborn, but he will listen and can change his mind. Sure, Maria's career is tremendously important to her, but she plans special times to be with me and shows me in other ways how much I mean to her (Brickman, Dunkel-Schetter, & Abbey, 1987).

As time passes, couples continue to assess their compatibility (Levinger, 1983). Are we right for each other? Is this the type of partner and the kind of intimacy I really want? Such questioning is natural and repeatedly occurs as the partners face the usual prob-

lems and issues that most intimates raise and try to resolve as their relationship develops.

The road to commitment is not smooth. Partners with similar interests or attitudes are likely to see each other as comfortable and attractive at the start of a relationship. Later, the partner's predictable sameness may become boring, leading some to look outside the relationship for a different person who, perhaps, offers a greater sense of excitement. However, among committed couples these forays away from a partner most often end in a greater appreciation of the common attitudes and shared experiences of the initial partner. Especially during times of stress, the old, comfortable relationship appears particularly attractive.

Misunderstandings about how committed each partner is to the relationship (''He keeps pushing to get married and I'm not ready''; ''She expects me to take her out every weekend like we're engaged or something'') as well as changes in one partner's belief in the commitment of the other (''I thought he loved me, but how can I believe that if: He wants to date someone else''; ''She decides to spend spring break with friends instead of me?'') are among the most commonly reported reasons for pulling away from a love relationship (Chelune et al., 1988).

WHAT MAKES LOVE LAST?

How do we know that the love we feel for someone or their love for us will last? Over the years social scientists have compared couples who remained together to those who later broke up. Several factors are identified as improving the chances that a couple will stay in love. Similarity in education level, age, attractiveness, and intelligence are related to the survival of a relationship (Hill, Peplau, & Ruben, 1976). So is frequency of interaction and physical closeness. Couples who spend time together often, share tasks, activities, and daily decision making, remain together longer than other couples (Berscheid, Snyder, & Omoto, 1989). Supportiveness is also important: couples who report relationship satisfaction self-disclose, listen to each other's problems, and provide sympathetic and compassionate support during stressful times (Davis & Oathout, 1987).

Other factors that influence the length of a love relationship include how couples fight and how they assess blame when things go wrong. Couples can disagree or argue about any number of issues in their relationship without destroying it, if they approach each other in a straightforward manner and express how they really feel (Gottman & Krokoff, 1989). Too often, partners hide their anger and discontent with the relationship and withdraw or refuse to talk about emotionally threatening issues. These hidden feelings do not go away. They remain underground where they grow into deeper resentments. Couples who can openly express their feelings in nondefensive and nonthreatening ways during disagreements report greater relationship satisfaction.

Moreover, couples who remain together over long periods of time are kinder in their assessments of each other's motivations. For example, when one of the couple has a bad day and is moody, distant, and angry, the partner does not rush to blame such behavior on embedded and unchangeable personality traits—selfishness, arrogance, inexpressiveness. Instead, one partner gives the other one the benefit of the doubt and looks for causes outside the person and the relationship: "The boss must have really let him have it"; "The traffic was probably more troublesome than usual"; "The client must have canceled her appointment again"; "She probably has one of her migraines" (Bradbury & Fincham, 1990). Happy couples more often attribute negative behavior to uncontrollable situations or circumstances and see positive behavior as acts of support and love.

Attachment

Attachment refers to the enduring bonds that develop between partners who love and care for each other. In addition to the factors already identified as important to staying together as a couple, psychologists Phillip

Shaver and Cindy Hazan believe that an individual's attachment style has a lot to do with the longevity of a love relationship. Building on the classic research on early attachment by Bowlby (1969, 1973, 1980) and Ainsworth and colleagues (1978), they compare adult love to the kind of attachment parents and infants have for each other. The same three attachment styles developed during infancy and childhood are also discernible in adult romantic relationships: *secure, avoidant,* and *anxious/ambivalent.* The following statements reflect how people with a particular attachment style typically think of their adult love relationships (Shaver & Hazan, 1988).

SECURE: I find it relatively easy to get close to others and am comfortable depending on them and having them depend on me. I don't often worry about being abandoned or about someone becoming too close to me.

AVOIDANT: I am somewhat uncomfortable being close to others; I find it difficult to trust them completely, difficult to allow myself to depend on them. I am nervous when anyone gets too close, and often, love partners want me to be more intimate than I feel comfortable being.

ANXIOUS/AMBIVALENT: I find that others are reluctant to get as close as I would like. I often worry that my partner doesn't really love me or won't want to stay with me. I want to merge completely with another person, and this desire sometimes scares people away.

Adults who experienced dependable, caring relationships as children are more likely to build secure, loving, and committed relationships throughout their lives, according to Shaver and Hazan.

In a study of 620 men and women, Hazan and Shaver (1987) found that secure partners (53 percent of the sample) described themselves as happy, trusting, friendly, and accepting and supportive of their partner, despite any faults the partner might have. Relationships of secure partners tended to last longer (10 years) than those of avoidant (6 years) or anxious/ambivalent (5 years) partners. Jealousy, fear of intimacy, and extreme swings in emotions were descriptive of the romantic experiences of avoidant partners (26 percent of the sample). Partners who described themselves as anxious/ambivalent (20 percent of the sample) reported that their love relationships were characterized by obsession with the partner, jealousy, extreme emotional swings, extreme sexual attraction, and a desire to have the partner reciprocate these strong feelings.

When asked how they viewed the course of romantic love over time, secure partners said they felt that romantic feelings rise and fall with time—sometimes reaching the intensity experienced at the beginning of the relationship or never fading from that emotional high. Avoidant partners believed that the romantic love depicted in the media didn't exist in real life. They described love as seldom lasting and felt that it was rare that one found another person to really fall in love with. Anxious/ambivalent partners said that they fell in love easily and often, but rarely found what they referred to as real love. They, like the secure partners, said that feelings of love rise and fall over the course of the relationship.

Though the model of love we learn as infants and children is certainly not fixed for life, it is possible that adult love relationships are to some extent influenced by those early attachment patterns. If later experiences in middle childhood, adolescence, and young adulthood mirror those of infancy, then love patterns would, of course, become more entrenched. If later experiences, however, differ from early ones, and should the individual purposely set out to alter earlier patterns of love behavior, change is likely.

Self-Esteem

Is *self-esteem*—a sense of self-worth—a prerequisite for being able to love someone? Will it make love last? Psychologist and therapist Nathan Branden (1980) has observed and interviewed couples who have remained in love for long periods of time. Individuals with good self-esteem, who feel competent, lovable, and deserving of happiness, have the best chance of connecting with a partner who is supportive of them and with whom they can build a close, intimate relationship, he believes.

Other investigators, however, question the notion of a direct link between self-esteem and successful love relationships. As far back as 1965, Elaine Hatfield speculated that people with low esteem might have a special need for affection and thus would most likely find romantic attachments more rewarding and fulfilling than those with high esteem. In a recent study of 150 undergraduate women and men, Kenneth and Karen Dion (1988) concluded that students with low esteem were less successful in their love relationships because they lacked social skills and thus had difficulty initiating and maintaining relationships with others. Stu-

dents with low esteem also reported that they more often loved others who did not respond in kind.

Interestingly, Dion and Dion also found that those students with low esteem actually appreciated their relationships and partners more than did students with high esteem. Low-esteem students voiced stronger feelings of love, liking, and trust for their partners and were more positive about their partners than were the other students. Perhaps, say Dion and Dion, "they have greater needs and appreciation for affection" (1988, p. 272).

The Dion's study shows that low self-esteem is certainly not a barrier to experiencing feelings of love, and, in fact, seems to enhance those passionate feelings. However, Dion and Dion studied students who were probably in the early stages of their relationships. As we have discussed, passionate love, often the result of a heightened state of physiological arousal, does not always lead to a long-term, fulfilling love relationship. Branden's study of long-term relationships suggests that low self-esteem does affect an individual's ability to sustain a relationship, despite the strength of the early attachment.

WHEN THINGS GO WRONG IN RELATIONSHIPS

Just because a relationship is loving and intimate, doesn't mean that it is free of problems and conflict. Over time partners must face and deal with relationship problems and negotiate some sort of mutual understanding if the relationship is to remain intact. When both partners are committed to a relationship and want it to work out, signs of trouble inevitably result in attempts to repair the rift. The couple looks for ways to bring the relationship back to its loving beginnings.

Signs of Trouble

What are some signs that a love relationship is in trouble? The first sign is when partners begin to communicate less with each other. They see each other less often and for shorter amounts of time. They begin to interact with friends less frequently as a couple. They find it increasingly difficult to plan joint activities. When they talk to friends about each other they more often make negative remarks. They portray the relationship as dissatisfying and troubled. "Feelings of at-

Diminished communication between partners is an early warning sign that a relationship is in trouble.

traction, warmth, and intimacy diminish'' (Miller & Parks, 1982, p. 130).

Couples in troubled relationships more often do and say things that serve as signs of rejection of each other. When they are together, they look at each other less frequently. When they talk, their tone of voice is cooler and less friendly and affectionate than it was in the beginning of the relationship. The partners experience longer periods of silence when they're together. They become involved in "acts of coercion—power plays, personal attacks, threats, guilt inductions. . . . Once conflict begins, participants have difficulty controlling it" (Miller & Parks, 1982, p. 139). This deterioration of the relationship typically leaves both partners anxious and upset.

Behaviors that lead to the deterioration rather than to the buildup of a relationship are discussed by Linda Thompson (1989).

Partners may fail to pay attention, discern another's needs, act in another's behalf, assert their own needs, speak in their own behalf, tolerate differences, see another's point of view, give credit to another, consider the consequences of their actions. Partners may say and do hurtful things, think only of their own needs, refuse to reveal their needs to another, misinterpret another's need, mistrust another's motives, insist on blaming another, lie, manipulate another with guilt, and silence another with anger or violence. (p. 13)

In most intimate relationships, partners at times question each other's motives and behavior: "Why does she act like that when she knows it hurts me?" "Why is he so self-absorbed and unmovable on issues I care so much about?" "Why can't I live without her?" "Why can't she ever make a decision on her own?" "Why do we fight about such trivial things?" "Why must he know where I am every minute of the day?" Partners attempt to answer these questions in order to better understand their relationship—its development, maintenance, or decline. But sometimes other factors get in their way. Two factors consistently associated with relationship problems are a need for control and jealousy.

Two Troublemakers in Love Relationships

Need for Control

We are attracted to others in part because they like us, share our attitudes, and provide us with emotional support when we're under stress, are afraid or lonely. Two separate people come together to begin a relationship. Interdependence develops over time as partners in an intimate relationship learn how and when to depend on each other. Each person strikes a balance between the need for dependency and the need for *personal control*—freedom to pursue one's own interests and goals (Fish & Fish, 1986). Couples must take into consideration each other's personal needs and desires as they pursue their own interests (Myers, 1987).

People who are inordinately concerned with being in predictable situations where they can feel secure, certain, in control, and powerful, may find it difficult to be intimate with others. Intimacy involves unpredictability, uncertainty, and the possibility of losing someone we care very much about. It requires giving up some personal control to our partner. People with a high need for control often experience difficulty admitting the slightest dependency on others and allowing themselves to show any emotional vulnerability— both essential to the development of intimacy. Phrases such as "falling in love," "being swept off my feet," or "being head over heels in love" can be upsetting to them. Such individuals say they fall in love less often than other people and take a more pragmatic, calculated approach to getting involved in a love relationship (Dion & Dion, 1988).

Another aspect of control is *relational control*—the extent to which one partner attempts to manipulate the actions of the other. One of the most destructive forces that affects trust in a love relationship is evidence that one partner is trying to establish a power base and dominate couple decisions. When this happens, the resistant partner generally pulls back from the relationship and, as a result, the couple fails to communicate effectively about relationship issues of control and dependency. To restore a sense of confidence and trust to their relationship, the couple must risk confronting the issues that stand in the way of intimacy (Holmes & Rempel, 1989, p. 215).

Jealousy

An additional factor that can also threaten a love relationship is *jealousy*—when individuals react with anxiety, mistrust, and suspicion because of fears that someone they love and care about may leave. Feelings of loneliness, betrayal, and uncertainty coexist with feelings of jealousy (Parrott & Smith, 1987). As one woman explained in a letter to investigators Peter Salovey and Judith Rodin (1989):

Jealousy is one of those things that even though you know it's a destructive emotion and it won't accomplish anything, you can't help but feel it. It grinds away at you like the horror of recognizing that all your worst fears are coming true. . . . It's an emotion so deeply embedded . . . that it's inescapable. (p. 222)

Though jealousy can be harmful—it has been linked to conflict, physical abuse, and even murder—it is an emotion that most people experience at one time or another. Jealousy acts as a reminder to us that certain of our relationships are very important to us.

Susan Pfeiffer and Paul Wong (1989) distinguish between normal jealousy and pathological jealousy. *Normal jealousy* is experienced when an individual sees a real threat to his or her relationship and because of this experience is moderately upset. *Pathological jealousy*, on the other hand, "might involve imagined threats, paranoid suspicions, a high degree of emotional upset and/or detective behaviors designed to check up on the suspected partner" (p. 185). This type of jealousy can lead to heated arguments or even violence and to relationship breakup.

Normal jealousy, according to Pfeiffer and Wong, can be either positive or negative for the relationship. On the positive side, the jealous partner may take her or his reaction as an indication of caring for the partner or that the partner is even more desirable because she or he is attractive to others. However, a high frequency of normal jealousy aroused, for example, when one partner constantly flirts, may have negative consequences similar to those evoked by pathological jealousy.

Jealousy usually begins unconsciously, as a reaction to behavior by our partner that we perceive as threatening. Once aroused, the threatened partner generally attempts to get a clearer picture of exactly what is happening and to estimate how their partner's behavior affects the relationship.

From their research, Buunk and Bringle (1987) conclude that jealous partners may feel losses in several areas. First, they may feel a loss of self-esteem from comparing themselves to their rivals—the rivals may be seen as being better looking, or more intelligent or successful. If the rival is evaluated as inferior, however, a jealous partner may still have a loss of self-esteem from having to face the fact that the partner "has bad taste and is not very discriminating" (p. 130). Second, jealous partners may feel their sense of "specialness" has been violated. Specialness is related to

The line between normal and pathological jealousy can sometimes be thin, as when a partner's frequent flirting provokes angry arguments between a couple.

how intimate the jealous partner perceives the relationship to be. For example, did the couple share thoughts, feelings, and activities exclusively, closing themselves off to others? Did they spend lots of time together and were they especially affectionate and loving toward each other? Third, and perhaps most important, does the jealous partner worry that the beloved may be lost entirely—that the relationship will be permanently dissolved?

Can normal jealous reactions be controlled? "Yes," say Salovey and Rodin. Jealous partners can use strategies such as refraining from saying things that they might later regret, maintaining a schedule of normal activities to keep their minds off their problems, not telling others about their suspicions until they are sure of the facts, and downplaying the situation until they have a chance to cool down and think more rationally. It also helps to identify what triggers the jealous reactions. What about the situation is really bothersome? What feelings surface when these things happen? Next, the jealous partner can ask, What about the relationship do I need to change? What do I want to be different? Why is this important to me?

Finally, the jealous person needs to discuss the situation with the seemingly guilty partner. How partners react is crucial. If the partner is committed to the relationship and wants it to continue, she or he will try to explain the offending behavior. Some partners say they are innocent—"It's all a simple misunderstanding"—and explain what happened. Others admit the offending behavior, but offer explanations—"I had no idea it would end up like this." "She kept forcing herself on me." Others try to justify their behavior by admitting guilt, but minimizing the consequences—"The fact that I told you only once shows how much I really care about you."

A more successful way for an offending partner to handle the situation is to apologize. An apology usually includes an expression of sorrow and guilt, recognition that the behavior was unacceptable, an assurance that it will not happen again, and a sincere attempt to make up for the hurt feelings (Buunk & Bringle, 1987). At this point it is necessary to agree about how future outside involvements will be handled—to establish new relationship rules ("I agree to see my women friends at lunch but not during the evening"). Most intimate relationships can withstand a bout of jealousy and survive, especially if both partners are committed to the relationship and one is not purposely manipulating the other.

In summary, love and intimacy are complex phenomena that are relevant to life satisfaction and relationship quality. What love is and the way individuals display love depend on personal, situational, cultural, and partner characteristics.

SUMMARY POINTS

■ There are two kinds of love—passionate and companionate. Passionate love is physical, nonrational, and quick to develop and dissolve. Companionate love develops slowly over a long period of time through shared thoughts, feelings, and experiences.

■ Robert Sternberg concludes that love consists of three components that form a triangle. Passionate love makes up one side of the triangle. Companionate love, consisting of intimacy and decision/commitment, completes the other two sides of the triangle.

■ Barriers or obstacles placed between lovers can stimulate their attraction for each other.

■ Some researchers believe that people mislabel fear or anxiety as passionate arousal because these three emotions are so similar.

■ Other researchers argue that love is not so fickle; that the intensity of our attraction for someone can be traced to the brain's release of phenylethylamine.

■ Views of love have changed across history. It is only within the last few centuries that romantic love has become associated with marriage. In America in the eighteenth and nineteenth centuries the affection, caring, and emotional bonding we currently associate with romance and marriage was found primarily between women. Marriage was seen as a duty or social obligation, not an emotional attachment.

■ Sociologist John Lee focuses on love as a socially constructed phenomenon influenced by cultural stereotypes and interpersonal interactions.

■ Gender roles have a powerful influence on how we choose to love someone.

■ Francesca Cancian, author of *Love in America*, believes that women and men love in different ways. Women identify love with emotional expression and talking about feelings; men, with providing help, sharing activities, and sex.

■ The power differential between women and men influences patterns of self-disclosure and consequently regulates the degree of intimacy in contemporary love relationships.

■ In contemporary America, love relationships are more often viewed as the mutual responsibility of both partners. Interdependent and equal relationships are increasingly valued as gender roles become more flexible.

■ Key components of intimacy include self-disclosure, equity, and commitment.

■ Intimacy is avoided by some individuals because they fear exposure of their faults and shortcomings, abandonment, discrediting attacks by others, engulfment by another person.

■ Self-disclosure happens slowly and cautiously over a long period of time and is guided by definite norms or guidelines.

■ Trust is built on believing that a partner will not take advantage of our vulnerabilities.

■ Couples are more satisfied in equitable relationships. Overbenefitted partners feel guilty. Underbenefitted partners feel depressed and angry.

■ Commitment is the desire to stay together long term, despite occasional conflict and inevitable problems.

■ Love is more likely to last for couples who spend time together; share tasks, activities, and decision making; and self-disclose, listen attentively, and provide compassion, support, and caring for each other.

■ Arguing and fighting do not mean the end of a relationship. Love can last for couples who openly discuss how they feel without getting defensive and give each other the benefit of the doubt when it comes to assessing blame or finding causes for marital problems.

■ Phillip Shaver and Cindy Hazan compare adult love to infant attachment. They identify three types of adult love relationships—secure, avoidant, and anxious/ambivalent.

■ Individuals with low self-esteem and/or a high need for control have difficulty establishing and maintaining intimate relationships.

■ Jealousy is related to a sense of loss—loss of self-esteem, loss of specialness, and in some cases loss of the partner.

KEY TERMS

Passionate love	*Trust*
Companionate love	*Equity*
Intimacy	*Equity theory*
Love triangle	*Overbenefitted*
Styles of loving	*Underbenefitted*
Eros	*Psychological equity*
Ludus	*Commitment*
Pragma	*Attachment*
Agape	*Self-esteem*
Mania	*Personal control*
Storge	*Relational control*
Self-disclosure	*Jealousy*

REVIEW QUESTIONS

1. Distinguish between passionate and companionate love. Describe how you feel physically and emotionally when in passionate love. Have you ever loved another passionately, only to have the passion fade? Explain.

2. Think of a romantic relationship you once had and draw a love triangle to represent the extent of your passion, intimacy, and decision/commitment. What shape does the triangle take? Which component—passion, intimacy, decision/commitment—was the most prominent; least prominent? Now draw your partner's love triangle. Which component was most prominent; least prominent? Are there differences between the two triangles? Do you think these differences had anything to do with the breakup of the relationship?

3. How does the "feminization of love" affect romantic relationships? What are some strategies cou-

ples might use to counteract this tendency in their own relationships?

4. Why is it important to self-disclose in relationships? What are the risks of self-disclosure? Have you ever been in a relationship in which your partner seemed to disclose too much, too soon? Describe the situation and how you felt. Is the relationship ongoing or did it end?

5. What is relationship equity? Equity theory? When an individual is underbenefitted in a relationship, how does he or she typically react?

6. What is the difference between normal and pathological jealousy? What causes a person to feel jealous? How does a person usually react when confronted by a jealous partner? Are there ways to keep normal jealous reactions under control?

4

Jacob Lawrence, *The Lovers*, 1946

Dating, Courtship, and Marital Choice

There is a growing desire for the intimacy of a close relationship—connecting in an interdependent way with another person. And, dating remains the primary way of meeting a potential partner. When the great-grandparents of today's teenagers were dating, it was referred to as "courting." To the average person today, however, "courting" suggests something formal that people used to do when "seeing someone" was specifically designed to end in a marital commitment. Courting gave way to the practice of dating, which came as a significant change from the older courtship practices. The date was planned by the young people themselves, and they were not to be chaperoned. Sexual intimacies were expected rather than forbidden, though there was a complex code specifying how far the young woman was allowed to go at each stage in the relationship. And there was no obligation to continue the relationship beyond the time of the date itself. Dating was a departure from the traditional courtship system in another important respect: Having fun became part of the serious business of choosing a partner.

In Chapter 3, we explored love, that most personal of experiences, in all its forms and described what fuels a loving relationship. In this chapter, we look at the social interactions in dating and courtship that may lead us to our selection of a marital partner. We explore, too, some of the problems encountered in dating and courtship which may lead to breakup.

THE CHANGING FOCUS OF DATING AND COURTSHIP

During the 1700s, decisions and rituals concerning courtship and marriage were considered too serious to be left to the couple. At stake were the disposition of property, the inheritance of goods, the continuity of

In some societies, a couple's freedom and privacy during courtship is not as important as it is in the United States. It is not uncommon in such countries for the couple to be accompanied to a greater or lesser degree by formal or informal chaperones.

bloodlines and, often, the forming of socially advantageous—or at least "suitable"—family alliances. In our society, the parents of any couple were heavily involved in these matters, considering the supervision of their children's courtship to be a great responsibility.

Today, most Americans would agree that the practice of parent-arranged marriages seems an invasion of a couple's freedom and privacy, but is still the rule in many other cultures. In such societies, the task of choosing an appropriate mate consists largely of matching up the status characteristics—including money, social position, wealth, health, and appearance—of the prospective bride with that of the groom. Parents or the professional matchmakers they hire, search for a prospective mate for their child, usually among the families of roughly equivalent status since, in the case of a daughter, they literally have to pay a price. Sometimes the transaction is explicit: A dowry, a sum of money or property (such as land or cattle), is

brought to the marriage by the woman. If a daughter is marrying into a higher-ranking family than her own, the dowry can be large. The exchange of money for social rank is universally considered a fair arrangement.

We learned in Chapter 3 that in contemporary India, marriage typically establishes an alliance between two kinship groups, in which the newly joined couple are the most conspicuous link. Marriage, then, is not simply an individual affair; the bride and groom not only marry each other, but all of each other's relatives. In societies where this kind of linkage is established, allowing two people from very different and unequal social classes to marry can cause the families embarrassment, because the families of the newlyweds do not consider themselves to be social equals. In addition, different assumptions about the roles and rituals of marriage by the marital partners themselves may encourage practical misunderstandings.

HOW ROMANTIC RELATIONSHIPS EVOLVE

Since Americans typically do not enter into arranged marriages, how do we meet and marry? Most Americans use some form of dating as a way of getting to know each other. If we do not find a person suitable, we move on to other dating relationships until we finally settle into a relationship that progressively develops into a marital commitment.

Courtship

To the average person, *courtship* describes the meetings between two people specifically designed to develop into marital commitment. In our society, courtship, until well into the 1800s, took place under the watchful eyes of the woman's parents, in their parlor or on their front porch (Bailey, 1988). Although it is difficult to imagine how two people ever got to know each other under those circumstances, it should be remembered that the setting played a role. In the stable, small-town environment where that courting usually took place, nearly every suitor was already acquainted with the young woman and her family before the courtship began. Today, by contrast, people frequently move from place to place, practicing a wide variety of lifestyles. Even if two individuals come from similar backgrounds, that is no longer any guarantee of similar marital expectations. As young people today postpone first marriage until their late twenties or early thirties, they increasingly emphasize that most dating relationships do not have commitment as an underlying goal. The majority, in fact, terminate without ever having discussed marriage. Perhaps this partly explains why today we do not use the word "courtship" as much.

Dating

Courting has long since given way in America to the practice of dating. Indeed, dating as we know it appeared in American culture at the start of this century, peaking in the 1950s and early 1960s, before reappearing again in the 1980s and 1990s. In contrast to a meeting during a courtship, the date was planned by the young persons themselves, and they went on it unchaperoned. But even with the freedom this entailed, an elaborate code of conduct governed the dating re-

lationship. One investigator (LeMasters, 1957) who studied the American courtship system in the 1950s identified a predictable sequence of six stages: group dating, random dating, steady dating, "pinning," engagement, and marriage. Certain symbolic acts, such as a young woman's wearing her boyfriend's high school ring to signify their going steady, or his fraternity pin to indicate their preengagement, marked each stage of the dating relationship. Each successive stage implied a deeper level of commitment and behavior, leading up to exclusively dating one person.

During the 1950s, dating encouraged other freedoms. Certain sexual intimacies, it was culturally agreed, were appropriate at each stage. More commitment meant that greater intimacy was permissible. And a specific sexual code governed each sexual stage of the courtship sequence as well. If the norms varied somewhat from region to region and from one age group to another, the rules nevertheless existed. This is what the system looked like to one contemporary young man:

> I often had the uncomfortable feeling that [passion was dispensed] by some sort of rule book. It had all been decided beforehand: the first date, so many kisses; the second date, lips part, tongue enters; fifth date, three buttons. . . . (Greene, 1964, p. 131)

At each successive stage it became more difficult to back out of the relationship. Breach of promise suits, although they had become a thing of the past by the 1950s, illustrate the traditional assumption that there was a definite commitment to marriage. Several generations ago, the presumption was that if her suitor broke the engagement, a young woman's reputation was damaged and her future prospects for marriage impaired.

In the 1980s and 1990s dating assumed new forms and incorporated new behavioral codes. The feminist movement and other societal changes such as dual-earner and single-parent families no doubt have made dating more egalitarian. For example, while it used to be improper for a young woman to call a male friend and arrange to get-together, today this practice is common. And while a fifties date used to be a special occasion planned by the male, who issued an invitation days in advance, now young men and women usually gather informally at parties or to see a movie or go to a game. Today, even the term "dating" is too formal for some people. Teenagers and young adults explain that dating is still common, but an informal practice known only as "getting together" is more descriptive of what they do. Casual contacts between people are not so likely to be defined as dates. Having fun has also become part of the serious business of choosing a partner, another departure from traditional courtship practices.

Regardless of which term is now more correct—courting, dating, or getting together—in virtually all societies, single women and men go through a formal process through which they choose a marital partner. And because whom we choose has an important effect on our later marital satisfaction and the quality of our marriages, much attention has been focused on how marital partners are selected.

Dating Expectations: Hers, His, and Peers'

Despite the increase in honesty between partners, one of the interesting aspects about dating as it has been practiced for at least a generation is that men and women often do not pursue the same goals. This difference reflects the fact that they have been socialized differently in regard to sexual expression and the desirability of marriage. Recent accounts of dating among college students suggest gender differences—especially about when sexual intimacy is appropriate—are apparently still common (Cate & Lloyd, 1992; Komarovsky, 1985; Knox & Wilson, 1983). Compounding the problem is that neither men nor women are likely to declare such expectations verbally to their dates.

To prove their masculinity, most males in this culture have been encouraged to express themselves sexually. They "characteristically prefer high levels of sexuality with a minimum number of dates" (Christopher & Frandsen, 1990, p. 89). In contrast, most women prefer to wait until there is some kind of emotional attachment. Also, they have been taught that self-respect and the respect of others depend on discretion in sexual matters. Family scientists Scott Christopher and Rodney Cate (1982) found that a man's decision about when to have his first sexual encounter depends primarily on peer influence; while a woman's decision is a personal one, based on the current status of her relationship. Nevertheless, peer pressure and social norms influence the dating behavior of women too.

> Couples who fall in love may feel sexual needs that have to be dealt with in a way that satisfies each of the partners and outside observers. . . . A couple's sexual habits are regarded as legitimate topics for gossip and peer pressure, such that couples will experience their own sexual needs not only in the context of the relationship itself but also in the context of the wider society. (Duck, 1988, p. 77)

But beyond its sexual and recreational aspects, dating also provides partners an opportunity to learn the social skills necessary to initiate and maintain a romantic relationship. It brings two people together to interact and discover if they want their casual relationship to develop into a closer and more intimate attachment. It is an apprenticeship in intimacy—an opportunity to learn about self-disclosure, mutuality, jealousy, and love. And it is a way to explore which social characteristics and personality attributes are important and attractive in a partner. Dating can, in addition, be a kind of window shopping with no obligation to buy, providing occasions for what sociologists refer to as status achievement. A young woman, for example, can sometimes raise her prestige image among peers by dating and being seen with a young man considered to be highly desirable—a star athlete, the most popular guy in class, and so forth.

A lot of time and energy are spent by experts and laypersons alike in attempting to understand why some people are able to establish intimate relationships which lead to marriage and others are not. Commonsense advice about how to find the right person is unreliable and contradictory. How often have you heard that you will know Mr. or Ms. Right as soon as he or she comes along? But the evidence suggests that, with rare exceptions, only in the movies is one's ideal partner revealed by a bolt of romantic lightning.

Dating can range from the most casual pairing within a group to an exclusive relationship. As the relationship moves toward exclusivity, the line between dating and courtship blurs. An examination of the courtship components of dating reveals that there are social, structural, and psychological factors that influence the choice of marital partner.

UNDERSTANDING MARITAL CHOICE: THEORIES OF MATE SELECTION

Despite the common notion that great romantic attractions begin unexpectedly, there seem to be unconscious as well as deliberately constructed selection criteria that enter the decision-making process. Three theories—compatibility, exchange, and interpersonal process—have been proposed by family scholars to explain how mate selection is refined as it progresses from initial attraction to casual acquaintance to serious dating to long-term commitment, and finally to marriage. Although in our society marital choice is considered a matter of individual preference, a variety of factors limit the *pool of eligibles*—group of available, compatible marriage partners.

Compatibility Theories

Theoretically, of course, we might be attracted to any individual. But, in reality, we rule out all but a tiny percentage for one reason or another. Clearly, in choosing a partner—even a dating partner—not just anyone will do. *Compatibility theories* assume that serious romantic partners assess each other's ability to meet various tests of similarity—"Do we have common interests?" "Do we share similar family values?" "Are we alike in our religious or spiritual beliefs?" "Do we see eye-to-eye on how marital roles should be carried out?" Such theories also assume that the process by which partners form a committed relationship is initially influenced by cultural and structural barriers or restrictions that narrow the pool of eligible marital partners (Cate & Lloyd, 1992).

Cultural Barriers to Partner Choice

You might guess that since ours is such a diverse society, individuals would frequently marry others who are different in education, family status, or race. Contrary to expectation, with remarkable consistency, it is actually people who are alike in important ways that more often marry each other. And one of the main reasons that they lean toward individuals that share the same social status, race, and education is that cultural barriers tend to block relationships between people from different backgrounds. *Cultural barriers* are societal norms and expectations that restrict the choice of marital partners to those with certain demographic or personal characteristics. Homogamy, the marriage gradient, and social networks are currently the three most influential cultural barriers (Surra, 1991).

Homogamy. The tendency to choose to marry someone similar in age, education, religion, social class, and race is called *homogamy. Heterogamy* refers to the ten-

Every culture sets up barriers that restrict marital choice. One of the most powerful cultural barriers is racial homogamy, even though this norm is becoming less powerful.

dency of people to marry others not like themselves on these same characteristics. According to recent Census Bureau statistics, homogamy remains the prevailing norm in American society, but heterogamy is becoming increasingly acceptable (Surra, 1991).

Racial homogamy is perhaps the strongest of all cultural norms that limit the field of marriageable partners. However, even the strength of this norm is weakening (see the "Changing Lifestyles" box). This is especially true for blacks, who rarely marry outside of their race. Age homogamy is also quite strong in American culture. Most married couples are usually no more than 3 or 4 years apart in age, except for black partners who are more likely to be further apart in age than are other races (Surra, 1991). The practice of marriage within one's own social group, *endogamy,* is another widely accepted norm (*exogamy* is the practice of marriage outside one's own social group). Traditionally, upper-class women, for example, marry upper-

CHANGING LIFESTYLES

Number of Black-White Marriages on Rise

The number of black-white marriages has more than tripled since 1970, according to the Census Bureau. And while interracial marriage is far more common between whites and members of other minorities, no pairing hits as raw a nerve as unions between blacks and whites.

"It has not passed the 'no blink' test," said Dr. Tom W. Smith, a researcher on social issues at the National Opinion Research Center at the University of Chicago. "It's clear that the majority of whites are not prepared to accept this as just another couple. The minimum you get is a look and a stare."

According to the General Social Survey, an annual polling of 1,500 American adults of all races directed by Dr. Smith, a significant proportion of whites—1 in 5—still believe interracial marriage should be illegal, as against 2 in 5 whites asked the question in 1972.

Further, 66 percent of whites said they would oppose a close relative's marrying a black person. Only 4 percent said they would favor it; the remainder said race was not a factor one way or the other. The margin of sampling error in the poll was plus or minus four percentage points, and seven percentage points for blacks.

No other ethnic or racial group engenders as intense a response from whites. About 45 percent of whites said they would oppose a close relative's marriage to an Asian or Hispanic person and 15 percent said they would oppose a marriage between a close relative and a Jew, according to the survey.

Blacks, on the other hand, exhibited indifference to intermarriage, with nearly two-thirds saying they would neither favor nor oppose a relative's marrying someone from another race.

To be sure, some white opposition has melted. The beaming faces of interracial couples appear with little protest on the wedding pages of Southern newspapers like The Augusta Chronicle in Georgia, a state where such unions were illegal until the 1970s. Television shows like "The Days and Nights of Molly Dodd" and movies like "Jungle Fever" have brought interracial relationships to living rooms and theaters, usually in a more realistic fashion than in the 1967 film "Guess Who's Coming to Dinner?"

But these new signs of openness do not necessarily translate into approval for most of these couples.

Teresa Johnson, a white social worker, has been married to Ralph Johnson, a black actor, for 17 years. They have two teen-age children and a house in the Hyde

class men. It is also the case that upper-class parents have more influence on their children's choice of partners than do parents from any other social classes—and they have more reason for it. Issues related to inheritance, maintaining the family financial structure, and even carrying on the family name are often extremely important to wealthy families, and are subject to a large degree of family control. In this way, marriage among the upper class resembles marriage in traditional cultures.

Even without family pressure, individuals from similar backgrounds tend to associate with people like themselves in more respects than not. Just as we shop in certain stores rather than others because they cater to our tastes, we limit our field of social contacts by associating with certain groups and by frequenting certain places where we meet members of these groups. Most of this delimiting takes place without our making any conscious decision to meet certain types

of people. We simply tend to feel more comfortable with people whose personal and social characteristics are similar to our own.

The Marriage Gradient. In keeping with the cultural expectation that in families the male should have higher status, another social barrier to choice of marital partner is the tendency in our society for men to marry women who are slightly younger, smaller, and of lower occupational and educational status. Sociologists call this tendency for men to marry down and women to marry up the *marriage gradient* (Bernard, 1982).

The major implication of the marriage gradient is that men have a wider range of acceptable partners to choose from. Another is that if men marry women with slightly lower education, occupational status, and family income, there will be some men who remain unmarried either because they can find no one who meets

Park section of Chicago. Her relatives are miles away in Cleveland, and all but the very closest of them know her by her maiden name; they think she is single and childless.

To protect this secret, she has not been to a family wedding or funeral since she married, for fear that the topic might come up. For years, only her parents knew. But they were horrified at the news and dared not let it slip. She did not even bother to tell them she was pregnant the last time.

"They were so upset about the first one," said Mrs. Johnson, 40 years old, "because that meant I wasn't turning back."

For years her parents would not let her children enter their house, preferring instead to meet them at the airport or at a pizza parlor in some other neighborhood. Now her parents let the children visit—but only at night so the neighbors won't see.

"To this day" said Mr. Johnson, "I can't go to their house because of the neighbors."

Mrs. Johnson said she felt caught in a cruel paradox because people cannot get beyond the color of her husband's skin. "Here we are, a typical middle-class family," she said. "Ralph's a Little League coach. He's on the local school council. I have cousins who have kids out of wedlock, who are juvenile delinquents and in the Hell's Angels. But I'm the one on the outs. If my husband was white and beat me, that would be O.K."

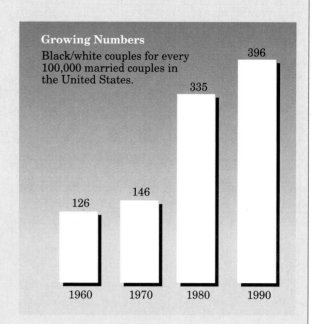

Growing Numbers
Black/white couples for every 100,000 married couples in the United States.

Year	Couples
1960	126
1970	146
1980	335
1990	396

EXPLORATIONS *Do you believe that in the next decade there will be greater cultural acceptance of interracial marriages? Why or why not?*

SOURCE: Excerpted from I. Wilkerson (1991).

these criteria or women do not choose them—they are, according to sociologist Jessie Bernard (1982), "bottom of the barrel" men. Conversely, many of the women who remain unmarried would be the ones who outrank men in social status categories, or as Bernard calls them, "cream of the crop" women.

This gradient effect is especially prominent for educated black women. Because many fewer black men attend college than black women, the social status hierarchy applied to white marriages is not nearly as evident in black relationships. Black women more often than women of other races choose to marry men who have less education than they do and who have been previously married (Taylor, Chatters, Tucker, & Lewis, 1991).

Social Networks. Despite their autonomy in choosing a mate and the erosion of homogamous marriages, most young people select partners not so dramatically different from those their parents might have selected for them. Our *social networks*—the people we recognize as being closest to us and most important to our lives—argue family scientists Catherine Surra and Robert Milardo (1991), influence the mate-selection process. We seem to care very much what these important others think about the people we date and plan to marry.

As a couple's commitment to each other grows and they spend more time together, they do tend to withdraw from some of their friends and acquaintances. But they continue to maintain strong relationships with their closest friends and kin (Surra, 1988). "In fact, participation with kin and close others actually may increase as partners formalize their commitments and absorb their partner's relatives and best friends into their own networks" (Surra, 1990, p. 851). If these significant others are nonsupportive of, and interfere with, the relationship, the couple's mutual commitment usually decreases (Johnson & Milardo, 1984).

Parents, for example, become increasingly involved, expressing approval or disapproval, as the couple become more serious (Leslie, Huston, & Johnson, 1986).

Social networks that include members who are closer and more involved in each other's lives probably act more strongly to suppress any new romantic involvements, if that involvement is viewed as threatening to the stability or quality of already established relationships within the network. Networks that are more distant—that include members who see each other less often and who are less involved in each other's daily activities—are less likely to influence marital choice. Networks in which members are not too close or too distant most likely offer the best balance between giving support and causing interference for a couple during the mate selection process (Surra & Milardo, 1991).

Structural Barriers to Partner Choice

The composition of the American population—how many women are born in a particular decade, compared to men; how many eligible singles live within driving and dating distance—is another factor limiting the pool of available marriage partners in our society. In Alaska and western states like Montana and Wyoming, for example, it is well-recognized that the shortage of marriageable partners of the appropriate sex, age, race, and background is a serious concern. Such barriers probably influence mate selection much more than we would like to admit.

Sex Ratio. After two decades of an oversupply of marriageable white women compared to men, the situation has reversed itself so that finding a woman to marry is expected to be more difficult for men throughout the 1990s (see Figure 4-1). One reason has to do with the *sex ratio*—the number of men per 100 women in a population. Today, white single men in their twenties outnumber white single women by a ratio of 122 to 100. For men in their thirties the ratio is even worse: 130 eligible men to 100 women (Bradsher, 1990). Men in their late twenties and early thirties say that they are often lonely and sometimes find it difficult to get a date. Moreover, women have historically married men older than they are, so the number of marriageable partners now available to younger men will probably be even smaller.

Already, some unmarried men ready for marriage are beginning to complain of a *marriage squeeze*—greater numbers of one sex looking for suitable marital

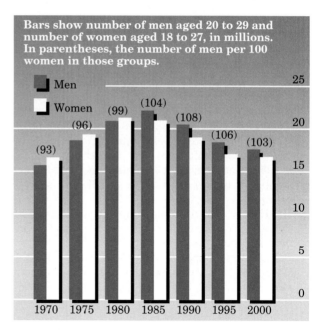

FIGURE 4-1
Women and Men: The Changing Balance
SOURCE: J. Fowles (1988).

partners. Even professional men with high-paying jobs are joining in to complain, although their main concern is having no time even to look for a date (Romance, 1990). (See the "Snapshots" box.) The marriage squeeze has not affected blacks in the same manner that it has whites. Because of an undersupply of black men, due to untimely and early death and incarceration, black females continue to experience a smaller pool of eligible partners. This situation has led to a wider gap in the ages of marriage partners in the black community, with black women tending to marry down—or black males tending to marry up (Surra, 1990). Thus we see among black couples another reversal of the white marriage gradient pattern.

Demographic trends are not the only influencers of the marriage squeeze. In Japan, for example, the squeeze is attributed more to ideological differences between men and women brought about by women's increased economic independence (see the "Diversity" box).

Propinquity. The choice of mate can be hampered by another structural barrier: *propinquity*—physical nearness or geographic closeness. Not having access to potential marriageable partners because they don't live

SNAPSHOTS

Too Many Men

After studying the effects of the marriage squeeze in several societies, social scientists Marcia Guttentag and Paul Secord (1983), in their book *Too Many Women*, discuss the consequences for women when they outnumber men. When the sex ratio favors men, the focus of dating tends to remain recreational, with males avoiding serious relationships and commitment to marriage. When women are scarce, however, monogamy increases and women's roles become more traditional; the age of first marriage drops, while birth rates climb. Moreover, under such circumstances, women receive less education and are less likely to be in the work force, or to divorce. As Guttentag and Secord's findings would predict, for the past two decades in America, with the sex ratio favoring men (too many women), women's roles have become more egalitarian, the age of first marriage has increased, birth rates have

dropped, and the divorce rate has soared. For the next decade and beyond, the marriage squeeze will reverse itself and there will be too many men. Sociologists are now considering whether international trends will continue to serve as good guides for changes in American dating, courtship, and marriage practices.

EXPLORATIONS *How do you think the new marriage squeeze will affect American society? Are there any signs that the preponderance of men is influencing a return to romance, monogamy, and traditional roles? Is there evidence that having too many men facilitates egalitarian trends—women gaining power in the dating and mating process, men agreeing to more equal marital roles, or the elevation of women's issues—sexual harassment, date rape, family violence, child care—to national attention?* ✺

close by can be a definite constraint. College students, for example, are more likely to develop friendships with peers who attend the same classes and sit nearby, or those in the same dormitory or apartment building. This tendency to date and marry individuals who live close by helps explain homogamy patterns. Blacks live in neighborhoods with other blacks, upper-class people live in the same suburbs as other upper-class people. Thus, without making a conscious decision to find partners whose characteristics match ours, we do, simply by choosing people who happen to live nearby.

In sum, compatibility theories of marital choice, based on cultural and structural barriers such as the ones we have identified here, are criticized because they give too much weight to unconscious demographic coincidences or conscious adherence to the expectations of others, while not emphasizing enough the role of personal characteristics and preferences. Stage theories of compatibility were developed to acknowledge the importance of personal choice factors in the selection of a marital partner.

Stage Models of Compatibility

From the viewpoint of a computerized dating service, cultural and structural compatibility factors have

the advantage of being the easiest to test and score— just fill out a questionnaire and wait for the computer to assign a dating partner who matches your wish list. Far more interesting to the rest of us, though, are the intangible qualities of marital choice that make a certain few people more attractive to us than anyone else. Compatibility theories that take these more personal issues into account are sometimes referred to as *stage models*. According to these theories, romantic partners actively test their compatibility on a variety of personal characteristics (Surra, 1991). Are partners that rational about their close relationships? Perhaps reading about two of the major stage models will help you decide.

Stimulus-Value-Role Theory (SVR). Sociologist Bernard Murstein (1980, 1987) has proposed the stimulus-value-role (SVR) theory of marital choice that describes a romantic relationship as developing through three sequential stages. In the *stimulus stage,* two people are attracted to each other before they actually interact, on the basis of physical appearance, social standing, reputation, dress, and so forth. The stimulus stage usually occurs during the first meeting, when each person has very limited data to use in evaluating the other. In the

DIVERSITY

Japan's New Marriage Squeeze

In strongly traditional Japanese society, where women have felt compelled to be married by the age of 25, many females are now balking at tying the knot. Apparently, while young Japanese women still want to have children, there is considerable doubt among them about whether they also need a husband. Beneficiaries of Japan's economic miracle, women clearly are taking their independence seriously.

Indeed, womens' opinions of men seem to have sunk to new lows. According to a recent poll, Japanese women rate three-fifths of all Japanese young men as "unreliable." Other adjectives women use to describe men are "self-centered," "boring," "predictable" creatures who, "spoiled" by their mothers, expect their wives to wait on them while they lie on the couch watching television.

How are Japanese men reacting to their lower status? Increasingly, they are bewildered, angered, and confused by the rejection. Many seem not to understand that they have to behave differently toward educated, employed women with independent pocketbooks and attitudes. For example, when his fiancee broke off their engagement, Takashi Takahashi, a 36-year-old marketing manager, was bewildered. Today, 4 years later, he still does not know why she ended their engagement, nor does he dare ask her.

Statistics indicate that this new tension between the sexes has already had serious consequences for Japanese society. In the last two decades, the number of unmarried men and women over the age of 30 has not only doubled but continues to rise. Simultaneously, the birthrate—at present 1.53 children per woman—has plunged. As a result, 17.4 percent of the country's pop-

ulation is now under the age of 15, or about half the 36 percent reported for most years prior to World War II. If this trend continues, it is estimated that by early in the next century Japan will be faced with an aging population. If this occurs, savings will have to go into supporting retirees instead of into factories, businesses, and other income-producing investments. It is no wonder then that the government is becoming seriously concerned about how to encourage a truce between Japanese women and men.

Meanwhile, in a society where being the head of a family remains a sign of male adulthood, some unmarried men are finding themselves the target of ridicule. Others have become resigned to their single state. Still others are creating new strategies to cope with desperate times. Thus, many young men are attending courses, which have sprung up across Japan, on how to understand women. Says one man who signed up for such a course, "I'm hoping these lectures will help me understand so I can persuade someone and then have a strong marriage."

EXPLORATIONS *Is it possible that ideological differences between women and men will contribute to the new marriage squeeze in America? Like in Japan, will increasing numbers of people remain single into their thirties? Will more women opt to have families without men, as single parents? Can you think of other social consequences of the marriage squeeze?*

SOURCES: K. Itoli & B. Powell (1992); and "New Social Struggle in Japan: Finding Marrying Women" (August 9, 1992). ✾

---

value stage, the partners discover whether they are compatible on the basis of shared basic attitudes and beliefs about politics, environmental issues, abortion, and the like. Suppose they both value academic achievement; this is a plus for their relationship. But suppose she is ardently pro-choice while he is militantly against abortion; then this is a minus for their relationship. If one or both partners believe there are too many minuses, the relationship will break up.

Value determinations usually occur between the second and seventh meeting. In the *role stage*, the couple evaluate how well they fit together in such roles as companion, friend, lover, potential husband or wife, and so forth. During this stage the focus is on behaviors. "Is she responsible?" "Is he supportive of me when I have a problem?" As each person sees how the other acts in these situations, comparison is made with one's expectations of a future spouse. If they fit, the relationship provides satisfaction and is more likely to progress toward greater commitment. Role evaluation usually occurs after the seventh meeting.

Wheel Theory. Instead of explaining, as Murstein does, the development of a relationship by its progress through distinct stages, sociologist Ira Reiss (1980) thinks of it as a wheel, consisting of four spokes and two rings. The four spokes represent the interpersonal elements that drive the relationship, while the rings represent the partners' sociocultural background and role conceptions—the context in which commitment develops. "Role conceptions define what one should do and expect in a love relationship. The sociocultural background in terms of education, religion, and such shapes the specific types of role conceptions that exist" (p. 129). (See Figure 4-2.)

The interpersonal elements, or spokes of the wheel, are rapport, self-revelation, mutual dependency, and intimacy need fulfillment. At first encounter, a feeling of rapport or ease in being with each other determines that the relationship will continue and leads the partners to reveal certain facts about themselves. Then, as the relationship progresses, the two people begin to feel mutually dependent. This happens, for example,

FIGURE 4-2
Wheel Theory of Relationship Development

SOURCE: I. Reiss (1980).

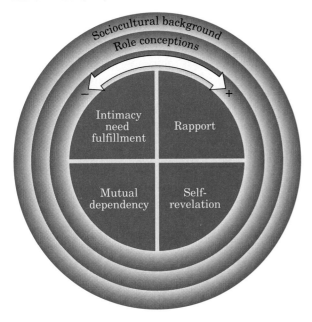

when she needs him as an audience for her jokes, or the two confide more deeply in each other.

The fourth spoke in the wheel, intimacy need fulfillment, comes into play when the partners fulfill each other's needs—"the need for someone to love, the need for someone to confide in, and the need for sympathetic understanding" (p. 128). These needs, when satisfied, are expressions of the close and intimate nature of the relationship, as Figure 4-2 shows.

Reiss calls his description a wheel theory rather than a stage theory because the four spokes can be regarded as elements of a single process. As the relationship develops, the wheel turns in a positive direction: More self-revelation leads to greater dependency, which, in turn, leads to more intimacy need fulfillment. With each turn of the wheel, the relationship becomes more intense and involves greater commitment. But the wheel can start turning backward at any point. Less rapport may make both partners somewhat reluctant to reveal anything more about themselves, which, in turn, may cause them to loosen their interdependency. If the wheel continues to turn backward, the relationship will eventually come to an end.

In most compatibility theories, couples who do not make it through the particular sequences or stages are considered at risk; they are viewed as likely to break up. Stage theories of mate selection have been criticized for ignoring that many potential marital partners have not yet learned to communicate at the highly intimate level needed to allow appropriate assessment of the similarity or "fit" of attitudes, values, and roles. Another fault of stage theories is that the boundaries between stages are not always clearly understood. The rationale for why particular stages precede or follow others are not always based on research findings. And in some cases, research has failed to verify that the stages occur in the order proposed.

Exchange Theories

Another way to describe how intimate relationships develop is to assess the costs and rewards of remaining in a particular relationship. The greater the rewards of the relationship the more likely it is to continue. According to exchange theorists, at the beginning of a relationship we evaluate the likelihood that the partner will be a rewarding companion—Will he or she reciprocate my interest and be willing to spend time in the relationship? Later we assess whether the relationship is rewarding enough to hold our interest over time—Are we being rewarded in the ways we deem important and necessary? When dating partners evaluate their relationship, they generally consider at least six types of resources: love, status, information, money, goods, and services (Foa & Foa, 1980). Partners typically are more satisfied with their relationship if they exchange love and information rather than money, services, or goods.

Equity theory is a variation of exchange theory, based on the idea that individuals desire fairness in their close relationships. Equity is defined as the feeling of fairness that is experienced when we evaluate the overall balance of rewards and costs of a relationship ("He shops for groceries, while I do the vacuuming"). Partners who feel that their relationship is fair are more willing to make a long-term commitment. They experience greater overall well-being and less distress than do couples in inequitable relationships (Fish & Fish, 1986).

As we discussed in Chapter 3, partners in equitable relationships are thought to be most content, partners who are overbenefited are slightly distressed (they are guilty and afraid of losing their superior position), and partners who are underbenefited (they feel angry and resentful) are most distressed. Elaine Hatfield and her colleagues (Hatfield, Traupmann, & Sprecher, 1985) propose that (1) equitable (versus inequitable) dating relationships are more likely to progress to higher levels of intimacy; (2) dating partners will be more content and less distressed in equitable relationships; (3) when inequity exists, intimate partners will try to restore equity; (4) following transitions or crises, couples will either work to reestablish equity or move toward breaking up; (5) equitable relationships are especially likely to be stable and to persist over time.

One criticism of exchange theory is that it overestimates how closely partners monitor their actions during mate selection. At the start of a relationship, people seem more tuned in to whether their partner reciprocates rewards and how costly certain traits and behaviors are, but as partners move toward greater intimacy and commitment there is more concern with meeting each other's needs (Berg & McQuinn, 1986). Individuals begin to think of their relationships as long term and trust that the partner will reward them, without needing to be so diligent about keeping track of who does what for whom. As long as the rewarding aspects of the relationship remain high and no better alternative appears, they stay committed. Some critics of exchange theory are also put off by the use of so-called hard-nosed economic theory (costs and rewards) to explain the loving, caring aspects of relationships.

Interpersonal Process Theories

It is clear that social constraints, compatibility, and equity are important factors in choosing a mate. However, the quality of the interpersonal interaction is also a critical element in the mate selection process. How often have you ended a relationship with someone who, when rationally assessed, was perfect for you, but the emotional connection never formed? *Interpersonal process theory*, which is currently gaining support among many family scholars, recognizes the key role of interpersonal interaction. It "acknowledges the importance of factors associated with the compatibility and exchange [theories of mate selection] but proposes that the interaction between individuals in a relationship to a large extent shapes the development of the relationship and choice of mate" (Cate & Lloyd, 1988, p. 420). This theory examines the progress toward mate selection and proposes that the choice of a partner depends on reaching a certain level of intimacy. If that is not achieved, the relationship unravels.

As we discussed in Chapter 3, couples self-disclose and interact in ways that help them decide whether to make a long-term commitment to each other and to the relationship. They develop beliefs about the quality of their relationship and decide if their commitment should include marriage. Interpersonal process theory, instead of viewing couples as moving from one clearly demarcated stage to another, views developmental change within relationships as continuous (Surra, 1991). Properties of relationships like interdependence and love—which we studied in Chapter 3—emerge and change over the duration of the relationship as intimacy develops. Perlman and Fehr (1987) propose that relationships develop over time in the following ways:

1 Partner interaction increases in terms of the frequency, duration, and number of settings in which it occurs.

2 Individuals gain knowledge of the innermost thoughts and feelings of their partners, the breadth and depth of shared knowledge expands, and partners develop unique communication patterns.

3 Individuals become more skilled at anticipating and understanding their partners' views and behaviors.

4 Partners increase their investment in the relationship—share time, give gifts, reveal values and beliefs, introduce the beloved to friends and family.

5 The interdependence and the sense of "we-ness" experienced by partners increase.

6 Partners come to feel that their individual interests are inextricably linked to the well-being and outcome of their relationship.

7 The extent of liking and loving and the sense of caring, commitment, and trust increase.

8 Partners' attachment grows, so they find it difficult to be apart; they long for each other when separated.

9 Partners see the specialness of their relationship—what they have that is unique and irreplaceable.

While other factors may influence mate selection, and can override the importance of the development of intimacy, this process is often critical to the evolution of a long-term relationship. To interpersonal process theorists, mate selection is less a choice and more a process.

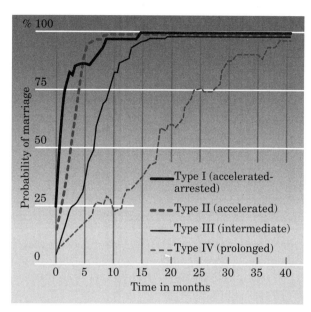

FIGURE 4-3
Relationship Types: Making a Commitment
SOURCE: S. Duck (1988).

Defining Relationships by Their Progress

In a study considering both interpersonal process and social networks, social scientist Ted Huston and his colleagues (Huston, Surra, Fitzgerald, & Cate, 1981) asked 50 newly married couples to draw graphs of the progression of their relationships toward marriage. The couples studied revealed three types of premarital relationship paths: a slow, rocky path; a path that began with a rapid acceleration to commitment and then slowed down; and a path that started more slowly but followed a steady track toward marriage.

In a later study based on in-depth unstructured interviews with another sample of 50 newlywed couples, Surra (1985) found four relationship types that were very similar to those previously identified: (1) an *accelerated-arrested* relationship in which the couple progress very quickly to a high level of commitment and then lose momentum; (2) an *accelerated* relationship in which the couple move smoothly and quickly to marriage; (3) an *intermediate* relationship in which the women report greater ambivalence than the men about commitment—the women have strong positive feelings, followed by feelings of uncertainty—but the couple then move slowly toward marriage; and (4) a *prolonged* relationship in which the couple take a long time to commit to marriage (see Figure 4-3). Partners in each

type of relationship give different reasons for changes in commitment.

Couples in the *accelerated-arrested* relationship more often gave *social network* reasons for the downturn in their progress toward commitment. Parents', neighbors', kin, or other influential third parties' negative responses toward the partner slow the couple's momentum. Partners using this type of reasoning might say: "He took me to meet his parents who didn't seem to like me," or "I didn't really fit into Shelley's group of friends at first, and that was a real problem." Important turning points in commitment were triggered by interference from the social network, but reevaluation led to reconfirmation rather than rejection of the partner.

Couples in an *accelerated* relationship report that turning points in their progress toward commitment, especially upturns, occur because they feel that it is the "right time" to make a stronger commitment to each other. Other reasons are the realization that the dating partner has the "right qualities" to be a good marital partner or that characteristics of the relationship match their preconceived standards of an ideal relationship. Partners using this type of reasoning might remark: "I graduated from college in May and I have a great job. Now it's time for me to find someone

I can share my life with," or "I knew from past relationships that she had all the qualities that were important in a marital partner."

Couples in *intermediate* relationships more often seem to have problems assessing each other's intimacy needs and understanding compatibility issues. "He told me he was falling in love with me and I got scared and backed off for a while," or "We fought about nearly everything at that point in time." Progress in intermediate relationships is usually interrupted by conflicts over differences in the partner's beliefs about what relationships should be like—how people should behave and interact when in committed relationships: How much self-disclosure is appropriate? Do our arguments mean that we really don't really love each other? How close should we be at this stage in our relationship? Are we seeing each other too much . . . or not enough?

Couples in *prolonged* relationships more often give *circumstantial* reasons for their progress toward commitment. Events or forces outside the relationship, they believe, are responsible for changes in their level of commitment. Partners in prolonged relationships might say: "I was so sick I could hardly move and John stopped by to see if I needed anything. He was so nice—brought me soup, took care of my cat, and made sure I was okay," or "I lost my job and that just seemed to put things on hold for a while," or "I didn't see him for two months over summer break." People who give circumstantial explanations for breaks in partner commitment usually mention factors such as fate, luck, accidents, actions taken by others such as bosses or friends, or predictable annual events like the beginning of school or Thanksgiving vacation.

The results of these studies indicate that dating couples take different pathways to long-term commitment and eventual marriage. For the most part, the couple progress steadily and continually toward commitment, but there are setbacks along the way. The ups and downs of relationships have to do with what happens between the partners—development of interdependence, trust, and intimacy as well as conflict over compatibility and equity issues. Progress is affected by how much support couples receive from their social networks; unexpected events that occur in their lives; feelings that the time is right for marriage; and perceptions of whether a partner fits their "ideal image" of a potential mate.

To summarize, although compatibility testing and exchange of resources may explain why some relationships fail while others develop, interpersonal processes are equally crucial to marital choice. The main criticism of interpersonal process theory is that most of the research supporting it is from studies in which individuals were asked to think back to when they were dating and provide step-by-step accounts. Few researchers have actually followed couples through the process of marital choice and observed and asked questions of partners at critical points along the way. It is possible, then, that partners' satisfaction with their current relationship may distort their memory of the early stages of their relationship. Another criticism is that although interpersonal process theory acknowledges the importance of cultural and structural barriers and takes personal choices into account, researchers using this theory typically do not ask study participants about these factors when they collect data. They mostly focus on how partners interact and how that interaction affects relationship progress toward commitment. However, Huston and colleagues (1981) seemed sensitive to this criticism and have taken these broader social factors into account. What may be needed to advance the study of marital choice beyond its current standing is the merger of all competing theories into an overall framework or "grand theory." We also need to study the process of marital choice as it unfolds across time and record the perceptions of each dating partner.

STRESS IN DATING RELATIONSHIPS

We like to think of romantic relationships as trouble-free and loving, but it is vital to dispel this myth and to identify and understand common problems couples may have before marriage. Premarital stressors have a way of spilling over into the marital relationship.

Inhibited Communication: Taboo Topics

One of the most common descriptions couples give of what lies at the root of a relationship problem is: "There was a misunderstanding." "Misunderstandings" cause everything from missed appointments to relationship breakups. With hindsight it usually turns out that, as the word suggests, the misunderstanding in question was due to a failure in communication. Either the wrong signal was sent or the wrong message was received. To a considerable degree, the progress of any relationship depends on how well the people involved communicate.

Even in close relationships, those you would expect to be most open, some degree of information control is likely. There are some topics one or both romantic partners are unwilling to discuss with each other. They may go so far as to resort to secrecy and deception or simply avoid talking about certain issues. Leslie Baxter and William Wilmot (1985), who specialize in communication research, studied these "off limits" areas, which they labeled taboo topics. They identify six such topics. Next to each topic is an example along with the percentage of respondents who considered it taboo.

The taboo most often mentioned was *state of the relationship* talk—discussing the current and future state of the relationship—"I think we've really gotten a lot closer lately." "I love you and want to get married soon" (68 percent). State of the relationship talk was considered taboo for a number of reasons. If the partners disagreed about their level of commitment to the relationship, such discussions, respondents feared, might lead to a breakup. "It would ruin a carefree relationship," indicated a male study participant. "At a minimum, we'd have to attach a label . . . a 'friendship' or that 'we're going together.' And that would bring all sorts of expectations and pressures with it" (p. 260). Relationship talk was also avoided because of a feeling that only in very close relationships should dating partners engage in such examinations. Talking about the state of a casual relationship would make it appear closer than the partners perceived it to be. According to one female, "The one thing we can't talk about is how much we really like each other; not in a romantic way or anything but just caring and liking. A serious talk about it would imply something neither of us wants. So we just joke around about it" (p. 262).

Others feared that the less committed partner might pressure them for greater commitment. As one woman noted, "For me right now, there's no way I'll get married, but sometimes I think he's more serious. . . . It's a sore subject and makes me feel on the defensive" (p. 259). Another reason given for avoiding relationship talk was individual vulnerability. As a male pointed out, "I just never talk about those kinds of things. Never. Big mistake . . . you leave yourself very vulnerable . . . your feelings can get hurt" (p. 261).

A second taboo topic was *extra-relationship activity*—talking about activities engaged in with other close friends or social network members—"Elaina and I talked for 2 hours yesterday and we've decided to go shopping together on Friday." "Michael wrote to me twice a week during summer vacation" (31 percent). Revealing extra-relationship activity was taboo because it could arouse a partner's anger or jealousy, compromise a need for privacy and independence, or lead to being put in the middle of a conflict of interest between a best friend and a partner. One female said: "I spent the summer in Guatemala and met this guy there. I write to him regularly, but I wouldn't tell this to my boyfriend because I don't want to hurt him . . . I don't want to make waves" (p. 262).

A third taboo topic was *relationship norms*—discussing the rules of behavior in the relationship—"You're so inconsiderate; I hate it when you talk to your friends and completely ignore me." "It seems to me that two people who have dated as long as we have should have an easier time talking to each other than we do" (25 percent). Bringing up relationship norms could end in arguments or embarrassment. Her partner's aggressive behavior, for example, was a taboo topic for one female. "It's an unpleasant thing to discuss with someone. If it came up he'd get mad and become very defensive" (p. 263).

Another off-limits topic was *prior relationships*—talking about past romantic relationships with others—"Travis was such a good dancer; I wish you would take me dancing sometimes." "Jennifer had this little rose tattoo on her left shoulder" (25 percent). That the past should be irrelevant to their present relationship, as well as a need to maintain a good impression, were the primary reasons given for not discussing prior relationships. "I don't think it matters what happened in the past," remarked a male research participant, "talking about past relationships places the emphasis on the past rather than on the present" (p. 263).

Also taboo were *conflict-induced topics*—pointing out how dissimilar or different the partners are—"Your family is so negative toward one another, while mine really cares about each other." "What is it about talking that is so great? Just because you have this great need to reveal all, does not mean that I have to" (22 percent). Discussing conflict-induced topics holds the risk of bringing to the fore basic ideological differences between the partners. These differences, respondents feared, could provoke arguments and perhaps ultimately precipitate a breakup. Emphasizing similarities in beliefs and attitudes was considered more productive in developing closeness than was finding differences.

A final taboo was *negative self-disclosure*—revealing

One issue dating couples today have difficulty talking about is AIDS. Couples may want to avoid disclosing their sexual pasts or even resort to deception. Or they may be uncomfortable about discussing the use of safe sex practices.

things that are damaging to one's personal image or unpleasant to discuss—"It's so difficult for me to talk about my father because he was never around while I was growing up." "I'm not proud of how I treated my younger brother and I've really tried to make it up to him" (17 percent). Respondents indicated that negative self-disclosure was taboo because such disclosure ultimately led to having the partner see them in a bad light.

Clearly, many dating couples tread carefully in addressing certain areas that they perceive could affect their relationship, and the reasons for their reticence vary. Baxter and Wilmot's research suggests that in some instances one partner will keep things from the other in an effort to protect himself or herself, the partner, friends, or the relationship itself. Whatever the reason, these researchers caution that although direct talk about the relationship is not a magic potion which can guarantee relationship health, it may be harmful to totally avoid it.

There is a time in the development of any committed relationship, most family scientists agree, when the partners must discuss their attachment, regardless of whether their discussion includes topics that may reflect negatively on either of them, or may seem threatening, risky, or distressing. How they handle such sensitive issues indicates how they will resolve similar dilemmas in a marital relationship. If both hide behind carefully manicured roles during courtship, neither

will be able to anticipate accurately how the other will behave in the daily reality of married life. (See Table 4-1.)

Dating Violence

Setting the Stage

Because serious dating relationships have tended to be viewed primarily as romantic attachments between committed partners considering marriage, it was not until the 1980s that scholars began to look at the darker side of dating. What they saw was that the system itself can set the stage for exploitation. Their observations about dating relationships indicate that the double standard remains a fundamental element. Not only are men's goals likely to be different from women's but males have more power in the relationship (Dilorio, 1989).

Since the early 1900s when dating became the main way to meet prospective marital partners, economics, physical attractiveness, and the ability to attract other eligible partners have become ever more important to the process:

> By the 1940s, a male partner's worth as a date has centered on: . . . his ability to "drive the right car" and go to "all the right places" . . . his worth was very

---

TABLE 4-1
Relationship Rules: How to Stay Close

After studying the essays of college students, Leslie Baxter identified these rules of behavior that dating couples expect to have their partners follow as a condition for them to remain committed to the relationship (listed in order of importance)

If individuals are in a close relationship, they should:

- Acknowledge one another's individual identities and lives beyond the relationship
- Express similar attitudes, beliefs, values, and interests
- Enhance one another's self-worth and self-esteem
- Be open, genuine, and authentic with one another
- Remain loyal and faithful to one another
- Reap rewards commensurate with their investments, relative to the other party
- Experience a mysterious and inexplicable "magic" in one another's presence
- Have substantial shared time together

Source: L. A. Baxter (1986).

directly related to how much money he spent on the date. Her worth, on the other hand, was related to her ability to generate as much competition as possible for her time. Ultimately, this meant that her worth was defined in terms of characteristics of her person [how physically attractive she was; how well she could please her partner; how much other men wanted her]. (Lloyd, 1991, p. 15)

The prevailing cultural expectation is that men should display traits and behaviors showing they are in control, while women should show their dependency on their partners and their relationships as measures of their worth. These expectations are not universal, of course, but represent threads of socialization, media portrayals, and gender stereotypes that influence certain individuals. According to family studies professor Sally Lloyd, a recognized expert on violence in courtship and dating, the more emphasis in a relationship on these themes of control and dependency as "the way courtship should be," the higher the potential for aggressive and exploitative behavior.

Gender-based stereotypes of control and dependency, Lloyd believes, lead to other common stereotypic beliefs about relationships: That men seek to avoid commitment and marriage, while women crave it, pressure for it, and lead terribly lonely lives without it; that to be a completely fulfilled person, a woman must be married—she will never be whole without the "right man"; that the success of the relationship rests squarely on the woman's shoulders—its failure must be *her* failure. And, finally, that it is men who leave relationships, while women cling to them, and to men.

The scene is set for deception and an escalating game of offense and defense if dating relationships are viewed as situations where women are out to trap reluctant men into marriage. In this scenario, men are expected to take the initiative, to make the first move both in showing their interest and in making sexual overtures. Women are expected to show that they like their dates and want to be asked out again, but not at the expense of losing their reputations. In devising their responses, women are left on their own about where to draw the line on sexual intimacy since parents, kin, and the larger community are no longer involved in the dating process. Yet intangible presences surround women: Parental expectations are that daughters will be popular, date frequently, but not let things "go too far." And, while men may initiate relationships, women are expected to maintain them.

The Role of Violence

Physical violence is the ultimate form of exploitative behavior. Between 33 and 50 percent of college students experience physical violence of some kind—hitting, slapping, pushing, punching—some time in their college dating careers (Bird, Stith, & Schladale, 1991; Lloyd, 1991). Women who have been physically abused during dates report that their partners' needs for control or domination precipitated the violence (Stets & Pirog-Good, 1987). When women hit men, it is almost always in self-defense, while resisting, or out of frustration and anger at their partners' attempts to control or dominate them (Emery, Lloyd, & Castleton, 1989).

Although there are many peaceful ways to handle disagreements, physical violence is used in an alarming number of cases. After surveying 400 students, family scientists Gloria Bird, Sandra Stith, and Joann Schladale (1991) found that in dating relationships where one partner tried to persuade the other to do things his or her way by using confrontational tactics—getting angry, blaming the partner for relationship problems—violence was most likely to occur. Refusal to communicate, verbal abuse, swearing, leaving the room, and withdrawing love and support were common in such relationships. If these failed, violence was often resorted to as a means of regaining control of the situation or of the partner.

What surprises many people is that as many as 40 to 50 percent of women who experience physical violence continue to date their abusive partners (Bird, Stith, & Schladale, 1991). Abused partners typically ignore, forgive, or make excuses for such behavior. They may justify the abuser's behavior in various ways such as: "He couldn't help it. He just got out of control—just sort of exploded," or "We were wrestling around and I accidentally elbowed her in the eye, then she slapped me so hard my teeth rattled. It really surprised me and I just reacted," or "He was under such stress. His favorite cousin had just died. On top of that, his father lost his job and then his grades dropped. When I said he couldn't spend the night, he just sort of went crazy." "He really loves me, you know. It's just that he's so jealous. It's hard for me to convince him that I have no interest in other men."

Sexual Aggression

Conflict between dating partners frequently revolves around sexual issues (Koss & Oros, 1982). Recent studies show that between 15 and 28 percent of women in dating relationships experience *rape*—forced intercourse (Garrett-Gooding & Senter, 1987; Lane & Gwartney-Gibbs, 1985). If other unwanted acts of a sexual nature are included—forced kissing and petting, for example—then 50 to 75 percent of women in colleges and universities say they have experienced some form of sexual aggression (Burke, Stets, & Pirog-Good, 1988; Muehlenhard & Linton, 1987).

Although they often suffer physical and psychological trauma from being forced to comply with their dating partners' sexual desires, women sometimes have difficulty labeling such coercive acts as rape (Lloyd, 1991). Rape is inconsistent with a close and loving relationship in which couples have been together for long enough to feel some degree of trust in each other. Why, then, does it happen? Both women and men tend to think of male sexuality in stereotypical ways, rather than basing their beliefs on the facts of human sexuality. Men are viewed as having urgent sexual needs. Women are expected to give token resistance to men's sexual pressure, to say "no" but mean "yes." Because the male is characteristically seen as having the right to control the sexual nature of the

relationship, this, in essence, gives him permission to use force to achieve his sexual goals.

The popular understanding of rape is as an act of forced intercourse with a stranger, or perhaps, in a dating situation, with a man who is a casual acquaintance. In reality, many college women are raped by men they have known for some time and feel comfortable and secure with (Koss, Dinero, Seibel, & Cox, 1988). That the perpetrator is the woman's dating partner with whom she has a close relationship can be as psychologically damaging to her as is rape by a stranger (Kilpatrick, Best, Saunders, & Veronen, 1988). (See the "Snapshots" box.)

As we discussed, some women forgive or excuse abusive behavior, and rape by a dating partner proves no exception. A woman's romantic ideals of what close relationships *should* be sometimes prevent her from realistically appraising forced sexuality. Such women tend to believe that in committed relationships men will not take advantage of them. "Romanticism," observes Lloyd (1991), "encourages reinterpretation of sexually exploitative actions as non-exploitative" (p. 18).

Rape prevention workshops are one way that colleges help both male and female students to become clearer about defining what is abusive sexual behavior, even by a dating partner.

SNAPSHOTS

Date Rape

"When a woman says 'no,' she doesn't always mean it."—say nearly half of the 2,092 high-achieving junior and senior high school students surveyed, *Roanoke Times & World News.*

"I thought it was all my fault, I felt so filthy, I washed myself over and over in hot water. Did he rape me?, I kept asking myself. I didn't consent. But who's gonna believe me? I had a man in my hotel room after midnight."—32-year-old Florida attorney in regard to an attorney she met while working on business for the Florida Supreme Court, *Time.*

"Juries don't have a great deal of sympathy for the victim if she's a willing participant up to the point of nonconsensual sexual intercourse."—Norman Kinne, a prosecutor in Dallas, *Time.*

"I felt violated. I felt like she was taking advantage of me when she was very drunk. I never heard her say 'No!,' 'Stop!,' or anything."—freshman student accused of rape at liberal arts college, *Time.*

"The bottom line is, Why does a woman's having a drink give a man the right to rape her?"—Dean Kilpatrick, director of the Crime Victim Research and Treatment Center at the Medical University of South Carolina, *Time.*

"When a woman says no, chances are that she means it. If the woman means no and the man persists, it is rape."—Charlene Muehlenhard, a psychologist at Texas A&M University, *Psychology Today.*

Four out of five rapes are committed by men who know the women they assault. Research data, results of court cases, commonly held attitudes about sexual activity and rape, and conflicting descriptions of the "attack" by the man and woman involved, make one thing perfectly clear—there is little consensus on the definition of date rape. Many persons do agree that when a woman says no, further sexual activity is rape, with no room for disagreement. But there are still many differing interpretations of the meaning of "No" within the context of male-female relationships.

EXPLORATIONS *If after a date and a drink or two, a man persuades a woman to have sex, even though she protests, is it rape rather than consensual sex? If she is initially unsure how to define what happened, and waits several months before filing a charge, is it rape? Is it possible for a man to believe he seduced a woman, and for her to believe that she was raped? Is there a communications problem between women and men that results in different views of the same situation? Do you think strict and specific laws are needed to resolve the question of date rape, or are there other alternatives?*

SOURCES: Excerpts from " 'Don't! Stop!' or 'Don't stop!' " (1989); K. Q. Miller (November 24, 1992); and N. Gibbs (June 3, 1991).

Reactions of Friends. Even though sexually aggressive behavior tends to be hidden from outsiders, the couple's peer group has a measure of influence. Friends and acquaintances of the dating couple can play into this idea that no rape really occurred. If the friends and peers of the sexually abused female have themselves been victims of forced sexuality, or her male friends regularly participate in such activity, then they are likely to be more accepting of such coercive acts as "normal" dating situations. Lloyd argues that such peer groups—she calls them sexually aggressive peer groups—are more likely than others to believe that men are entitled to sex in serious dating relationships. Men are reinforced in the belief that forced sex is acceptable if they frequently associate with others who engage in forced intercourse and other sexually exploitative acts with women (Boeringer, Shehan, & Akers, 1991; DeKeseredy, 1988).

On college campuses, unlike in the general population, forced sex more often occurs between brief acquaintances—for example, women and men who meet at planned social functions on campus. One study of some 850 university students identified four types of rape:

> *Stranger rape,* the stereotypical image of rape; *party rape,* in which the victim and perpetrator are strangers but are part of the same social situation; *acquaintance rape,* in which victim and perpetrator are actually acquainted (e.g., friends, dormmates, classmates); and *date rape,* in which victim and perpetrator are seeing one another in a dating relationship, which can range from first date to boyfriend-girlfriend. (Ward, Chapman, Cohn, White, & Williams, 1991, p. 66)

Most campus rapes occur in dorms, apartments, and fraternities. Many of the attacks are "party-related": the attacker has been drinking and knows the victim only casually. But in 30 percent of attempted rapes and in 33 percent of completed rapes, the perpetrator is the woman's boyfriend (see Figure 4-4 and Table 4-2). In 73 percent of completed rapes, forced sex occurred despite repeated verbal and/or physical protests.

Forced sexuality does have serious, long-term consequences. Women who have been raped by a date or someone they know find it difficult to trust another male partner and to love and be intimate in their closest relationships for years afterward (Emery et al., 1989). Raped women need help in dealing with their emotions, in rebuilding their self-esteem, and in restoring their capacity for trust if they are to build a new relationship based on mutual respect.

BREAKING UP

Most relationships go through troubled times. Why some survive while others fail has been an enduring subject for poets, playwrights, and novelists. It has also engaged the attention of scholars, who have examined some of the factors that can underlie a couple's determination to part.

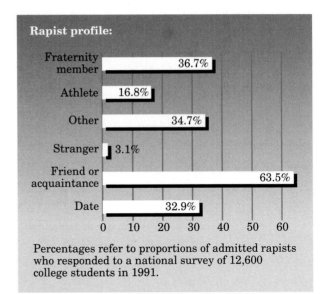

FIGURE 4-4
Rape on Campus
SOURCE: D. Winston (1991).

Reasons for Breaking Up

A study by Baxter (1986) identifies eight reasons college couples gave for the breakup of their dating relationships. These reasons involve compatibility, equity, and interpersonal process issues. They are cited in order of frequency (pp. 295–297):

> *Desire for autonomy* (37 percent): "She was upset whenever I went out with friends . . . she even expected me to put her in front of my family . . . I felt trapped by her possessiveness."
>
> *Lack of similarity* (30 percent): "We began having serious disagreements on our ideas and beliefs about things. . . . The differences between us were very apparent."
>
> *Lack of supportiveness* (27 percent): "He never seemed to be listening to what I had to say. He was inconsiderate and thoughtless about my feelings. He felt he could do whatever he wanted and I'd be there. I began to feel like I was a convenience put on earth for his benefit."
>
> *Lack of openness* (22 percent): "I wanted him to talk about his feelings. I had been dating him for more than a year and I couldn't understand his emotional withdrawal. . . . I oscillated between understanding his probably masculine aversion

TABLE 4-2
Risk Factors for Date Rape

FACTORS THAT ENHANCE THE PROBABILITY OF SEXUAL ABUSE

Male has strong needs for power and control in the relationship.

Miscommunication about sex: He misinterprets his partner's behavior as indicating a desire for sex.

Emotional incongruence: When she says no, he thinks that she "led him on," or he becomes angry at being turned down; these emotions lower his inhibitions toward sexual force.

Sexual arousal.

Imbalance in power between the partners: He initiates the date, provides transportation, plans the activities, pays all expenses, and is allowed to take a dominant role during the date (he does most of the talking; she defers to his opinions and decisions).

FACTORS THAT REDUCE MALE'S INTERNAL INHIBITIONS AGAINST RAPE

Attitudes

- He has traditional gender-role attitudes.
- He accepts violence against women as sometimes warranted.
- He endorses rape myths—for example, women who are "loose" or who "lead men on" are "asking for it"; women always put up "token" resistance, but they really "want it" as much as men.
- He believes that male-female relationships are usually adversarial—antagonistic, hostile, or oppositional—so he expects to have to push for what he wants; that he will pressure his partner and she will resist but eventually give in.

Prior abusive acts

- He has been abusive in other relationships.
- He was abused as a child or adolescent.

FACTORS THAT REDUCE MALE'S EXTERNAL INHIBITIONS AGAINST RAPE

Location of date: Some men interpret a woman's willingness to go to certain locations as an indication that she's interested in sex—*his* home or apartment or other private or secluded places.

Mode of transportation: Alone in his car.

Date activity: The more sexual the surroundings, the greater the likelihood that he will interpret the situation as arousing ("parking" in a secluded area; going to a party where other couples are pairing off and going to bedrooms; attending a sexually explicit movie or a movie that portrays women as reacting positively to aggressive or forced sex).

Alcohol or substance use: Such activity does *not cause* rape, but it gives him an "acceptable" excuse to act less responsibly; if she drinks too, people are more likely to "blame the victim"—degrade her character and make her more responsible for what happens on the date.

SOURCE: P. Lundberg-Love & R. Geffner (1989).

to feelings and thinking everything was my fault."

Failure to maintain loyalty/fidelity (17 percent): "I felt tremendous guilt because I was intimate with another person at the same time we were going together. . . . I couldn't face my girlfriend to tell her, so I just broke it off cold."

Reduction of shared time (16 percent): "Some people

may be able to get by on letters, phone calls, and vacation visits, but to me, that's not what a relationship is all about."

Absence of equity (12 percent): "I felt that I wasn't getting as much energy put back into the relationship as I was putting forth. I was giving without getting. . . . Being in this relationship was not benefitting me in any way."

Absence of romance (10 percent): "All I know is that something was missing—the same old feeling wasn't there anymore. The magic was gone."

Women, more frequently than men, report that autonomy, lack of openness, and lack of equity are the biggest reasons they decide to break up with a dating partner. In contrast, men more often break up due to a lack of romance in the relationship.

Making the Decision: Whether to Repair or End the Relationship

It is impossible to maintain a high level of satisfaction throughout a relationship despite having chosen a supposedly "ideal" partner. All close relationships have their ups and downs. There has been a lot of interest in how couples react to dissatisfying relationships. Two theories in particular have received great attention.

Breaking Up as a Strategy: Exit, Voice, Loyalty, or Neglect

After conducting several studies, social psychologist Caryl Rusbult (1987) identified four strategies that people use when faced with relationship dissatisfaction: exit, voice, loyalty, and neglect. Some partners decide that the best way to deal with a dissatisfying relationship is to *exit*. They have little to lose and believe that the relationship is not worth saving. Such partners are usually unhappy with the state of the relationship, have little invested in its development, believe that they have good alternatives for finding another partner, and are faced with what they regard as serious relationship problems. These individuals actively attempt to harm the relationship by talking about leaving or by saying and doing things that they know will upset their partner and eventually lead to a breakup.

Other partners use *voice* as a means of handling relationship dissatisfaction. They make active and constructive attempts to improve relationship quality by asking the partner what is wrong and trying to change, discussing problems, compromising, seeking advice from a counselor or clergy member, and suggesting solutions to problems. Voice is an attempt to rescue a valued closeness that is in danger of being lost. It is used more frequently by a partner who has been highly satisfied with the relationship, invested heavily in its development, and is faced with relatively serious relationship problems.

Out of *loyalty* some partners passively "hang in there," waiting for conditions to improve without putting much effort into changing things. They wait and hope that things will improve without active intervention. Such partners tell themselves that it is best to "give things some time." While they wait for improvement, they continue to be supportive of their partners, hold back on criticism, and continue to have faith that the relationship will somehow heal itself. Loyalty primarily maintains the status quo (that is, Why try to fix a basically good thing?). Dissatisfied partners generally respond with loyalty when there is a history of high overall relationship satisfaction. They have invested much in their relationships, have few alternatives for replacing their partners, and truly believe that their problems are relatively minor.

Other dissatisfied partners *neglect* their relationships and passively allow them to deteriorate. They typically ignore their partners by arranging their lives so they spend less time as a couple and more or less just let things fall apart. When issues arise, neglectful partners refuse to discuss problems, treat their partners badly emotionally or physically, criticize their partners for things unrelated to the real problem, chronically complain without offering solutions to problems, and sometimes become sexually involved with other people. Neglect occurs when a partner has not been satisfied with the relationship in a long time, has invested little of himself or herself in the relationship, and is not motivated to do much of anything about what most couples would consider relatively minor problems.

Although Rusbult describes these strategies as distinct and separate choices of dissatisfied partners in romantic relationships, they may overlap and occasionally blend as partners try different methods of keeping their uneasy relationships alive or decide to end them. She points out that women more typically react to problems in their relationships by voice and loyalty, while men tend to rely on neglect.

Breaking Up as a Process: A Stage Theory

Loren Lee (1984) is particularly interested in relationships that employ the "voice" strategy, which is the healthiest way to end a relationship. His stage theory looks at the dissolution of relationships where negotiation is key to the process. Lee is concerned with both interpersonal behaviors and social network behaviors (see Table 4-3).

In Stage 1, the *discovery of dissatisfaction,* one or both

TABLE 4-3
Stages in the Breakup of Romantic Dating Relationships

Stage	Couple Process	Individual Behaviors	Social Network Behavior
1. Discovery of dissatisfaction ■ Recognition of significant problems, conflicts or dissatisfaction	■ Couple's tensions are concealed. ■ Couple's interaction is passive or subvertive rather than supportive. ■ Couple make effort to maintain a balance in the face of undisclosed conflict.	■ Dissatisfied partner copes with mounting discontent and frustration. ■ Evaluates strengths and weaknesses of relationship and of partner. ■ Makes the decision to expose dissatisfaction or confront partner.	■ Peers/family members may promote or otherwise influence partner dissatisfaction. ■ Others with a romantic interest in one of the partners may provide reasons or reinforcement for the breakup.
2. Exposure ■ Dissatisfactions are brought up to partner	■ Dissatisfied partner deliberately confronts other partner or "leaks" information to let other partner know of discontent.	■ Emotions are expressed —shock, relief, anger, hurt. ■ Attempts are made to protect self or partner by minimizing the problem or bringing up problems other than the "real" issues causing the discontent.	■ Partners make efforts to explain "leaks" to peers, or . . . ■ Attempt to conceal conflict from them.
3. Negotiation ■ Discussion of issues of dissatisfaction and course of action	■ Couple find a way to negotiate their differences. ■ Efforts are made to placate the partner through bargaining; conflict escalates. ■ State of the relationship talk continues; both partners jointly assess the relationship and the consequences of breaking up.	■ Efforts are made to formulate/communicate views and needs. ■ Evaluates partner's point of view. ■ Copes with stress and ambivalence while working out reasonable options.	■ Consultation with peers and family members; professional aid (e.g., therapy) occasionally sought. ■ Available support network considered and entered into "breakup" evaluation.
4. Resolution ■ Decision reached concerning relationship	■ Dissatisfied partner decides to end relationship, or . . . ■ Both partners resolve to compromise on a resolution to the problem.	■ Attempts to maintain "integrity" and a personal balance despite impending change in the relationship. ■ Copes with fear, anger, and confusion.	■ Friends are given new attention and importance in anticipation of transition in romantic relationship.
5. Transformation ■ Actual changes executed in relationship	■ Couple go through parting rituals like making "farewell addresses" to each other. ■ Couple meet less frequently and for shorter periods; interaction becomes less intimate.	■ Mourns for the loss of the relationship; recovers from traumatic emotions. ■ Reflects on the lost relationship.	■ Support network helps absorb the shock of the breakup. ■ Network of peers/ friends is given a full account of the rise and fall of the relationship.

SOURCE: L. Lee (1984).

partners become unhappy with the relationship. A triggering event or a general sense of dissatisfaction leads to a reevaluation of commitment. During Stage 2, *exposure,* the partner or partners bring the dissatisfaction out in the open for discussion. In Stage 3, *negotiation,* the troubling issues are discussed seriously, along with what might be done to save the relationship. In Stage 4, *resolution,* a decision is reached about continuing the relationship. Finally, during Stage 5, *transformation,* the couple break up and each partner goes through a period of adjusting to the loss of the relationship.

Although it is often only one partner who is unhappy and initiates the breakup, ultimately both are forced to come to a decision. And, as we have seen in several other instances in this chapter, the couple's social network becomes involved in the dissolution process. It is to the network that partners first confess their dissatisfaction, and the reactions of friends and relatives play a significant role in whether a partner decides to continue or end the relationship. The network also gives support during the breakup and as the partners adjust after the relationship ends.

Complete disengagement from the relationship can be difficult. Some couples shift back and forth between withdrawal and intense reconciliation. When one partner wants to leave, and the other wants to keep the relationship going, breaking up is especially challeng-ing. "Bringing one's partner down—'cooling the mark,' " as Lee calls it, "may involve several tries to achieve the desired break" (p. 65). Throughout, each partner must cope with a host of intense emotions that can run the gamut from anger and guilt to pain, shock, sorrow, and, in the end, relief or resignation.

Many changes have occurred in courtship and dating patterns since colonial times. Decisions concerning marital choice have moved from the realm of parents into the hands of the individual partners. Selecting a marital partner is still serious business, but has been delayed until later in the life course. There is now casual dating (getting together to have fun) and serious dating (going out for the purpose of forging a close relationship that moves toward exclusivity and commitment). Women's and men's roles in the dating and marital choice process have become more egalitarian, just as they have in marriage, although cultural expectations still persist and sometimes result in relationship stress. Because marriage continues to be viewed as a significant long-term commitment—"happily ever after"; "till death do us part"—potential partners are ever more interested in what factors influence people to develop close attachments, and what processes during dating lead to commitment versus breaking up. Individuals are beginning to recognize that quality and stability begin in the premarital stage of the relationship.

SUMMARY POINTS

■ The term "courtship" is now used mainly to describe a dating relationship in which the partners are interested in a long-term commitment that includes marriage.

■ In other societies, the main function of parent-arranged marriages is the alliance of two kinship groups rather than the individual happiness of two partners.

■ Dating has several functions, including the facilitation of learning about the social responsibilities and intimacy requirements of a close romantic relationship.

■ Women prefer to delay sexual involvement until a relationship develops some degree of emotional intimacy. Men, on the other hand, tend to be more influenced by peer pressure and push for sexual contact earlier in a relationship.

■ Three major theories are used to describe how dat-ing progresses toward long-term commitment—compatibility, exchange, and interpersonal process.

■ Compatibility theory assumes that mate selection is influenced primarily by cultural and structural barriers, as well as personal choices.

■ Social barriers to marital choices include homogamy, the marriage gradient, and social networks.

■ Structural barriers to marital choices include the sex ratio and propinquity.

■ The marriage squeeze describes a particular point in time when the sex ratio of the population is such that women or men of a particular era or generation do not have enough available marital partners.

■ Stage models of marital choice are compatibility theories that rely on the assumption that partners' similarities arise out of choices they make; that partners actively seek out certain demographic and personality characteristics in possible mates and then test their compatibility on a wide range of traits and roles.

- Stimulus-value-role theory and wheel theory are examples of stage models of marital choice.

- Exchange theories assume that costs, rewards, resources, and perceptions of equity influence our choice of marital partner.

- Interpersonal process theory assumes that mate selection is a *process* that relies heavily on what happens between the partners—how they communicate, handle conflict, jointly create feelings of intimacy—interdependence, mutuality, trust, and love.

- Catherine Surra identifies four different paths to commitment among dating couples—accelerated-arrested, accelerated, intermediate, and prolonged.

- Sally Lloyd contends that the control/dependency theme in dating relationships sets the stage for aggressive and exploitative behavior.

- Dating partners who use confrontational tactics during arguments and who are verbally and emotionally abusive when trying to convince another to change certain attitudes or behaviors are also more likely to use physically violent means of controlling their relationships or their partners.

- Most date rapes occur in dorms, apartments, and fraternities.

- Forced sex by a boyfriend is rape. And, women who are raped by their boyfriends feel a violation of trust, love, and intimacy so great that it sometimes takes months or even years for them to be able to trust another male partner.

- Taboo topics in dating relationships include state of the relationship talk, extrarelationship activity, relationship norms, and prior relationships.

- Dating couples typically break up because of perceptions that their partners are too controlling of them, do not share similar values and beliefs, are not supportive, or are not open with them.

- Strategies used to reduce relationship dissatisfaction include exit, voice, loyalty, and neglect.

- When a premarital dating relationship ends, it generally progresses through five stages of dissolution. Each stage is accompanied by reactions from the couple, each dating partner, and members of their social network.

KEY TERMS

Courtship	*Propinquity*
Pool of eligibles	*Stage models*
Compatibility theories	*Stimulus-value-role theory (SVR)*
Cultural barriers	*Wheel theory*
Homogamy	*Exchange theory*
Heterogamy	*Equity theory*
Endogamy	*Interpersonal process theory*
Exogamy	*Physical violence*
Marriage gradient	*Stranger rape*
Social networks	*Party rape*
Structural barriers	*Acquaintance rape*
Sex ratio	*Date rape*
Marriage squeeze	

REVIEW QUESTIONS

1. How has mate selection changed since the 1700s?

2. In what ways do the dating expectations of women and men differ?

3. Which theories do you believe best identify how people choose each other as marital partners in the 1990s?

4. Has your social network—family, friends, or peers—ever influenced you to stop dating someone? Describe their reactions and how and why you responded the way you did.

5. Talk to a married couple you know. Ask them to describe how they first met and the progress of their relationship toward marriage. Draw a graph like the one in Figure 4-3 to illustrate the path their relationship took toward commitment. Which of Catherine Surra's relationship types does their marital path most resemble?

6. Think back to a past romantic relationship. Write down the topics considered off limits or taboo. Do the topics fit the categories discovered by Leslie Baxter? Which ones? Did you discover a new taboo topic not found by Baxter? If so, what would you call it?

7. How do dating expectations set the stage for relationship violence, including sexual exploitation?

8. Have you ever experienced the breakup of a serious romantic relationship? If so, how well do you think Loren Lee's stage theory reflects your own situation? What, if anything, would you add to the model in Table 4-3?

5

Fernand Léger, *Three Women*, 1921

Interpersonal Lifestyles: Singles in the Land of the Married

Singles are a diverse population, including the never married, the separated and previously married, and the widowed. While the number of married couples has risen 19 percent since 1970, singles have grown by 85 percent—49 million Americans over age 25 are now single (DeWitt, 1992). Despite the growing number of singles, they are not often surveyed by social scientists because, in the past, singlehood was considered a short transitional stage between adolescence and first marriage or a brief interlude between one marriage and another. As these stages or interludes have lengthened from months to years, family scientists are being encouraged to take a more evaluative look at singlehood, especially young singlehood.

The timing of our lives today is quite different from that of our grandparents: Formal education lasts longer, marriage comes later in the life course, the childbearing period is considerably shorter, and life expectancy is much longer (see Figure 5-1).

New life stages develop in response not only to social changes, but also to modifications of the life cycle. Adolescence, for example, became defined as a life stage as the need for child labor decreased and the demand for a better-educated work force increased. The growing acceptance of delayed marriage may mean that yet another stage, young singlehood, is being inserted between childhood and marriage.

In this chapter, we describe the lifestyles of singles, giving special attention to cohabitors, as well as partners in gay and lesbian relationships. We identify the kinds of problems singles face in our marriage-oriented society and also describe the satisfactions of people in each of these interpersonal lifestyles. This chapter focuses on never-married singles (see Chapter 14 for a discussion of divorced singles and Chapters 8 and 15 for information on singles with children). We begin by addressing why increased singlehood causes some concern about the future of marriage and iden-

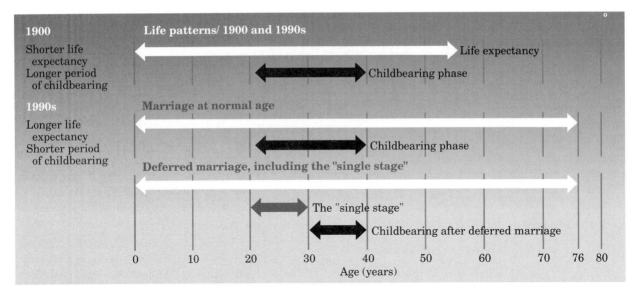

FIGURE 5-1
Life Patterns: 1900 and 1990s

tifying how cultural norms and expectations create the social and historical context within which public opinion operates.

THE SINGLE LIFE: IS IT A THREAT TO MARRIAGE?

As the Census Bureau releases its latest reports on individual and family demographic trends for the 1990s, the increase in young never-married singles has prompted some social critics to wonder if marriage is less relevant to Americans today. Fewer Americans were married in 1992 (61 percent) than at any time since 1890—the peak rate was in 1960, when 74 percent were married (Usdansky, 1992). Part of this decrease is due to higher divorce rates, but most is caused by the growing number of Americans who delay their first marriage. Young people, it appears, are postponing marriage much longer than their parents and grandparents did, with the median age of first marriage being 26 for men and 24 for women—the highest age at first marriage ever recorded for women (see Figure 5-2).

If this tendency toward later marriage seems to represent only a modest change, consider the number of people who now remain single well into their twenties. The percentage of women aged 20 to 24 who have not married almost doubled between 1970 and 1991. The same upward trajectory is evidenced for all young adults, regardless of race or ethnicity, including those in their early thirties. The percentage of black adults in their twenties who have never married, however, is substantially higher than for other population groups. Among black adults in their thirties, both male and female, the percentage who have not married is about twice as high as the corresponding figures for whites and Hispanics (see Figure 5-3).

Marrying later, social analysts contend, has major social implications. People who postpone marriage usually do so to take advantage of educational and employment opportunities. This decision, in turn, affects other areas of their lives, for example, childbearing decisions. Men and women who marry later are more likely to conceive a child outside of marriage. "During the 1980s, out-of-wedlock childbearing was the second most common source of new family formation" (Wetzel, 1990). Marrying later is also associated with having fewer children throughout the marital life course. Choosing to have fewer children and to have them later in the life cycle has resulted in today's families being smaller than ever before.

Observation of these trends in conjunction with an increase in cohabitation has led one social commentator to remark, "after three decades of profound social change, the venerable institution of marriage no longer seems quite so inevitable" (Landers, 1990). Why does

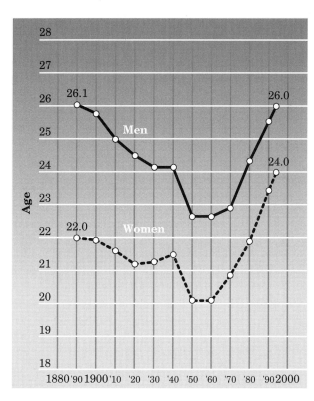

FIGURE 5-2
Increase in Median Age of First Marriage

<small>Source: R. K. Landers (1990).</small>

tually marry (Vobejda, 1991; Wetzel, 1990). Moreover, 90 percent of those surveyed in the latest Gallup poll (1989) responded that having a "good family life" was very important to them.

One study shows that after 2 years of living together, 37 percent of cohabitors decided to marry, 23 percent broke up, and 40 percent decided to stay together, but delayed marriage (Thornton, 1988). In another study, 60 percent of first-time cohabitors eventually got married (Landers, 1990). This research suggests that most cohabitors make long-term commitments to their relationships, with many marrying over time. Furthermore, research indicates that people who marry later in life tend to have lower divorce rates when compared to those who opt for earlier marriages. And most people who postpone childbearing end up having children; they simply wait longer than what might seem typical.

Another important point to remember when attempting to sort out the meaning of recent trends is that individuals in gay and lesbian relationships, who comprise a significant minority of the single and cohabiting population, are not legally permitted to marry. Many gays and lesbians, however, believe that this right should be extended to them. Further, it is becoming more common for this population to have

this comment and other like it create worry and concern for some Americans? Family sociologists Philip Blumstein and Pepper Schwartz (1989) explain that these are normal reactions when something valued and relied on is threatened. We depend on the institution of marriage to provide us with feelings of security and stability. "An institution is a way of life that is very resistant to change. People know about it; they can describe it; and they have spent a lifetime learning how to react to it," write Blumstein and Schwartz. "Institutions set up standards and practices that let people fall neatly into niches, giving them roles and rules that help interaction proceed smoothly" (p. 267). People take comfort in knowing what is expected in some domains of their lives.

If marriage is no longer as relevant today as it was for our parents and grandparents, then are we in trouble as a society? To bring some perspective to this question, we can look at long-term demographic trends which show that 90 percent of Americans even-

In American society, there is growing acceptance of later marriages. Indeed, people who marry later in life, perhaps because of their greater maturity, are less likely to divorce than those who marry at a young age.

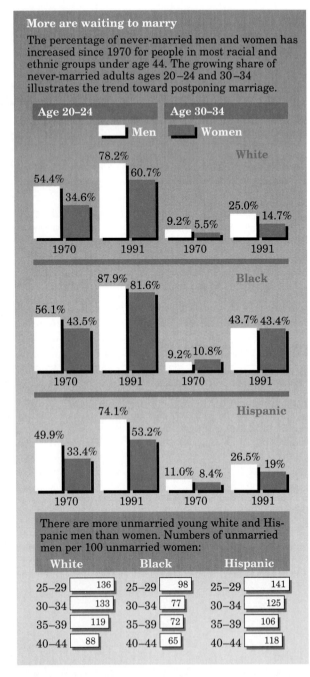

More are waiting to marry

The percentage of never-married men and women has increased since 1970 for people in most racial and ethnic groups under age 44. The growing share of never-married adults ages 20–24 and 30–34 illustrates the trend toward postponing marriage.

There are more unmarried young white and Hispanic men than women. Numbers of unmarried men per 100 unmarried women:

	White		Black		Hispanic
25–29	136	25–29	98	25–29	141
30–34	133	30–34	77	30–34	125
35–39	119	35–39	72	35–39	106
40–44	88	40–44	65	40–44	118

FIGURE 5-3
The Proportion of Never-Married Women and Men Is Increasing

SOURCE: M. L. Usdansky (1992).

children within their current relationships or to bring children with them from past relationships. It would seem, then, that couples, regardless of their lifestyle, continue to value marriage and family.

MARRIAGE AS AN AMERICAN NORM

Pressure to Marry

For those in their twenties, the pressure to marry has eased off considerably, but there are still strong expectations toward marriage. In the 1990s, parents, kin, and friends generally wait until an individual reaches his or her early thirties before intensifying the marriage questions: "When are you going to bring Emanuel home to meet us?" "You stopped seeing Marlee? She seemed so right for you." "You really should meet Randy's friend. I'm sure the two of you would mesh perfectly." "The old biological clock just keeps on ticking, you know." "You say you're 35 and not married, hummmmm."

Clearly, there is more social support now than there was a generation ago for people who choose to remain single. Stereotypes, however, sometimes persist and imply a certain stigma. One public example of the pressure to marry is when the lifestyle of the 50-plus bachelor, David Souter, caused some debate when he was nominated to the U.S. Supreme Court. Although he passed the confirmation hearings with great ease, his ability to be a competent jurist was questioned by some critics who feared that he would not be able to relate to the many family issues that come before the court. Where and how he lived, including information about former dating partners, became public knowledge. Another example is the intensive media attention afforded long-term celebrity singles who wed. It seems we must publicly examine their somewhat reluctant entrance into marriage and family life and record their acknowledgment of how much better married life is than singlehood: Warren Beatty, Bonnie Raitt, and Candice Bergen are examples.

Although the pressure to marry is often blatant, it can be more subtle (see Table 5-1). Regardless of how the notion is gotten across, however, the message behind those pressures is the same: People have a responsibility to get married. In the American culture, marriage has been regarded as an obligation.

TABLE 5-1
Pushes and Pulls Toward Singleness or Marriage

Peter Stein (1981) discusses the complex assortment of pushes and pulls that result in ambivalent feelings as we try to decide in favor of singleness or marriage. Pulls are positive factors in marriage or singlehood that attract us toward that choice. Pushes are pressures or negative things in our lives that also influence our choices.

FROM SINGLEHOOD TOWARD MARRIAGE	
(−) Pushes (Negatives that drive us)	*(+) Pulls (Positives that attract us)*
Need for economic security	Parents' example
Influence of mass media	Desire for family
Pressure from parents	Example of peers
Need to leave home	Romanticization of marriage
Interpersonal and personal reasons	Love and intimacy
Fear of independence	Physical attachment
Loneliness	Emotional attachment
Alternatives not attractive	Security, social status, prestige
Cultural expectations, socialization	
Regular and safe sex	
Guilt over singlehood	

FROM MARRIAGE TOWARD SINGLEHOOD	
(−) Pushes (Negatives that drive us)	*(+) Pulls (Positives that attract us)*
Involvement in suffocating one-to-one relationships	Career opportunities
Feeling trapped	Variety of life experiences
Obstacles to self-development	Self-sufficiency, autonomy
Boredom, unhappiness, anger	Sexual availability
Role playing and conformity to cultural expectations	Exciting lifestyle
Poor communication with partner	Freedom to change and experiment
Sexual frustration	Mobility
Lack of friends, isolation, loneliness	Close, sustaining friendships
Limitations on mobility and available experience	Supportive groups
Influence of mass media	Men's and women's groups
Abusive partner	Group living arrangements
	Specialized services
	Singles-only apartments, vacations, and clubs

SOURCE: Adapted from P. Stein. (1981).

Marriage as a Privilege and Obligation

So thoroughly are we influenced by the values of our marriage-oriented society that it may be surprising to learn that marriage in western culture has not always been a universal norm.

Europe: In Historical Time

In Europe in the Middle Ages only individuals who had earned economic security could hope to marry, and since land and shops were scarce, gaining economic security was difficult. "Marriage was, in brief, a kind of privilege, a prerogative, a gift bestowed by the community," writes sociologist Jessie Bernard. "One had to wait until there was a house or cottage on the commons. A place had to be vacant, land for the luckier ones, or a bakery, a joinery, a loom, or some other productive property" (1973, p. 123). Journeymen and apprentices were not allowed to marry, and the younger sons of the landed aristocracy typically joined the church, which demanded celibacy, or the military.

Medieval society was rich in opportunities for unmarried women. Upper-class unmarried women could join convents. Women dominated several craft guilds, most notably the brewers and spinners. This was, in fact, the origin of the word "spinster," which had no negative connotations until the eighteenth century, when the growing textile industry removed spinning and weaving from the home to the factory, turning unmarried women who remained at home from economic assets into liabilities (Watkins, 1984). More remarkable even than the economic limitations on marriage was the generally low estimate of it in medieval culture. The church regarded celibacy as holier than marriage. It was not until much later that marriage came to be regarded as a model of the good life.

The American Pattern: Couples Only

From colonial times, American marriage patterns have differed from the European model. Economic conditions, far from compelling young people to remain single, encouraged them to marry, for land was limitless and large families were needed to settle the new country. Nor was there any religious tradition of celibacy; the Puritans, in fact, placed an especially high value on marriage and family (Mintz & Kellogg, 1988). In many New England towns, bachelors had to pay extra taxes, on the theory that "sin and iniquity . . . ordinarily are the companions and consequences of the solitary life" (Morgan, 1966, p. 133).

The impetus to marry remained strong even after Puritanism declined. Economic opportunity, social pressure, and the hardships of life on the frontier all contributed to a pattern of early and nearly universal marriage in America. As Jessie Bernard summarizes the American trend through the 1950s:

> Marriage in the twentieth century was no longer dependent on a competence, on property, nor even on maturity. One did not have to wait until one could set up an establishment or manage a large household. Marriage was no longer a class privilege. And the trend in the United States since 1890 has been, until the late 1950s, for marriage at an even earlier age and for a larger proportion of persons. In fact, the most important characteristic of the American pattern has been the freedom to marry which it encompassed. (1973, pp. 112–113)

The more a culture idealizes marriage, and the higher the percentage of people who marry, the greater the pressure on everyone to conform to this model. From the mid-1960s and continuing throughout the 1970s, the percentage of never-married people who remained single increased dramatically, but the "lonely loser" stereotypes of the unmarried woman as a thin, dried-up cranky old lady and of the unmarried man as a fussy eccentric, probably fixated on his mother, remained alive and well—coexisting somehow with a newer image of "swinging singles." The "swinging singles" image was capitalized on by advertisers and the media from the late 1970s through the 1980s. "Swinging singles" were portrayed as young, active, and affluent. According to stereotypes, they lived in "singles only" apartment complexes, hung out at the pool, bar hopped most evenings, and enjoyed sexual pleasures with a variety of others until the early hours of the morning.

At the same time, there was another, very different theme in some of the articles and advertising written for and about singles. Much of the advertising aimed at singles played on a fear of loneliness. The same magazines and advertisements that helped to create the image of "swinging singles" conveyed another message too: the lifestyle of singles is lonely and desperate. The "lonely loser" could best be helped by finding a partner, or so the ads implied.

In the 1990s, however, these stereotypes are beginning to erode as a more realistic picture of who makes up the singles population emerges from current research and writing.

THE SINGLE LIFE TODAY

In the 1990s, to marry or not to marry has become a realistic question in many people's lives. No longer is it a foregone conclusion that marriage, undertaken at a relatively early age, is the only way for most adults to live. *Singles:* The label itself, as in tennis, suggests something more vigorous and perhaps more fun than doubles. But a rather idealized image of what singles do and how they live is not the same as their reality. Living alone in a society where the traditional locus of affection, intimacy, even human wholeness has been marriage poses some difficult problems. Why, then, are more people choosing to remain single?

Reasons for Choosing the Single Life

The motivations to remain single are complex, and often obscure even to those who make this choice. In recent years, two general factors have contributed to the growing appeal of the single life. The first—a historical shift in values—made the single life increasingly desirable. The second—a growing number of practical alternatives, for example, greater opportunities for women—made it increasingly possible.

Shifting Values: Encouraging Singlehood

Since the 1950s, perceptions of marriage have changed several times. These 40-plus years of observing and experiencing marital life in contemporary times has very much influenced deferred marriage.

Reality versus Idealized Images of Marriage. It is difficult to chart value changes with any precision, but popular images of marriage and family life clearly differ from what they were a generation ago. People who do not marry, as well as people who do, are influenced by cultural pressures even if they are not consciously aware of them. The generations that married in the 1950s and 1960s, for example, were probably unaware of the strong external pressures urging them to marry. Couples who married during those decades, if asked why they were getting married, probably would have responded, "Because we love each other," *not* "I have been influenced by idealized images of marriage in books and magazines, on television, and in the movies for as long as I can remember." And yet both factors contributed to their decision.

So a key reason for the choice of the single life in later generations may have been the awareness of young adults of the gap between what was promised and the reality of their parents' marriages. In the 1950s and 1960s, the nuclear family, complete with children and two cars in the garage of a suburban house, was a widely recognized symbol of the "good life." It may have been the idealization of marriage during those years that contributed to its decline afterward. Since "everyone was led to expect a marriage that was a great personal achievement, like the celebrated love affairs of history," some disappointment was almost inevitable (Bird, 1972, p. 35).

Growth and Change versus Culturally Set Roles. A second shift in attitudes about the desirability of marriage among young adults—it began in the 1970s—was the tendency to value growth and change over stability and long-term commitment. Quotations from some of the single people interviewed by sociologist Peter Stein record this shift. For example, a young man explains his divorce: "It's simplistic to think that one person is always going to fill all my needs and that I'm not going to change and she's not going to change." Stein concluded that the most important motivation in the decision to remain single in the 1970s was the belief that marriage was "a restriction and obstacle to human growth" (1975, pp. 10–11).

By the early 1980s, claims Wanda Urbanska, in her book *The Singular Generation* (1986), romance was dead, replaced by "an era of pain, confusion and sometimes outright warfare between the sexes," in which "we came to understand that love and sexual passion are not only fleeting but that they can backfire" (p. 86). Determined to raise the quality of their relationships, younger adults, beginning in the 1970s and continuing into the 1980s, tended to evaluate themselves not by fixed external standards—roles and norms—but by internal criteria—personal needs and goals. Urbanska explains,

> To us, the trappings of romance—the candlelit dinners and the "you are the only one for me" and "I couldn't live without you" routines—struck a false note; they seemed corny and false. . . . We knew that one *could* live without the other, and that he or she probably *would*. (p. 86)

At the same time, more liberal sexual and social standards were gaining acceptance. Improved contraception made sex without marriage less risky and cohabitation more probable.

Great Expectations versus Settling for Something Less. A third change in values that has encouraged the popularity of the single life is that Americans today expect more from marriage and life in general than formerly. In the contemporary view, marriage is expected to provide meaning and satisfaction in life.

Marriage in the 1990s centers on the idea that two independent and autonomous people will come together, and as a couple will promote the mutual growth of *both* partners through the development of an interdependent and intimate relationship, as discussed in detail in Chapter 3. Couples today, then, seem more conscious of the complexities and compromises of marriage. They have lived through the mistakes of the past generation and seem determined to learn from those miscalculations. This generation appears content to delay marriage until it has accomplished some individual goals and then to commit to a more interdependent coupling that meshes the needs and desires of both partners.

Reduced Stigma. As attitudes toward early marriage have changed and the number of singles have increased, their public image is changing as well. The old stereotypes picturing either lonely, rejected misfits or the sexually liberated, fun-loving singles have, in fact, not much to do with how most singles live. These stereotypes have generally given way to a new recognition of singleness as a valid lifestyle. Indeed, recent use of the label "singles" reflects changing perceptions. Many Americans apparently perceive the single life differently today, and fear of singleness is no longer a strong motivation to marry. The millions of young adults who are single have become increasingly visible, especially in large cities, where they tend to be concentrated: New York, Washington, Chicago, and Los Angeles.

Growing Number of Practical Alternatives

Some factors contributing to the increase in singles have less to do with value and attitudinal shifts and more to do with additional opportunities and practical alternatives in support of the single lifestyle.

Women's Changing Economic and Social Needs. Contemporary women, for the most part, do not find early marriage as attractive as being single. As their educational avenues and job opportunities have widened, so has their embrace of singlehood. As Martha Riche (1991), director of policy studies at the Population Reference Bureau, explains: "People who can support themselves . . . have less need to depend on one another" (p. 45). If men no longer need wives to keep their houses, neither do women need husbands to support them economically as they once did. Marriage becomes more of a mutual choice and less of a mutual obligation based on economic and social need.

We as a society are much more accepting of the notion that women can take care of themselves. The new autonomous woman of the 1990s has gained the right to live on her own, unmarried, away from her protective family. Not long ago, women were expected to remain in their parents' homes until they married. The only other accommodations for single women were hotels, boarding houses, or residences for females only. Today, although a surprising number of single people between the ages of 25 and 34 still live with their parents—20 percent of women and 32 percent of men—there are thousands of studio apartments designed for one person in most urban and suburban areas (Gross, 1991). Women also share apartment space with roommates to save money and gain safety.

And, increasing numbers of middle-class single women are buying condominiums and houses.

Anonymity and Sexual Freedom. Singles tend to move to large cities, with the wide range of jobs, services, social contacts, and housing offered there. Cities offer anonymity as well as the freedom to pursue a social life outside of marriage without the pressure of traditional standards and gossiping neighbors. In fact, greater acceptance of sex outside of marriage is another reason for the growing popularity of the single life. When sex outside of marriage was widely frowned upon, many people married to enjoy sexual fulfillment in a socially respectable way. Now, with more permissive sexual standards, young people need not marry to have sexual relationships.

Convenience. With more people choosing to remain single, the single lifestyle has become much more convenient. Even without knowing their exact numbers, the signs of the growing singles subculture are visible everywhere: apartment complexes that discourage or even prohibit occupancy by families with children; vacation packages and resort facilities designed for the unmarried; and organizations, clubs, and church gatherings for "singles only."

Entrepreneurs, ever alert to new trends, have produced a wide range of new products for the singles market. Single servings of everything from frozen entrees to desserts and wine are today almost as easy to find in supermarkets as "family packs." As they advertise their products, businesses sell the single lifestyle as well. Perhaps the most influential of mass media messages are ones that portray idealized images of masculinity and femininity—images that underscore the allure of the single life.

Of course, there are many varieties of singles, and not all have the opportunities and alternatives of the young middle class. It is important to explore some of the more obvious differences in singles by age and social status to get a broader picture of the singles lifestyle.

THE VARIETY OF SINGLES

Between 1960 and 1990, the proportion of households consisting of one person increased from 13 to 24 percent (Wetzel, 1990). Although these households are all the same for census purposes, they include a large variety of lifestyles, individuals of different ages, and people who are living alone for very different reasons. The lives of most of the people in such households do not correspond to the image that usually comes to mind when the word "single" is used—that is, a young, not-yet-married person. For example, 42 percent of all one-person households are maintained by people aged 65 or older (Exter, 1990).

Psychologist Eleanor Macklin (1987) reminds us that most of the information currently available about singles and their lifestyle choices originates from research on young, white, highly educated, middle-class urban professionals or white middle-class retirees (see the "Changing Lifestyles" box). Who are the other singles, and what do we know about them?

Singles in the Black Community

One group that has captured recent interest is black singles. Throughout the first half of the century, black Americans married earlier than whites. The past 40 years or so has seen a reversal of that long-standing trend (Staples, 1981). Today, at every educational level, and especially among women, the percentage of never-married black adults is substantially higher than it is for whites (O'Hare, Pollard, Mann, & Kent, 1991). Why do blacks more often than whites remain unmarried? If we look at the age groups in which most of the mate selection takes place, we see that the mortality rate of black males is substantially higher than it is among whites; black women begin to outnumber black men by age 18. As noted in Chapter 4, black women face an unbalanced sex ratio, and one that creates a relatively restricted field of eligibles (see the "Diversity" box). The most dramatic change in marital patterns during the past generation, however, is in the proportion of relatively uneducated black women who remain unmarried.

The situation is also difficult for well-educated black women. Because college-educated black women considerably outnumber college-educated black men, many are unable to find mates with similar backgrounds. Educated black women expand their pool of eligibles in various ways. Contrary to normative expectations, they marry men who are either younger or substantially older than they are; they choose mates who have previously been married; they choose someone less educated; or they choose someone of another race. In ever-increasing numbers black women have also decided not to marry at all (Surra, 1991; Taylor, Chatters, Tucker, & Lewis, 1991).

Because there are many more college-educated black females than college-educated black males, some of these women expand their pool of eligible mates by marrying men who are younger or much older, less educated, or another race, or have previously been married.

Family life has come to depend less on marital ties and more on the mutual-assistance patterns of the black extended kin network (see Chapter 10 for more details). No one explanation is entirely satisfactory to understanding why so many adult blacks are unmarried, but this distinctive pattern of the black subculture may be a rational and adaptive response to demographic and economic realities.

Older Single Women of the Working Class

Social class also influences differences among singles. Although we tend to view singles primarily from a middle-class perspective—most of the research on singlehood either uses samples of young adults or women

Some Older Singles Live an Affluent Lifestyle

America is an aging society. More and more people in their fifties and sixties have living parents, aunts, and uncles, as life expectancy extends to the late seventies. Advocacy groups many times portray older Americans with a rather negative image—almost everyone existing on low incomes, at risk of chronic health problems and poverty. In contrast, advertisements for automobiles, housing developments, and cruise ships present images of silver-haired seniors who are affluent, energetic, and vital. Similarly, services generally associated with younger singles, such as dating services, are now finding a market of older singles, particularly among women.

Both images are accurate depictions of older persons, representing the poorest 20 percent and wealthiest 20 percent of households, respectively. The affluent are often overlooked by social scientists—but not by those in marketing and sales. While they remain a minority today, many are still actively engaged singles, as this excerpt demonstrates.

He was a perfect gentleman—tall and handsome—and he wanted desperately to take LaRuah Robertson on a cruise to the Caribbean. But the 95-year-old Portland, Oregon, widow would have none of it.

"That man pestered the life out of me to get me to go on that trip," Robertson says. When she refused, "he went on the trip and met some lady who was dying to get a boyfriend, and now he's moved in with her. Nobody's going to move in with me."

Robertson would tell you that the singles scene for seniors isn't always swinging. But in an age of rising travel costs and risks, more single seniors seek companionship when they hit the road.

"I've traveled by myself, and it's not a pleasant experience," says Jens Jurgen, founder of the Travel Companion Exchange in Amityville, New York, which pairs up single travelers. "You want to share your memorable times with somebody you like." Many seniors also feel safer in groups. Jens Jurgen has a dating service-like list of 2,000 people who are seeking fellow travelers. Most of Jurgen's clients are 45 and older, and most are women. "We are always looking for mature men," Jurgen says. "They get snapped up very quickly."

Jurgen represents Melvin, 68, a divorced male who says, "my health exceeds my looks, but there are worse things in this world than not being handsome." He might want to meet Jane, 70, a "witty widow with wanderlust." Jane wants to go to the Orient and Africa, and she will go "ballooning anywhere!" Some weddings have resulted from the travel companion service.

LaRuah Robertson is a rarity—she doesn't mind traveling alone. Since her husband died in 1965, she has crisscrossed the globe by herself. But dinner can be a lonely affair on the road. And "women can do almost everything by themselves on a cruise, but they can't dance," says Mimi Weisband of Royal Cruise Line.

Royal offers mature men a chance to cruise for free as "hosts." Hosts schmooze, play bridge, and dance with women who travel unattached. "They don't have to be Fred Astaire or Cary Grant," says Weisband. But it helps if they can foxtrot. The cruise line requires hosts to bring a tux and a white dinner jacket, and often requires that they spend up to 5 hours. "One guy with a pacemaker had to drop out of the program because it was too grueling," she says. The program is in its tenth year, and Weisband knows of women who book the cruise solely because of the hosts.

Romance is only one reason singles seek each other out on trips. Safety is another major factor. "As a single person, I don't always feel secure enough to go by myself," says Millie Wiener, a 70-something widow from Lake Oswego, Oregon. "If I'm going to China, I want somebody to run interference for me."

Assigned roommates can also save travelers a lot of money. "Everything in the travel industry is double occupancy," Jurgen says. "We do try to match people up with roommates," says spokeswoman Sherry Bounnell. "They save money and have automatic companionship."

EXPLORATIONS *Besides safe accommodations and trustworthy travel companions, what are some other needs of middle-class older singles? How do their needs compare to those of singles at mid-life? To singles in young adulthood? In what ways do the needs of working-class and low-income older singles differ from those of more affluent singles?*

SOURCE: Excerpted from D. Fost (1992).

Singlehood among Black Women: Lifestyle Choice or Mate Availability?

Black women are marrying later and significantly fewer are choosing to marry, compared to white women. Although the trend of black women remaining single is for some a lifestyle choice, closer examination indicates it is due more to sociological and demographic factors.

While social scientists offer differing explanations, most agree that the economic and social problems affecting young black males are a primary factor. According to Joyce Ladner, a sociologist at Howard University, institutional racism—"the combined factors of joblessness, low skill levels, a lack of education, the social problems of substance abuse, alcoholism, imprisonment, all lead to reducing the pool of individuals who would be able to earn a living and support a family" (Vobejda, 1991, p. Fl). The high homicide rate among young black men further reduces the pool of marital partners. Ladner goes on to say that black women clearly and realistically make a great distinction between having a partner versus a husband—someone able to provide for his family. Therese Poku, a single, 29-year-old corporate sales director agrees: "For a small percentage of women, it's a matter of choice not to marry. For a large percentage, it's a matter of availability" (Vobejda, 1991, p. Fl).

In a study comparing poor and middle-class teenage mothers, black adolescents had the same expectations as whites—that a husband and father should be able to provide emotional and financial support to his family. Most black teens were unwilling to compromise their ideals and marry someone who did not fit these expectations. Black adolescents described the fathers of their children variously as being immature, unemployed, and uninvolved in parenting responsibilities (Farber, 1990).

Various solutions are suggested in response to the trends of increasing singlehood and single parenting among black women. One is to increase the educational and employment opportunities for black men to encourage their willingness to be economically and emotionally supportive marital partners and fathers. Another is to improve the educational and employment opportunities for black women; so, if they choose to remain single, they can better provide for themselves—and their children.

EXPLORATIONS *Which of these proposed solutions do you favor? Why? Can you think of other alternatives? What is one alternative?*

SOURCES: N. Farber (1990); and B. Vobejda (1991).

---

from middle-class backgrounds—one recent study by family scientist Katherine Allen is an exception. For her research, Allen initially interviewed 104 working-class single women in their seventies. Of those, 30 were selected for additional in-depth interviews, 15 had never married, and 15 had been married but were later widowed. In her book *Single Women/Family Ties* (1989), Allen notes that never-married women in the working class tend to follow traditional familistic norms and live at home, caring for widowed aging parents. Working-class families across history have had fewer resources and thus less economic independence, compared to their middle-class counterparts. A sense of family obligation and survival of the family unit, rather than thoughts of individual needs, is the rea-

soning behind the willingness of such women to remain single.

For the most part, despite giving much of their lives to parental caregiving, the women seemed unaware of the significance of what they had accomplished. The caring work provided and the personal sacrifices made seemed invisible to both women and their kin, and consequently was underappreciated. Allen writes:

They kept people alive, they provided relief from day-to-day responsibilities of married siblings. . . . Yet, the stereotype of the old maid persisted. . . . In their recollections, they described realistically the complex emotions associated with caring for families: the missed opportunities, the bitterness and disappointment, the heartbreak of separation and loss, and the rewards associated with intimate attachments over their life course. (pp. 132–133)

Working-class lives are parallel but uniquely different in some ways from middle-class lives. Even today, in working-class families, economic security depends to a large degree on a strong kin network and attention to family rather than individual needs. Personal fulfillment and professional achievement are more characteristic of the middle-class than the working-class life course.

Single Men 40 and Over

Another group of singles that is typically neglected by researchers is the approximately 2.5 million never-married American men over 40—10.5 percent of men aged 40 to 44 have not married, compared with 7.1 percent in 1980. By the time a man reaches 40, there is only a 12 percent possibility he will marry; at 45, the likelihood is 1 in 20. This trend is even more pronounced for never-married black men, who by age 40 are about twice as likely as white men to remain single.

Contrary to the stereotypes of older single men as unsatisfied, rejected, "bottom of the barrel" males who lack self-esteem and well-being, a recent study by psychologist Charles Waehler finds that many neither need nor want marriage ("40-and-older," 1991). Half of the men surveyed liked their single status and reported being successful, happy, and content with life. The other half were regretful of being single at age 40, but said they were too set in their ways to try marriage now. Most were successful professional men who lived alone. The majority owned homes and described themselves as pro-female and pro-marriage. In fact, 90 percent had considered marriage at some point before they reached age 40 and over 60 percent insisted that they were likely to get married "sooner or later" ("40-and-older," 1991).

Waehler concludes that for most men over age 40, singlehood has become a lifestyle. The "sooner or later" response, he views as a type of defense mechanism that keeps critical others at bay while reducing any personal anxieties about singlehood the men may have. Marriage at this stage of life really runs counter to already established life routines, as well as individualism and self-reliance. Most men over 40, he contends, "need a relationship but they don't need marriage" (p. E8).

Single Women at Mid-life

Single women at mid-life are also largely ignored by social researchers. The few available studies focusing on single women at this age suggest that they are more anxious, depressed, and less satisfied with their lives than are married women. One major investigation, however, questions this assumption. Social scientists Grace Baruch, Rosalind Barnett, and Caryl Rivers surveyed 300 mid-life women between the ages of 35 and 55. Their study, *Lifeprints: New Patterns of Love and Work for Today's Women* (1983), sheds light on the pleasures and sources of self-esteem of single women.

Single women, the researchers found, must work harder than married women to seek out sources of connection and intimacy in their lives. Despite this disadvantage, they do not view themselves as "failures," somehow inferior to other women. They see themselves as "competent and valued human beings" (p. 212). Single women who fared best in this study were those with jobs. "A single woman in a high-prestige job has a good chance of achieving high well-being," conclude the authors (p. 213). In fact, having an unsatisfactory job is more depressing to a never-married woman than being single.

The majority of women accepted their singlehood as positive, had satisfactory jobs, and, consequently, reported high well-being. Only those women who defined their singlehood as rejection—not being chosen—suffered in terms of well-being. Such women felt stigmatized by their singlehood. Feelings of dissatisfaction seemed to subside with age. By mid-life, one woman said:

> I don't know whether it's my age, or society changing. I was definitely out of step in my twenties. Then, everybody was getting married and having children. But nowadays, nobody thinks about whether you're unmarried. Nobody thinks everybody has to be a couple anymore. So it's easier now. (1983, p. 230)

Baruch, Barnett, and Rivers draw a composite picture of today's employed single woman in middle adulthood: someone who is active, involved in her work, and who maintains close ties with extended family members. Such a woman has close friends, and may be involved in a romantic intimate relationship. She may feel a certain degree of deprivation, but it neither destroys her self-esteem or her satisfaction with life.

Clearly, there are many varieties of single people, and most report more social support now than in the

Until her recent marriage, Senator Carol Mosley Braun was an example of a single black woman who had achieved the kind of high status that makes finding a black male mate of the same level of accomplishment difficult.

past as they choose to defer marriage or permanently remain single. It is too early to predict with confidence how many people in the 1990s will never marry, but we do know that many will choose to live together first. In fact, the current increase in unmarried young adults should probably not be interpreted as an increase in the singlehood lifestyle because many are cohabiting at almost as early an age as they did before marriage rates declined (Bumpass & Sweet, 1991).

COHABITING LIFESTYLES

Cohabitation—living together—has become increasingly acceptable as well as a more widespread practice over the past decade, and represents the most significant modification of the courtship process since the invention of dating. But one important question remains about its implications: Is the experience of living together an occasion for compatibility testing—or is it a permanent alternative to marriage?

In the 1970s, when cohabitation began to attract attention, some observers were very much concerned about it. They extrapolated from the growth curve of the previous decade and concluded that if it continued, cohabitation might replace marriage entirely. But subsequent evidence suggests otherwise. There has certainly been an increase in the number of older cohabitors, many of whom no doubt consider living together a long-term alternative to marriage. If, however, we look mainly at the living-together phenomenon among young people, and particularly at its significance among college students, cohabitation is not regarded as the equivalent of marriage, nor as a lifelong marriage alternative.

Singles today more often cohabitate as a way of satisfying their desire for a more emotionally intimate lifestyle than dating provides. Parents, concerned about their adult children's welfare, often ask what cohabitation implies. Does it mean going *very* steady, or is it a type of trial marriage, or is it simply a convenient living arrangement with no strings attached? Cohabitation has a variety of meanings. If it is precisely that flexibility which makes cohabitation attractive, the possibility that it may mean different things to the people who are living together also creates new problems.

In fact, cohabiting college couples typically cannot recall any specific decision to live together. Compared to the carefully calibrated stage-by-stage development of relationships of past generations, cohabitation usually begins quite casually. One of the most common reasons that college students mention for living together is that they like it better than dating. Compared to those who date, cohabitors report more intimacy and self-disclosure in their relationships (Risman, Hill, Rubin, & Peplau, 1981).

How Many Cohabitors?

It is difficult to get an accurate count of the number of cohabitors for several reasons. First, the term itself is vague. If, for example, two people maintain separate residences but spend most of their time together, are they cohabiting? Perhaps the most useful definitions are those, such as the one proposed by Macklin (1987), which specify a minimum amount of time that two people must spend together in order to qualify as cohabitors, thus distinguishing them from people who sometimes stay together. Macklin counts as cohabitors those who go to bed together for at least four nights each week for at least three consecutive months. She also thinks that "the degree of emotional involvement and commitment to the relationship" is important in sorting cohabitors from noncohabitors (p. 321).

Types of Cohabitors

There are at least five types of cohabiting relationships according to Macklin:

Temporary casual—sharing living space because it is convenient and cost-effective; no romantic attachment.

Affectionate "going steady"—living together because it is satisfying to both, but long-term commitment is not expected.

Trial marriage—living together is a test of compatibility for marriage.

Temporary marital alternative—looking for the "right time" to marry; commitment is established.

Permanent alternative to marriage—living together is a long-term commitment and the couple are devoted to one another, but marriage is not in the picture.

Because various researchers use these different definitions of cohabitation, estimates of the number of cohabitors vary widely. A second problem in assessing the extent of this trend is that the Census Bureau's estimate of the number of unmarried men and women living together in a single household undoubtedly underestimates the actual number of cohabitors. Many people simply will not reveal their lifestyle on a government form.

At any one time, approximately 5 percent of all unmarried couples are cohabiting, about one-third of whom have children (Sorrentino, 1990). The best estimates of the incidence of cohabitation among undergraduates in the United States suggests that the number of cohabitors has increased three times since 1970. Although we tend to think that the largest group of cohabitors are in college communities, living together is actually more common among the less educated—40 percent of whom have children (Bumpass & Sweet, 1991). Unmarried college graduates are 64 percent less likely to cohabit than are high school dropouts (Landers, 1990). Cohabitation is also more prevalent among previously married persons and black Americans (Riche,1991). Further, people over the age of 65 comprise 5 percent of cohabitants (U.S. Bureau of the Census, 1988). And, while most cohabitors over age 25 expect to marry their partners, there is substantial disagreement (between partners) about the quality and satisfaction of the relationship (Bumpass & Sweet, 1991).

Two studies found that over half the couples sampled had cohabited before marriage (Bumpass & Sweet, 1989; Gwartney-Gibbs, 1986). Another indicated that almost 50 percent of the 30-year-olds surveyed said they had cohabited at some time in their lives (Landers, 1990). Surprisingly, there do not appear to be marked regional differences in cohabiting. However, cohabitation is more common and more accepted in European countries (Macklin, 1987).

The United States and Other Countries: A Comparison

One way of putting the living-together phenomenon in perspective is to compare what has happened in this country with recent patterns in Europe, where there also has been a sharp increase in cohabitation since the 1970s. It is particularly revealing to look at the contrasting experiences of Sweden and France and to ask which more closely resembles what is happening in this country.

In Sweden today, virtually all couples live together before marriage. Judging by the sharp drop in the Swedish marriage rate, it appears that for a substantial number of couples, living together now means forgoing marriage. And, almost 50 percent of all births are to unmarried mothers. Social scientist Constance Sorrentino (1990) writes,

> Nonmarital cohabitation is regarded legally and culturally as an accepted alternative, rather than a prelude to marriage. This is reflected by the fact that the average period over which Swedish couples remain unmarried lengthens each year, with a growing number never marrying at all. (p. 48)

France offers a contrasting pattern. There, cohabitation is a common, but far from universal, practice— 8 percent of the population cohabits. In contrast to Sweden, fewer French couples who are living together have children—1 in 5 children are born to unmarried mothers.

Which country provides the better guide to interpreting cohabitation patterns in the United States? One good reason to conclude that our pattern will not soon resemble the Swedish experience is that in the Scandinavian countries it is traditional for couples to live together before marriage, particularly among rural Swedes, since marriage is regarded as a private matter. In America, the idea that marriage should begin with a public ceremony, and one that invokes the authority of the church as well as the state, has had widespread support. In several respects, the American experience with cohabitation more closely resembles the French pattern, with cohabitation a temporary stage in the courtship process that is widely tolerated if not yet completely accepted. And, it is not yet acceptable in France or in the United States, as it is in Sweden, for cohabiting couples to have children.

Some Consequences of Cohabitation

Cohabitors identify many benefits of their lifestyle including increased communication and emotional and sexual intimacy, reduced financial burdens, greater safety, and heightened opportunities for compatibility testing. Living-together couples also encounter problems, some of which are common to those in any intimate partnership, including marriage.

Emotional Involvement

As Macklin (1987) sees it, the primary emotional issues for cohabitors include a tendency to grow overinvolved and feel a subsequent loss of identity. Additionally, cohabitors report a lack of opportunity to participate in activities with friends and family members or to socialize without their partners, and an overdependency on each other. "As in marriage, achieving security without giving up the freedom to be oneself, and growing together while leaving enough space so that both individuals may also grow, may well be central to success in the relationship" (Macklin, 1974, p. 30).

Parental Approval

Getting a parental endorsement can also prove difficult. Although living together is at least tolerated in many campus communities, where neither college administrators nor landlords are interested in preventing it, one of the most common problems is differences in attitudes between students and parents. Many couples try to hide their live-in relationship from parents because of anticipated disapproval. Parents sometimes cause rifts between the cohabiting couple because of their strong feelings and disruptive actions. Even in the 1990s, many parents still object to their children, especially their daughters, living with a person without being married. They fear that the cohabiting partner will somehow take advantage of their child. Perhaps parental anxiety is inevitable in a society where young people have the freedom to choose their own marital partners and parents can only stand by, hoping their children will make the right choice.

Level of Commitment

Ease of relationship dissolution is an additional concern. Cohabiting relationships can be terminated more easily than marriages. They may provide a fairly realistic testing ground for compatibility without the expectation of lasting "till death do us part." Even engagement is a less reversible step toward marriage than cohabitation. In general, cohabiting couples are less committed to the idea of marriage. Young singles, in particular, behave more like singles who happen to live together than partners in "trial marriage." For example, many cohabitors do not pool their financial resources or make major purchases together (Blumstein & Schwartz, 1983). Restrictions of this kind may serve, in part, to limit commitment and make it easier to move apart. In the long run, living together may provide a better means of testing compatibility than dating, but this does not mean that those who cohabit are necessarily more satisfied, or more likely to stay together once they marry.

Although cohabitation may have a variety of meanings, depending on the couple involved, the one essential element is that two unmarried people share the same household.

Cohabitation and the Likelihood of Divorce

In one study, sociologists Larry Bumpass and James Sweet (1989) found that after 10 years of marriage, of those who divorced or separated, 36 percent had lived together before marriage and 27 percent had not. Couples who had cohabited before marriage espoused less traditional family attitudes and were uncertain about the quality of their relationships. Two other investigations substantiate these findings. Thomson and Colella (1992) and DeMaris and Rao (1992) conclude that couples who cohabit before marriage are less committed to the institution of marriage, hold more individualistic views of marriage, and are more likely to divorce than noncohabiting couples.

Other researchers, however, have noted no connection between cohabitation and divorce. For example, when two researchers conducted a follow-up study 4 years after they first interviewed more than 100 couples who applied for marriage licenses in Los Angeles County, they found that cohabitors were no more likely to have divorced than noncohabitors. Both groups were equally satisfied with their marriages (DeMaris & Leslie, 1984; Newcomb & Bentler, 1981).

More recently, after studying the responses of over 8,000 women and men, sociologists Jay Teachman and Karen Polonko concluded that "once allowance is made for the total time spent in a union, there is no difference in the rate of marital disruption by cohabitation status" (1990, p. 217).

A certain caution is appropriate in interpreting the results of any study that compares cohabitors and noncohabitors, for they tend to be somewhat different types of people. Cohabitors have more liberal attitudes about family life, tend to have had more diverse sexual experiences, and regard themselves as more competent and self-reliant than do noncohabitors. Cohabiting couples divide household work on a fairly equal basis, except for child care, which is less likely to be equitably shared—women do more of it (Waldrop & Exter, 1991). Each of these characteristics has some bearing on the likelihood of divorce.

What appears to have happened since 1970 is that rather than replacing marriage, cohabitation has become institutionalized as part of the premarital and remarriage sequence. Most cohabiting couples either marry or separate within a few years. The picture that emerges is that cohabitation is increasingly regarded, except by young adults, as a quasi-family status in which commitment to the partner and quality of the relationship are valued, but less so than in marriage.

GAY AND LESBIAN LIFESTYLES

Many *gay and lesbian relationships*—male and female same-sex couplings—include cohabitation because marriage, as indicated, is not a legally available alternative. Some couples draw up legal contracts and others even arrange social or spiritually guided ceremonies to publicly announce their commitment to one another. Laws are on the books in a handful of cities to recognize *domestic partnerships*—cohabiting couples, who either live together out of a desire to remain single or because they have no other legal alternative—for the purpose of extending to them certain economic and social rights (see the "Dilemmas and Decisions" box for additional information).

Gay and Lesbian Relationships

Research over the past 25 years supports the view that most people, regardless of sexual orientation, want a secure and intimate love relationship. When questioned about the relative importance of nine relationship goals, for example, lesbians, gays, and heterosexuals all rank affection, personal development, and companionship as most important (Ramsey, Latham, & Lindquist, 1978). Moreover, each of the three groups rate honesty, affection, and intelligence as the most sought-after qualities in a romantic partner. Money and physical attractiveness rank much lower (Laner, 1977). When Kurdek and Schmitt (1986) sampled heterosexuals, gays, and lesbians, they found that all scored similarly on how satisfying their relationships were and on feelings of love for their partners. "Revealing intimate feelings, spending time together, holding similar attitudes, having an equal-power relationship, and having sexual exclusivity" are important qualities that most individuals desire in a romantic relationship (Peplau & Gordon, 1991, p. 482).

Clearly, there are few differences among lesbian, gay, and heterosexual couples on indicators of love and affection, relationship satisfaction, and in the qualities each partner looks for in a romantic partner. There are differences, however, in how perceptions of power

Many gay men and women use friendship as the model for an intimate relationship. Thus they look for a partner who is about the same age and is willing to share power and responsibilities equally.

influence the relationship and in the role behavior of couples. Like heterosexual couples, most lesbian and gay couples are in dual-earner relationships. Having an equal say in how the relationship progresses and in the give-and-take of making daily decisions that affect the relationship is valued by the majority. But, this is more of an ideal than a reflection of reality for most. When asked how power is actually distributed in their relationships, 38 percent of gay men, 40 percent of heterosexual men, 48 percent of heterosexual women, and 59 percent of lesbians say their relationships are about equal in power (Peplau & Cochran, 1980). In the three relationship types that include men, the partner who earns more money generally has greater power (Blumstein & Schwartz, 1983).

Among gay couples, in particular, income, education, and age have considerable influence on which partner will have more power (Peplau & Gordon, 1991). It is a major issue in gay relationships when one partner has considerably more resources and is thus the more powerful. If things are too lopsided, the partner with greater power generally has difficulty respecting the other partner, who may be viewed as less ambitious, less competitive, and less willing to make a commitment to the workplace—traits men have traditionally expected of each other. The less powerful partner is more likely to leave the relationship out of frustration because he feels undervalued and not appreciated (Blumstein & Schwartz, 1989).

DILEMMAS AND DECISIONS

Living Together: What Are the Legal and Financial Issues?

When two singles decide to cohabit, they initially focus on their changing relationship and learning to live together. What they are not likely to consider are the legal and financial aspects of cohabiting. Although society has become much more accepting of cohabitation, the legal system has barely begun to contemplate the ramifications of nonrelated persons combining the management of their finances. Lawyers who counsel cohabiting couples indicate they have no legal protections if they separate or one dies. To protect the rights of each individual—should the relationship fail, a health emergency arise, or in case of the death of one partner—precise plans and decisions should be made.

Two lawyers, Ralph Warner and Toni Ihara, with over two decades of experience in living together, suggest writing a living-together agreement (LTA). In their book *The Living Together Kit* (1990), they describe the agreement as a means of clarifying financial and property rights. They suggest spelling out the contribution—household services and/or money—which each partner brings to the relationship. Partners may agree to split expenses 50-50, regardless of the proportion of income earned, or divide them according to the actual proportion they contribute.

The LTA also details how or whether the couple will share ownership of major purchases such as a home, cars, and household goods. If they choose to be joint tenants with the rights of survivorship, as most married couples are, the survivor owns the items upon the death of the other. If, instead, they choose to be tenants in common, each owns only their own predecided portion of each item. If they own a home, for example, one may sell his or her portion or leave it to a family member at death. The LTA also spells out how assets would be divided if the couple separate and whether one partner would retain responsibility for the financial support of the other. It is important to update the agreement as necessary. The absence of such an agreement could result in a long and expensive court battle to prove who owned what property.

Cars may be owned together, but partners must search for an insurance company that agrees to sell one policy to two unrelated people. However, it may be easier if cars are owned separately and each has his or her own separate policy. In fact, it may be wiser to avoid joint ownership of most other purchases, such as furniture, electronics, appliances, and personal items, if the partners are not willing to enter into a formal LTA.

It is in the areas of income taxes and employee benefit programs that cohabitors are particularly penalized. Only married couples may file joint tax returns—cohabitors may not claim the higher standard deduction or the personal exemption for the partner that is allowed for marrieds. In addition, the income of single persons is taxed at higher rates.

Cohabitants are not entitled to their partner's health insurance, retirement, or Social Security benefits. Only a few cities and corporate employers have instituted programs to provide limited benefits, particularly health insurance, to the partners of unmarried employees. Unemployed partners and even many who are employed, do not have access to health insurance. Also, only a few health insurance companies will issue individual policies to cover unmarried partners. Life insurance can be a problem too, as employers are reluctant to pay life insurance benefits to unmarried partners of deceased employees. Life insurance companies generally refuse to sell individual policies on the life of a nonrelated person. In that case, each partner could buy a policy on herself or himself and make the partner the beneficiary.

The LTA does not take the place of estate planning for cohabitors. A will provides for the distribution of property upon one's death and has precedence over any other written or oral agreements in providing for the distribution of property to the partner. Thus, a will is more difficult to challenge in court by family members of the deceased.

EXPLORATIONS *Do you think that passing a national law to legalize "domestic partnerships" for cohabiting couples, as a legal counterpart to marriage, would be appropriate? Explain.*

SOURCES: C. V. Clarke (1989); J. Larson & B. Edmondson (1991); and R. R. Roha (1990).

Lesbians, in contrast, tend to work hard to avoid the effects of income on power in their relationships. It is important to them that money not be the deciding factor in making one woman dependent on the other (Blumstein & Schwartz, 1983). When power is more equal in a lesbian relationship, women report that they are more satisfied, have fewer problems, and remain together longer (Caldwell & Peplau, 1984). Among lesbian couples there is a strong desire to be independent—to be able to take care of oneself. Blumstein and Schwartz (1989) point out that lesbians are often caught in a double bind: wanting, on the one hand, an emotionally intense home life, but, on the other, a strong, independent, and ambitious partner. They want to give a lot, but only if their partner gives equally. They demand a great deal, but no more than they can reciprocate. They do not want to be the provider, nor do they desire to be the one provided for.

In contrast to heterosexual couples, partners in gay and lesbian relationships do not typically adopt husband-wife roles. According to psychologists Letitia Peplau and Susan Cochran (1990), they specialize in certain tasks, but rarely does one partner perform most of the "feminine" chores while the other performs most of the "masculine" activities. Friendship is the model for a majority of gay and lesbian relationships—with expectations that partners be similar in age, equal in power, and fair in the division of life responsibilities. Rather than follow predetermined cultural expectations of how roles should be enacted in their relationships, gay and lesbian couples are more likely to base their patterns of behavior on the unique individual characteristics of the partners (Peplau & Cochran, 1990) (see the "Snapshots" box).

Differences Between Gay and Lesbian Couples

Despite the experience of sharing a similar lifestyle, gay and lesbian relationships are not alike. There are some interesting distinctions.

Numbers and Ideologies

Historically, researchers have documented fewer lesbian than gay relationships. One reason is that what women do in a society, compared to what men do, has until recently been of less interest to those who observe and study human behavior. Moreover, women, because they have consistently had to rely on men for economic support, have been unable to afford to live together as same-sex couples unless they had careers or had inherited money. Therefore, it has taken longer for women to recognize and develop their own identities as lesbians and to form distinct lesbian subcultures. It is also true that love and affection between women has traditionally received societal approval, so such behavior among lesbians has, for the most part, escaped the stigma of being labeled homosexual.

The series of events that most recently served to advance the lesbian lifestyle occurred as part of the women's movement. While leaders of the movement have taken care to separate feminism from lesbianism, the women's movement undeniably allowed *all* women to gain greater educational, economic, and legal advantages in American society. In so doing, it simultaneously facilitated the more rapid emergence of communities of lesbian women.

Although many women are motivated to self-identify as lesbians because of their sexual orientation, a significant minority say that their choice of a relational partner is based on an ideology of support and empowerment of women. Such women are often referred to as "political lesbians" because they "engage in lesbian relationships out of feminist solidarity" (Buunk & van Driel, 1989, p. 80). Philip Blumstein and Pepper Schwartz write:

> Women are less likely than men to view their sexual acts as a revelation of their "true sexual self," and female sexual choice seems to be based as much on situational constraints as on categorical desire. Desire seems to be aroused frequently by emotional intimacy rather than by absolute erotic taste. (1990, p. 310)

Gay men have no similar ideology. Compared to lesbians, gay males self-identify at a younger age and *come out*—reveal publicly one's gayness—for more personal and less situationally and socially motivated reasons. Once *out*, however, many gay men are publicly active in the movement to reduce discrimination and intolerance toward homosexuality in American society.

Sexual Frequency, Monogamy, and Stability

Overall, as is typical among all types of couples, sexual frequency among gay and lesbian couples decreases with length of time in the relationship. There is, however, a definite gender difference in how often same-sex couples have intercourse, with males reporting greater frequency. The primary reason, most ex-

SNAPSHOTS

Gay and Lesbian Relationships

"My involvement with other men is always like we are buddies, or at least that's what I strive for. . . . I very much want to have a man-to-man relationship with my friend and I value this element of masculinity. . . . I believe masculinity can be realized as readily through another man as it can through a woman." —A GAY MAN.

"In a heterosexual relationship, you are playing a role . . . in a gay relationship, you don't have that. You have two people on an equal level living together, sharing responsibilities. In a heterosexual relationship you are not going to get it 50-50 (division of labor). You'd be lucky if you get it 60-40, so there is a certain amount of role playing that you are going to have in a heterosexual relationship that you don't have in a gay relationship." —A LESBIAN.

"I see differences and I see similarities between gay and straight couples. A big difference is that gays are less frequently obliged 'to stay together.' Ed and I don't have the kids, the high cost of divorce, the in-laws, and the financial entanglements to keep us together. We also don't have all the support systems that straights enjoy." —A GAY MAN.

"Marje and I are no different from any straight couple. We've got a lot of problems to work out. And the problems aren't any different from the problems straights have: financial, sexual, in-laws. . . . However, what's different is that we don't have a lot of the structures straights have to help them solve their problems. We have to do it on our own, and so it's harder for a gay couple to stay together and make their relationship work." —A LESBIAN.

These descriptions of gay and lesbian relationships (Peplau & Gordon, 1991), indicate both similarities with and differences from heterosexual marital relationships. Peplau and Gordon note that like lesbians and heterosexuals, gay men prefer enduring relationships, which is quite contrary to stereotyped portrayals. Lesbian and gay couples also appear to be as "well adjusted" as heterosexual couples.

A common concern is that lesbian, and particularly gay relationships, don't last as long as heterosexual ones. Although the U.S. Bureau of the Census has accurate records on heterosexual relationships, there is no comparable information available on lesbian and gay

relationships. But the length of any relationship is rather subjective. Even among heterosexuals, 3 months may be a long-term relationship for adolescents, just as 2 years might be a relatively long-time for 25-year-olds to be together, or 25 years for 50-year-olds.

EXPLORATIONS *What are the "structures" and "support systems" available to heterosexual couples that are not available to encourage gay and lesbian couples to stay together? What could take their place?*

SOURCE: Quotes excerpted from L. A. Peplau & S. L. Gordon (1991).

perts agree, is that men in American society are socialized to desire and initiate sex. Their sexuality, compared to women's, is less constrained by the risks of reputational damage or pregnancy. So, regardless of the type of relationship men are in, heterosexual or gay, they expect more, negotiate for more, and consequently experience more frequent sex.

Lesbians, in contrast, have been socialized to be

more receptive than aggressive in sex, explain sociologists Blumstein and Schwartz (1990). Thus, both partners share a reluctance to seize the sexual initiative, which may result in less frequent sex. Another factor that contributes to the lower frequency of sex among lesbians is that some women strongly believe that sexual intercourse is much less important than other aspects of their relationship. They equate sexual assertiveness with male-dominated relationships where one partner typically has greater power over the other. To avoid power and dominance issues in their relationships, "higher standards of relationship satisfaction are demanded in order to legitimate sexual intimacy" (p. 316).

Gay couples are also less monogamous than lesbian couples. Mutual sexual exclusivity is rare in long-term gay relationships, because of the traditional subculture focus on sexual experimentation and release (Buunk & van Driel, 1989). Until AIDS became a prominent issue in the gay community, sexual norms facilitated casual sex. Gay men have traditionally separated sexual desire from intimacy and love, evolving instead a norm of having relationships that permit occasional or a lot of sex outside their primary love relationship (Blumstein & Schwartz, 1990). Compared to lesbians, 71 percent of whom believed in monogamy, only 35 percent of gay men thought monogamy was important in a 1983 study conducted by Blumstein and Schwartz. After AIDS, monogamy increased in importance and relationship commitment has been more strongly encouraged in the gay community.

But exclusivity is still an issue among gay couples. In fact, long-term partners must find ways of dealing with this issue in order to remain committed to their relationship. Blasband and Peplau (1985) suggest that gay couples considering a long-term commitment discuss their personal beliefs about monogamy, needs for sexual variety, feelings about autonomy and intimacy, and jealousy. What is most critical is that the partners agree about these issues (Peplau & Cochran, 1990).

When Blumstein and Schwartz (1983) studied large groups of gay and lesbian couples for their book *American Couples*, they followed some of the sample for 18 months and found that couples who had been together for 10 years or more rarely broke up. But, among couples who had lived together for less than 10 years, 16 percent of gay and 20 percent of lesbian couples ended their relationships. This research runs counter to most other studies, however, which indicate that lesbians are less likely than gay couples to break up (Peplau & Cochran, 1990).

Lesbians and gays are generally engaged in relationships that last an average of about 3 years (Harry, 1983). Whereas three-quarters of the lesbians in the classic study by Bell and Weinberg (1978) lived in stable relationships, only half of the gays did. One explanation is that little institutional encouragement existed, until recently, for stable partnerships in the gay culture. There are fewer incentives for staying together and fewer barriers to breaking up. In marital relationships, the presence of children, jointly held property and other financial investments, one partner's greater financial dependence on the other, and the monetary costs of a divorce act in concert to keep the relationship intact (see Chapter 8 for information on gay and lesbian parents).

The images of singles and cohabitors in our society say less about the way people actually live than about the ambivalence toward these interpersonal lifestyles in a marriage-oriented society. One way of moving beyond these stereotypes is to view singles and cohabitors, regardless of sexual orientation, as people who seek to meet basic human needs for companionship, enjoy satisfying sexual lives, and experience stable intimate relationships outside the framework of marriage. We should not assume, however, that these interpersonal lifestyles are a replacement for marriage or that marriage is no longer relevant in American society. The evidence presented does not support those conjectures.

SUMMARY POINTS

■ Young people today are postponing marriage, but like past generations, over 90 percent will eventually marry.

■ The number of black adults who remain single within any age group is about twice that of white adults.

■ Individuals who marry later generally have fewer children because they begin their families later in the life cycle.

■ The pressure to marry has lessened over the past two decades. Parents, friends, and significant others now wait until young adults are in their early thirties before getting concerned about wedding plans.

■ Even today, however, singles suffer a certain amount of stereotyping and stigma. Our culture still looks upon marriage as a rite of passage into a mature and responsible life.

■ Marriage has not always been a norm in western culture. In medieval times marriage was considered a privilege that had to be earned by demonstrating that one was a productive community member with land and earnings enough to support a family.

■ The "swinging singles" and "lonely loser" stereotypes are fading as the portrayal of singles becomes more realistic and less punitive.

■ Two factors have contributed to the growing appeal of the single life: a historical shift in values and a growing number of practical alternatives. Shifts in the following value systems have been noted: reality has replaced some idealized images of marriage, growth and change are preferred over culturally set roles and responsibilities, and great expectations have gained ground over settling for something less. Practical alternatives are enhanced by changes in women's lives, increasing anonymity, greater convenience, and reduced stigma.

■ Young adults do not make up the majority of singles—42 percent are age 65 and older. Nevertheless, most of what we know about the singles population comes from studies that focus on young, white, middle-class professionals.

■ There has been a substantial increase over the past generation in the number of college-educated black women who remain single. The same trend has also been noted among less well-educated black women. As a result, family life in the black community has become less dependent on marital ties and more dependent on kin and community support networks.

■ Single middle-aged women fare best if they look at their singleness as a lifestyle choice, have satisfactory jobs, feel independent and in control of their lives, and are involved with family and friends in mutually supportive relationships.

■ Women of the working class more often than middle-class women remain single out of a sense of family obligation. Much of the lives of working-class women is spent caring for parents. Such work, though greatly beneficial to families, is typically invisible, unpaid, and undervalued.

■ Eleanor Macklin describes five types of cohabitors: temporary casual, affectionate "going steady," trial marriage, temporary alternative to marriage, and permanent alternative to marriage.

■ Cohabitation is more prevalent among people with less than a high school education and among the previously married than among college students.

■ In Sweden over 95 percent of couples cohabit prior to marriage, while in the United States about 30 percent cohabit at some time in their lives.

■ The rewards of cohabiting are an increased sense of intimacy and emotional support; costs include becoming too emotionally involved, having parents disapprove of your lifestyle, and being in an intimate relationship that is easily terminated.

■ Although cohabitation may partly account for the recent upturn in people postponing marriage, it is not an alternative that is intended to replace marriage entirely.

■ Gay and lesbian couples, like heterosexual couples, value secure and intimate love relationships that include affection, honesty, and companionship.

■ Though lesbian, gay, and heterosexual couples are similar in many ways, they differ in how power is handled in their relationships and in how they perceive and enact their roles as intimate partners.

■ Most women who identify as lesbians do so because of their sexual orientation, but a minority of "political lesbians" base their self-identification on a personal ideology of support and empowerment of women.

■ Gay couples engage in more frequent sex, are less monogamous, and have less stable relationships than lesbian couples. These gender differences are consistent with variations in the ways women and men are socialized.

KEY TERMS

Singles	*Domestic partnerships*
Cohabitation	*Come out*
Gay and lesbian relationships	

REVIEW QUESTIONS

1. Is the single life a threat to marriage?

2. How would you describe the "institution of marriage"?

3. Locate a single person between the ages of 26 and 28, another between 35 and 40, and still another between 45 and 50. Ask each of them if they:

    a. have considered remaining single (never marrying)

    b. have experienced any direct or subtle pressure from parents, relatives, or friends to marry

    c. have ever had people make remarks stereotyping them as strange or unusual because of their singleness

Compare your findings with your classmates' results. Do you notice any differences among interviewee responses by gender, age, or social status? Explain any differences you observe.

4. If you were to develop a profile of cohabitors, what characteristics would you include?

5. What are the differences among patterns of cohabitation in the United States, Sweden, and France?

6. If you were asked by your instructor to write a one-paragraph description of gay and lesbian relationships, based on what you have read in this chapter, what would you say?

6

Gaston Lachaise, *Couple (Dans la Nuit),* 1935

Sexuality: Patterns and Attitudes

Social scientists are not sure how much people's sexual behavior has actually changed in the past generation, but there has been a notable shift in the tone of public discussion about sexuality. The 1990s seems to be a decade of introspection for the American public as they search for reasons as well as solutions for pressing social problems—many of which appear to be intertwined with changes in sexual attitudes and behaviors. Over the past few years, adolescent sexuality, perennially a private concern and a source of tension between parents and children, has become a prominent public concern as well. Troubling questions are raised by the upward trajectory of premarital sex among even the youngest of today's teenagers and the inexorable spread of *AIDS* (Acquired Immune Deficiency Syndrome)—a viral infection transmitted by blood or semen that suppresses the immune system.

In this chapter, we identify recent changes in premarital sexual behavior and examine four different sexual standards, each of which has its adherents on college campuses today. We find out if knowledge of AIDS has affected sex among adolescents, on the college campus, as well as within gay and lesbian and marital relationships. In addition, we explore the significance of sex in marriage and ask how it has changed over the past several decades. But first we examine how sexual thinking is influenced by cultural norms and explore some of the reasons for recent changes in sexual standards.

THE SOCIAL CONTEXT OF CHANGING SEX STANDARDS

Sex appears to be one of the most natural of human functions, but it is mainly a learned behavior that is channeled by cultural expectations and shaped by the symbolic environment.

Sexual Norms/Sexual Scripts

Sexual attitudes and behaviors are strongly influenced by cultural norms. As Albert Klassen and his associates remind us in *Sex and Morality in the U.S.*, a *norm* is:

> . . . a behavior-regulating rule that individuals, as members of a society, share and believe they share with others. It is a morally binding rule that ordinarily elicits both external social and internal psychological sanctions. *Sexual norms*, then, are shared conceptions stipulating what sexual conduct is culturally prescribed, preferred, and permitted. In most social situations there is usually a substantial but varying degree of consensus about what is right and what is wrong. (Klassen, Williams, & Levitt, 1989, p. xxvii)

Although we may be biologically ready for a sexual encounter in early adolescence, social controls typically prevent or delay such behavior. Family, religious, and educational institutions provide us with norms for sexual conduct and perspectives from which to understand how sexuality impacts on our personal development as well as in our relationships with other people. Together, these social institutions intervene in our lives to provide a system of informal control. There are also formal controls on our sexuality, enacted through the legal system, concerning who is allowed to have sex with whom, under what conditions, and at what age. At the individual level we adopt *sexual scripts*—guidelines that we learn so well that they become a mostly unconscious pattern of thinking about sexual behaviors and interactions. For example, how we prepare for an upcoming date and the sequence of thoughts and actions that eventually lead to a sexual encounter are part of our sexual scripts (Reiss, 1986).

Sociologists Edward Smith and Richard Udry (1985) have identified a sequence of behaviors performed by adolescent couples as they move toward sexual intercourse. The process begins with necking and progresses to touching breasts through clothing, touching breasts directly, touching sex organs indirectly, touching the genitalia directly, to intercourse. This general script is subject to individual modification, of course. Moreover, when these researchers compared black and white adolescents they found that white adolescents seem to have a longer sequence of expected sexual behaviors prior to actual intercourse. Black adolescents much more often skipped from necking and petting through clothing to intercourse.

For marital partners, sexual scripts imply a subtle understanding of how a sexual encounter should be initiated and by whom, how long a sexual tryst should last, when orgasm should occur and for whom, which sexual positions are sanctioned, and whether masturbation and other forms of sexual pleasuring are appropriate. Scripts also assist people in evaluating the meaningfulness and satisfaction of sexual encounters. Additionally, they help establish the level of responsibility individuals take for their partner's safety, esteem, comfort, and pleasure during and after intercourse.

Masters and Johnson (1986), in their book *Sex and Human Loving*, suggest that a satisfying sexual relationship rests on the ability of marital partners to communicate and educate each other concerning their sexual needs, desires, and preferences. Individual sexual expectations and personal scripts for sexual behavior are negotiated by couples through communicating their expectations and adjusting to each other's sexual perspectives.

Gender also affects sexual scripts. How we respond to sexual messages, how we feel about ourselves as sexual beings, how we define the quality of our sexual relationships—all of these things are influenced by our identification as women or men.

Gender and Sexual Scripts

Male Scripts

Males and females typically are taught to attach quite different meanings to sex. For men, sexuality is closely tied to masculinity—taking on the adult male role. Sex is a symbolic "rite of passage" from boyhood to adulthood. Traditionally, it has been the male's responsibility to initiate sex. He is expected to be in control of the sexual encounter—to know the techniques and mechanics of sex and to perform by getting an erection and having an orgasm. The goal of sex is not intimacy, but orgasm. During adolescence, male sexuality is largely oriented toward impressing same-sex peers. Adolescent males learn from their peers to regard sex as recreation, an occasion for proving one's prowess.

Among college students, men continue to seek approval for their sexual exploits from other men and are more likely to talk about their sexual experiences than are women. When sex takes place in casual relationships with little emotional commitment, one of the main rewards for young men comes from telling oth-

For teenage males, scoring with young women in front of peers (or telling the "guys" about their sexual feats) is a way of proving themselves sexually.

ers. Males receive more peer approval than females do when they talk about their sexual involvements. These differences dissolve, however, when sex takes place between two people who are in love or have plans to live together or marry. The sexual scripts of both men and women regard the private sexual moments of intimates as off limits to others.

Participating in sexual activities also makes men vulnerable, but their vulnerability has much to do with competency: Is he a good lover? Did he satisfy his partner? How does his performance compare to that of other men? Men's vulnerability also has to do with responsibility. Will introducing sex into the relationship mean that his partner will expect more of him? Will she want greater intimacy, self-disclosure, exclusivity, commitment? Will he need to be a more willing participant in decisions about safe sex and birth control? In the event of pregnancy, how involved will he be in decisions about having a child and caring for it? Social researchers Blumstein and Schwartz (1990) write:

Male sexuality in our cultural view is shaped by the scripts boys are offered almost from birth, by the cultural lessons they learn throughout the life course, among them, the belief in a sometimes overpowering male sex drive and the belief that men have immutable sexual needs that are manifested over and above individual attempts at repression. (p. 310)

Female Scripts

The sexual script taught to most females, in contrast, emphasizes the relational aspects of sex, not the recreational or specifically genital ones. Social analyst Carol Vance notes:

Women—socialized to keep their dresses down, their pants up, and their bodies away from strangers—come to experience their own sexual impulses as dangerous. Self-control and watchfulness become necessary female virtues. As a result, female desire is suspect from its first tingle, questionable until proven safe, and frequently too costly when evaluated within the larger cultural framework which poses the question, Is it really worth it? (1984, p. 4)

Women are more comfortable expressing their sexuality within the context of an intimate relationship that fuses sex with love. Sex, they tend to believe, is an intimate activity that symbolizes affection, trust, and commitment.

Having a sexual relationship makes a woman vulnerable in several ways. First intercourse, for her, means passing the point of no return to the status of nonvirgin, which is less important today than it was two decades ago, but still carries emotional and psychological implications. Being sexually active also makes her vulnerable to reputational damage through rumor and innuendo. Our cultural norm is still that it is good for men to be sexually active, but questionable for women. In addition, a sexual relationship exposes a woman to *STDs*—sexually-transmitted diseases, which in women are more difficult to detect and diagnose—and possible pregnancy. And such activity increases a woman's sexual knowledge and abilities, which may lead future partners to believe that "she's been around" (Vance, 1984). Unfair as it may seem, when a man thinks about a woman in this way it puts her at greater risk of sexual exploitation.

According to Blumstein and Schwartz (1990), women's sexual scripts are closely linked to love, and sexual desire is more often a result of feeling emotionally attached to their partners. They argue that when women experience sexual pleasure prior to emotional attraction, they are less likely to continue the relationship. If the attraction is powerful, a deeper emotional commitment is sought to sustain and justify the continuing sexual feelings. Women's sexuality, then, is organized around emotional rather than physical signals.

Gender Differences

By noting the differences between the sexual scripts that males and females typically follow, a better understanding is gained of how the erotic responses of the two sexes differ. Indeed, one might conclude, as several researchers have, that most of what is normally defined as pornography, such as erotic pictures or hard-core films, might more accurately be labeled *men's* pornography; whereas the stimuli that often produce intense arousal in women, such as Harlequin romances and Danielle Steele novels, are not normally considered pornographic. The typical pornographic film overlooks precisely that aspect of eroticism that the romantic novels dwell upon—the seduction: the creation of suspense about the outcome of some male-female encounter. To the extent that women have been taught to respond sexually to romantic overtures, hard-core pornographic films that focus narrowly on genital contact are less likely to arouse women sexually than the romantic novel.

Gender differences in sexual scripts are evident even in what would seem to be the most private and nonsocial form of sex, *masturbation*—self-stimulated sexual pleasure. Masturbation is a nearly universal practice among males from early adolescence; among females it typically begins somewhat later and is not practiced by quite so many. Moreover, while masturbating, males usually fantasize about imaginary encounters—sexual experiences they would like to have—whereas females recall actual pleasurable experiences. Thus, the masturbatory fantasies of males seem to follow a recreational script, while those of females seem more relational in content (Ellis & Symons, 1990).

As relationships increasingly become the focus of life satisfaction, sexual scripts are expected to become less gendered. Sexual maturity, after all, is influenced by changes in culture and socialization practices and is a life-long developmental process that unfolds as illustrated (Sarrel & Sarrel, 1990):

1 Developing a positive sense of body image and gender identity
2 Learning to handle the leftover feelings of guilt and shame connected with sexual thoughts and actions from childhood and adolescence
3 Discovering what stimulates sexual enjoyment
4 Understanding and appreciating one's sexual orientation
5 Achieving a satisfying sex life
6 Becoming increasingly aware of one's sexual nature and how sexual intimacy benefits intimate relationships and satisfaction with life
7 Accepting sexual intimacy as a mutual responsibility of both partners with each having the right to experience sexual satisfaction
8 Gradually increasing one's ability to experience companionate as well as passionate love as aspects of an intimate relationship

Although the first stage of sexual maturity occurs during childhood, it is not until early adolescence that parents and the general public become involved and begin to observe and comment on individual behavior. A cultural change in sexual maturity that is currently stirring up societal anxiety is the tremendous increase in premarital sex among the youngest of adolescents.

SEX AND THE ADOLESCENT

Changes in Premarital Sexual Behavior

Few topics are as difficult to discuss with any objectivity as adolescent sexuality. Many adults who defend the traditional form of *premarital sexual abstinence*—refraining from having sexual relations before marriage—use the language of crisis and collapse in discussing contemporary sexual norms. Young people, caught up in the atmosphere of changing sexual standards, fight back by condemning the hypocrisy of their elders. The debate continues and escalates and becomes even more emotionally charged.

In this climate, communication and understanding are difficult. Social scientists generally agree, however, that the most significant change in sexual attitudes and behaviors is that premarital sex is now widely regarded, especially by young people, as a legitimate choice. Over the past decade, racial, ethnic, and social status differences in adolescent sexuality have narrowed considerably. During this period, white upper-income adolescents have accounted for much of the increase in premarital sex rates, according to the Alan Guttmacher Institute which is known for its outstanding research in the area of adolescent sexuality (Waldrop, 1991).

Another important change in premarital sexual behavior is that sexual activity is beginning at earlier and earlier ages. The so-called sexual revolution seems to have moved from the college campus to the high school, judging by the sexual activity among 15-year-olds—27 percent of females and 33 percent of males have had intercourse. Approximately 78 percent of American females and 86 percent of males first experience sexual intercourse while they are still teens (Pratt, 1990; Sonenstein, Pleck, & Ku, 1989).

Family researchers Brent Miller and Kristin Moore (1991) observe that adolescent females typically have their first sexual experience with adolescent males about 3 years older than they are—fewer than 10 percent of the males are age 23 or older. The first sexual partners of young women are persons they are steadily dating, and their initial sexual experience is unplanned or "just happens." But, as the authors of several studies point out, it should not be assumed that young adolescents are *sexually active*—have sexual relations on a regular basis. Sexual activity among teens tends to be sporadic, with over 60 percent averaging about 6 months between sexual encounters (Sonenstein et al., 1989).

Parents, policymakers, educators, and others are trying to understand why adolescents are increasingly involved in premarital sex despite the threat of AIDS and admonitions from family, church, and school.

Why the Change in Adolescent Sex Patterns?

Several factors have contributed to the rise in premarital sex, including an increase in social pressure, the lengthening of adolescence, the erotic environment, and various family influences.

Increased Peer Pressure

Adolescents aged 14 to 17 report feeling increased peer pressure to engage in sexual activity. When polled by Harris and Associates (1986), 73 percent of the females and 50 percent of the males identified social pressure as the primary reason for having intercourse

for the first time. In another survey, social scientists John Billy and Richard Udry (1985) also examined the impact of peer influence on the sexual behavior of black and white adolescents and discovered that white females were often influenced by their best friends. Having a sexually active close friend was strongly linked to increased sexual experimentation. White adolescent males admitted choosing friends partly on the basis of their experiences with sex—sexually active people were more often sought out as desirable friends. In comparison, neither friend choice nor friend behavior seemed to affect when black adolescents decided to become sexually active. Peer relationships did, however, encourage fatherhood. The more children a young black man had fathered, the higher was his social standing among peers (Francoeur, 1987).

Other research indicates that the earlier adolescents date and the sooner they have a steady dating partner, the sooner they will have sexual intercourse (Miller, McCoy, & Olson, 1986; Thornton, 1990). Adolescent females reveal that they have intercourse for the following reasons—peer pressure (34%), pressure from boys (17%), "everyone is doing it" (14%), curiosity (14%), love (11%), and sexual gratification (5%). Boys, in contrast, say their reasons for having intercourse are peer pressure (26%), curiosity (16%), "everyone is doing it" (10%), sexual gratification (10%), and love (6%) (Stark, 1989).

Almost Endless Adolescence

Another factor making premarital sex more probable is the lengthening of the period between the end of childhood, as marked by sexual maturity, and the beginning of adulthood, signified by entry into the world of work and accompanied by the privilege of full sexuality.

Until about a century ago, 16-year-olds were still biological children, both in physical size and sexual development. A relatively short period elapsed between the onset of physical maturity and marriage. But today, teenagers mature sexually at a much earlier age, long before they are intellectually or emotionally mature, and long before they are allowed to marry. Much of the concern about premarital sex might be regarded as a response to this pattern of earlier sexual maturation.

Thus, the beginning of adolescence comes earlier, while its ending, postponed by various social pressures and particularly by added years of formal education, comes later. In this "almost endless adolescence," persons who in most other cultures should long since have experienced the privileges and responsibilities of adult life, live in situations (for example, with parents, in a campus culture) that prolong their dependence. Between these two factors, earlier sexual maturity and postponed adulthood, adolescence has become about twice as long as it was a century ago, making premarital abstinence that much harder to maintain.

The Erotic Environment

An additional factor that may substantially influence sexual norms is the frequent exposure to erotic stimuli experienced by adolescents. Television programs and movies are becoming more sexually explicit, and many of the estimated 70 advertisements that the typical person pays some attention to every day are erotically highlighted. Sex has become commercialized. Products of all kinds, even detergents and automobile tires, are advertised with the promise of improving the buyer's sex appeal. Probably one of the few settings that advertisers do not picture as sexy is marriage. In most advertising, sexuality is portrayed as being *outside* the marital relationship—a message that, when repeated so often, may have a special impact on premarital sex.

All the media today carry more unreserved and adventurous discussions of sex than they did in earlier generations. Popular magazines frequently include articles on *sexual dysfunctions* (physical or psychological impairments that make erection or orgasm difficult or impossible), sexual fantasies, *sexual aids* (tools or devices used to enhance sexual pleasure), and other such topics that would never have been discussed in public in previous decades. This cultural atmosphere in which almost anything goes is a potent force for revising sexual standards. Sociologist Ira Reiss, author of *An End to Shame: Shaping Our Next Sexual Revolution* (1991), maintains that society is, in effect, giving adolescents permission to have sex.

Family Factors

Family structure, behavior within families, as well as family characteristics such as amount of education, social standing, and race also contribute to changing premarital sexual norms. For example, adolescents in single-parent families engage in sexual activities at younger ages than do adolescents in other family types (Forste & Heaton, 1988; Newcomer & Udry, 1987). Most single parents must seek full-time employment to support their families. They typically have no at-

home partner to help with parenting responsibilities. Unfortunately, the strengths of the single-parent family, including self-directed family members and a cohesive family unit, may contribute to earlier sexual encounters (Visher & Visher, 1988). Single parents may be less available to directly supervise their adolescents' behavior and thus depend on their children's ability to be autonomous and make good decisions.

Another reason for early sexual activity among adolescents in single-parent families is that single parents may be dating and adolescents could be modeling some of the adult behaviors they observe, despite efforts on the part of most parents to maintain privacy and be good role models. As one teenager said upon finding her mom's Friday night date at the kitchen table for Saturday morning breakfast, "How can she preach to me about premarital sex?" ("New Teen-Age Codes," 1989, p. B11). According to family researchers Brent Miller and Kristin Moore (1991), "Adolescents and parents who have experienced divorce have more permissive attitudes about sexual intercourse outside of marriage" (p. 310).

Families have a great deal of influence on adolescent values and goals. When parents and adolescents get along reasonably well, family values are usually transmitted successfully, regardless of whether parental values are liberal or conservative. Adolescents with more highly educated parents generally postpone sexual intercourse. So, too, do adolescents who receive good grades in school and have future plans that include graduation from high school, followed by college attendance. Cultural norms and sexual scripts about premarital sexual activity have historically differed by family socioeconomic status. Sexual activity at early ages as well as early pregnancy are behaviors traditionally linked to lower socioeconomic status (Moore, Simms, & Betsey, 1986), but that trend is changing. As we mentioned earlier, most of the change in premarital sex is now occurring among adolescents from middle-class families (Waldrop, 1991).

An additional factor associated with changes in premarital sexual activity is race. Although black adolescents have always had earlier sexual experiences than adolescents of other races, this trend is increasing and is more frequently leading to teenage pregnancy. This change is attributed to a drop in the overall importance of marriage in the black community, with greater tolerance for unwed pregnancies. Some see this as the result of demographic and social changes related to racism (as we have discussed in Chapters 4 and 5) (Taylor, Chatters, Tucker, & Lewis, 1991). Summing up a study that followed nearly 400 primarily black adolescent mothers over a 20-year period, sociologist Frank Furstenberg concluded that the young women interviewed "had a general leeriness of early marriage and a greater acceptance of out-of-wedlock childbearing" (in Kantrowitz, 1990, p. 78). Social scientist Stephen Thomas reasons that:

> A major reason black teens are sexually active is due to the unavailability of traditional symbols of adulthood. What do young adults do? They go to college or get a job. But as access to educational and employment decreases for black youth, sexual intercourse remains one of the few rites of passage into adulthood still clearly defined and available. . . . If you can't get a job or go to college, your only entry into manhood and womanhood depends on your ability to be sexually active and produce a child. (in Randolph, 1990, p. 50)

William Oliver, professor of criminal justice at the University of Delaware adds, "many of our boys make the passage from boyhood to manhood by defining manhood as sexual promiscuity, toughness and thrill seeking" ("Facing Grim Data," 1990, p. A14). The black community is very concerned and increasingly frustrated by this image. Across the nation, over the past several years, black scholars, ministers, and community leaders have been meeting and discussing solutions to what they see as a major concern for black youth and their families.

To summarize, there are several factors that have created an atmosphere in which early premarital sex continues to flourish. Parents, educators, health-care providers, and other professionals who work with adolescents are especially concerned about the increase in premarital sex, especially now that AIDS is in the picture. Demographer Judith Waldrop (1991) argues that AIDS has not affected the rate of intercourse among adolescents. Even though most high school students understand AIDS and how it is transmitted and realize that AIDS places them at risk, many falsely believe that there will soon be a cure. Others incorrectly assume that they can detect someone with the AIDS virus by observing their physical appearance. Others just don't seem to know or care about the consequences of unprotected sex. As one 17-year-old said, "We don't need no condom because he says he loves me" (Adler et al., 1991, p. 52).

Reiss (1991) likens premarital sexuality to a mine field of potential disease, pregnancy, and emotional entanglements. He explains, "It's not as if you can just tell them not to step on a mine, you've got to tell them how to avoid the mine" (in Painter, 1991, p. D8). Sex education programs and programs to make contraceptives more accessible are two measures designed to reduce premarital sex or make it safer, but they sometimes produce fierce public debate.

Contraceptives: Why They Don't Solve the Problem

Condom use has increased by over 50 percent in the past decade, but there is still much room for improvement, particularly among adolescents (Sonenstein et al., 1989). Between 1982 and 1988 the share of women aged 15 to 19 who used contraception during their first sexual experience rose from 48 to 65 percent (Waldrop, 1991). And, 80 to 90 percent of adolescents who were sexually active—had sexual relations on a regular basis—used a contraceptive of some type (Moore & Peterson, 1989).

We still have a way to go before it can be assumed that most adolescents are both adequately informed and equipped to manage their sexual activities. The youngest of adolescents who engage in premarital sex are often the least informed about contraceptives and the most ambivalent about their sexual activities. To choose an effective contraceptive or even to seek counseling on the subject is an admission of sexual activity that is difficult to make, precisely because premarital sex, though widely practiced, is not as widely condoned for adolescents. Moreover, many doctors are reluctant to deal with sexually active minors, especially without their parents' consent.

Contraceptive use among adolescents does increase with age. "Older teens have more information about birth control, including where to obtain a method, are less likely to fear having their parents informed, and are more likely to have access to money and transportation so that they can obtain contraception" (Miller & Moore, 1991, p. 313). Buying contraceptives can be very embarrassing for an adolescent. This embarrassment fades as they age and become involved in a steady dating relationship (Hofferth, 1987). Older adolescents, compared to younger ones, can more easily accept themselves as sexual beings and thus can more consciously plan for their sexual involvement. Self-acceptance and planning are two important prerequisites for the use of contraceptives (Winter, 1988). When adolescents convince themselves that sex "just happens" and is "beyond their control" they may feel less anxiety and guilt over their sexuality, but they run a much higher risk of problems.

When parents accept and approve of their adolescents' sexuality, contraceptives are more often used (Hayes, 1987). Table 6-1 describes some additional factors linked to adolescent women's nonuse or inconsistent use of contraceptives.

Sex Education: In the Home and in the Schools

If you wonder why adolescents have so little accurate knowledge about sex and contraception, consider the process by which most children learn about sex. In American society since the turn of the century there has been a marked tendency toward more positive attitudes about sex. Today's parents are more likely to accept the normality of children's sexual impulses. But the early sexual lessons taught by parents are still typically admonitions intended to prevent early intercourse and pregnancy. These traditional sanctions against premarital sex do not curtail sexual activity, but rather inhibit the flow of information that would allow adolescents to act more knowledgeably.

Even today many parents are uncomfortable talking about sex with their children. Apparently because of the anxieties that parents express in answering sexual questions, rarely do these queries continue into adolescence. One reason for parental reluctance is their fear that such discussions might be interpreted as an acknowledgment of their children's right to be sexually active. Another is a lack of knowledge about sex on the part of parents and the absence of a suitable vocabulary for talking about sexual functions.

The latest Kinsey Institute study which examined the sexual knowledge of nearly 2,000 adults, ranging in age from 18 to 80, revealed an appalling sexual illiteracy (Seligmann, 1990). None of the respondents answered all 18 questions correctly, and 55 percent flunked the test, giving the correct answer for less than half the questions. The questions covered topics that are important for making informed decisions about sexual behavior, such as contraception, AIDS, sexual stereotypes, and personal sexual health. Just 18 percent were aware that 60 to 80 percent of all women have masturbated. Half of the respondents thought that AIDS was transmissible through anal intercourse, even if neither partner was HIV positive.

The survey also showed a surprising lack of knowledge about contraception. Half of those surveyed thought that impregnation was impossible during menstruation. Fifty percent were unaware that baby oil and petroleum jelly should not be used with con-

TABLE 6-1
Adolescent Women Who Don't Use Contraceptives: Factors That Influence Their Decisions

DEMOGRAPHIC FACTORS
■ Is less than 18 years old.
■ Has low income.
■ Does not plan to attend college.
■ Has fundamentalist Protestant religious preference.
■ Is black or Hispanic.

SITUATIONAL FACTORS
■ Is not in a steady, committed dating relationship.
■ Has unplanned intercourse that does not happen regularly.
■ Has a high-stress lifestyle.
■ Has a poor mother-daughter relationship.
■ Lacks access to a confidential, free family planning service.
■ Lives in a poor neighborhood.

PSYCHOLOGICAL FACTORS
■ Has low educational/occupational achievement and goals.
■ Has expectations of having children in the future.
■ Has attitudes of risk taking, alienation, personal incompetence, powerlessness, fatalism, low self-esteem, dependence on others.
■ Does not accept reality of own sexual behavior.
■ Has poor communication skills with partner about sex and contraceptives.
■ Lacks partner cooperation.
■ Fears contraceptive side effects and possible infertility.
■ Is not aware of family planning services.
■ Thinks she is at "safe time of month."

Source: Adapted from C. Chilman (1990).

doms and diaphragms because they can cause tiny holes in the latex within seconds. As June Reinisch, the director of the Kinsey Institute points out, "No wonder we have the highest teenage-pregnancy rate in the Western world. No wonder the rate of sexually transmitted diseases continues to grow. And no wonder the AIDS crisis has not abated" (in Seligmann, 1990, p. 74).

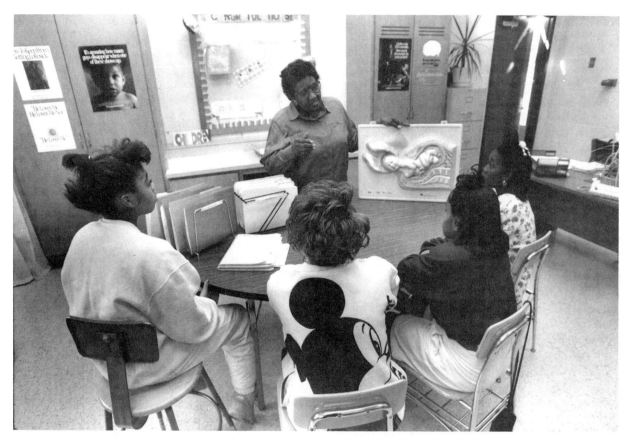

For a number of reasons, sex education courses in American public schools impart only a superficial knowledge about issues such as contraception that are critical to students' lives.

Reinisch goes on to call for a new emphasis on sex education from kindergarten through the first 2 years of college.

The majority of Americans (85%) support sex education in school (Harris & Associates, 1988). But partly because of the 15 to 20 percent of parents who object, and by reason of their lack of training in this specific area of study, teachers are at times reluctant to teach sex education. Today 80 percent of states either require or encourage sex education as part of the public school curriculum. But, according to a nationwide survey by the Alan Guttmacher Institute, sex education in the U.S. public schools usually consists of superficial discussion of human biology and "family life" issues. Many sex education programs, in fact, have no instruction in birth control methods, only emphasizing abstinence from sexual relations (Glazer, 1989).

Since some adolescents are sexually active by age 13, sex education courses offered at the high school level probably come too late. Even where those courses

are offered to junior high school students, some question the effectiveness of classroom instruction in this area.

How Effective Is Sex Education?

For years some critics have argued that teaching sex education promotes more sexual activity and thus increases adolescent pregnancy. Yet most research over the last 10 years has failed to show such a connection, except in cases where adolescents are taught to "just say no" without any other type of instruction. Social scientists F. Scott Christopher and Mark W. Roosa (1990) recently completed an evaluation study of an abstinence, or "just say no" program. The researchers were particularly interested in the adolescents who dropped out of the six-session program. Three hundred and twenty adolescents participated in the study (61 percent were female, 39 percent were male). Most were age 13; 69 percent were Hispanic, 21 percent were black, and 8 percent were white. The researchers concluded that pregnancy prevention programs that use only one approach, such as teaching abstinence, may be ineffective. Adolescents who dropped out of the program probably needed it most because they reported being more sexually active. Such students "may be turned off by a message that suggests they have done something bad or wrong" (p. 72). Other studies using a "just say no" format show similar results.

The United States has a higher rate of adolescent pregnancy than do other western nations, even though the level of sexual activity of their adolescent citizens is very similar. Why is there such a difference? Most other western nations, Christopher and Roosa (1990) argue, emphasize abstinence, yet provide effective contraceptives as an alternative to those who become sexually active.

One American program with a similar approach is available through The Johns Hopkins University School of Medicine in Baltimore. The hospital offers medical services and counseling at a clinic near area junior and senior high schools. The purpose of this outreach program is to delay the student's first sexual experience and to provide contraceptive services. Classroom presentations and personal counseling of individual students are the methods used to reach students. Over a 2-year period, pregnancy rates at the targeted schools dropped by 30 percent. "The program postponed students' first sexual encounter by about 7 months . . . the frequency of sexual activity also declined among those already sexually active" (Glazer, 1989, p. 345).

Family scientist Catherine Chilman worries that much of the current sociological literature ignores the point that most adolescent sexuality is "healthy." Adult preoccupation with the problem-laden nature of adolescent sexual development, she thinks, can lead to confusion on the part of adolescents about how to incorporate sexuality into their broader life concept. Adolescents who are sexually healthy are proud of their developing bodies. "They accept their own sexual desires as natural but to be acted upon with limited freedom within the constraints of reality considerations, including their own values and goals and those of 'significant others' " (1990, p. 124). Chilman advocates that educational programs for adolescents be based on accurate knowledge of their emotional and developmental needs and an avoidance of a "sex-as-sin" approach.

Although early sexuality, use of contraceptives, and access to sexual knowledge are the sex issues of young adolescents, college students struggle with how to adjust their sexual behavior to incorporate concerns for AIDS and issues of sexual equality.

SEX AND THE COLLEGE STUDENT

In contrast to adolescents, who are showing an increased level of sexual activity with seemingly little concern for contracting AIDS, young adults over age 18 do report that they are changing their sexual behavior. As one young man told Stephen Thomas, Director of the Minority Health Research Laboratory at the University of Maryland, "This may sound shallow, but the truth is . . . the first thing that attracts me to a woman is the way she looks. But, I'm not going to risk my life no matter how fine she is" (Randolph, 1990, p. 48). A woman who recently graduated from college agrees, "I always insist a man wear a condom—no exceptions" (p. 49). In fact, more young women today are buying condoms, with some brands even targeted specifically to female buyers, an indication that concern about AIDS has caused modifications in sexual behavior. In a recent New York Times/CBS poll, 40 percent of 18 to 29-year-olds report that fear of AIDS caused them to change their sexual behavior, mostly by limiting the number of sexual partners and increasing the use of condoms (Kagay, 1991). Those reporting changed behaviors varied by race, sex, and age, with those most at risk showing the most inclination to change (see Figure 6-1).

Yet, another survey of California college students showed that less than 20 percent of sexually active students with multiple partners used condoms (Adler et al., 1991). While this pattern may be unique to California, it is consistent with the evidence that young people are less likely to change their behaviors in response to the AIDS epidemic. Given the wide age range of the New York Times/CBS poll, it is difficult to determine how many of the 40 percent who did report altered sexual behavior were in the younger age range. It may be that the safer behaviors are being exhibited by those aged 21 to 29, who have graduated from college, while college students are as oblivious to the consequences of unprotected sex as high school students. (See the "Dilemmas and Decisions" box.)

Sex Standards on Campus

To construct a profile of the sexual standards and behavior of today's college-age populations, we draw on

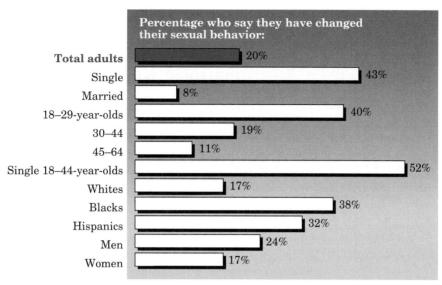

Percentage who say they have changed their sexual behavior:

Total adults	20%
Single	43%
Married	8%
18–29-year-olds	40%
30–44	19%
45–64	11%
Single 18–44-year-olds	52%
Whites	17%
Blacks	38%
Hispanics	32%
Men	24%
Women	17%

Based on telephone interviews conducted June 3 to June 6 with 1,424 adults nationwide.

FIGURE 6-1
Sexual Behavior and Fear of AIDS

SOURCE: M. R. Kagay (1991).

a number of studies. It can never be assumed, of course, that what people say they do is what they actually do, especially in so personal and emotionally charged an area as sex. A further caution is that most studies of sexual behavior have been conducted with small samples of college students from middle-class backgrounds; there is little reliable information about the premarital sexual behavior of young people in other social classes. Table 6-2 illustrates how college students compare with other groups on some indicators of sexual activity.

Abstinence

Despite the popular assumption of almost universal permissiveness among college students, some endorse the tradition of premarital abstinence. The most common reasons for adopting this standard, other than religious ones, are family training and the desire to wait until after marriage, as well as what has been referred to as the triple threats of infection, detection, and conception.

If reasons for adopting the abstinence standard have not changed much over the years, the percentage of young people who subscribe to it has altered substantially. Although the precise percentage of young people who indicate support for abstinence varies somewhat from survey to survey, there are at least three conclusions that we can reach from such studies:

1 There is very little support for abstinence.

2 Virginity becomes less important with age; college seniors are more likely than freshmen to say that it is unimportant to them.

3 College students who believe in abstinence support a position with which a majority of their peers disagree.

The Double Standard

Apparently one of the most significant changes in sexual norms that has taken place over the past two decades is the erosion of the *double standard*—the belief that premarital sex is more acceptable for men than for women. Studies conducted at various campuses across the country over the past few years find that most college students reject the notion (DeLamater & MacQuordale, 1980; Jacoby & Williams, 1985; Sprecher, 1988; Williams & Jacoby, 1989). In one study of 246 students, Williams and Jacoby (1989), however, did find that regardless of gender, sexually experienced students preferred less-experienced individuals as potential dates or marital partners. The researchers called this the "selfish standard": It was perfectly acceptable for *them* to be sexually experienced, but questionable for anyone they chose to date.

And what do the adults in the general population think of the double standard? Roughly 75 percent of

DILEMMAS AND DECISIONS

Does Asking Questions Lead to Safe Sex?

Virtually everyone past the fourth grade has received information on AIDS and safe sex. Despite this unprecedented level of awareness of a fatal disease and the means to avoid it, extremes in sexual behavior continue, ranging from doing everything possible for protection, to leaving safety in the "hands of providence."

One precaution advocated by magazines, newspapers, and television news programs is for dating partners to ask questions of each other concerning sexual history. However, this question-and-answer approach to dealing with AIDS is not always the safest way to minimize the risks (see inset), for nearly half of college men and 40 percent of women indicate it is all right to lie about the number of previous sexual partners. So getting reliable information may be difficult. Another problem is uneasiness or discomfort in communicating about sex and disease. Both women and men worry about offending their partners by insisting on condom use. They fear it indicates a lack of trust or raises suspicion that they are infected themselves. One 20-year-old woman, a peer-counselor, found that college women hesitate to talk about condoms: they fear being labeled "sexual" and having men pursue them for that reason. A further complicating factor is that men and women do not feel equally responsible for contraception and prevention of AIDS and other STDs. This as-

What to Ask Your Partner

- Have you been tested for HIV or other STDs?
- How many sex partners have you had?
- Have you ever been with a prostitute?
- (For a woman to ask a man): Have you ever had sex with another man?
- Have you or your sex partners ever injected drugs?
- Have you ever had a transfusion of blood or blood products (particularly before 1985, when blood wasn't screened for HIV)?

pect of sex has traditionally been left to women, who typically did not select condoms. Now, in the age of AIDS, many men and some women still avoid using condoms, saying they are uncomfortable, lessen spontaneity, and reduce sexual pleasure.

EXPLORATIONS *Is it ever appropriate to lie about or distort one's sexual history? Why do you think college students feel less vulnerable to AIDS and other STDs? Are there AIDS educational or counseling programs on your campus? Do you think they are effective?*

SOURCE: J. Adler et al. (1991); and M. R. Kagay (1991).

those surveyed by the Roper Organization in 1985 reported that single women should enjoy the same sexual freedom as single men. However, when asked about the existence of a double standard, about 80 percent of both sexes said that different sexual standards are still applied to men and women. Adults also admitted applying more traditional sexual standards to their college-age daughters than to their sons. They do so not because they believe that males should have greater freedom, but because they fear that their daughters will be judged more harshly for their premarital sexual activities.

The Modified Double Standard

A more contemporary standard, the modified double standard, on the other hand, allows sexual freedom to men and an acceptance of premarital sex for women

also, but only when deeply in love, engaged, or planning to marry. When a woman is in a committed relationship, sex is considered to be her right as much as it is his. Although this is a popular standard now among college students regardless of sex, males tend to be more accepting of it (Williams & Jacoby, 1989).

The most important change in premarital sex attitudes among college students is the recent acceptance of the newer, more permissive sex-with-affection standard. This is the standard that a near majority of college students affirm when they agree, "If two people care for each other, it's all right for them to have sex, even if they haven't known each other for a long period of time."

Reports from colleges across the country indicate that a substantially higher percentage of young women than ever before are now having premarital sex. At the

TABLE 6-2
Sexual Behavior by Social and Demographic Characteristics

Of 1,400 women and men surveyed concerning sexual activity in the past year, 22 percent were abstinent. The average number of partners in 1 year was slightly over one, with more than seven since age 18. Of those married, only 1.5 percent had a partner other than their spouse. Overall, 7 percent are at relatively high risk of contracting AIDS.

Characteristic	Average No. of Partners in Past Year	% Abstinent in Past Year	Average No. of Partners since Age 18	No. of Times Had Intercourse in Past Year
All	1.16	22.1	7.15	57.4
Gender:				
Men	1.49	14.1	12.26	66.4
Women	0.91	28.0	3.32	50.6
Education:				
<High school	1.07	37.5	4.59	45.6
High school	1.20	20.3	7.50	60.6
Jr. college	1.13	11.4	6.84	66.8
College	1.19	14.2	8.40	64.2
Marital status:				
Never married	1.84	24.6	8.67	54.9
Married	0.96	9.2	5.72	67.3
Widowed	0.21	85.9	3.01	5.7
Divorced	1.31	25.9	13.30	55.2
Separated	2.41	20.0	11.75	66.1
Age:				
18–29	1.76	12.9	6.08	77.8
30–39	1.25	7.3	8.38	78.3
40–49	1.27	10.3	9.71	66.9
50–59	0.97	21.4	9.28	46.1
60–69	0.68	40.4	4.65	22.6
≥70	0.35	68.1	3.51	8.2
Race:				
White	1.11	22.3	7.30	66.0
Black	1.64	21.6	5.84	68.2
Other	1.08	18.2	7.18	63.1

SOURCE: T. W. Smith (1991), p. 103.

same time, there is no apparent increase in premarital sexual activity among college males. Thus, attitudes and behavior seem to be converging toward a single pattern (Pratt, 1990). Under the sex-with-affection standard, sexual relations are no longer reserved mainly for the engagement period. Intercourse is now more likely to happen for the first time earlier in the relationship, when the couple is dating. This does not mean that "anything goes," but rather that a single standard allowing sex for both males and females in affectionate, stable, and loving relationships is now more widely accepted. What has changed most is the relatively recent emphasis on integrating sex into the overall relationship.

Many people assume that the "sexual revolution" ushered in an era of unlimited sexuality. A popular image of the college campus is that, in the absence of adult restrictions, sex has been reduced to a form of interpersonal recreation. There is little evidence that the sex-without-affection standard has grown substantially in popularity during the past few years. In fact, a higher percentage of young males and females view promiscuity as immoral, compared to students in the mid-1970s (Robinson, Ziss, Ganza, & Katz, 1991).

Most college students of both sexes do not believe in sexual abstinence.

New Standards: Conflict and Confusion

While a majority of adults no longer assert categorically—as they did in the 1970s—that premarital sex among college students is immoral, neither is there a consensus about the circumstances in which premarital sex is condoned, or about its effects. Young adults tend to believe that the more relaxed sexual patterns, despite the risk of AIDS, will help people choose better marital partners and develop more honest relationships. But, as the "Point of View" box indicates, some apparently feel that AIDS is cheating them of some measure of sexual freedom. Many parents, on the other hand, worry that their children are too sexually permissive and would prefer they have a monogamous live-in relationship rather than multiple sex partners (Klassen et al., 1989). How people define permissive today seems to be closely linked to changes in the sexual environment (AIDS). This issue is among the most difficult facing Americans today. The difficulty is compounded by the fact that college students and their parents often take very different positions.

Typically, research and media accounts of premarital sexuality focus on sex among adolescents or young singles or sexual patterns on campus. But they largely ignore the sexual expectations and practices of gays and lesbians. The advent of AIDS has changed that.

GAY AND LESBIAN SEXUALITY

Cross-Cultural Comparisons

Drawings, sculpture, and pottery from early civilizations including those of ancient Rome, Greece, Egypt, China, as well as American Indian tribes illustrate that *homosexuality*—being sexually attracted to same-sex partners—has a history as long as *heterosexuality*—being sexually attracted to partners of the other sex. It

POINT OF VIEW

Coming of Age in the Time of AIDS

Young adults coming of age during the 1960s and 1970s experienced a sexual freedom unlike any previous generation. Freed by the pill from fear of unwanted pregnancy, millions of women and men fully participated in an unprecedented time of casual sex. Sex in the 1990s cannot be described as fearless or casual. It may be a return to earlier, more monogamous sexual attitudes and behaviors, as this excerpt indicates.

I was 12 years old when AIDS was first identified, and my entire generation came of age under its shadow. It existed during our first kisses, first dates, and first relationships, bringing to an end a decade or two of sexual freedom. AIDS put my generation in a position closer to that of our parents and forced us to become responsible for our actions before we really wanted to.

Most people have experienced a time when sex did not mean risk. AIDS changed their behavior; it formed mine.

The years between the pill and AIDS were a time of freedom and casual relationships, when pregnancy was not an issue, when most things you could catch from a partner could be fixed with penicillin.

Those days are over, at least among the responsible and informed. So my generation missed out on the entire period of sexual freedom. The idea of casual sex is as inaccessible to me as it was to my mother when she was my age—but with a difference. It probably never occurred to her, while for me it is a lost possibility.

In the 25 years between her youth and mine, the world changed twice. After the pill freed women from the fear of unwanted pregnancy, "free love" and sexual exploration were condoned. Then along came the plague, and the world has reversed itself again—but with a new twist: men are also at risk. Suddenly, they are as willing to make commitments as women traditionally have been, and monogamy is back in style.

I have heard this described as a "return to morality." A return to fear would be more accurate.

This is the world my peers and I entered when we became adults. My mother married my father at exactly the point of life I'm at now. My life, however, appears very different from hers, for I have lived with my boyfriend for 2 years while she moved directly from her parents' house to her husband's. The fear of pregnancy no doubt reinforced her decision to commit herself to my father at an early age, just as the fear of AIDS has strengthened my commitment to my boyfriend.

I am even more controlled by sex than she was, since she faced a bad reputation or unwanted pregnancy while I face death. Perhaps it is because of AIDS that my parents accepted my early commitment to my boyfriend. It was better to see me living with someone at 18 than risking my life with multiple partners.

I am a member of the first generation to mature under the shadow of AIDS. Perhaps I shouldn't complain about how AIDS has affected my life, having lost few friends to it. But its existence has shaped my life, controlled my behavior, and locked me into a situation I might not have been in otherwise.

My boyfriend, who is several years older than I, assures me that the promiscuity and wild times were not as exciting or fun as they may appear to have been. Still, he admits he finds it hard to imagine spending his entire life having known only one partner.

I do not regret my early commitment to my boyfriend, as my mother did not regret her marriage to my father. But I live with the knowledge that AIDS has cheated my generation of the freedom recently known by men and women.

EXPLORATIONS *Has the threat of AIDS changed the dating patterns and sexual behavior of anyone you know? Do you consider the lessening of sexual freedom a missed opportunity for your generation? Are there benefits as well?*

SOURCE: Excerpted from K. Vermeulen (1990).

appears that gay and lesbian sexual activity has existed in all cultures, but the extent to which it has been condoned has varied enormously. One survey of preliterate societies determined that in 49 out of 76, some form of gay or lesbian activity was regarded as normal or acceptable, although it was seldom sanctioned (Ford & Beach, 1951).

The early Greeks approved homosexuality under certain social and spiritual circumstances. Special duties and responsibilities were often reserved for homosexuals in roles as caregivers, medical or herbal experts, entertainers, and spiritual leaders. Among the American Indians, supernatural powers were attributed to men who appeared to be homosexual in orientation. Such men were typically assigned the tasks of tribal historians or keepers of the culture (Wales & Kluckhohn, 1974).

Today in some regions of Africa, homosexuality among men is embedded in the process of socialization for all adult male roles. Male rituals exist for same-sex *fellatio*—oral stimulation of male genitals—and intercourse for the purpose of transferring semen, valued for its role in the development of various masculine characteristics. From puberty to young adulthood among some groups it is taboo to look at or touch women. This taboo changes during adulthood when men are then expected to marry and become exclusively heterosexual (Stoller & Herdt, 1985).

One group of Pacific Islanders condones homosexual behavior between adult males and male adolescents or between two male adolescents. Men are expected to marry around age 20 and then practice heterosexual relations from that point on, though extramarital homosexual encounters are still considered appropriate behavior. Among the Aranda in Australia, males are socialized to be exclusively homosexual during adolescence but bisexual after marriage.

One of the most extreme examples of socialized homosexuality is seen in the Etoro in Papua–New Guinea. In this society, it is believed that semen is a powerful life force that contributes to a man's vitality. Each boy is born with a limited supply of semen and is taught to preserve this semen by avoiding heterosexual intercourse. Homosexuality is preferred because the Etoro believe that adolescent boys must acquire semen from older men through oral intercourse to grow into men and to gain enough semen to give life force to their children. Thus, homosexual acts are considered to be as important to the reproductive process as heterosexual sexual behavior (Kottak, 1991).

Homosexuality is also more readily accepted in Denmark and the Netherlands, compared to America. In the Netherlands, a vast majority believe that there should be no legal restrictions on homosexual behavior. And, since 1973, it has been legal for consenting adults to have homosexual or heterosexual relations as long as the participants are over age 16. In the modern world, gay and lesbian sexual activity has perhaps nowhere been more harshly condemned than in American society, in which criminal sanctions have applied

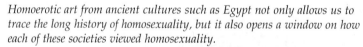

Homoerotic art from ancient cultures such as Egypt not only allows us to trace the long history of homosexuality, but it also opens a window on how each of these societies viewed homosexuality.

to gay and lesbian acts, and homosexual activity was long regarded as a form of mental illness.

Sexual Identity—Its Meaning and Significance

According to most estimates, somewhere between 5 percent and 10 percent of the American population today is gay or lesbian—approximately 25 million people. But such figures raise as many questions as they answer, because they imply that everyone can be categorized as either homosexual or heterosexual. In truth, the words "gay" and "lesbian" are social labels. Sexuality is much more complex than these words imply. First, it is important to distinguish between a person's sexual orientation, sexual behavior, and sexual identity. As Ritch Savin-Williams explains in his book *Gay and Lesbian Youth* (1990):

> A homosexual *sexual orientation* consists of a preponderance of sexual or erotic feelings, thoughts, fantasies, and/or behaviors desired with members of the same sex. Homosexual activity connotes *sexual behavior* between members of the same sex. *Sexual identity,* by contrast, represents a consistent, enduring self-recognition of the meanings that sexual orientation and sexual behavior have for oneself. (p. 3)

The distinction among these three terms is important, but sometimes causes confusion. To further clarify, we need to understand that just because a person has thoughts and fantasies of gay or lesbian sexual activity or is involved in homosexual behavior does not mean that she or he would identify with being gay or lesbian. There are far more people who engage in homosexual activities than there are people who identify themselves as gay or lesbian. "Gay or lesbian identity is the sense that a person has of being a homosexual/gay male/lesbian . . . a very personal sensation, experienced as a recognition of 'who I am' " (Cass, 1990, p. 246).

In the pioneering work of Alfred Kinsey and his associates only half the total studied could be regarded as exclusively heterosexual, as defined by both sexual acts and feelings since puberty. Of the males, 13 percent had experienced homosexual sexual desires that they had not acted upon, and 37 percent had experienced at least one gay contact in which they reached orgasm. About 18 percent of the men had had as much gay as heterosexual experience, and 8 percent had spent at least 3 years since adolescence in exclusively

gay relationships. However, only 4 percent of the males had been exclusively gay throughout life (Kinsey, Pomeroy, & Martin, 1948).

In contrast, there was considerably less lesbian sexual activity among the women that Kinsey (Kinsey & Gebhard, 1953) studied: 15 percent had experienced lesbian desires but had not acted upon them, 13 percent had experienced some lesbian contacts, but only about 2 percent of the female population said they were exclusively lesbian. In a more recent study, 20 percent of those sampled in a nationwide survey said that they had experienced gay or lesbian sex at least once in their lifetime (Fay, Turner, Klassen, & Gagnon, 1989). And, in another study of 262 lesbians, 75 percent reported having sex with men since age 18. Of those, 43 percent indicated that they had always identified themselves as lesbians even though they had sex with men (Sanders, Reinisch, & McWhirter, 1990).

As you can see, the majority of people who engage in gay or lesbian behavior do not continue this practice throughout their adulthood nor do they identify themselves as homosexual. Of those who identify as gay or lesbian, many continue to have sexual relationships with others of the opposite sex.

Before Kinsey's research on sexuality, homosexuality and heterosexuality were seen as dichotomous: a person was either gay or straight. "Some allowed for a third category of *bisexual*—being sexually attracted to partners of either sex, but others believed that a bisexual was a homosexual in disguise (trying to pass for heterosexual) or a heterosexual who was experimenting" (McWhirter, Sanders, & Reinisch, 1990, p. xxi) (see the "Changing Lifestyles" box). Kinsey challenged those notions of sexuality. From his studies, he developed a continuum of sexuality that ranged from 0 to 6 (see Figure 6-2). For present purposes, we are interested mainly in that group whose sexual orientation is predominantly or exclusively homosexual, and whose sexual identity is gay or lesbian as well.

The Process of Self-Identification

Though sexual identity is usually set by age 4 or 5, self-identification as gay or lesbian is a long process that consists of at least six stages. Individuals differ in how quickly they move from one developmental stage to the next during this process. All gays and lesbians, in fact, do not progress through the entire six stages. Some never leave stage 1, others go on to stage 3 or stage 4 and then stop. Many, however, do complete all stages.

CHANGING LIFESTYLES

Bisexuals Enter the Spotlight

In a world where sexual orientation is polarized into heterosexuality and homosexuality, bisexuality comes as a disturbing challenge, at once a riddle and a discomfort. . . . Bisexuals often inspire nervousness, distaste and hostility in both straights and gays and are all but ignored by scholars.

Lately, however, bisexuality has been hard to overlook. Bisexual characters are the newest twist in movies and TV shows, most notably *Basic Instinct* and *L.A. Law*. . . .

But the issue has been more than fodder for gossip columns. The advent of AIDS has made bisexuality a matter of medical concern. Bisexual men who practice unsafe sex with male and female partners may help speed the spread of HIV through the heterosexual community. "Up until the time of AIDS, the term bisexual was hardly even used," says anthropologist Carmen Dora Guimarães of the Federal University of Rio de Janeiro, "but with the spread of AIDS, we are now trying to flush out this enigmatic character."

Fearful of stigma and discrimination, bisexuals across the U.S. and Europe are becoming more organized and politically active, networking in such groups as BiNet and BiPAC. They are also challenging gay organizations, with which they have had an uneasy alliance, to focus more on bisexuality.

The activism has sparked a new debate about sexuality in general. Are people essentially either straight or gay, with bisexuality being merely the unnatural by-product of confusion and repression among some homosexuals? Or is bisexuality a third distinct orientation? Is sexuality governed by biology or culture? Is it fixed, an identity that is set early and endures through life? Or is it fluid, shifting with time and temptation?

In truth, sexual identity is a complex weave spun of desire, fantasy, conduct and belief; pulling on any one thread distorts the fabric. Even defining one's own sexual orientation can be difficult. Avowed lesbians sometimes sleep with men, and men who describe themselves as straight engage in sex with other man. . . . Moreover, sexuality is as much a state of mind as an act of body. People may be attracted to someone but unwilling to act on their desires out of guilt or shame; conversely, others may act contrary to their true feelings.

Statistics on the number of bisexuals are unreliable since people who engage in such behavior often do not call themselves bisexual. But the ability to respond erotically to both sexes seems to be a common human trait. . . .

The most common perception is that bisexuals are basically straights with a taste for exotic adventure or essentially gays who are unable or unwilling to acknowledge their true orientation. To growing numbers of bisexuals, however, as well as therapists and researchers, this is nonsense. They insist that bisexuality is not a walk on the wild side or a run from reality but has a legitimate identity of its own. Explains John Craig,

Remember that self-identification is a very individual process that is probably not as orderly as we present here. There is most likely some backtracking and sometimes a stage may be skipped altogether, or stages may be taken out of order because of individual needs or special circumstances. Social scientist Vivienne Cass (1990) describes the stages of gay and lesbian sexual identification as follows:

Stage 1: Identity Confusion. This stage begins when sexual behavior, feelings, or thoughts are recognized as being gay or lesbian in nature and ends with the individual admitting "I *may* be homosexual." During this stage, people question and explore the possibility that they may be gay and either reject the view; accept it, but view it as unwanted and not a desirable choice; or accept it as correct and desirable. Confusion, fear, and denial are typical reactions at this stage.

Stage 2: Identity Comparison. During this stage the broader implications of being gay or lesbian—how it will affect relationships with family members, career choices, and friendships—are explored. Feelings of social isolation and alienation are not unusual as the individual compares previous heterosexual experiences with what will likely result if a commitment is made to self-identify as gay or lesbian. By the end of stage 2, the individual begins to think "I am *probably* homosexual."

a 40-year-old writer in Amherst, Mass., who organizes weekend retreats for bisexual men: "I want to experience contact with a man's body and with a woman's body. That's just a basic part of who I am.

Because of society's reluctance to recognize their existence, bisexuals often face an even more torturous struggle than gays in coming to terms with their identity. Unlike gays, bisexuals lack an established community or culture to help ease the process. For men, the confusion seems to surface during adolescence and early adulthood. Al, 38, of Chicago, recalls that during his troubled college years "there was almost no place I could go where bisexuality was part of the norm." Having "bought into the myth that bisexuality was a political cop-out," he swung betweeen describing himself as straight and gay. But his distress was so great that "I went through a period of a year or two where I called myself 'unlabeled.'"

Some bisexual women travel a similar path. Sarah Listerud, a member of a large Catholic family, arrived at Oberlin College believing marriage for her was a "given." During her sophomore year, she fell in love with a woman. She had subsequent lesbian liaisons but remained attracted to men. . . .

For other women, bisexuality is a late discovery. "Many never had any sexual attraction to other women," notes psychiatrist Tim Wolf of San Diego. "But now they are in their 30s or 50s, and they fall in love with a particular woman." . . . Wolf speculates that women come to a realization of their bisexuality later than men do because women tend to be more physically affectionate with each other throughout their lives and this closeness camouflages the sexual desire. . . .

Some bisexuals have a stronger physical passion or romantic longing for one sex. Eric, 31, a journalist in San Francisco, has sex with women and men, but "I experience more emotional intensity with men." Other bisexuals, like John Craig or Sarah Listerud, find that attraction varies over time, even taking on an almost cyclical quality.

To Eric, bisexuality "enhances the human experience. You get a fuller, richer sexual life. Other men plow through life without understanding the parts of themselves that are feminine." Bisexuals often claim to be more sensitive and empathic lovers. . . .

Still many bisexuals, especially men, are racked by discomfort and conflict. About two-thirds of bisexual men are married, . . . and discovery that a husband is involved with other men can easily wreck a marriage. The husband feels humiliated, and the wife betrayed, not so much by his having sex with men as by his having gone outside the marriage. . . .

Answers to the puzzle of bisexuality are becoming more urgent. As the threat of AIDS intensifies, more precise information regarding bisexuals' prevalence and practices is desperately needed. As agitation for bisexual rights increases a clearer understanding of sexuality's origins is pivotal to the debate. One thing is already evident: more even than gays, bisexuals used to live in the shadows. Now they are entering the spotlight.

EXPLORATIONS *Do you think people are either straight or gay or is bisexuality also a distinct orientation? Why? Do you think one's sexual identity is fixed and unchanging throughout the life cycle? Why?*

SOURCE: Excerpted from A. Toufexis (1992).

Stage 3: Identity Tolerance. By the end of this stage, thinking changes to "I *am* homosexual." Recognition of this fact and experiencing the consequences of that reality are the primary tasks of stage 3. But, the focus is on tolerance rather than acceptance. There is still no full commitment to being gay or lesbian. During this stage other gays and lesbians are sought out and the individual rehearses his or her newly admitted identity in the more secure environment of supportive company, in order to gain a clearer picture of what it would be like to make a full commitment.

Stage 4: Identity Acceptance. Self-identification becomes clearer and more determined at this stage. Increased

contacts are made with others in the gay community and a network of friends is developed. The individual feels more comfortable and secure now, but hesitates to self-disclose to others outside the support network. It is still more comfortable at this stage to "pass" as heterosexual and avoid conflict.

Stage 5: Identity Pride. During this stage, positive personal attitudes toward being gay or lesbian conflict with the prevalent societal view of homosexuality as deviant. Feelings of gay pride coexist with those of anger about the stereotypical societal reactions and the low status accorded gays and lesbians. A rigid "them versus us" mentality can develop as a means of self-protection. Disclosure of identity of-

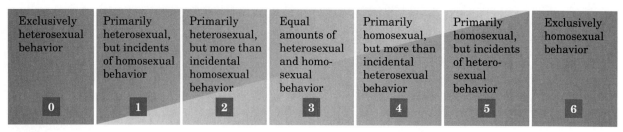

Exclusively heterosexual behavior	Primarily heterosexual, but incidents of homosexual behavior	Primarily heterosexual, but more than incidental homosexual behavior	Equal amounts of heterosexual and homo-sexual behavior	Primarily homosexual, but more than incidental heterosexual behavior	Primarily homosexual, but incidents of hetero-sexual behavior	Exclusively homosexual behavior
0	1	2	3	4	5	6

FIGURE 6-2
Kinsey's Continuum of Sexuality
Rather than treating people as either heterosexual or homosexual, the Kinsey group placed individuals along a continuum divided into seven categories, as this figure shows.
SOURCE: Adapted from A. Kinsey, W. Pomeroy, & C. Martin (1948), p. 638.

ten ends in conflict and confrontation at this stage, reinforcing those conflictual feelings.

Stage 6: Identity Synthesis. The "them versus us" stance is abandoned as feelings of anger and pride become less intense. At this point there is recognition that gays and lesbians are part of a minority group that is regularly discriminated against—attacks on homosexuals are seen as less personal and more political. Feelings of security and comfort increase. Disclosing sexual identity to others becomes easier. Contacts in the gay community are enlarged to include a broader range of friends and acquaintances from the straight world. Feelings of peace and well-being are more common.

The process of identity formation for gays and lesbians is clearly complex. It involves discarding certain cultural norms and socially learned attitudes and behaviors, while learning new ones that fit the gay or lesbian lifestyle (Herdt, 1990).

Coming Out

As discussed in Chapter 5, gays and lesbians who decide to publicly acknowledge their sexuality are described as "coming out" (of the closet). It is not an easy decision because of the risks of rejection, condemnation, discrimination, and *gay bashing*—emotionally and physically abusive behavior from others including name-calling, beating, attacking with weapons, and engaging in other injurious activities. Reasons for not coming out include fear of the unknown; the desire not to disappoint people one loves, especially parents; and an avoidance of rejection by parents as well as peers. Positive results of coming out are experiencing a sense of freedom, claiming one's real self, no longer living a lie, and finding real acceptance (Savin-Williams, 1990).

Coming out is typically a significant life event. As one gay male reveals, "Gay men and lesbians 'come out' for a lot of reasons—by force, for political objectives, for pride—but there is only one 'good' way to 'come out' and that is for ourselves." He continues, " 'Coming out' is a choice that is personal, sometimes public, and always political. It is not a point in time, but a continuum—a beginning" (Wilson, 1987, p. 8).

Stereotypes and Their Effects

In 1973, when the American Psychiatric Association approved a resolution that "homosexuality per se cannot be classified as a mental disorder," that decision reflected a widespread tendency in recent years to reconsider the nature of gay and lesbian sexuality. There are several reasons why the American Psychiatric Association decided that gay and lesbian sexuality should no longer be included on its list of recognized forms of mental disorder. The primary one, however, is that there is no convincing evidence that there is any more pathology among gays and lesbians than among heterosexuals (McWhirter et al., 1990).

One of the most significant changes that has taken place in recent years is that it is becoming more common for gays and lesbians to be regarded as a minority group that has experienced many of the same types of prejudice as members of racial and ethnic minorities. Stereotypes about gays and lesbians serve the same purpose as stereotypes about other minorities—to distort their characteristics so as to justify continued discrimination. Accounts of gay and lesbian lifestyles allow a more objective view and challenge the belief that all gays and all lesbians are alike. Many of the older misconceptions are being tested, such as the idea that most gays and lesbians have disturbed personalities, or that they are identifiable by mannerisms, body types, or the way they dress.

Over the past two decades, gays and lesbians have become more visible, partly because of the activities of such groups as the Mattachine Society and the Gay Activists' Alliance, which have organized events such as "Gay Pride Week." On many college and university campuses, Lambda, an activist and support group, provides a forum for examining and presenting gay and lesbian issues on campus. The goal of such groups, and the aim of much of the recent literature that depicts gays and lesbians sympathetically, is to gain legal rights and prevent further discrimination on the basis of an individual's sexual orientation.

Unquestionably, there is a far broader awareness of gay and lesbian concerns today than there was in the early 1970s, when the gay rights movement began. Major political figures now routinely appoint representatives to the gay and lesbian community. In many cities, there are gay and lesbian churches and a wide variety of businesses operated by gays and lesbians. In recent years, television shows and movies have increasingly depicted gay and lesbian characters. More recently, the characters are presented as normal, healthy individuals, although there is still a tendency to overemphasize stereotypes.

Homophobia

Nevertheless, *homophobia*—irrational fear or hatred for gays and lesbians—is still a major problem in our society. Such feelings are related to misinformation and misunderstanding about the causes and consequences of being homosexual. They fuel incidents of "gay bashing" that result in gays being several times more likely than the average citizen to experience a criminal act or other violence.

Recent research concludes that up to 92 percent of gays and lesbians have experienced verbal abuse including threatening remarks, while 24 percent have been physically attacked (Herek, 1988). "Telling 'queer' jokes and belittling homosexuality expresses an element of hostility that is part of the homophobic" (Crooks & Baur, 1990, p. 325). Because of homophobia people lose careers, opportunities for advancement, homes, and friends.

Although men and women tend to be more prejudiced toward homosexuals of their own sex, heterosexual men are particularly inclined to be homophobic. It has to do with the process of socialization whereby boys and men are taught that any feminine traits in themselves or in other men are unmasculine, unwanted, and in need of adjustment. It is not so much a distaste for the sexual nature of the gay lifestyle that promotes homophobia, rather it is the feminine characteristics that are stereotypically attributed to all gay males that result in homophobic responses. Homophobia is linked to hesitancy on the part of some heterosexual males to display any sort of emotional attachment or closeness to other males. Ways of dressing, making love, and even communicating are carefully monitored to exclude anything that seems remotely unmasculine.

Men and women who display homophobic tendencies usually subscribe to more rigid gender-role preferences, more often attend fundamentalist religious services, come from rural areas, and feel greater guilt from experiencing sexual pleasure (Herek, 1988; Kurdek, 1988). Many psychologists maintain that deep dislike toward homosexuals may be an attempt to deny or suppress one's own homosexual feelings (Crooks & Baur, 1990).

Prepared under the auspices of Kinsey's Institute for Sex Research, the book *Homosexualities: A Study of Diversity among Men and Women* (Bell & Weinberg, 1978) makes the point that there are many different gay and lesbian lifestyles. Based on interviews with about 1,500 gays and lesbians, it provides evidence that contradicts many of the familiar stereotypes. The majority of gays and lesbians in this sample supported themselves in stable jobs—and not in stereotypically gay fields such as hairdressing or interior design. And, contrary to the popular stereotyped notion that gay males are incapable of any enduring relationships, this study concludes that almost all of the respondents had experienced long-lasting committed love relationships.

Overall, perhaps the most revealing aspect of the Bell and Weinberg study is that its authors were less concerned with understanding the origins of gay and lesbian sexuality than they were with pointing out what gays and lesbians have in common with heterosexuals—such concerns as making a living, being in a loving and committed relationship, and achieving sexual compatibility with their partners. These findings were confirmed in a second book published by the Kinsey Institute, *Homosexuality/Heterosexuality: Concepts of Sexual Orientation* (McWhirter, Sanders, & Reinisch, 1990).

The Influence of AIDS

Until the onset of AIDS, gays and lesbians were making significant strides toward acceptance in the

The increasing willingness of many gays to openly declare their sexual orientation has no doubt contributed to increased public awareness of gay and lesbian issues.

community at large. When Morton Hunt (1974) replicated the classic Kinsey study on sexuality, he found that the percentage of people who expressed tolerance of gay and lesbian behavior was about twice as high as it had been a generation before. About one-quarter of the people in Hunt's sample agreed that "being homosexual is just as natural as being heterosexual." Surveys taken in 1980 revealed that a 60-percent majority agreed that "homosexuals should be guaranteed equal treatment under the law in jobs and housing" (Barron & Yankelovich, 1980, pp. 120, 125).

After AIDS became a public health concern in the early 1980s, acceptance and tolerance of gays declined markedly. Today, public attitudes toward gays and lesbians are once again more tolerant. A Gallup poll shows that 59 percent of the adults surveyed thought that sexual relations between consenting adults should be legalized—up from 47 percent in 1987 (Salholz, 1990). Reasons for these more accepting attitudes stem, in part, from public recognition, respect, and empathy for how the gay community has handled the AIDS

health crisis. For gays, in particular, there is a link between receiving information on AIDS and a change in sexual attitudes and behavior (Adler et al., 1991). It is also explained by the greater involvement of the gay community in politics and public relations.

So far we have focused on the sexual attitudes and behaviors of adolescents, college students, and gays and lesbians. An attitude of concern and restraint seems to prevail in these groups. By contrast, major issues in marital sexuality revolve around mutual satisfaction, quality of performance, gender differences, sexual equality, and marital fidelity.

CHANGING IDEOLOGIES ABOUT MARITAL SEX

The idea that spouses should share the pleasures of their sexuality is a relatively recent one. Our knowledge of the typical sexual satisfactions of marriage in other ages and cultures is scanty and unreliable, but it is not unlikely that marital sex provided much mutual satisfaction for most couples. For both spouses, sex had far more to do with the performance of conjugal duties than of mutual pleasuring.

Sex as Sin

Like most of the western European cultures, American society is emerging from a past of strong antisexual feelings. The predominant sexual script in nineteenth-century America defined procreation as the only legitimate motive for sexual activities between spouses. Marital sexuality has long been regarded as no better than a shameful necessity by some religious groups. If pursued mainly for pleasure, sex between marital partners was still regarded as morally wrong.

Religious teachings combined with other social currents to create an extremely repressive, sex-as-sin ideology. In several respects, sex in contemporary America has been secularized and demystified. Since the first few decades of this century, religious restraints have eroded, and our sexual scripts have been revised very rapidly. There is a considerably greater tendency now than there was a generation ago to regard sex as having dual functions: a way of expressing and receiving pleasure—a very individual and self-centered fulfillment; and a means of communicating caring and love within an intimate relationship—a more mutual and couple-centered fulfillment. For many married couples, the image of sex as sin has been replaced by the image of sex as play.

Sex as Play

The studies of human sexuality published by Alfred Kinsey and his associates in 1948 (*Sexual Behavior in the Human Male*) and 1953 (*Sexual Behavior in the Human Female*) had a profound effect on how married people thought about sexuality. One of Kinsey's accomplishments was to demonstrate that sex could be studied just as we study other behavior. Among his discoveries, Kinsey found that fewer than half of the orgasms experienced by married men came in intercourse with their wives. Many of his readers were shocked at the considerable evidence of sexual activities in childhood, premarital sex, homosexual encounters among apparently heterosexual men, and extramarital sex. A majority of most men's sexual experiences, in other words, were socially disapproved and many were illegal (1948, p. 568).

Writing about the Kinsey studies in 1954, sociologist Nelson Foote noted that, according to the reports, a great deal of sexual activity was going on, and very little of it concerned reproduction. The most common motive, rather, was pleasure. Thus Foote suggested the most appropriate metaphor for sex is that of *play*, an activity engaged in for its own sake and one that generates rules allowing it to continue.

Today, there is greater acknowledgment of the equal sexuality of married partners. The recent emphasis on women's equal right to sexual pleasure and multiorgasmic potential, substantially revises the traditional belief that sex is a man's pleasure and a woman's duty (Allegeier & Allegeier, 1991). Today, because of the availability of more effective contraceptives, conception can be more reliably controlled, thus minimizing the risk that sex might lead to pregnancy. This allows married couples to define sex as play, something engaged in for its own sake, and allows them to have less anxiety about its possible consequences. New expectations for sexual pleasure, however, have created a new intolerance of humdrum sexuality (boring sex), or sex that offers pleasure to one partner but not to the other. This aspect of marital sex has convinced some partners that sex is work.

Sex as Work

Since sex is now widely accepted as a form of play, it follows that if it is not fun there must be something wrong with the way you are doing it. To correct the situation, you must work at it. The first lesson in many sex manuals and articles in the popular press is that sex requires careful preparation. The second lesson is that sex, like any demanding job, requires competence. The thinking is that there are certain technical skills that must be mastered for a proper performance. Some married partners believe that these written guides to sexuality emphasize performance to the detriment of pleasure. Others think that it is important to know the basics in order to extend the most pleasure to oneself and to one's partner.

One reason people buy "how to" manuals and read articles on sexuality is undoubtedly that they seek some standard against which to judge competence and normality. They want to find out "how they're doing." What they typically find is that the range of sexual behavior from one individual to another is enormous. Consider women's orgasms, for example. June Reinisch, director of the Kinsey Institute, notes that about

SNAPSHOTS

Is There Sex after 80?

Young adults usually cannot envision their parents having a sex life, and grandma and grandpa still "doing it" would be totally unimaginable. The following is an excerpt from a study of more than 200 men and women between the ages of 80 and 102, living in an apartment building for retirees.

■ The most common sexual activity was touching and caressing without intercourse, reported by 82 percent of the men and 64 percent of the women. Masturbation was the second most common activity, reported by 72 percent of the men and 40 percent of the women. Sexual intercourse was third: 63 percent of the men and 30 percent of the women reported doing it.

■ 70 percent of the men and 50 percent of the women said they often or very often fantasized or daydreamed about intimate relations with the opposite sex.

■ Retirement home living did not preclude sex, according to 63 percent of the people, and 42 percent felt that it actually increased their chances for sex.

■ 47 percent of the men and 70 percent of the women had no regular sex partners; of those who did, 80 percent of the men and 64 percent of the women were mildly happy with their partners as lovers.

■ About 25 percent of the men and almost twice as many women reported no interest in sex.

Men of every age said they were much more interested in sex and more sexually active than women. As men moved from their eighties to their nineties, their frequency and enjoyment of sexual touching and caressing declined. Women reported no such decrease.

EXPLORATIONS   *Were you surprised that touching and caressing were considered sexual activities? Do older people fantasize about and participate in sex more or less than you imagined?*

Source: Excerpted from P. McCarthy (1989).

---

10 percent of women have never experienced an orgasm, and between 50 and 75 percent who are orgasmic do not depend solely on penile thrusting during intercourse (1990). Some women have one orgasm during a sexual encounter while others have two, three, or more. Over a range this wide, averages are obviously not very meaningful. Sex therapists Virginia Masters and William Johnson characterize the sex-as-work approach to marital sexuality as problematic. As early as 1976, in *The Pleasure Bond,* Masters and Johnson titled one chapter, "Why 'Working' at Sex Won't Work." More recent publications allow greater room for spontaneity and picture sex as more playful and less work intensive than older writings did (Dennis, 1992; Masters & Johnson, 1986).

Sex over the Life Course: From Early Marriage to Old Age

In a 1983 nationwide study of some 3,600 married and unmarried couples, Blumstein and Schwartz found that "married couples are having more sex, and having it more regularly than we might have expected" (1983, p. 195). Other studies indicate that spouses commonly practice a variety of coital positions, with women playing an active part and regularly experiencing orgasm. A recent study also found that more marital partners are practicing oral sex, anal sex, and mutual masturbation than ever before (Allegeier & Allegeier, 1991).

According to Blumstein and Schwartz, most marital partners continue to have sex at least once a week into the middle years of their marriage. Only a few couples—6 percent of those married 2 years or less, and 15 percent of those married more than 10 years—have sex once a month or less. It is clear from this research that sex is a "steady and continuous part of married life for short- and long-term couples" (1983, p. 195).

Frequency of marital intercourse reaches a peak for those between the ages of 25 and 29 and declines thereafter (Bachrach & Horn, 1987). By the time married couples are in their late twenties and early thirties, frequency has decreased to about one to two times per week; and by their fifties, frequency of intercourse declines to about once a week. But interest in sex continues well into old age, as the "Snapshots" box indicates.

In one study of 100 couples (all considered themselves to be happily married), sociologists Ellen Frank and Carol Anderson (1991) divided the marital life course into three sexual stages—early marriage, middle years, and later years. They discovered that the early years of marriage were viewed as sexually satisfying. The major task of the sexual relationship at that stage involved pleasuring each other. And, the main sexual complaint concerned women's arousal and orgasmic difficulties. Women in early marriage said that their husbands were unaware of what pleased them (the women) sexually. In contrast, men said that their wives knew how to please them (the men). *Premature ejaculation*—inability of the male to voluntarily control the discharge of seminal fluid—was a concern for couples at this stage of marriage.

In the middle years, marital partners became distracted from their sexual relationship by other activities and responsibilities. "More than one-third of the men and 40 percent of the women at this stage of marriage reported that there is too little foreplay in their sexual relationship" (p. 188). Despite this dissatisfaction, most were satisfied with the sexual part of their marriage.

By the later years, couples had sex less frequently. "Men reported less trouble with premature ejaculation, but had more difficulty in both getting an erection and maintaining it," noted Frank and Anderson. Women at this stage reported greater dissatisfaction with the sexual relationship than at any other time in the marriage. "They described themselves as less excited, less confident, and more resigned . . . about 50 percent of women still reported difficulty getting excited and having orgasms" (p. 189). But, as in earlier stages of marriage, couples maintained that they were mostly satisfied with the sexual part of their marriage. It was the feelings of being cared for and loved rather than the quality of the sexual performance that mattered most.

In early marriage, wives seem to be more sensitive about what pleases their husband sexually than their husbands are about what pleases their wives.

In another study, social scientist Cathy Stein Greenblat (1991) interviewed 97 people who had been married 5 years or less. Her most striking finding involved frequency of intercourse. "The men reported monthly frequencies from 1 to 43, while women's reports ranged from 2 to 45" (p. 176). This represents a wide range of sexual activity which was not affected by age, education, previous marital history, or previous sexual experiences. After the first year of marriage, children, jobs, commuting, household chores, and finances all collectively conspired to decrease the level of sexual interaction. No action seemed to increase it.

A woman in Greenblat's study comments on the effect of children on marital sex:

> The first year it was between five and seven times a week, but Danny's working two jobs right now. Since the baby's been born and with Danny's schedule, we do it when we can. . . . So maybe once or twice a week. But, it's not out of choice, but out of circumstances. She's not a very good sleeper at all—she wakes up quite frequently. I would say the baby is the main reason, and lately since Danny's been working an early morning job he's very, very tired at night. (p. 181)

Another woman prefers to see the decline in frequency as a positive circumstance:

> Maybe it's not a necessity anymore. We have other ways of expressing our feelings, and intercourse is one of the ways. When we first got married we thought it was the only way, and now we realize it's not and the quality of our sex life has improved. Now it gives us so much satisfaction, it's not really necessary that we have it every single night. (p. 182)

Sex seems to decrease in importance after the first year of marriage as other marital roles and responsibilities became more intense. Study participants described sex as important but emphasized that sex was not the only way to show love. Companionship, tenderness, emotional closeness, and other demonstrations of affection—hugs, kisses, back rubs—were more important.

The emphasis on shared sexual enjoyment in marriage, like other heightened expectations in contemporary marriages, does not appear to lead to greater marital dissatisfaction. Though sexual pleasure is often regarded as a right to which both spouses are entitled, it is important to think of it too as a result of intimacy, which typically takes a while to acquire. And when things do not work out as planned or hoped for, couples seem to cope by looking at the sexual part of their relationships as more than the sex act. Marital satisfaction encompasses a broad range of interactions between partners. Love, affection, and caring are expressed in many different ways.

Despite evidence gained from these and other studies that sex is only one component of marital quality, many people incorrectly attribute the seemingly natural decline in frequency of marital intercourse to trouble in the relationship. Some even wonder if marital fidelity is somehow connected to frequency of sex.

EXTRAMARITAL SEX: THE QUESTION OF MARITAL FIDELITY

Do Americans Approve of Extramarital Sex?

The ideal of fidelity in marriage is still considered important to most people. When asked about *extramarital sex*—having intercourse with someone other than the marital partner—a large majority of adults respond that it is wrong. Indeed, the answers to this question have been remarkably consistent over time.

Between 1972 and 1988 "there was an increase from 84 to 91 percent of the adult population reporting that extramarital sex was always or almost always wrong" (Greeley, Michael, & Smith, 1990, p. 41). Although a solid majority of all Americans disapproves of extramarital sex, it is noteworthy that older people and those with less education most consistently disapprove. Noting that young, well-educated adults are least likely to disapprove of extramarital sex, we might speculate that this signals the beginning of a trend. Yet disapproval of sexual relations with anyone other than one's marital partner appears to increase with age. Monogamy is a strongly held moral ideal, even if some do not adhere to it.

Do Attitudes Match Behavior?

In 1983, the authors of one of the few reliable studies of extramarital behavior concluded that, after 10 years of marriage, some 30 percent of men and 22 percent of women had at least one extramarital experience (Blumstein & Schwartz). When asked about their extramarital behavior in the past year, 11 percent of the husbands and 9 percent of the wives reported being nonmonogamous. This study took place before the AIDS crisis began to receive media attention (see Table 6-3).

In 1990, Andrew Greeley and his associates re-

TABLE 6-3
Monogamy among American Couples

PERCENTAGE REPORTING AT LEAST ONE SEXUAL ENCOUNTER OUTSIDE THEIR RELATIONSHIP IN THE PREVIOUS YEAR	
Husbands	11%
Wives	9
Male cohabitors	25
Female cohabitors	22
Gay men	79
Lesbians	19

SOURCE: P. Blumstein & P. Schwartz (1990).

ported, after interviews with a randomly selected sample of 1,500 adults, that among single and married adults who were sexually active during the previous year, 82 percent were monogamous—86 percent of women and 78 percent of men. Married partners reported an even higher rate of monogamy (96 percent). Tom Smith (1990), using a similar sample of adults, noted the same trend. Of married people surveyed, only 1.5 percent reported having a sexual encounter with anyone other than their spouses in the year preceding the interview. Smith also asked how many sexual partners these married respondents had experienced since age 18; they averaged six partners. In summarizing his findings, Smith concluded that the vast majority of American couples today appear to be monogamous.

Typically, there are differences in the number of extramarital liaisons experienced by men and women. Fewer women have affairs, but the gap is narrowing. One reason is that women today have more opportunities for extramarital sex because of their involvement in the work force. As Laurel Richardson (1986) explained, after studying 700 women who had affairs:

> By not altering the usual routines, she can see her lover fairly frequently and openly. . . . One woman routinely stays late at the office with her lover and accompanies him on business trips . . . another, a teacher, continues to spend considerable public time preparing for classes with her lover, a member of her teaching group. Both believe their romances are totally camouflaged by the cloak of routine work activity. (p. 25)

"Meaningful" Affairs or Lust: Motivation and Consequences

Some couples make it clear to each other that if either ever has a sexually intimate relationship with someone else, the marriage will terminate. Other couples acknowledge the possibility of an extramarital affair, but work at maintaining an exclusive, emotionally satisfying relationship. A few couples admit openly considering the possibility that one or the other may become sexually involved with another person. The partners may even discuss the conditions under which an affair may proceed, coming to some type of mutual agreement (Allegeier & Allegeier, 1991).

Macklin (1987) describes involvement in an extramarital affair as dependent on the following factors:

1 *Perceived opportunity*—having an available partner and a private place to meet.
2 *Readiness to take advantage of the opportunity*—having unfulfilled needs for independence, emotional closeness, and/or physical intimacy, and being willing to satisfy them outside of marriage.
3 *Expectation of satisfaction*—being attracted to someone and thinking, based on past experience or from talking to others, that the affair will be pleasing.
4 *Expectation of negative consequences*—believing there is little chance of the partner or anyone else finding out, or that having someone find out would have few negative consequences.

When researchers ask men and women who have engaged in extramarital affairs to characterize them, only a few (11 percent in Blumstein and Schwartz's study) describe them as "meaningful"—the participants have developed a deep affection and caring for each other. This finding is in conflict with Richardson's (1986) work, based on in-depth interviews with women. Her research, however, was concerned less with establishing how frequent extramarital relations are than with what they mean. She observed that sex was not the most important activity in many of the affairs. Neither was it what kept the parties involved. Such relationships provided an occasion for intimate friendship, for sharing secrets and mutual vulnerability. Because the women's involvements were unknown to friends or family, they were not judged or tested by outsiders. There was more freedom, then, to imagine the relationship as "ideal" and the partner as "special." This feeling of specialness resulted in deeper involvements than the women had originally intended. Once again we may be seeing evidence of gendered socialization, whereby women have learned to associate sharing and emotional and physical closeness with intimacy.

Ten years ago, some family scholars found that a minority of people who had affairs, or whose partners had affairs, expressed feelings of marital dissatisfaction (Blumstein & Schwartz, 1983). Lynn Atwater found similar results in a separate study, which was carried out about the same time (1982), of 50 women who had had extramarital encounters. Most of these women were not unhappy in their marriages and were motivated to experience sex outside their marriages purely by curiosity and a desire for personal growth. The majority reported few negative consequences from their behavior, and claimed that such experiences increased their enjoyment of sex and enhanced their self-image. Of these 50 women, 93 percent noted feeling more powerful, resourceful, autonomous, and self-confident as a result of their extramarital sexual activity. Today, with the threat of AIDS hovering over every new sexual encounter, curiosity and personal growth may not be enough motivation to venture outside the bounds of a satisfactory, marital sexual relationship.

Despite the fact that Atwater's subjects reported few negative consequences occurring as a result of their extramarital affairs, this type of behavior can be very destructive to the marital relationship. This is especially true if the spouse discovers the other relationship, and there has been no prior agreement allowing for extramarital activity. After all, marriages represent companionship, shared experiences, and a trust based on mutual disclosure and emotional attachment. An affair threatens marital bonds of affection and responsibility. The offended or betrayed partner is typically portrayed as feeling devastated, shamed, rejected, angry, resentful, jealous, and inadequate. As one woman explained to Shere Hite in an interview for her book *Women and Love* (1987):

> How do I feel? Mad as hell. I am angry and it hurts. It is like having some kind of sickness that is slowly eating away at me. . . . He does not satisfy me sexually because I have this constant competition with this other woman in my mind. . . . I feel horribly betrayed. (p. 414)

Such feelings are more pronounced, of course, if the affair is "meaningful."

In some cases, an affair brings marital partners closer together by motivating them to discuss their marital expectations and how they feel when those expectations are not being met. Sometimes this process of discussion and the search for sources of marital dissatisfaction can lead to an improved marriage. But, many times, discovery of the infidelity leads to divorce. Whether the affair is a "cause" of the divorce or a symptom of a marriage already in trouble, depends on the circumstances of each particular marriage. One of the main questions about the future of sex in marriage is how the tensions between expectations of intense erotic satisfactions and exclusivity will be resolved.

SUMMARY POINTS

■ Sexual norms are behavior-regulating rules about sexual conduct that are provided by family, religious, and educational institutions as a way to guide and informally control individual sexuality.

■ Sexual scripts are mostly unconscious patterns of thinking that we adopt concerning appropriate sexual behavior and sequences of interaction between sexual partners.

■ Gender-role expectations affect our sexual scripts. Historically, the sexual script of males has focused on the recreational aspects and mechanics of sex. The sexual script of females, on the other hand, has been concerned with the relational aspects of the sexual encounter—affection, trust, commitment.

■ Having a sexual relationship makes both women and men vulnerable, but in different ways.

■ Two of the most significant changes in sexual attitudes and behavior are that premarital sex is now widely regarded as a legitimate choice and that sexual activity begins at a much earlier age than in past generations.

■ Adolescent women typically have their first sexual relationships with adolescent males who are about 3 years older.

■ Premarital sexual standards have changed because of an increase in social pressure, a lengthening of adolescence, the erotic environment, and various family factors.

■ Between 80 and 90 percent of sexually active adolescents rely on some form of contraception, but only about 65 percent use a contraceptive during first intercourse.

■ Older adolescents, in contrast to younger ones, more often seek birth control because they are less embarrassed by their sexuality and less fearful of their parents finding out that they are sexually active.

■ Parents today are more accepting of their children's sexuality, but still find it easier to admonish their children about what they should *not* do than teach them about sex and intimate relationships.

■ The overwhelming majority of American adults support sex education at school.

■ Sex education programs that use multiple approaches rather than a single "just say no" message are more successful in delaying adolescent sexuality.

■ The predominant sexual standard on campus is the sex-with-affection standard.

■ Sex as play and sex as work are still major ideological influencers of marital sex today.

■ Though sex is a steady and continuous part of married life, sexual frequency drops off over the life course and sexual problems are not necessarily resolved in the early years of marriage. Regardless of the quality of sexual performance, however, couples at each stage of married life say that they are basically satisfied with their marriages.

■ Approximately 91 percent of adults believe that extramarital sex is always or almost always wrong.

■ Two recent studies by Andrew Greeley and Tom Smith indicate that monogamy is on the rise within marital relationships.

■ Extramarital affairs typically threaten marital bonds of affection and trust; however, some marital partners report strengthened relationships as a result of their affair.

■ Four factors that increase the likelihood of an extramarital involvement are perceived opportunity, readiness to take advantage of the opportunity, expectation of satisfaction, and expectation of few negative consequences.

KEY TERMS

Acquired Immune Deficiency Syndrome (AIDS)
Norm
Sexual norms
Sexual scripts
Sexually-transmitted diseases (STDs)
Masturbation
Premarital sexual abstinence
Sexually active
Sexual dysfunctions
Sexual aids
Double standard
Homosexuality
Heterosexuality
Fellatio
Sexual orientation
Sexual identity
Bisexual
Gay bashing
Homophobia
Premature ejaculation
Extramarital sex

REVIEW QUESTIONS

1. Discuss how sexual scripts differ by gender.

2. How has adolescent sexual behavior changed over the past two decades? What are some reasons for these changes? Will AIDS eventually affect adolescent sexual attitudes and patterns? How and when?

3. How do family characteristics influence premarital sexuality among adolescents?

4. Why have these two approaches—teaching about sex at home and sex education in the classroom—failed to affect the age of first intercourse and frequency of adolescent sex? How could each approach be improved so that these goals might be achieved?

5. Ask three college students and three mid-life adults which of the sexual standards introduced in this chapter they most agree with, and why. Compare the responses you receive with those of other students in your class. Do you notice any pattern to the responses by age, ethnicity, or gender?

6. What is the difference between sexual orientation and sexual identity? Describe the process of self-identification among gays and lesbians. How do you think stereotypes, homophobia, and gay bashing affect ease of self-identification?

7. Describe how ideologies about marital sex have changed across time.

8. When frequency of marital sex decreases, satisfaction with marriage is negatively affected and divorce is soon to follow. True or false? Explain your answer.

9. What motivates a person to initiate an extramarital liaison and what are the consequences for the marital relationship?

PART III

Family Roles
and
Relationships

7

David George Marshall, *Old Couple,* 1980

Marriage over the Life Course

Marriage is both an individual matter and a social concern. For society, marriage is an *institution*—a socially structured means of providing for certain recurrent cultural needs. As society interprets marriage, it is a system of role obligations and duties as well as rights and privileges legalized by a binding arrangement, a civil contract, that can be dissolved if the two parties agree to do so. For the individual, marriage means connecting in an intimate and committed way with a loved one. The bond between the couple celebrated in the public wedding ceremony is thought of as a commitment to create with a partner a relationship defined by love, care, trust, and emotional and sexual intimacy. The dissolution of this bond is costly in human and financial terms.

In this chapter we describe marriage as a process that begins with a loving promise and ends with death (divorce, the other primary means of dissolving marriage, is discussed in Chapter 16). We view the marital process as taking place within a historical context, and as being influenced by prevailing social norms. We consider how individuals and their marital tasks change across time as new situations appear that require alterations in behavior. In addition, we discuss marital success: Under what conditions do couples rate their marriages as satisfying or happy and why do they stay together? We begin with an explanation of *developmental theory*—a theoretical perspective that views people, and the marriages and families they are members of, as changing over the life course as circumstances and responsibilities alter.

ADULTHOOD AND MARRIAGE AS DEVELOPMENTAL PROCESSES

Adult Development

Until about a decade ago, social scientists paid relatively little attention to adulthood. Psychologists focused their attention on infancy and childhood and showed almost no concern for mapping the progression of adult development. The thinking was that most development occurred in the early years of a person's life. Adulthood was merely an extension of earlier, more critical stages of development. Because children and adolescents matured in fairly predictable patterns, adults were believed to evidence similar discernable stages of development—but less obvious and thus less essential to their behavior. Even today, it is difficult to pinpoint specific patterns of adult development that fit most individuals, but scholars continue to try.

Much of the early research on adult development was initiated to determine how people change over the course of their lives. An attempt was made to link various traits and developmental tasks to specific age periods or stages. The pioneering proponent of a stage theory of adult development was psychiatrist Erik Erikson. In 1963, he proposed an eight-stage theory of adult development, but his work has been criticized for focusing almost entirely on individual issues and ignoring evidence that most people are in relationships as marital partners, parents, and friends, and that these relationships also help set the tone for much of how we develop as adults.

Psychologist Daniel Levinson (1978) found support for Erikson's work when he interviewed 40 men aged 35 to 45. Using these interviews and supplementing them with information gleaned from the biographies of great men and from literature containing accounts of the lives of prominent male characters, he and his colleagues proposed "Levinson's Ladder"—another model of adult development.

Levinson found that for about 80 percent of study participants, the mid-life transition—which began at the age of 40 and lasted for about 5 years—was a time of considerable personal turmoil. At mid-life the sense of limitless possibilities that an individual felt in youth began to fade. Instead, one had a tangible reminder from the physical changes of middle age that time was beginning to run out. By the time most men reached their late forties or early fifties, they had reached the peak of their career advancement. Some men in middle age, having met cultural expectations and invested themselves heavily in their work, looked over their shoulders at what they had accomplished, and wondered if it was worth the effort.

During this period, men in Levinson's study typically questioned the pattern of their lives, engaged in a personal reappraisal, and made certain modifications in their lives. It was not that middle age was without its satisfactions for these men. The tyranny of social demands for success and achievement began to subside, and many males began to yearn for a more balanced life. If there was no longer the same preoccupation with proving one's success that tended to concern younger men, this period was normally accompanied by the realization of the disparity between one's dreams and one's accomplishments. This was also a time when relationships underwent considerable change, including a man's relationship to his children, who were then adolescents or young adults. Although several other researchers and a popular book, *Passages* (1976) by journalist Gail Sheehy, have continued to promote the stage theory of adult development, debate continues over its reliability (see Table 7-1).

One criticism of stage theories is that most are based on studies of white middle-class men born before or during the Depression. Using the responses of this particular group of men as a model for all individual development has, some believe, led to many incorrect assumptions about adult development in general and women's development in particular. More recent studies have attempted to correct this problem, but the majority focus on gender differences and continue to ignore race and class as possible key factors. Psychologist Carol Gilligan (1982, 1988), for example, concludes that women's development, more than men's, is based on relationships. Women seem to organize their lives around developing and maintaining close connections to others, while men organize their lives around workplace roles. For men, the responsibilities of work and family roles are similar and overlapping—to be a "good provider" is also to be a "good family man." For women, work and family roles are very different and combining them frequently causes role conflict and personal stress.

While men at mid-life may be at a point of reflection and renegotiation of roles, women may have negotiated a similar period in their thirties, during which time they may have had a child, divorced, returned to

TABLE 7-1
Adult Developmental Tasks

Early Adulthood (ages 20–40)	Middle Adulthood (ages 40–60)	Late Adulthood (ages 60+)
1. Psychological separation from parents. 2. Accepting responsibility for one's own body. 3. Becoming aware of one's personal history and time limitation. 4. Integrating sexual experience (homosexual or heterosexual). 5. Developing a capacity for intimacy with a partner. 6. Deciding whether to have children. 7. Having and relating to children. 8. Establishing adult relationships with parents. 9. Acquiring marketable skills. 10. Choosing a career. 11. Using money to further development. 12. Assuming a social role. 13. Adapting ethical and spiritual values.	1. Dealing with body changes or illness and altered body image. 2. Adjusting to middle-life changes in sexuality. 3. Accepting the passage of time. 4. Adjusting to aging. 5. Living through illness and death of parents and contemporaries. 6. Dealing with realities of death. 7. Redefining relationship to spouse or partner. 8. Deepening relations with grown children or grandchildren. 9. Maintaining longstanding and creating new friendships. 10. Consolidating work identity. 11. Transmitting skills and values to the young. 12. Allocating financial resources effectively. 13. Accepting social responsibility. 14. Accepting social change.	1. Maintaining physical health. 2. Adapting to physical infirmities or permanent impairment. 3. Using time in gratifying ways. 4. Adapting to losses of partner and friends. 5. Remaining oriented to present and future, not preoccupied with the past. 6. Forming new emotional ties. 7. Reversing roles of children and grandchildren (as caretakers). 8. Seeking and maintaining social contacts: companionship vs. isolation and loneliness. 9. Attending to sexual needs and (changing) expressions. 10. Continuing meaningful work and play (satisfying use of time). 11. Using financial resources wisely, for self and others. 12. Integrating retirement into new lifestyle.

SOURCE: C. A. Colarusso & R. A. Nemiroff (1981).

school, or started a new job. Women, then, may reassess their role commitments earlier in life than men. By their forties or early fifties, women with jobs or careers have typically achieved some occupational security, if not success, and can anticipate with varying degrees of satisfaction another 10, 20, or more years of employment. Some scholars believe that men, too, may no longer pause to reflect at mid-life. As psychologist Carol Ryff (1986) speculates, mid-life for today's middle class—the first generation to be well-educated and in dual-career marriages—may offer sufficient challenges that middle age will not be a period of personal reflection marked by the so-called crisis of past generations.

Another criticism of stage theories is that the year we are born may be much more important to our individual development than our chronological age. Some social scientists like Bernice Neugarten strongly advocate an *age cohort* explanation for how we develop—that people born during the same year or during a specific 5-, 10-, or 20-year period exhibit similar developmental characteristics based on the historical events they collectively experience. For example, people born during the Great Depression are said to look at life through a different lens than do the "baby boomers" born after World War II or "baby busters" born in the late 1960s and 1970s. The big news today is that the "boomers" have reached middle age. And the "busters" have graduated from college and are facing a bleak job market and a very real possibility that they will not be as economically prosperous as their more successful parents (see Table 7-2).

Finally, other researchers like Albert Bandura and Walter Mischel caution us not to ignore the way *events* in our own lives also affect how we develop. Getting a divorce, being fired from a valued job, going back to school, being widowed—any of these personal events can alter the course of an individual's life.

Adult stages cast development as unidirectional, hierarchical, sequenced in time, cumulative, and irreversible—ideas not supported by commanding evidence. The facts, instead, indicate that persons of the same age, particularly beyond adolescence, and the

TABLE 7-2

Profile of Baby Boom and Baby Bust Generations

The following profile of the baby boomers and baby busters are broad generalizations, a recognition of trends rather than exact descriptions of all members of those groups.

Baby Busters	Baby Boomers
■ Born between 1965 and 1975.	■ Born between 1946 and 1964.
■ 46 million, large enough group to fuel economic growth in mid-90s.	■ 80 million, largest generation ever, whose needs re-shaped society.
■ Grew up in two-earner households, or with separated, divorced parents.	■ Grew up in two-parent homes, mother was home-maker or employed parttime.
■ Feel angry, shut out, neglected, pessimistic about prospects for the future.	■ Overly credited with nation's successes, blamed for its ills. They are now the establishment, with one of their own as president.
■ Poor job prospects; recession, unemployment, fewer jobs after graduation.	■ Virtually unlimited job prospects after graduation.
■ Many are underemployed in low-paying service, "McJobs."	■ Many are in career or professional positions; some careers are peaking, others are crashing in the recession.
■ Return home to live with parents, fear they'll never own a home, are postponing marriage, are less family-oriented than boomers.	■ Delayed marriage and childbearing; have young children and older parents needing care and financial support.
■ Money spent on clothing, eating out, entertainment, travel, and other discretionary expenditures. Shop for quality and value, more conservative in finances than boomers.	■ Money spent on children's needs, saving for college, and own retirement. Family-, sports-, health-, and fitness-oriented expenditures.
■ Have a postindustrial thrift-shop look, flannel shirts, ripped or baggy jeans, and baseball caps.	■ Wear L. L. Bean, J. Crew, Dockers, and old blue jeans.
■ Like Grunge music; Nirvana, Red Hot Chili Peppers, Ice-T.	■ Are moving from rock and roll to country music; Garth Brooks, Trisha Yearwood.
■ Read *Spin, Details, Sassy, Entertainment Weekly.*	■ Read *Rolling Stone, Countryside.*
■ Socially liberal, comfortable with ethnic diversity, friendships with opposite sex.	■ Socially and politically more liberal than parents or children. Often uncomfortable in opposite-sex friendships.

SOURCES: L. F. Bouvier & C. J. De Vita (1991); L. Zinn, et al. (1992).

same historical period are undergoing different changes; one person may show an increase in certain attributes while another shows a decline in the same aspects of behavior and personality. (Brim & Kagan, 1980, p. 31)

It is very likely that future studies will verify the importance of stages, ages, and events in explaining our development as adults. It seems logical that when we are born, the structure of our lives—whether we marry, have children, are employed, as well as the people (relationships) and the circumstances we encounter along the way—all play a role in our development during adulthood (see the "Point of View" box). "Our adult years are marked by our shifting perspective on ourselves and our world—who we think we are, what we expect to get done, our timetable for doing it and our satisfactions with what we have accomplished" (Rosenfeld & Stark, 1987, p. 64).

Marriage and Family Development

The course of family life, like that of our individual lives, is also regarded by many as occurring in stages—the *family life cycle*—with each stage representing the

POINT OF VIEW

Suddenly I'm the Adult?

Several years ago, my family gathered on Cape Cod for a weekend. My parents were there, my sister and her daughter, too, two cousins and, of course, my wife, my son and me. We ate at one of those restaurants where the menu is scrawled on a blackboard held by a chummy waiter and had a wonderful time. With dinner concluded, the waiter set the check down in the middle of the table. That's when it happened. My father did not reach for the check.

In fact, my father did nothing. Conversation continued. Finally, it dawned on me. Me! I was supposed to pick up the check. After all these years, after hundreds of restaurant meals with my parents, after a lifetime of thinking of my father as the one with the bucks, it had all changed. I reached for the check and whipped out my American Express card. My view of myself was suddenly altered. With a stroke of the pen, I was suddenly an adult.

Some people mark off their life in years, others in events. I am one of the latter, and I think of some events as rites of passage. I did not become a young man at a particular year, like 13, but when a kid strolled into the store where I worked and called me "mister." I turned around to see whom he was calling. He repeated it several times—"Mister, mister"—looking straight at me. The realization hit like a punch. Me! He was talking to me. I was suddenly a mister. . . .

The day comes when you suddenly realize that all the football players in the game you're watching are younger than you. Instead of being big men, they are merely big kids. With that milestone goes the fantasy that someday, maybe, you too could be a player—maybe not a football player but certainly a baseball player. I had a good eye as a kid—not much power, but a keen eye—and I always thought I could play the game. One day I realized that I couldn't. Without having ever reached the hill, I was over it.

For some people, the most momentous milestone is the death of a parent. This happened recently to a friend of mine. With the burial of his father came the realization that he had moved up a notch. Of course, he had known all along that this would happen, but until the funeral, the knowledge seemed theoretical at best. As long as one of your parents is alive, you stay in some way a kid. At the very least, there remains at least one person whose love is unconditional.

For women, a milestone is reached when they can no longer have children. The loss of a life, the inability to create one—they are variations on the same theme. For a childless woman who could control everything in life but the clock, this milestone is a cruel one indeed. . . .

One day you go to your friends' weddings. One day you celebrate the birth of their kids. One day you see one of their kids driving, and one day those kids have kids of their own. One day you meet at parties and then at weddings and then at funerals. It all happens in one day. Take my word for it. . . .

One day I made a good toast. One day I handled a headwaiter. One day I bought a house. One day—what a day!—I became a father, and not too long after that I picked up the check for my own. I thought then and there it was a rite of passage for me. Not until I got older did I realize that it was one for him, too. Another milestone.

EXPLORATIONS *What events or "rites of passage" have occurred in your life to remind you that you are getting older?*

SOURCE: Excerpted from R. Cohen (1987).

performance of certain tasks and the accomplishment of certain goals (Mattessich & Hill, 1987). One of the tasks of early marriage, for example, is the establishment of the couple's own, independent residence. Later on, parental roles must be accommodated within the marital relationship.

Family Life Cycle Stages

There is no consensus among social scientists about the number of stages in the course of marriage. Most proponents of the family life cycle, however, use the age of the oldest child as a marker and identify four to eight stages. For example, Joan Aldous (1978) and

Mattessich and Hill (1987) discuss a family life cycle with seven stages: (1) newly established couples (childless couples), (2) childbearing families (families with infants and preschool children), (3) families with school-age children (one or more children are of school age), (4) families with adolescents (one or more children are adolescents), (5) families with young adults (one or more children are age 18 or older), (6) families in the middle years (children are launched from parental household), (7) aging families (parents are in retirement).

Here, we collapse these seven life stages into four to facilitate discussion of how the demands of parental roles affect marriage: the *newlywed marriage,* a relatively short period ending with the birth of the first child; the *parental marriage,* which lasts until the oldest child reaches adolescence; the *mid-life marriage,* sometimes called the empty-nest period because at this stage children go through adolescence and leave home; and the *later-life marriage,* which begins at retirement and ends with the death of either spouse.

Evelyn Duvall (1988) describes each family as having eight basic *developmental tasks*—responsibilities that must be accomplished to ensure the family's operation as a unit at all stages of its development (p. 131):

1 Providing physical care
2 Allocating resources
3 Determining who does what
4 Assuring that members are socialized
5 Establishing interaction patterns
6 Incorporating and releasing members
7 Relating to society through its institutions
8 Maintaining the morale and motivation of members

At various times in family life, events occur—parenthood, launching children, retirement—that, according to Duvall, shake up a family, compelling them to change the way they handle developmental tasks. These *critical transition points* are markers that occur just prior to each stage of the family life cycle as the family mobilizes for the next step in their development. Each stage is accompanied by particular tasks and stressors—problems that cause feelings of anxiety, frustration, or depression—that family members must learn to cope with.

As with theories of adult development, there has been some criticism of looking at the course of marriage from a stage perspective. Some family scientists

argue that each married couple is unique in certain ways and that the stage framework fails to take this into account. Not all couples, for instance, are the same age when they marry; some choose not to have children; with others, family size or the spacing of children creates unusual patterns. In fact, some individuals never marry at all, while others divorce and remarry and have children in both marriages.

Evaluating Stage Theories

Stage theorists agree that not all marriages go through the same stages, but they maintain that there is a fairly predictable progression of expansions and contractions in the size and complexity of most families, and that looking at how families negotiate and support these transitions is important (Carter & McGoldrick, 1989). Paul Mattessich and Reuben Hill (1987) argue that the life-cycle model applies to between one-half and two-thirds of all American families. Moreover, these authors have developed life-cycle models to show that single people and single-parent and remarried families, like intact two-parent families, progress through stages or sequences of development. They have also identified life-cycle stages of development in black families to provide evidence that race need not be ignored when using the family development approach to marriage and family studies. Black Americans, for example, are less likely to marry than are other population groups, and many black women have children but remain single for years or never marry. For these families, parenting is the first stage of the life cycle, followed by marriage as the second stage, with the third and all following stages very similar to those of other married groups (Mattessich & Hill, 1987). Most stage models continue to ignore possible socioeconomic influences on life stages.

Studying marriage from a family life cycle or developmental perspective provides a way of categorizing families who are experiencing similar events, facing similar transition points, and attempting to accomplish similar developmental tasks. The focus of the life cycle is on the process of change. Stages in the life cycle are identified not because they occur during the same chronological time frame in all families, but because they are marked by a distinctive role structure which clearly separates them from other periods in family life.

Because marriage and family life begin with the wedding ceremony, we start with an exploration of the symbolic nature of weddings and examine the social norms surrounding marriage and the implications of these norms for today's marital partners.

THE MARITAL AGREEMENT: A SOCIAL AND LEGAL COMMITMENT

About 30 years ago sociologist William Stephens (1963) defined *marriage* as a socially recognized sexual union, begun with a public announcement or ceremony, defined by an explicit contract, and undertaken with the intent of permanence. It might be added that marriage provides the social legitimation for bearing children. And in our own society, marriage is limited to unions between two heterosexual partners.

In the traditional wedding ceremony still followed by most couples, each of the elements in Stephens's definition is expressed symbolically. The ceremony functions as a vivid reminder of the power of tradition, the historical significance of the past. Almost all the symbolic details of the wedding ceremony have ancient roots—flowers, veil, rice, bridesmaids, and processional. The couple is *not* free to attach whatever meaning they please to the marital relationship. The wedding ceremony is more than a public announcement of a new status. It is society's way of reminding the bride and groom that obligations as well as rights are attached to their new status.

In the excitement and the pleasant confusion surrounding a wedding, not many people step back to notice the symbolic meaning of marriage. If they did, they might realize that the traditional commitment is not at all what many young couples today have in mind when they say "I do."

The Wedding Ceremony

The large congregation of family and friends who come together to help celebrate a marriage performs an indispensable function just by being present. Love, romance, sexual attraction—all the things that lead up to marriage—are private matters. But the wedding ceremony is a public act. It asserts that marriage creates new social bonds, as the presence of family members from both sides, whether or not they ever get together on any other occasion, demonstrates. During courtship, young couples typically have a great deal of freedom to do as they please, to withdraw temporarily from certain obligations and constraints. The friends

and family members assembled for the wedding are witnesses to the fact that the status of the couple has changed, that they have publicly entered into a commitment of considerable significance, one that cannot be casually dissolved. The vows between husband and wife are thus announced in public, which impresses upon them, as well as on those who attend the ceremony, the significance of the status transition.

Typically, the vows indicate more explicitly than any other part of the ceremony what the marital agreement is. The vows suggested in the Book of Common Prayer, for example, require the spouses to make a commitment that is both permanent and exclusive. He is asked: "Wilt thou love her, comfort her, honor her, cherish her, and keep her; forsaking all others, cleave thee only unto her, so long as ye both shall live?" She is asked to make the same commitment, with just one addition, to "inspire him." An important element of the contract is that it specifies rights, obligations, and role responsibilities. This is most explicit in the Jewish wedding, where the reading of the *Ketubah*—the Jewish marriage contract that specifies the obligations of the groom and what he can expect in return from the bride—serves as a reminder of the solemnity of the occasion and the gravity of the obligations that the newlyweds are agreeing on.

Traditionally, the wedding ceremony recognizes that the woman's status changes far more than the man's in the eyes of the community and the law. Notice that the father of the bride gives her away to the husband, and then the bride takes the husband's last name. Both acts symbolize the transfer of ownership. As writer Marcia Seligson points out, this assumption was expressed even more vividly in some marriage ceremonies in the past. In Russia, the father would hit his daughter gently with a new whip, and then hand the whip over to the groom (1974, p. 22). If the *patriarchy*—the social custom of recognizing the father as head of the family—implied in the act of giving the bride away can be dismissed as a curious antique, several other symbols in the traditional wedding fly in the face of contemporary beliefs and realities. For example, the ring placed on the bride's finger was originally a token of purchase. The rice showering down on the newlyweds as they leave the ceremony signifies fertility. And the veiled bride, dressed in white, is a symbol of virginal purity.

Weddings, after all, reflect the social, political, and economic tenor of the times. In recent years, some couples have noticed the gender bias implied by the symbolism in the traditional ceremony and have made alterations. In many ceremonies today fathers are not asked to escort the bride down the aisle; she walks alone or with both parents. Wedding dresses come in a variety of colors and styles, some with hats or floral hair accessories instead of veils. Bird seed or flower petals have, in some cases, replaced the rice. Rings are exchanged by both partners and vows are more often written and read by the couple themselves. Some of these changes reflect the concerns of today's older newlyweds, who want their wedding to reflect their unique relationship and mutual commitment. Parents are increasingly being displaced from positions of direct control as the bride and groom assume a more active role in financing and planning their wedding. Finally, many women are choosing not to change their last name.

But some elements of the traditional wedding remain basically the same, even if they take a slightly different form today. One implied constant is that marriage is a socially recognized sexual union. In certain cultures in the past, as Seligson notes,

> the wedding night involved public participation as much as the events preceding. Guests would follow the couple into the bedroom, the male attendants undressing the groom and tussling to capture the bride's garter; the parents would make elaborate fertility toasts over the bed; and cowbells, having been surreptitiously affixed to the mattress, would make joyful noise unto the activities that followed. It was not unusual for the "witness" to hang about outside until the first consummation was completed and the husband gave some public sign of satisfaction. (1974, p. 25)

Lustful, ceremonial sexuality remains a crucial part of the honeymoon plans of most newlyweds.

The Requirements of the Law

If many of the symbolic details of the wedding ceremony reflect ancient assumptions rather than current realities, so do the laws pertaining to marriage and family. It is an agreement undertaken not just between two individuals, but also between them and a silent third party, the state. Marriage is different from a civil contract, in which the contractors are free to define circumstances as they please and dissolve the agreement whenever they choose.

In the past, according to sociologist Lenore Weitzman (1985), there were five central principles or characteristics of a legal marriage (pp. 2–4):

1 Basic rights and obligations of husbands and wives were based on gender, creating a sex-based division of roles and responsibilities.

2 The husband was the head of the family; his wife and children subordinate to him.

3 Husbands and wives were constrained by moral vows to remain sexually faithful to one another.

4 Marriage was permanent: It was a joining together, for better or worse.

5 Spouses were engaged in a joint enterprise with the woman devoting herself to being a wife, homemaker, and mother in return for her husband's promising lifelong financial support.

All five provisions were based on the assumption that certain obligations and privileges should be assigned to men and others to women, regardless of their individual preferences or capabilities.

Until recently, then, marriage was no equal partnership in the eyes of the law, but rather an arrangement in which there was a strict division of labor according to sex. In various ways, the law stepped in to define the nature of the marital relationship. To justify state intervention in the marital relationship, jurists referred to landmark cases in which the state's "compelling interest" in marriage and family arrangements was first articulated.

But by the 1970s, popular conceptions of the "obligations and liabilities of marriage" had changed, and gradually the laws began to change to accommodate those newer conceptions. In 1979, a significant advance toward "gender-neutral" laws took place when the Supreme Court ruled that state laws specifying that husbands but not wives may be required to pay alimony were unconstitutional because they violated the equal protection clause of the Fourteenth Amendment. According to the majority opinion, written by Justice William Brennan, "The old notion that generally it is the man's responsibility to provide a home and its essentials can no longer justify a statute that discriminates on the basis of gender" (in *The New York Times*, March 6, 1979, p. A11). In one way or another, all states have changed their laws to make gender-based roles in marriage obsolete, though these changes do not prevent couples who wish to conform to traditional marital roles from doing so.

When couples marry today, each owes the other financial support. The courts recognize that couples may prefer the traditional arrangement, and allow them to decide in such cases which person—the male or the female—will be regarded as the "dependent spouse." In effect, the obligation of mutual support is a negative one. Neither the husband nor the wife may allow their spouse to become a public charge as long as he or she has the ability to support the spouse.

So the laws regarding marriage and family have changed dramatically since the 1970s. By suspending traditional assumptions about the proper roles for each spouse, the new laws allow a greater range of decision making for today's married couples. (In Chapter 14, we take a closer look at how these new legal arrangements affect divorce, child support, and the division of marital property.) For example, the marital pair now share more power within the marriage, reflecting the more equal earning capacity and greater economic independence of the spouses. Men of the nineties are more likely than their fathers to share household chores, child care, and daily decision making with wives. The "new man" is more cognizant of how personal well-being and marital satisfaction are tied to family roles. Women are more disposed than their mothers to negotiate for changing gender roles within the family. They are more often approaching the marital partnership with a recognition of their own worth as family providers and are less willing to accept as a given the overload of responsibilities connected with having a job and a family.

Individual Marriage Contracts

Looking at the divorce rate as an index of the number of failures produced by our present system of marriage, some have suggested that marital vows be written in the form of a legal contract—a *prenuptial agreement*. It appears that more couples have begun to specify in such a contract what their understandings and assumptions are regarding the marriage into which they are about to enter. In the past, such agreements were used mainly in cases where at least one of the partners had a substantial amount of money and did not want that estate to pass to the spouse or the spouse's family in case of death or divorce. Today, they are often used to protect the more economically powerful marital partner—the Donald and Ivana Trump divorce highlighted this use of an agreement. The purpose, in this case, was to limit how much money the ex-wife received. Such agreements usually contain provisions concerning support and living expenses, custody and child-care responsibilities, and division of property. The contracts are extensions of what we do every day in our free enterprise system.

Most courts, at first, were reluctant to allow prenuptial agreements to play more than a limited role in regulating the affairs of married people, so such agreements were rare. As long as marriage was regarded mainly as a status, it was the responsibility of the state—not of the couple about to enter into marriage—to define their obligations to each other. Recently, however, courts have begun to uphold such prenuptial contracts as legal and binding.

Another more informal way of defining individual expectations for the relationship is the *relationship agreement*. Couples who use this type of agreement seem to prefer it because it contains warmer and more flexible language, and is more lovingly crafted than a prenuptial agreement. It simply consists of the written expectations of the couple, put on paper where they can be read, then discussed and negotiated. It is not intended to be a binding, legal agreement. The most common goal of couples who choose to write their own personal marital agreement is to define such basic issues as economic expectations, plans for children, and career intentions. A potential advantage of designing a relationship agreement is that role responsibilities can be adapted to personal preferences and abilities, rather than the dictates of tradition.

New Priorities, Satisfactions, and Problems

New purposes and redefined functions have transformed the institution of marriage. One of the most significant elements of that transformation as discussed in Chapters 3 and 4, is an increasing emphasis on love and intimacy. As couples strive for a deeper understanding of one another, communication and shared roles become more important in marriage. In the past, companionship between spouses was not nearly so significant. As recently as the 1920s, this observation appeared in a report on life in a typical American city: "In general, a high degree of companionship is not regarded as essential for marriage. There appears to be, between husbands and wives of all classes when gathered together in informal leisure-time groups, relatively little spontaneous community of interest" (Lynd & Lynd, 1929, p. 118).

Over the past few decades, however, with the increasing emphasis on self-disclosure, negotiation, shared responsibilities, and mutual satisfaction, we are now influenced by a different set of ideals and assumptions. Without a doubt, many people derive from today's marriages a level of emotional closeness that

Spending leisure time together in a jointly pleasurable activity enables many marital partners to achieve a degree of companionship possibly not even desired by most couples in earlier generations.

yesterday's marriages only rarely delivered. It is also true that the demands placed on the marital bond vary across the marital life course, which makes living together and maintaining a satisfying intimate relationship more tenuous.

THE FAMILY LIFE CYCLE: MARKING THE MARITAL LIFE COURSE

The Newlywed Marriage: Creating a Partnership

People make many personal adjustments when they marry. Spouses accept certain cultural prescriptions for husband and wife roles—*role taking*—while working out discrepancies between each other's marital assumptions. They also actively create marital roles based on their own individual and couple values, needs, and goals—*role making*. As marital partners,

they must communicate expectations and negotiate workable strategies for resolving the inevitable differences that arise between them. There are other tasks of the newlywed period as well, such as establishing a pattern of sexual and emotional intimacy, deciding on the appropriate balance of marital and job responsibilities, and forming a new set of ties with the family and friends of one's spouse. In-laws, in particular, can exercise both a positive and negative influence on early marital adjustment. While supportive in-laws can advance the status of the marital pair within the extended family, lack of support can lead to trouble. At least four types of problems can arise in marriages due to in-law influences:

1 *Transition Dilemmas*—inability to make the transition from child status to adult status; hesitancy of the parents to release their married child from dependency.

2 *Boundary Disputes*—difficulty maintaining appropriate distance; parents constantly phone or drop by,

asking personal questions that invade the privacy of their adult child.

3 *Cultural Conflicts*—problem of parents objecting to new family rituals and/or religious practices instituted by their married child and his or her partner.

4 *Time Allocation*—problem of parents putting pressure on their adult child to spend time with them to the exclusion of other family members or friends.

The fact that divorce is more likely to happen in the earliest years of marriage than later on indicates that some couples discover their role-making incompatibility very quickly. One problem appears to be that new couples expect this process to occur naturally and immediately, not realizing that this activity requires work and continues throughout the marital life course.

In *The First Year of Marriage: What to Expect, What to Accept and What You Can Change* (1989), Samuel Pauker and Mariam Arond note that 49 percent of newly married couples have serious marital problems. They interviewed 346 women and men who had been married for between 1 and 18 months and found that 37 percent admitted that they were more critical of their partners since marriage and 29 percent said that they argued more often now than when they were dating. Further, 41 percent reported that they found marriage harder than they thought it would be.

These authors describe the beginning stage of marriage as a time when partners have to deal with their changing perceptions of each other and of the relationship (see the "Point of View" box). Partners start out idealizing each other and the marriage, then become disappointed as they face daily reality together, and, finally, come to realize that marital success depends on reconciling their dreams with the facts of married life. Marital partners, as opposed to mere dating partners or cohabitors, may feel entitled to certain advantages. For example, before marriage a man may have been proud and supportive of his beloved's frequent business trips to exotic cities. He may have phoned with romantic words of encouragement while she was away and, on her return, eagerly awaited descriptions of her adventures. As a married man, he may resent such frequent intrusions, extra household responsibilities, and missed supportive dinner discussions: "Shouldn't a wife be here when I need her?" Before marriage a woman may have accepted the bachelor evenings with the guys and football Mondays as rituals that revealed her beloved's masculine side. Once married, she may feel left out and lonely: "Shouldn't

a husband care about family time?" Spouses may also make some unsettling discoveries about each other: He's a "neatnik," while she's a slob; she likes vacations at the beach, while he prefers hiking and mountain camping; he thinks Sundays are for hanging out with his brothers at his parents' home—eating fried chicken or roast beef dinners and playing cards or pool, while she prefers bed-and-breakfast weekends and reading the Sunday paper until noon.

As Pauker and Arond write, "We enter marriage with great expectations, but marriage carries a high degree of scrutiny with it, so disappointment is inevitable" (p. 10). Newlyweds in successful relationships resolve their differences and eventually adapt to married life. They learn to tolerate imperfections in their partners and make a commitment to remain married and work through their problems as a couple.

Despite the inevitable disagreements and disappointments that greet most couples early in marriage, the satisfactions of this beginning phase of marriage are considerable. In fact, this stage of marriage is probably considered the happiest. Early marriage is in many ways a continuation of courtship. If the newly married couple discovers that they do not agree with each other in as many ways as they thought, they still enjoy many pleasures together, particularly shared activities and companionship. They prize individual responsiveness and have few role responsibilities that conflict with their being together. Because both have jobs in the majority of young couples, their combined income generally allows a more comfortable living than will be possible later, in the parental marriage.

The Early Parental Marriage: Is There Love after Baby?

For most couples, the newlywed phase is relatively brief compared to other marital stages. Before long, the couple's first child arrives. At this point, primary role responsibilities change abruptly, and so does reported marital satisfaction (Glenn, 1990). Most studies confirm that women report significantly greater marital dissatisfaction than men do at this stage, probably because of their greater responsibility for parenting.

The relationship between husband and wife changes in important ways with the birth of children. In the newlywed marriage, as we saw, interactions between marital partners are person-centered, stressing the individual traits of the spouses and how they mesh; parents, in contrast, soon begin responding to

Marriage Is No Longer "Two-Someness"

Columnist Ellen Goodman describes the difficulty wives and husbands face in maintaining their personal identities after marriage, while learning to create a couple identity.

We have been to weddings this season, a flight of them. The children of friends are getting married. The churches that we visit ring out with words about union, togetherness, two people becoming one.

At times, it sounds as if the style of marriage is still as rooted in tradition as the bridal gowns. A costume of lace and pearls appropriate for exactly one day.

Sitting in my place, a veteran witness of marriages—both first and second—I have come to wonder how much even our fantasies about perfect marriages have changed.

Once, the dream of an ideal union meant that a wife would follow her husband in obedient contentment. A successful marriage rested, or so it was said, on her willingness to fold her life into and under his.

A generation ago, the fantasy of marriage was rather like that of simultaneous orgasm. The marital achievement manuals said that a husband and wife should be in such perfect harmony that their bodies reached mutual pleasure whenever they touched.

Today, we don't approach relationships quite the same way. We leave more room for reality and for differences. Two people may become one couple but, even for those who stay attached, the coupling is looser than it once was.

Our new version of the fantasy is that two people can lead lives that are both separate and together, independent and synchronized. With a proper sense of timing, we want to believe that each of us can have whatever we individually want out of life—including each other.

Our daydreams, if we have them, conjure up scenes in which his chance to work in Oregon will be just what she dreamed about in her office in Missouri. That what they would choose for themselves is also happily best for each other. No one will have to be selfish. No one will have to be sacrificed.

each other more in terms of roles—in some cases even calling each other mom and dad. The responsibilities of parenthood often take precedence over the partners' relationship to each other. As one new father stated, "I keep asking her to get a sitter so we can go out for a quiet dinner, but she always finds a reason not to. It's like being turned down for a date week after week" (Cowan & Cowan, 1992, p. 61).

At least in this early phase of child rearing, when spouses are coping with the transition to parenthood and when infants make particularly heavy demands on the time and attention of their parents, husbands and wives commonly experience very mixed feelings. Many discover that they have underestimated the demands and difficulties of parenthood and the problems involved in balancing family and work commitments. Sociologist Norval Glenn (1991) notes that idealized expectations of marriage and uncertainty about the division of household chores and child care are two key

factors that contribute to marital dissatisfaction. Gender equity is an issue that arises again and again in these contemporary marriages, as the mother of a 6-month-old noted:

He wasn't being a chauvinist or anything, expecting me to do everything and him nothing. He just didn't *volunteer* to do things that obviously needed doing, so I had to put down some ground rules. Like if I'm in a bad mood, I may just yell: "I work eight hours just like you. This is half your house and half your child, too. You've got to do your share!" Jackson never changed the kitty litter box once in four years, but he changes it now, so we've made great progress. I just didn't expect it to take so much work. We planned this child together and we went through Lamaze together, and Jackson stayed home for the first two weeks. But then—wham—the partnership was over. (Cowan & Cowan, 1992, p. 63)

Wasn't this the marital success story that Michael and Hope left behind on the last episode of "Thirty-something"? The centrifuge of modern life threatened even this "perfect couple." They were spinning out of control—he to California, she to Washington, their marriage to divorce.

But at the last moment, the crash was averted. Magically, her need to work folded symbiotically with his need to break from work. The happy ending came without conflict or compromise. But real life doesn't always wrap up in the nick of time. The seams in our lives tend to show, stretch, and rip even the very models of seamless unions.

We face what Alva Myrdal, that remarkable Swedish woman of the world, called "the problem of two-someness."

A central theme in the stunning memoir that ethicist Sissela Bok has written about her mother, Alva Myrdal, touches on this: how difficult it is to lead a questing and individual life in context with another.

Alva and Gunnar Myrdal were in their lifetime the most heroic version of a contemporary marriage. Separately each had a brilliant career, indeed each a Nobel Prize. Together they had three children and a marriage that spanned 60 years, until her death in 1984.

They were defined publicly and often as a perfect modern couple. Yet Alva Myrdal, who began her marriage under the ideal of oneness in work and love, came to doubt that possibility. A writer, ambassador and cabinet minister who focused her formidable intellect to dilemmas ranging from family to disarmament, she came to describe herself and Gunnar more like "consort battleships, crisscrossing the world but stronger together."

Yet the question Myrdal repeatedly pondered was, "How do I become myself?" Her pursuit of "self" struggled within marriage and strained its bounds. Here is how her daughter describes the dilemma: "This problem arises each time two persons join their lives together: To what extent does each one then remain a separate person while also becoming part and parcel of the other's existence."

These are not words heard in a marriage ceremony. Weddings celebrate union. Today, the bride and groom are told, two people become one.

Well, not exactly.

It seems to me that sometime before the fifth or 10th or 20th anniversary, "couples" come to see themselves as fellow strugglers. And the best of them try hard to keep the seams from splitting under the pressures and pleasures of "two-someness."

EXPLORATIONS *What do you think makes the difference between the fantasy of "two-someness" in marriage a generation ago, and the reality of "two-someness" today?*

SOURCE: Excerpted from E. Goodman (1991).

Study after study document the fact that women are overwhelmingly and disproportionately responsible for the care of their children. "Women, especially those in the working class, report that their husbands are less likely to be confidants—to be there to talk to when needed—after the birth of the first child" (Ross, Mirowsky, & Goldsteen, 1991, p. 349).

What should not be overlooked is the growing sense of partnership that also develops between many spouses. In a recent study, a team of researchers looked at what happens to couples from the time a child is born until he or she is 3 years old. Much of their findings confirm the results of previous investigations. They observed a modest decline in the overall quality of marital life, especially in the period immediately after the birth of the baby. Although women reported more of a decrease in marital satisfaction than their husbands, both agreed that the romantic aspects of their marriages had dwindled significantly. "As they acquire a new role and the joys and burdens of that role," reported one of the investigators, psychologist Jay Belsky, "something's got to give. What gives is the marriage." But there is a growing sense of closeness as well. In Belsky's words, "Couples seem to give up romantic intimacy as they gain another source of affection" (*The New York Times,* January 6, 1985, p. C1).

What can new parents do to maintain intimacy and retain satisfaction with their marriage? Psychologists Carolyn Cowan and Philip Cowan, authors of *When Partners Become Parents* (1992), make some suggestions:

- *Share expectations:* Talk about each other's images of the ideal family. Discuss hopes and anxieties for the future. Do not be afraid to disagree on some key issues—knowing about differences as well as similarities better prepares partners to cope with both the positives and negatives of child rearing.

- *Plan regular interpersonal "checkups":* Bring up prob-

With the arrival of a child, romance between husband and wife may take a back seat, but for many there is the compensation of greater closeness.

lems and issues for discussion as they arise, but pick a time when both partners can have a quiet, uninterrupted talk. Avoid talking about issues when either partner is stressed out or overly anxious. Discuss only one problem at a time and give each person an opportunity to talk.

■ *Schedule time together:* Plan a time each week when both partners can spend an hour or two together. Make a date with each other and keep it.

■ *Regard problems as normal and negotiable:* Consider an argument about a program as a sign that something is amiss in the relationship. Take time to listen and gain information about what is wrong. Keep a positive attitude about your ability to work out differences.

■ *Do not ignore sex and intimacy:* Understand that a drop in sexual frequency is normal after childbirth. Find ways to express love and intimacy in a nonsexual manner. Hugs, cuddles, hand holding, and lingering touches are affectionate means of expressing love and caring in the harried, time-constrained first months of parenting. Call on supportive others who love babies and then take some time out.

■ *Find support outside the marriage:* Talk to friends or

find a support group. Sharing information with others in a similar situation gives strength.

■ *Find a balance:* Remember that children develop best in a home environment where parents are satisfied. Take time to meet personal and relationship needs. All family members need nurturing.

Parents at Mid-life: The Sandwich Generation

As a result of two trends—a more compressed childbearing period and a longer life expectancy—the couple who marry today can anticipate spending between 40 and 50 years together, many of them during middle age. The third stage of marriage, which begins when the oldest child is an adolescent and continues until all children eventually exit from their parents' home, has been referred to as the postparental period, the launching stage, and the empty-nest phase. All these expressions call attention to the transitions in parenting status that accompany mid-life. The term most often heard today is the more encompassing *sandwich generation*—referring to the mid-life couple positioned between the needs of adolescent children and the needs of aging parents. Adolescents seek greater autonomy and free-

dom from parental supervision, while retired parents face possible moves, health concerns, and the death of a spouse. The couple at middle age has the potential of experiencing stress, transmitted both up and down the generations (Preto, 1989). Meeting these new demands brings about shifts in marital, parental, and work roles. Compounding the nature of this dilemma is the realization by the couple of their own aging process.

The mid-life couple can look forward to a much longer period of being alone together than they enjoyed as newlyweds—over half their married lives will be spent with no children in the house. Time alone may cause new problems or allow new freedoms and a renewed sense of intimacy. Many couples report a revitalized kind of rapport that is most common among newlyweds, and marital satisfaction soars.

There is also reason to conclude that the mid-life marriage is a somewhat different experience for couples in different socioeconomic circumstances. Among working-class couples who have fewer financial resources than their middle-class counterparts, one of the major changes in the postparental years is that they are relieved of the financial burdens of child rearing. As a consequence of greater discretionary income, there is a discernible improvement in their lifestyle at this point. In families of lower socioeconomic status as well as among black and Hispanic families, the extended family network is a more prominent feature of family life. There is a greater likelihood in these families that grandparents will provide care for grandchildren and some economic support for the mid-life couple as well (Raup & Myers, 1989). Regardless of family

economics, however, parents report that adolescence is the most stressful period of child rearing and increased marital satisfaction is the result of the empty nest.

The Empty Nest: Is It a Syndrome?

There is much discussion about women experiencing an *empty-nest syndrome*—feelings of worry, dissatisfaction, loneliness, depression, and a sense of uselessness triggered by the departure of children. Indeed, it is women who have committed themselves primarily to the roles of wife and mother who may find themselves facing an empty nest with feelings of grief and sadness. Often, with little preparation or cultural support, they enter a period of their lives defined by a sense of rolelessness—of having fewer defined roles and responsibilities. At this time, such feelings are short-lived if women become more involved in community activities, return to school, or return to the workplace—replace mothering responsibilities with other satisfying activities. Overall, the departure of children does not typically cause any long-lasting psychological problems for mid-life homemaker mothers. For women who have been in the labor force for much of their adult lives, the transition to the postparental household is likely to be easier than it is for homemakers. The majority of employed women do not appraise the "empty nest" as traumatic. Their attitude is generally one of anticipation and pleasure of the additional time and energy available for personal, marital, and employment interests (Raup & Myers, 1989).

Today it is more difficult to know when children are truly launched. Studies indicate that there is little

The empty-nest syndrome is neither inevitable nor long lived. Indeed, many working mothers look forward to the redistribution of their emotional time and energy.

or no consensus among parents regarding what norms mark the transition to the empty nest. Most parents seem to view the launching of children as a gradual weaning process which begins in late adolescence and is punctuated by events like graduating from high school, leaving for college, finding a career, getting married. For most parents, however, the transition to empty nest is marked by their own perception of their child's movement toward independence and adulthood. Often, these perceptions are relatively independent of events like graduation or marriage (Barber, 1989).

Very little research exists on the empty-nest transition among men. The usual assumption is that men are relatively unaffected. Some men, however, report distress when their children leave home. Mainly they regret lost opportunities—not taking a more active fathering role. When sociologist Robert Lewis and his colleagues (1979) interviewed fathers about the empty nest, they found that most expressed either neutral feelings (35 percent) or some degree of happiness (42 percent). Nearly one-quarter, however, reported feeling unhappy. Fathers who had the most difficult time adjusting were those who had the most to lose. They tended to be older and thus had fewer years to share with their children; had fewer children and were more emotionally connected to each; perceived themselves as more nurturing, caring, involved fathers who felt a loss of identity when the caregiver role was gone; or

had less satisfying marriages and felt emotionally lonely once their children departed (Lewis, Freneau, & Roberts, 1979).

Most parents expect the empty nest to be irreversible. That is, once children leave home they rarely, if ever, return. This assumption is not being confirmed in the 1990s.

Children Returning Home: The Boomerang Kids

A trend that shows no sign of changing is the tendency of grown children to return to the parental home. Among mid-life parents aged 45 to 54, 45 percent have an adult child living at home (Aquilino, 1990) (see the "Dilemmas and Decisions" box). Returning children can interfere with marital satisfaction and some of the other positive aspects of mid-life—leisure and social activities, spousal interaction, employment responsibilities (Mancini & Blieszner, 1991). At this stage, then, it may be the *loss* of the once empty nest that causes problems both for parents and for their adult children. On the one hand, parents at mid-life must adapt to their children leaving home to lead autonomous, independent lives. On the other, once parents begin to enjoy the benefits of such changes in individual and marital roles, they may experience the returning adult children as a financial and emotional burden (Schnaiberg & Goldenberg, 1989). It is the unanticipated nature of these renewed responsibilities that presents the most problems. Parents know their children must eventually leave, so they anticipate, rehearse for, and adapt to this loss. When children return, it can be an unexpected event and thus may require another period of adjustment (Neugarten & Neugarten, 1987).

Is the return of an adult child always seen as a negative event? In a recent article, Aquilino and Supple (1991) explore that question using interviews with 609 mid-life parents. They conclude that when an adult child returns home, conflict may occur because the child wants to be treated with full adult status. Parent and child roles must then be renegotiated. This renegotiation can set the stage for closer parent-child relations when the child once again leaves home. Parental satisfaction is greater and the family functions better when parents join with their adult children in pleasurable activities and when children are more independent.

Aquilino and Supple indicate that race has no effect on the level of satisfaction experienced by mid-life parents when their adult children return home. Black

DILEMMAS AND DECISIONS

Boomerang Kids

"Your parents want you out of the house. They really want you out of the house. They are worried about you. They love you but, God, they want you out of the house." These sentiments were included in commencement addresses by comedian Bill Cosby at several universities (Wilcox, 1992, p. 83). The humor is directed at the trend of young adults in their twenties and thirties returning home to live with their parents—the "boomerang" kids. The reality is that for many "boomerang" children, financial independence is more difficult to achieve in this depressed economy.

The percentage of young adults living with parents is at the highest level in over 30 years, but the increase for men is much greater than for women (see inset figure). Some observers believe that more men return home so they can indulge themselves in a better lifestyle, while being pampered by their mothers, who do the cooking, cleaning, and laundry. Fathers are said to berate their sons for taking advantage of such mothering. These observations may have some validity in the case of homemaker mothers, but according to other

reports, boomerang males do their share of the household work and many pay rent to their parents.

The reasons for returning home are many and varied. Some are unable to find employment or do not earn enough to allow independent living. Others like paying low or no rent or utilities, so they can splurge on luxury goods. Single women are more inclined to share expenses with roommates rather than return home. Some "boomerang" children move home out of loneliness, others are not ready to be on their own, and a small number return to care for an ill parent.

Parents have decidedly mixed feelings regarding children returning home. They have more trouble adjusting to this change than do the children. Fathers usually have little understanding of the realities of the job market in the 1990s, and how it differs from their own youth, and tend to believe their sons are simply not trying hard enough to find jobs. Many feel the son should take a minimum-wage job after college if a career position is not immediately available. Single mothers, in contrast, appear to particularly benefit from a son's return. Sons in single-parent families share the household work and provide enjoyable companionship and a greater sense of safety for their mothers. Parents tend to allow sons more freedom to come and go and stay out late. Daughters experience more restrictions and parental concern with their safety and well-being.

Parents are torn between the desire to help their children and the loss of their own independence, but as Cosby said, most really do want their children out of the house!

EXPLORATIONS *Why are daughters more reluctant to return home? How might the family situation be different for them, compared to sons? Should parents and adult children come to some kind of binding agreements prior to living together, on sharing household work and expenses and putting a limit on how long the children can stay at home?*

SOURCES: J. Gross (1991); and M. D. Wilcox (1992).

All adults 25 to 34 years old, married and single, who were living with parents.

20%
15
10
5
0

1960 1970 1980 1990

Men
Women

mothers do have more disagreements with their adult children compared to mothers of other races. And even though black fathers experience greater conflict with their returning children, they also share more activities and report having more enjoyable times with their children than do fathers of other races.

Moreover, education has an important influence on a father's satisfaction in living with adult children. More highly educated fathers are less satisfied with "boomerang" kids. This is probably because these fathers have higher expectations for their children's success in beginning careers and achieving self-sufficiency. "Fathers may harbor stronger achievement demands for children than mothers." It is also possible that among middle- and upper-middle-class fathers "adult children create an impediment to midlife parents' desires for self-development" (Aquilino & Supple, 1991, p. 24).

Relationships with Grown Children and Grandchildren

The first wedding of an adult child sets in motion all kinds of feelings—reflections accompanied by strong emotions is the norm for mid-life couples at this time in their lives (McCullough & Rutenberg, 1989). The birth of the first grandchild is another milestone for marital partners at mid-life. Couples generally feel more content as grandparents when it happens "on time" in their lives—between the ages of 42 and 57. Early grandparents are more likely to be uncomfortable with their new role and to say that it interferes with their daily activities (Bengtson & Robertson, 1985).

Sociologists Andrew Cherlin and Frank Fursten-berg (1986), after interviews with 510 grandparents identified three styles of grandparenting:

1 *Remote*—interact with grandchildren in an unattached and distant way; have little direct contact with them

2 *Companionate*—interact with grandchildren in a relaxed, affable manner, but take almost no direct responsibility for them

3 *Involved*—take an active role in raising grandchildren, exercise considerable influence on their socialization and express definite expectations for their behavior

After surveying 99 grandfathers, gerontologist Vira Kivett (1985) concluded that most feel close to the grandchildren they have the most contact with. The grandparent role, however, is rated as less important to men than are their other life roles. The older the grandchild, the less close is the grandfather/grandchild relationship.

Overall, grandmothers seem to enjoy grandparenting far more than grandfathers. The more involved the grandmother is in the daily lives of her grandchildren and the younger the grandchildren, the greater is her satisfaction with her grandparenting role (Thomas, 1986). This is not to say that the interaction between grandparents and school-age children and adolescents does not provide sources of satisfaction. When adolescents are asked about their relationship with grandparents, they respond that grandparents play two significant roles in their lives—as a confidant, someone to discuss personal matters with (80 percent), and as a companion, someone to share activities with (70 percent) (Dellman-Jenkins, Papalia, & Lopez, 1987). All adolescents seem to share these views on the role of grandparents, regardless of race or ethnicity (Burton & Bengtson, 1985; Flaherty, Facteau, & Garver, 1987; Schmidt & Padilla, 1983; Wilson, 1984). Grandparents and grandchildren who see each other at least three times a year seem to enjoy a special bond that, unlike the parent-child relationship, is uncomplicated by duties, responsibilities, and conflicts.

Black grandparents, in contrast to white, tend to be more directly and actively involved in raising their grandchildren (Cherlin & Furstenberg, 1986). This is probably because more black grandchildren live in three-generation families where grandparents have greater parenting responsibilities (Beck & Beck, 1989). Black families, which are more often headed by separated, divorced, or never-married single parents, rely on grandparents as significant sources of family support (Taylor, Chatters, Tucker, & Lewis, 1991). Cultural norms in the black family appear to promote the giving and receiving of assistance and emotional sustenance both up and down the generations. Such support has a definite positive effect on grandchildren's educational and employment aspirations and achievements (Taylor et al., 1991; Wilson, 1989).

Parental Caregiving

Although the majority of older persons are relatively healthy and lead independent lives, increasing numbers of elders aged 75 and older means that more mid-life children are assuming caregiver responsibilities. Families are the "inner circle" of primary support for our oldest citizens, 90 percent of whom live in the community, not in nursing homes (Soldo & Agree, 1988). Usually, spouses care for each other as long as possible, and then an adult daughter or daughter-in-law takes responsibility.

Caregiving occurs within a context of family history. Because family members of all ages care for each other in a variety of ways, caregiving roles in mid-life are not necessarily unusual or unique, but are extensions of an existing family support system. Most families provide for each other both up and down the generations, and most adult children do not consider caring for their aging parents an overwhelming burden when they think of it from this perspective (Mancini & Blieszner, 1991; Walker & Pratt, 1991). Of course, caregiving responsibilities do have some negative aspects, and women tend to experience these negatives more directly because they, rather than men, are more

As the numbers of older Americans increase, the strain of caring for those who need help will become greater on their adult children of both sexes.

often responsible for helping parents (Dean, Kolody, Wood, & Ensel, 1989). But husbands of caregivers, too, feel the strain. Daily schedules, vacation times, and spousal interaction suffer and can negatively affect marital satisfaction (Kleban, Brody, Shoonover, & Hoffman, 1989).

Although many women are in the work force, the amount of caregiving they do themselves or make other provisions for has not substantially diminished (Walker, Thompson, & Morgan, 1987). According to a national survey on long-term care, 44 percent of women caregivers are employed and 12 percent gave up their jobs to care for an aging family member (Stone, Cafferata, & Sangl, 1987). Still, more frequently than in the past, families are working as a team to make decisions and take action rather than making these tasks the responsibility of one family member (Matthews & Rosner, 1988). It also helps that business and government are beginning to step in to provide more caregiver services for dependent family members. Some companies, for example, offer caregiver/companions who live in or work day or evening hours caring for older adults in the older adults' own homes. It is generally the older client's children who decide to hire such help. Mid-life children also make use of *adult day care*—staffed centers that provide care for certain hours each day, week, or month for an hourly fee (Ostroff, 1991).

Marriage in Later Life

Many more men than women are married after age 65 (see Figure 7-1). Women more often live alone (41 percent), with a relative (17 percent), or with a nonrelative (2 percent) ("A profile of older Americans," 1990). Fewer women are married for two basic reasons. First, 7 out of 10 outlive their husbands by several years and have less opportunity to remarry because of the marriage squeeze for the elderly (Treas & Bengtson, 1987). Their pool of eligibles is smaller because of the social trend for women to marry older men (who after age 65 are either already married or no longer living). Second, it is more socially acceptable for older women to live alone than in past generations. Older women today are more likely to have the income needed to sustain a single lifestyle (Smeedling, 1990). Most older people actually prefer to live alone rather than with relatives. This preference for single living extends across racial and ethnic groups. When gerontologists Judith Treas and Vern Bengtson (1987) asked older people whether they would prefer to live alone or with their children, 98 percent of whites, 83 percent of blacks, and 72 percent of Hispanics wished to live singly.

FIGURE 7-1
Living Arrangements of Persons over Age 65

SOURCE: A profile of older Americans. (1990). American Association of Retired Persons, p. 4.

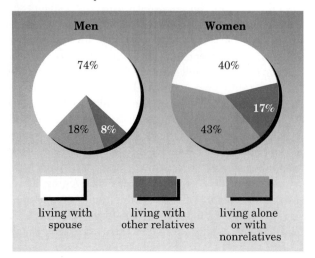

Family relationships continue to be very important in later life. Of older persons who are married and living with their spouses, most describe their marriages as providing a great deal of companionship and emotional support (Brubaker, 1991). They typically have had a long marital history together and have accumulated experience in dealing with various life events and transitions. Having been each other's companion for many years, in a variety of situations, and having developed unique ways of communicating and coping with stress as a team gives them a special bond (Brubaker, 1990). Two of the key adjustments faced by couples in later life are retirement and the loss of a spouse.

Retirement

The nature of the marital relationship before retirement will impact on how the couple adapts to increased husband-wife interdependence after retirement. At retirement, most men and increasing numbers of women reorient their interests and activities after years of making heavy investments in their occupational roles. Retirement generally means a substantial redefinition of household routines and responsibilities, except for full-time homemakers who really never experience retirement or a significant reduction in role responsibilities. For many couples, retirement means that husband and wife spend more hours together each day than they ever did before; even more than they did in the early years of marriage. Various studies describe retired men as less concerned about power, more reflective, and more oriented to the present than the future. They are also more interested in companionship and in turning toward the family (Zube, 1982).

We know far less about women's than men's retirement patterns because it is only recently that significant numbers of women were employed for much of their married lives and did, indeed, retire with pension plans and other financial perks of the workplace. We do know that most women and men look forward to retirement, though it brings a radically reduced standard of living. They find retirement satisfying, provided they are in reasonably good health and have an adequate income.

Retirement offers the hope of renewed intimacy, and many married couples report increased closeness in the later years of marriage. In fact, there is an interesting reversal that often takes place in this phase of marriage. Young married men frequently desire their partner's companionship less than young married women do. But in the retirement years, the tables turn. Researchers find that men who have been married for many years depend increasingly on their wives to organize their social lives after retirement. Such couples spend more evenings at home and enjoy more leisure activities together.

Many wives, however, feel that this is too much of a good thing. Blumstein and Schwartz describe a couple married for 33 years, and quote the wife on her surprise at realizing that she now has an overabundance of her husband's company:

> It's not like it used to be, I can tell you that. Used to be I would have to call around trying to find out where he was. Now he is just Mr. Homebody. I tell him to go out and look up those old buddies because I don't think he should be dependent upon me all the time. I don't need him to be around all the time. . . . Whoever thought I'd be complaining about too much of Manfred? (1983, p. 177)

Many family scientists have noted the shifting of power in marriages in later life. Men tend to become more affiliative and less competitive after they retire while women become more assertive and autonomous. Men more often look toward their family for close relationships while women more frequently look outside the family. Adult children also gain power with the extended family network as they provide more services to older adults within the family.

Nearly 50 percent of older adults have chronic health conditions that limit their activities (see Figure 7-2). Managing the costs of long-term health care can cause worry and anxiety for couples. Whichever spouse becomes the caregiver, the burdens on both partners can severely test the social and emotional bases of the marriage (Gilford, 1986). Of the many older women who give care to their ailing spouses, over 80 percent report that this role is stressful (Beckman & Giordano, 1986).

Other problems of the retirement years result from a legacy of stereotypes about what it means to grow old. Among the most serious misconceptions about old age—one that many older people share—is that sexual interests are abandoned as the years go by. It is often assumed that older men can no longer perform sexually. Jokes about sex among "golden agers" often reveal our squeamishness about a sensitive topic. Older couples sometimes take these attitudes to heart and feel guilty about their sexual urges.

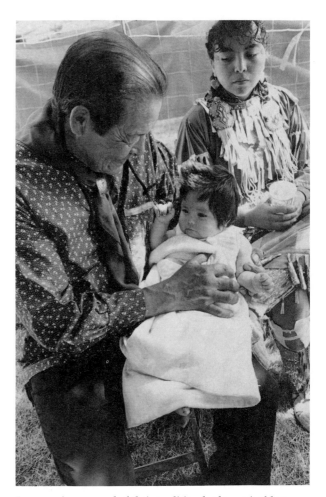

In a seeming reversal of their traditional roles, retired husbands tend to assign increasing value to close familial relationships while wives seek to extend their emotional lives beyond the family.

Couples in good health and with adequate incomes say that leisure and social activities are important to their life satisfaction. John Robinson (1991), a sociology professor at the University of Maryland, recently completed 600 interviews of people 65 and over for The Americans' Use of Time Project. He describes retired men as having 25 extra hours per week for leisure; women have 18 extra hours. Where does the extra free time go? Older men nearly double the time they spend on household tasks. Men aged 65 and older do over 40 percent of the chores, compared to 33 percent among men from 18 to 64. They cook an average of 24 minutes and clean about 18 minutes per day. Older Americans also tend to sleep longer. Nap time almost doubles for people over 65. But, surprisingly, television picks up the largest share of the older person's

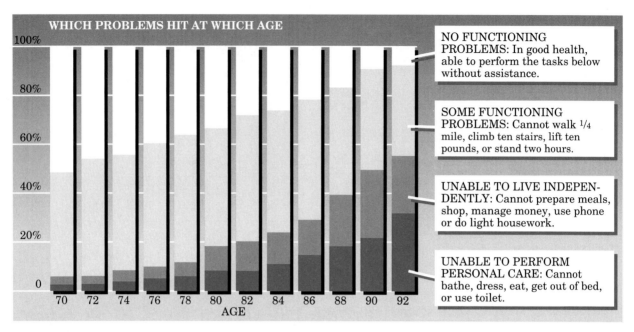

FIGURE 7-2
Health and Well-Being of Elderly Americans
Most people in their seventies are healthy enough to live independently; by their eighties, however, many need help. About 42%
of 70-year-olds live to be 85. But only one-quarter of 85-year-olds are in good health.
SOURCE: B. O'Reilly (1992).

free time (50 percent). Older men watch television 25 hours each week (older women watch it 22 hours) or nearly half their free time and 20 percent of the amount of time they are awake. Meal times also increase by almost 50 percent after retirement, but less time is spent eating out. On the other hand, older Americans spend more time walking than younger people do. Surprisingly, hobbies, outdoor sports, recreational activities, and visiting and socializing occupy about the same amount of time as they did in their earlier years. Increasing numbers are employed part time or do volunteer work. As people live longer and lead healthier lives, society's definition of old is being altered to incorporate a more active image.

Widowhood

As we discussed earlier, many marital partners eventually face the death of a spouse. This is not an easy adjustment, but the patterns of communication and support learned during marriage function to reduce distress during widowhood (Brubaker, 1991). Sociologists Gloria Heinemann and Patricia Evans (1990) propose that the process of adjusting to widowhood occurs in three phases (Figure 7-3). They emphasize

that adjustment occurs over an extended period of time and varies from individual to individual.

Phase One: Preparation. This period actually begins relatively early in life as individuals learn to cope with various life problems and crisis situations—moving to a new community, breaking off an old friendship, or divorcing a once-loved partner, to name a few. The skills and abilities accumulated from dealing with these earlier stressors prepare people to cope with later stressful circumstances. Individuals with more education and greater annual incomes seem to adapt better to widowhood. The main reason is that this group has more resources and thus more alternatives for solving life's problems.

During mid-life it is not unusual for individuals to begin to become concerned about the health and well-being of a spouse—to begin to anticipate loss. Loss may be sudden and unanticipated or gradual and expected. Partners who plan and make some changes in their lives in preparation for the eventual loss of one spouse, adapt more successfully to widowhood (Remondet & Hansson, 1987). Anticipating a loss may not affect the intensity of grief, but it positively affects

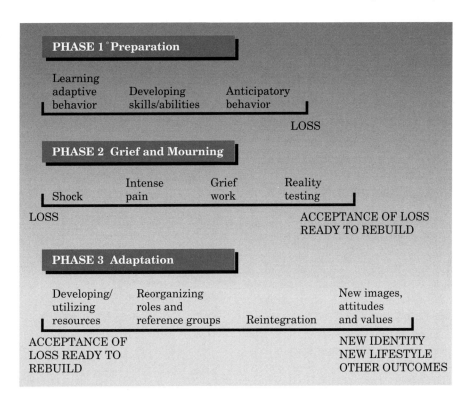

FIGURE 7-3
A Process Model of Loss and Change
SOURCE: G. D. Heinemann & P. L. Evans (1990).

long-term adaptation to the loss (Heinemann & Evans, 1990). Adult children and close friends and relatives, however, may resist an individual's need to plan for or anticipate loss because of their negative reactions to discussions of death and dying (Heinemann, 1982).

Phase Two: Grief and Mourning. This period begins with the shock of the loss and ends with acceptance and a resolve to rebuild one's life. During this phase of widowhood it is important for individuals to express the emotional and physical feelings of the loss by talking to others. Throughout this process, the widowed partner attempts to understand the loss and its consequences. Individuals who are not supported in this "grief work" have difficulty moving on with their lives and can remain in phase two for an extended period of time.

Phase Three: Adaptation. This is the time when individuals begin to set new goals and develop new skills and abilities for rebuilding their lives without

the spouse. Life regains meaning. Gradually, social roles and kin, friend, and community contacts are resumed. New values and attitudes may also emerge. The majority of widows adapt well and reestablish happy and meaningful lives; others "get by"; while a minority never recover from their loss. It is important to remember, caution Heinemann and Evans, that coping with loss is a very individual matter. And although there may be some differences in how women and men adjust to widowhood there are far more similarities. Both must establish new life patterns and both experience higher well-being if their health is good and their finances adequate.

The family development perspective is one way of studying marriage and families and the changes they undergo from the time they are formed until they dissolve (Aldous, 1990). The family life cycle is especially valuable in identifying events that normally happen within families—child birth, launching children, retirement, widowhood—and cause increased stress for family members. Most family members cope successfully with these predictable transitions in their lives.

And a majority report that their marriages remain satisfying over the life course.

OF TIME AND DISENCHANTMENT: THE SATISFACTIONS OF MARRIAGE

In previous sections of this chapter we raised the question: What happens to individuals and marriages over time? We looked at stages of adult development as well as the various stages of the family life cycle, and drew upon descriptive accounts to understand the characteristic stresses and rewards of each of these stages. Our next questions are: What happens to marital satisfaction over time? What are the ingredients of successful marriages? If we could identify the elements of a successful marriage, wouldn't it be possible to avoid less-than-successful ones?

Mary Anne Fitzpatrick (1988), Director of the Center for Communication Research at the University of Wisconsin-Madison, notes that marital success is usually defined as "marital stability" or "marital satisfaction." *Marital stability* is interpreted as whether a couple in a given marriage remain together, instead of separating or divorcing. *Marital satisfaction,* in contrast, refers to how marital partners evaluate the quality of their marriage. It is a subjective description of whether a marital relationship is good, happy, or satisfying. Various names are used to identify satisfaction in marriage: marital happiness, marital quality, and marital adjustment are employed most frequently. Hundreds of studies of marital satisfaction have been published since the 1970s. If these studies are at least a generally accurate portrait of marital satisfaction, they provide impressive and consistent evidence that most American couples rate their marriages as very satisfactory. Moreover, the research over the years agrees that the key factor determining feelings of satisfaction or dissatisfaction, for both males and females, is the stage of life that they are passing through; more specifically, whether or not they have children and if those children have left the parental home (see Figure 7-4).

As we saw earlier, marital satisfaction begins to decline after the unscripted spontaneity of the newlywed period. As the marital partners become more involved in parenting and take on expanded job responsibilities, companionship declines along with common interests and demonstrations of affection. Eventually marital satisfaction increases after the children are launched and the parents have the house to themselves again.

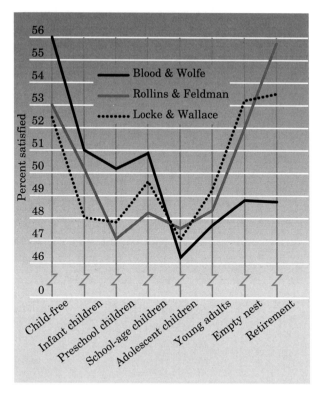

FIGURE 7-4

Marital Satisfaction over Stages of Family Life Cycle
Several investigators (Locke & Wallace, Rollins & Feldman, and Blood & Wolfe) have reported that satisfaction declines in the middle years of marriage, but returns to its previous high level during the postparental period.

SOURCE: Adapted from B. C. Rollins & K. L. Cannon (1974).

As Glenn concludes, the "relationship between family stage and some aspects of marital quality is about as close to being certain as anything ever is in the social sciences" (1990, p. 823). More specifically, Glenn contends, "The percentage of persons still married who say their marriages are 'very happy' goes steadily and appreciably downward . . . for at least the first 10 years and maybe for 25 years or longer" (p. 825).

In recent years, researchers have tried to identify the specific connection between the presence of children and marital dissatisfaction. According to Glenn, when couples have children, the level of spousal interaction decreases, family finances are strained, and the division of labor becomes more traditional—husbands share fewer of the household tasks.

It may be that in a society in which values are highly individualistic . . . and in which marriage is expected to involve a high degree of emotional and sexual intimacy and to be the spouses' primary source of companionship, there is an inherent tendency for children to lower marital happiness and satisfaction, whether or not they are planned and wanted. Children tend to interfere with marital companionship and to lessen the spontaneity of sexual relations, and their presence in the family creates the potential for jealousy and competition for affection, time, and attention. (Glenn & McLanahan, 1981, p. 420)

Many couples stay together during the parenting stage of marriage "for the sake of the children." They balance the needs of the family against their own personal needs and persevere out of a faith in the future—things will get better over time as the children mature, finances improve, and they have more time to spend together. As the years go by, personal satisfaction with the marital relationship comes to depend less and less on one's partner. It may not be because of a lower estimate of the spouse but because there are alternative sources of satisfaction both inside and outside the marriage—children, kin, friends, colleagues at work, and so forth.

Another reason for declining marital satisfaction is that spouses interact more in terms of roles—husband/wife, mother/father—than in terms of their unique personalities. She has a need to feel in control of everyday events; he feels distant by the end of the week and wants lots of affection and togetherness on weekends. In many of the marital enrichment programs that have been initiated across the nation in an attempt to revitalize marriages, one of the objectives is to help spouses remain personally sensitive and responsive to one another. Spouses who manage to maintain companionship and emotional commitment continue to respond to each other's personal traits and needs, despite the demands of occupational and parental roles.

Problems in Assessing Marital Success

Among the many criticisms of the research on marital success, two stand out. First, any assessment of success in marriage depends on self-reports. That is, the subjects themselves judge how satisfactory their marriages are. But how accurate are their subjective judgments? How honest are their answers to personal questions asked by strangers? Some people do candidly admit a lack of satisfaction; but studies based on self-reports undoubtedly underreport marital dissatisfaction.

A second criticism of such studies is that the con-clusions reached are heavily influenced by the specific meanings they attach to key words. What one person means by expressions such as "marital success," "adjustment," "happiness," or "satisfaction" is probably quite different from what those words mean to another person. Since there is no general consensus about the meanings of these words, researchers try to give them a fixed definition—but not necessarily the same definition applied by other researchers.

The success of a business enterprise or baseball team can be measured by a single, widely agreed-upon goal such as profits or games won. Marriages, however, have many different goals, not all of them consistent with each other. Attempts to measure such illusive qualities have not always been well received. There are many difficulties in applying an objective yardstick to so subjective an experience.

Fitzpatrick (1988) points out that surveys on marital satisfaction generally ask questions about the amount of spousal conflict; extent of partner agreement on the importance of certain beliefs, views, or values; how often the couple do things together; how happy the partners rate the marriage; and whether they think the marriage will last. One of the most frequently used scales for measuring marital satisfaction is the Dyadic Adjustment Scale (DAS) (Spanier, 1976). The DAS defines marital satisfaction as having four components: consensus, cohesion, expressions of affection, and satisfaction. As Fitzpatrick explains (p. 34):

- *Consensus* deals with the couple's perception of how much agreement they share on 15 important marital issues, including philosophy of life and child rearing.

- *Cohesion* refers to how often a couple work together on a project or have a good time together.

- *Expressions of affection* deal with whether a couple ever have disagreed about sex or other displays of affection.

- *Satisfaction* includes an estimate of how often spouses have serious disagreements in the marriage, and also how committed each person is to remaining in the marriage.

One of the major shortcomings of the DAS is that the scale assumes that marital disagreements, leaving the house after an argument, or being too exhausted for sex are harmful to marital satisfaction. Not all couples or all researchers see these factors as negative. Conflict, in many marriages, means partners are trying to work out their problems. Leaving the house after an argument is endorsed by some stress theorists and marital therapists as a positive way to cool down when anger gets in the way of resolving an argument—as long as the withdrawal is temporary and the problem is eventually dealt with. Being too tired for sex is a normal circumstance for dual-earner couples with young children.

In her own research, Fitzpatrick has found that the primary factor that separates happily from unhappily married couples is how well they communicate with each other. People who report being happily married can resolve their problems and communicate their feelings to each other. Such couples interpret each other's nonverbal communication very accurately (see Chapter 11 for a detailed discussion of marital communication). Differences of opinion about how to define and measure marital success will continue as researchers search for ways to assist couples who wish to maintain successful relationships.

Marital Stability and Marriage Type

One way of learning more about marital satisfaction is to study marriages that have lasted over time and gather useful information that can be passed on to other couples. A few researchers have identified people in long-term marriages, surveyed them, and then drawn conclusions about marital success. The consensus is that there is no one type of marriage that has consistently been found as more likely than others to remain stable and satisfying over time. Many marriages are not satisfactory to the marital partners, yet they last for many years. Other marriages are considered satisfactory by the partners but for one reason or another break up.

One of the first attempts to identify marriage types and relate them to marital success was conducted by John Cuber and Peggy Harroff (1968). They interviewed a sample of over 400 married upper-middle-class Americans, between the ages of 35 and 55. Using data from the 211 people who had been married at least 10 years without ever having considered divorce or separation, they were able to describe five marriage types: (1) *conflict-habituated*, (2) *devitalized*, (3) *passive-congenial*, (4) *vital*, and (5) *total* (see Figure 7-5).

Remarkably, these authors concluded that marital partners were not all looking for the same qualities in marriage. As long as their personal needs were met by the marriage, they were relatively content and rated their marriages as satisfying. Cuber and Harroff found

FIGURE 7-5
Marriage Types

SOURCE: Adapted from M. A. Fitzpatrick (1988).

Utilitarian	
Conflict-Habituated	• Fight often, but rarely settle anything.
	• Incompatibility and tension are pervasive
Devitalized	• Were once close, now have no "spark."
	• Time together is routine, mostly involving duties and responsibilities.
Passive-Congenials	• Rarely argue, find marriage convenient and orderly.
	• Share common interests, are involved in community, children, and careers.
Companionate	
Vitals	• Are intensely bound together in life matters.
	• Thoroughly enjoy each other's company and prefer activities that they can do together.
Totals	• Are more intensely and intimately involved than vitals.
	• Share every aspect of each other's lives; whenever possible, do everything together.

SNAPSHOTS

Making Love Last

"Although we were considered a close couple, it was very important to the both of us to have private time, our own interests, and our own friends outside of the marriage."

"Next to communication, I think that taking good care of myself and my own needs was the most important thing in making our marriage work."

"I'd have to say that being able to say 'I'm sorry or I was wrong,' and being able to compromise was the most important thing in our marriage."

When older widows who reported being in "happy" marriages were asked what made love last, their comments reflected two common themes: partners should have independent interests, finding fulfillment both inside and outside the marriage; and communication and compromise keep marital partners from drifting apart.

EXPLORATIONS *Do you think these women's comments are still relevant for young couples today?*

SOURCE: Excerpted from V. J. Malatesta (1989).

that 5 percent of the marriages they studied were total, 15 percent were vital, and the remaining 80 percent consisted of the other three types—referred to collectively as "utilitarian." Utilitarian marriages were described as practical arrangements that offered a considerable amount of security and stability. These types of marriage may be well-suited to the social and historical climate of contemporary times. They may also be a reflection of how marital needs change across the life course. The vital and total marriage types seem especially appropriate to the early and later years of marriage when couples spend more time together and the needs for partner companionship and intimacy are greater. The devitalized and passive-congenial marital types seem to describe couples in their middle years, when parenting, work, and community roles seem to take precedence over marital roles. For parents, the utilitarian marriage may be exactly right. Employed parents may cherish practicality, dependability, and stability. It could be that educated, financially comfortable, middle-class couples without children (or whose children have been launched) have the best chance of building vital or total marital relationships.

In a more recent study, Robert and Jeanette Lauer (1986) surveyed 351 couples who had been married for 15 years or more. The couples were asked what factors

accounted for the success of their long-term marriages. Those who rated their marriages as happy thought of their partners as "best friends" and were highly committed to maintaining the relationship. When asked what spousal qualities were most important to marital success, they replied, "caring, giving, honesty, and having a sense of humor" (p. 387).

Although happy couples noted high and low points in their relationships, they were willing to tolerate hard times and work through the difficulties. When solving marital problems, the couples recommended "attacking the issue and not the mate, maintaining calmness and flexibility, and keeping the issues in perspective" (p. 388). Happy marriages were not problem-free or untroubled. The key to their marital success was the partners' refusal to allow early dreams of successful marriage to be undermined by the realities of marital problems (see the "Snapshots" box for the reflections of some middle-aged and older widows on marital success).

Many of the problems in marriage today stem from the high expectations that people bring to it. In societies where spouses do not expect to be friends, companions, lovers, and otherwise emotionally interdependent partners, marital dissatisfaction is far less likely to cause problems. But most Americans would look at such marriages as empty and unfulfilling, devoid of intimacy. Perhaps as people approach marriage with somewhat more realistic expectations, greater awareness of its complexities and deeper understanding of how individual and family needs and tasks vary as the marriage progresses over the life course, they will be better prepared for the continual adjustments required. As family historian Tamara Hareven (1987) explains:

Changes in the structure of the household and in the age of its members are affected to a large extent by the movement of family members through their prescribed roles over the course of their lives. . . . Studying the family life cycle offers an effective way of examining the family as a collective unit, engaged in various activities and decisions, which change in relationship to the roles and the social characteristics of its members and in response to external conditions. (p. 45)

SUMMARY POINTS

■ The developmental perspective for explaining behavior is based on the assumption that individuals as well as marriages and families change throughout the life course.

■ Erik Erikson and Daniel Levinson were among the first researchers to propose stage theories of adult development.

■ Researcher Carol Gilligan maintains that stage theories of adult development are based on studies of men and thus fail to take women's perceptions into consideration.

■ Among the criticisms of stage theories of adult development are complaints that the effects of history on age cohorts and the impact of life events on individuals are not given adequate consideration.

■ Evelyn Duvall was among the first scholars to suggest that the family life cycle was a good representation of marriage and family life across time. The family life cycle offers a way of studying the systematic shifts that occur in marriage and family life.

■ Developmental tasks are the basic responsibilities that family members must take on in order to operate effectively as a family unit.

■ Critical transition points refer to events that occur just prior to each stage in the family life cycle. For example, the birth of a child signals the movement of a family from the newlywed stage to the parental stage of marriage.

■ The family life cycle is usually conceptualized as having four to eight stages. This chapter discusses the marital relationship across four stages: newlywed marriage, parental marriage, mid-life marriage, and later-life marriage.

■ Marriage is not only a personal commitment between partners, it is a social and legal commitment to the larger community.

■ The wedding ceremony has many symbolic details—a veil, rice, the processional, the father "giving away" the bride—that are based on traditions from past generations.

■ The marriage license is a contract between partners that specifies rights, obligations, and role responsibilities.

■ When couples marry, each partner is held accountable for the financial support of the other.

■ Marriage today is based less on carrying out the traditional roles of husband/father, wife/mother and more on provision of emotional intimacy through communication, shared roles, and interdependence.

■ Marital satisfaction drops off with the birth of the first child and rises again after children depart from the parental home.

■ Sometimes the mid-life couple is called the sandwich generation because married partners not only have their own mid-life developmental needs to meet, but are also called upon to meet the needs of their children and those of their aging parents.

■ The mid-life crisis, or empty-nest syndrome, is mostly based on modern stereotypes of the struggles of past generations of middle-class men and women in traditional marital roles.

■ Sociologists Andrew Cherlin and Frank Furstenberg identify three types of grandparenting: remote, companionate, and involved.

■ Caregiving is something most family members do for one another. It has been stereotyped as an extremely burdensome activity that is carried out only for dependent elderly family members.

■ In later life, men become less competitive and more relationship-oriented while women become more assertive and independent.

■ In later life, many individuals feel a need to discuss and plan for their eventual death. Younger family members may find it difficult to listen to and cooperate with their elders at this time, but it is important to overcome such feelings for the sake of the older family members.

■ Marital satisfaction refers to how a person describes and evaluates the quality of his or her marriage.

■ Married couples who interact more on the basis of roles rather than on personal characteristics and individual needs usually rate their marriages as less satisfactory than do other couples.

■ The Dyadic Adjustment Scale is the most frequently used instrument for measuring marital quality, but it has been criticized by some researchers.

■ Cuber and Harroff found five basic types of marriage: conflict-habituated, devitalized, passive-congenial, vital, and total.

■ Currently there is no one type of marriage that can accurately be described as more stable than others, but family researchers continue to ask partners in long-term marriages for the "secrets" to their marital success.

KEY TERMS

Institution	*Marriage*
Developmental theory	*Ketubah*
Age cohort	*Patriarchy*
Family life cycle	*Prenuptial agreement*
Critical transition points	*Relationship agreement*

Role taking	*Companionate grandparent*
Role making	*Involved grandparent*
Sandwich generation	*Adult day care*
Empty-nest syndrome	*Marital stability*
Remote grandparent	*Marital satisfaction*

REVIEW QUESTIONS

1. What is developmental theory and how does it apply to the individual? To families?

2. Why are stage theories of adult development criticized?

3. What is the difference between "baby boomers" and "baby busters"?

4. What is the family life cycle and why is it criticized by some observers?

5. Discuss how marriage is a social and legal commitment as well as a personal choice.

6. Describe how the newlywed marriage differs from the parental marriage.

7. Why is the couple in a mid-life marriage sometimes referred to as the sandwich generation?

8. Is the "empty-nest syndrome" real?

9. What does the term "boomerang child" mean? What is the effect of this phenomenon on parents? On adult children?

10. Describe the three styles of grandparenting. Identify gender differences in grandparenting.

11. How does retirement affect marriage in later life?

12. What is marital satisfaction? If you were to investigate marital satisfaction, how would you proceed? What questions would you ask? What groups would you study?

8

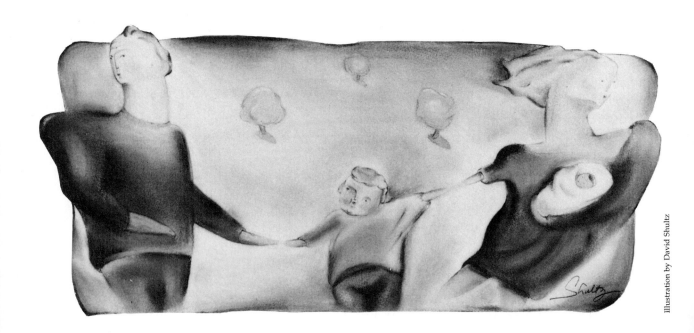

Parenthood

Until recently, one could hardly speak of marriage without implying parenthood. For married couples, having children was less a choice than an inevitability. Both the sacrifices and the satisfactions of parenthood were largely taken for granted. The prevailing image of parenthood in America consisted of a married mother and father and their biological children. During the last three decades, this reference family has undergone change and their definition has been broadened by the realities of contemporary times, making the lives of parents and children today far different. Household living arrangements, child-rearing attitudes, and parenting behaviors have been irrevocably altered by a number of demographic, social, and economic trends. Today, it is no longer easy to take the institution of parenthood for granted, or to assume a certain constancy in how each generation performs the task of preparing for the next.

Accordingly, much of this chapter is a study in contrasts, a profile of differences between the postwar generation and the current generation. In many ways, the parents of these two generations have made remarkably different decisions about such matters as family size, the timing of childbirth, and child care. We consider child-rearing patterns and how they have changed, discuss new options for parents, and explore parenthood without marriage. We begin with a snapshot of the postwar generation and the factors that have contributed to the much heralded baby boom, and then compare the assumptions and patterns of that generation with the current one.

FERTILITY: A STUDY IN CONTRASTS

The Baby Boom

The big news in 1946 was not just that things were returning to normal after World War II. Aspirations that had been bottled up for more than 15 years—through the Depression years as well as the war—were being revived. Chief among them was the desire for families, *big* families. Throughout the 1920s and 1930s, American fertility had declined. In fact, not enough women were born during the Depression to replace the women who were leaving the childbearing age. There was ominous speculation at the time about "incipient decline," about the implications of a dwindling population. By the end of the war, that concern was widely shared. In the words of the editors of *Life* magazine, "without exception, every country in the Western world is dedicated to the policy of 'more babies.' "

When, in 1946, 3.4 million babies were born in the United States—an all-time high, 20 percent more than in 1945—that was regarded as very good news. The following year, American births soared to even greater heights, to a grand total of 3.8 million. Then, when the birth rate slipped back in the next 3 years to somewhat lower levels, demographers speculated that the postwar baby boom was over, that American families had accomplished what they had deferred during the war years. But as the events of the next few years would prove, the postwar surge in births was no short-term phenomenon. Instead, it was the first manifestation of a demographic tidal wave that would affect all classes and races in American society for nearly two decades.

Several trends combined to create what would soon be dubbed the "baby boom," among them sustained prosperity and a renewed faith in the future. Not only were more Americans marrying, but they were marrying younger. The median age of marriage for women declined sharply after the war, to a historic low of 20.1 in 1956. More American women were prepared to have babies during the physiological peak years for childbearing, ages 20 to 24, thus allowing larger families. Moreover, the typical couple of that era didn't wait long to begin childbearing. By the late 1950s, the median interval between marriage and first birth declined to 13 months—an all-time record.

That era is accurately described as the age of the *procreation ethic* (Jones, 1980). In a variety of ways—from subtle, unspoken assumptions about the obligations of married couples to bear children, to blatant paeans to motherhood—pronatalist pressures were everywhere. To be sure, most societies encourage couples to have children. But during the postwar years those themes were particularly pronounced. It was often assumed that the lives of men as well as women were incomplete if they did not have children.

Throughout the 1950s, as the baby boom accelerated, in the words of *Fortune* magazine, "Americans are merrily reproducing themselves at an unprecedented rate." In each year between 1954 and 1964, more than 4 million babies were born. All told, some 76 million babies—almost one-third of the nation's current population—were born between 1946 and 1964. Ever since, the influence of that unprecedented childbearing binge has been pervasive. And its effects will continue until sometime after the middle of the twenty-first century, when the last member of the baby-boom generation dies.

The Baby Bust

The postwar era of the procreation ethic was followed by a period in which childbearing came to be regarded in a distinctly different way. By the early 1970s, due in part to the increased use of new contraceptive technologies, more people began to think of childbearing as a matter over which parents could exert a good deal of control. Whatever the source of the new ideas about childbearing and family size, preferences changed dramatically. In 1973, 43 percent of Americans favored families consisting of three or more children; by 1990, that was the preference of only 29 percent. Since the early 1970s, surveys have shown a growing preference for families that consist of no more than two children (Gallup & Newport, 1990) (see Figure 8-1).

Moreover, there is more support now for couples who choose to have no children. Still, voluntarily childless couples are rare. The Census Bureau currently projects that only about 10 percent of married women deliberately forgo childbearing. The main reason for the decline in the childbearing rate is not that many couples have decided to forgo having children, but rather that most couples are having fewer children than their parents.

Despite the decline in fertility after the mid-1950s, in the late 1960s and 1970s there was anxious speculation about a *population bomb*—the large number of women of childbearing age, the products of the baby boom. Its explosive potential was explained by observers who pointed out that in 1980 there were about 1 million American women aged 44; in comparison, there were about 2 million women aged 24. If the women of the younger generation chose to have babies at anything like the rate of their mothers, there would be a baby boom of staggering proportions. Some referred to it as an echo effect, and worried about the shock waves it would send through the schools and

In the United States, the baby boom was fueled by peace, prosperity, and optimism.

then the rest of the society. But by 1986, when the youngest members of what came to be known as the "baby-bust" generation turned 21 and entered their peak childbearing years, it was clear that there was little reason for concern. The birth rates of the current generation have turned out to be far lower than those of the previous generation.

When a husband and wife decide to have no more than two children, it may not seem a particularly important decision. But when an entire generation decides to do so, the implications extend far beyond family life. The typical mother of the baby-boom era had more than three children. The fertility rate reached its postwar peak of 3.7 children per woman, on average, in 1957 (U.S. Center for National Health Statistics, 1976). Then it steadily declined. In 1972, the rate fell below 2.1 children per woman, which is defined as the *replacement level*—the number of children one generation must have in order to replace itself with a generation of equal size. The rate remained below 1.9 until 1988 when it rose slightly. Today the fertility rate re-

mains below 2.0 (National Center for Health Statistics, 1992).

What has happened, then, is a striking reversal of several of the childbearing patterns of the postwar era. The typical parents of the current generation not only are choosing to have fewer children but are choosing to have them later. *American Demographics* magazine predicts that the number of families with children will decrease 12 percent between now and the year 2000 (Exter, 1990) (Table 8-1). Recent reports from the Census Bureau show that older women—those between 30 and 34 years of age—are the only ones whose rate of childbearing has been rising. This group of women who delay childbearing includes a high percentage of unusually well-educated women. The majority are established in their careers and after giving birth return quickly to the workplace. As might be expected, the longer a woman postpones motherhood, the fewer children she ultimately has.

It takes some time for lower fertility rates to translate into population decline. Even though the fertility

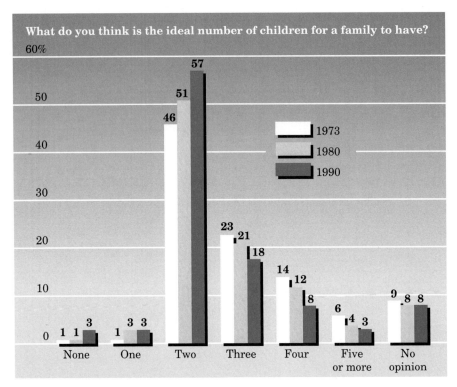

FIGURE 8-1
Changes in Ideal Number of Children
SOURCE: G. H. Gallup & F. Newport (1990).

rate may remain low compared to what it was in the 1950s, the U.S. population will continue to grow because the number of women in their childbearing years is so much larger than it was in the past. At the current fertility rate, which is below the replacement level, the American population will continue to grow until at least the middle of the next century. These trends differ slightly, depending on racial and ethnic patterns (see Figures 8-2 and 8-3).

The Contraceptive Revolution

One of the chief reasons fertility rates have declined so rapidly over the past two decades is that effective contraceptive methods have come to be so widely used by married couples. In 1965, the leading contraceptive methods were the pill, condoms, the rhythm method, and the diaphragm. The last three of these rank among the less effective contraceptive methods, with relatively high failure rates.

In just 8 years, from 1965 to 1973, the proportion of married couples using more effective birth-control methods (sterilization, the pill, or the intrauterine device) soared from 38 to 69 percent. Since then, although there has been an increase in the use of sterilization and a decrease in the use of the pill, roughly 7 in 10 couples continue to use one of the more effective contraceptive techniques (Pratt, Mosher, Bachrach, & Horn, 1984).

That shift in contraceptive practice has had dramatic results. Unplanned pregnancy still occurs among all social groups, and is especially common among the very young, the poor, and the uneducated—people who are more likely to use unreliable contraceptive methods and to use them carelessly or intermittently. But among married couples, unwanted or mistimed pregnancy is far less common than formerly.

The trend since the mid-1960s has been toward wider use of more reliable contraceptives. Indeed, the contraceptive revolution has not just had a profound effect on average family size; it has also given women a new measure of control over their lives.

TABLE 8-1
Married with Children, 1990–2000

Percent of married-couple families with and without children under age 18 at home, by age of householder; in thousands, 1990–2000.

	1990 (%)	1995 (%)	2000 (%)
ALL AGES			
With children	45.6	42.1	37.7
Without children	54.4	57.9	62.3
UNDER 25			
With children	51.9	51.6	51.4
Without children	48.1	48.4	48.6
25 TO 44			
With children	76.6	74.5	72.5
Without children	23.4	25.5	27.5
45 TO 64			
With children	24.3	20.4	16.4
Without children	75.7	79.6	83.5
65 AND OLDER			
With children	1.3	1.1	0.9
Without children	98.7	98.9	99.1

SOURCE: T. Exter (1990), p. 55.

FIGURE 8-2
Birth Rates by Race/Ethnic Group
SOURCE: M. L. Usdansky & M. Puente (1991).

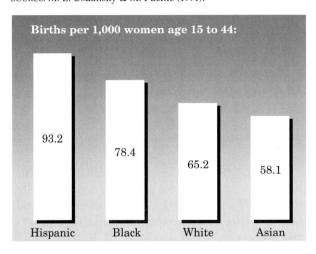

Births per 1,000 women age 15 to 44:

Hispanic 93.2
Black 78.4
White 65.2
Asian 58.1

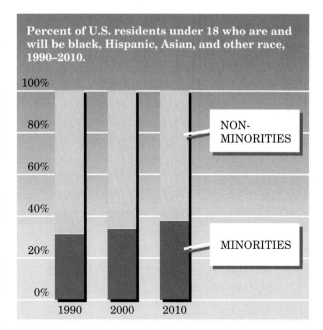

Percent of U.S. residents under 18 who are and will be black, Hispanic, Asian, and other race, 1990–2010.

NON-MINORITIES

MINORITIES

1990 2000 2010

FIGURE 8-3
Growth of Minority Children
Minorities will grow from 31% of the nation's children in 1990, to 34% in 2000, and 38% in 2010.

SOURCE: Ethnic babies come to toyland. (1991, June).

Reasons for Having Fewer Children

The marked decline in unwanted births tells us something about the control that most couples exert over the number of children they have, but it reveals little about *why* most people stop at one or two children.

Let us assume for a moment that most couples engage in some sort of cost-benefit analysis before deciding whether to have children, and if so, how many. The first item on that list might be the considerable financial expense of raising a child for 18 years or more (see Figure 8-4). Among the emotional costs, as we saw in a previous chapter, are a slight decline in marital satisfaction and an increase in marital conflict that commonly accompany the early child-rearing years.

What about the rewards? Some of the traditional benefits of parenthood have lost their allure. Children are no longer an economic asset, as they were in agricultural societies, where they worked in the fields and the kitchens. Neither can children be counted upon to provide a pension for their elderly parents. It is rare today for parents to have children so they can perform religious rituals, although this may still be a factor in some Jewish families, where a son is needed to say the

FIGURE 8-4
The Costs of Raising a Child
The cost of having a baby and providing for it for the first year of life has doubled in the past 30 years. And this initial cost continues to expand as the child grows to adulthood. If consideration is given to money, time, and career opportunities forgone, children are indeed expensive. By one estimate, a middle-class family with two children will spend approximately $100,000 per child by the time each reaches age 18 (Rauch, 1989). By another estimate, rearing a child to age 18 and then sending him or her to a 4-year state university would cost $232,000 (Belkin, 1985).

SOURCES: L. Belkin (1985); J. Rauch (1989); and B. Cutler (1990).

kaddish for his deceased father. As family name and lineage have become less important, we are less likely to have children in order to extend the chain of generations.

Social factors, too, figure prominently in a couple's decision to limit the size of their family. If everything else were equal, we might assume that those who are better educated would choose to have larger families. After all, they typically earn more and are in a better position to afford more children. Yet the actual pattern is just the reverse. For some years, it has been true that those with more education (and higher family income) have smaller families. This pattern holds true regardless of race or ethnicity. The effect of more education is especially striking among black women.

The labor-force status of women also has a strong impact on preferences about family size. While having a job or career doesn't convince many women to forgo childbearing entirely, it is a factor in convincing them to have fewer children than they otherwise would. By providing income, a satisfying role, and outside interests that women might have to give up (at least temporarily) when children are born, a job creates certain disincentives to childbearing. This is a key reason for the expectation that fertility rates will remain substantially lower than they were in the baby-boom era. As we will see in Chapter 9, women are involved now to a much greater extent in the work force. It is highly unlikely that many women would (or could afford to) give up their work roles in favor of larger families.

Another reason for today's lower fertility rate is that improvements have been made in infant health care. In the eighteenth and nineteenth centuries, women bore many children to assure that a few might survive. The infant death rate was over 50 percent (Mintz & Kellogg, 1988).

According to a recent report by the National Commission on Children, more than 9 in 10 couples have at least one child, and most parents and children describe their relationships as close ("Despite Troubles," 1991). After interviewing 1,700 parents and their 900 children the commission reported that 90 percent of parents believed that it was more difficult to be a parent today than in past generations. They also thought that parents today have a more difficult time providing economically for their children. Of the parents interviewed, 6 out of 10 wished they could spend more time with their children; 2 out of 10 worried about their children misusing drugs or alcohol, having sex at too early an age, getting AIDS, or being shot; and most said they make a point to play with, read to, and eat with their children regularly.

When asked about their relationship with their children, two-thirds of parents said it was excellent while one-third said it was good. Only 3 percent rated it fair or poor. Of the children interviewed, 9 out of 10 named their mother and father as special adults in their lives.

Not only do employed women have fewer children, but occupational demands also cause them to devote less time to child care.

More than one-third said that they talked with a parent about their concerns at least once a week.

For most parents, providing nurture and being needed by one's children are sufficient rewards for parenthood. As difficult as it is to characterize the satisfactions of child rearing, they are considerable. Of parents surveyed, 93 percent said they would do it all over again. When asked what the greatest plus or thing gained most from having children was, the most common responses were the love and affection children bring (12 percent); having the pleasure of watching them grow (11 percent); the joy, happiness, and fun they bring (10 percent); the sense of family they create (7 percent); and the fulfillment and satisfaction they bring (6 percent) (Gallup & Newport, 1990). One grandmother commented, "Many parents are unaware of the amount of commitment necessary to be a good parent. It's a 24 hour a day job for a long time. But I loved it and found it very satisfying" (p. 8).

PARENTHOOD TODAY

It was not long ago that books on parenting either excluded entirely or spent very little time discussing fathers. In fact, many prominent authors wrote exclusively of motherhood. If the word "parent" appeared in the title of a book or article, it was the mother who was interviewed and who remained the focus of the study. Parenthood is a term that has emerged along with the notion that both mothers *and* fathers have an influence on a child's development. Even today, however, we still look at parenting as consisting of two distinct gender-based roles, motherhood and fatherhood.

Motherhood

Despite evidence that being a mother has *opportunity costs*—in other words, it "restricts freedom, increases workload, raises monetary needs, and generally complicates and constrains life"—Americans still strongly believe that all married women should be parents (Goldsteen & Ross, 1989, p. 505). And the majority of women make this choice willingly and with few regrets. Traditionally, mothering has been considered something quite different from fathering. While the mother is supposed to raise and care for the child—providing unconditional love and attending to the child's needs as reflected by societal expectations—the father is supposed to provide a model of achievement and success in the outside world.

Should anything happen to cause anxiety for a child or to indicate less than satisfactory development—some below-average grades on a report card, a child who expresses unhappiness over his or her popularity with schoolmates, for example—the mother almost always feels some degree of inadequacy and guilt. Why? Because it is the mother who is typically held responsible by members of the extended kin and friend network, the school system, and representatives of the mental health profession if all is not operating smoothly in her child's life. Perhaps this explains, at least partly, why we tend to hear very little praise, appreciation, or positive feedback directed toward mothers, except, possibly, on Mother's Day each year. And even then, romanticized views of motherhood predominate. Media profiles highlight the lives of "supermoms," testimonials appear in local newspapers and national magazines from mother-of-the-year award winners, and greeting cards filled with loving poetic tributes are prominently displayed in every department and discount store in town.

As a society, then, we have traditionally given mothers almost the sole responsibility for shaping the next generation. We seem to ignore that other socialization forces like the school system, the media, religious institutions, and the community also surround and influence children. Nor do we emphasize that children also have some degree of choice as to which path they eventually follow. The many other factors that intervene between the type of mothering provided and how children turn out are similarly played down, such as how involved the father is in child rearing, the economic well-being of the family, and the accessibility of quality child-care supports. This romantization of motherhood assumes that children are best able to develop to their full potential under the tutelage of the mother. This stereotypical view puts tremendous social pressure on mothers and results in intense scrutiny of the mother-child relationship.

Is a Full-Time Mother Necessary?

How much care or attention do children need? Does it make any difference who supplies that attention? Dr. Benjamin Spock's answers to these questions contributed to the domesticity and emphasis on full-time motherhood that characterized the 1950s. In the first edition of his tremendously popular *Baby and Child Care* and in every revision until recent ones, Spock

equated proper child care with mothering, and described mothering as a full-time job. Only in recent revisions does he suggest that, at least in some families, both the child's and the mother's needs might be better served by some other arrangement than full-time mothering (Spock & Rothenberg, 1985). The shift away from full-time mothering is well worth examining because it represents a fundamental change in our ideas about what is proper parenting.

The first edition of *Baby and Child Care* was written during a period when researchers and clinicians such as the British psychoanalyst John Bowlby (1953) were devoting considerable attention to the problems that arose from inadequate mothering. For people who were influenced by the idea of maternal deprivation in the 1950s, there were very practical implications for mothers. Based on what appeared to be well-founded advice from clinicians and researchers, many concluded that continuous, full-time mothering was required to guarantee the proper development of the child. Like Spock, Bowlby equated proper child care with mothering, and he advocated full-time motherhood.

Other writers, such as the widely respected American psychiatrist Theodore Lidz, brought the argument full circle. Not only do children need full-time mothering, but women need to bear children. Lidz wrote that woman's

> biological purpose seems to require completion through conceiving, bearing, and nurturing children. . . . Her generative organs seem meaningless unless her womb has been filled, her breasts suckled. . . . The woman's creativity as a mother becomes a central matter that provides meaning and balance to her life. (1968, p. 443)

This statement affirmed the existence of a maternal instinct, and the practical implications of such a thing are enormous. If there is a maternal instinct, one need not ask who should take care of children. As Bowlby and Lidz suggested—and Spock assumed—mothers are uniquely qualified for the task. If mothering is not learned but instinctive, then all women must have an interest in and aptitude for child rearing. And if infants and young children need their mothers' undivided attention and care, then a mother should not work outside the home, even part time; and day-care centers—no matter how well equipped and staffed—may be harmful to children.

In recent years, however, both the idea of maternal deprivation and the belief in a maternal instinct have been widely criticized. There are certain ways in which mothers and infants are biologically predisposed to a mutual attraction. There are certain unlearned maternal responses that are conducive to a close mother-child bond. For example, the crying of an infant triggers the secretion of the hormone oxytocin, which in turn causes nipple erection and prepares a woman for nursing (Rossi, 1977). But to acknowledge the relevance of such biological facts to an understanding of the mother-child bond is only to say that biology shapes what is learned, which is a very different thing from assuming that "blind" instinct leads women to conceive, bear, and nurture children. Most of what we mean by mothering is learned, not instinctive. Some women are good at it, and others are not—which is true of any acquired skill.

The emphasis that Bowlby and Spock placed on full-time mothering seems quite strange, moreover, when we compare it with child care in other societies, particularly traditional societies. There, child care is generally regarded as a part-time activity, one that women pursue while carrying out other tasks such as food gathering or crafts. In very few societies can women afford to devote most of their time to child care. (For a detailed discussion of employed mothers, see Chapter 9.)

Fatherhood

Until just a few years ago, most discussions of child rearing referred to the father's role only in passing. It was not a matter of dismissing fatherhood, but rather of concluding that it was a supporting role. Today, there is another quite different theme in much of what has been written and said about fatherhood. According to this new perspective, the male is expected to play a more active role, to take a direct hand in nurturing his children. What is now frequently referred to as "the new fatherhood" signals a redefinition of parental roles.

Traditional Fatherhood

Throughout the nineteenth century and the first half of this century, as we saw in Chapter 1, men and women occupied distinctly different spheres. The man's primary role was to provide the family with an income by working outside the home. Under that system, men's roles at home consisted mainly of certain

Until relatively recently, Americans have traditionally emphasized full-time mothering, but in many societies economic necessity has driven many mothers to divide their time between work and child care.

duties such as setting the standard of morality and acting as disciplinarian. It was not assumed that child rearing was a man's proper task or that men were temperamentally suited to it. As reflected in court decisions from the mid-nineteenth century on, when a guardian had to be specified, the mother was almost automatically given custody of the children by virtue of her temperament as well as her experience.

That assumption persisted until well into the twentieth century. Consider, for example, how fathers were depicted in the popular media in the 1930s, 1940s, and 1950s. Typically, they were caricatures, figures of fun like Ozzie Nelson in the radio and television show "The Adventures of Ozzie and Harriet." In their domestic roles, men were frequently portrayed as well-intentioned bumblers who were humored, cajoled, and patronized by their long-suffering wives and clever children.

The New Fatherhood

But just as popular images of women's roles have changed since the 1970s, so too have popular images of men's roles. What caused the change? Sociologist Ralph LaRossa and his colleagues (1991) argue that fathers are now expected to be more competent and knowledgeable about their children and to participate in child rearing to a greater extent than ever before, for three reasons. First, the declining birth rate has meant there are fewer children at home and each child is seen as a developing individual with critical needs to be met. Second, more mothers are in the workplace, thus they have less time for child rearing without cutting back on other essential family and work responsibilities. And third, there is a strong and growing so-

cietal belief that child rearing be shared—that fathers should be equally responsible for their children. LaRossa calls this the *egalitarian ethic*. Others refer to this new trend as being on the *daddy track*.

Whatever the reasons, the way we think and feel about men and parenthood is shifting. In various ways, fathers are now being told that they should participate directly in the raising of their children. In many communities, there are classes for new fathers where men get together to learn about diapering, feeding, and taking care of an infant. Ads for baby products show fathers bathing their babies and changing their diapers.

There is widespread evidence that many men have taken this new ideal of fatherhood to heart and become more involved with their children than their fathers were. One manifestation of a more direct involvement is that, over the past decade, the idea that fathers should be present at the birth of their children has gained wide acceptance.

Ideals vs. Reality

Still, there is a disparity between actual behavior and the idea of an involved father who takes on half or more of the management of the children when he gets home. As Ralph LaRossa (1988) reminds us, mothers are still the primary caregivers of children. Even in dual-income families it is the mother who attends to most of the children's needs. Studies have shown that most fathers rarely spend as much as 30 minutes a day interacting directly with their children. Significantly, researchers have also found that most men take almost no responsibility for such tasks as taking their children to the doctor (Baruch, Barnett, & Rivers, 1983).

LaRossa believes that fathers should be more strongly encouraged to participate in child rearing. When men offer excuses like "I'm not good at taking care of the baby" or "I can't be with Tommy now, I have to go to the office, the store, to sleep, mow the lawn, or pay the bills," women should listen attentively and question whether these statements are legitimate reasons, rationalizations, or merely tired excuses. According to LaRossa, "only when men are forced to seriously examine their commitment to fatherhood (versus their commitment to their jobs and avocations) can we hope to bring about the kinds of changes that will be required to alter the division of child care in this country" (1988, p. 456). Flexible work schedules and paternity leave will encourage such change.

What few studies there are of men's behavior with their children indicate that fathers and mothers contribute to the development of their children in somewhat different ways. While mothers typically respond similarly to male and female children, fathers apply somewhat different standards to their sons and daughters. Fathers typically feel more responsibility toward the male child, and they give boys more independence training (Gilbert, Hanson, & Davis, 1982). With young children the father's main role is that of playmate, and the play between fathers and their infants is typically less verbal and more tactile than is play between mothers and their children. As contrasted to mothers, who characteristically stimulate their children verbally, fathers more often engage in physical activities such as rough-and-tumble play (Parke & Sawin, 1977).

Why are so many fathers—even those who would like to be closer to their children—unable to do so?

Lack of support from the larger society is one reason. As one father put it: "I can think of nothing that our society does to help families who want to try something new" (Broberg, 1988, p. 81). Another reason is that fathers feel unprepared for the parental role. Family researcher Brent McBride suggests: "Fathers often have little exposure to parental role models, few social opportunities to prepare for fatherhood, limited institutional supports for the parental role, and a lack of father-child interaction" (1990, p. 250). Other social scientists believe that many men have trouble reconciling the demands of active fatherhood with their careers. Today's middle-class father is supposed to do housework, change diapers, and be emotionally involved with his children—all without slighting his work responsibilities. As many men have discovered, that is a very demanding ideal, and one that is often accompanied by guilt about what they haven't done—both at home and at the office. This situation is complicated by the fact that most men become parents at the same time they are establishing themselves in their occupations. "These are crucial, formative years for both my child and my career," says one man, a professor and father of a 2-year-old daughter. "In some sense, I want to put in overtime on both. It's a very difficult conflict" (in *Newsweek,* March 31, 1986, p. 56).

An increasing number of fathers say they would welcome the opportunity to take parental leave. In a 1991 study the Bureau of Labor Statistics found that only 20 percent of large companies offered leave (see the "Snapshots" box). Money is one obstacle; not every father can afford unpaid leave when they typically earn one-third more than their wives. A research chemist at Du Pont says, "I'm the main wage

Where Paternity Leave Is Catching On

Before the Parental Leave Act of 1993 was passed by Congress and signed by President Clinton (see Chapter 9 for more information) several large companies described their experiences with parental leave in an article in Business Week. *The general conclusion was that more fathers were choosing to take leave.*

LOTUS DEVELOPMENT

One of a few companies to offer men paid leave: up to 4 weeks, depending on length of service, plus another 4 weeks unpaid. In 1990, some 23 men took leaves, compared with 29 in the previous 2 years combined.

AETNA

Gives men up to 6 months off, without pay, for major family obligations. Ten men took leaves last year, up from three in 1989; 20 are expected to do so this year.

3M

Twenty-four men may take unpaid leaves this year, up from four in 1986. Male attendance is also up sharply at company-sponsored lunchtime parenting classes.

EASTMAN KODAK

Grants up to 17 weeks unpaid leave. In 3 years, 61 men have taken leaves, compared with 812 women in the same period. Average length of leaves, about 11 weeks, is the same for men and women.

AMERICAN TELEPHONE & TELEGRAPH

Men account for 1 of every 50 employees taking family leave. A decade ago, they accounted for 1 in every 400. Parents can take up to 12 months unpaid leave. Last year, some 82 percent of men on leave, a higher rate than for women on leave, took 3 months or longer.

EXPLORATIONS　*How do companies benefit from offering paternal leave? How do fathers and their families benefit? What are the costs to companies and families for fathers taking leave?*

SOURCE: Excerpted from H. K. Hammonds & W. C. Symonds (1991). Reprinted from April 15, 1991 issue of *Business Week* by special permission; copyright © 1991 by McGraw-Hill, Inc. ✳

earner in our family, and I don't think our budget could afford my taking six months off" ("Taking Baby Steps," 1991). But, if the U.S. experience is anything like that of European countries, paternal leave should become an increasingly popular option. In 1975, for example, Sweden passed a law mandating that paternity leave be available to all new fathers. That year only 2 percent of eligible fathers took it. But in 1991, 27 percent asked for leave. Money is one obvious obstacle; there are other obstacles, too. A man who takes a few months off is likely to be regarded as shirking his responsibilities at work.

Quite conspicuously, then, the 1990s father feels the tensions between two competing expectations. He is still expected to be the primary wage-earner and to do what is necessary to establish and advance his career.

But with the advent of "the new fatherhood," he is also expected to invest more of his time, energy, and emotion at home as an active partner in nurturing his children. In the decades to come, it will be interesting to see how men's behavior changes—at work and at home—as they try to reconcile the competing demands of work and family.

Parenting Styles and Strategies

Few parents today are either trained or prepared for the experience of having and rearing children. Thus, it is not at all uncommon for people to feel inadequate as parents. Moreover, a substantial number of parents apparently feel that they do not have any secure guidelines about how to raise children. Although child-rearing manuals have been a staple of American life for years, bookstores now carry advice books on nearly every aspect, from toilet training to raising a child's IQ. There is no way of knowing whether such books create more anxieties than they allay. Their popularity, though, does seem to be symptomatic of deep concern and insecurity among parents.

Raising Children by the Book—a History

Dr. Spock's first book, *Baby and Child Care,* came out in 1945. Like other child-care manuals, which had been available for more than a century, Dr. Spock's entry was a how-to book about the art and science of parenting. It gave information and advice about hundreds of practical matters from toilet training to left-handedness, from the medical problems of infants to their nutritional needs. It reached the bookstores just in time for the postwar baby boom, and for some reason it captured this huge market. Since its publication it has sold millions of copies, achieving the status of a standard reference work in middle-class homes. It is no exaggeration to say that *Baby and Child Care* has had a considerable influence, either direct or indirect, on most of the postwar generation. This book—including the revisions in each of the successive editions—can be used as a prism through which we examine what is most distinctive about parenting in America.

One of the interesting things about the success of this and other child-rearing manuals available today is that it was written by an "expert," someone who presumably knows better than we do about how to bring up children. For centuries, women learned how to be mothers from *their* mothers, who knew the traditional answers, passed down from one generation to the next, to the questions that mothers were likely to ask. Fifty years ago, parenting was easier because there was more consensus about what parents should do. But now there is no general agreement about what characteristics best serve children as they grow to adulthood. Thus, child-rearing advisers have taken over from grandmother the task of giving advice—but in the process, it seems, mothers and fathers have become more anxious about whether they are doing the right thing.

Looking back over the various expert instructions on child rearing, we see a substantial shift in the adult personality that socialization practices were supposed to produce. At the turn of the century, an adult with good moral character was the objective. The ideals of honesty, orderliness, and industry were supreme. To-

day, most child-rearing manuals take an independent, spontaneous adult as their goal.

The shifting currents of advice are revealed most clearly when parents refer to the books to find out how strict they should be, and how they should deal with such matters as toilet training and misbehavior. In the 1920s and 1930s, they were told to enforce rigid feeding schedules and early toilet training and to restrain themselves from rushing to the baby's side when it cried. John Watson, an early behavioral psychologist, advised parents that immediate gratification is not in the child's interest and warned against excessive displays of affection, too.

By the 1940s, however, parents were encouraged to be more indulgent. Spock advised mothers to feed infants when they were hungry. Rigid toilet-training schedules were no longer in fashion. The baby's needs achieved a new priority. Thumb sucking and masturbation, which earlier had been considered pernicious habits to be broken, were now regarded as wholesome expressions of the child's needs for exploration and experience.

Today it is widely assumed that parents should gratify an infant's need for food, sucking, and reassurance, and should allow children to satisfy their curiosity by exploring. Parents are also advised to avoid physical punishments. Overall, studies of how children develop into responsible and self-reliant, uninhibited but not overly aggressive, people suggest that parents should combine warmth and encouragement with firm but not harsh control and discipline.

Child-Rearing Guidelines

Students of human development have discovered very few rules that would suggest a specific list of things parents should or should not do to produce a particular type of child. There are, however, some general guidelines derived from social learning theory and research in cognitive development that parents have found useful.

Developmental Readiness. Parents are understandably eager to teach their children new skills as early as possible. But it is important to be aware of the child's limits—both psychological and physiological—at each stage of development. To attempt to teach a skill that the child is not yet ready to learn is to invite frustration. For example, since young infants have no sense of time, they are incapable of learning patience or respect for regularity because of being fed on a set schedule.

Toilet training is another area in which parents should be aware of the child's readiness. Since most children cannot develop adequate control over their sphincter muscles until about 18 months, no amount of cajoling at an earlier age will work.

Praise over Punishment. For several reasons, punishing a child when he or she does something wrong is not often a very effective way of dealing with undesirable behavior. From the child's perspective, punishment often seems arbitrary, and is interpreted as a sign of rejection. When punishment is necessary, it should take place immediately after the behavior in order that the child clearly understand the connection. The parent should explain the punishment and offer some alternative behavior that is more desirable. Children learn more effectively when the consequences of their actions are fairly and reasonably explained. Some form of positive reinforcement generally works best, because it poses no threat to the bond of affection between parent and child and bolsters the child's self-esteem. Physical punishment is not recommended by either the American Psychological Association or the American Medical Association because it is an expression of family violence and leads to negative feelings for both parents and children—fear, disgust, hate, anger, resentment, misery, anxiety, and so forth.

Love and Respect. When correcting a child's behavior, comment on the behavior, not the child's traits. If the message is "I don't love you when you act like that," the child may well feel rejected. Putting negative labels on anyone, but particularly on a child, is destructive because it attacks the self-concept. Being told who you are in negative terms is much harsher than being informed of something specific you did wrong. Parents need to model respect and kindness as well as firmness. One of the most important functions that parents serve is to provide models with which children can identify.

Clarity and Consistency. It is confusing to a child if the parent ignores a certain behavior on one occasion and punishes it on another. Parents should be very clear about family rules and the consequences for breaking them. Threats and unkept promises confuse children.

Open Communication. Understanding is heightened by mutual self-disclosure. Keep in mind, however, that listening is as critical to communicative ef-

It is far more effective to focus on children's behavior ("You said you were going to stay in school late, but you were really at John's") than to damage their self-esteem by criticizing who they are ("You're a liar").

fectiveness as is talking (a thorough discussion of communication is found in Chapter 11).

Reasonable Consequences. One of the most common dilemmas of parenthood is to decide when children can safely make certain choices and learn from their own mistakes. As long as the consequences will not be physically harmful or psychologically devastating, children need this freedom in order to learn how to solve problems and make decisions.

There is a susceptibility of American parents to feelings of guilt and inadequacy, as they hear child-rearing experts endorse the idea that each child has a certain "potential" that can be realized only with the right kind of parental guidance. The parent is thus made responsible not just for the child's physical welfare, but also for his or her personality as well. If the child grows up with any personality flaws, the parents (and the mother in particular) are held responsible.

We do not have to look very far back in history or very far afield in the variety of cultural practices to see how peculiar this attitude is. Until recent times the attitudes of parents toward their children were quite pragmatic. Of course there were bonds of affection between parents and children in times past, but parents were not so personally invested in their children's psychological development as they are now. The emphasis on the quality of parenting is largely a contemporary phenomenon.

Parenting Myths

Societal endorsement of the belief that somehow there is a recipe for the perfect child has influenced us to idealize parents' roles in child development. E. E. LeMasters and John DeFrain, in their book *Parents in Contemporary America* (1989), discuss some commonly held myths that exert enormous pressure on modern parents, causing them undue anxiety and distress.

Rearing Children Is Fun. Actually child rearing is hard work; it is frequently distressing, involves enormous responsibility, requires skills and abilities that take time to develop, and takes long-term commitment and dedication. There is no way to say, ''Well, I've tried being a parent and it just did not work for me. Here, please take this child back.''

Children Are Sweet and Cute. Because of this myth new parents usually go through a process of disenchantment after the birth of their child, during which they deromanticize their parental expectations—that is, they come to terms with the work side of parenthood.

Children Will Turn Out Well If They Have ''Good'' Parents. Parents cannot guarantee happiness and success to their children. Because society is complex and complicated, parents are not in control of all aspects of their children's lives.

Children Improve Marriage. Though we might like to believe that this is true, the presence of children does not improve intimacy or interaction between marital partners. More often than childfree couples, parents are dissatisfied with family finances and the household division of labor. Couples consistently say that they are less satisfied with their marriages after the birth of their child.

If You Rear Them Right, They Will Stay Right. Most parents set good examples for their children only to find that these examples are not always appreciated or followed. There is no recipe for the perfect child. It is not unusual for parents with several children to remark that most thrived and grew into healthy, successful adults. Many parents, however, will talk with dismay about one or more of their children who took a more difficult and troubled path to adulthood.

The Nature of the Child Being Reared Is Really Not Very Important—Good Parents Can Manage Any Child. Most parents of more than one child say that each of their children was born with a distinct personality or temperament. A child's temperament is very relevant to how she or he is parented and how she or he gets along in the larger society. Some children are born with extremely difficult temperaments; others are cooperative from the beginning. In the end, children seem to have as much effect on parents as parents have on shaping them.

Today's Parents Are Not as Good as Those of Yesterday. Societal expectations of parents have risen dramatically since the 1700s and 1800s. It is difficult to know the exact guiding philosophy of most parents in ''the good old days,'' but it seems likely that they were not superparents, but simply fathers and mothers doing the best they could under the prevailing social circumstances.

There Are No Bad Children—Only Bad Parents. Parents are consistently blamed for the ills of modern America; while children, their teachers, and other child caregivers are portrayed as the ''good guys,'' ever vigilant, nurturant, and protective.

Parents Are Adults. Not all parents are adults; some are adolescents. But even among adults, simply reaching the age of 21 does not automatically bestow maturity, responsibility, unselfishness, empathy, and diligent parenting abilities upon an individual with children.

Children Today Really Appreciate All the Advantages Their Parents Are Able to Give Them. Children sometimes take for granted, and perceive as their inherited "right," many of the advantages conferred upon them by parents. "Parents, then, may feel guilty when they cannot deliver the goods" (p. 261). As a result, some parents derive little satisfaction from providing "extras" for their children because "extras" have a way of becoming the expected.

The Hard Work of Rearing Children Is Justified by the Fact That the Children Will Make a Better World. This myth has more to do with our dreams and hopes for the future than with the realities of life.

Parenthood Receives Top Priority in Our Society. Most parents have to take care of their child's needs within the time frame and opportunity structure of our culture—parental responsibilities are expected to be sandwiched in between other role responsibilities. The work role comes first, according to most employers, and it is usually inflexible in terms of time. Nurturing the marital relationship, being involved in community affairs, attending school functions, finding time for leisure pursuits—all of these and many other activities vie for parental time.

Love Is Enough to Guarantee Good Parental Performance. Love is, of course, important in any parent-child relationship, but it must coexist with knowledge, insight, trust, respect, cooperativeness, and self-control.

Parents Alone Should Rear the Young. Parenting is a big job that deserves support and cooperation from others like grandparents, friends, the community, the work environment, the political and legal systems, and others with a stake in future generations.

Influence of Social Class on Parenting

As various studies have shown, the question of obedience has very different meanings to parents at different social class levels. Imagine the following situation. You are the parent of a 4-year-old girl, and she is supposed to be taking a nap. When you check on her you find that she has gotten out of bed and discovered a paint set that was stored in a closet. At this point she has succeeded mainly in covering herself with paint,

but she is intent on her creation, a nondescript finger painting that adorns the wall.

As with most of the situations that parents confront every day, there are several ways you might respond. Furious at the mess and angry at the child's disobedience, you might slap her for "painting all over the wall" and pronounce a rule: "Don't ever play with those paints again!" If the child should ask why, you could answer: "Because I said so!" Another response would be to approve the child's absorption in such "creative" play, irritated though you might be at the mess. In this case you would probably also encourage your daughter by example to clean up, scold her for not being in bed, and explain why an afternoon nap is so important.

As several studies have shown, the style of parenting that is characteristic of the middle class today is different from that of blue-collar or working-class families. There is no right way of responding to a situation like the one we just described, but there are ways characteristic of each social setting, and they reveal different assumptions about the good child and the roles parents should take.

The first response exemplifies the so-called traditional or *authoritarian* pattern, which was more common in the past and today is more characteristic of blue-collar parents. The second response exemplifies the so-called *authoritative* or "democratic" style of child rearing commonly advocated in child-rearing books and usually put into practice by the middle-class parents who read these books. It is difficult to describe these two patterns without implying that the second one is preferable, but we can show that it has disadvantages as well as advantages.

Authoritarian Parents

For parents who follow the authoritarian pattern, a good child is one who has learned obedience, neatness, and cleanliness. The aim of this style of upbringing is to control the child's impulses, not to explore or express them. Traditional parents view themselves as unquestioned authority figures who have a right to give orders and lay down unexplained rules. It is assumed in such families that the children should adjust to their parents' needs and preferences, not vice versa. Setting limits and making rules is assumed to be an important part of the parents' role. And when the children break these rules, physical punishment is often considered appropriate.

Authoritative Parents

Parents who follow the authoritative pattern, in contrast, make different assumptions about what constitutes the good child and the proper parental role. Such parents prize curiosity, creativity, happiness, ambition, autonomy, consideration, and achievement in the child more than obedience. The child's impulses are often accepted and encouraged; in a number of respects, in fact, these families are far more child-centered than are those of the other type. When 4-year-old children invent fictitious friends and imaginary animals, middle-class parents are more likely to approve of them as signs of a fertile imagination. The parental role, according to this model, is that of counselor, not disciplinarian. As many child-rearing manuals advise, parents explain rules to children, and children are encouraged to understand this reasoning and apply it for themselves. This verbal style of discipline and direction can be frustrating for parents who discover that the cool voice of reason does not always persuade an unruly 4-year-old. This style of parenting is more egalitarian than the traditional style. The middle-class parent is more concerned about the child's development than his or her obedience. Social class differences in parent-child relations also show up in adulthood (see the "Diversity" box).

Why have child-rearing patterns changed so dramatically? One explanation is that in an era of rapid social change parents can no longer say, "Do as I have done." They have to prepare their children for a future that is substantially different from the present. It is partly because there is no consensus about what type of behavior will be best suited to tomorrow's realities that the parents' role is so complicated today.

Ethnic Diversity and Parenting

Along with social class, race and ethnicity also influence parenting practices. For example, in Hispanic and Asian families the father is generally considered the main authority figure, but both parents are accorded greater respect than in most other American families. Even in adulthood, parents and older brothers and sisters have greater familial responsibilities, with part of their role being to carry on family rituals and traditions and be good role models for younger family members (Mindel, Habenstein, & Wright, 1988).

Although ethnicity and race do not produce identical parenting characteristics, there are some similar-

ities. Most ethnic families view education as the primary means for their children to achieve and advance in society. To facilitate educational opportunities, the majority of such families have more than one member in the work force. Parents typically socialize their children to understand and appreciate their cultural heritage, with most believing that having a sense of ethnic identification gives a child strength, security, and self-esteem. Such an identification is particularly critical in black and Native American families where prejudice and stereotyping can quickly undermine a child's sense of self-worth (McAdoo, 1986, 1988; McAdoo & McAdoo, 1985). Ethnic socialization can provide a child with ways of self-protecting in the face of discrimination and racism (Taylor, Chatters, Tucker, & Lewis, 1991; Vega, 1991). (See Chapter 1 for a review of ethnic diversity and socialization effects.)

OPTIONS FOR PARENTHOOD

Couples today have many decisions to make regarding parenthood: Do they want to have children? If they are diagnosed as infertile, will they use modern technology to increase their chances of becoming parents? Should they adopt? Should they postpone parenthood until later in life? Is it okay to have one child?

Voluntarily Childfree

For many years The National Alliance for Optional Parenthood and the National Organization for Non-Parents (NON) have provided advice and support for couples who wish to remain childless. Voluntarily remaining childfree is not easy. Even in the 1990s there is some stigma attached to this choice. A strong cultural expectation exists that all married adults over age 30 should be parents (Menaghan, 1989). In fact, over 90 percent of American adults do have children. According to sociologists Karen Goldsteen and Catherine Ross (1989), Americans strongly believe in the positive effects of childbearing and child rearing. Women without children are especially thought to feel lonely, empty, and unfulfilled (p. 505). Joe Pittman and his colleagues agree: Married couples are frequently not even identified as true "families" until they have children; in fact, parenthood is seen by many as the cul-

Mothers and Daughters: Differences by Social Class

Historically, mothers and daughters, regardless of race and class, have had one of the closest family relationships, often even surpassing the intimacy and emotional connection of the husband-wife relationship (Boyd, 1989). Today's daughters are likely to choose a different path from that of their mothers: to have premarital sex at an early age, cohabit, marry at a later age, be coproviders of the family income, have fewer children later in life, and divorce. These divergent ways of living, however, do not appear to permanently undermine the special mother-daughter bond (Fischer, 1991). There is a "sense of mutual responsibility and protectiveness" for each other with mothers and daughters moving "back and forth between mothering and being mothered" (Boyd, 1989, p. 207).

Lucy Fischer, research scientist and author of *Linked Lives: Adult Daughters and Their Mothers* (1986) concludes that there are major differences between middle-class and working-class mother-daughter relationships. The connection between middle-class mothers and daughters is based on *change*. Because middle-class daughters have had more education and job opportunities and often made different choices than their mothers, one of their primary relationship responsibilities is to bridge the gap in values and goals between themselves and their mothers. Most daughters, for example, bring their mothers up to date on current issues and concerns of contemporary women and their families—sexual harassment, family leave, single parenthood. Middle-class daughters also help their mothers change with the times by doing things like counseling them on family and marital problems, encouraging them to go back to school, or asking them to reconsider and reevaluate their belief systems and life goals.

In working-class families, mothers and daughters base their primary bond on *acceptance*. They help each other accept what they cannot change about their lives. Together, they face "their fate as women": that women have very little power to change things at work or in the family (Fischer, 1991, p. 244). In other words, men have certain ways of doing things, definite ideas about how the family and work worlds should operate; and since they control most of what happens in life, women may as well learn to live with it.

Because they view the world as changeable, middle-class daughters and mothers support each other in their efforts to gain more power for themselves and other women in the family and workplace as well as in the large society—through marital negotiation, political action, community involvement, the court system, and by other means. Again, as we have seen in previous chapters, because of their greater access to resources, they have a different view of the world than do working-class women. They feel that they have some control over what happens in their lives and believe that they can implement change (Barnett & Baruch, 1987).

EXPLORATIONS *Do you think that the relationship between fathers and adult sons differs from that of mothers and adult daughters? How? Would social class differences be as obvious among fathers and sons? Explain.*

SOURCES: R. C. Barnett & G. K. Baruch (1987); C. J. Boyd (1989); and L. Fischer (1986, 1991).

minating event in adult socialization (Pittman, Wright, & Lloyd, 1989).

One might think that childfree couples are somehow maladjusted and otherwise unhappy because parenthood is so strongly associated with adult well-being. Actually, they typically score higher on measures of psychological well-being and life satisfaction than do parents (McLanahan & Adams, 1987; Umberson & Gove, 1989). This may be because such couples have avoided the additional responsibilities and resultant daily stress involved in the parenting role.

Why do some couples decide not to have children? When sociologist Karen Seccombe (1991) examined the reports of approximately 800 childless men and women, she found that women more often mentioned their age as a reason to remain childfree. They also expressed greater concern than men about parenthood being stressful and anxiety-producing. Men, in contrast, gave economic and financial issues greater weight. After reviewing 29 studies of childfree couples, Houseknecht (1987) concluded that the most often used rationales for remaining childless are freedom from child-care responsibilities, greater opportunity for self-fulfillment, and unhampered mobility (79 percent); more satisfactory marital relationship (62 percent); woman's career opportunities (55 percent); and economic advantages (55 percent). Lesser-used rationales included concern about population growth (38 percent); a general dislike of children (38 percent); doubts about ability to parent (31 percent); concerns about childbirth and recovery (24 percent); and concern for children, given world conditions (21 percent).

The decision to remain childless seems to occur in one of two ways. Some couples read about and observe parents, compare the experiences of parenthood with those of nonparenthood, and eventually decide that not having children is the best choice for them. For other couples, nonparenthood consists of a gradual process of disenchantment based on a series of postponements of childbearing. Couples go through four basic stages of postponement (Veevers, 1979):

1 The couple delay childbearing to meet some important objective like completing their education or saving money for a house.

2 The couple find it difficult to say exactly when they will have a child. They grow increasingly reluctant to set a time and remain vague about their reasons for doing so.

3 The couple debate the pros and cons of parenthood, giving the cons increasing weight in the final decision.

4 The couple make their final decision not to become parents.

In childfree marriages, Veevers points out, the husband is a big source of support for the wife, who must withstand more of the cultural pressures and sanctions for the couple's childfree lifestyle. His support buttresses her self-concept, coping efficacy, and life satisfaction.

Today, having children is more of an option and less of a mandate than in the past. Couples more carefully and thoughtfully examine the costs and benefits of parenthood. Should they decide against having children, the methods for remaining childfree are very effective. Estimates of the extent of childlessness in the 1990s vary. Some believe that 5 percent of American couples will never have children (Pratt, Mosher, Bachrach, & Horn, 1984); others say the figure will be more like 10 percent (Veevers, 1990); while a third group of researchers cite figures between 15 and 25 percent (Bloom & Trussell, 1984; Kenkel, 1985). Whatever the figure, the main point is that childlessness by choice is increasing.

In some cases, childlessness is not a choice, however. Some couples want children very much, but are unable to conceive.

Involuntary Childlessness

Of all married couples in the United States in which the woman is of childbearing age and is not contraceptively sterile, about 10 percent are *infertile*—have not conceived after trying, without protection, for 1 year (Abbey, Andrews, & Halman, 1991; Mosher, 1990). Causes of infertility include previous episodes of sexually transmitted diseases, damaging infections related to use of intrauterine devices to prevent pregnancy, and exposure to toxic drugs and chemicals. Smoking, nonnutritional diets, low body weight, and excessive exercise can also reduce chances of pregnancy.

Infertility, no matter the cause, puts lots of stress on the marital relationship. Women seem to experience the most distress because of the importance our culture attaches to motherhood (Veevers, 1990) and the tendency to attribute infertility problems to the female, regardless of the actual source (Miall, 1989). Moreover, women, in particular, mourn the loss of the parenting role. Typical reactions include depression, guilt, anxiety, helplessness, and fear (Abbey, Andrews, & Halman, 1991). As one woman reports:

> It affects your ego. It has an immense effect on self-concept, in all kinds of crazy ways. You ask "How can I be a real woman?" By affecting the self-concept, it affects sexuality, and it affected work for me for a while. "How can I be good at this; I'm not a normal person?" (Greil, Leitko, & Porter, 1988, p. 181)

Men tend to be disappointed but much less so than their wives, as this man's testimony demonstrates:

> My personal infertility has never tormented me. I've sometimes wondered if I have some sort of mental problem or something that it hasn't. It's never really

eaten away at me. Maybe I've just permanently flipped the switch to think about other things or something like that. Maybe subconsciously I am tormented, but I've talked myself out of feeling tormented or something. I don't know, but I just don't feel that sorry for myself. (Greil et al., p. 182)

The source of a man's disappointment is less related to his inability to have children and more connected to how it affects his wife and his relationship with her. Men regret the loss of a satisfying, enjoyable marital companion, as is illustrated by this man's words:

I love my wife dearly and desperately, and as long as she's less than happy I'll never be really happy. I think that her lack of happiness is the main stumbling block in my life. Otherwise, my life is quite satisfactory. (Greil et al., p. 183)

Women often become so depressed by their infertility that they have great difficulty focusing on anything else for very long. Their unhappiness tends to permeate most other life roles. Even the act of making love may become work rather than pleasure because so much emphasis is placed on the sex act as a test or treatment or cure for infertility. Women, more than men, become engrossed in reading materials related to infertility—its causes and cures—and seek out other infertile couples to befriend. They tend to take charge of whatever treatment plan is initiated, even when the treatment involves only the husband. As they immerse themselves in the problem and how to resolve it, women frequently become upset with their partners for seemingly taking less interest. Despite these difficulties, in most cases, the initial disagreements between the couple eventually culminate in a greater understanding of each other's feelings and a renewal of intimacy and closeness as they work through their anxiety and frustration.

Affected couples may pull closer together because they find it difficult to tell outsiders about their infertility. Their reluctance is based on their conviction that fertile friends cannot fully understand their problem. Lack of understanding often leads to hurtful remarks and probing questions. For example, it is not unusual for infertile couples to be asked for sexual details about their relationship or be called upon to assign blame. "Whose fault is it, yours or your husband's (wife's)?" is a query they commonly hear from friends, acquaintances, and family members. Consequently, infertile

couples may shut themselves off from other people and come to rely solely on each other for support.

Sociologist Charlene Miall found that the majority of the infertile couples she studied used several strategies to protect themselves from gossip and prying. Some couples avoided certain people entirely, or interacted with them but avoided conversations about pregnancy and child rearing. Said one respondent, "My whole approach is to be as low key as possible, not to get excited, to show we are normal" (1989, p. 396). Sometimes a couple carefully chose seemingly trustworthy friends to talk to but revealed things to them selectively—a bit at a time—to test their reactions and gauge whether to tell them more or to pull back. A few couples disclosed their problems with infertility to family and friends as an emotional release, as part of the process of emotional healing: "In a couple of situations we just blurted it out and I don't think we did it very well. And yet every time we talked about it we felt better" (p. 397). Another protective strategy that couples used was to say they had a medical problem: "It was a medically open and shut case" (p. 397). This strategy tends to work by keeping people from making remarks like, "Well maybe you're not doing it right." Practiced deception is a final strategy that infertile couples employ. With this strategy the couple disclose they are infertile, but remain vague about which partner has the problem. One couple explained:

We agreed to present it as a joint problem of trifling proportions individually but enough to ensure that we as a couple would not be able to have our own children. We left them with the suspicion that with someone else we could [have children]. Love keeps us together, see? (p. 399).

Another couple agreed, "We fudge the issues and pretend it's both of us. . . . I don't think that it's any of their business" (p. 399).

Infertility is complicated by our cultural bias toward parenthood and the consequent stigma we attach to being childless, whatever the circumstances. The support of family and friends can be crucially important to the infertile couple. Another important source of support are self-help groups. The national organization RESOLVE is one such group. Infertile couples can receive counseling, gain referrals to reliable treatment sources, and meet other couples like themselves (Higgins, 1990). In the end, 50 to 60 percent of infertile couples do eventually conceive. Although some conceive without biotechnical aids, others rely on artificial insemination, *in vitro* fertilization, embryo transplants, or surrogate mothers.

Biotechnology and Surrogate Parenthood

Surrogate Motherhood

In his novel *Brave New World*, Aldous Huxley imagined a society where children are mass-produced in state-run "hatcheries" and "conditioning centers." When Huxley's novel was published in 1932, that seemed a distant prospect. But in 1978, when the world's first "test-tube" baby was born in England, Huxley's vision of a society in which sex and procreation are entirely separate no longer seemed so improbable. In one of the most widely publicized episodes in medical history, Dr. Patrick Steptoe and Dr. Robert Edwards removed a ripe egg from the ovary of a woman whose Fallopian tubes were blocked, fertilized it in a petri dish with her husband's sperm, and implanted the developing embryo in the woman's uterus. This experiment in *in vitro fertilization (IVF)* led, in July 1978, to the first human birth from an egg that was fertilized outside the mother's body.

A new industry has subsequently grown up around the procedure. In 1989, there were 169 IVF clinics in the United States. But while the heart of the fertility industry is *in vitro* fertilization—the making of "test-tube babies"—many of these clinics offer a range of services, including ultrasound and sperm-enhancement procedures. Some of them also serve as centers for *surrogate motherhood,* in which a husband fathers a child with another woman via artificial insemination because his wife cannot carry a child to term. This surrogate gives the baby, after it is born, to the couple to raise as their own (see the "Snapshots" box).

In 1986, when the case of "Baby M" first attracted nationwide attention, the practice of surrogate parenthood sparked a loud and contentious debate about the manipulation of basic life processes and the redefinition of motherhood. In recent years, as the number of infertile couples has increased, the practice of hiring women to bear babies has become more common. It is estimated that over 500 such children have been contracted for since the early 1980s. What was unusual about the case of Baby M was not that a woman—in this case, Mary Beth Whitehead of New Jersey—was hired to bear a child she conceived through artificial insemination, and then turn the baby over to its bio-

As in vitro *fertilization has become more common, some of the ethical debate concerning it has died down.*

logical father, William Stern, and his wife Elizabeth. It was, rather, that when Ms. Whitehead saw the baby she had given birth to, she was, according to her husband's testimony, overpowered by her emotions and convinced that she could not relinquish the baby. She refused to sign the documents that would formally clear the way for the Sterns to gain custody of the child.

The case ultimately went to court, where the judge had to weigh the sanctity of the contract between Mr. and Ms. Stern and Ms. Whitehead against her claim as the biological mother. With few legal precedents to guide his decision, Judge Harvey R. Sorkow had to determine whether Baby M (as she was referred to in court documents) should live with her biological mother and her husband or with her biological father and his wife. Finally, after a protracted trial, Judge

SNAPSHOTS

Surrogate Mothers

The science involved in the birth of a child through *in vitro* fertilization and a surrogate mother is relatively easy compared to defining and accepting the legal and ethical aspects of such births. In a California case, the surrogate mother bore a child created from the egg and sperm of the genetic parents, and in turn received a payment of $10,000. The judge granted full parental rights to the genetic parents, emphasizing the importance of heredity in determining legal parenthood.

While empathizing with the plight of the surrogate mother who claimed to have bonded with the child, the judge "found evidence about the bonding of the baby to the gestational mother to be less clear" (*Los Angeles Times*, 1990, p. A6). Her role was compared to that of a "foster mother, who feeds, nurtures and may grow at-tached to the baby, but may be required to relinquish the child to the natural mother." She was denied visitation rights.

The judge noted, "It's not an adoption ruling case. It's not a baby-selling case. It's not a Baby M case where we had natural mothers on both sides."

EXPLORATIONS *To what extent do you believe surrogacy transactions should be closely regulated by law? Should surrogate mothers have visitation rights and be recognized as the child's "second" mother? What do you think about recent cases where the surrogate was the real grandmother and gave birth to her own grandchild?*

Source: *Los Angeles Times* (1990, October 23), p. A6.

Sorkow ruled that the contract between the Sterns and Ms. Whitehead was valid, and he granted custody to the Sterns, with visitation rights for Ms. Whitehead. The New Jersey Supreme Court subsequently allowed her 6 hours of unsupervised visitation per week.

Other courts and state legislatures will grapple with the larger question of surrogate parent contracts. Should affluent couples such as the Sterns be allowed to hire women to bear their children? Does a natural mother's right to her child outweigh that of the natural father? How should the best interest of the child be determined in such cases?

Reproductive Technology: New Dilemmas

In March 1987, the Vatican stepped into the debate on the new methods that are being used to combat infertility. In an effort to influence laws in this area before they are passed, the Vatican issued a lengthy statement condemning virtually all forms of test-tube fertilization, the use of surrogate mothers, and experimentation on human embryos. The document is an appeal for a simpler, more "natural" ethic in which marriage, sexuality, and procreation are parts of an indivisible whole.

The authors of the Vatican statement on human reproduction had in mind not only options that are cur-rently available but also technologies that are on the medical horizon. Medical researchers predict, for example, that within a generation a totally extrauterine birth will be possible, in which fetuses develop in an artificial womb, with their nutrients, hormones, and temperature controlled by computer.

Most people agree that new reproductive technologies should be pursued if they help infertile couples to procreate. And almost everyone is against procedures that would make babies into commodities. But where in this unfamiliar moral terrain should the line be drawn?

The new reproductive technologies are emblematic of the great array of choices available today in marriage and family life—choices that pose new dilemmas and call into question the very foundations of family life. As several observers said of the Baby M case, it redefined the meaning of the term "mother," and in doing so took away a reference point.

After trying unsuccessfully to conceive, many infertile couples decide to adopt a child. Not all couples who adopt, however, are infertile. The majority of adoptive parents do so out of a love for children, a need in their own family (for example, a family member dies), or a socially conscious desire to provide for a child who otherwise might not have a family.

Adoption

Most adopted children are born in the United States, although overseas adoptions increased during the 1970s and 1980s. About 1 million children in our society live in adoptive families (National Committee for Adoption, 1989). The number of children adopted is expected to decrease in the 1990s as overseas adoptions become more difficult and the supply of American-born adoptive children continues to decline, because of better contraceptives and a decrease in the number of mothers willing to give up their children (Bianchi, 1990).

Most adoptions (41 percent) are arranged through a public agency, but private agencies and private lawyers also arrange for 35 and 25 percent of adoptions, respectively (Bachrach, Adams, Sambrano, & London, 1990). Most couples adopt children as babies—82 percent of children are under 1 year of age. Children of all ethnic and racial backgrounds have about an equal chance of being adopted, with black children more often adopted by an extended family member. More white than black or Hispanic couples adopt, but interracial adoptions are less common today owing to protests by various ethnic and racial groups over possible harmful effects to children (Bachrach et al., 1990). There is a growing concern that interracial adoptions lead to loss of identity and cultural heritage.

We tend to think of adoption as a private matter between an individual, couple, or family and an agency or lawyer. Once the adoption process begins, however, not much about the adoptive parent or parents remains unexplored. Values, beliefs, goals, and attitudes are scrutinized along with living arrangements and finances. It often takes years for the entire process to unfold. Adoptive parents, compared to other parents, tend to be older, well-established financially, and have longer-term marriages. Because of this advantaged living situation, most adoptive children are healthy and have high well-being in their early years. We know less about older children because hardly any longitudinal research exists on adoptive families.

Let's Wait: Delaying Parenthood

As a consequence of the recent tendency to defer marriage and childbearing, it is not uncommon today for couples to decide to have their first child as late as their mid-thirties. The timing of first birth is partly a matter of personal preference, of course, but it is also a question of biological capability. Although it is commonly assumed that age 35 is the biological boundary for women to bear their first child, there is no reason to conclude that the risks of childbearing increase dramatically in any given year. However, the woman who waits much past the normal age of first marriage to bear children does take a greater risk, both to her own health and the baby's, and that risk gradually increases with age.

One age-related factor in both males and females is *fertility,* the capacity to bear children. Fertility depends upon the proper coordination of both partners' reproductive systems. In order for conception to occur, the woman has to be able to release healthy eggs; her Fallopian tube must allow the passage of the fertilized egg into the uterus; and the lining of the uterus must be prepared for the implantation of the embryo. The man has to be able to produce healthy sperm capable of propelling themselves up the uterus to the Fallopian tube where they meet the ovum, and those sperm must be compatible with the chemical balance of the woman's reproductive system. Anything that restricts the production of sperm and eggs or impedes their interaction lowers the chances of conception.

The fecundity of men and women declines after age 30. Although male fecundity declines more slowly than that of females (some men father children as late as their seventies or eighties), aging does have an effect on their reproductive ability. With increasing age men produce fewer sperm and less active ones. The fecundity of women is typically highest in their mid-twenties, then it declines gradually during their thirties and more rapidly in their forties. The main reason why the fecundity of women decreases with age is that ovulation—which does not necessarily accompany each menstrual cycle—takes place less frequently. Women who have experienced irregular menstruation, repeated abortions, or prolonged use of the pill (which suppresses the function of the ovaries) may have special difficulties in conceiving during their thirties and forties.

The most common fear about late pregnancy is that it may produce retarded or deformed children. Although recent developments in obstetrics have reduced the risk of late childbearing, the chance of producing a child with congenital abnormalities does increase with the age of the parents. A genetic defect known as *Down's syndrome* is one of the most widespread abnormalities associated with aging parents.

Down's syndrome is the single most common form of mental retardation and often involves severe heart defects. Among mothers in their twenties, the chances of producing a child with Down's syndrome are very low—about 1 in 1,500. Those odds change to about 1 in 800 for women in their early thirties, to about 1 in 280 for women in their late thirties, and then to about 1 in 100 for women in their early forties.

In the case of other abnormalities, such as *Klinefelter's syndrome*—a condition in which male children are born with two X chromosomes and abnormally small testes that make them incapable of producing sperm—the age of the father seems to be an important factor. And there are other abnormalities associated with advancing parental age, such as the fact that women who give birth for the first time in their early thirties have about twice as many stillbirths—about 112 per 1,000 deliveries—compared with women who are in their early twenties. It is also important to note that the risk to the mother increases as she gets older. Delivery is more often complicated, and the risk of maternal heart failure and cervical cancer increases with age.

Childbirth at a relatively late age is safer for women today than it was a generation ago because parents can now avail themselves of a relatively new diagnostic technique, *alpha-feto protein (AFP) screening*—a blood test that detects various genetic abnormalities. Should this screening prove positive, then *amniocentesis* or ultrasound is typically used (Kolata, 1989). This procedure allows early diagnosis of Down's syndrome, spina bifida, and *Tay-Sach's*—a genetic disorder found in Jewish families—as well as other congenital disorders.

Amniocentesis, which can be performed 14 to 16 weeks after conception, involves the insertion of a thin needle into the womb to remove fluid and cells for analysis. If such examination indicates the presence of Down's syndrome or other genetic disorders, the mother can seek an abortion. It also allows doctors to determine the sex of the unborn child.

However, parents who intend to use amniocentesis should be aware of its limitations. It cannot yet be used to detect the presence of all birth defects. It is a relatively expensive procedure, and the results of the test are not available immediately after the test is taken. And although medical researchers at the University of California concluded on the basis of a study of 3,000 women that the procedure is safe and extremely accurate, many doctors are still concerned about the possibility that amniocentesis may damage the fetus. One

procedure that is sometimes preferred to amniocentesis is *chorionic villus sampling (CVS)*. This technique is considered safer because the needle is inserted through the abdomen or cervix to remove some of the embryonic membrane. It can be performed several weeks earlier than amniocentesis, when treatment is safe (Kolata, 1987).

Although the risk of producing a congenitally malformed child does increase with age, those risks are still fairly low for a woman in her mid-thirties or early forties who is married to a man no more than about 10 years older than she is. For the prospective mother of this age who uses the facilities of a well-equipped medical center to minimize possible birth complications, there is little reason for concern about the special risks of late childbearing.

Another available medical procedure is *ultrasound*—using high-frequency sound waves to create an image of the fetus within the uterus. A competent radiologist can view the results—called a *sonogram*—on a monitor, similar to a home-computer screen, and determine critical information about the developmental progress and location of the fetus. The sex of the fetus can even be determined during later stages of a pregnancy.

When One Is Enough

"It's better to give one child the best than to give two children half as good," said a mother in a recent interview. "One is affordable. One is manageable. One is a handful as it is" (Dreyfous, 1991, p. E1). Such is the reasoning of a rising number of couples in the recessionary 1990s. Scaling back on the essentials includes, for some couples, cutting back on the number of children they have. Census Bureau demographer Martin O'Connell points out that between 1978 and 1990 the number of women aged 40 to 44 years who had one child doubled and at the same time the number of women aged 30 to 34 years who planned to have one child also almost doubled, rising from 1 million to 1.7 million; 22 percent of American parents now have one child (in Dreyfous, 1991).

Why has the one-child family become a small but growing minority of American families? Besides the obvious economic costs of raising a child, today there is less social stigma attached to having one child. Though parents often hear stories about the only child who is demanding, self-centered, antisocial, dependent, and lonely, when they look around at the only children among their friends and neighbors, these stereotypes are just as likely to prove false as to ring true. There are also books like Susan Newman's *Parenting an Only Child* (1989) and Toni Falbo's *The Single-Child Family* (1984) as well as recent articles and interviews in the popular press that reject these stereotypes.

As middle-class, educated couples increasingly delay parenthood until their thirties, there is less opportunity to have a second child. These dual-income parents often get caught up in the reality of finding quality child care, paying escalating day-care costs, and managing the time crunch related to providing good parenting while simultaneously maintaining a career and a marriage. Many find that they have postponed having a second child either purposefully or unintentionally until the physical, emotional, and economic consequences have grown too costly. One-child families are even more common among the divorced—35 percent of single children live in divorced families—because many people delay marriage and then divorce prior to having children (Kantrowitz, 1986). By the time they marry a second time and start their family, most are well into their thirties. Again, it is the postponement model at work. Reduced fertility is the result.

Another parenting trend is having children outside of marriage. This emerging phenomenon has changed the structure of contemporary families.

PARENTHOOD WITHOUT MARRIAGE

Our cultural beliefs prescribe getting married before having children; nevertheless, increasing numbers of older, middle-class, educated single women and young adolescents are saying, "No, I don't think so." Our society, on the other hand, insists that marriage *not* be allowed for one group, gay and lesbian parents, who are increasingly likely to have children. The theme underlying such social prescriptions is "what is best for the child," but in contemporary society it is increasingly difficult to have guidelines for parenting that apply to all situations.

Single Mothers

Single-parent families are created in a variety of ways—through births to never-married mothers, separation, divorce, and widowhood. And single-parent families, regardless of how they are created, are overwhelmingly female-headed; fewer than 10 percent are headed by a male (U.S. Bureau of the Census, 1991). Single mothers usually live alone with their children; only 22 percent live with a relative or with others in a nonfamily situation (Rawlings, 1989). And despite folklore to the contrary, most single mothers are not on welfare, sitting at home and having babies to increase their allotment checks (Pear, 1991). Single mothers have more child-care options today than in the past, which enables a larger number to be employed. The Census Bureau reports that 53 percent of new mothers are in the work force—up from 38 percent in 1980. Among single mothers with 4 years of college, 68 percent are employed, compared to 32 percent of mothers with a high school education. Mothers with less than a high school education have greater difficulty providing for their families. Among single mothers, they are at greatest risk of living in poverty (see the "Point of View" box for a discussion of the politics of single motherhood).

Poverty is to a large extent a result of the economic and social vulnerability of women. Single mothers have less access to jobs that pay good wages and as women without marital partners they are disproportionately responsible for the well-being of their children (McLanahan & Booth, 1991). Children in single-parent families live on one-third the family income of two-parent families. Half live in poverty, compared with 10 percent of children in two-parent homes. "Around 75 percent of single-parent children will sink into a spell of poverty before they reach age 18, versus 20 percent of children from two-parent families" (Magnet, 1992, p. 43).

Because of delayed marriage and because women's intimate relationships more often begin in their adolescent years and include sex, adolescents are at greater risk of out-of-wedlock pregnancy. Most single mothers (66 percent) become pregnant by accident and then decide not to marry. Because the largest increase in single-parent families in the last decade has been among unmarried women and most of the current social concern is focused on adolescent single mothers, we begin our discussion with that group of mothers.

Adolescent Pregnancy

Social Concerns

Though American adolescents are no more sexually active than their counterparts in most industrialized

POINT OF VIEW

The Politics of Single Motherhood

A major concern of social scientists and family advocates is whether the increase in mother-only families is a sign of social progress or decline. Of further concern is the feminization of poverty. The following excerpt explores these concerns.

Single motherhood is a highly politicized subject that involves conflicting values and competing gender, class, and race interests. First and foremost, single mothers are women, and therefore their prevalence and material condition have relevance for debates over inequality between men and women. The poverty of single mothers highlights the economic vulnerability that is inherent in women's role as mothers and calls attention to the relatively low earning capacity and disproportionate responsibility for children that is shared by all women.

Single mothers are also disproportionately poor; hence their condition is relevant to debates over inequality across social classes. Although many of these women were poor prior to becoming heads of household, the plight of mother-only families has attracted the nation's attention and raised questions about the fairness and efficiency of our social programs. How can a society with such a high standard of living account for the fact that about 20 percent of its children are living below the poverty line? For policy makers and analysts who support greater equality across classes, the mother-only family has become a rallying point.

Finally, a large number of single mothers are black, which means that discussions of the trends in family disruption and nonmarriage are inevitably linked to discussions of racial inequality and discrimination. The politics of single motherhood are perhaps nowhere more evident than in the debate over the black mother-only family, which dates back to the 1960s. At that time single mothers were cited as evidence of a growing pathology in the black family and as a critical link in the intergenerational transmission of poverty. This characterization of the black family was widely criticized by many black scholars and liberal politicians for being implicitly racist and for "blaming the victim." More recently, some of these issues have reemerged. Now, as then, the political and intellectual dilemma is how to develop an analysis that stresses the economic and social disadvantages faced by poor single mothers without reinforcing negative stereotypes about their lifestyles and values.

What should be done to reduce poverty and income insecurity in mother-only families? Should we move in the direction of private solutions, such as increased child support and employment opportunities? Or

nations, they have substantially higher pregnancy rates—twice that of France, England, and Canada; three times that of Sweden; and seven times that of the Netherlands (Timberlake & Carpenter, 1990, p. 87). In 1988, 472,000 adolescents younger than age 20 gave birth. Of these births, 179,000 were to adolescents under age 17 and 10,000 were to girls under age 14. Today more young women age 15 and under are getting pregnant and more are also keeping their babies. Among this group of adolescents there were 949 abortions for every 1,000 births (National Center for Health Statistics, 1992).

The majority of adolescent births are to white mothers (65 percent), but the mother-headed family type is

more prevalent among blacks and Hispanics. Black adolescents, who make up 15 percent of the adolescent population, give birth to approximately 30 percent of the babies (Adams, Adams-Taylor, & Pittman, 1989). Demographer William O'Hare and his colleagues write:

Socioeconomic differences between blacks and whites explain much of the difference in their fertility levels. Birth rates are similar among black and white women within the same level of educational attainment, for example. . . . Two glaring disparities in the childbearing patterns of blacks and whites, however, are causes for concern: black babies are nearly four times more

should the state provide support directly, in the form of children's allowances, subsidized child care, or a minimum child support benefit? It would appear that we need a mix of public and private programs. It is unreasonable to expect taxpayers to increase public subsidies for single mothers unless parents themselves are contributing their fair share. Thus, the implementation of a publicly guaranteed child support minimum benefit is likely to be accompanied by a strengthening of the private child support system. Similarly, support for subsidized child care is most likely to be linked to programs that promote mothers' employment, especially mothers currently on welfare.

Will enforcing child support obligations reinforce women's traditional dependence on men and/or push low-income minority fathers (and their new families) into poverty? Will increasing public sector benefits create new dependencies on the state? The best way to protect poor fathers from economic hardship is to make child support obligations a percentage of current income. Then if the father is poor or unemployed, his obligation will also be low. Another way is to designate a minimum income that is not subject to the child support tax. Both solutions are preferable to exempting all fathers from child support on the grounds that it may impoverish a few.

The best way to minimize single mothers' dependency is to (a) redistribute their sources of support across a broader array of institutions, including the family, the market, and the state; and (b) extend support to a wider population. Dependency itself is not the problem, but rather the loss of power and the feeling of helplessness that often accompanies it. Distributing support across multiple institutions minimizes the degree of dependence on any one person or organization. It is one thing to depend on the ex-spouse or the state for 90 percent of one's income; it is another to be 20 percent dependent on each of these institutions and to be 60 percent dependent on a paid job. Extending support to a broader population would mean making programs such as child support, child care, and pay equity available to all women (as opposed to those who are poor).

Ultimately, a full solution to the problems faced by mother-only families will necessitate a reorganization of the sexual division of labor, which at present places a disproportionate share of child care responsibilities on women and in doing so restricts their earning capacity and economic independence. In the meantime, achieving the goal of economic security for single mothers will require the coming together of different interest groups in support of multiple policies aimed at solving the problems of both middle-class and poor mother-only families.

EXPLORATIONS *How would you divide the responsibility for finding solutions to decreasing poverty for single mothers and their children among public or government agencies, family members, or private businesses? Should single mothers be required to accept job training and/or employment in return for receiving public assistance?*

SOURCE: Excerpted from S. McLanahan & K. Booth (1991).

likely to be born to a single mother, and three times more likely to be born to a teenage mother. (O'Hare, Pollard, Mann, & Kent, 1990, p. 11)

Frank Furstenberg, who has studied adolescent pregnancy and childbirth for over 20 years, explains that the number of births to adolescent mothers reached a high in the early 1970s and has recently declined from 19 to 13 percent. He adds, "but the issue of teenaged childbearing as a social problem did not go away" (1991, p. 130). One reason for the concern is that in the United States premarital sexual activity is often regarded as an indicator of public morality. Some point to statistics that show that 800,000 adolescent females still become pregnant each year and argue that many of the pregnancies lead to births that dramatically affect the lives of mother, father, child, and the kin network (Christopher & Roosa, 1990).

Adolescent Mothers

Adolescent mothers typically leave school. Among high school dropouts, one-half of the females were mothers and almost one-third of the males were fathers (Adams et al., 1989). Not having a diploma means that these young people will have difficulty finding a job that pays much more than the minimum wage. Since 1960, the earnings of high school dropouts, compared to those who graduated from high school, fell

22 percent. Adolescents who become pregnant often have one or more of the following characteristics in common—academic failure, despair over future opportunities, or a desire to use sex as a means of strengthening a relationship with a boyfriend (Furstenberg, 1991).

From his study, focusing mainly on black adolescent mothers, Furstenberg (1991) concludes that sometimes having a child can give direction and purpose to young women who are unsure if they will ever rise out of poverty. Moreover, some teens reported that childbearing raised their status among family and friends. Over a 20-year period, many of the adolescent mothers Furstenberg interviewed eventually managed to go back to school, find steady jobs, and leave the welfare system.

Although many social analysts fear that there may be a *cycle of adolescent childbearing*—a situation in which the daughters of adolescent mothers become adolescent mothers themselves—over 65 percent did not repeat their mother's behavior and most finished high school. When Furstenberg was asked how the daughters avoided following in their mothers' footsteps, he credited individual families and the way they dealt with the pregnancy, the school system, the teens themselves, or just luck itself (in Kantrowitz, 1990). Despite the eventually positive responses of most adolescents and their families, many young women still viewed their pregnancy as poorly timed, an error, and a calamity for their parents who were sometimes reluctant or economically unable to assume the burdens of child care.

Most adolescents say that their pregnancies were unplanned and unwanted (Forrest & Singh, 1990). Similar to earlier generations, they do not typically begin contraception at the same time that they initiate intercourse. Instead, they seek contraceptive methods only after they become sexually active, and thus risk pregnancy in their early sexual encounters, when the possibility is highest. In most cases, first intercourse is not expected to happen when it does; without planning, there is no provision for contraceptives. Such preparations are particularly unlikely when one's first sexual experience is with a partner to whom there is little emotional commitment and when young people cannot fully accept the implications of their own sexuality (Bachrach, 1984; Kisker, 1985).

Adolescents are typically unhappy and fearful when they discover their pregnancy. Their families, when they find out, are usually negative about the situation. But, by the time of birth most adolescents and their families are mildly to overwhelmingly positive (Furstenberg, Levine, & Brooks-Gunn, 1990). Stress theorists would probably explain that these families when faced with a crisis situation—the pregnancy—successfully coped by changing their perception of the situation from negative to positive. Coping in this manner allows the family to accept the pregnancy as inevitable and thus prepare for the future and offer support to the pregnant adolescent.

The Role of Fathers

And the fathers of the children born to adolescent mothers—What is their role? There is considerable disagreement about how much such fathers are involved with their children. Some family researchers have concluded that only a relatively small number are "hit and run" victimizers who never support the mother or child in any significant way. Even experts may have severely underestimated the degree of support unmarried fathers provide, particularly among minorities where informal systems often substitute for legal paternity systems (Adams et al., 1989) (see the "Changing Lifestyles" box on teaching young men to be fathers).

Furstenberg (1991) believes that the studies conducted so far with adolescent fathers are biased by small sample size, how the sample was selected (volunteers were used), or by the fact that the fathers were only observed or interviewed soon after childbirth. Based on his longitudinal study of adolescent mothers, he concludes that fathers seem to play an important part early in their children's lives, but, as time passes, paternal bonds typically weaken. By the time their children reach adolescence, only a small minority of fathers write to, talk with, or visit their children regularly. An even smaller number give substantial financial support.

The Growing Reluctance to Marry

Thirty years ago when a single woman became pregnant the usual reaction was to tell the father and head for the altar. This is no longer the case. One in four women who give birth today are not married. Among adolescents the figures are even higher. Of black adolescent mothers, 90 percent are unmarried. Among whites, 66 percent are unmarried—a doubling of the rate since 1970 (U.S. Bureau of the Census, 1991) (see Figure 8-5). Even among mothers with higher incomes, one-half give birth without being married. In

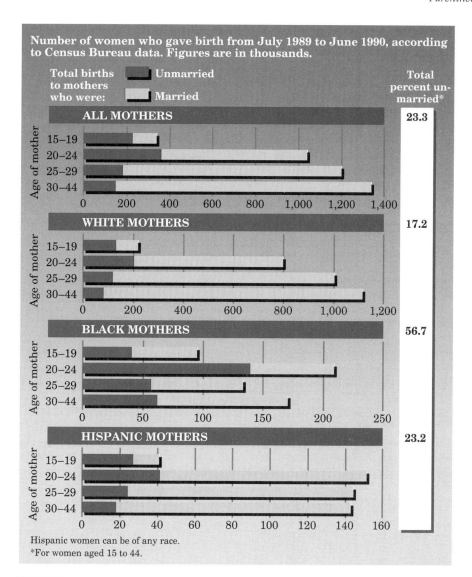

FIGURE 8-5
Single Mothers Giving Birth
SOURCE: R. Pear (1991).

some cases—about 25 percent of the time—the child is born into a two-parent family, but the parents are co-habiting rather than married. About one-third of adolescents marry within 5 years of giving birth.

Why would a pregnant young woman decide against marriage? Recently, sociologist Naomi Farber interviewed a sample of unmarried black and white mothers aged 15 to 20 years from middle-, working-, and lower-class families. She asked mothers how they felt about men as potential husbands, their hopes and expectations about marriage, and various other questions designed to get to the bottom of why adolescent mothers were increasingly reluctant to marry the fathers of their children. To her surprise, nearly all of the study participants, regardless of race or class, believed in marriage, wanted to marry, and thought that the ideal way to rear children was within marriage. As one adolescent mother said:

Teaching Young Men to Be Fathers

Revitalizing the black community through restoring the family is the goal of a number of community groups across the United States. One of the core strategies of these programs is teaching young men how to be fathers and be involved in the lives of their children. The following article describes one such program and its successes.

Two years ago, Paul Smalley found himself getting sucked into a stereotype. At 21 he returned home from military prison a frustrated, unemployed young black man who also happened to be a brand-new unmarried father. His son and namesake was already 4 months old, and Smalley was so unfamiliar with his new role that he thought he could not touch the baby without permission. "I was asking if I could pick him up," he says. "I just didn't feel like a father."

Smalley worried because he could see a familiar pattern forming, born of his shame over not being able to support his child, the feeling of inadequacy and the strain on his relationship with the baby's mother. He resisted joining the ranks of young black fathers who cut out on their kids because they will not face the pressures of parenthood, but he could not see how to break the cycle—until he learned from a friend about the Responsive Fathers Program at the Philadelphia Children's Network.

While social-assistance programs have long been available to teenage mothers, little effort has gone into helping young fathers. The Responsive Fathers Program is one of a growing number of groups across the United States seeking to fill the vacuum. The programs try to help young unmarried men become better fathers, providers, and mates through counseling services, particularly assistance in a job search. The 61 participants in the Philadelphia program, who range in age from 16 to 26, meet in group sessions once a week and discuss child rearing, self-esteem, male-female relationships, and the job market. "The program helped me to open up," says Smalley. "It gave me the drive to want to do things. I've learned how anger affects my child and about how he needs both parents."

Fathers come to the program either by referral from a hospital, community center, or probation office or, like Smalley, by word of mouth from a friend. Thomas J. Henry, 47, the program's director, says that many young fathers just need help cutting through the bureaucracy: filling out forms, standing in the correct lines

When I got pregnant and I decided to bring Joshua home with me, it didn't seem nice . . . for a little boy or little girl to have one of what he should have—you know, half of what he should have. . . . I wouldn't wish that on anybody. A child was meant to have a mother and a father. . . . I can't imagine myself having only my mother. My life wouldn't be the same without my mother and my father. (1990, p. 54)

Most of the mothers in the study expressed similar views. So why did they remain single? The reasons that Farber uncovered were multiple and diverse and varied by race and class. Farber writes, "Each teen offered a scenario that included the influence of her family, the baby's father, subsequent boyfriends, and her own beliefs, goals, and desires" (p. 54).

Mothers from middle-class and working-class homes said that the babies' fathers were not ready for marriage. The fathers encouraged them to terminate the pregnancy or, failing that, to put the child up for adoption. All middle-class and working-class mothers received some kind of support from their own parent(s). This support was not contingent on marriage. Rather, it was given along with the advice *not* to marry. No pressure was applied by the women's other adult kin or friends to marry. Both the mother and her parents believed that, by marrying, the couple would be making one more mistake. Some parents felt that marriage would threaten the mother's future education and job opportunities. At the time of the interviews, most of the middle-class and working-class mothers had steady boyfriends and planned to marry one day.

for public assistance, and dealing with unresponsive bureaucrats. "This system encourages fathers not to be there," he says. "'You have many fathers declared absent when they are actually present. People think they're just making babies and don't have any feelings attached to that act. Everyone says, 'We want you to be a responsible father,' but we give them nothing to be responsible with."

The Responsive Fathers Program is part of a study being conducted by Public/Private Ventures, a nonprofit public-policy research organization that focuses on youth development. Using five other similar programs from across the country, PPV launched the study last year to try to discover whether it could get young unwed fathers to come forward and seek help, identify their needs, and direct them to the services they require. The group aims to provide information to policymakers responsible for family welfare programs so that as they debate decisions concerning young mothers, they will keep young fathers in mind as well.

"It is important for families that we begin to consider the role of fathers," says Bernadine Watson, director of individual and family support at PPV. "Our work has shown that these men, even though they are young and do not have the educational background or employment skills, are very interested in being good parents."

Henry believes the Philadelphia program will make a difference because it is willing to take the 3 to 6 years needed to "put things right" in a young man's life. Such philosophy and time frame contrast with government programs offering quick-fix solutions, but Henry believes in taking a pay-now-or-pay-later approach. His goal for the fathers is true self-sufficiency, by training them for jobs in areas such as printing, building maintenance, and computer programming. This is no easy trick; the program has a hard time persuading employers to give the young men a chance.

The young men say they enjoy the sessions because they can vent their feelings of frustration, often born of their sense that society perceives them as bad parents. The black male has become the focal point of blame for the deterioration of the African-American family. But in many cases such blame is misdirected. Devon Shaw, 24, whose three children range in age from 6 months to 4 years, was just out of high school when his first child was born. He doesn't like the way the system "lets you know what we're doing wrong, not what they're doing wrong." Smalley, who now works as an animal-care technician and goes to school at night, admits that many of his friends simply cannot function as fathers: "Some don't even try. Some don't care. They just turn to drugs or drug dealing as their way out." But he stresses that there are many more who are trying to be responsible, who want their kids to have two parents, a good education, and a safe place to live. "It's just we have so many obstacles to becoming decent men," he says. "But it is inside of us. It's in the black men out there."

EXPLORATIONS *How does the Responsive Fathers Program differ from traditional social services programs?*

SOURCE: Excerpted from S. C. Gregory (1992).

Lower-class mothers were not as confident as other single mothers that they would eventually marry; most did not have a steady dating partner. Many poor black mothers could see no advantage to marriage over single parenthood. As one said:

Marriage doesn't make any difference. 'Cause my sister, you know, when she had her first child she was alone. Her second child, she was married . . . but it still was like she was on her own. Because no one can really help as much as yourself. (p. 59)

Many black lower-class women expected less of men in general. According to Farber, they want their man's commitment, but anticipate that such hopes will probably not be realized and so prepare themselves for this possibility. As one 16-year-old black mother confided:

Well, I don't think I will get married, but I'll just have a boyfriend or something. . . . No, most boys don't stick around. All they be doing is talking. I guess most of the boys think that it makes them feel like a man. "Hey, I've got a son" and all this stuff, and one coming and all. Just makes them look stupid if they ain't taking care of it. (p. 60)

Another point made by black mothers is that the fathers are usually unemployed. They cannot find work and as a result are unable to provide for themselves, let alone their out-of-wedlock child. Some social critics like William Wilson (1987) propose that discrimination has reduced job opportunities for urban black men and consequently has influenced a reduction in the marriage rates and a rise in illegitimacy and single-mother families in poor black communities.

The major difference Farber observed between the white and black mothers she studied was that the white mothers were more optimistic about getting married "someday." Although many black women were in stable relationships with men, they were ambivalent about the lasting power of such relationships. According to Farber, in the last two decades adolescent women in poor urban communities have observed many failed relationships and separated marital unions, have lived through similar difficult family situations in their own homes, and have had personal relationships that repeated the same pattern of dissolution. The result may be a cynical outlook on their chances of "having it all"—a committed relationship that includes marriage to a man who will be there as a parent to their children.

The Fate of the Children

Children born to unwed mothers of any age are more likely than others to be raised in circumstances of economic need (McLanahan & Booth, 1991). But becoming a mother is typically a far more difficult thing for a teenager than it is for a more mature woman. Because teenage girls are physically less mature and often do not receive adequate prenatal care, those who bear children face a greater risk both to their own health and to that of their babies. In addition, some adolescent mothers have to manage social disapproval along with the tasks of caring for and financially providing for their children. Children have higher well-being if their mother is emotionally and physically healthy, has at least a high school education, and is older—at least in her late teens (Dubow & Luster, 1990).

Many children of adolescent mothers fare well. One study by Eric Dubow and Tom Luster (1990) indicates that children with average or better intelligence cope better with the stress of their disadvantaged circumstances. Intelligent children, these authors suggest, are better problem solvers and thus deal with life's difficulties more successfully. They are also better able to understand homework assignments and participate in school activities, and consequently achieve greater academic success.

High self-esteem also reduces stress for these children. Children with high self-esteem usually are independent, inquisitive, and assertive. They are generally well-liked by peers, which adds to their sense of

self-worth. The mother's parenting style is seen as the main contributor to children's self-esteem. Mothers who "emphasize setting clear limits, enforce those limits consistently, and respect the child's right to make decisions within those limits" have children with higher self-esteem (p. 403). The life courses of parent and child are intertwined. When mothers are able to supply emotionally supportive and intellectually stimulating home situations, children thrive. In addition, children's own personality traits and learned behavior patterns also affect how they deal with stressful life circumstances and their relative disadvantage.

There is almost universal agreement that adolescent mothers and their children need additional economic help, encouragement to stay in school, and advice about how to avoid another pregnancy.

> Teens need compelling reasons to believe that delaying pregnancy and parenthood is in their best interest. Teen decisions about sexual activity and use of contraception are tied to their perceptions of the opportunities open to them. Teens with strong achievement orientations and clear goals for the future are less likely to become sexually active at early ages and more likely, if sexually active, to be regular and effective contraceptive users. (Adams et al., 1989, p. 226)

Preventive measures require at least a tacit acceptance of adolescent sexual activity, and such measures invite fierce debate about the most delicate of topics—abortion, access to contraceptives, and sex education.

Gays and lesbians are another group of parents seldom discussed without reference to stereotypes and misinformation.

Gay and Lesbian Parents

It is estimated that 20 percent of gay men and women are parents, though there are no accurate figures available (Bozett, 1987). Because their numbers are low and owing to their need for privacy, only recently has much research focused on gay and lesbian parents. Results of the studies completed suggest that gay and lesbian parents do not differ significantly from heterosexual parents in regard to parenting style or ability to parent (Bigner & Jacobsen, 1989; Pies, 1990).

Most gay and lesbian parents have been married and their children were conceived within the marriage. They face special challenges as parents because of the social taboos and stereotypes attached to their lifestyle (see the "Changing Lifestyles" box). They worry more than their heterosexual counterparts about finding a partner who will accept parenthood as a goal of the relationship and will remain committed to raising a child. Lesbian mothers, compared to heterosexual mothers, are more concerned about whether cohabiting with a female partner will make them vulnerable to neighborhood criticism and jeopardize their rights to custody—in custody cases, only about 15 percent of lesbians win (Bigner & Jacobsen, 1989). When lesbian partners choose to have a child, it requires considerable planning and coordination—who will be the donor, what method will be used to induce pregnancy, who will be told and when, and how will legal issues be resolved—are only a few of the many questions that must be addressed (Pies, 1990). Lesbian mothers also struggle with many of the same issues that heterosexual mothers confront, such as time, jobs, emotional support from their partners, attitudes of family and friends, and raising a child who is emotionally and mentally healthy.

Heterosexual fathers, compared to gay fathers, espouse more traditional parental values. For example, they more often mention becoming fathers out of a need to continue the family name, a desire to have someone to care about them when they grow old, and a hope to pass along family traditions to a new generation. Gay fathers more often talk about how fatherhood conveys acceptance as an adult member of society—that parenthood is a rite of passage into adulthood (Bigner & Bozett, 1990).

What happens when children find out that their parent is gay? Most children, according to social scientist Frederick Bozett (1988), respond in a positive manner. Children's acceptance is due to several factors: that gay parents make a special effort to teach their children to be accepting of individual differences; that children are unlikely to reject a parent who has provided years of care and affection; and that finding out a parent is gay may help the child better understand why his or her parents are separated or divorced (most are) and thus relieve them of any personal burden of guilt, blame, or responsibility for the split.

Of course, a few children do take a negative view of their parent's lifestyle. One child said, "I'm embarrassed that my father is gay. A lot of times I would just like him to go away." Another child said, "Sure, I'd prefer for my dad to still be in the closet. There's no conflict (that way)" (Bigner & Bozett, 1990, p. 162). The main concern voiced by children is that their friends and peers will react badly upon finding out;

that they will assume that the child is gay too. To protect themselves, children cope by using several different strategies (Bozett, 1987). They sometimes ask their parents to conceal their sexuality around their friends, or they avoid being seen in public with their parents when accompanied by their gay partners or gay friends, and keep friends away from the house to protect them from accidentally finding out about their parents. Some children cope by never disclosing to anyone that their parent is gay. Others selectively tell their most trusted friends about their parent. "The less obtrusive the child believes the parent's homosexuality to be and the more feelings of mutuality or connectedness the child has with the parent, the less often the child will use these coping strategies" (Bigner & Bozett, 1990, p. 163).

To ensure more positive responses from their children, it is best if the parent has come to terms with his or her own sexual orientation. Otherwise, parents could inadvertently pass along a sense of negativity or shame. Care should be taken to fit the words and terms describing sexual orientation and lifestyle to the age of the child. If at all possible, it is better for parents to discuss gayness with the child before he or she suspects or finds out from someone else. Finding out from someone else can be upsetting because this may violate the sense of trust between a parent and child (Bigner & Bozett, 1990).

When and how the child is told is important. Bigner and Bozett (1990) advise parents to pick a safe and quiet setting, free of interruptions. Parents, these authors believe, should take a positive and sincere approach. If possible, a gay parent should try to find another gay parent who has gone through the experience with positive results. Talking to that parent about his or her approach could be helpful—what worked, what did not. It is important to assure the child that nothing has changed; that the parent is the same person as before. Finally, the parent should be prepared for questions and rehearse possible answers. For example, the child might ask, "Why are you telling me this?" "What does being gay mean?" "What makes a person gay?" and "Will I be gay, too?" Gay parents involved in stable and caring relationships who are open about their sexual orientation tend to be more involved parents than those who hide their gayness or remain married despite knowledge of their sexual orientation (Bozett, 1987).

The prevailing societal attitude toward gay and lesbian parents is one of prejudice and homophobia. Pub-

CHANGING LIFESTYLES

Sarah's Parents

Sarah is in most ways your basic 5-year-old: a watcher of Charlie Brown videos, a reader of Richard Scarry books, a crayoner of cotton-puff clouds and fat yellow suns with Tinkertoy-spoke rays. Like every other piece of kindergarten artwork ever made, her portrait of "My Family" contains stick-figurey construction paper people, all holding hands and looking jolly. Except her family is a little different: there's Sarah, there's "Daddy," there's "Mom-my" . . . and there's Amy, Mommy's lover.

Sarah's "cubby" at school is special, too. While the other kids hang their windbreakers and lunch boxes next to photos of one parent, or two, Sarah has three. She takes this embarrassment of riches in stride—which is to say, without any embarrassment at all.

Not that she isn't a very savvy little girl about the precisely calibrated degrees to which the many adults in her life fit into the larger scheme of things. If you ask her about the members of her "whole" (that is, extended) family, she will tick off various grandmothers and cousins on her fingers. "Francie [her biological mother's ex-lover and now best friend] is in my family, too," she adds. "But Richard [her father's new boyfriend] isn't *exactly* in my family . . . yet." The adults around her would probably say the same thing, in many more words.

Amy, Nancy, Sarah, and their two cats live down the street from Doug in an adobe house with a yard full of mesquite trees. Amy and Doug have pooled their resources and opened a café. He does most of the cooking, she takes care of most of the business end. Nancy meanwhile teaches at a nearby college. All three contribute to Sarah's expenses, although Amy—because she lives with Sarah and has a more flexible schedule than Nancy—is the primary caregiver in terms of time at the moment.

"It confuses people," Amy notes cheerfully. "People come into the restaurant, and they see that Doug and I are partners, and then they see this little kid running around after school relating to both of us. Not surprisingly, they assume that Doug and I are married—which, of course, we both hate. Usually, I sit them down and just explain the story." Some people still don't quite get it. For Sarah's sake, the adults tend to like to deal with the gay issue up front, where it can be defused if need be. "When it came time to get a pediatrician, all three of us marched in—we didn't want some situation later on where the doctor didn't realize that all of us were in on this. It's the same thing now that we've been looking at elementary schools for next year. At interviews our position is, "This is our situation, and it's very important that Sarah gets support on that if she needs it.' " At one school they considered, they got more than they asked for—several faculty members discreetly came out to them.

Doug and Richard have occasionally hinted that Sarah gets away with too much at Nancy and Amy's house, and the women have occasionally felt a financial

lic fears revolve around whether children in such families can develop successfully without role models of each sex living at home, whether the children will grow up to be gay, whether lesbian mothers will provide enough quality time to their children, whether gay and lesbian relationships will remain stable, and whether children will be subjected to sexual abuse. None of these fears has a basis in research findings. In fact, all have been disputed by various studies (Bigner & Bozett, 1990; DiLapi, 1989; Hoeffer, 1985; Lewin & Lyons, 1982; Pennington, 1987; Steckel, 1987; Strong & Shinfeld, 1984; Weitz, 1984). Children of gay and lesbian parents seem no more likely than other children to have difficulty with mental health or sexual identity. It is the quality of the parent-child relationship rather than the sexual orientation of parents that seems most important. Children with parents who are secure with their own identity, committed to their parental role, and buttressed by a supportive network of friends and family fare best.

Parenting cannot be classified as a completely positive or negative experience. Judgment of the balance of positive and negative effects varies day by day, week by week, and year by year depending on the parent's economic situation, marital status, and access to supportive others. Age and personality of the child and the parents as well as the life-cycle stage the family is passing through are also critical factors in assessing

pinch when Doug is casual about paying his share of the child support money on time. But the splits are minor, and they're by no means consistently boys versus girls.

But Amy and Nancy are quick to note that almost all their minor difficulties—from scheduled sex to sporadic conflicts about child raising—are typical of those encountered by all parents.

But when you ask them all if there's anything they would do over differently, the answer is: not much. "I'm glad I did it with a father that I know, and not a sperm bank," says Nancy. When Sarah was an infant, Nancy did go through a spell of jealousy over Doug's relationship with their child. "I didn't want to share her with him; I hardly knew him," she admits. "Then I told myself to just cool out and think of what was best for Sarah." Nancy adds that she might be less enthusiastic if Doug were an absentee father. "There's this whole Daddy Thing; Daddy gets to be Daddy, and all that that represents, no matter what he does or doesn't do, and kids—all kids—just plug into that. But in fact, Doug *is* lovely with her."

Of all the adults in Sarah's life, Amy is the one in the most vulnerable position. She has no legal claim on Sarah if she and Nancy ever break up (although gay civil rights groups are fighting for the rights of nonbiological lesbian mothers who are thus left with no recourse). Nancy and Doug's wills specify, that if they were to die, they would want Amy to have custody, but it's a wish that grandparents or even the state could challenge in court. "It's too devastating to think about," says Amy. "So I don't."

She also finds terminology a problem. "I'll be at the grocery store and some clerk will ask me if Sarah's mine. Well, she *is*, damn it, even if that's not what they meant. I periodically sit Sarah down to make sure she's okay with this stuff. Like I recently said to her, 'You know, I'm not your mother, but I'm sort of like your parent.' She nodded and said, 'Right. Mommy is my mother. But I *am* your daughter.' "

At the preschool Sarah currently attends, the other kids tend to announce "Your Amy is here to pick you up." There are several other children in Sarah's class who have gay parents, and in one of the more open families, the nonbiological mother also happens to be named Amy. It's becoming a sort of generic honorific: Sarah and her friend Rex both go off after school with their Amys.

Perhaps things will be more awkward when Sarah is older, the adults say. But perhaps they won't be. Or, more likely, they will be, but only because most teenagers find *something* about their parents that's like, totally gross. So far, so good.

Sarah's only recorded worry about the future is one that she shared with Nancy one day when she was trying to figure out how she could be a doctor and stay home with her own sick child. Nancy assured her that such things were eminently doable; she herself could baby sit. Sarah sighed with relief, her grown-up life secured.

"But," she suddenly asked, "where will I find a Daddy and an Amy?"

EXPLORATIONS *How does Sarah benefit from having a "nontraditional" family? What additional issues and concerns, related to their unique family patterns, might Sarah's parents encounter as she progresses through middle childhood and adolescence?*

SOURCE: Excerpted from L. V. Gelder (1991).

parent-child well-being. Most parents value children and take their parenting role seriously. They worry about how to be good parents and whether their children will become successful adults. Parents basically raise their children as best they can, given their circumstances and the condition of their neighborhood and community (Demo, 1992).

SUMMARY POINTS

■ 1946 marked the beginning of a "baby boom" in America which continued until 1964. During this almost two-decade period, couples married younger, had more children at a younger age than previous generations, experienced economic prosperity, and expressed a renewed faith in the future.

■ During the "baby-boom" years a procreation ethic dominated family life. Pronatalism—societal pressure for couples to have children—was at a peak. Motherhood was increasingly viewed as a fulfilling lifetime career. Without children, men were portrayed as having lost their place in history.

■ A "baby bust" was underway by the early 1970s, due in part to a renewed preference for smaller families, the availability of reliable methods of birth control, and a concern over a swelling population—the echo effect of the "baby boom."

■ The preferred number of children for most couples today is two.

■ Minority groups accounted for 31 percent of the nation's children in 1990 and will account for 34 percent in 2000 and 38 percent in 2010.

■ By one estimate, it costs almost $6,000 to provide financially for a baby in the first year of her or his life; $100,000 from birth to age 18; and $232,000 if a college education is included.

■ Despite the financial costs of rearing a child, and regardless of the fact that 90 percent of parents believe that it is more difficult to be a parent today than in past generations, most would do it all over again.

■ Parents describe the most rewarding aspects of having children as the love and affection children bring, the pleasure of watching children grow, the happiness and fun they bring, the sense of family they create, and the fulfillment and satisfaction they create.

■ Maternal deprivation and maternal instinct are two ideas about motherhood that have been widely criticized. We tend to romanticize and idealize motherhood to such an extent that much unnecessary anxiety and distress accompany the parental role for women.

■ Fathers today are expected to be more involved in child rearing for three reasons: successful child development is believed to rely on meeting the needs of the child at critical points in time; mothers are likely to be in the work force and to have less time for parenting; and the society expects the "new" father to be an involved father.

■ The *egalitarian ethic* or *daddy track* refers to the emerging cultural belief that fathers should be equally responsible (with mothers) for their children.

■ Mothers and fathers are often uneasy and anxious about bringing up children. In the past, they looked to grandmothers and other members of the previous generation for answers to their questions about child rear-

ing. Today, parents increasingly rely on child-development specialists and other experts for parenting advice.

■ Though there are some general guidelines that will help most parents with child rearing, there is more than one right way to raise a child.

■ Voluntarily childfree couples score higher on measures of psychological well-being and life satisfaction than do parents.

■ Many childfree couples go through a four-stage postponement process as they decide against having children.

■ Among infertile couples, women more often mourn the loss of the parenting role, while men regret the loss of their wife's companionship and what was once a satisfying marital relationship.

■ Infertile couples use several strategies to protect themselves from gossip and prying remarks: remain low key about their problem; talk to a trustworthy friend or two; say their problem is a medical one; or refuse to give specific reasons for their infertility, blaming it instead on a combination of things that affect *both* equally.

■ New reproductive technologies bring new choices as well as ethical and moral dilemmas.

■ Though there is a higher chance of abnormal births to mothers in their late thirties and forties, the risks have been lessened by new diagnostic and birthing methods.

■ The single-child family has been stereotyped as deviant and dysfunctional for children, despite research to the contrary.

■ The vast majority of single parents are mothers. Most unmarried single mothers become pregnant by accident and then decide not to marry.

■ American adolescents, though no more sexually active than adolescents in other developed countries, have substantially higher pregnancy rates.

■ Adolescent pregnancy has decreased considerably since the 1960s and 1970s, but approximately 800,000 adolescent girls still get pregnant each year.

■ Though children of adolescent mothers are at greater risk than other children of being economically disadvantaged, many are able to cope successfully with their situation because of their mother's parenting style and their own intelligence, self-esteem, and resourcefulness.

■ More than other mothers, single, poor black mothers are ambivalent about marriage. Sociologist Naomi Farber believes that this is because the mothers have observed many failed relationships within their communities and, as a result, have developed a cynical but realistic outlook on poor black mens' ability to provide for and parent their children.

■ Though gay and lesbian parents do not differ significantly from heterosexual parents in regard to parenting style or ability to parent, they do face special challenges as parents because of prevailing social taboos and stereotypes concerning their lifestyles.

KEY TERMS

Procreation ethic
Population bomb
Replacement level
Opportunity costs
Egalitarian ethic
Authoritarian parenting
  style
Authoritative parenting
  style
Infertility
In vitro *fertilization*
  (IVF)

Surrogate motherhood
Fertility
Down's syndrome
Klinefelter's syndrome
Alpha-feto protein (AFP) screen-
  ing
Amniocentesis
Tay-Sachs
Chorionic villus sampling (CVS)
Ultrasound
Sonogram
Cycle of adolescent childbearing

REVIEW QUESTIONS

1. Trace the history of fertility and parenthood from World War II to the present.

2. Ask two sets of mothers and fathers with young children what they find most rewarding and most frustrating about being a parent. In class, compare your findings with those of other students. What are your conclusions?

3. List ways our society romanticizes and idealizes motherhood. Discuss the special problems created for mothers by the prevailing cultural ideology. Think of things that mothers might do to counteract and otherwise deal with this cultural bias.

4. Look over the child-rearing guidelines suggested in this chapter. Would you add any additional guidelines for parents of adolescents? And for parents of young adults?

5. Why do you think voluntarily childfree couples are happier and more satisfied with their marriages than are couples with children?

6. Of the methods available for infertile couples to have children, which do you find the most morally or ethically problematic? Why?

7. You have been asked to give a 30-minute talk on adolescent pregnancy to the local PTA. Outline the points you would want to make during your presentation.

8. Explain why single black women are increasingly bearing children without benefit of marriage.

9. A gay father calls the hot line of the local mental health agency while you are on volunteer duty. He asks for information about gay parenting. What would you tell him? Are there any books or articles you would recommend?

Jacob Lawrence, *Images of Labor*, 1980

Family and Work Roles: Redefining the Relationship

One of the most significant changes in family life in the last 50 years has been the sharp increase in the number of employed married women. American society may still think of a woman's place as in the home, but the reality is that well over half of all women are employed—75 percent of women aged 25 to 44. Women's employment has been linked to critical alterations in gender role attitudes and behaviors, including men's greater involvement in family roles, the advancing divorce rate, and increased public interest in providing improved family services to employees (Menaghan & Parcell, 1991).

The average family income is $47,000 when a wife is employed, compared with $30,000 when she is not (U.S. Bureau of the Census, 1992). As women contribute more of the family income, their evaluations of marital fairness tend to decrease because the work load at home remains inequitable. Recent headlines attest to women's rising dissatisfaction with the status quo. "Women Get Mad" was the title of one article focusing on women's increasing frustration with working a *second shift* at home after putting in a full day on the job (Townsend & O'Neill, 1990).

Next to their disappointment with the amount of money they earn, the help they get with household work is the biggest cause of frustration in women's lives. When asked what would make life better, the top five responses are more money, more control over the way things are going in my life, more household help from my husband, more leisure time, and more household help from my children (Roper Organization, 1990). A continuing challenge of contemporary married life is adapting to the two-paycheck family.

This chapter examines how marriage and family life have been affected by women's expanded employment roles, and by the economic pressures that have made dual-earner families a prominent feature of American life. Couples are exploring new ways of combining work and family responsibilities. There are also new choices for society as a whole, as we try to decide what responses are appropriate on the part of employers and government to help couples care for young children and elderly family members. We begin with a historical look at how work and family roles have changed.

WORK AND FAMILY: YESTERDAY AND TODAY

Women in the Work Force

Long before the nineteenth century, women worked outside the home whenever it was necessary to provide economic support for their families. By the early years of this century, it was common for women to work as teachers, in the sweatshops of the garment industry, in textile factories, and—in increasing numbers—as salespeople and clerical workers. But most women who worked before the 1940s were young and single, with the proportion of employed women rising only slightly between 1910 and 1940 (Anderson, 1988).

World War II: A Defining Event

World War II was the event that caused a dramatic change in the employment patterns of women. The jobs vacated by men who joined the armed forces were filled by women. Before the war, only 15 percent of married women worked; by the time it ended, nearly 25 percent of all married women were employed. For the first time, there were more married women in the labor force than young, single women (Marshall & Paulin, 1987).

Despite some feeling that women who were employed during the war should give up their jobs to returning veterans, most women continued working, encouraged by a variety of factors. During the postwar years there was a shortage of young people entering the labor force because of low birth rates during the Depression. Furthermore, government-sponsored programs were designed to encourage returning veterans to attend college, and many of the young men who would have reentered the labor force went to school instead. At the same time, the economy was expanding very rapidly. Most of the demand for new employees occurred in white-collar occupations—such as clerical or secretarial work—that were defined as women's work (Mintz & Kellogg, 1988).

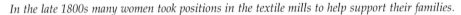

In the late 1800s many women took positions in the textile mills to help support their families.

Women's Jobs: A Profile

The percentage of employed married women has increased steadily, from 22 percent in 1948 to 65 percent by 1992 (Ahlburg & De Vita, 1992). And the proportion of female earners is even higher among women between the ages of 25 and 44 and among mothers of school-age children (75 percent). Employed women, however, still tend to be concentrated in low-paying jobs.

> The ordinary working woman is typically a working mother in her thirties; she attended and probably graduated from high school. . . . She works, for example, in the typing pool of a large corporation, on the assembly line of a manufacturing firm, or she is a file clerk in an insurance company. She is the woman who waits on you when you shop for clothing . . . who serves you at your favorite restaurant, cashes your check at the bank . . . washes and cuts your hair. (Fox & Hesse-Biber, 1984, p. 97)

The proportion of employed black women is nearly equal to that of white women. This was not the case at the beginning of this century, or even 20 years ago when black women's labor-force participation rates were about 10 percent higher. The employment rate of Hispanic women continues to be slightly less than that of blacks or whites.

Black Americans generally earn less than white Americans and are excluded from some jobs because of racial discrimination, so it sometimes takes contributions from several family members to support the household. White women working full time earn about $19,000 annually, black women make close to $17,000, and Hispanics are paid approximately $15,000 (U.S. Department of Labor, 1992). Black men's jobs have traditionally been less stable than those of white men—many are seasonal or part time. As a result, black families have traditionally viewed employment as one of women's expected family roles (Anderson, 1988).

A majority of intact families now have two earners (see Figure 9-1) and a majority of women of all social classes express a preference for combining work and family roles. There are several reasons to assume that this trend will continue. Women are catching up with men in educational attainment: 52 percent of the college graduates in 1992 were women. And women are earning a steadily increasing percentage of advanced degrees—including over one-third of the degrees in law, business, accounting, and computer sciences. This is highly significant, because the more educated a woman is the more likely she is to be employed—82

FIGURE 9-1
Families in the Labor Force

Source: D. A. Ahlburg & C. J. De Vita (1992).

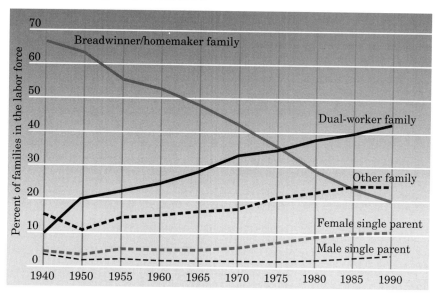

percent of female college graduates are now employed (Ahlburg & De Vita, 1992).

Women constitute over one-half of those employed in professional, technical, and sales occupations. They occupy 40 percent of all executive and managerial positions, up from 28 percent in 1979. The median salary of employed women is 70 percent of men's, up from 60 percent in 1980 (Kelly, 1991). Because family size is smaller than it once was and life expectancy is somewhat longer, young women who prepare for many years in the workplace are being realistic about their futures.

Benefits of Women's Job Commitment

The majority of women, including those employed as waitresses and factory workers, are committed to their jobs and would not leave them even if they did not need the money (Roper Organization, 1990; Scarr, Phillips, & McCartney, 1989). Most view their employment as an extension of their family roles.

Women work for many reasons: to keep their families from the edge of poverty, to earn money for family necessities like house and car payments, and to finance their children's educations. Their paychecks are an important contribution to the family's economic well-being. Married women employed full time contribute over 40 percent of the total family income (U.S. Bureau of Labor Statistics, 1990). Moreover, dual-earner families earn 50 percent more than couples in which the wife is not employed. This figure jumps to 60 percent for Hispanic families and 98 percent for black families (Ford Foundation, 1989).

The majority of employed wives, whatever their reasons for working, derive some satisfaction from their jobs. The employment role strongly influences good health (Hoffman, 1989; Ross, Mirowsky, & Goldsteen, 1991; Verbrugge & Madans, 1985). Employed women, compared to other women, have fewer physical health problems and suffer less from depression and various other symptoms of emotional distress. These benefits help balance the costs of employment, which include having less leisure time and being responsible for most of the household chores and child care (Barnett & Rivers, 1992).

Women Working at Home

Women have always worked. It is the pattern and place of work that have changed. Work is generally defined as something that takes place outside of the home for pay. Housework, then, is unpaid labor that takes place in the context of today's smaller families, ready-made clothing, electricity, appliances, convenience foods, and with the support of outside institutions like schools and hospitals.

The Impact of False Assumptions

The rise in technological developments and community services leads many to falsely conclude that household chores no longer consume much of women's time and energy. The home is more often envisioned as a place for leisure activities rather than as a place of work. Such notions have changed how women's roles at home are culturally viewed, leading to an increase in anxiety and depression among women whose main identity comes from the roles of wife and mother (La Croix & Haynes, 1987; Ross et al., 1991). Although it is inaccurate to conclude that *all* full-time homemakers are distressed or that this role necessarily makes women miserable, the fact remains that homemaking is often associated with personal distress.

Why Homemaking Can Be Stressful

Studies have found that various aspects of the housewife/mother role are troublesome. To begin with, today's homemaker is more isolated from other adults than was yesterday's. In the past, women commonly spent many of their daytime hours around other adults who were either members of the extended household or neighbors. More of the day-to-day do-

Some mothers are convinced that staying home with their young children is the best choice.

mestic tasks were shared. Today, in contrast, few of the tasks involved in child care or housework are typically shared with other adults; thus, homemakers no longer have easy access to role models or well-defined performance standards against which to measure their efforts.

Additionally, despite the widely shared notion that women should be happiest when at home with young children, women who actually stay at home with preschool children are unusually susceptible to depression and physical symptoms of distress—headaches, back pain, difficulty sleeping (Barnett & Rivers, 1992; Gore & Mangione, 1983). One reason the caretakers of young children report being under greater stress is that they are subject to the demands of others to an unusual extent. Many full-time mothers feel that their children's problems are *their* problems—thus making them vulnerable to feelings of inadequacy and incompetence (Barnett & Baruch, 1987). Even though nonem-

ployed mothers are convinced that staying home full time allows them to bond more strongly with their children, and most enjoy child care, they still experience some internal conflict. As one mother puts it, "sometimes I feel that I'm just a mother and not a person" (Farber, Alejandro-Wright, & Muenchow, 1988, p. 172). It is sometimes difficult for women to stop and enjoy leisure time or to rest, even when ill.

"I don't hate my work—often I am neutral about it—it's part of how I give to my family," says one homemaker. Another notes, "I do enjoy taking care of my family and home. At times things seem tiring and boring, but on the whole it is a fulfilling job to me" (Berheide, 1984, p. 49). Detracting from these emotional benefits, however, is the fact that most household work is invisible—done while the rest of the family is away from home or preoccupied with other activities—so that the work accomplished often goes unrecognized and unappreciated.

CHANGING LIFESTYLES

The Mommy Wars: Is It Time for a Truce?

The mounting tensions between full-time and working mothers have escalated into what has been dubbed the "mommy wars." During the 1992 presidential campaign, Hillary Clinton defended her decision to combine motherhood and a career, while Marilyn Quayle boasted about putting aside her own legal career to raise three children. Below are portraits, sometimes in their own words, of mothers on opposite sides of the mommy wars.

Mrs. Jaffe was a career woman and, at the nursery school, it is the mothers who have full-time careers with whom Mrs. Jaffe most identifies herself, at least in her own head.

She used to be a political campaign consultant in California, and was starting a software consulting business—the business cards were already printed—when she decided to stay at home to raise her daughter, now 7, and her son, 5.

"I'd wake up in the morning and I'd look at my daughter and I'd look at the list of phone calls I was supposed to make and they didn't seem that important."

Now her life is more like that of her mother, a homemaker who raised 12 children.

"A lot of women take stock of what their man is about, whether he has a lot of drive, and we fill the vacuum left," said Mrs. Jaffe, whose husband is a research manager for International Business Machines. "I know some whose husbands have very little drive and initiative so the women develop really good careers. My husband has a lot of drive and I fill in the space where he isn't. The hidden thing is that even those of us who are feminists tend to respond to the needs of others."

Mrs. Jaffe said she tends to gravitate these days to women who also stay at home, "only because I still feel a little inadequate with women who have a career, especially when I hear about their jobs."

"It's like show-and-tell time," she said, "and I don't have anything to show and tell."

Mrs. Jaffe says that for her one of the rewards of motherhood is the look on her children's faces when she is baking, particularly if the cookies are oatmeal and chocolate chip.

Laurie Hander Leahy is the mother of 5-year-old Max and a caterer, a career she began dreaming about when she was 12. "My entire life is not about watching his first step," she said. "My life is about him but also working."

Economic freedom has always been one of her goals. When she and her husband, Richard, the owner of several appliance stores in Westchester County, decided to have a child, it was only after they agreed they could afford, first, a 24-hour baby nurse to feed and change diapers, and then a live-in nanny.

"It was interesting and a bit disturbing," write the authors of one book, "to see how closely the self-esteem of full-time housewives is tied to their husbands' approval. The women appear to be judging themselves by how their husbands see them" (Baruch, Barnett, & Rivers, 1983, p. 64). While it is natural and in many ways desirable to look to one's spouse for approval, what concerns these observers is how precarious it is for anyone to tie their self-esteem to the judgment of just one other person. Women who invest themselves exclusively in the role of homemaker and isolate themselves from other people and activities tend to have more difficulty managing problems in their daily lives and may rely too heavily on their immediate families for the majority of their emotional fulfillment.

Homemaker Strains Are Not Inevitable

None of the strains of the homemaker's role are inevitable. Much of what has been written and said about this role during the past two decades has been so negative that it may come as something of a surprise to learn how positively many full-time homemakers regard the work they perform (see the "Changing Lifestyles" box). Women at home can choose to expand their roles by cultivating friendships with others outside the family and becoming involved in neighbor-

"I knew I would never stay home full time with a child," said Ms. Leahy, who is 37. "There are times I have regretted it. I've missed a lot. Sometimes I think, 'Wouldn't this be great to spend more time and be here?' But you can't have both."

"My father treated us as he would have treated boys," said Ms. Leahy, the daughter of an accountant in West Orange, NJ, and a mother who raised three girls. "He encouraged the same education, the same aspirations for career. What he taught us was that working hard was a good thing and I interpreted working as working outside the home. I never thought about being a mom. In the back of my mind, I figured one day eventually, it would come with the territory of being female."

It is the little things, Ms. Leahy said, that bring out the differences between mothers who stay at home and mothers who are employed, things like how much they talk about domestic issues and children. For the last 2 years, she worked on the nursery school's financial committee and was the driving force behind a raffle that set records for the school, raising $3,000 each year.

"They had ridiculously low goals and I pushed them," she said. "They just weren't realistic in dealing with money because they're not making it."

Bobbi Ornstein has tried to reconcile the conflict by working part time. "I didn't want to be away from him so much," the 42-year-old physical therapist said of her 3-year-old son, Douglas. "He might adjust to it better than I would but it would be hard for me."

Mrs. Ornstein works, she said, because she and her husband, Robert, a psychoanalyst, can use the money. And she has little sympathy for women who are not driven to work full time by economic necessity.

"Since mothers haven't been working full time for that many years, we have yet to see the results of the upbringing of the children," she said. "We don't know what these children are going to be like but it's hard to imagine it's going to be terrific."

Mrs. Ornstein grew up in a middle-class family in the Mill Basin neighborhood of Brooklyn, where her father was a textile salesman and her mother stayed at home to raise her.

"Although I wasn't a strong feminist, I did believe I would work, but I would do it differently than my mother did," Mrs. Ornstein said. "She was a very dependent person and I never wanted to be in that position. I wanted to do everything to counter that."

Mrs. Ornstein considers herself a late bloomer in many ways. She started her career as a physical therapist after her first marriage ended when she was in her late-twenties. She was married for the second time at age 36. She give birth to Douglas at age 39.

It was not until she was pregnant that she realized how strongly she felt about devoting time to motherhood, even though she said she loved her work.

"I guess something happened from the time that I was pregnant and he was born that changed my thinking," she said. "I couldn't leave this baby full time. It was too important to me. I couldn't leave him with a stranger."

EXPLORATIONS *After reading these excerpts, do you think each mother has something to protect? If so, what is it? Some social analysts think the mommy wars represent our failure to come to terms with changing family patterns and the realisms of family diversity in the 1990s. What do you think?*

SOURCE: Excerpted from L. Richardson (1992).

hood and community activities. They can define themselves in ways that are not limited to routine household tasks and encourage family members to show appreciation and respect for the work they do.

Men, Work, and Family

Despite the view that most men are much more involved in work than family roles, the majority of recent studies show that men's psychological well-being depends on their satisfaction in *both* roles (Barnett & Baruch, 1987; Barnett, Marshall, & Pleck, 1992; Pleck, 1987). It is only among the minority of men who are highly educated and attain significant success through money, power, and prestige that employment roles take precedence. And, even among men of high job status, those who choose to be excessively involved in their work while neglecting family roles are still rare (Pleck, 1985).

Men's Roles Change

For men, work has traditionally served a dual purpose. By being employed, a man was not only providing economically for his wife and children, but was fulfilling his role as a good family man. He, in effect, got dual credit for one very important activity. Recent

More than ever before, fathers are expected to demonstrate commitment to family as well as work roles.

changes in women's roles have triggered redefinitions of men's family roles, creating new ambiguities and tensions as well as opening up new opportunities for self-fulfillment. Men's roles now include being cooperative, expressive, supportive of their wives' employment activities, and appreciative of the contribution women make to the family income. Increasingly men are encouraged to take an active role in child care and housework. There is widespread agreement today—among men as well as women—that child care and other household responsibilities should be shared by husband and wife (Hiller & Philliber, 1986; Roper Organization, 1990).

While men are expected to demonstrate some of the "softer" emotional qualities that have historically been regarded as feminine traits, they are still obligated to be successful in their primary role as wage earner. In a sense, the "job description" for a successful man today is more demanding than it was for his father or grandfather. He is still expected, as men of previous generations were, to be a successful earner. But, he is expected to take a more active role at home as well. Moreover, since women's entry into the workplace is often accompanied by greater marital power, he is being asked to share the position of "head of the household" with his marital partner.

Men's Ambivalence Toward Change

Many men welcome their wives' participation in the work force. However, much of men's support for women's new roles is highly qualified. One writer, Anthony Astrachan (1986), conducted some 400 interviews with men in various regions of the country. He reported that men in various occupations and social classes expressed positive feelings about changes in women's roles, ranging from pride and admiration to relief when the wife's salary helps to pay the bills. Many males agreed that men should become more involved at home. They felt that their employed partners deserved more help. Frequently recalling that their own fathers were not available emotionally when they were children, many men agree that it is desirable for males to play a more active role at home.

Still, the striking thing about Astrachan's interviews was the hostility expressed by some men. "Even men who have demonstrated support for women's equality," writes Astrachan, "display negative feelings about women's entry into traditional masculine occupations or about women's changing roles. Those feelings include anger, fear, and envy" (p. 401). Although blue-collar men expressed the most overt hostility to changes in women's roles and the changes they require in men, resistance from middle- and upper-middle-class men also appeared. What is the source of men's fear of and hostility toward changing gender roles? One of the themes that appears in Astrachan's interviews is the worry that the wives of "real men"—which is to say successful men—should not have to work. From this perspective, the source of men's concern is what their wives' entry into the labor force reveals about their own inadequacies as providers.

More pervasive is the fear, in Astrachan's words, that "woman's work will end our dominance, or the shade of advantage that we like to feel even when we have given up any thought of being lord and master" (p. 208). An employed wife means far more than an additional paycheck. There is a potential here for tipping the balance of marital power. Lucia Gilbert (1987) found that the issues with which husbands of employed women typically struggle include lost marital power, decreased freedom in making occupational decisions (for example, when to change jobs, where to seek employment), and increased involvement in "women's work" in the family. *Wall Street Journal* reporter Susan Faludi, in her book *Backlash* (1991) concludes that young blue-collar men are especially negative about women becoming major income providers, seeing it as a serious invasion of their domain as the family breadwinners. Given these concerns, how do employed couples successfully combine work and family roles?

WORKING COUPLES: REINVENTING THE MARITAL RELATIONSHIP

Distinguishing Between Careers and Jobs

In *dual-career marriages* both partners are employed in careers—view their employment as a way to earn money, but also as an avenue to personal fulfillment and identity formation. In *dual-earner marriages* both partners are employed in jobs—view their employment primarily as a means of earning money to support their families.

A *career* is generally defined as a succession of professional positions, each related to the next. Anyone pursuing a career usually moves in a predictable sequence from positions of lower prestige and responsibility to those that confer more authority, prestige, and income. Careers typically require more education and training than do jobs, they make more time demands, and they require greater personal commitment (Voydanoff, 1987b). "Most management and executive careers command complete loyalty and submission to organizational goals with total submersion into corporate structure. . . . Deadlines are not flexed to accommodate family and personal schedules" (Kelly, 1991, p. 83). The lines between personal and private matters get blurred as companies act as if all employees, men as well as women, either have no families or have spouses at home to take care of all family responsibilities.

A *job,* unlike a career, does not necessarily require strong individual commitment to the work role or regular updating of knowledge to stay current with the

field. It is good to keep in mind, however, that many people in earner positions are in the process of acquiring the educational and technical credentials to move into career positions, so the distinction between jobs and careers occasionally becomes blurred. Dual-earner couples represent the majority of American couples; however, the number of dual-career couples is rising quite rapidly as increasing numbers of women and men pursue advanced degrees.

Increasingly, people are interested in how dual-earner and dual-career families differ. After lengthy interviews with 50 dual-earner and dual-career families, sociologist Arlie Hochschild (1989) concludes:

> The working class tends toward the traditional ideal, and the middle class tended toward the egalitarian one. . . . The problems of the two-job family are tougher in the working class, but they are difficult in a different way. . . . What exacerbates strain in the working class is the absence of money to pay for services they need, economic insecurity, poor daycare, and lack of dignity and boredom in each partner's job . . . in the upper-middle-class it's the instability of paid help and the enormous demands of the career system. (p. 189)

It is important to remember that Hochschild was referring to upper-middle-class families when she spoke about hired help. Many, if not most, dual-career families are middle-class teachers, social workers, nurses, midlevel managers and others who, although employed in careers, cannot afford hired help except for day care.

Even though there are many satisfactions and rewards from being in dual-earner/dual-career marriages, partners in these relationships feel pressure and stress as they go about balancing work and family roles.

Dual-Earner Marriages

Dual-earner men and women generally work in positions where advancement, achievement, and financial success are limited, regardless of job commitment.

> These mothers and fathers talk compellingly about their commitment to family life and the importance of working hard for the sake of their families. . . . They are troubled about the futures of their children. They worry about how to protect their jobs and the benefits their jobs confer on their families. (Lein, 1979, p. xi)

Wive's Concerns

Women in dual-earner families almost always make less money than their husbands and their work tends to be regarded as optional rather than as a demonstration of family responsibility. The home remains their primary responsibility and they do most, if not all, of the household work and child care. Because traditional gender role expectations generally guide dual-earner couples, it is the wife who more typically refuses time-intensive job assignments and stays home from work, quits her job, or cuts back to part-time work when family obligations conflict with demands. In order to accommodate family needs, women often take jobs that offer few fringe benefits, are less satisfying, and pay less.

Dual-earner women are often overloaded with work and family tasks. They get approximately one-half hour less sleep per night than do homemakers (Pleck & Rustad, 1980) and when time spent doing household chores is added to hours of employment, they spend 50 percent more hours working than their husbands (Rexroat & Shehan, 1987). They also spend 15 fewer hours at leisure each week than their husbands (Skow, 1989).

Despite these disadvantages, women hesitate to complain or ask their husbands for help (Holder & Anderson, 1989). When husbands do provide assistance with family work, earner women typically consider it a sign of support and feel deeply appreciative (Ferree, 1991). Studies indicate that a husband's help greatly decreases a wife's distress and improves her sense of well-being (Bird & Fremont, 1989). Housework is seen by many dual-earner women as a means of compensating family members for the costs of taking on an outside job. Some feel that one way to pay back family members for tolerating their employment away from home, and to win them over if they disapprove, is through housework (Ferree, 1987).

In the dual-earner family, the wife's employment serves to shield the family from some financial risk when the husband faces cutbacks in hours or layoffs. However, because earner women are considered to be "secondary" workers who put family needs first, they often suffer discrimination from employers in terms of pay, promotions, and benefits. This further puts dual-earner families at risk (Ross et al., 1991).

Husband's Concerns

Blue-collar men are more likely than career-oriented men to feel that if their wives are employed they have somehow failed as the "family provider" (Staines, Pottick, & Fudge, 1986). They are often stuck in unrewarding and unchallenging jobs that offer little control over the work environment. Their dedication to their families many times prevents them from changing jobs, which would very likely threaten job seniority as well as health and retirement benefits.

Men of the working class often live with a fear of cutbacks in their hours, reduction of pay, and layoffs. Many have little job security because of fluctuations in economic conditions (Mortimer & Sorensen, 1987). When blue-collar families face economic problems, it is not unusual for husbands to work overtime or take a second job. Working more hours makes them less available to family members, but protects the family from financial hardship (Piotrkowski, 1978; Piotrkowski, Rapoport, & Rapoport, 1987). During these times, wives pick up the slack by taking care of most other family responsibilities.

Dual-Career Marriages

Facing Corporate Barriers

In most marriages, even today, it is taken for granted that the husband's job activity is more important than the wife's. It is a foregone conclusion that a woman should accommodate her plans to the needs of her husband and children. However, in dual-career families there is a need to accommodate *both* of the spouses' careers and jointly take care of family roles. Family responsibilities, nevertheless, are expected to remain invisible at work. When professional couples compromise career goals in favor of families, colleagues and supervisors at work are likely to regard this as an indication that they are not seriously engaged in their professions. This negative evaluation can have severe career consequences.

Even when couples agree among themselves to share both family and work roles in an egalitarian manner, and given the fact that career spouses have more power, prestige, status, and earnings than most other couples, there are still many social barriers to their occupational success that are worrisome. For example, most corporations value independence in their employees, while most career couples embrace mutual cooperativeness and try to balance their career activities to coordinate with each other's personal goals and with family needs. Couples also find that the wife faces more intense discriminatory hiring and promotion practices, which, even when acknowledged by the husband, can cause friction. Because of these and other barriers, dual-career couples may discover that they are unintentionally advancing his career over hers, creating tension, and fostering competition between spouses (Bird & Bird, 1987).

Adapting to New Roles

Lucia Gilbert (1985, 1987, 1988, 1993) has authored several articles on dual-career families and written three books, *Men in Dual-Career Families, Sharing It All,* and *Two Careers, One Family.* From her research and professional observations as a therapist, she concludes that men in dual-career families generally have high self-esteem, are achievement-oriented, and are supportive of their wives' careers. They are more likely than other men to share family roles and to view their wives' employment as an opportunity rather than as a liability. Because dual-career men tend to have less traditional beliefs about gender roles than do dual-earner men, they are more likely to appreciate and applaud their wives' career achievements, even though they also perceive costs. As one man noted: "Sometimes I think, 'my father didn't do it that way, my friends don't do it that way, why should I?' But then I realize that those rules aren't in effect" (Gilbert, 1988, p. 63).

Dual-career women expect their husbands to be partners in a relationship unlike those of other employed women. "They want someone to look across at, not up to . . . [they] look beyond what a man can provide economically. Sensitivity, emotional depth, and companionship mean much more," concludes Gilbert (1988, p. 60). This is not to say that those expectations are always met or that it is easy for men to give up what Gilbert calls "feelings of male specialness" and "sense of entitlement." As one successful male writer revealed in an interview: "When I hold my daughter or brush out her hair or tell her stories, I am frightened by the side of me that wants to push ahead at her expense. At the same time, I feel that by taking on more of my wife's load I am losing ground in my career; it's like swimming with rocks in my pockets" (1988, p. 65).

Wives Who Outearn Their Husbands

Because of traditional gender role attitudes that it is acceptable for husbands to outearn wives, but detrimental to marriages if wives outearn husbands, earnings are an issue in some families. The wife may feel pressure not to exceed the husband's accomplishments and guilty if she does (Gutek, Repetti, & Silver, 1988). When the wife earns more, some research shows that she may overcompensate by doing most of the household chores and by being especially nurturant and supportive of her husband (Wampler & Kingery, 1985). She may also define her situation as temporary ("He will eventually earn more than I do"), downgrade her skills and abilities ("I'm really just lucky—I was in the right place at the right time"), or exaggerate the husband's abilities ("He's actually much more intelligent and resourceful than I am"). Sometimes women even reject promotions and try not to appear as successful as they really are (Sekaran, 1986).

Couples with contemporary gender role attitudes more often define themselves as *interdependent*—believe that the benefits gained by one partner profits the other as well. This way of thinking increases feelings of intimacy and commitment and keeps down competitiveness (Bird & Bird, 1987). Men in interdependent relationships generally have strong senses of self-esteem, confidence in their own abilities, and are able to view their partners' earnings as nonthreatening. Husbands are affected only slightly, if at all, when they feel satisfied with their own accomplishments and perceive their wives as supportive, understanding, and fair (Gilbert, 1988).

The Family as a Partnership

One woman explained the changing ideology of how a woman should combine work and family roles:

> In the 1970s, she was supposed to bring home the bacon, fry it up in a pan, and never, never let her husband forget he's a man because she's a woman—a superwoman. In the 1980s, she was supposed to "balance" her career, family, and civic obligations with the finesse of an acrobat spinning plates on sticks. Now, in the 1990s, she is supposed to "manage multiple priorities" using a business management model. (Kang, 1991)

A more satisfying model for combining work and family roles may be the family partnership model. Rather than making women almost solely responsible for family matters, the partnership model promotes the idea that all family members should act as a team in resolving work and family dilemmas.

One reason most dual-career families struggle so

hard to negotiate a fair distribution of the costs and benefits of work and family roles is that most come to the realization that perceptions of fairness and mutual supportiveness is the key to a successful marriage. And, although many men have problems adjusting to changes at home—and women to the work environment—over time the problems become routine and easier to handle. Partners who work long hours at career tasks report that they are in "supportive marriages that involve partners doing favors for each other, listening and offering advice, and altering habits and ways of doing things to please the other" (Guelzow, Bird, & Koball, 1991, p. 160). Moreover, couples who are mutually supportive have less marital and professional distress.

When both marital partners are involved in careers there is a potential for high stress levels because careers require considerable time, effort, and energy. Some have suggested that career-oriented partners may be competitive with each other and much less involved in family roles than are other employed couples. Research, however, disputes this. Greenhaus (1988), for example, found that when both marital partners are highly involved in careers, they indicate *low* levels of work-family stress. He concludes, "Perhaps, two partners who are each highly job-involved understand each other's needs and aspirations, provide support to each other, adjust their expectations regarding each other's role involvements, and develop a system of mutual accommodation" (p. 151). Similar results were observed by Guelzow, Bird, and Koball (1991) in a survey of 150 dual-career couples.

Gains for Both Partners

Women benefit from being part of a dual-career family by gaining the opportunity to develop professionally, attain economic independence, and achieve greater autonomy and higher self-esteem. They also gain a greater sense of power in the family. Most women in dual-career marriages indicate that they would experience a sense of loss if they had to give up their careers. Moreover, their husbands are usually interested in and proud of their work (Gilbert, 1985). In relationships where careers entail similar activities in the workplace, spouses have much to talk about at the end of the day. For these couples, the listening and lively interaction enhances their enjoyment of the relationship.

Men gain freedom by not having to shoulder the total economic responsibility for the family. They also gain the opportunity to involve themselves in parenting and to give care and nurturance to their children. An additional gain for men is learning to accept women as peers and supervisors in work settings and to recognize women's abilities outside the home. Moreover, wives' earnings often allow husbands to search for new career opportunities, go back to school for further education or training, and work fewer hours—all without fear of family financial collapse.

The results of several recent studies support the view that it is possible to have a dual-career marriage that works to the advantage of both partners, but because few role models exist and the work environment as well as gender role socialization practices operate against such a relationship, it takes determination and resolve from each spouse to succeed. In cases where husbands and wives fail to negotiate a mutually satisfying resolution to work/family conflicts, divorce is likely. Both spouses' economic independence enables them to more readily leave an unsatisfying relationship.

THE STRAIN OF "HAVING IT ALL"

A person involved in several roles simultaneously—such as worker, parent, marital partner—is said to have *multiple roles.* People with multiple roles gain benefits from each of their roles, including a sense of competence, self-esteem, positive feedback, and financial gain (Gutek, Repetti, & Silver, 1988). These benefits help balance the strain of taking on additional roles. *Role strain* refers to the difficulties, challenges, conflicts, or problems experienced as a result of being in a particular role and attending to the tasks and activities required in that role. Two types of role strain are prevalent in dual-earner and dual-career families: role overload and role conflict.

Role Overload

Role overload is feeling like there is too much to do and never enough time to accomplish everything that needs to be done.

Starting a Family

Dual-earner families with young children are particularly affected by role overload. As one woman explains:

Before we had children, we would work hard and play some, too. We used to go out a lot together, sometimes to a different movie every night. We bicycled weekends. But when our [law] practices got up to 55 hours a week and Kevin was born, we went into a state of siege. No one tells you how a child turns your life around. For a while, we were just surviving, very little sleep, no sex, little talk, delight in Kevin, and adrenaline. We just say hello in bed before dropping off. (Hochschild, 1989, p. 209)

It is not unusual for couples to feel exhausted when they get home and guilty about being so tired when their families need them—dinner must be prepared, dishes washed, children fed and bathed, and so on. When both partners feel tired and drained of energy and neither really relishes doing chores, or when one partner is expected to do most of the family work, marital tension is almost inevitable. This condition of bringing home the fatigue and residue of emotions and moods stirred up on the job is referred to as *work spill-over*.

Heavy Work Schedules

Heavy work schedules mean that employed couples have to schedule or plan family time as well as time to be together as a couple or other activities will

It can be difficult to keep work demands from spilling over into family time.

quickly consume those hours. Both partners may be in the time- and energy-demanding "launching phase" of their careers, yet also engaged in the joint process of managing a household and raising young children. Each partner craves the haven from tension that family life is supposed to provide; neither may have the time to bring reality to that desire.

For women who choose a career, there are still tensions between the kind of commitment needed to achieve success and the commitment they expect to make to their families. Paradoxically, the prime years for establishing a career are also the prime years for starting a family. Although the lives of married men and women are becoming more similar, important differences remain in their career expectations and behavior. Moreover, despite the fact that employed women are contributing an increasing percentage of total household income, the man's job may still take precedence in the household and be given more weight by employers. When dilemmas result from conflicting demands on both spouses, wives still bear most of the responsibility for resolving them (Bird, Goss, & Bird, 1990; Gilbert, 1988; Holder & Anderson, 1989).

Because women are more likely than men to subjugate career needs to family needs, employers often infer that they are not as dedicated to their work. Putting husbands' careers first "reinforces stereotypic assumptions about the marginal commitment of professional women to their work roles. This, in turn, intensifies institutional constraints against the advancement of women, setting the stage for conflict and stress" (Gupta & Jenkins, 1985, p. 153).

Marriage and children are typically considered by employers to be burdens to a woman's career development, but assets to a man's career. Companies usually expect the wife to perform most of the supportive functions for the dual-career couple—make child-care arrangements, attend company functions, and make contacts in the community through volunteer work (Voydanoff, 1987a). Colleagues and supervisors at work may expect her to be the perfect "corporate wife" (Gupta & Jenkins, 1985). All of these extra tasks can accumulate and lead to role overload.

Role Conflict

Role conflict occurs when the demands of one role interfere with doing what needs to be done in another role.

Feeling Neglectful

Employed parents sometimes find it difficult to stay at home to care for a sick child or to always be available for school- or community-related activities because of rigid, demanding work schedules. This situation creates conflict. On the one hand, a person wants to be an involved and dedicated employee. On the other hand, being a caring parent is also a priority. Caring for one's child may mean risking being viewed as an uncooperative worker. Going to work may mean being labeled a neglectful parent. Guilt is the end result in either case.

Deflecting Other's Expectations

Another source of role conflict for employed couples is dealing with disparities between how they choose to plan and organize their lives as family earners, household members, and parents versus how neighbors, relatives, and people at work *expect* them to behave. Demands imposed by others—parents, children, bosses, child-care providers, the school system—often conflict with what the couple think is best for their family. For example, a husband may share the household chores and all is well until his parents visit. When they observe their son doing the laundry or vacuuming, they may make negative comments—"George's wife works, but he never does any housework. Don't you resent it?" "I guess Jenny just can't handle a job *and* the kids, maybe she should quit." These comments and others like them frequently cause tension between the marital partners as they struggle to define family roles according to their own needs.

Fighting Internalized Norms

Discontinuities between what the couple was socialized to believe about family life and how they are currently managing their family responsibilities can also cause role conflict. Employed parents, for example, worry about having enough time to parent their children the way they believe children should be parented, about whether their job involvement is harmful to their children's development, and about finding adequate child care. Men who share household work and are supportive of their wives' employment sometimes worry that going against traditional gender role socialization may mean that they are somehow failing to live up to their masculine image as the family provider. Women, by comparison, worry that the attitudes and behaviors necessary for building a successful career and fending off discriminatory practices at work may stifle some of their nurturant, empathetic, and caring qualities.

Making Time for Kin and Friends

Couples also mention that they feel conflicted about their inability to maintain close contact with kin and friends due to heavy work and family responsibilities. Some make friends with people at work who have similar lifestyles. Within these friendships, they feel safe and protected because someone understands and appreciates their way of handling work and family matters. Because dual-earner couples do not operate like other families and have very little time for socializing, they sometimes have a difficult time fitting into traditional social networks. And since they may move more often than other couples, they may have difficulty maintaining close kinship networks where daily tasks and family events can easily be shared (Schnittger & Bird, 1990).

Moving or Having a Commuter Marriage

Pressure to move also creates role conflict for dual-career couples. In many organizations the expectation is that employees will be mobile and that promotions to higher levels of job responsibility will require transferring to new locations. These relocations can disrupt the careers of both spouses and cause stress in the family. Even though some change has been noted, it is usually the woman's career that suffers the most in these situations (Bird & Bird, 1985).

Sometimes a couple decides to have a *commuter marriage*—an arrangement whereby each spouse lives and works in a different location, meeting at prearranged times, for example, on weekends. But these arrangements are usually best suited to childfree couples with high earnings. A commuter marriage is typically a short-term solution to a chronic work or family problem. For instance, a family decides that the husband will return to college for a master's degree, but rather than move for 2 years, he will commute. Or, one spouse gets transferred and the other wants to stay put for another few months or years. In most cases, the commuting couple move back together relatively soon. Commuter couples report having satisfying marriages and say that their separations, rather than causing deterioration, actually strengthened their marital relationships (Gerstel & Gross, 1985).

Strain in the Work Environment

Overload can also happen at work, where it is most often related to feelings of time pressure—that the overall work load is heavier than can comfortably be handled. Careers are more time demanding than jobs. Employers expect people in career positions to work until the task is done. It is not unusual for dual-career partners to work late at the office and then bring paperwork home and receive calls there. Career activities can compete with family activities in the evening hours and on weekends. Travel might also be expected as part of the job. Such rigid, typical expectations by businesses and organizations lead to stress. A common solution to this problem is to delay childbearing. By age 40, 90 percent of male executives have children, while only 35 percent of females are mothers (Kelly, 1991).

Work strain also arises from other pressures in the work environment—underutilization of skills, *role ambiguity* (being uncertain about what the expectations are for the job taken on), and lack of control—all of which are linked to poor mental health and decreased job and family satisfaction (La Croix & Haynes, 1987). When individuals believe that their skills are appreciated, understand what is expected of them, and have some control over their work environment, they experience less stress. For example, dual-earner couples who work long hours and whose schedules are inconvenient have less stress if they have some say over when their hours are scheduled. Job flexibility allows them to better mesh family activities and child-care responsibilities with work (Lewis & Cooper, 1988).

Women experience additional work strain from discriminatory management attitudes and practices. Women are more often judged as less suitable and less deserving when evaluated at work than men (Nieva & Gutek, 1980). Many face a *glass ceiling*—an invisible, but effective corporate barrier than limits professional potential and puts women at risk (see the "Dilemmas and Decisions" box).

Sexual Harassment

Another strain for employed women is *sexual harassment*—unwelcome sexual behavior, which includes requests for sexual favors and verbal remarks, if compliance is required as a condition for employment or as a basis for promotions and raises. It includes behavior that creates a hostile working environment that is intimidating, offensive, or interferes with a person's ability to work. Because male employees are only rarely pursued in this manner, we refer to the targets as female as we discuss this issue (see Table 9-1 for examples). Sexual harassment affects between 45 and 90 percent of all employed women (Kelly, 1991).

Traditionally, charges of sexual harassment have been trivialized by such statements as "Women can't take a joke," "If women want to do a man's job, then they should act and work like a man," or "If women don't like pornographic or 'centerfold' types of pictures, they don't have to look at them." Sexual harass-

TABLE 9-1
Examples of Sexual Harassment

People of both genders draw the line in different places as to what behavior constitutes sexual harassment. The following are examples of behaviors which, depending upon the total circumstances, may constitute sexual harassment:

VERBAL HARASSMENT

- Using language of a sexual nature
- Whistling at someone, cat calls
- Making sexual comments about a person's body
- Making sexual comments, innuendos, or kissing sounds, howling, etc.
- Turning work discussions into sexual topics
- Telling sexual jokes or stories
- Asking or telling about sexual fantasies, preferences, or history
- Making unwanted sexual compliments, innuendos, or suggestions
- Telling lies or spreading rumors about a person's sex life

NONVERBAL HARASSMENT

- Looking a person up and down in a suggestive fashion
- Staring at a person
- Blocking a person's path
- Following the person
- Giving unwanted personal gifts
- Displaying sexually suggestive visual materials

PHYSICAL HARASSMENT

- Giving an unwanted massage around the neck, shoulders, or back
- Unwanted touching of a person's clothing, hair, or body
- Touching and/or rubbing oneself sexually around another person
- Standing close or brushing up against a person

DILEMMAS AND DECISIONS

Breaking through the Glass Ceiling

The "glass ceiling" refers to the invisible workplace barriers limiting equal employment opportunities for women—having gender differences viewed as negative attributes rather than valued characteristics, having to follow traditional male career tracks but particularly blocking promotion to the highest levels of corporate management.

Women make up over 50 percent of the work force, yet only 3 percent of senior corporate executives are women, and promotion of women to senior positions is still considered a novel and newsworthy event. Most male and even many female executives continue to deny that discrimination occurs in their companies, but a study by the U.S. Department of Labor confirms that gender-related bias exists in most companies (Segal & Zellner, 1992). A *Business Week*/Harris poll found that 70 percent of women executives express frustration with a "glass ceiling" at their companies and with a male-dominated culture that slows their advancement (Vamos, 1992). There is little recognition of the potential damage the glass ceiling imposes on women and no universally accepted solutions to institutionalized discrimination against women.

The personal and professional experiences of Bill and Hillary Clinton, the first baby-boomer occupants of the White House, may represent a significant model for change. Like so many other couples of their generation, they juggled the demands of two careers—he as the governor/chief executive officer (CEO) of a state and she as an influential corporate lawyer—with parenting roles. As more men and women with experiences similar to the Clinton's reach CEO positions, corporation policies affecting the employment and advancement of women will undoubtedly reflect those experiences, further encouraging "equal" access to employment opportunities.

Women's gains will also be achieved through other, more direct, means. For example, there is an increase in legal action to remedy what has often been blatant discrimination. One common situation concerns women who are passed over for promotion in favor of younger, less experienced males, often trained by those same women. There are also more lawsuits resulting from women being paid less than men for doing the same work, for exhibiting what were viewed by supervisors as "unfeminine" characteristics (ones generally praised as appropriate for men), or for being fired after complaining of sexual harassment or taking maternity leave.

An increasing number of corporations are formally instituting programs to aggressively recruit, retain, and promote women in managerial and other top-level positions. Some programs were begun somewhat defensively as a result of high-profile lawsuits, while other policies were initiated because companies more quickly realized that policies that are good for women are also good for the corporation. There is recognition of demographic changes in the work force, of an increase in the availability of women and minority employees, and a subsequent decline in the proportion of white males. There is a growing recognition that ignoring qualified women is not only discrimination, but is also bad for business.

EXPLORATIONS *What are the costs to women of "hitting the glass ceiling"? How is having a glass ceiling bad for business?*

SOURCES: A. Saltzman (1991); A. T. Segal & W. Zellner (1992); and M. N. Vamos (1992).

ment involves much more than the simple telling of sexual stories, displaying pictures, making a pass, or even inappropriate touching. Instead it is an abuse of power against workers who depend on their jobs for financial and/or professional survival. Harassers direct their attacks primarily at women in lower-paid blue-collar jobs, but women in professional positions are also targeted.

The televised testimony by law professor Anita Hill and Supreme Court nominee Judge Clarence Thomas in the 1991 Senate hearings was most notable and unprecedented in focusing national attention on sexual harassment. Examination by the Senate confirmation committee of professor Hill brought out an all-too-familiar line of questioning. The all-male panel asked why she had waited 10 years to tell her story, and if she had been harassed by Judge Thomas while working for him at one agency, then why did she follow him to another agency, where the alleged harassment continued. Her poignant answer was the same as that of many others. Ten years earlier, sexual harassment was not taken seriously by managers, in government or in business; it was her word against his and, without any evidence, the harasser wins. Finally, it came down to financial and professional survival—she needed his good will, if not his recommendation, to advance professionally. Even though the public was divided in its assessment of the hearings, sexual harassment quickly moved to the forefront of workplace issues. Lynn Martin, former Secretary of Labor, declared that "sexual harassment is not only a women's issue, it's a business and labor issue. A positive work environment is critical to both personal satisfaction and productivity" ("What to do," 1992).

A year after the hearings, when the Equal Employment Opportunity Commission reported a 50-percent increase in harassment claims, it was clear that companies must become more involved, that sexual harassment was *not* an interpersonal problem but a workplace issue. It was also apparent that sexual harassment flourished when management failed to address the issue or made only a token effort to contain it. Numerous high-profile lawsuits with multi-million-dollar awards to women have convinced many companies that it is preferable to establish training programs for all employees, not just managers. As managers and employees alike struggle amid confusion to understand how to conduct themselves, a critical key to success is the message from the top executives that sexual harassment will not be tolerated.

Two federal court decisions have been advanced that protect the rights of harassed employees. A judge in a California court ruled that the law covers remarks or behaviors that a "reasonable woman" would find objectionable, and that a man's perception is likely to differ from a woman's. The judge also noted that because women are much more likely to be victims of rape and sexual assault, they have a "stronger incentive to be concerned with sexual behavior" (Painton, Sachs, & Reid, 1991, p. 54). A Florida federal court provided additional clarification, ruling that the "standard for what's offensive is based on the perception of a 'reasonable woman,'" so that employers must consider sexual harassment from the perspective of a reasonable woman (Garland & Segal, 1991, p. 32).

When a woman is approached in an unwelcome sexual manner, she should immediately make it clear to the harasser that she does not like his behavior. The definition of sexual harassment is based on the fact that the behavior is not welcome. In addition, she should keep a written record of the details of the behavior and tell a trusted person about the incident. The next step is to tell her boss and insist that a record of the incident be made and an investigation begun. Finally, if management does not respond appropriately, she should take legal action by contacting an attorney or the Equal Employment Opportunity Commission. Sexual harassment is a problem in other countries as well. Companies in Japan, for instance, are beginning to take the issue more seriously as women become increasingly vocal in their complaints (see the "Diversity" box).

In addition to experiencing the same work strains as other employed couples, black dual-earner couples must deal with daily evidence of prejudice and discrimination in all aspects of their lives. Because "black women are expected to assist in the empowerment of black men, whatever power men seem to lack in the broader society, the relationship is expected to provide" (Peterson, 1992, p. 14D). Dual-earner women in black families sometimes suppress their own needs in their attempts to help their husbands deal with the effects of racial barriers at work. These employed couples are pioneers in the sense that they have had to develop new ways of integrating family and work roles to reduce role strain and create unique coping strategies for dealing with stress within a societal atmosphere of bias. Dual-earner couples in other minority groups share this experience.

Black women face the usual strains of dual-earner family life coupled with the added burden of overcoming racial barriers.

DIVERSITY

Revenge of the Japanese "Office Ladies"

For one executive at a prestigious Tokyo company, it started about a year ago. She found notes on her desk alluding to her sex life. Her male colleagues pinned up a nude centerfold resembling the woman. Another time, they wrote the woman's name at the top of a diagram of a human brain, indicating which lobes drove her sexual obsessions. When she protested, management advised patience. This spring, she was transferred to a less challenging post, while the men were not disciplined. "I spent half my energy just trying to cope with the humiliation," recalls the woman. "My bosses just acted as though it was my problem."

For many years, the only recourse for Japanese women in such situations has been *naki-neiri*, or quietly crying themselves to sleep. Now, that is changing. An unprecedented number of female workers are taking on Japan's male-dominated corporate society. They are accusing companies of condoning sexual harassment—or *seku-hara*—in the workplace and of sexist discrimination regarding promotions and pay.

SURPRISE RULING

As the cases proliferate, some are starting to get results. Last April, a former employee at a small publishing company in Fukuoka, 700 miles southwest of Tokyo, became the first person ever to win a sexual harassment case in Japan. In that case, a female employee claimed that her boss spread rumors about her alleged pro-

miscuity. When she complained, she was forced to quit. The surprising ruling has breathed fear into some companies, while the Japanese news media have stirred a national debate on sexual behavior in the workplace. Two days after the case ended, the Tokyo government issued 10,000 copies of a booklet on sexual harassment, and all were quickly snapped up. Says Yukiko Tsunoda, a lawyer who was involved in the decision: "This case showed that sexual harassment is the company's responsibility. If they don't take measures to prevent it, they will be sued."

Indeed, they are. Currently, Hitachi Ltd. faces a $437,000 wage-discrimination suit in which nine women charge that men with similar employment histories were routinely paid from 10 to 74 percent more. Hitachi denies the charges. At Sumitomo Life Insurance Co., two dozen women have accused the company of delaying the promotions of married women. Says a Sumitomo official: "We don't believe there was any discrimination."

Japanese companies in the U.S. are also becoming targets of harassment cases. Trading company Sumitomo Corp., for example, faces a complaint before the Equal Employment Opportunity Commission that its Chicago office abused Kimberly Carraway, a U.S. citizen who worked as a sales assistant. She charges that Japanese managers allowed pornographic materials to be circulated and that one manager repeatedly asked her for photos of herself in a bathing suit. Meanwhile,

COPING: MEETING THE CHALLENGES, REDUCING THE STRESS

The actions and perceptions adopted by employed couples to alleviate role strain are described as *coping strategies*. (An in-depth discussion of stress and coping is found in Chapter 13.)

How Women Cope

Employed women cope by prioritizing their activities and doing the most important things first, planning their time, consciously leaving work problems at

the workplace, and negotiating with husbands and children to share more of the household tasks and child care (Bird & Bird, 1987). They also limit community and leisure activities and use *cognitive restructuring*—focus on the good things about being in a dual-earner family ("We have enough money to provide our children with some of the advantages we never had"); define situations and events within their families as favorable ("The staff is very well-trained and when I pick Martyn up from day care, he is happy and full of stories about his day"); believe that the benefits of their lives outweigh the costs ("Sure I get stressed out sometimes, but my work is challenging and it's an important part of who I am") (Schnittger & Bird, 1990).

she claims, she was given only token promotions. A lawyer for Sumitomo declined comment. And trading firm C. Itoh & Co. is trying to reach an out-of-court settlement with the female employees at its New York office who have initiated a class action, claiming sex discrimination. A C. Itoh lawyer declined to comment.

In Japan, it's nothing new for women to find themselves stuck at the bottom of the corporate ladder. The first barrier to success is Japan's two-track hiring system, which leaves fewer than 3 percent of the professional positions at blue chip companies open to women. As a result, ambitious women who fail to secure one of these full-time jobs often end up as "office ladies" who file, wear uniforms, and politely bow while serving tea to guests and male colleagues.

Women lucky enough to land a professional job may run into a second barrier—a hostile corporate climate. A Labor Ministry poll indicates that 43 percent of all women in management positions complain of sexual harassment. Another hurdle is customers' tendency to feel slighted if a company does not send a man as its representative. Although women's rights to equal employment have been protected by Japanese law since 1986, "companies still expect women to get married and retire," says Masaomi Kaneko, labor consulting chief for the Tokyo Metropolitan Government.

But now, women in Japan are starting to speak out. On June 27, the weekly magazine *Gendai* ran an essay— ironically preceded by a six-page glossy pictorial of a nude woman—by the woman who won the $13,200 judgment in April. And female employees at an apparel company in Tokyo recently protested when the firm insisted they all wear a new miniskirt the company was trying to promote.

DOUBLE STANDARD

Even sophisticated companies in Japan can be blind to sexual harassment. Take ad giant Dentsu Inc. Its 1992 recruiting brochure, aimed at college seniors, features a drawing of the typical Dentsu "Working Girl," covered with what are intended as playful, handwritten comments. But they focus on her physical charms and seductive powers instead of her intellectual and creative talents. One message notes that her breasts are "pretty large." Another draws attention to her "rather soft" bottom. A drawing of the Dentsu Working Boy also pokes fun, but makes almost no comment on his physical qualities. A Dentsu official says that "we were not trying to say especially that she was cute or sexy. It was partly meant as a joke." He says that the brochure has been withdrawn. Still, several prospective employees have received copies within the past two months.

Even though Japanese women are starting to hit back, few if any companies are setting up procedures for formally dealing with discrimination and harassment. "They'll make things look pretty," says lawyer Tsunoda, "without dealing with real problems." If that's what happens, it will only create more complaints, court battles, and pressure on corporate Japan to guarantee women an equal deal.

EXPLORATIONS   *Why do you think sexual harassment policies in Japan lag behind those enacted in the United States?*

SOURCE: Excerpted from T. Holden & J. Wiener (1992). Reprinted from July 13, 1992 issue of *Business Week* by special permission, copyright © 1992 by McGraw-Hill, Inc.   ✿

In addition, women rely on social support. They count on family members for encouragement and make friends with other employed women.

When asked how they relieve stress at the end of the day, women say they watch television, listen to music, or take a bath or shower. Figure 9-2 has additional information on women's other workday stress-reduction activities. They are least likely to have a cocktail at home (22 percent) or go to a bar (12 percent). Asked about how they reduce stress at day's end, men report employing a much smaller range of activities than women. They most often read (53 percent), take a bath or shower (53 percent), or go for a walk (50 percent). The only stress reducing activities men use

more often than women are having a cocktail at home (33 percent), going out to a bar (24 percent), and exercising—jogging, aerobics, swimming (42 percent).

How Men Cope

Men's coping strategies for reducing chronic, long-term role strain include putting career goals on hold to make additional time for family responsibilities, postponing tasks at work, and establishing barriers against intrusions on their time, for example, saying that their schedules are already full and that they can't possibly take on anything else at this time (Bird & Bird, 1986). They also prioritize and plan their activities.

When under stress, men are more likely to use self-

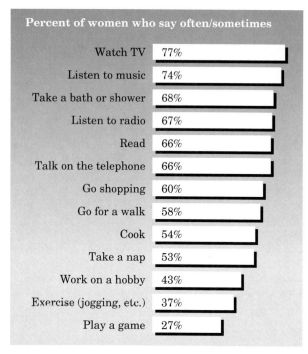

Percent of women who say often/sometimes

Activity	Percent
Watch TV	77%
Listen to music	74%
Take a bath or shower	68%
Listen to radio	67%
Read	66%
Talk on the telephone	66%
Go shopping	60%
Go for a walk	58%
Cook	54%
Take a nap	53%
Work on a hobby	43%
Exercise (jogging, etc.)	37%
Play a game	27%

FIGURE 9-2

Stress-Reduction Activities: How Women Relieve Stress

SOURCE: Roper Organization (1990).

control—keep their feelings in check and just concentrate on what they have to accomplish. Women, by comparison, more often express frustration and resentment when confronted with the pressures of role overload and role conflict (Wakat & Bird, 1990). But, contrary to what you might expect, the majority of women and men report coping effectively with the various strains of work and family roles and indicate low to moderate stress levels.

Couples who balance work and family roles most successfully express a commitment to jointly work through the issues and problems that arise in their marriages and strive to solve problems in a way that brings satisfaction to *both* marital partners. One dual-earner father described his family this way: "There's never a dull moment in our lives. No sooner do we take care of one problem than another situation arises waiting to be resolved. . . . But we seem to be able to handle the problems without too much distress in the family" (Sekaran, 1986, p. 13). By resourceful handling of the problems and challenges that occur, families gain a sense of confidence and competence. Their well-being is enhanced by being able to focus on the benefits of their lifestyle.

HOW DO THE CHILDREN FARE?

Mothers, in particular, feel responsible for the continuing success and happiness of their children and often blame themselves and face social stigma when anything goes wrong in their children's lives. For many years the prevailing stereotype has been that mothers' employment has adverse effects on children's development. After reviewing 50 years of research on employed mothers, a National Academy of Sciences panel found that employment was only one of the many factors that influenced children's well-being, and not the most critical one (Kamerman & Hayes, 1982).

Psychologist Lois Hoffman has studied the effect of mothers' employment on children for over 30 years and is well-known for the books and articles she regularly publishes on this topic (Hoffman, 1979, 1984, 1989). She and other noted scholars conclude that when parents are sensitive to children's needs and loving, consistent, substitute care is available, children's development is not harmed. The quality of parent-child relationships depends more on whether a woman wants to be a parent and how satisfied she is at work than on simply being absent from the home because of employment. Women who are satisfied with their lives are more nurturing of their children, regardless of their employment status (Barnett & Rivers, 1992; Scarr, Phillips, & McCartney, 1989).

Children report no differences in feelings of closeness to their mothers regardless of their employment status (Piotrkowski & Repetti, 1984). Both the daughters and sons of employed women exhibit more egalitarian gender role expectations. They are more likely to perceive women's and men's roles as being similar, have fewer stereotyped beliefs about appropriate male and female behavior, approve of women being employed, and view women as competent at work and at home (Hoffman, 1989; Mortimer & Sorensen, 1987). Daughters of employed mothers tend to be more self-confident, achieve better grades, and more frequently pursue careers than do daughters of other mothers.

Children with employed parents benefit by having contact and involvement with both parents, being exposed to fewer gender role stereotypes at home, and developing a greater sense of independence and competence through sharing family responsibilities such as household chores (Hoffman, 1989). Children exhibit higher self-esteem when they are given the opportunity to help the family and feel that their work is important and makes a difference.

When family scientist Patricia Knaub (1986) asked adolescents and young adults about their lives, they responded that the greatest benefits of living in a dual-earner family were having positive role models, feeling financially secure, and having the opportunity to develop as independent and autonomous individuals. Hochschild (1989) also interviewed older adolescents and young adults and got similar responses. Benefits of dual-earner life included "the education, the family vacations, the financial needs their parents' wages met." Most responses were like those of one college student who replied: "It's sure made me self-reliant. I can cook for myself, do my homework without prodding. I wouldn't be so independent if my mom had been home all the time" (p. 264).

Although it seems that there can be costs for families in which both parents are employed—lack of time, scheduling problems, role overload, use of day care—the results can be rewarding as well. For many couples a main concern is how to reconcile the conflicting role expectations of being a good parent with those of being a good professional (see Table 9-2). Men as well as women experience such conflict as the social and marital pressure increases for sharing the load (see the "Snapshots" box).

TABLE 9-2
Good Parent versus Good Professional

Many of the qualities that businesses expect of successful professionals are at odds with the characteristics cultivated by nurturing parents.

Qualities Needed to Succeed in Chosen Career	*Qualities Needed to Meet Needs of Child*
Long hours and one's best energy	Time to be together as a family and energy for the hards tasks of parenting
Mobility	Stability
A prime commitment to oneself	Selflessness and a commitment to others
Efficiency	A tolerance for chaos
A controlling attitude	An ability to let go
A drive for high performance	An acceptance of difference and failure
Orientation toward the future	Appreciation of the moment
A goal-oriented time-pressured approach to the task at hand	An ability to tie the same pair of shoelaces 29 times with patience and humor

SOURCE: S. Hewlett (1991).

SHARING THE LOAD: ARE MEN DOING THEIR FAIR SHARE AT HOME?

Are husbands sharing more of the work at home to offset wives' increased work load outside the home? Although changes in men's family roles have lagged behind changes in women's employment roles, men have stepped up their participation in household chores and child care (Barnett & Baruch, 1987). Between 1965 and 1985, men's share of the total time spent on household chores and child care rose from 20 percent to 30 percent (Pleck, 1987). And, in the intervening years, there are indications that their share has remained near that figure or slightly above (Stripling & Bird, 1990).

Negotiating for Change

Despite these encouraging statistics, the reality is that it is usually up to women to negotiate for more sharing from husbands. Much of the work of negotiation involves emphasizing the importance of the marriage as

a *partnership*. Sociologist Cynthia Epstein concludes that women who are more successful at managing multiple roles "experience the least guilt about delegating tasks at work and at home . . . and feel comfortable letting their husbands take on parenting responsibilities that other women tend to guard more jealously" (1987, p. 30). Most women with strong feelings about sharing the family work either marry men who plan to share these responsibilities or actively go about encouraging their husbands to view family roles as a shared enterprise. As one woman put it, "We went into this marriage, both working, and we did it together. We are partners" (Lubin, 1987, p. 60).

Women use various other strategies to encourage husbands to increase their involvement in family roles. One woman bought her husband a cookbook.

> He didn't know how to cook. . . . He didn't know about products. . . . It may sound ridiculous, but you have to take time to explain. . . . I bought him *The Sixty-Minute Gourmet* and told him, "I'm not going to cook now. I can't leave work to come home and cook." He just took to it, started with the first recipe and worked his way through. (Lubin, 1987, p. 61)

SNAPSHOTS

An Unusual Advocate for Child Care

Richard Stolley, a 63-year-old grandfather, is an unusual crusader, working to make child care a national priority. A very traditional noninvolved father to his own children, he became aware of child-care issues only when they affected the lives of his four daughters. He then used his position as an editorial director of three national magazines to encourage articles on child care and supported development of a day-care center for employees' children. He is also president of the Child Care Action Campaign, a national advocacy organization focusing attention on the problems of child care, saying:

I want to get other men involved. . . . Child care will

not become a national priority unless we get men involved. Our institutions, in too many cases, are controlled by men who are uninformed or unsympathetic to the problems of child care and dismiss it as a woman's problem.

EXPLORATIONS *When Stolley concludes that child care is not a women's issue or a family issue, but a national issue, what does he mean? What are the advantages of considering child care a national concern?*

Source: C. Lawson (1992).

Another refused to do the laundry: "If his socks are dirty, there is no reason why he can't put them in the washing machine. We both work. So when he didn't have any clean socks, he figured out what to do" (Lubin, 1987, p. 62). A husband responds:

If she asks me, I don't have much problem doing it. I think most women have a level of expectation about what someone ought to do without being asked. I don't have a whole lot of role models. . . . I know my father, even though my mother worked—just passed through our lives. My mother was supposed to raise the kids. (p. 63)

Women also teach men to clean bathrooms, vacuum, and load the dishwasher. They purposely leave some household tasks for husbands. In the process, women change their perceptions of how meals should be prepared, groceries bought, and clothes washed to better fit with husbands' ways of doing things.

Women, however, continue to take the management role in the household—keep track of when things need to be done, plan family activities and events, make lists, and remember to call the plumber, pediatrician, and so forth. Even women who contribute substantially to the family's standard of living, status, and social prestige and are financially independent may not have equal marital partnerships. The smaller the discrepancy between what a woman earns and what

her husband makes, however, the more equal the marital power structure and the more egalitarian the family decision making (Bird & Bird, 1984).

Men Receive Mixed Messages

Despite their traditional upbringings, many men are beginning to voice agreement with the notion that men have an obligation to be more involved in the daily life of the family. Arguing from a male perspective, Pleck (1985, 1987) notes that men get mixed messages about their involvement in family roles. Even though there is a general societal belief that men's family involvement is good, other attitudes limit their contribution. Many believe, for example,

that men's primary responsibility is breadwinning, and family involvement is good only as long as it does not interfere with this prior obligation . . . that men are more fulfilled in, or more psychologically suited for paid work than family roles; that it is demeaning or psychologically harmful to men to expect them to perform traditionally female family work. (Pleck, 1985, p. 280)

According to Pleck, men get very little support from supervisors and peers at work for being family-oriented. Men who more actively participate in family roles must usually cut back on productivity at work.

For many men, especially those in blue-collar positions, this puts their family economic survival at risk. Policies and practices at work and societal attitudes must change in order for men to invest more heavily in family roles. The major result of this imbalance in family roles is that employed wives experience significantly greater role overload than husbands.

Why Men Resist

Several other reasons why men resist increasing social and marital pressures to share the work load at home have been proposed. Hochschild (1989) concludes that men's resistance is related to three underlying fears: fear of losing decisioning power in the family; fear of losing face with family members, their kin network, and community members; and fear of being bossed around and told what to do. For men who are "failing at work, or otherwise feeling badly about themselves, avoiding work at home is a way of 'balancing' the scales with their wives" (p. 200). Some men also decline household chores as a way of compensating for wives' career progress. Women who get too far ahead are seen as gaining too much power in the relationship. Another reason for resisting sharing is men's reluctance to give up the benefits of having a homemaker wife. They feel privileged when their wives take care of them—look after, listen to, and otherwise nurture them. Men also insist that they were not raised to believe that family roles are in their domain of responsibility. In any case, they believe that their jobs are really too demanding or stressful to allow the addition of any new responsibilities.

Strategies of Resistance

Men's strategies of resisting change are typically unconscious and not intentionally manipulative. Faced with change, a usual reaction is to "drag one's feet" and thus gain the time needed to adjust and regroup psychologically. Other delaying tactics include doing the chores in a distracted way—forgetting important events like parent-teacher conferences, carelessly burning the family dinner, feigning ignorance of where the vacuum is stored. Hochschild (1989) calls these strategies "a male version of playing dumb" (p. 201). An additional delaying strategy is for a man to wait for his wife to ask for help. Asking is a chore that women do not relish. Rather than ask, some women will just go ahead and do the work themselves.

Men may also respond to requests for help by being disagreeable, getting irritated, and otherwise indicating a bad mood. These negative responses make wives uncomfortable about bothering husbands with such onerous tasks. Sometimes men bargain to delay or completely avoid certain tasks: "Well I really can't do the laundry right now, but as soon as I finish this diagram I will walk the dog"; "I can't watch Elizabeth on Saturday morning, I have to pay the bills, but I will take her to the beach in the afternoon." An additional strategy men use is to ignore requests for help and try to "outwait" their wives.

> It is acceptable for fathers, but not for mothers, to say that their wage work keeps them from their children or that they are impatient or incompetent in child care. Other reasons that stand for fathers but not mothers—inexperience, tiredness, clumsiness, and squeamishness. . . . Their jobs are too demanding or they were not "brought up" to do housework. (Thompson, 1991, p. 192)

Many men believe that women have more time to do the family chores. They think that women have accumulated skills as well as an inherent talent for doing household work. Women, according to some men, enjoy such tasks much more than they do (Komter, 1989). Men may presume that women somehow have a greater need for clean clothes, household order, and balanced meals. They reason that this greater need results in women doing more of the household work.

Why Women Accept the Status Quo

Relationships are important to women. They basically enjoy the satisfying feelings gotten from keeping the family operating smoothly and free of tension and conflict. Husbands' "help" is in many ways a symbolic expression of care and loving support. Besides sharing household work, women look for other signs that men are being responsive parents and marital partners. Husbands who are supportive of their wives' employment, appreciative of the extra work women do on the "second shift" at home, attentive listeners and comfort givers, and who also take care of the children when their wives really need it, are considered engaged and helpful partners (Thompson, 1991).

Women often compare their husbands to friends' husbands or to their own fathers and grandfathers and observe that their spouses do considerably more. Moreover, they have a difficult time viewing themselves as economic partners with their husbands in earning the family living, which results in them thinking that their husbands' roles are somehow of greater importance than their own. They may feel lucky to have a job they like and guilty about inconveniencing the family when they are at work.

Some women do bargain for more equitable family arrangements. In Hochschild's (1989) study, for example, 20 percent of the couples shared household work and child-care responsibilities about equally. Women in sharing relationships have certain identifiable characteristics (Thompson, 1991). First, they refuse to be *superwoman*—a woman who manages work and family roles by doing everything herself, despite the overload. Superwoman tend to deny their own needs and compare themselves to other women, beside whom they feel better organized and more energetic.

Women in egalitarian marriages, in contrast, compare themselves to their husbands: "Compared to Rick, I do much more of the household work and have almost no time for myself." This comparison usually culminates in a resolve to negotiate for change. Women who negotiate for sharing also recognize the value of their work to family well-being and thus feel entitled to a fairer distribution of the family work. Finally, they question gender-based justifications for maintaining a traditional division of the work load at home. Comments like "Women are better at folding clothes and making dinner," "Women enjoy doing the cooking and cleaning—to them, it symbolizes love," and "Men are clumsy, careless, and incompetent parents," are not given serious consideration by egalitarian, sharing couples. Men who share have more androgynous gender role attitudes and see their increased involvement as the fair thing to do, given the family work load (Bird & Bird, 1984; Guelzow et al., 1991).

Impact on Well-Being

For a woman, having a supportive husband is the key to success and well-being. Employed women with higher well-being (fewer depressive symptoms, less anxiety, greater life satisfaction) indicate that their husbands have positive attitudes toward their employment and cooperate by doing their fair share of the household tasks and child care (Stripling & Bird, 1990). Moreover, "If child care is accessible and husbands share in it, women's depression levels are low. In contrast, employed mothers without accessible child care and with sole responsibility for it have extremely high depression levels" (Ross & Mirowsky, 1988, p. 370).

Some people have speculated that having an employed partner would result in greater levels of anxiety and depression among men because of increased pressure to adopt new roles or change old ones. Pleck (1987) reports that although men's mental health has decreased relative to women's over the past 20 years, this change is unrelated to having an employed wife. In fact, the more money a wife earns, the less distressed her husband reports being (Ross et al., 1991; Wethington & Kessler, 1989). Likewise, the problem does not seem to be that husbands of employed women perform more housework and child care and thus are more anxious and depressed. Men who share more of the family work are *less*, instead of more, distressed. According to Pleck, men who are the most distressed remain steadfastly traditional in their gender role attitudes and behavior and try hardest to resist change.

Role transitions can be especially difficult for older men who grew up in a time when most women were homemakers. *Role flexibility*—maintaining an open, nonresistant attitude toward role change—seems the key to successfully combining work and family roles. Individuals and families, however, can do only so much. Other social institutions such as the workplace must also do their share to promote family well-being.

MAKING THE WORKPLACE "FAMILY FRIENDLY"

A growing number of businesses are attempting to accommodate employees with family obligations, but change is slow. Over 50 percent of employed women have paid pregnancy leave, but the benefits are usually available to women in the large corporations rather than the small companies for which many women work (Schroeder, 1989). Fewer firms offer any leave to fathers. Many companies do not guarantee that parents will get their jobs back if they are off work for longer than 6 to 8 weeks. In Europe, most mothers get 3 months' paid maternity leave and many corporations are considering increasing that to 6 months (see Table 9-3).

The Family and Medical Leave Act

The Family and Medical Leave Act signed by President Clinton in February 1993 requires companies with 50 or more employees to grant them up to 12 weeks of *unpaid* leave after childbirth or adoption. The leave is also available to people who have a personal illness or who must care for a seriously ill child, spouse, or par-

TABLE 9-3
Maternity Leave Policies in Other Countries:
Guaranteed by Law

	Maximum Weeks Allowed	Percent of Salary Replaced
Sweden*	51	90%
France	16–38	84%
Italy	20	80%
Britain	18	90%
Canada	15	60%
Germany	14	100%
Japan	14	60%
Netherlands	7	100%

* For both parents combined.
SOURCE: S. Caminiti (1992).

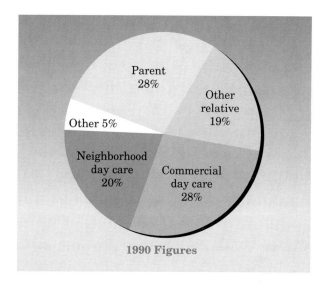

FIGURE 9-3
Who Cares for the Children?
SOURCE: S. Caminiti (1992).

ent. To qualify for leave, an employee must notify the company 30 days in advance and provide a doctor's certification. Companies are allowed to substitute an employee's earned paid vacation days for part of the leave, and can refuse the leave requests of employees who have not been with the company for one year nor worked 1,250 hours, or more than 25 hours a week in the past year. Companies can also exempt the highest-paid 10 percent of employees from leave because of the economic hardship imposed by losing key personnel. An employee taking leave is guaranteed the same job or a comparable position upon his or her return and is entitled to receive health-care benefits while on leave (O'Brien, Gupta, & Marsh, 1993).

Because 95 percent of all American businesses employ fewer than 50 employees and the leave is unpaid, the act is seen by some as having a placebo effect on solving the problems of working families (O'Brien et al., 1993). In the long run, antifamily policies hurt business. Companies that ignore family needs have higher rates of employee absenteeism, tardiness, and job dissatisfaction.

Reliable Child Care

Finding reliable child care is probably one of the most difficult, anxiety-producing problems for parents (see Figure 9-3 for information on how children of employed parents are cared for). Caring for sick children, making arrangements for temporary sitters when the regular caregiver is unavailable, and getting children to and from medical and dental appointments contribute to employees being absent, late, or departing early from work (U.S. Bureau of National Affairs, 1986). A

small, but growing number of companies offer on-site child care because they recognize that the availability of such care is critical to employed parents.

Despite the growing sensitivity to employed parents, a certain bias still exists in many companies. When words like "unreliable" and phrases like "uncommitted to the team" are used in employee evaluations, the consequences can be devastating. Bosses who frown on using sick leave to care for an ill child, in effect, tempt employees to be deceptive in order to be good parents. Only a few communities have emergency day-care facilities and many families do not have access to friends or relatives who can step in during an emergency. Many parents, faced with a feverish child, are on their own. And in the majority of cases it is the mother who stays home with the child. Most families continue to view the man's job as the most important and continue to believe that parenting is better left to the mother. Among couples whose goal it is to be more egalitarian in dividing family responsibilities, deciding who stays home with a sick child may trigger a confrontation that results in resentment and erodes marital satisfaction (Crosby, 1991).

The "Mommy Track"

One of the most helpful things a company can do is expand its definition of what it takes to be a successful employee. Women's career paths are very often different from men's. They are less linear (a straight path to

DILEMMAS AND DECISIONS

The Mommy Track

A proposal was made in 1989 for business to create two separate training and career paths for women, a "career-primary" path and a "career-and-family" path, later labeled the "mommy track." Since then, a long-running controversy has emerged with advocates and critics taking sides. One problem with the mommy track is the suggestion that women be identified early in their professional lives by their career paths. Those expected to remain dedicated to advancing their careers (like the career track for traditional males), would be given different training and promoted faster. Many fear that under this system, "career-and-family" women will not be taken seriously, ultimately being relegated to a "female job ghetto."

As a practical matter, most career-employed women do not know for sure which track is most appropriate for them until they become mothers. Childless women often do not realistically foresee the life changes brought about by becoming a parent, believing that setting priorities, planning, and organization will resolve all problems. Many mothers are, in fact, able to keep their careers on track after having a first child, especially if their husbands are supportive and involved in parenting. It is typically the birth of a second child that causes them to pursue their own version of a mommy track.

The mommy track was originally proposed as a means of reducing a company's investment in the training and promotion of women who would not benefit the company as continuing, long-term employees. Proponents failed to consider that many men and women who are highly committed to careers do not remain as lifelong employees of a single company. Nor was there recognition that younger fathers are becoming interested in taking brief leaves from work, from a few days to a few months, to be at home with their newborn children.

There appears to be little support for the mommy track. One-fourth of women and men surveyed favor the arrangement, with 55 percent of women and 45 percent of men believing it is a bad idea (Roper Organization, 1990). A majority of women (63 percent) and men (57 percent) believe the mommy track would mostly benefit business. Fewer than 10 percent of those polled believe that women would be the primary recipients of benefits if the mommy track were implemented. Heated discussion of the mommy track continues, often in conjunction with concern over the glass ceiling (see "Dilemmas and Decisions" box, Breaking through the Glass Ceiling, p. 252).

A growing number of employers, aware of the changing demographics of the workplace, have been listening seriously to these and other women's concerns. Fearful of losing talented and productive women, they have instituted new policies directed to family needs such as maternity leave, flexible work hours, part-time employment, and transfer to positions that allow women to devote more time to family needs until they are ready to resume focusing more time and energy on their careers. Some become frustrated with fighting the system and drop out until their children are grown, or they start their own businesses, often in their homes, to create their own balance between work and family.

Many women have pioneered changes on the job by arguing that flexibility works to the advantage of both the employee and the company. A recent examination of women in alternative career tracks indicates that careers do not suffer from periodic reductions in responsibilities or institution of flexible scheduling (Kantrowitz & Wingert, 1993). Good managers were found to remain successful, even while working part time. Some received promotions soon after returning to full-time employment. Others changed career goals, using this period of flexibility to move to positions that demanded less of their time or were more satisfying.

The greatest career risk for many women is financial. The immediate effect of taking extended leave or part-time employment is the loss of wages, vacation pay, and automatic raises, which affects the level of future income. A related issue is the loss of employment benefits, such as health and life insurance and contributions to retirement plans. These issues are of particular concern when the income and benefits are critical to the needs of the family.

EXPLORATIONS   *In what ways would the mommy track benefit women? How might it further erode women's positions in the work force? How could the proposal be revised to be less threatening to its critics?*

SOURCES: E. Ehrlich (1989); B. Kantrowitz & P. Wingert (1993); and Roper Organization (1990).

TABLE 9-4

Workplace Alternatives: Advantages and Disadvantages

Alternative	Advantages	Disadvantages
Flextime:		
Flexible arrival/exit time: can arrive at work anytime during a 2- to 3-hour grace period.	The most stressful time of day is the "rush hour" getting to and from the workplace—flexibility reduces this stress.	Studies indicate single women are the users, not parents. Flextime is not considered appropriate for supervisors and managers of personnel.
Compressed work week: most common ones are 40 hours in 4 days or 32 hours over a weekend.	Allows parents one or more full days of access to businesses, schools, and medical facilities. Weekend shifts popular among nurses.	High fatigue among workers. Adds the need for special child-care arrangements for the extended working days.
Part-time work:		
Part-time professionals: work less than 32 hours per week yet receive prorated amount of benefits afforded to full-time employees.	A parent spends more time on child care without losing "professional status."	May not have access to the more important projects and tasks given to those who are available through the entire workday.
Part-time partnership tracks: accomplished based on total number of billable hours, total amount of income, or total number of hours worked.	Allows professionals like doctors and lawyers to keep on a partnership track during child-rearing years.	May take twice as long to gain partnership as a traditional track. Many professions are project-oriented so may often work more hours than contracted.
Job sharing: two or more people share one job either simultaneously or alternatively.	Well-received by helping professionals like teachers and counselors—avoids burnout and helps maintain creativity. Affords the most flexibility in time spent at work.	Must be done on a voluntary basis. With professionals, employer will get more than "half" of their energy and talents—employee gets half the pay.
Extended leave:		
Maternity leave: extended leave for mothers of newly born or adopted children.	Helps women make the adjustment to motherhood while still guaranteeing her job at work.	Does not offer men the opportunity to learn and practice primary child-care responsibilities.
Paternity leave: same as maternity leave but for fathers.	Promotes bonding of father to child at birth and fosters new role development for fathers.	Although the job is guaranteed, maternity or paternity leave may result in loss of positioning for key promotions.
Parental leave: same as maternal and paternal.	If each spouse could take turns, the time period for which a full-time parent is available is doubled.	This system can work only if both have access to leave—an unlikelihood today.
Homework:		
Telecommuting	Allows women to combine home care, child care, and work for pay in the home. Saves time and cuts the cost of commuting and day-care tuition. Also allows flexibility of scheduling.	The isolation of home-based work keeps women from networking and prevents positioning for key opportunities. Also, without physical boundaries, can result in even more role strain and overload.

SOURCE: R. M. Kelly (1991).

higher levels of status and responsibility), having more interruptions along the way (usually for childbearing). This pattern of halting careers for childbearing and resuming them after children are older is called *sequencing*. Some critics suggest a *mommy track* as the remedy—a career ladder designed especially for mothers. But there are differences of opinion about the value of such a track (see the "Dilemmas and Decisions" box). What may be needed is a less gender-based career ladder, the "parent track." Work assignments would be less intense and career advancement less rapid until family responsibilities abate, but the track would not be for women alone nor would it be used as a way to identify and label workers as less committed or less promotable.

Elder care is another worry voiced by employees as a growing number of individuals reach age 80 or older and become the responsibility of their employed adult children. Employees who care for aged or ill parents, like employees with child-care responsibilities, experience greater stress and an increased incidence of absenteeism and lateness (Ford Foundation, 1989).

Flexible Work Hours

An additional issue for employees is the traditional work schedule. Only a few companies offer flexible work hours—*flextime*. Some women work part time because flextime either is not available or does not allow sufficient freedom to take care of family needs. For example, employees who are allowed to work over the lunch hour or come in an hour early, may not be permitted to come in 2 hours early or stay late. It is sometimes easier and more cost effective for companies to offer part-time employment than to change policies to incorporate flexible hours. Part-time workers can be paid less per hour and often do not qualify for health insurance or pension plans. Another cost to em-

ployees is that many upper-level jobs require a full-time commitment; thus, part-time employees find their options limited to a few jobs without the potential for promotion. *Telecommuters*—employees who, with the aid of a computer and fax, work at home—are another growing segment of the work force. For additional information on these and other workplace options see Table 9-4.

Businesses definitely feel the impact of increasing numbers of dual-earner and dual-career families and say they expect to respond to the need for family-oriented changes. However, there is confusion about exactly how companies will address work/family needs. Impatience has led some employees to charge that companies are giving lip service to family policies instead of actually putting them into practice.

As the 1990s unfold, most American couples will continue to be in dual-earner families. To build successful relationships, they will need to negotiate a work/family structure that fits their own marital situations and learn to cope with the unique strains that accompany their lifestyles. They will also need support from the larger society in the form of family friendly workplace policies as well as flexible cultural attitudes concerning what constitutes a good parent, marital partner, and employee.

SUMMARY POINTS

■ Only after World War II did significant numbers of married women enter the work force.

■ Compared to other women, employed women suffer fewer physical health problems and experience fewer symptoms of emotional distress.

■ Because household work is not valued as much today as it was in past generations, homemakers sometimes have a difficult time feeling good about what they do.

■ Men's psychological well-being depends as much on family roles as on work roles.

■ Typical concerns with which husbands of employed women struggle include lost marital power, less freedom to make occupational choices, and more involvement in household chores and child care.

■ Jobs and careers have different characteristics and

it is those discrepancies that distinguish dual-earner from dual-career marriages.

■ Taking on most of the housework is sometimes viewed by dual-earner wives as a means of rewarding family members for any inconveniences experienced because of their employment.

■ Dual-career couples tend to have more egalitarian marriages than dual-earner couples, but their relationships are still far from equal in terms of roles and responsibilities.

■ Among couples in which the wife outearns the husband, having an interdependent ideology increases feelings of intimacy and commitment.

■ Dual-earner families that subscribe to the family partnership model of combining work and family roles believe that all family members should act as a team to resolve problems and reduce stress.

■ Role overload and role conflict are two types of role strain that affect dual-earner families.

■ The glass ceiling and sexual harassment are examples of work environment strains that create barriers to success for employed women.

■ Employed women and men use various coping strategies to reduce stress: prioritizing activities, planning and organizing their time, using cognitive restructuring, postponing certain responsibilities, and establishing barriers to intrusion.

■ To reduce the stress they feel at the end of a long workday, men and women rely on similar strategies.

■ Parents' employment generally has no long-lasting harmful effects on children. The quality of the parent-child relationship and the satisfaction gained from being employed are two critical factors in predicting children's well-being in the dual-earner family.

■ Employed women typically must negotiate for change in the division of household tasks. Men are reluctant to share household responsibilities and resist women's efforts.

■ Women with sharing husbands refuse to be superwomen. They compare their efforts directly to their husbands' and believe in the value of their work as coproviders of the family living. Men in egalitarian marriages are less likely to use the traditional male justifications for escaping family tasks.

■ Employers are beginning to understand the need for a "family friendly" workplace, but are slow in enacting policies and practices to make it so.

■ The mommy track is one management suggestion proposed as a means of acknowledging women's obligations to their families, but most critics view it with suspicion.

KEY TERMS

Second shift	*Role ambiguity*
Dual-career marriage	*Glass ceiling*
Dual-earner marriage	*Sexual harassment*
Career	*Coping strategies*
Job	*Cognitive restructuring*
Interdependent	*Superwoman*
Multiple roles	*Role flexibility*
Role strain	*Sequencing*
Role overload	*Mommy track*
Work spillover	*Flextime*
Role conflict	*Telecommuter*
Commuter marriage	

REVIEW QUESTIONS

1. What is the second shift?

2. Why does women's work in the home get little recognition or societal praise?

3. Why are some men threatened by having an employed wife?

4. Discuss the similarities and differences between dual-earner and dual-career marriages.

5. How does having an interdependent outlook on life help couples cope with having a wife outearn her husband?

6. Explain how the family partnership model could be the answer for dual-earner families trying to resolve work/family conflicts.

7. What role strains do employed couples typically face and how do they cope?

8. What constitutes sexual harassment?

9. Give some examples of physical, verbal, and environmental sexual harassment.

10. Why do men resist becoming more involved in the daily running of the household? What strategies do they use?

11. Compare women who accept the status quo with women in more egalitarian marriages.

12. Using the knowledge gained from reading this chapter, create a profile of men in egalitarian marriages. What characteristics might distinguish these men from their more traditional counterparts?

13. Discuss the advantages and disadvantages of flextime, part-time employment, and telecommuting.

14. How can companies make the workplace more "family friendly"?

10

Jacob Lawrence, *Builders—Family*, 1974

Kin and Friends: A Support Network for Families

Perhaps the documents that best reveal the type of society we live in are the ones we carry around in our wallets. Social Security cards, credit cards, hospitalization and health care cards, plastic ID cards—all are peculiar to modern society and reveal one of its basic features, for as recently as the 1920s they were unnecessary. Then it was the family, not some impersonal bureaucracy operating with nine-digit ID numbers and computerized correspondence, that was supposed to provide assistance.

One of the most telling facts about the family today is that it is no longer called upon to perform certain family caregiving functions. Most of us, for example, will never be expected to take care of a cousin who is temporarily unemployed, an autistic brother, or a grandfather who has Alzheimer's disease. These traditionally family responsibilities are increasingly given over to outside institutions.

Credit cards tell the same story. Formerly, your face, name, and family reputation were all the identification you needed. But in today's large-scale society, ID cards bearing your photograph and signature are often necessary because the members of a particular group—a company, a club, or college—do not necessarily recognize one another.

For several generations, one of the preoccupations of sociologists was to describe this shift from traditional to modern society. "Time was," as Peter Laslett writes in *The World We Have Lost*, "when the whole of life went forward in a circle of loved, familiar faces, known and fondled objects, all to human size. That time has gone forever. It makes us very different from our ancestors" (1965, p. 6). It was commonly argued that industrialization caused the breakup of the extended family, which consisted of grandparents and collateral relatives—aunts, uncles, cousins. Judging from the size of most modern households, many sociologists concluded that it had dwindled into the smaller, portable, isolated nuclear family consisting of a husband and wife and their children.

It was also assumed by many sociologists that the bonds of kinship had eroded; family members no longer depended on one another as they had in the past. The modern family, according to this view, was considered to be little more than a launching pad for the children, who would soon be in their own orbit at some distance from their parents and kin, both geographically and emotionally.

But is this really what happened? Clearly, something significant has changed. We no longer live in a society where the bonds of kinship are commonly considered more important than the marital union, and it is tempting to conclude that the ties of kinship have eroded almost completely for many American families. And yet studies conducted since the 1950s have repeatedly demonstrated that kinship ties still have value.

If most American families have not really abandoned their kin, however, there is another respect in which many families today are somewhat isolated. Compared with family life in the past, it is common for today's families to be relatively isolated from their neighbors and the surrounding community. The household has become a more self-contained and self-sufficient unit, and family life has become a more private affair. Many people have complained about the feeling of isolation that such private households promote.

There are indications that people are interested in exploring new forms of connectedness and breaking down the fences that have been erected around the nuclear family. In many cities, there are "hotlines" or "dial-a-shoulder" services for potential suicides, alcoholics, even for people who want a dating partner. There are youth centers bearing names like Project Trust and Sanctuary where troubled youngsters can go to find help.

In addition to exploring some of the problems associated with the relative isolation of family life, this chapter acknowledges the social ties that extend beyond the family. Accordingly, it includes a discussion of friendship ties.

THE BONDS OF KINSHIP

Until just a few generations ago, a person's family name was her or his fate. Like skin color or finger-

prints, it could hardly be changed. Much of what anyone might ask about you could be answered by saying "I am the son or daughter of X, the cousin of Y." Especially in small towns where a few dozen families had lived together for generations, it was assumed that your family name said much about who you were. Here, for example, is Harper Lee's description of the life of a small town in the south during the Depression, from her novel *To Kill a Mockingbird:*

> The people who had lived side by side for years and years were utterly predictable to one another: they took for granted attitudes, character shadings, even gestures, as having been repeated in each generation and refined over time. Thus the dicta "No Crawford minds his own business," "Every third Merriweather is morbid," "The truth is not in the Delafields," "All the Bufords walk like that," were simple guides to daily living: Never take a check from a Delafield without a discreet call to the bank; Miss Maudie Atkinson's shoulder stoops because she was a Buford; if Mrs. Grace Merriweather sips gin it's nothing unusual—her mother did the same. (1962, p. 134)

In such towns, your family name was your credit card—unless, of course, you happened to be a Delafield.

Kinship was an important factor even in large cities. Edith Wharton's novels, for example, describe "good society" in New York at the turn of the century as an almost tribal community consisting of five or six great families, each related to the others through marriage.

In many societies other than our own, kinship provides the very basis of the social fabric. In contrast to our own language, which has few kinship terms—and not very precise ones at that—most preliterate societies are characterized by a complex kinship vocabulary. In such societies, the kinship system indicates a precise code of responsibilities, rights, and obligations. People function not as autonomous individuals but as members of certain kinship groups. Virtually all relationships are defined by the type and degree of kinship that exist between two people.

Because we place such a high value on individual freedom and personal autonomy, societies that are organized around the principle of kinship seem confining to us. The American population now mainly resides in metropolitan areas, not small towns. Family name and kinship ties are no longer as essential as they were (see the "Point of View" box).

Is the Nuclear Family Isolated?

Like most people, scholars sometimes mistake frequently repeated beliefs for established fact. Early theorists, for example, all stressed the differences between folk and urban society. They believed that much of the history of the family could be understood as the decline of the large, extended family unit and the rise of the nuclear family. Theorists pointed out that the modern family had been stripped of many of its old functions, and explained that the strong bonds of the extended family were not consistent with the needs of modern society.

What, exactly, had caused the extended family to break down? Several influential theorists answered the question by pointing to the process of industrialization. Here, for example, is Raymond Firth's explanation of why industrialization ushered in the nuclear family:

Industrial employment alters the occupational structure, lessens the time spent together by family and kin members, attracts able-bodied men away from their natal homes, loosens the bonds of obligation and control in respect to their elders, gives them a personal cash income which is easily convertible to their own purposes. Able to induce their wives to follow them to their place of employment or to obtain wives away from their home and the conventional local ties, they can form family units of an independent character, and take the responsibility for the support of their own wives and children. (1964, p. 74)

And, it was argued, this small nuclear family is ideally suited to the requirements of industrial society. In such a society mobility is necessary, and the nuclear family is a portable unit that also provides a refuge from the competitive pressures of industrial society. It is well suited to a society in which individual achievement is more important than the accident of birth into a particular family and kin group.

The idea that the distinguishing feature of the modern family is its isolation from the bonds of kinship seemed so plausible that it was accepted as self-evident truth. It was an attractive hypothesis that gained the status of accepted fact without having been subjected to the test of inquiry.

The hypothesis of the isolated nuclear family seemed especially plausible in American culture, which had been characterized since the colonial period by rapid mobility. Americans were—and still are—more rootless and mobile than other people. Nineteenth-century English novels usually end as two people get married, and that ending symbolizes not only the triumph of romantic love, but also the fact that the couple has found a place in the established social structure. By contrast, American novels of the same period are more likely to end with the hero riding off into the sunset.

In nineteenth-century America there was a saying, "If you can see your neighbor's chimney, it's time to move on." One of the most persistent themes in our folk songs is the idea of freedom and loneliness, the necessity of leaving family and friends, and moving on. For Americans, the self-made man became a cultural ideal. The phrase itself suggests how far we have moved from those societies of the past in which one's name was one's fate.

Kinship in Contemporary Society

It is no doubt true that kinship plays a less dominant role today than it has in the past, and that the mobility characteristic of American society since the colonial period has created social patterns unlike those in western Europe. But research conducted since the 1950s suggests that the theorists who drew a sharp contrast between folk and urban society, and thus concluded that kinship is no longer important in modern society, inaccurately represented both the present and the past.

First, these theorists incorrectly assumed that the typical household of the past consisted of an extended family. That may have been true of the wealthier households in eighteenth- and nineteenth-century Europe, but in North America and Britain and among poorer families especially, the typical household of the past contained the same members we find in most families today—a husband, a wife, and their children.

The assumption that industrialization and urbanization caused the breakdown of the extended family has also been challenged over the past few decades as historians have assembled evidence showing that the nuclear family structure was common *before* industrialization, and indeed that its existence was a key prerequisite for industrial development. (Hareven, 1987; Mintz & Kellogg, 1988). Students of contemporary kinship systems have, therefore, turned their attention to the specific types of assistance that kin offer each other and to the meanings attached to kin networks by people of different races and social class backgrounds. Kinship patterns in black families is an example.

POINT OF VIEW

Grandpa's Family Circle

In 1883, a 14-year-old youth named Michael Tenzer arrived in New York City from Europe with only $4 in his pocket and, even worse, not a scrap of family.

He soon made up for both, most strikingly with a clan of Biblical proportions, begetting seven children who produced 15 grandchildren, 32 great-grandchildren, and a fifth generation that now numbers 29.

What makes his story different from those of most other immigrant Americans is that his more than 200 descendants and other relatives have managed to stay in touch, even as they have scattered across much of America. They have done so through a little known but historically significant institution called the family circle or association, a phenomenon that began in the mid-nineteenth century as families of the early American settlers found themselves dispersing ever westward.

FORMALITY, BURIALS, AND SALAMI

Experts say there are hundreds of these associations still functioning. Cutting across many ethnic groups, they hold regular meetings with parliamentary formality at which they assist faltering relatives, resolve family crises, arrange burial plots, trace clan history, and, in the case of Mr. Tenzer's family, dispense charity.

During World War II, for example, the Tenzers wrapped packages of salami and candy to send to their sons fighting overseas, and they rescued dozens of relatives in Poland from the Nazis.

The Michael Tenzer Family Circle has clung together. They have done so in a way that recalls a time when families had their social life, not in front of a television set or at nightclubs, but simply with each other.

So yesterday, 75 Tenzer relatives gathered in a midtown Manhattan kosher restaurant, Lou G. Siegel's, to celebrate the family circle's sixty-fifth anniversary, and their enduring affection for one another.

"Not only do we have relatives, but our relatives are our very good friends," said Bernard Tenzer, a 70-year-old grandson of Michael.

Fred Wilson, a fourth-generation cousin, said: "You know your roots; you know the people who make up your family. If you need help you know they're there."

As they sang the American and Israeli national anthems and lunched on stuffed cabbage and matzoh ball soup, they shared stories about the clan's stern but tender patriarch and the gentle matriarch, Rose. They marveled again at how vigorous the three surviving children, Eva Pion, 96, Estelle Schiff, 89, and Herbert Tenzer, 86, continue to be.

They remembered the Passover seders when 50 relatives, living within blocks of each other in Crown Heights and Flatbush, would crowd into a Brooklyn apartment, and a scorching glance from Grandpa Michael would silence all mischief.

"There wasn't a weekend we didn't go to Grandpa's and Grandma's," said Bernard Tenzer. "Those brothers

---

The Role of Kin Networks in Black Families

While many accounts of family life acknowledge the persistence of close ties among kin who do not share the same household, particularly in the black community and other economically disadvantaged groups, it is often assumed that such kin networks are mainly a survival mechanism, a way of coping with poverty—and that families no longer rely on that kin network when their economic circumstances change.

But studies suggest that kinship ties—as indicated by visiting patterns and the exchange of aid—continue to function strongly among blacks (Cantor, 1979; McAdoo, 1988; Mutran, 1985). These studies point to the significance of a distinctive cultural tradition among blacks that emphasizes the bonds and obligations of kinship, regardless of the socioeconomic level of the family. (See the "Diversity" box for an example of the same trend in Hispanic families.)

There is considerable interdependence among the members of the black extended family, including financial assistance and the provision of help on an ongoing basis as well as in emergencies. There is more shared responsibility for all the children in that kin group, resulting in fosterage of small children and adolescents. Similarly, there is more shared responsibility for aged parents and grandparents. And the extended

and sisters were inseparable. All of their social life was in each other's houses."

VIRTUES AND ECCENTRICITIES

The family stories, capturing the virtues and eccentricities of their relatives, have served to thicken the family bond, even if some have been considerably embroidered with time.

The monthly family-circle meetings were carried out with near-congressional protocol. There was a salute to the American flag and the reading of minutes. There were officers, including a sergeant-at-arms who disciplined unruly children. There were dues—at first $5, now $10—that along with bequests and funds raised through parties added up to thousands of dollars, which was dispensed to organizations like the Jewish National Fund and Fight for Sight. And there was a periodic newsletter, the Standard Bearer, currently edited by Estelle Schiff, that kept everyone informed about weddings, illnesses and deaths.

With nourishment from Aunt Eva's and Aunt Estelle's sandwiches of egg salad and tuna salad, there were also games of pinochle and gin rummy, funny hat parties and shows produced by the children, who met separately in a family "junior league."

"It was to make sure that the children inherited the sense of family," said Bernard's wife, Shelley Kitzes Tenzer. "Naturally, it doesn't happen. You have to get together and do things as a family."

The family circle was born at Eva Tenzer Pion's tenth wedding anniversary in 1927, which she celebrated, of course, with her entire family.

"We decided it was such a lovely gathering that we ought to have a family circle," Eva Pion remembered.

The numbers of circle meetings, held in recent years at the American-Israel Friendship League in midtown Manhattan, have dwindled from monthly to three or four a year as more members, heeding the call of marriage or career, have settled in places like Wisconsin and Alaska. Robert S. Herbst, a 33-year-old Manhattan lawyer who is a fourth-generation cousin, points out that with the tribe's growing affluence and education, "we don't need the support of family because people are making it on their own."

And Eva, who has a great-granddaughter at Brown University and a great-grandson at Vassar, lamented: "Unfortunately the younger generation is not as interested. They have the time, but they devote their time to other things."

But at the celebration yesterday, relatives like Mr. Herbst and Gloria Batkin Kahn, a Westchester psychologist, suggested that they would work to keep the circle going. Beyond necessity and economics, Ms. Kahn said, it's simply "good to have cousins and family around."

Mr. Herbst added: "I have my wife, my friends. I watch the Giants on Sunday. Life goes on without it. But it's a treat to have something like this."

EXPLORATIONS *Why is it newsworthy that a family in the 1990s would attempt to keep their ties vital and ongoing? On what occasions does your extended family gather? Does your family have any stories it passes down from generation to generation? Does it have other means of reminding members of their connectedness? What are they?*

SOURCE: Excerpted from J. Berger (1991).

family commonly includes *fictive kin*—individuals not actually related who assume the obligations and enjoy the privileges of blood relations. For many single, black mothers who are part of extended families spread over several households—including a mother, a brother, an aunt, and other relatives who actively provide financial as well as emotional support and share the childrearing tasks—the kin network commonly provides a more enduring bond than does marriage itself.

Adaptable kin networks represent a real strength that enables black families to function well even in economic adversity. But they also pose certain diffi-

culties for their members, for example when loyalty to the group conflicts with individual ambition. Consider the dilemma faced by an older couple in one such network. When the couple inherited $1,500, their intention was to use the money as a down payment on a house. But their plans changed when others in their network made requests that they could not refuse. One relative needed $25 to pay an overdue phone bill; another faced eviction if she did not pay her rent; several others needed train fare to attend a funeral. Within a matter of weeks, the windfall was gone—and very little was spent by the couple who received the inheritance (Stack, 1974). Accounts of kin networks among

Family Ties Can Bind

There are no reliable statistics on how many Hispanic students who enroll ultimately graduate, but educators note that only a small percentage of college graduates are of Hispanic descent.

"It doesn't come easy," David Arredondo, the associate admissions officer at Oberlin, said of recruitment and retention efforts. "It takes a lot of work to do both, and sometimes some of the kids don't make it."

College officials say they continually bump into one obstacle they had not fully grasped until recently: the Hispanic culture, in which the family comes first, often frowns on a son or daughter leaving home to attend school.

Once enrolled, Hispanic students are more likely than others to drop out to take jobs to help support their families, admissions officers say, and others leave because they cannot function outside an extended family.

Retention rates are also kept low by academic problems, as some students are unable to do college work. That is not surprising, college administrators say, because a preponderance of Hispanic students attend public schools in underfinanced districts that cannot afford the college-preparatory courses.

Some students say that racism also takes its toll. At the University of Notre Dame last year, Lonni Limon, then a freshman from Austin, Tex., said a classmate who was giving a party called him a wetback and threw him out.

"I called my Mom and told her I wanted to come back to Austin and go to U.T.," said Mr. Limon, referring to the University of Texas. He turned to Hispanic classmates for support. "If I hadn't been strong," he said, "I would have left."

"Catholic institutions have an easier time because of the Catholic tradition most Hispanic families share," said Mary Pat Nolan, president of the Catholic College Admissions Association.

A recruiter from Notre Dame recounted how the parents of a student in El Paso had refused to let her attend the University of North Texas, 600 miles from home, but had readily agreed to let her enroll at Notre Dame, about 1,500 miles away, because of its Catholic affiliation.

Increasingly, the Ivy League institutions, the so-called public Ivies, like the University of Michigan, and other colleges say their representatives or alumni recruiters are making sweeps through the Southwest and West, where most of the nation's Hispanic population lives. Notre Dame does that and more by dispatching Maria Fuentes to cultivate recruits.

"When parents look at me, they see their daughter or son," said Ms. Fuentes, 25, a Notre Dame alumna whose fluency in Spanish helps overcome barriers. Ms. Fuentes said that despite the built-in advantage of Notre Dame's Catholic ties, "the problem I have to deal with is parents think their son or daughter won't care for them or their family as much when they go away to school."

Notre Dame's efforts have resulted in a Hispanic enrollment of more than 400 students out of a student body of about 7,600, compared with about 200 five years ago.

But recruiting students may be just a battle half won. Pepperdine University in Malibu, Calif., has learned that to retain Hispanic students it needs to offer extra academic and emotional support. It created the Cultural Enrichment Center 18 months ago to give minority students tutoring, counseling and a place to meet socially.

For Angel Maldonado, a freshman from McAllen, Tex., the university's services were crucial. "At first I was very homesick," said the 19-year-old accounting major. "It was difficult for my family, too. My sisters wanted me to come home every weekend. But the program helped me meet other people and make friends. And my parents, as much as they miss me, now want me to finish."

EXPLORATIONS *Which specific family values are being tested when Hispanic students are recruited by colleges? What other life decisions might result in kin resistance in Hispanic families? Are there other ethnic or racial groups that would probably react similarly? Explain.*

SOURCE: Excerpted from W. Celis (1993).

low-income blacks, such as the one just described, suggest how difficult it is for any individual in these networks to raise their standard of living until everyone is able to do so.

In the black family, the role of *kinkeeper*, traditionally assigned to one of the most respected and dependable family members, has gone to an elderly woman—usually a grandmother or aunt. Kinkeepers help maintain family continuity by serving as family historians, being role models of family morality as well as living examples of what is good about the family as a whole, espousing a theme of family unity by confronting any family member who is disruptive of it, and making sure that family members are supported in times of need. Kinkeepers prepare folk remedies for ailing family members, give advice and counseling, and mediate family quarrels.

Kinkeeping may also include the assumption of a surrogate-parent role to a single unmarried mother or to grandchildren whose parents are chronically ill or otherwise unable to continue their parenting responsibilities (Burton & Dilworth-Anderson, 1991). Though the surrogate-parent role is seen as a positive adaptation of the black family to the realities of modern family life, the cost to black women may be high. "Many find themselves overburdened by juggling the care of their own children and grandchildren with work, school, and maintaining personal relationships outside the family" (Burton & Dilworth-Anderson, 1991, p. 320).

The Bond between Parents and Adult Children

In our society today, the norm is that a married couple should be financially independent, needing little assistance from their parents or kin. There is a clear message that married children should be separate from their parents, but not completely cut off. "The desired relationship is a very subtle blend of dependence and independence" (Finch, 1989, p. 169). Nonetheless, a majority of young married couples struggling to maintain their lifestyle do take substantial assistance from parents.

Rather than providing continuous financial help, parents more frequently offer assistance in the form of no- or low-interest loans or money for inexpensive vacations or household equipment. Like gifts given on ceremonial occasions such as anniversaries or birthdays, assistance of this sort is less threatening to the young couple trying to maintain their independence than regular subsidies would be. Parents usually give the most financial aid early in their children's marriages. This type of aid diminishes quickly, while provision of services—babysitting, preparing food, repairing autos—remains high until the grandchildren have reached school age. Middle-class parents more often provide money; working-class parents are more likely to provide services (Finch, 1989).

Parents and other kin are also called upon for assistance in times of emergency. When people are in trouble or need help, they turn to relatives more readily than to friends. The bonds of kinship are still considered by most people to involve certain "inalienable rights" as well as obligations. When struck by major disasters such as fires or floods, victims seek help from their relatives even before they turn to outside agencies (Goetting, 1990). The more impersonal forms of assistance—hospitalization plans and government relief for disaster victims—are used, but relatives are still called upon in times of need. Blue Cross will not take care of the children when a woman is hospitalized, but her mother frequently will.

Parents whose children have formed their own households clearly indicate that they want to remain a significant part of their children's lives. Judging from the assistance that is offered, it is evident that parents and their adult children often maintain close ties. Summarizing his studies of the relationships between adults and their parents, one researcher concludes that "most adult children feel very close to their elderly parents, and vice versa." He found minor variations, such as the fact that daughters feel closer to their elderly parents than sons do, and that individuals at higher socioeconomic levels typically feel somewhat less close to their elderly parents. However, the overall pattern—generally positive feelings between adults and their elderly parents—is consistent and significant (Cicirelli, 1981).

Such studies demonstrate that the "family" is considerably more than a "launching pad" for children. The ties of kinship—particularly those between parents and children, and brothers and sisters who once shared the same household—still endure in today's society. When researchers returned in the late 1970s to Muncie, Indiana, to replicate the "Middletown" study, conducted 50 years earlier, they were surprised at how little the bonds of kinship had changed. "The single most important fact about the nuclear family in contemporary Middletown," they found, "is that it is *not* isolated." In fact, no other bond "directly links as many of the city's people to other people in or near

Middletown. . . . Middletown people see more of their closest relatives than of their closest friends, and they do more with them" (Caplow, Bahr, Chadwick, Hill, & Williamson, 1982, p. 168).

Women more often maintain close relationships with their parents than men do. As the proverb says, "A son's a son till he takes a wife; a daughter's a daughter for all her life." Ours is a society in which the family name is traditionally transmitted through the male line. But judging by continued bonds between parents and their offspring, we more closely resemble a matrilinear pattern, in which the female line is more important. Kinship studies confirm not only that women take a more active part than their husbands do in maintaining kin relationships, but that the mother-daughter bond is closer than either the father-daughter bond or that between parents and their sons (Rosenthal, 1985). Perhaps this is one consequence of the emphasis on childhood socialization of male independence. As one expert explains:

> Caring is "given" to women: It becomes the defining characteristic of their self-identity and their life's work. At the same time, caring is taken away from men: not-caring becomes a defining characteristic of manhood. Men are marked out as separate and different from women because they are not involved in caring for (and with) others. Their sense of self is achieved by doing things for (and by) themselves. (Graham, 1983, p. 18)

The In-Law Connection

The closeness of the mother-daughter bond helps to explain that common family complaint: in-law problems. The most typical in-law conflicts occur between women and their husband's mothers and fit our cultural stereotypes that the mother-in-law tends to interfere, criticize, and be possessive and overprotective.

The universality of mother-in-law jokes suggests that the special attachment between mother and child is difficult to sever. The situation is further complicated, as sociologist Ann Goetting points out, because no clear guidelines exist for relationships of this type:

> Western ideology dictates that the solidarity of the marital tie should supercede claims of the extended family, and there are no clear roles involving in-laws. This means that an in-law is someone we should feel attached to—but we are uncertain as to how to express this closeness. (1990, p. 68)

Like these two daughters leafing through the family photo album with their 83-year-old mother, most American women are the kinkeepers for their families.

The lower status of in-laws (son's parents) is evident from observing support patterns in families. The wife's parents provide greater financial assistance to newly married couples. Her parents are usually the ones called on during times of personal crisis. And though mothers and mothers-in-law are about equal in giving loans, money, and gifts, "mothers-in-law are somewhat more likely to *give* things, whereas mothers are more likely to *do* things" (p. 81).

Moving On: How Mobility Affects Kinship Ties

The average American moves about 14 times in a lifetime. Even if many of those moves are from one residence to another within the same city, long-distance moves have become a more common fact of life over the past few decades. In professional or technical occupations or in managerial positions, geographical mobility is commonly required for career advancement.

How is it possible, as we have noted, for most Americans to see their relatives as often as they do in the midst of such a high rate of geographical mobility? The answer is that despite the extraordinary amount of moving about that Americans do, most families do not move so far that they are deprived of relatively easy access to their family. When asked if relatives live nearby, 90 percent of respondents report at least one household of relatives within ready access; 60 percent visit with relatives at least once per week. Combining those people with no nearby relatives with those who see nearby relatives less than once a month, David Blankenhorn (1989) concluded that about 30 percent of the American population appear to have very little personal contact with their relatives.

Several studies conducted over the past several decades help us understand the effect of mobility on kinship bonds. It has been found, for example, that mobility has one meaning for lower-class and blue-collar families and another for middle- and upper-middle-class families. The mobility pattern of lower-class and blue-collar families is illustrated by Lewellyn Hendrix's study of families that moved from a small town in Arkansas. Hendrix found that over one-half of the people who left moved to cities where kin were already living. Typically, those who had first settled in the new location helped their kin to follow by offering the newcomers assistance in finding jobs and a place to live (Hendrix, 1975). Social historian Tamara Hareven noted the same patterns of migration in her study of working-class life in Manchester, New Hampshire. Hareven explains:

> Relatives acted as major brokers between the workers and the industrial corporations. Kinship networks also facilitated the movement of job seekers from one industrial town to another. Within the textile factory, kin also offered their relatives basic protection on the job, initiated the young and the new immigrants into the work process, and manipulated the machinery and work procedures. . . . In this way the family developed its own defenses and brought its cultural traditions to bear on work processes and relations among workers, and between workers and management. (1987, p. 43)

These studies, like others, demonstrate a pattern of *chain migration* for many lower-class and blue-collar families. Most industrial cities contain clusters of families that have migrated from the same town or region in the south. This pattern of migration might be compared with that of nomadic peoples in other societies, who move as a group and establish new settlements that retain many of the characteristics of the older one.

Upper-middle-class couples, however, move for somewhat different reasons. Having more specialized vocational skills, they are more likely to move for occupational advancement and not just to find another job. Nor are they likely to move to a location where relatives have already settled. This pattern has been demonstrated in various studies: the more education a person has, the more likely he or she is to live some distance from kin (Fischer, 1982).

For middle-class couples more than lower-class or

Most blue-collar and ethnic families socialize and celebrate with relatives.

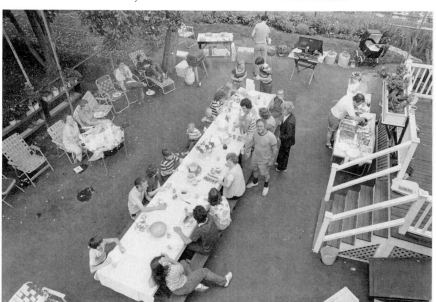

SNAPSHOTS

Granny Dumping: Are Families Deserting Kinship Responsibilities?

One elderly woman was left sitting in a hospital driveway as a car sped away. Another was wheeled into an emergency room with a note saying, "Please take care of her," pinned to her purse. Emergency-room workers call it "granny dumping," a phenomenon that they say is becoming more familiar across the country as families crumble under the strain of caring for relatives who are living longer than ever.

. . . More commonly, the elderly person is brought in or transferred in by a landlord or nursing home under pretext of illness. Then, when the emergency room is ready to send the patient home, there's suddenly no one in sight, the boarding room is taken or the nursing home place is gone. . . . The patients that are most typical are the people who have sort of been abandoned by life. They get too sick to stay in the shelter and they're not quite sick enough to stay in the hospital and they don't have friends or relatives or resources to take care of them.

EXPLORATIONS   *Is this situation an indication of family deterioration, and yet another reason for believing that we are becoming a nation of individuals with no sense of responsibility or obligation toward extended family? Or, is "granny dumping" a reflection of other societal problems like a health-care system that has cracked under the strain of so many needy elders? What social trends have led to "granny dumping"? What would help families and social institutions regain their ability to be responsible caregivers?*

SOURCE: Excerpted from M. Locke (1992).

blue-collar families, moving from one place to another often causes feelings of isolation. Ties of kinship are typically less intense than they are for lower-income families and some ethnic groups, in which family social life largely consists of events and activities involving relatives. But many middle-class couples still consider kinship to be part of their lives. Air transportation and phone calls enable kin to keep in touch despite the wide distances separating them. Both emotional attachment and certain patterns of assistance can be maintained even though the amount of direct contact is reduced.

That extended family identification remains strong even when people are geographically distant reveals feelings of obligation to stay in touch with relatives. Yet, as we would expect, family members who are physically separated from one another have much less face-to-face contact (Lee, 1980). And less face-to-face contact translates into reduced awareness of each other's lives. As sociologist Jesse Sprey points out:

What happens in such extended families is *not* that people stop caring for one another, but rather that individual members, depending on their circumstances, become less aware and less a part of the deeper content of each other's daily lives. (1991, p. 233)

It is no doubt useful to know how frequently family members call upon one another for certain forms of assistance, and important to dispel the notion that the bonds of kinship have eroded entirely. But it still cannot be denied that compared to most societies in the past, kinship bonds are not a critical resource for many families in today's society (see the "Snapshots" box). The majority of middle-class nuclear families are relatively independent. As social scientist Janet Finch so clearly demonstrates in her book, *Family Obligations and Social Change*:

most people see their kin as a "last resort" rather than a first. . . . You can fall back on your relatives—especially your close kin—if all else fails. Even then you cannot assume that assistance will be given automatically. . . . For most people the desirable situation is never to have to use the safety net except for relatively minor assistance which can be repaid easily. (1989, p. 240)

THE FAMILY: AS REFUGE AND RETREAT

If, with regard to kinship, we must characterize most families as only relatively independent, there is another sense in which they might well be considered more isolated. While some ties to the extended family remain, connections with the local neighborhood and community have eroded to a greater degree. Gradually, family life has become a more private affair.

The family began to be idealized as an island of harmony and a retreat from the outside world just when the most rapid urbanization was taking place, about the middle of the nineteenth century. If the rise of the modern city and its bustling heterogeneity were threatening to many people, family life could provide a refuge. The simple virtues of domestic life began to be celebrated in the inscription that can still be found on many kitchen and living room walls: "Be it ever so humble, there's no place like home."

Historian John Demos vividly described how Americans in the early 1900s began to divide their private lives from the impersonal world outside.

> The family stands quite apart from most other aspects of life. We have come to assume that whenever a man leaves his home "to go out into the world" he crosses a very critical boundary. Different rules, different values, different feelings apply on either side, and any failure to appreciate this brings, inevitably, the most painful kind of personal distress. The contrast has, of course, a pejorative character. The family becomes a kind of shrine for upholding and exemplifying all of the softer virtues—love, generosity, tenderness, altruism, harmony, repose. The world at large presents a much more sinister aspect. Impersonal, chaotic, unpredictable, often characterized by strife and sometimes by outright malignity, it requires of a man that he be constantly "on guard." It goads and challenges him at every point, and occasionally provokes response of a truly creative sort; but it also exhausts him. So it is that he . . . retreats periodically within the family circle. (1970, p. 186)

The Private Family

Kinship Patterns Influence Family Roles

When social anthropologist Elizabeth Bott (1957) conducted a study of urban working-class families in England in the 1950s, she noticed something that helps to explain the intensity of family life in American middle-class suburbs today. Among many of the families she studied, husbands and wives did not expect to be friends; masculine and feminine roles were highly segregated. After inquiring about many aspects of these marriages, Bott concluded that the definition of marital roles is influenced by the social environment surrounding the family. Where there is a close-knit network of relatives, friends, neighbors, and coworkers, many of whom know each other and interact frequently, marital roles are more likely to be segregated.

But why does the social environment of the family have such a striking effect on the definition of male and female roles within a marriage? Bott suggests two reasons for it: (1) wives with a close circle of friends and relatives can depend on them rather than their husbands for assistance; and (2) close-knit groups tend to agree on certain norms and put pressure on individuals to conform. Thus, where there is a close-knit family network, both males and females are under pressure to conform to traditionally masculine or feminine roles.

When families moved away from these close-knit groups, marital roles were frequently redefined. Bott found that the typical couple soon developed a marriage with certain middle-class characteristics, including more companionship between spouses and less role segregation. As couples moved away from close friends and relatives, they were forced to "seek in each other some of the emotional satisfactions and help with familial tasks that couples in close-knit networks can get from outsiders" (1957, p. 60).

Bott's research provides a major insight into the changes that have taken place in the family and how they are affected by the kinship network and the community in which the couple lives. As walls of privacy are erected around the nuclear family, spouses come to depend on each other for many of the social and emotional satisfactions that used to be provided by a number of friends, relatives, and neighbors. Children come to depend almost entirely on the good will of their parents. Often there are no other adults around to serve as a safety valve.

Walls Protect the Private Family

Even town planning and house design lend themselves to the pursuit of the private family. Around the turn of the century, most middle-class houses were built with front porches. What took place on those porches was fairly public behavior. The neighbors, who spent a good deal of time on *their* front porches, could see and hear much of what went on. But over the next few decades, new architectural conventions reflected changing social ideals. The relatively public front porch gave way to the more private screened back porch, sun room, or deck. In most suburban middle-class communities today, the front lawn, which is carefully mowed and manicured, is mainly for ceremonial display. Not much of family life is visible from the street. Outdoor activities take place in the backyard, which is far more private than the front porch was in our grandparents' generation.

And, as certain walls of privacy have been erected around the nuclear family, private spaces have been created within the household as well. Unlike the all-purpose rooms of sixteenth- and seventeenth-century households, most of the rooms in suburban middle-class homes are designed for particular uses. Indeed, "family rooms" would not be necessary if the other rooms were not special-purpose rooms. One of the main objectives of the architects who design such homes is to ensure privacy. Design criteria for the houses in which today's families live both reflect and encourage the belief that maximum privacy, not only between the family and the surrounding community but within the house as well, is something that is highly desirable.

Three Decades of Backlash

After centuries of increasing privacy for the family, the reaction against this tendency that was so prominent in the late 1960s and early 1970s was considered by some, such as Philippe Ariès, as a kind of "prison revolt" (Ariès, 1975). The communal experiments of that era represented attempts to open up family life, to reverse the tendency toward a small, emotionally exclusive family. Significantly, many of the young people who showed the most interest in communes and other group-living arrangements came from middle-class homes that epitomized the nuclear family characteristics we have been examining.

As the emphasis on self-development increased throughout the 1970s and early 1980s, so did the number of critics who claimed that the need for privacy was being pursued to such an extent that the *individual* rather than the family was becoming the primary focus of American life. Scholars like Christopher Lasch in *Haven in a Heartless World* (1977) and *The Culture of Narcissism* (1979) and Robert Bellah and colleagues in *Habits of the Heart* (1985) argued that the emphasis on personal satisfaction was undermining family ties as well as an interest in neighborhoods and communities. They worried that we were fast becoming a society of isolated, self-centered individuals unconcerned with maintaining strong bonds either to family or friends and labeled the 1970s the "me decade." Though other family scholars [e.g., Mary Jo Bane in *Here to Stay* (1976), Theodore Caplow and colleagues in *Middletown Families* (1982), Francesca Cancian in *Love in America* (1987), and Joseph Veroff and colleagues in *The Inner American* (1981)] offered evidence to the contrary, their voices were essentially drowned out.

Arlene Skolnick (1992) in her recent book, *Embattled*

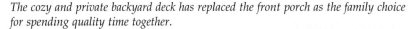

The cozy and private backyard deck has replaced the front porch as the family choice for spending quality time together.

The communes of the 1960s represent the first backlash against the privatization of American families.

Paradise: The American Family in an Age of Uncertainty, envisions the 1980s as a period of backlash against the "me decade" and the era of self-development. The election of Ronald Reagan, says Skolnick, was an effort to bring back the traditional family values of the 1950s. She writes, "By the late 1980s it was clear that the Reagan era's politics of nostalgia had not restored the "traditional family" (p. 179). Indeed, as the 1980s ended, they became increasingly known as a decade of greed and corruption.

So where are we in the 1990s? Skolnick concludes:

> Numerous surveys show that despite talk about the disappearance of the extended family, family ties beyond the nuclear family persist. Regardless of mobility, most Americans have ready access to members of their family. . . . Clearly the image of contemporary Americans as isolated and rootless is far from reality. . . . Rather than yearning for an elusive perfected family, we would be wiser to consider new social arrangements that fit the kinds of families we now have and the kinds of lives we now lead. (pp. 222–224)

In the 1990s, there is a greater willingness to accept the realities of how families have changed since the 1950s, along with a growing understanding that individual development is best achieved within the nurturing confines of committed, enduring relationships. Family ties remain strong as is illustrated by the continuing significance of rituals such as annual holiday celebrations (see the "Snapshots" box) and the family dinner hour (see the "Changing Lifestyles" box). Ties to friends also continue to be pivotal to personal and family well-being.

FRIENDS: THE OTHER SUPPORT NETWORK

Like kin, friends serve as a valuable support network for family members. When Rubin (1985) asked 300 women and men to describe the difference between family and friends, most said that friends are easier to confide in. While they could tell a close friend almost anything, they were more careful around family members, taking precautions to protect them from knowing the true depth of their pain and anxiety. Study participants reported relying on family in times of crisis—during emergencies or in cases where chronic problems endangered mental or physical health. Most admitted that it was less threatening to have disagreements with family than friends because of the stability and reliability of kinship bonds. Friendships were more likely to break up when conflict arose.

From family, individuals gain a sense of emotional attachment and permanence. From friends, they realize a sense of belonging and a feeling that they have a niche—someplace they "fit in"—other than with immediate family. People tend to look to friends when they need reassurance that their problems and concerns are "normal." Both family and friends are sources of personal well-being, but we seem to appreciate the importance of family and neglect the impact of friends on our lives (see Table 10-1). As social psychologist Sharon Brehm (1992) notes:

> Often, friendship is something we appreciate mainly in its absence. When we move to a new place and have no friends, then we realize how much having friends contributes to our lives. Or when we suffer the loss of other significant relationships, then we are aware of how much we need good friends. The problem with such an approach to friendship is that if we do not make the effort to maintain our friendships during good times, we may find ourselves without friends during those bad times when our need for them is greatest. (p. 362)

Almost one-half (48 percent) of the 1,226 adults surveyed in a recent Gallup poll said they have between one and five close friends, not counting relatives. Most (74 percent) had telephoned a friend within the past day or two, 67 percent had visited or done something special with a friend in the past week, and about half (54 percent) had talked with a friend about a private and personal matter during the past week (DeStefano, 1990). Most middle-aged respondents were in friend-

SNAPSHOTS

Family Rituals: How Important Are They in the 1990s?

Celebration of Christmas is nearly universal in the United States. Ninety-four percent of Americans celebrate Christmas. Hanukkah is observed by 1 in 20 adults (5 percent), and most of those who observe the Jewish holiday celebrate both Christmas and Hanukkah. Five percent say "Bah! Humbug!" to the whole season and celebrate neither religious holiday in December. A wide variety of activities contribute to the making of an American Christmas. Gallup polled 1,153 adults who usually celebrate Christmas and found that family traditions are at the heart of the American Christmas celebration.

For nearly two out of three, everything about Christmas day (the place, people, food, and activities) is the same from year to year. About as many (58 percent) spend Christmas eve in much the same style each year.

A young woman from New York who always spends Christmas at her parents' house described an old English pub drink her father makes every year on Christmas eve: "That is a constant. If he didn't do that, we'd boycott Christmas."

Others say their celebrations would be incomplete without "dinner at Grandmom's," "a family game of charades on Christmas day," "oyster stew on Christmas eve," "a family football game pitting the young against the old," or "a candlelight Christmas eve church service with the family."

Among the key findings from the poll on how people celebrate Christmas:

■ The Christmas celebration is a family event for the vast majority. At least 9 in 10 spent Christmas eve and Christmas day with family last year. About 1 in 20 spent Christmas eve or day with friends only, and even fewer were alone on Christmas eve (3 percent) or day (2 percent).

■ The traditional Christmas eve celebration is usually a close-knit family affair spent at home. Last year, just over half (52 percent) of those celebrating Christmas spent Christmas eve at home and of those 62 percent spent that evening with the immediate family only (spouse, parents, children, or siblings).

■ Dinner on Christmas day is more inclusive. Last year nearly 4 in 10 (38 percent) sat down to a Christmas dinner with grandchildren, cousins, aunts and uncles, or nieces and nephews.

EXPLORATIONS   *Does your family have any special rituals that play a key role in celebration of the December holidays? What are they? Have any new traditions been initiated in your family over the years? What are they? Do you think family celebrations of such holidays as Christmas and Hanukkah serve important purposes? If so, what?*

SOURCE: Excerpted from L. DeStefano (1989).

---

ships that had endured across distance and time: 50 percent had kept in touch with at least one friend from high school days; many others had maintained ties with college friends.

The Changing Nature of Friendship

In *Habits of the Heart*, Bellah and colleagues (1985) describe how the concept of friendship has changed since colonial times. Traditionally, friendship consisted of three basic components: enjoyment of each other's company, usefulness to each other, and a shared commitment to bring out the best in each other and do things for the good of the community. In some cases, friends are still chosen because they are useful in some way, but friendship today primarily involves enjoyable activities and good conversation. "Friends are those we take pleasure in being with" (p. 115).

The component of friendship that has almost completely disappeared in modern times is the idea that friends are responsible for bettering each other and encouraging contributions to the larger community. In

TABLE 10-1
How Kin and Friends Influence Personal Well-Being

What Kin and Friends Do	*Impact on Personal Well-Being*
■ Give unconditional support and commitment.	■ Builds trust and security; establishes feelings of attachment and belonging.
■ Affirm that one is known, valued, and accepted for his or her "real self."	■ Gives a sense of personal worth and self-esteem.
■ Provide an opportunity to help, nurture, and influence someone.	■ Develops empathy, respect for others, altruism, and caregiving skills.
■ Provide exposure to individual differences in feelings, attitudes, beliefs, and goals.	■ Develops tolerance, respect for differences, and openness to others.
■ Provide sources of social comparison and a safe setting for trying out new roles and gaining feedback and support.	■ Allows opportunities for self-appraisal and builds self-esteem; provides a frame of reference against which one can judge one's own abilities.
■ Furnish information and intellectual stimulation through ideas, jokes, and gossip.	■ Increases knowledge level which helps in making informed decisions and in choosing appropriate strategies for dealing with life problems.
■ Act as role models.	■ Teaches social skills and norms for appropriate behavior in life roles.
■ Act as stress buffers.	■ Lowers anxiety and depression.
■ Act as companions.	■ Allows involvement in activities (games, sports, parties, dinners, vacations) that would be difficult to do alone; increases stimulation and enjoyment and decreases boredom.

SOURCES: M. Cochran, M. Larner, D. Riley, L. Gunnarsson, & C. R. Henderson (1990); and R. B. Hays (1988).

colonial America, where small communities were the norm and face-to-face meetings typical, people participated mutually in enterprises that furthered the common good. Today we focus more on our own individual well-being and that of our closest family members and best friends, sometimes stretching this focus to encompass the good of the companies that employ us.

Types of Friendship

All friendships are not equal, probably because people choose friends to meet different personal needs. Some friendships develop rapidly over a short period of time because they are task-oriented or instrumental in nature. For example, friendships are formed for specific purposes like participating in leisure activities—walking or jogging, going to sports events, drinking, eating, making casual conversation. Other friendships are coveted for the sense of intimacy and emotional closeness they provide. These commonly unfold in a gradual process of self-disclosure and a buildup of intimacy. Friendships of this type provide caring and affection, mutuality, interdependence, and commit-

ment. As one woman said in an interview with Lillian Rubin, author of *Just Friends* (1985):

> There are a lot of people I can play with, but the people I call my real friends are the ones I can talk to also. I mean, they're the people I can share myself with, not just my time. (p. 61)

Five categories of friends have been identified from interviews with 2,000 people:

Convenience friends: A relationship develops because of the exchange of goods or services (e.g., lawyer and client, nurse and patient).

Doing-things friends: People become associated through their work or leisure activities.

Milestone friends: The friendship is mostly based on memories of past experiences; periodic contacts maintain the connection (e.g., classmates, war buddies, old neighbors).

Mentor friends: People come together because one person has exceptional ability, knowledge, and/or talent that he or she is willing to share. Once the subordinate person begins to approach equality, the

CHANGING LIFESTYLES

Dinner Time: Is It Still Family Time?

It's a contemporary image of the American family: children eating dinner in front of the television set, Mom and Dad drifting through the kitchen at whatever odd hours they come home from work to fix individual meals, the nuclear family reduced to bouncing particles.

But the image may be all wrong. According to a New York Times/CBS News poll, the vast majority (80 percent) of Americans with children say that on a typical weeknight most of their family eats dinner together.

Interviews with 31 respondents after the poll revealed that despite the pressures on single parents and on families in which both parents work outside the home, families go to great lengths to eat dinner together. Nearly all of these people said eating dinner together provided a peaceful respite from the frenzy of their day. Without it, many said, they would no longer feel as though they were a family.

Among the poll findings was that on a typical weekday most American families eat dinner at relatively early hours. Nearly half (49 percent) said they eat between 6 and 7 P.M. More than a quarter (26 percent) eat dinner between 5 and 6 P.M. A fifth (17 percent) eat between 7 and 8 P.M.

The poll found that 48 percent of families spent half an hour at dinner and 20 percent spent even less time. Thirty-one percent spent more than a half hour. In a surprising finding, given the proliferation in recent years of single-serving foods and the popularity of having foods prepared "your way," most families (81 per-

cent) reported that everyone at the table ate the same food. In only 32 percent of the families did children ever prepare their own dinner, and the majority of these children were older than 13.

A complex portrait emerged of what a "family dinner" means to Americans. While some families think of dinner as a formal meal at home, others meet at fast-food restaurants after work. While some families prohibit television at the dinner table, others use the opportunity to watch the news and other programs.

A majority, however, reported that conversation was the main activity. Less than half (42 percent) said they watched television during dinner. The majority (56 percent) said they spent dinner time talking without the television on.

What is clear is that eating dinner together is extremely important to American families and appears to be a powerful symbol of the family itself. Seventy-four percent of the respondents said getting the family together for dinner was "very important."

"Clearly, the symbolic meaning of dinner has not changed very much," said Thomas S. Weisner, an anthropology professor at the University of California at Los Angeles who has studied 20 families and the place of dinner in their lives. "Even though it may not be enacted every day, the family dinner is still there as a cultural ideal."

In interviews, it became clear that the ideal of the family dinner was so important that many respondents

---

friendship changes (e.g., teacher and student, scout leader and scout).

Close friends: A relationship develops out of choice; the friendship is based on being of equal status, having shared values and beliefs, and being mutually self-disclosing—with intimacy expected as part of the relationship (Block, 1980).

How Friendships Develop and Why They Dissolve

To find out the ways individuals go about making friends, communication researchers Dorothy Miell and

Steve Duck (1986) interviewed first-term college students to discover how they got to know others and what they chose to talk about as a friendship developed. Several stages of friendship formation were identified.

When meeting someone new, an individual typically uses the *new acquaintance script*—cautiously gathers information about the potential friend and discloses a few basic facts to appear friendly and responsive. If what is learned about the other convinces either individual that a relationship should not be pursued, then the second script—the *restricting script*—is activated to prevent further friendship de-had to be pressed to admit any deviation. They talked about these occasions differently, as if these more haphazard meals did not count and certainly did not represent their family's traditions.

In the survey, nearly half of the respondents (47 percent) said that when the family did not eat together it was because of the parents' schedules. Nineteen percent said the children's schedules sometimes interfered, while 17 percent said it was both the parents' and children's schedules. Sixty-six percent said, however, that everyone in the family had dinner together the previous evening.

If one thread bound the 31 families interviewed after the poll, it was the passion with which they embraced the concept of eating dinner together. Respondents spoke of dinner as the linchpin for the day, a respite from the chaos and separation in daily life. A kind of indignation accompanied the suggestion that some families are too busy to share the evening meal, as if eating dinner together was as integral to family life as fidelity is to marriage.

Many of those interviewed spoke of the extraordinary efforts that having dinner together required.

What was eaten or where varied widely. Although many families said in follow-up interviews that they cooked meals with a main course and two vegetables, there were just as many who spoke of going to McDonald's or opening a box of macaroni.

Clearly, there is something precious to American adults about the dinner hour, something they have taken from their own childhoods. In the poll, 85 percent of the respondents with children remembered that when they were children their family usually ate dinner together, too.

"Dinner says a lot about our society," Dr. Weisner said. "Our notions of equality and everyone sitting around a single table, eating from the same dishes, consuming the same food." He noted that in some societies men and women do not eat together and children eat last.

The notion of a family dinner in American culture dates from the mid-nineteenth century and the Industrial Revolution, when men began working outside the home and eating lunch, once the principal meal, on the job. Dinner became a celebration of the breadwinner's return and it took on great ceremony.

It is that reaffirmation of the family that is the most dramatic conclusion of the survey, said John R. Kelly, a sociologist in the Department of Leisure Studies at the University of Illinois at Urbana-Champaign.

"Despite all the pressures, the priority of the family in people's lives is clear," he said. "Dinner together is one of the absolute, critical symbols in the cohesion of the family."

"Frankly, I'm surprised," said Robert Bellah, a professor of sociology at the University of California at Berkeley who has written about the pressures on the American family. "But I'm also heartened."

EXPLORATIONS *Did it surprise you that the majority of American families continue to have dinner together? What do you think drives the stereotype of the uninvolved, overcommitted, neglectful American family? Are most Americans right to put so much emphasis on the family dinner? Why?*

Source: Excerpted from D. Kleiman (1990).

velopment. If, however, each person has positive impressions about what she or he initially finds out, and a friendship is suggested, the goal of each partner changes in the direction of getting to know the other person better and activates the *friendship script.* At this point the two potential friends meet more frequently, talk about a wide range of topics in greater depth, while observing each other's reactions and gaining insight into the values, attitudes, and beliefs that each espouses. If all goes well, they continue their interactions and move into the *intensifying script.* If not, the restricting script is reactivated again (see Figure 10-1).

Several criteria are used to determine the future of a friendship: "how similar he or she is, how trustworthy, how easy-going, how easy to talk to, and how available" (Miell & Duck, 1986, p. 137). As people become closer, discussions turn to different aspects of their personalities, what worries them, as well as their fears, hopes, and ambitions. Potential friends become more relaxed and less polite to each other. Trust grows enough for each to admit some basic differences on important issues.

Greater closeness in the form of self-disclosure and interdependence also increases the chances that disagreements and disenchantment will occur. "Arguments are most common among young adults under

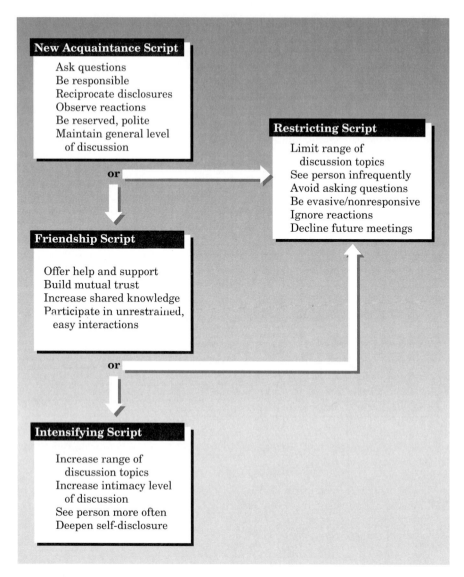

FIGURE 10-1
Four Friendship Scripts
Source: Adapted from D. Miell & S. Duck (1986).

age 30 and become less frequent as people get older" (DeStefano, 1990, p. 26). Friendships are governed by social rules, and violations can lead to friendship dissolutions (see Table 10-2).

Benefits of Friendship

As the friendship continues to develop, individuals focus less on what they are getting out of the relationship and concentrate greater energy on how the friendship benefits *both*. A unique characteristic of close friendships is that the people involved usually give help to one another without expecting reciprocity. Should a friend need help of some kind, the personal satisfaction of helping becomes the primary focus of the relationship, because from past experience each knows that eventually the other will return the favor; a pattern of give-and-take has been established. Close

TABLE 10-2
Rules of Friendship

Michael Argyle and Monika Henderson (1985) propose that all relationships are governed to a certain extent by social rules or guidelines about appropriate behavior. When they asked people how they thought friends should behave toward each other, study participants identified the most important rules of friendship as:

- Volunteer help in time of need.
- Respect the friend's privacy.
- Keep confidences.
- Trust and confide in each other.
- Stand up for the friend in his or her absence.
- Don't criticize each other in public.
- Show emotional support.
- Look him or her in the eye during conversations.
- Strive to make him or her happy while in each other's company.
- Don't be jealous or critical of his or her other relationships.
- Be tolerant of each other's friends.
- Share news of success.
- Ask for personal advice.
- Don't nag.
- Engage in joking or teasing with the friend.
- Seek to repay debts, favors, and compliments.
- Disclose personal feelings or problems to the friend.

When study participants were asked why friendships broke up—what distinguished good friends from lapsed friends—most identified the following factors:

- Being jealous, critical, or intolerant of the friend's other relationships.
- Discussing with others what was said in confidence.
- Not volunteering help in time of need.
- Not trusting or confiding in the friend.
- Criticizing the friend in public.
- Not showing positive regard.
- Not standing up for the friend in his or her absence.
- Not showing emotional support.
- Nagging.

SOURCE: M. Argyle & M. Henderson (1985).

friendships occur more rarely and the individuals involved in them are often referred to as best friends. A *best friend* is described as:

> a confidant with whom one can share very private information, a critic/advisor whose counsel is acceptable, a standard against which to measure oneself, an ego support whose affection and respect for one are known and reliable, an understanding ally, and a moral support in times of crisis. (Ritchey & Ritchey, 1980, p. 537)

College-aged friends described the following benefits of their friendships: companionship, having a confidant, emotional support, information exchange, material or task assistance, and self-esteem (Hays, 1985). Other major benefits derived from friendship include gaining a sense of who we are and that we are worthy of trust and confiding in; sharing world views: acquiring new skills or interests; gaining an opportunity for unselfish giving; receiving emotional support and understanding; and accepting each other as unique individuals (Bell, 1981). The most frequently mentioned disadvantages of friendship are: time, money, added responsibilities, emotional aggravation, loss of independence, negative influence of friend on self, and negative effects of friendship on other close relationships (Hays, 1985).

It is obvious that friendship and romantic love have many elements in common. Both close friends and romantic partners view each other as accepting, enjoyable, respectful, helpful, and trustworthy. But close friends are not as passionate about or as preoccupied with each other as are romantic partners (Davis & Todd, 1982; Sternberg, 1986). Each type of relationship fulfills an individual need and each contributes uniquely to personal well-being.

Gender Differences in Friendship Patterns

Just as women and men define intimacy in dissimilar ways, so do they characterize friendship differently. Women's friendships tend to be face to face, while men's tend to be side by side (Wright, 1989).

Women: Up Close and Intimate

In friendships, women more often emphasize shared confidences, trust-building conversations, and emotional revelations. Women would much rather talk when they get together with a friend. They are more comfortable disclosing personal information to friends and prefer being with one or two people at a time rather than socializing in larger groups where intimate interaction is more difficult. From their friends women gain self-esteem and affirmation of themselves, their ideas, and their beliefs (Wright, 1985). "Talk creates for female friends an elaborate and ongoing mosaic of non-critical listening, mutual support, enhancement of self-worth, relationship exclusiveness, and personal growth and self-discovery" (Johnson & Ariès, 1983, p. 358). Women report feeling closed off and lonely when they are deprived of the company of friends and when friends fail to self-disclose.

Women derive great pleasure from and place great value on the interaction process itself and the sense of communality it represents. To women, friendships have a therapeutic value. They offer a safe place to discuss personal problems and receive advice and emotional support. If a friendship is in trouble, a woman will typically talk to her friend and try to find the source of strain in the relationship.

Men: Doing Is Caring

Male friendships, in comparison to female friendships, focus more on shared activities (Caldwell & Peplau, 1982; Hays, 1988). For men, establishing friendships through participation in sports and other similar activities is a continuation of their earlier socialization patterns (Winstead, 1986). From an early age, males are encouraged to become involved in group activities as a means of learning appropriate gender roles, developing leadership skills, and gaining cooperative, team-building abilities. Men derive much less enjoyment than do women from expressing their feelings and participating in any type of "relationship talk." A man, faced with a troubled friendship, will generally distance himself from the problem, preferring instead to disregard and work around it (Wright, 1989).

Social psychologist Drury Sherrod (1989) suggests that men's friendship preferences differ from women's for one of three reasons:

> Either males fail to report accurately the true intimacy of their friendships because high intimacy is seen as inappropriate for the male sex role, or males express intimacy through different dimensions than self-disclosure and emotional expressiveness . . . or men simply do not seek the same degree of intimacy from same-sex friendships that women seek . . . men are satisfied with less intimacy than women because they prefer less intimacy than women. (p. 174)

Despite these differences, both men and women say that empathy and altruism are more necessary components of friendship than is companionship (Fox, Gibbs, & Auerbach, 1985). And both report that trust is what they value most in a friend (Bell, 1981).

Cross-Sex Friendships: What Makes Them Different?

Cross-sex friendships differ from same-sex friendships in several ways. Compared to same-sex friends, cross-sex friends communicate less often, share fewer confidences, and provide less emotional support and instrumental aid (Davis, 1985; Rose, 1985). Cross-sex friends also tend to be more alike in age, social class, and education (Parlee, 1979). When status, earnings, or other resources are heavily skewed in favor of one friend over the other, power may become an issue that undermines the relationship. Despite these differences, "there is no less trust, respect, acceptance and spontaneity in same-sex and cross-sex friendships, and the

Male friendship and intimacy is typically expressed through participation in competitive sporting events and other shared group activities.

level of enjoyment of each other's company is similar" (McAdams, 1985, p. 30).

Marriage and Friends: Are You Asking for Trouble?

Even today, married people who establish cross-sex friendships must deal with the social stigma of going against cultural norms. In American society, friendships are supposed to be less important than romantic or marital relationships. Time devoted to friends is frequently seen as either detracting from other close relationships or putting them in jeopardy—as if sharing personal information and emotional closeness should occur only between romantic or marital partners (Davis & Todd, 1985). When a married woman in one study was asked if she had any male friends, she replied:

No, I don't have men friends. Even if I wanted to, Ray's so jealous he'd kill me. I understand how he feels, because I sure wouldn't like him to have some woman for a friend either. (p. 156)

Her husband agreed:

Friends with women? You've got to be kidding. It's nothing but trouble for anybody that cares about his marriage. (p. 156)

Besides the social stigma and reluctance of marital partners to approve of such friendships, cross-sex married friends also say that they must deal with the issue of their sexuality and any sexual tensions that occur

from their togetherness. Men and women are socialized to be attracted to one another. Rarely are they taught how to relate to each other as friends instead of potential lovers. As one man relates:

The whole idea of friendship with women as opposed to a sexual relationship is a puzzle. It's not codified; you don't know what the rules are. And it's not something that's celebrated as any ideal in movies or books or anything. How do you get to be friends with a woman and not have to come on in any way? Friendship is almost in opposition to the love relationship game, which is what makes it so hard for men and women to be really good friends. If you're a friend you don't have to use any kind of a line, or play any kind of a role, or act some part. (Rubin, 1985, p. 149)

A woman talks about her ambivalent feelings about having cross-sex friends:

I'd like to have friendships with men, but I don't seem to be able to pull it off very well. If you get sexually involved, it ruins whatever friendship was possible, and if you don't, there's all that gaminess that goes on. (p. 150)

Even if a married woman and man become friends and manage to avoid any sexual involvement, many in their social circle will continue to assume that their relationship includes sex. The assumption is that friendship involves interdependence, caring, and commitment. With all this emotional attachment how can sex fail to be part of the package? Another societal assumption is that there must be a problem in marriages where partners have cross-sex friends; otherwise wouldn't their respective spouses be providing all they need of friendship? In one survey, only a small percentage of married couples (17 percent of men and 13 percent of women) indicated that their spouse was their best friend (DeStefano, 1990).

Keeping Sex Out of Friendship

Although there is not much a person can do about gossip, the following four relationship guidelines are offered to assist women and men in keeping their cross-sex friendships at a platonic level (Lasswell & Lobsenz, 1983):

1 Tell your friend that you are married or already involved with someone you care about in a romantic way; this helps make your expectations for the friendship clear.

2 Allow the relationship to develop slowly. Don't self-disclose too freely in the beginning.

3 Should sexual overtones develop, clear this up immediately with frank discussions. If your romantic or marital partner displays any signs of jealousy, reassure him or her that the friendship can in no way substitute for the special relationship the two of you have; silence helps to increase suspicion and uncomfortable feelings.

4 Know what you expect from a cross-gender friendship; it is dishonest to have the secret aim of sexuality.

The Value of Cross-Sex Friends

Even though they have fewer cross-sex than same-sex friends, men say they value those friendships very much (Davis & Todd, 1985). It is within such friendships that men more frequently self-disclose and give and receive emotional support. Women seem to have an exceptional capacity for encouraging men to "open up" and talk about themselves and their concerns (Derlega, Winstead, Wong, & Hunter, 1985). Moreover, people who have women friends report that they are less lonely than other people (Reis, 1986). One man says about his women friends:

> My women friends are very bright, have strong personalities, a sense of humor and are also very sensitive

people. They are people I completely trust. This is not something I would say about all of my male friends. With these women I would and have revealed anything to them. Not the same things to all of them, but only because it has never been relevant. If anything, I probably reveal too much about myself. This is something I don't do with my male friends. (Bell, 1981, p. 111)

When asked how they benefit from cross-sex friendships, women report receiving more instrumental than emotional support. As one interviewee notes:

> There is a hard edge you come up against in dealing with a man that I appreciate sometimes. I don't quite know how to say it, but there's a kind of safety in it. It doesn't let you forget who you are. . . . It's not that I think men are smarter than women, but their intellectual style is so different that it's easier to deal with sometimes. In some ways I can take criticism and give it more easily with a man friend. We women are always worried about a relationship or hurting someone's feelings—thinks like that—so things can sometimes get irritatingly mushy and messy. (Rubin, 1985, p. 163)

Friends and Well-Being

It seems natural to seek out friends in times of trouble. They assist by listening and helping to devise coping strategies to combat stress. Their intervention reduces vulnerability to illness and contributes to an overall sense of well-being and life satisfaction (Hays, 1988). In times of stress the type of support needed from friends varies with the magnitude of the problem, the suddenness of its onset, and whether it is seen as a challenge or as a threat. If the problem is not overwhelming or sudden in its arrival (its onset was expected), can be considered a challenge rather than a threat (the consequences are not too risky or dangerous), then contact with a friend will most likely help in at least three ways. First, a friend can listen and by empathizing reduce the emotional distress connected with the problem. Second, a friend can provide some useful advice or do something that will make a difference. Finally, a friend can provide a diversion from the problem by offering temporary distractions—arranging a night out with pals, staying close by until the worst is over, and so on.

The Constraints of Time

Almost one-third of adults complain about not having enough time to be with friends and 26 percent say that they are sometimes lonely. Individuals who feel most lonely for friends are employed women, women with children at home, and adults aged 30 to 49 (DeStefano, 1990). Loneliness is also more prevalent among the divorced, widowed, and separated—especially if they have no children at home.

Most people say they have no problem making friends if they have adequate time. About one-fourth of adults, however, find it fairly to very difficult to make friends. Because friendship is essential to well-being, human service professionals, individual and marital therapists, and family studies scholars are often called upon to provide information and recommend strategies to help people develop friendship networks. Most professionals advocate a mix of techniques, both cognitive (helping people think more positively about themselves) and behavioral (teaching social skills) (see Table 10-3). The desire for friendship is a very individual matter so there is no one "recipe"

that will have positive results for everyone in every situation (Blieszner & Adams, 1992).

Friendship can be a two-edged sword. From one perspective, friends provide a valued emotional connection outside the family, as well as beneficial support services; from another viewpoint, friends place many demands on time and personal resources (Ellison, 1990). Women, in particular, say that they are sometimes exhausted by the needs of their friends (Ross, Mirowsky, & Goldsteen, 1991). And negative encounters with friends can reduce personal happiness and life satisfaction to such an extent that later attempts to revive good feelings through positive interaction, emotional support, and shared activities prove very difficult.

Despite historical changes in family structure and functioning, kin and friend networks continue to provide valuable support services. They offer a place to turn when family members need care and understanding. They furnish stability and commitment in an ever-changing society.

TABLE 10-3
Friendship Anxiety and How to Overcome It

In their book *Adult Friendship,* Rosemary Blieszner and Rebecca Adams (1992) describe feelings and behaviors that get in the way of making friends and how individuals can improve their friendship skills.

FEELINGS AND BEHAVIORS THAT GET IN THE WAY OF MAKING FRIENDS

- Lack of confidence in one's conversational ability.
- Difficulty introducing oneself to others, making phone calls, and joining groups.
- Unrealistic expectations about how friendships develop and what kinds of behavior is appropriate in a friendship.
- Fear of being entrapped or "closed in" by the needs and demands of someone else.
- Difficulty in trusting other people.
- Anxiety about being a likeable person who is worthy of another's attention, caring, and nurturance.

TO IMPROVE FRIENDSHIP SKILLS

- Think positive thoughts. Give yourself credit for what you have to offer as a friend. This will reduce anxiety and give you greater confidence in your ability to begin and maintain a friendship.
- Create mental images of yourself meeting new people. Practice what you might say and do in such situations. Know that the most useful skills in friendship include expressiveness, assertiveness, empathy, and flexibility.
- Remember not to rush things. Moving from the getting-acquainted stage of friendship to a stage of greater closeness depends on the development of trust, which takes time to grow.
- Understand that friendships are characterized by emotional closeness, but that each person in a friendship needs to maintain some autonomy and self-direction.

SOURCE: R. Blieszner & R. Adams (1992).

SUMMARY POINTS

■ Until relatively recently, kinship, the family name in particular, helped define an individual's social status and afforded opportunities for success in the larger community.

■ Kinship ties continue to be salient today, but individual attributes and behaviors are more critical to achievement than is birth into a particular family or kin group.

■ Black families, regardless of social class, have historically emphasized connections and obligations among kin. The role of kinkeeper usually goes to an older woman who acts as the family historian and as a role model and counselor to the larger kin network.

■ Parents and their adult children struggle to maintain a blend of independence and dependence, with parents using occasions like birthdays, anniversaries, and other holidays as legitimate times for giving.

■ Women take a more active role in maintaining kinship ties than do men; consequently, the husband's family is generally visited less often and communication through the male family line tends to be constricted.

■ In-law conflicts most commonly occur between a woman and her husband's mother. One reason for this sometimes troubled relationship is that there are no clear norms concerning how in-laws are supposed to behave toward one another.

■ Despite high rates of mobility, most people live near at least one relative and most are in contact with some member of their family on a regular basis.

■ Lower-class and blue-collar families rely on a system of chain migration. Relatives facilitate geographical moves from one area of the country to another by helping family members locate jobs, homes, and community services in their new neighborhoods.

■ Middle-class professional couples rely less on relatives for job location and advancement. They more typically live some distance from kin, socialize more often with friends than relatives, and, when in need, contact close relatives for help only if all else fails.

■ Families are more private today than in past generations; nuclear families are supposed to meet many of the emotional and social needs once fulfilled by a larger network of kin, friends, and community members.

■ In colonial times, friendship consisted of three components: enjoyment of each other's company, usefulness to each other, and a commitment to bring out the best in each other while working for the greater good of the community. Today, friendship is more often based on companionship and enjoyable activities.

■ Friendships generally progress through at least four developmental stages during which individuals employ different interactional scripts.

■ Friendships are governed by a set of social expectations or rules that, if broken, can lead to dissolution.

■ Men usually make friends through participation in group activities—doing things together. Women build friendships through conversation—sharing confidences and feelings.

■ Same-sex friends typically communicate more, share more confidences, and provide greater emotional support and instrumental help than do cross-sex friends.

■ Cross-sex married friends must usually deal with negative societal views of their friendship, anxious or jealous spouses, and issues of physical attraction and sexuality.

■ Having friends reduces life stress and increases mental and physical well-being, but friends also place demands on time and other personal resources.

KEY TERMS

Fictive kin	*Restricting script*
Kinkeeper	*Friendship script*
Chain migration	*Intensifying script*
New acquaintance script	*Best friend*

REVIEW QUESTIONS

1. Why do black and other minority group families, low-income families, and blue-collar families tend to place more emphasis on connections and obligations among kin than do other American families?

2. Does your family have a kinkeeper? How is his or her role defined within the family? What special things does he or she do to keep the family together? Do you have regular family meetings?

3. In what ways are contemporary families more private than were families in past times? Describe the backlash that has developed against the privatization of family life.

4. Are there rules of kinship in your family—guidelines about appropriate behavior toward immediate and extended family members? Describe them. Are in-laws treated differently from other "regular" family members? Why or why not?

5. Was dinner time family time in your home? What was a typical evening meal like when you were a teenager? Were there other times during the week that family members made a special effort to be to-

gether? Do most American families have rituals and celebrations in which they regularly take part? Give examples.

6. What were the three components of friendship in colonial times? How does friendship differ today?

7. Describe the process most people go through when making a new friend.

8. Think of one of your friendships that broke up. What were the factors that caused its dissolution? Were they similar to those identified by Argyle and Henderson in Table 10-2, "Rules of Friendship"?

9. Discuss how cross-sex friendships can be beneficial as well as problematic.

10. How does gender influence the development and maintenance of kinship and friendship networks?

11

Susan Walp, *The Couple*, 1981

Communication and Conflict Resolution

Couples today place greater emphasis on the expression of feelings than they did a generation ago. In an examination of "advice" articles that have appeared in popular magazines over the past few decades, sociologists Francesca Cancian and Steven Gordon found that as recently as the 1950s spouses were advised to avoid conflict and follow traditional gender roles. But, beginning in the mid-1960s, there was a significant shift—from the notion of love as self-sacrifice to that of self-expression. From that point on, magazine articles mirrored changing cultural norms by advising husbands and wives to express both love and anger and to encourage their spouses to do likewise.

According to these new emotional ground rules of marriage, disagreements among spouses are normal. Indeed, talking about problematic events and bringing up personal concerns are measures of the strength of the relationship, not signs of its weakness (Cancian & Gordon, 1986, 1988). It would be almost impossible to have a lasting relationship without conflict.

All partners in close relationships eventually behave badly. It is inevitable that in responding to the irritation and dissatisfaction of everyday life, one or the other partner eventually will engage in a potentially destructive act—being thoughtless, yelling at the partner, or not spending adequate time at home. (Rusbult, Verette, Whitney, Slovik, & Lipkus, 1991, p. 53)

At the same time, it is important to keep in mind that the ideal of expressive marriage in which spouses continuously share their thoughts and feelings does not correspond to the reality of most people's lives. In one national survey the researchers asked, "How often have you wished that your spouse understood you better?" Not surprisingly, a majority of the respondents answered either "often" or "sometimes" (Veroff, Douvan, & Kulka, 1981, p. 169). In another study, it was only one type of married couple, out of three, that regularly communicated according to the ideal of *emotional expressiveness*—the ability to share one's most private positive and negative thoughts and feelings with one's partner (Fitzpatrick, 1988).

In this chapter we examine marital communication patterns by observing how subtle and significant these patterns are. In marriage, even more than in other close relationships, the simplest gestures are loaded with meaning. It is often more difficult to communicate effectively with intimates than with people who are not so close to us—and in this chapter we begin to understand why. We also describe how these difficulties may be overcome through such elements of effective communication as self-disclosure, clear and consistent messages, empathy, and useful feedback.

This is also a chapter about marital conflict. No two spouses ever agree completely about basic values, claims to certain privileges or scarce resources, or the precise meaning of role responsibilities. Airing and resolving these differences are a crucial part of any relationship; the absence of bargaining about differences may signal the presence of real problems. It is through effective communication and successful conflict resolution that relationships are maintained—retain their vitality and remain satisfying to both partners.

Another theme we explore in this chapter is gender differences in communication styles. Since, as we noted in previous chapters, men and women continue to be socialized differently, it is not surprising that they differ in how they communicate. Gender differences in communication patterns emerge from norms learned from, and reinforced by, parents, peers, and others from early childhood (Maltz & Borker, 1982). Women and men come together as participants in different cultures and the knowledge and rules for mixed-gender communication are not well-specified. Considering these differences, it is hardly surprising that intimates often misinterpret each other's messages.

COMMUNICATION PATTERNS: IS THERE A GENDER GAP?

If we listen carefully to conversations between women and men, gender differences in styles of communication show up clearly and consistently:

SHE SAYS: You listen but you don't hear what I'm saying.

HE SAYS: You're always telling me what to do.

SHE SAYS: You never tell me anything; you expect me to read your mind.

HE SAYS: You never get to the point; you want to talk too much about things. (Tannen, 1992).

Hierarchy versus Intimacy

From childhood, girls are taught to be skilled in verbal interaction and the kind of emotional sharing that form the basis of intimate relationships. Boys are taught *not* to express their feelings, but instead to attend to an objective reality that they are expected to master in order to succeed in their work. Sociolinguist Deborah Tannen proposes that as a result of this socialization process there are two underlying themes that explain most of the conversational differences between men and women. Men want to know: Who is in power? Who is up and who is down? Women want to know: Are we close or far away? Are we connected to each other or distant? According to Tannen:

> For most men, talk is a primary means to preserve independence and negotiate and maintain status in a hierarchical social order. This is done by exhibiting knowledge and skill, and by holding center stage through verbal performance such as storytelling, joking, or imparting information. . . . For most women, the language of conversation is primarily a language of rapport: a way of establishing connections and negotiating relationships. Emphasis is placed on displaying similarities and matching experiences. (1990a, p. 77)

When men are together they tend to make demands, push and pull at each other verbally to establish some kind of hierarchy of status, protect their autonomy, and deflect challenges. They talk more loudly than women and use words like "uh" to fill in gaps in the conversational flow to prevent another individual from interrupting. Women, in comparison, try to create intimacy. They believe that talk is the glue that holds a relationship together. Women carefully monitor closeness and distance from each other and make adjustments (Tannen, 1992). They are better judges of body language and are more accurate in identifying the meanings behind voice tones and facial expressions (Hall, 1984).

Advice Giving versus Troubles Talk

Conversational themes and talk rituals of men and women frequently create misunderstandings and cause conflicts in relationships. For example, when a woman comes home from work after a frustrating day, she expects to talk about it in detail with her partner. What she wants is to be listened to and given support. Her male partner, however, may try to give her advice. A man thinks: If she's telling me this, she must want advice. But if he gives advice she may be disappointed. To her, listening, understanding, supportive nods, and verbal acknowledgments indicate involvement—that her partner cares about her. Tannen calls this *troubles talk*.

Tannen (1990b) relates the story of a female college student who was frustrated by her boyfriend's inattention to her request that he listen to her. Whenever she told him that she wanted to talk, "he would lie down on the floor, close his eyes, and put his arm over his face. This signaled to her, 'He's taking a nap.' But he insisted he was listening extra hard" (p. A4). When she questioned him further, she found out that he covered his eyes to keep from being distracted by other things in the room and to concentrate on what she was saying.

When women talk to each other, they usually align themselves face-to-face so that when they speak they can attend to both verbal and nonverbal conversational cues. They typically talk at length about one or two topics during a conversational episode. Men, on the other hand, sit at angles to each other, avoid looking directly at each other, and move quickly from topic to topic. When men fail to make eye contact and switch from topic to topic in their conversations, women think they are not listening attentively. Moreover, Tannen points out, women "make more listener noise, such as 'hmm,' 'uhuh,' 'yeah,' to show 'I'm with you.' Men more often give silent attention" (p. A4). Their silent listening is often taken as evidence that men do not attend well to what women say.

Showing Agreement versus Being Challenged

Another example of gendered communication patterns: If there is an issue that comes up in the relationship (something bothers one partner and he or she wants a change), a woman will usually want to talk it through. She typically feels that if both partners keep talking about the issue, the relationship is working and involvement and care are being shown. A man is more likely to talk about the issue once and then think that things are resolved. If his partner brings the issue up

1992 Cathy Guisewite. Reprinted with permission of Universal Press Syndicate. All rights reserved.

again, he may take it as a sign that the relationship is in trouble.

Another complicating factor is that as the partners seek to solve their problem the woman will expect to hear supportive statements and observe some signs of agreement with her views. A man, in contrast, believing that a good listener points out alternative explanations and gives advice, may challenge some of his partner's observations and make corrective suggestions. To a woman, this is a challenge to her esteem and a threat to intimacy. Being challenged is a sign of disloyalty and a failure to be supportive. The man, thinking that he is doing his conversational duty, may then feel frustrated and confused when his attempts seem unappreciated (Tannen, 1992).

This gender gap in communication also affects how women and men interact in the workplace and places women in a double-bind situation. If women conform to cultural norms when at work—use indirect tactics for getting what they want—they are ignored and viewed as modest and unassuming. Colleagues then judge them as likable but not very capable in terms of knowledge and leadership abilities. If women, on the other hand, use masculine tactics—ask for the floor, portray themselves and their work in the best light possible, use assertive bargaining tactics, and otherwise try to compete with men—they are seen as arrogant, opinionated, and aggressive "dragons" who are

taking liberties that are inappropriate for women (Burgoon & Miller, 1985).

Women and men today are more concerned than ever before about *how* to talk to one another in ways that will protect and enhance their relationships. Reflecting this interest, Tannen's book, *You Just Don't Understand* (1990a), became a best seller. Moreover, the popular press regularly runs feature stories and advice columns on how to improve communication skills. Gender issues are the focus of many such columns (see the "Snapshots" boxes). Gender socialization is a common source of marital tension. As a consequence of misunderstanding what each other is saying and meaning, as well as some confusion over how women and men should go about communicating what they want in a relationship, couples may habitually avoid issues that need resolution and suffer a decrease in marital satisfaction (Thompson & Walker, 1991). And, as we see later in this chapter, socialization affects how couples self-disclose to each other.

EFFECTIVE COMMUNICATION: PROMOTING UNDERSTANDING AND VALIDATION

Making an attempt to understand what your partner says and indicating appreciation for his or her viewpoint signals a willingness to communicate. Effective communication benefits all couples by increasing relationship satisfaction and stability (Noller & Fitzpatrick, 1991). But communication is a very complex process. A communication consists of a sender, a receiver, and a message. After being sent, a message must be interpreted. The receiver always has to make some judgment about what the message means, for even plain words mean different things in different contexts.

You're Not Listening to Me: Sending Clear Messages

Common sense leads us to believe that the more time partners spend together, the better they will understand each other, but differences in conversational style can still create problems. The same interaction can sometimes be viewed quite differently. Imagine a woman who complains to her husband at dinner that she is "very tired." What those words mean depends

Barbra Streisand is famous for being a film director who uses masculine tactics. She has been publicly criticized and professionally punished for her so-called aggressive and arrogant style.

on the way they are said. He may assume that the real message is that she is fatigued. But, when the same couple is in bed later on and she responds to his tentative caresses with the words "I've very tired," he may interpret them as a rejection and conclude that she no longer finds him attractive.

Trying to understand the message in some communications is like watching a foreign-language film without subtitles. You know something is happening, but you can't figure out what it is. In the following example, notice that what the spouses actually say to each other conveys very little of their real message:

> A husband and wife, driven to the point of spontaneous combustion by their three small children and a few dozen other eroding pressures, escape for the evening to a party in their neighborhood. They have been looking forward to this evening for a week. The party is great. In about an hour, however, the wife develops a headache. After waiting a short while to make sure that the headache is not going to leave her, she dismays her husband with the entreaty, "You'd better take me home." He resists momentarily. "Every time we start having fun, you seem to get a headache." She doesn't feel like arguing. "You take me home and then you come back to the party." He pauses, rehearses in his mind all the reasons why he should return to the party and says, "Okay, let's go." They are both quiet during the drive home. Arriving home, he escorts her into the living room, asks her if there is anything to do to help her get comfortable, and announces his departure. "Where are you going?" she asks. "I'm going back to the party." He notices the pained expression and a small tear welling up in the corner of her eye. "What's the matter now?" "You're leaving me alone." "But you told me I should go back to the party." "I know, but if you really loved me, you wouldn't want to. . . ." (McCroskey, Larson, & Knapp, 1971, p. 169)

In this common example of faulty communications, it is easy to see what has gone wrong. Neither spouse pays much attention to the other's preferences or needs. The wife tacitly assumes the husband would not return to the party without her, but he takes her words literally and criticizes her for contradicting herself. Both avoid the real issue: Which is more important, her care or his fun? He may be thinking, "I know what her headache *really* means. It's her way of depriving me of something I enjoy." Then, as if this were not enough, she accuses him of not loving her. Now he knows she will feel hurt and rejected if he returns to the party and will probably respond with anger or hostility. Although probably not very significant in itself, the episode has really raised one of the basic issues in any relationship—how much the partners care for each other and how they demonstrate it.

Most students of marital communication patterns agree on the necessity of *leveling*—communicating where one stands, airing grievances, and expressing real feelings about the relationship. Partners should be clear in communicating where they stand and candid about what they expect from each other. Unlike with a casual acquaintance or a business associate where leveling is usually inappropriate and even costly, with a loved one, leveling generally enhances interdependence and intimacy.

Are You Sure That's What You Mean?: Deciphering Nonverbal Cues

Faulty communication can also result from mixed messages. Most commonly, a verbal message contradicts a *nonverbal message*—the silent system of communication consisting of facial expression, posture, tone of voice, eye movement, and rapidity of speech. The sender of mixed messages is not aware of what he or she is doing, and the receiver is, of course, confused. Here are two examples of mixed messages. In the first example, a wife responds to a suggestion made by her husband with the words "That's a good idea." At the same time, however, her voice is anxious and strident: her body stiffens and her hands clench into white-knuckled fists. Which is the real message, the verbal message or the nonverbal one?

In the second example, a family is sitting in a therapist's office, the father next to his daughter. When the therapist asks the father how he feels about his daughter, he replies, "I love her. She means the world to me." But while making this statement his legs are tightly crossed, he does not even glance at his daughter, and he speaks in a flat tone. The father's actions appear to contradict the verbal message he apparently intended to convey. Which message is more accurate? Because nonverbal communication lacks precision, it can create confusion and misunderstanding. How, for example, would you distinguish a nonverbal expression of anger from one of determination or one of disgust from one of contempt?

An essential communication skill is gaining an awareness of the range of meaning in nonverbal mes-

SNAPSHOTS

He Says

Tom Arnold, writer, producer, actor, comedian (and real-life husband of Roseanne), advises men to follow carefully certain basic rules of marital communication:

■ Listen to your wife. Listen all the time. And *let her know* you are listening. Because if she thinks you don't listen to her enough, she'll think you don't love her.

■ Talk to your wife. Talk to your wife even if you have nothing to say. Think up conversational topics when you're not around her and write them down. Because if she thinks you don't talk to her enough, she'll think you don't love her.

■ Look at your wife. Look at her even when her back is turned. Look at her eyes, her clothes, her feet. Because if she thinks you don't look at her enough, she'll think you don't love her.

■ Spend time with your wife. Think of things you both love to do. Do them. Think of things she loves to do

that you can tolerate. Do them. Think of things she loves to do and you despise. Do them. Because if she thinks you don't spend enough time with her, she'll think you don't love her.

■ Romance your wife. Send flowers, write notes, apologize. Romance her when you're tired (after the game). Romance her when you're really tired (after working out). Romance her when you're really, really tired (after *The Arsenio Hall Show*). Because if she thinks you don't romance her enough, she'll think you don't love her—and if she thinks you don't love her, *you will pay.*

SOURCE: Excerpted from T. Arnold & R. Arnold (1992).

sages. In the communication of an emotional message, 55 percent of the impact is due to the speaker's facial expression, 38 percent to tone of voice, and only 7 percent to the words themselves (McKay, Davis, & Fanning, 1983; Noller, 1984). When two people misunderstand each other, it may be because the communication was not sent clearly or because the partner failed to receive it accurately. Differences in communication style are exacerbated by cultural differences (see the "Diversity" box).

I'm Listening: Giving Feedback

For an individual to communicate effectively, he or she must receive *feedback*—a summary or restatement in different words of what was said or revealed nonverbally. Feedback allows communicators to know if their words are being interpreted clearly and accurately. It is important for partners to be aware of the messages they may be sending with their bodies, faces, and words, and of the possible interpretations of these

behaviors. It is equally critical for message receivers to check to be sure of the accuracy of these interpretations.

One of the most common conversational patterns is what philosopher Abraham Kaplan once called a *duologue,* two people taking turns at separate conversations, neither listening nor responding to one another. A husband, for example, might be discussing his upcoming business trip, while his wife responds by recounting her day at the office and her worries about a big project that is due in two days, and he responds by saying he needs more time to prepare for his trip. It is not really a communication because neither one is providing feedback to the other; nothing that either one says really modifies what the other will say next. Effective communication involves not only careful listening but also inquiries about how the other feels, or whether the listener has understood correctly. Phrases such as "Do you mean . . . ?" or "You sound discouraged about that . . ." or "Would it help if you . . . ?" indicate that the other person was listening to what

SNAPSHOTS

She Says

Roseanne Arnold, actor, comedian, producer, and writer advises women:

- Men are simple. Even though we have suspected this for years, popular wisdom (created, of course, by men) encourages us to ignore the facts. Don't.

- Because men are simple, they are not physically capable of handling more than one task at a time. Women can easily cook dinner, feed the baby and talk on the phone all at once. Were a man to try this, he would probably explode. So don't ask him to (after all, you're the one who'll have to clean up the mess).

- Men do not converse as well as women do. Men don't even speak English as well as women do. Their language consists of grunts, sighs, and a handful of offensive noises left over from their teenage years. Forget about deep, meaning-of-life conversations—if he speaks to you for an uninterrupted 5 minutes a day, consider yourself lucky.

- Oddly enough, while men cannot remember basic facts—like your dress size or your anniversary—they can recite from memory every statistic from every football game that took place during the last 6 years. The trick, then, is learning how to relate important events in your life to football.

- Men have no experience "taking hints." Your attempts at subtlety—which work so well with your female friends—will get you nowhere with your husband. Put aside your feminine wiles and ask directly for what you want. He'll be so happy that, for once, he understands you, he'll give you anything you want.

EXPLORATIONS: *How well do you think Roseanne and Tom Arnold's comments reflect the realities of communication patterns among American couples? Would you add anything to Tom and Roseanne's basic rules of marital communication? What?*

SOURCE: Excerpted from T. Arnold & R. Arnold (1992).

---

was said and recognizing the speaker's thoughts and feelings.

You Can Trust Me: Protecting Self-Esteem

One reason it is often more difficult to communicate effectively with family members than with strangers is that the people who are closest to us affect our self-concepts most powerfully. It is in intimate relationships, where we reveal more of ourselves, that we are most vulnerable to attack, ridicule, and criticism. Because spouses (and other family members) play such a significant part in either confirming or denying our sense of self-esteem, communication among family members is a tricky business.

As therapists often suggest, one of the most important interpersonal skills to learn is how to express pos-

itive judgments as well as negative ones, thus bolstering the self-esteem of one's partner, and how to express criticism in descriptive rather than judgmental terms. Couples show love, acceptance, and trust by talking about the positive aspects of their relationships and what they like about each other. Don Dinkmeyer and Jon Carlson, authors of *Time for a Better Marriage*, advise partners to use phrases such as I like . . . ; I appreciate . . . ; I enjoy . . . ; I value . . . ; and I respect . . . (1984, p. 74).

How Much Must I Tell You?: Making Appropriate Self-Disclosures

According to current social norms, intimacy requires self-disclosure; therefore, making judgments about how much disclosure is appropriate in specific situations, and with certain people, is a key element in our

One of the most important aspects of communication is body language. Proximity, posture, and facial expression are usually more telling than the actual verbal message.

communications. From an early age, most of us learn *not* to disclose certain judgments—particularly negative evaluations of other people—just as we learn that it may be inappropriate to act spontaneously in all situations. But we also learn that love requires the open expression of feelings and that relationships without "real" communication are doomed to be unsatisfying and unhappy arrangements prone to decay and dissolution.

Intimate relationships are increasingly defined as those in which partners feel free to talk about aspects of themselves that they normally keep hidden, yet research continues to show that there is not a consistently high level of self-disclosure in all romantic relationships. In most relationships, women are more forthcoming about their personal feelings and opinions (Peplau & Gordon, 1985). "Women often say that they have to pull things out of their husbands and push them to open up" (Thompson & Walker, 1991, p. 77). Men protest that women never seem to be satisfied, regardless of how much they disclose. They are reluctant to reveal aspects of themselves that partners may not regard as desirable. Furthermore, men tend to demonstrate intimacy through acts rather than words (Cancian, 1986; Rubin, 1984).

Self-disclosure in a relationship, then, appears to be a gender issue. To be a good communicator seems to require one to behave in ways that sometimes go against strongly ingrained gender preferences. Perhaps the best tactic, under the circumstances, is to appreciate that women and men differ in how much intimacy they need and in how much they believe must be self-disclosed to ensure intimacy.

I Understand: Showing Empathy

Empathy—the capacity of seeing things from another's viewpoint—is particularly valuable in marital communications. One of the stock cartoons about married life shows a man hiding behind his newspaper over coffee in the morning while his wife tries without much success to attract his interest. This picture typifies a grievance among wives about the empathy they receive from their husbands.

> To him, reading the paper is an essential part of his morning ritual, and his whole day is awry if he doesn't get to read it . . . a woman who objects is trying to keep him from doing something essential and harmless. It's a violation of his independence—his freedom of action. . . . She perceives his behavior as a failure of intimacy. He's keeping things from her; he's lost interest in her; he's pulling away. . . . All her life she has had practice in verbalizing her thoughts and feelings in private conversations with people she is close to; all his life he has had practice in dismissing his and keeping them to himself. (Tannen, 1990a, pp. 82 & 83)

Various studies suggest that because of boredom, indifference, or the mistaken belief that one already

DIVERSITY

Cultural Differences in Communication Style

The success of any relationship depends on two things, what we say and how we say it. People who grow up in other countries, or even in different parts of the United States have different conversational styles based on their unique ethnic, religious, or socioeconomic backgrounds. Understanding these differences improves communication as well as the quality of relationships.

■ A Greek man married to an American woman accused her of speaking in an irritating monotone, especially when their tempers were strained. She felt terrible about this newly discovered failing, and wondered why no one had ever mentioned it before. It never occurred to either of them that he found the tone of her talk monotonous because he was listening for the extreme shifts in pitch typical of Greek speakers, especially Greek women. And her American habit of muting her expression of emotion when she was upset seemed unnatural to him.

■ An American woman visiting England was repeatedly offended when Britishers ignored her in settings in which she thought they should pay attention. For example, she was sitting at a booth in a railroad station cafeteria. A couple began to settle into the opposite seat in the same booth. They unloaded their luggage; they laid their coats on the seat; he asked what she would like to eat and went off to get it; she slid into the booth facing the American. And throughout all this, they showed no sign of having noticed that someone was already sitting in the booth. The omission of such talk seemed to her like dreadful rudeness. The American couldn't see that another system of politeness was at work.

■ An American man who had lived for years in Japan explained a similar politeness ethic. He lived, as many Japanese do, in frightfully close quarters—a tiny room separated from neighboring rooms by paper-thin walls. In this case, the walls were literally made of paper. In order to preserve privacy in this most unprivate situation, his Japanese neighbors simply acted as if no one else lived there. They never showed signs of having overheard conversations, and if, while walking down the hall, they caught a

neighbor with the door open, they steadfastly glued their gaze ahead as if they were alone in a desert . . . the intention was not rudeness, but politeness.

■ Most Americans think it's best to "get down to brass tacks" as soon as possible, and not "waste time" in "small talk" or "beating around the bush." But this doesn't work very well in business dealings with Greek, Japanese, or Arab counterparts for whom "small talk" is necessary to establish the social relationship that must provide the foundation for conducting business.

■ A woman from Texas went to Washington, DC, for a job in dormitory administration. When the dorm staff got together for meetings, she kept searching for the right time to break in—and never found it. Although back home she was considered outgoing and confident, in Washington she was perceived as shy and retiring. When she was evaluated at the end of a year, she was told to take an assertiveness-training course because of her inability to speak up.

■ A white office worker appeared with a bandaged arm and felt rejected because her black fellow worker didn't mention it. The (doubly) wounded worker assumed that her silent colleague didn't notice or didn't care. But the coworker was purposely not calling attention to something her colleague might not want to talk about. She let her decide whether or not to mention it; being considerate by not imposing.

EXPLORATIONS: *Have you ever been in a situation where you were misunderstood because of cultural differences in communication style? Explain.*

Source: Excerpted from D. Tannen (1986).

knows how the other feels, spouses often overestimate their understanding of each other. Misunderstandings may therefore arise because a husband does not make his feelings or preferences known, while his wife is not even aware of what he is doing. Real communication is replaced by a guessing game in which husbands and wives make certain assumptions about each other rather than seek out further information that might lead to real understanding. "Empathy," writes Dinkmeyer and Carlson (1984), "allows us to enter our partner's perceptual world and to spontaneously feel what our partner feels. Empathy may not result in agreement, but it allows us to demonstrate understanding" (p. 75).

Happily married couples seem to be more effective communicators than couples who seek marital counseling (see Table 11-1). Happily married couples talk more frequently with each other, understand what their spouses are saying, are more sensitive to each other's feelings, and are more aware of nonverbal cues as well as direct messages (Retzinger, 1991; Schaap, 1984).

THE PROCESS OF CONFLICT: HOW IT BEGINS, BUILDS, AND ENDS

When events occur that threaten or damage intimate connections with a partner, it seems natural to attempt to alleviate the strain by bringing up what is troublesome. Couples try to talk things through and restore

TABLE 11-1
Happy versus Unhappy Couples: Differences in Communication and Conflict

The way couples communicate and resolve conflicts has much to do with whether they are content or distressed in their relationships. Recent studies identify the following factors as significant in distinguishing happily from unhappily married couples:

Happy Couples	Unhappy Couples
■ Get along well, are satisfied with their marriages	■ Have frequent conflicts, express marital dissatisfaction
■ Keep discussions focused on the issues and keep the boundaries of conflict limited to specific differences	■ Are more likely to use coercion and personally rejecting statements; cross-complain; interrupt each other
■ Show positive affect—empathetic smile, warm voice, affectionate touch	■ Get caught up in a cycle of escalating aggression, then withdraw from each other
■ Approve of and agree with each other	■ Overlook positive behavior of partner
■ Use reconciling acts—change the subject, use humor, accept the other's ideas	■ Show negative affect—inattention, lack of eye contact, silence, or loud talking
■ Are responsive/facilitative—acknowledge and praise, affirm each other's feelings, describe partner favorably, paraphrase and summarize partner's remarks	■ Display coercive acts—leave the room, deceive, threaten, induce guilt, make disparaging remarks
■ Display supportive behaviors—agree with process and outcome of disagreements	■ Give negative feedback—turnoffs, put-downs, criticism
■ Sit close together	■ Are defensive—disagree with the process and/or outcome of conflicts
■ Are egalitarian about sharing power, control and assertiveness—use directions, instructions, suggestions, or requests that bring about change in the behavior of the partner	■ Have struggles over power, control, and assertiveness
	■ Engage in long, drawn-out conflicts; expand issues by using words such as *always, never, all,* or *none*
■ Resolve conflicts through problem-solving acts—compromise, offer to collaborate in planning, probe, seek and give information	■ Violate relationship norms—fail to live up to each other's expectations; make unfair demands and requests
■ Use almost no coercive acts—demands, inducing guilt, threats, disparaging remarks	■ Rebuff each other—fail to respond to partner's requests
■ Are flexible to changes in the relationship	■ Place blame on each other for all relationship problems; crucialize (If you really loved me, you would . . .)

SOURCES: A. Holtzworth-Munroe & N. S. Jacobson, 1985; D. R. Peterson, 1983; P. Noller, 1987; H. Raush, W. Barry, R. Hertel, & M. Swain, 1974; S. M. Retzinger, 1991; C. Schaap, 1984

harmony to the relationship. Conflictual interaction, then, is a signal that something in their relationship is not functioning properly, that there is a need for change. Most family scholars consider it healthy for couples to admit their differences and air their grievances. They view conflict as a means of restoring relationship bonds. Couples who engage in conflict, in fact, often report that the outcome includes a greater understanding of each other's perceptions and higher marital satisfaction (Knudson, Sommers, & Golding, 1980; Noller & Fitzpatrick, 1991).

Nevertheless, not all conflicts are resolved to the satisfaction of both partners. Sometimes conflict escalates to the point where it threatens the continuation of the relationship. Sociologist Suzanne Retzinger, author of *Violent Emotions: Shame and Rage in Marital Quarrels*, distinguishes between constructive and destructive conflict, arguing that conflict sometimes may be destructive, eroding relationships, and culminating in violence. "When further alienation rather than unity occurs it can be destructive" (1991, p. 5). Therapist George Bach proposes that since fighting is inevitable between intimates, couples should learn how to disagree in a manner that is constructive rather than destructive to their relationship (see the "Dilemmas and Decisions" box). Perhaps conflict can best be understood as a process that has three distinct stages—a triggering event, engagement, and termination (Peterson, 1983).

The Triggering Event

The *triggering event* is something one partner does or says that is particularly irksome to the other and sets off a protracted disagreement. Four triggering events are identified by couples as especially problematic: criticism, illegitimate demands, rebuffs, and cumulative annoyances (Peterson, 1983).

Criticism ("You're never here when I need you"; "You never listen to what I say.") elicits a sense of injury and injustice, which brings on emotional responses like anger and hurt. Such feelings are hardly conducive to the cooperative and caring spirit that leads to conflict resolution. Instead, the offended party seems compelled to reciprocate the perceived insult with some negativity of his or her own. In their book on communication and conflict, Dinkmeyer and Carlson (1984) give an example of how criticism leads to additional conflict.

HE SAYS: I'm in a hurry. Where did you put the car keys?

SHE SAYS: I haven't driven your car, nor do I know where your keys are. You're always misplacing things.

HE SAYS: Don't blame me. You're responsible for the house. I always put the keys on the desk and they aren't there. You must have moved them.

SHE SAYS: I'm not the only one responsible for this house, and I'm certainly not responsible for your keys. You're the one who leaves stuff lying around. If you weren't so messy you could find something now and then.

HE SAYS: You are always making me late. . . . If you really want to help me, keep track of my things. (pp. 51, 52)

In this example, the man complains that the car keys are missing and it is his partner's fault. He expands the complaint and further criticizes her for not taking appropriate responsibility for the household work and, as a consequence, she is "making him late." She responds by reminding him that he is always losing

Criticizing, cross-complaining, and blaming are not conducive to the satisfactory resolution of a disagreement.

DILEMMAS AND DECISIONS

Fifteen Suggestions for Constructive Conflict

When something happens to trigger a fight between marital partners, it is important to keep the disagreement as constructive as possible by avoiding detrimental communication patterns. In their classic book, Pairing, *therapists George Bach and Ronald Deutsch give some guidelines for constructive conflict.*

1 Be specific when you introduce a gripe.

2 Don't just complain, no matter how specifically; ask for a reasonable change that will relieve the gripe.

3 Ask for and give feedback of the major points, to make sure you are heard, to assure your partner that you understand what he [or she] wants.

4 Confine yourself to one issue at a time. Otherwise, without professional guidance, you may skip back and forth, evading the hard ones.

5 Do not be glib or intolerant. Be open to your own feelings, and equally open to your partner's.

6 Always consider compromise. Remember, your partner's view of reality may be just as real as yours, even though you may differ. There are not many totally objective realities.

7 Do not allow counterdemands to enter the picture until the original demands are clearly understood, and there has been a clear-cut response to them.

8 Never assume that you know what your partner is thinking until you have checked out the assumption in plain language; or assume or predict how he [or she] will react, what he [or she] will accept or reject. Crystal-ball gazing is not for pairing.

9 Don't mind-rape. Don't correct a partner's statement of his [or her] own feeling. Do not tell a partner what he [or she] should know or feel.

10 Never put labels on a partner. Call him [or her] neither a coward, nor a neurotic, nor a child. If you really believed that he [or she] was incompetent or suffered from some basic flaw, you probably would

not be with him [or her]. Do not make sweeping, labeling judgments about his [or her] feelings, especially about whether or not they are real or important.

11 Sarcasm is dirty fighting.

12 Forget the past and stay with the here and now. What either of you did last year or month or that morning is not as important as what you are doing and feeling now. And the changes you ask cannot possible be retroactive. Hurts, grievances, and irritations should be brought up at the very earliest moment, or the partner has the right to suspect that they may have been saved carefully as weapons.

13 Do not overload your partner with grievances. To do so makes him [or her] feel hopeless and suggests that you have either been hoarding complaints or have not thought through what really troubles you.

14 Meditate. Take time to consult your real thoughts and feelings before speaking. Your surface reactions may mask something deeper and more important. Don't be afraid to close your eyes and think.

15 Remember that there is never a single winner in an honest, intimate fight. Both either win more intimacy, or lose it.

EXPLORATIONS: *Are there other suggestions you would add to this list? Which of the 15 suggestions do you think are most critical to constructive fighting?*

Source: Excerpted from G. R. Bach and R. M. Deutsch (1974).

things and criticizes him for being a messy person. After the initial volley is fired, this couple plunges into a cycle of criticism, cross-complaining, and blaming.

A second triggering event, the *illegitimate demand*, involves the awareness of one partner that the other is

asking for too much—that the request exceeds the boundaries of what should reasonably be expected in their relationship. One couple interviewed by sociologist Arlie Hochschild (1989) fought for years over division of household tasks:

Tom left all housework and care of their four sons to his wife, a school administrator. He said his wife reasoned with him about it, then she argued with him. Then she tried lists. When that failed, she tried therapy. When that failed she left. . . . As he explained: We had this formal thing about Tuesday, Wednesday, Thursday—whose turn to do dishes, whose turn to do the laundry . . . we went to one of those marriage encounters and came up with a definite way of splitting up housework. . . . I wasn't doing any. I always felt I'd been railroaded into doing it against my will . . . I still remember blowing up and stalking out of the house. (pp. 212, 213)

This couple ended up divorced after 7 years because they were never able to resolve what each felt was an illegitimate demand on the part of the other. She expected fairness in how marital tasks were divided and he expected to leave their original marital bargain unchanged—that she would be in charge of the household work.

This example also illustrates a third triggering event, the *rebuff*—which occurs when one partner feels devalued because the other fails to meet his or her expectations. The wife felt rebuffed because the husband refused to share the household work despite her obvious need and in spite of her use of multiple strategies to persuade him. He, in turn, felt rebuffed because she would not accept his fervent belief that a man should not be expected to do household chores that are "women's work."

A fourth triggering event is *cumulative annoyance* in which the "abrasive but unwitting actions of one person produce a progressively increasing state of irritation in the other" (Peterson, 1983, p. 372). Finally, "some threshold is exceeded. 'That does it!' . . . and the fight is on" (p. 371). For example, one couple quarreled as they drove to visit her parents:

Paul was in the back of the station wagon reading. I was driving. We were on the Turnpike, and I asked him to move to the side. I wanted to pass and I couldn't see through him. He told me to look out of the side mirror or turn around and look. I'm accustomed to using the rearview mirror and I didn't feel I should have to change my driving habits when he could move to the side a little so I could see. A little later I said, "*Will* you move? I can't see through you." He just sat and glared. Twice more I asked him to move and finally he blew up and told me to pull over so he could drive . . . Paul kept on with some nasty remarks. I told

him he was making a big deal out of this and it was ridiculous to fight about and that I thought he really was going overboard about the whole thing. (p. 360)

Sometimes, despite cumulative annoyance, a fight may be temporarily postponed, as in the following exchange between a husband and wife:

We were in our car en route to a family gathering. The last few days had been going well, including this particular morning, until I asked her to sit next to me in the car, to which she sarcastically replied, "I'm fine." This brought up all sorts of old feelings of resentment within me but rather than try to settle a dispute at a family function, I decided to can it for another time. Later I smoked a couple of cigarettes (which I'm not supposed to do according to an agreement, but why adhere to an agreement like this when everything else is shitty between us). Upon discovering this, she promptly walked up and put out the cigarette plus announcing that I was not to smoke in front of her. (This was in the presence of other people.) Again I did nothing. (p. 372)

The man in this instance has decided that the damage the conflict will do in this particular family situation outweighs his distress and humiliation. But, later in the day, they end up in a very emotional confrontation when he thinks she has encouraged their daughter to interrupt his nap. He says: "When it got to the point she encouraged Susan to disturb me, I *got pissed!*" (p. 373).

When unresolved differences are allowed to pile up, couples frequently use withdrawal as a means of avoiding confrontation. From her study of blue-collar marriages, sociologist Mirra Komarovsky confirms that husbands more often than wives simply leave the house. Wives more typically withdraw psychologically, resorting to a sullen silence. Not unexpectedly, the failure to air grievances often leads to later engagement in the form of a blowup. As one man explains, "You don't quite know what you feel, you're just sore and mad so you don't say nothing and it gets worse, and after a while you blow up" (1967, p. 195).

Engagement

During engagement, one of two things usually happens: the couple negotiate (negotiation is discussed in detail in Chapter 12) to resolve the issue, or the conflict escalates. If the conflict escalates, the participants generally get angrier and angrier and deliver more verbally hurtful messages. Both parties increasingly rely on threats, coercion, and distortion of the facts to make their points. Each may blame the other for past and present slights. Each may focus on behavior and characteristics of the other that are especially loathsome (You never . . . ; You always . . . ; You are a . . . ; You act like a . . . ; Why don't you ever . . .). Cross complaining and other destructive fighting methods replace more cooperative attempts to listen, understand, and validate what the partner is saying.

Destructive Fighting

Many couples who lack the skills or desire to resolve conflict resort to tactics that are detrimental to their relationship. By examining some of these tactics it may be possible to understand why some fights resolve conflict, while other fights produce greater anger and differences.

Character Analysis. One popular negative tactic is *character analysis*—the "I know you better than you know yourself" tactic.

SHE SAYS: I'm telling you, you're just fooling yourself. You'll never get that job.

HE SAYS: That's ridiculous! I know what I'm doing. I'm qualified and I'm going to apply.

SHE SAYS: I know you inside and out. You're totally unaware of how you come off. There is no way they will take you seriously.

Character analyses of this sort are particularly infuriating because they disqualify what the other person says or does. An exchange that begins like this is likely to lead only to further insistence on the part of the husband that he really does know what he's doing.

Labeling. Another destructive tactic is *labeling*—telling someone that he or she has the stereotypical characteristics of a very troubled individual—a sadist, psychotic, neurotic, or alcoholic, for example. This tactic is depersonalizing and will likely lead to an exchange of insults. Comments of this sort may be made under the assumption that they will help change a partner's behavior, but using derogatory labels is particularly destructive because they attack the other's sense of self-worth. Communications researcher Donald Baucom (1987) describes a conversation he had with a husband who regularly resorted to negative labeling

and stereotyping in fights with his wife. When called on it, he replied: "Well, I have to do that. First of all, that is the only way to get her attention. Second, she loves to prove me wrong. So if I say these bad things about her, then she just might change, just to prove I'm wrong" (p. 198).

In general, the partner who is the target of such attacks responds with an angry self-defense. Being told who you are in negative terms is much harsher than being informed of something specific you did that displeased your partner ("I was really hurt last night when you . . ."). Moreover, such labeling is unlikely to resolve any specific issue.

The "Kitchen Sink" Fight. Another typical type of conflict couples engage in is the *kitchen sink fight*—literally, almost every marital issue, past and present, is brought up. For example, a married couple meet for a dinner date. The wife arrives 20 minutes late.

HE SAYS: Why are you late?

SHE SAYS: I tried my best.

HE SAYS: Yeah? You and who else? Your mother is never on time either.

SHE SAYS: That's got nothing to do with it.

HE SAYS: The hell it doesn't. You're as sloppy as she is.

SHE SAYS: (getting louder) You don't say! Who's picking whose dirty underwear off the floor every morning?

HE SAYS: (sarcastic but controlled) I happen to go to work. What have you got to do all day?

SHE SAYS: (shouting) I'm trying to get along on the money you don't make, that's what.

HE SAYS: (turning away from her) Why should I knock myself out for an ungrateful bitch like you? (Bach & Wyden, 1968, p. 3)

In this destructive volley, there is no specific grievance or issue, but rather a mess of complaints and accusations. This example shows how many things can go wrong in a destructive fight where no specific issues are raised. In comparing his wife to her mother, the husband throws in an irrelevant barb from the past. The wife counterattacks by accusing him of being a bad provider; in return, he questions her usefulness and calls her a bitch. Both overload the other with grievances and nothing is resolved.

Placing Blame. People who blame their partners while taking no (or very little) responsibility for their own negative behaviors and feelings, tend to find themselves in relationships in which conflicts remain unresolved and the same pattern of arguments appears over and over again. The simplest issue may escalate into a heated disagreement that threatens the entire relationship. Such a couple face the prospect of having almost every argument turn into a bitter quarrel that results in emotional distancing and withdrawal of care and affection. They jointly feed into a cycle of defensiveness and escalation of other negative emotions—each giving tit for tat.

When a conflict escalates, it is usually because one partner leads and the other reciprocates, each building off the emotions and behaviors of the other. Typically, the couple find themselves in a prolonged argument without much hope of resolution. They seem to become entrapped in their struggle, each needing to extract himself or herself, but each also needing to save face—the first one to withdraw might somehow be labeled the loser, so each remains in the argument. As Retzinger (1991) describes it:

> . . . communication barriers increase. Anger increases, and perceptions of the other side become increasingly inhuman . . . use of threats and coercion generate counterthreats and aversive behavior. . . . When threats are used, the attacked individual feels forced to behave in a more menacing manner in order to save face. (pp. 7, 8)

As previously indicated, both what we say and how we say it are essential parts of the communication process. In order to understand what is being communicated, both the words used and the manner of their delivery must be observed. Because of the complexity of these dual messengers—voice and gesture—communication is often misinterpreted. When couples argue, the conflict generally does not come from the issue at hand, no matter how weighty, but from the inability of the couple to establish effective ways of managing and resolving conflict.

How does a couple move from an emotionally intense cycle of blaming, cross-complaining, and even open hostility to a more cooperative state?

A Conciliatory Act

If insulting remarks have been exchanged and anger raised, it is difficult to move from confrontation to the rational problem-solving activity required for resolution. "Before negotiation can begin under these conditions, an intermediate step is needed. This step usually takes the form of a *conciliatory act*, intended to reduce negative affect and to express a willingness to work toward resolution of the problem" (Peterson, 1983, p. 377). A conciliatory act is one way of admitting that the problem has gotten out of hand, that to save the relationship the couple must step back for a moment and regroup.

At this point, one partner might suggest that they refocus on the offending event or issue that started the whole mess and try to take a more realistic approach to resolving it. This partner also typically tries to widen the responsibility for the problem to include both of the participants by saying something like, "This argument is partly my doing. I would like to do whatever I can to help resolve it." If the other partner agrees, heated emotions begin to subside. Attention is redirected toward the specifics of the issue and to problem solving rather than to criticizing and blaming each other. Both partners concentrate on putting an end to the disagreement.

Termination

There are several ways to end a disagreement. The most frequently used are separation, domination, compromise, and integrative agreements, each of which will be briefly described (Peterson, 1983).

Separation

The couple may decide to separate or withdraw from each other in order to have some time alone to think and "cool off." When anger subsides, the couple may be able to come back together and negotiate more cooperatively. Unfortunately, as some couples leave the scene of the argument, they hurl "parting shots" at each other that make reuniting more difficult. Others come back together but fail to move from blaming, cross-complaining, and criticizing to more positive strategies and, thus, cannot bring closure to the issue. Still other couples come to the conclusion that they simply will never agree on a particular issue. When it becomes obvious that they will probably never agree, couples sometimes "agree to disagree" and try to avoid future discussions of the issue.

How to Break a Deadlock. In a few instances, couples get stuck in running disagreements. Unable to ignore the issue raised or agree to disagree, they fight the same battles repeatedly. As we saw in Chapter 7, for some couples, conflict is a way of life. John Cuber and Peggy Harroff call such marriages conflict habituated and describe them as relationships in which incompatibility is pervasive, conflict is ever potential, and an atmosphere of tension permeates the togetherness. One of the women interviewed by the researchers looks back over her own marriage and characterizes it as "a running guerrilla fight. . . . It's hard to know what it is we fight about," she says. "You name it, and we'll fight about it. . . . We don't really agree about anything" (1968, pp. 44–45). As the authors suggest, in such cases it is reasonable to assume a deep need by both spouses to maintain the psychological battle. For conflict-habituated people, the differences may actually serve as a cohesive factor that keeps the marriage together.

For most couples, however, conflict is not cohesive. It is anxiety-producing and energy-depleting. Rather than relish it, couples try to come to some kind of agreement that is satisfactory to both partners. Couples who reach a stalemate in their conflict are advised to ask themselves a series of questions to facilitate breaking the deadlock (Dinkmeyer & Carlson, 1984):

- How did this impasse develop?
- What do I want from this discussion?
- How can I communicate what I want more effectively?
- Does my partner know that he or she is the most significant person in my life?
- How will this impasse affect the overall quality of our relationship?
- What is the worst possible thing that could happen if we don't resolve the conflict exactly as I want it resolved?
- Can I live with another decision?
- What is my underlying fear about this decision?

Often, answering these questions results in a renewed determination to try again.

Domination

Another way for a conflict to end is in domination or conquest. One partner pushes very hard for his or her perspective and the other eventually gives in. There is a definite "winner" and a definite "loser." Most usually, the "winner" controls more resources

and, thus, has more power in the relationship (power is discussed more fully in Chapter 12). But partners who consistently win disagreements may eventually end up the losers, if they regularly ignore their partners' wishes in order to win "at all costs" and fail to take opportunities for constructive change. Such individuals usually end up in distressed and unhappy relationships. "The powerless, disenfranchised partner feels cheated and resentful, and whether aware of it or not, usually seeks ways to even the score" (Duncan & Rock, 1993, p. 51).

Compromise

Some couples *compromise*; both are "winners." They come to a mutually acceptable agreement that takes some parts of each partner's proposals into consideration. In the following example concerning a family summer vacation, she needs to work through June to complete an important project on time; he wants to vacation at the beach during June because it is the only time he can arrange to rent their favorite cottage for 3 consecutive weeks. After much back-and-forth discussion, they agree to limit the June vacation to 2 weeks and she will bring her work along. He volunteers to take the children to the beach each day and supervise their care and play activities until their 2 P.M. nap time. She will work until nap time, when she will join him for some private time and remain with the family until the children go to bed. Then, it's back to work.

Integrative Agreement

In a few rare instances, couples are able to satisfy the original proposals of both partners by coming up with an *integrative agreement*—both are "winners" of the argument, but no one compromises. For example, a dual-earner couple argues continually about their two children. He thinks they are being neglected because she is employed. She refuses to leave her job because of the family insurance benefits and needed income it provides. He is a nurturing father who takes on a large share of the child rearing, but he hates the idea of day care. She has tried staying home but despises it. Homemaking leaves her depressed and resentful. They eventually come to an ageement that satisfies both. Although it means that they will see each other less often, they agree to work a split shift for several years until both children are in school. She will continue working days at her job in a local plumbing supply store and he will switch to the night shift at the auto factory. This, by the way, is a decision that many blue-collar families actually make to cut day-care costs and allow both partners to keep much needed jobs.

Honoring the Agreement

Issues have to be recognized and resolved for conflict to be constructive. Learning how to fight might be compared with learning how to dance. Both processes involve certain mutual understandings, including the premise that in the long run the two partners receive the greatest satisfaction from performing together. Any constructive conflict ends with some negotiating over potential solutions. In marital bargaining as in international diplomacy, if there is little underlying trust to begin with or if one party feels that concessions are not being fairly reciprocated, it is unlikely that differences will be resolved to the satisfaction of both. The outcome of today's argument, then, rests to a large extent on what the partners experienced during and after previous conflicts. If, in the past, the couple negotiated from positions of cooperativeness and flexibility and neither exploited nor took advantage of each other, chances are good that other disagreements will be handled in a similarly constructive way. It is the process of negotiating and the honoring of the agreement that brings most couples closer together.

COMMUNICATION AND MARITAL SATISFACTION

We hear much about couples in unhappy marriages who cannot or do not communicate with each other, but most couples in distressed relationships are actually "communicating clearly, concisely, intensely, and decisively. The consequence of the messages may be painful, disabling, intolerable, mean, and ugly, and the marriage may break apart, but not because the couple did not in some way clearly convey their dissatisfaction" (Norton, 1988, p. 315).

Relationship Maintenance through Communication

When they see things going wrong in their relationship, the majority of couples attempt to restore things to normal or make changes to ensure marital stability. When we talk about *relationship maintenance* we are referring to "preventive efforts to keep a relationship

Relationship maintenance is best attained by being a generally rewarding person who is warm, interested, attentive, supportive, and understanding.

healthy before the onset of real problems" (Baxter & Dindia, 1990, p. 188). In order to maintain a relationship, one must prefer it to other relationships, and also have the skills and abilities to reward the partner and keep him or her actively involved (Duck, 1988).

Respecting Marital Rules

From the first days of any partnership, the two people involved are deciding how they are going to behave with each other and what kinds of communication they will foster or prohibit. Each relationship has its own language, myths, and taboos which, because they serve the participants well, seem right, logical, even inevitable. The bonds that tie relational partners together consist of an intricate web of shared realities, interdependent roles, and certain intimate secrets. The most satisfying relationships are those in which each partner respects the norms and behaviors that the other partner typically believes in.

Marital rules are a kind of recipe or formula developed by couples for maintaining satisfaction in their particular partnership (Argyle & Henderson, 1985). Rules develop over time from a tapestry of thousands of individual episodes in which partners talk to each other about their expectations for each other and for the marriage itself (Montgomery, 1988). Rules for individual relationships also operate within a larger framework of cultural rules. At the societal level, a rule may specify "Be open. A couple within that society might find, however, that they do better by modifying that standard: Be open only when it will not hurt the other's feelings" (Montgomery, 1988, p. 353).

Relationship rules can make life easier. In recurring situations, we know what to do without having to negotiate everything from scratch. Marital guidelines simplify life by limiting options to the few we find acceptable. If there is a drawback to having marital rules, it is that they also maintain the status quo. By always staying within the acceptable boundaries, part-

Remembering anniversaries, Valentine's day, birthdays, and other personal and special events keeps relationships vital and satisfying.

ners may find their options too limited when change is needed in the relationship.

Couples like to feel that they are in control of what happens in their relationships. They want to believe that the work they do on behalf of the relationship holds it together, not luck or chance. Creating a unique system of rules helps the couple feel that their relationship is special and satisfying; that they have the power to take their own needs into consideration. They decide which types and sequences of behavior are appropriate and inappropriate, beneficial and costly, satisfying and unsatisfying. They decide what qualifies as good versus poor communication and, ultimately, sets the tone of their relationship. According to Argyle and Henderson (1985), the most significant marital rules are (p. 147):

- Show emotional support.
- Share news of success.
- Be faithful.
- Create a harmonious home atmosphere.
- Respect each other's privacy.
- Keep confidences.
- Engage in sexual activity with each other.
- Stand up for the partner in his or her absence.
- Disclose personal feelings and problems to the partner.
- Inform the partner of your personal schedule.
- Be tolerant of each other's friends.
- Don't criticize the partner publicly.

Communicating Interest and Support

When communication researchers Kathryn Dindia and Leslie Baxter (1987, 1990) asked couples how they kept their relationships vital and satisfying, 49 separate *maintenance strategies* were identified, ranging from "share my feelings," "talk about my day," "refrain from criticizing," and "allow my spouse time to be alone or to do things with other people," to "try to be a better listener," "remember my spouse's birthday, our wedding anniversary, Valentine's day," and "compliment my spouse." Other strategies were "reminisce," "do a favor," "kiss and make up," and "give compliments." Couples who had been together longer used fewer strategies. It may be that the longer a relationship lasts, the better communicators the partners become and consequently the more accomplished they are at understanding each other and meeting each other's needs and expectations.

SUMMARY POINTS

■ The hallmark of a successful contemporary marriage is emotional expressiveness—the ability to share both positive and negative feelings and thoughts with one's partner.

■ According to Deborah Tannen and other communication researchers, there are definite differences in the communication styles of women and men. Men in conversation are more concerned with maintaining independence and establishing a hierarchy of status. Women, in comparison, are more intent on establishing close relationships and creating intimacy.

■ A communication consists of a sender, a receiver, and a message. Messages are interpreted by the receiver from the sender's verbal and nonverbal cues.

■ Effective communication consists of clear and consistent messages that project empathy and understanding. It is the partner's responsibility to listen and indicate whether or not the message was understood.

■ Happily married couples, compared to unhappily married couples, are more sensitive to each other's feelings, display more supportive behaviors, and are more flexible and cooperative during arguments.

■ Conflict is a process that progresses through three recognizable stages: a triggering event, engagement, and termination.

■ The triggering event is something one partner does that causes the other to be upset: criticism, illegitimate demands, rebuffs, and cumulative annoyances.

■ When faced with a triggering event, the couple either avoid conflict or actively engage in it. If the couple engage, the issue is either resolved in some way or the conflict escalates—takes a destructive turn, and gets out of control. Should conflict escalate, destructive fighting—blaming, cross-complaining, character analysis, or kitchen sink fighting—typically occurs.

■ A conciliatory act is generally needed to bring things back to normal after a destructive argument. The act most frequently consists of one partner accepting partial responsibility for the fight and attempting to redirect the disagreement back to the real issue.

■ A conflict ends in one of four ways: separation, domination, compromise, or through an integrative agreement.

■ Past negotiations and outcomes have a great deal to do with how future conflicts are conducted and resolved. Constructive conflict requires trust, fairness, flexibility, and a cooperative spirit.

■ Relationship maintenance refers to the multitude of efforts that couples make to prevent the normal problems of daily life from eroding their otherwise satisfying relationship.

■ Couples interested in maintaining their relationships work to reward their partners by showing warmth and interest in them, listening, giving advice and help, and respecting the norms and rules of the relationship.

■ Marital rules develop over time through day-to-day interaction as couples negotiate the terms of their particular relationship. Some of the most important marital rules are: show emotional support, share news of success, be faithful, respect privacy, and keep confidences.

■ When Kathyrn Dindia and Leslie Baxter asked couples to identify strategies they used to maintain their relationships, the couples listed many useful tactics including: share feelings, talk about your day, and refrain from criticizing.

KEY TERMS

Emotional expressiveness	*Cumulative annoyance*
Troubles talk	*Character analysis*
Leveling	*Labeling*
Nonverbal message	*Kitchen sink fight*
Feedback	*Conciliatory act*
Duologue	*Compromise*
Empathy	*Integrative agreement*
Triggering event	*Relationship maintenance*
Illegitimate demand	*Marital rules*
Rebuff	*Maintenance strategies*

REVIEW QUESTIONS

1. Describe a time in a recent cross-sex friendship or romantic relationship when you and your partner seemed to be on different wavelengths—misunderstood each other's intentions and failed to comprehend clearly what the problem was. Looking back now, after reading about Deborah Tannen's work, do you think gender differences in communication styles explain part of the problem? Do you think women and men have different expectations for emotional intimacy and self-disclosure in relationships? Explain.

2. How important is effective communication to relationship satisfaction? What are some characteristics of effective communication? What are some pitfalls to avoid?

3. How do the communication patterns of happily and unhappily married couples differ?

4. Describe the process of conflict. How does it begin, build, and end?

5. How do conflicts with your parent(s) usually end—separation, domination, compromise, or integrative agreement? How do conflicts with your best friend usually end? And with your romantic partner, how are conflicts generally terminated? Do you notice any similarity in how conflicts end across relationships? Are there obvious differences in how conflicts end across relationships? What do you think explains the similarities? What explains any differences?

6. Which fighting tactics do you consider most destructive to a relationship? Why?

7. How do you feel when someone you care about fails to honor an arrangement you both agreed to at the conclusion of a conflict? In what ways has his or her negligence affected subsequent disagreements?

8. List three of the most important rules you expect your relational partner to honor. Why do you think these rules are so meaningful to you? What would happen if your partner broke a rule?

9. What maintenance strategies do you use to keep your romantic relationship vital and satisfying? And your best friendship—how do you go about keeping it vital and satisfying? Do you use similar maintenance strategies for each relationship? Explain.

PART IV

Stress, Dissolution, and Rebuilding of Intimate Relationships

12

Illustration by Ted Wolter

Power and Violence

Even though people are encouraged to think of intimate relationships as emotional sanctuaries, retreats from pressure, anxiety, and stress, this portrayal does not necessarily match the reality of daily life. Many couples find solace, support, and physical renewal in each other's company, but behavior that contradicts this image is largely ignored. Indeed, mounting evidence suggests that the relationships we look to for satisfaction of our most intimate needs are also the ones most commonly characterized by power inequalities and conflicts and by violence.

Power is customarily associated with the world outside the family—for example, in politics, at work, in the court system. Acknowledging that relationships characterized by love and intimacy also have to do with power and, in some cases, aggressive actions is uncomfortable. Such a viewpoint opens the door to the possibility that one partner may have the potential to determine the behavior of the other (Meyer, 1991). Further, it raises the issue that relationships can also have a dark side.

In this chapter, we define power and discuss how it is used to influence others to listen to reason, reevaluate decisions, consider alternatives, or change behavior. We also identify types of power, explore gender differences in the use of power, and discuss the connection between power and violence. Further, we address several questions raised by evidence that there can be a violent side to marriage and family life: How common is marital violence? What other forms of violence exist in families? If, as research suggests, violence is not a rare or isolated phenomenon, but rather a recurrent pattern in millions of households, how can we explain why the family is such a crucible of extreme behavior?

WHAT IS POWER AND HOW IS IT USED IN RELATIONSHIPS?

Defining Power

Power is sometimes regarded as a personal strength—the ability to make one's own decisions and operate independently—or a personality characteristic—the extent to which an individual is motivated to want power. But social scientists more often think of it as an aspect of a particular relationship. For example, *parental power* is the ability of parents to influence their child's beliefs and behaviors; *offspring power* is the capacity of children to influence their parent's attitudes and actions; *sibling power* is the capability of brothers and sisters to sway each other's ways of thinking and behaving; and *kinship power* is the reciprocal influence that exists between particular family members and their extended kin (McDonald, 1980). In this chapter we confine our discussion to *dyadic power*—the ability of an individual to pursue her or his own interests in the face of a partner's resistance (or to resist the partner's influence) (Szinovacz, 1987; Winter, 1988).

Understanding Dyadic Power

An example of dyadic power in process would be the case of a female student, also a wife and mother, who wants her husband to spend Saturday mornings looking after their two school-aged children and doing some light household chores (sort and start the laundry, vacuum the living room) while she goes to the library to study. He, of course, can think of many other things he would rather do and believes it is unfair that he must give up every Saturday morning because of her educational commitments. Should either spouse change his or her position and move toward agreement with the other, this movement would be considered a result of power—the ability of one partner to influence the other to reevaluate and change direction despite resistance.

It is sometimes forgotten that love and caring can operate to take the edge off of the dominating and controlling force that power implies. For this couple, the wife has, in the past, agreed to similar arrangements at her husband's request so he could pursue work commitments. Neither especially likes putting individual desires on hold, but each understands that over the years things usually balance out, and their long-term mutual goals include having a happy marriage and being good parents. In interdependent relationships, couples more often act on the basis of mutual interests rather than self-interests. Their overall intent is to improve relationship satisfaction by taking each other's views into consideration and maximizing the rewards of *both* partners. More powerful partners frequently resist the urge to promote their own aspirations in favor of enhancing their loved one's success and happiness.

As marriages have become more interdependent, egalitarian norms have begun to take hold in middle-class American society, and an increasing number of marital and family issues are being negotiated rather than taken for granted. For many couples, there is less often a basic "recipe" for who makes what decisions in the family or whose interests are always given priority in certain areas (if it involves work, he decides; if it pertains to family and home, she has the final say). Negotiation, cooperation, and fairness in decision making are the hallmarks of contemporary relationships.

And having the final say is less important to some couples than how the process of deciding unfolds: Were each partner's concerns heard? Was the opinion of each valued? Can each rely on the other to keep the bargain? Democratic methods of deciding are, in the long run, more satisfying and lead to more fulfilling relationships. Achieving equity in power relations requires that partners demonstrate patience, trust, understanding, and empathy because resources are rarely evenly distributed among relational partners and imbalances can create tension and resentment should the advantaged partner always be favored.

Just how resources translate into power has been a subject of much study. Although there are several theories of how power is achieved and used, most scholars agree that availability and distribution of resources are critical to understanding dyadic power.

Power Bases

Power is gained through *power bases*—resources available to each partner, but usually more accessible to one than the other. The power realized from a particular resource is determined by how valuable it is to the partner as well as how easily he or she can find replacements or alternatives (Foa & Foa, 1980). Resources include, among other things: income, social status, love and affection, understanding and supportiveness, companionship, and sex. In a classic study, sociologists J. T. French and Bertram Raven (1959) categorized resources into six major groups and described how they operate (see Table 12-1).

Whether and how partners use these resources to gain power depends on personality (some people have a high need to exert power); trust (when partners do not trust each other, they make more attempts to control each other); family composition (less powerful family members sometimes pool their resources and form coalitions to gain additional power); and ideology (partners who believe in egalitarian relations strive for equity in power).

Gender also complicates the power process. Women and men seem to bring different needs and expectations to their love relationships, and our society accords men more resources.

THREE TYPES OF POWER AND SOME GENDER DIFFERENCES

Today, with so many couples coveting equal relationships and shared power, how close does reality approach the ideal? Research examining dyadic power suggests that, although couples initially report making key marital decisions in an egalitarian manner, decisions are quite one-sided, with men having greater influence, as revealed in in-depth interviews. Based on her work with married couples, sociologist Aafke Komter (1989, 1991) concludes that power operates in three ways to bring issues forward for discussion or prevent them from being raised.

Social Power

The first type of power is *social power*. This power has social or cultural origins and refers to the norms and expectations that guide our beliefs about how power should be allocated between partners in intimate relationships. Social power has traditionally favored men by granting them greater status and authority compared to women.

The prevailing cultural beliefs that the husband should "head" the family, or that the male partner in a romantic relationship has the right to "lead," generally give men a power advantage. This imbalance of power is further influenced by the resources available to each partner, such as education and income (men

TABLE 12-1
Power Resources and How They Operate

Resource	Power Conferred	How Power Operates
Rewards	Reward power	Partner promises to provide something valued (more time together; a weekend at the beach); promises to remove something negative or disliked (do the grocery shopping; stop complaining about the broken garage door).
Costs	Coercive power	Partner threatens to take away something valued (financial support, sex); do something known to displease (be late for dinner; refuse to allow stepchildren to visit).
Authority	Legitimate power	Partner is recognized as having authority (social, religious, or government status) based on cultural norms and expectations; she or he asks for compliance based on that status. ("Because I am your wife, you should . . ."; "As your husband I have the right to. . . .")
Love and respect	Referent power	Partner exhibits love and says he or she cares and is committed to the relationship and asks that these behaviors be reciprocated. ("Because you love me, you will understand that I need . . ."; "You know I wouldn't do this if I thought it would hurt you in any way.")
Expertise	Expert power	Partner has greater expertise in a particular area and thus should have the last say. ("As a tax consultant, I advise . . ."; "Because of my position on the city council, I must. . . .")
Knowledge	Informational power	Partner persuades by using knowledgeable explanation. ("I have thoroughly researched the alternatives and believe . . ."; "I understand from reading *Consumer Reports* that. . . .")

SOURCE: J. T. French & B. Raven (1959).

Men's greater social power is often as taken for granted as their place at the head of the dinner table, their exclusive right to a favorite chair in the family room, and the expectation that dad drives when the family goes to the movies.

are usually better educated and make more money than their partners). Another factor influencing the power imbalance is the involvement and dependency of the two partners. Women are socialized to define and sustain their self-concepts through relationships, so they tend to invest more time in the attentive and supportive aspects of coupling (Cancian, 1987; Peplau & Gordon, 1985; Thompson & Walker, 1991).

In several ways, then, women are at a power disadvantage. As sociologist Jessie Bernard notes in her seminal book on the future of marriage:

> Take a young woman who has been trained for feminine dependencies, who wants to "look up" to the man she marries. Put her at a disadvantage in the labor market. Then marry her to a man who has a slight initial advantage over her in age, income, and education, shored up by an ideology with a male bias . . . then expect an egalitarian relationship? (1972, p. 146)

In sum, social power is based on culturally induced differences in how women and men perceive themselves and their relationship and how they go about explaining the nature of their activities.

When Komter (1989) asked 60 married couples with children living at home to describe themselves, their perceptions coincided with stereotypical gender roles—men are like this, women are like that; men do this, women do that. Many of the couples believed that marital roles were naturally divided by gender and both men and women saw greater value in male roles. Not only did women place less value on themselves and their roles in the family, but they expressed greater respect and regard for their husbands' competencies than their own. Husbands expressed similar attitudes. The result of these perceptions was that men had higher self-esteem than women and were granted more power in the marriage.

There was an exception to this general trend. When women were employed, they gained self-esteem and exerted more influence in their relationships. This finding is confirmed by a more recent study by family scientist Gloria Bird and family therapist Gudrun Freeman (1993). Employed women reported higher self-esteem and indicated use of fewer manipulative tactics during marital decision making than women who were not employed. Instead, these employed women relied on cooperative tactics like bargaining and reasoning.

But the impact of employment on women's power also depends on whether women think female power is legitimate and how they choose to act on that belief. If a woman has traditional gender role attitudes, views her work as secondary to her husbands, and fails to take credit for the impact of her earnings on family well-being, she will assert less influence in the marriage, regardless of her resources.

Many couples unconsciously justify or legitimize traditional marital roles by placing limits on how much power the female partner can have. When, for example, couples argue over how to divide household tasks or who should care for the children, both women and men tend to accept culturally driven explanations for maintaining the status quo. "Well, of course she does more because:

> She has more time available; He has no feeling for it; He is not born to it; It does not fit his character; She has more talent for it; It is a woman's natural duty; She has chosen to be a housewife and mother; and She enjoys it more than he does. (Komter, 1989, p. 209)

Despite these standard rationalizations about why women are responsible for 70 percent of the housework and much more of the parenting, when asked how much they enjoyed these tasks, women more often talked about the stress and strain and their frustrations with trying to "do it all." "Wives," Komter noted, "were less contented than husbands in all areas studied" (household work, parenting, financial management, sexuality, and leisure activities) (Komter, 1989, p. 209). They also expressed greater desire for change.

Some couples are able to negotiate less gendered ways of interacting. They tend to be more aware of the unfairness of current cultural frameworks that divide marital roles into *his* and *hers* and give one partner a hidden advantage in negotiating marital roles and responsibilities. Within their own relationships, they try to value the work done inside and outside the family as necessary and valuable and strive to change their own patterns of behavior to equalize power and decision making (Thompson, 1991).

Latent Power

A second type of power is *latent power*—when the needs and wishes of the more powerful partner are anticipated and taken care of without discussion, or change is not attempted because a negative outcome is expected. One partner, in effect, is indirectly influencing the other because of the couple's past history together (Komter, 1991).

Men, in particular, are beneficiaries of latent power. In some cases, women believe that their partners are entitled to special treatment because of their position in the family and that it is part of women's family responsibility to anticipate husbands' needs. In other cases, a history of long and unproductive marital dis-

agreements leads to the belief that further discussion on certain issues is pointless. A partner may decide that the end result is always the same, so why fight it. Or the partner may know from experience that, should he or she "win" the disagreement, the spouse will retaliate in ways that will, in the end, be even more costly or painful, so why go through the process. In still other cases, some people decide not to negotiate for change or state an opposing view because they fear that their partners will leave. To them, this cost would be too great. And finally, it is difficult for women to bring up issues that may cause conflict because they value intimacy and connection. They struggle to keep marital ties strong and any threat to the relationship causes them much anxiety.

Manifest Power

The third type of power is *manifest power*. This power reveals itself through overt and deliberate attempts to influence someone's behavior. These attempts are also typically referred to as *power strategies*—the tactics used to encourage others to understand and support one's attitudes, beliefs, goals, or actions. Much of the research on power centers on identifying such strategies and judging their success.

POWER STRATEGIES

The simple fact of loving another person and trying to establish a committed, intimate relationship means that conflicts of interest are bound to occur. No two people will have perfectly compatible goals, and both cannot always have their way. Being in conflict means being involved in each other's lives.

When resolving relationship issues results in conflict, change is usually involved—what one partner desires the other is reluctant to provide, or finds difficult to provide, or would like to provide but cannot seem to manage. When faced with such an impasse, the partner desiring the change attempts to move the other in the preferred direction by various means. The other partner tries to maintain the status quo. Perceptions and use of power strategies during this process of attempted change are affected by gender.

One of the first studies to investigate the use of power strategies relied on a sample of 200 male and female university students. They were asked how they went about influencing their romantic partners to "do things their way." Thirteen power strategies were identified and collapsed into four types: direct-cooperative, direct-uncooperative, indirect-cooperative, and indirect-uncooperative. Directness indicates the extent to which the strategies were straightforward or obvious. Cooperativeness indicates whether individuals considered only themselves (uncooperative) or also considered their partners (cooperative) in their influence attempts (Falbo & Peplau, 1980).

Types of Strategies

Partners who use *direct-cooperative* strategies approach a problem in a straightforward manner (do not "beat around the bush") and include the partner in the process of resolving the issue ("I like the green sofa best. What do you think? Should we buy it?"). These strategies include bargaining and compromising, and garner positive and satisfying results. (Both partners have a say in deciding the issue.)

Direct-uncooperative strategies—simply saying what is needed or telling a partner what has been decided—are also straightforward tactics, but are used in situations in which a person knows what a partner's reaction will probably be and believes that further communication is unnecessary (or is not wanted). For example, Anthony knows that he will be out of town on Thursday, his usual night to stay with the children while Roseanne goes to night class. He simply informs her of the need for a change in plans and says that he will ask his sister to fill in for him that evening. His responsibility is covered and he expects no protest from Roseanne.

Indirect-cooperative strategies, such as being especially affectionate or using "sweet talk," are used in situations in which resistance is expected and, consequently, the partner is approached from a positive but more subtle position. The strategy is considered cooperative because the partner is invited to participate in the discussion, but he or she is rewarded with affection and caring during the process to "soften the blow." A conversation might go like this: "Here, let me rub your back. Have you read the evening paper? May I get it for you? Oh, by the way, I hope you won't mind, I know how you dislike Katherine, but she asked to stop by this evening. I promise she will be here only a few minutes, and then we can cuddle up on the sofa and watch our favorite video. I stopped by and picked it up after work. But, if you really, really hate having her here, I can call and cancel. What do you think?"

Indirect-uncooperative tactics like pouting, remaining silent (giving the "silent treatment"), or leaving the room (or house) are one-sided and considered among the most negative of power strategies. They cut off interaction with the partner and punish her or him by withdrawal of caring and communication.

Gloria Bird and her colleagues (Bird, Stith, & Schladale 1991; Bird & Freeman 1993) revised and expanded Falbo and Peplau's list of 13 power strategies to 25 and asked 400 university students and 249 married couples to respond. The power strategies were found to cluster into seven distinct groups: reasoning, bargaining, telling, persuasion, coercion, manipulation, and threatening (see Table 12-2). Gender was found to influence power strategy use.

Gender Influences

One of the earliest studies to examine gender differences in the use of power strategies uncovered two essential distinctions. Men are more likely to exert direct power by openly and overtly stating what they want or issuing requests, while women more often employ indirect power tactics, the goal of which is to soften or conceal their attempts to influence. In addition, men are more likely to bargain with concrete resources like money, authority, and knowledge; while women tend to employ personal resources such as love and affection or approval that depend on personal relationships for their maintenance (Johnson, 1976).

Later studies confirm that these gendered styles of interacting continue to be endorsed in American society (Szinovacz, 1987). Komter (1989, 1991) found that women use more indirect power strategies—hinting, grumbling, giving sly digs. They also rely on "step-by-step" strategies as is illustrated by this woman's remark: "I really proceed very slowly. I want to change things in a gradual way. You have to be very careful . . ." (1989, p. 204). Such indirect strategies tended to be very ineffective for women because they were so subtle that many partners did not even detect the need for change. And change may be what the woman required to remain in the relationship.

Even when women used more direct strategies, they were less successful in negotiating change than their male partners. Komter (1989) writes:

A husband who repeatedly did not keep his promise to be at home for dinner in time was offered a cold meal. Some women refused to take care of buying certain essential household supplies their husbands had

TABLE 12-2
Power Strategies Used in Intimate Relationships

Gloria Bird and her colleagues have identified seven power strategies partners use in intimate relationships to influence each other on important issues.

REASONING

- I use my expertise; claim I have a lot of experience in such matters.
- I say it is in her or his best interest.
- I appeal to a sense of fairness; say it's the only fair and right thing.
- I use logic and reason; give all the reasons my way is best.

BARGAINING

- I try to negotiate something agreeable to both of us.
- I bargain or compromise to resolve our differences.
- I say how very important my request is; how much it means to me.
- I say what I would be willing to do in exchange.

TELLING

- I simply ask for what I want or need.
- I talk about it; discuss our differences and my needs.

PERSUASION

- I try to persuade.
- I repeatedly make my point until he or she gives in.
- I do some fast talking.

COERCION

- I discuss the issue heatedly; use harsh, angry words.
- I get very emotional; let him or her see how this affects me.
- I insult or swear at him or her.
- I am especially disagreeable.
- I leave the room, house, and so on.
- I withhold something I know she or he takes pleasure in.

MANIPULATION

- I ignore her or him; refuse to respond until she or he sees reason.
- I bring it up in an indirect way; hint or make suggestions.
- I am especially affectionate; I am loving and romantic.
- I withdraw; become cold and silent.

THREATENING

- I threaten to move out.
- I threaten to break up (or get a divorce).

SOURCES: G. W. Bird, S. M. Stith, & J. Schladale, 1991; F. Gryl, S. M. Stith, & G. W. Bird, 1991; G. W. Bird & G. Freeman, 1993.

promised to provide. Or, they left the kitchen in a mess for days, hoping that their husbands would, in the end, clear away the rubbish, as they promised. As the husbands did not seem to be bothered very much, the strategy was scarcely effective. (p. 204)

When men used direct strategies, however, they got results. Komter continues:

Some lower-class men sanctioned their wives for their lack of sexual interest by threatening to "go to another woman." Or they criticized their wives for not having done the laundry by scattering the dirty laundry around the room. Or again, in the lower class, when women told their husbands that they wanted to look for a job, their husbands threatened to [spend long hours in cafes and recreation/beer halls]. An upper-class husband's reaction was to make the proposition of resigning from his own job, so that his wife would have to support the whole family. (p. 205)

In another study of over 200 married couples, Bird and Freeman (1993) found that when women used direct strategies like simply telling their partners what they needed and wanted, it was easier for the couples to reach agreement on important marital issues. Women reported that when direct strategies were used during marital negotiations issues were settled more fairly and their needs were more often taken into account. They also indicated feeling greater love for their husbands and reported being more committed to their relationships than women who used indirect strategies. When husbands had been flexible and willing to listen in past marital negotiations, wives more often used logic, reasoning, and bargaining in present negotiations. These strategies are direct and inclusive of the partner.

How partners use power is crucial to relationship health and satisfaction. Use of coercive and threatening tactics are associated with lack of self-confidence, low self-esteem, and declining relationship satisfaction. Reliance on such strategies may lead to even more aggressive behaviors.

POWER STRATEGIES AND VIOLENCE

Trying to influence one's partner is neither positive nor negative in itself. Power is a facet of any relationship. When a problem arises or beliefs conflict, each partner naturally attempts to be understood and negotiate a constructive resolution to the issue. Because partners are usually committed to having their relationship continue, care is usually taken to keep the interaction as rewarding as possible.

Scholars of family interaction speculate that use of power strategies ranges on a continuum from positive to negative, with cooperative strategies being the most advantageous for a relationship and physical aggression being the most detrimental. Bargaining, telling, reasoning, and persuasion are cooperative power strategies. They are, for the most part, direct and to-the-point attempts either to inform the partner of an important change that may affect his or her regular routine or to convince the partner to reconsider his or her position on an issue. Should these attempts fail to achieve results, more competitive strategies such as coercion or manipulation may be employed—using harsh, angry words; insulting or swearing; withholding rewards; becoming cold and silent. Next, threats may be implemented as a last ditch effort to convince the partner of the seriousness and importance of the issue ("I'll move out"; "I'll get a divorce.").

In some relationships physical aggression represents the final stage of conflict, when interaction escalates from verbal means of negotiation to physical means. Physical aggression is employed when other power strategies are unsuccessful and "may be an indication of faulty conflict management . . . the ultimate resource" (Lloyd, Koval, & Cate, 1989, p. 128). Aggression conveys few rewards, but inflicts many costs (humiliation, shame, physical pain, erosion of self-esteem). When one partner resorts to such tactics, the other may very well retaliate in self-defense or out of anger at being treated so negatively (Scanzoni & Polonko, 1980).

In the end, if physical aggression succeeds in producing changes in attitudes or behavior and increases one person's power over the other without too many negative consequences, it may be used repeatedly as a means of exerting control. The physically abusive partner wins the argument without taking the other's desires and needs into consideration. In future disagreements, the *threat* of aggression by itself may be sufficient to inhibit partner resistance. In the face of threats, a partner may increase efforts to placate by attempting to remove all sources of irritation and stress from the path of the other. Women report trying harder to keep the house clean, quiet the children, have dinner ready on time—anything to keep the negative actions from recurring (Pagelow, 1981; Walker, 1984). Physical aggression as a means of exerting power serves to make a relationship very one-sided and lowers the happiness and well-being of both partners.

VIOLENCE WITHIN RELATIONSHIPS

Definitions and Some Statistics

Violence (also referred to as physical aggression, physical force, physical abuse, or battering) is "an act carried out with the intention or perceived intention of causing physical pain or injury to another person" (Gelles & Cornell, 1985, p. 22). Until relatively recently, such phenomena as wife battering and child abuse did not go completely unnoticed, but when acknowledged, these practices were often regarded as the behavior of a small group of disturbed individuals. For decades, even knowledgeable social scientists ignored evidence of domestic violence. For example, an analysis of articles that appeared in the *Journal of Marriage and the Family* between 1939 and 1969 shows that there was not even one title in which the word "violence" appeared (O'Brien, 1971). But, since the early 1970s, family violence has attracted a great deal of attention in both the popular press and professional journals (there is now a *Journal of Family Violence*), and there has been widespread recognition of how different the ideal of the family as haven is from reality.

Although this chapter focuses on physical abuse, it is also clear that *emotional abuse*—communicating verbal and nonverbal messages with the intent of causing psychological pain (calling names, making cutting remarks, refusing to speak, destroying personal property)—is a form of violence, and its effects can be devastating to mental health. As is reflected in one man's account of the abuse he suffered in his family, "cuts and bruises heal, but to this day I can hear my father yelling at me. That's what really hurt, it was the yelling . . ." (Straus & Sweet, 1992, p. 346). Despite the stereotype that women are more emotionally abusive and men more physically abusive, research shows that women and men are equally as likely to resort to emotional battering.

The nation's police spend one-third of their time responding to domestic violence calls. Attacks by husbands on wives cause more injuries than rapes, muggings, and automobile accidents combined. In the United States, over 25 percent of all murders involve members of the same family, and in about 15 percent of all homicides one spouse kills another. Each year

Domestic violence, usually in the form of wife battering, accounts for a large part of the daily work of police departments across the nation.

"some 4 million women are beaten and 1,320 murdered in domestic attacks" (Gibbs, 1993, p. 41). In almost 70 percent of violent deaths due to domestic conflicts, women are killed by their male partners. "Over half of *all* women homicide victims are murdered by current or former partners" (Walker, 1989, p. 697). Clearly, family violence is not a rare or isolated phenomenon.

Even with these crime statistics, it is difficult to get a real picture of the extent of family violence because such behavior usually occurs within the privacy of the family home and people feel ashamed of it and are thus reluctant to acknowledge it. Therefore, the records kept by law-enforcement agencies in this area are not very accurate because instances of family violence are the most underreported of crimes. Studies of family violence undoubtedly underestimate the severity and incidence of the problem as well. Still, research at least allows us to get some estimate of the range and level of violence in families.

The Incidence of Family Violence: Two National Studies

In 1975, a team of researchers led by Murray Straus, Richard Gelles, and Suzanne Steinmetz conducted the First National Family Violence Survey and published the results in a book, *Behind Closed Doors: Violence in the American Family* (1980). The survey was based on a sample of 2,143 couples (147 were black). In 1985, Straus and Gelles conducted the Second National Family Violence Survey, which they wrote about in several books and articles (for example, Gelles & Straus, 1988; Straus & Gelles, 1986). For this survey, data were collected from 6,002 couples (576 were black) (Hampton & Gelles, 1991). After the second study, the authors concluded that about 16 in every 100 couples had been involved in at least one violent episode in the preceding year. About one-third of those incidents consisted of severe violence, such as the threat or actual use of a knife or gun (Straus & Gelles, 1986). They also reported that rates of marital violence had modestly declined between 1975 and 1985, perhaps as a result of heightened awareness of the problem and the tendency of police departments to treat marital violence as a crime.

The first study found that black women were four times as likely as white women to report being physically abused. This research also provided evidence that there were few differences between black and white families in incidents of severe child abuse. When rates of violence were compared between the First and Second National Violence Surveys,

severe violence toward black children remained stable in comparison to the statistically significant decline found among the entire sample; and violence toward black women declined significantly, while it remained unchanged among women in the entire sample. (Hampton, Gelles, & Harrop, 1989, p. 974)

The types of abusive behavior reported by parents were essentially the same regardless of race, except that black parents were more likely than other parents to say that they threw things at or hit or tried to hit their child with an object (Hampton & Gelles, 1991).

It is crucial to refrain from making sweeping generalizations based on the findings of the two national surveys and other smaller surveys, some of which have reported racial differences in family violence and some of which have not. Black Americans are "highly diverse in regard to economic status, family structure, occupational pursuits, and lifestyle" and studies often do not take these differences into consideration (Lockhart, 1991, p. 15). When studying family violence, not only should race and social class be considered, but also cultural norms, gender role preferences, and communication patterns. For example, do some marital issues provoke more volatile reactions than others; are particular sequences of events during the process of resolving differences more likely to produce violent exchanges between partners? Taking a broader perspective than race is critical to understanding family violence.

Contributing Factors

Studies of violence reveal that it is more common in households where the father is recently unemployed or high stress exists because of poverty, chronic family problems (illness, disability), or close relatives or friends live some distance away (Gelles & Cornell, 1990). And, although studies have found a distinct connection between the use of alcohol and drugs and family violence, it would be misleading to conclude that much of the violence among family members can be attributed solely to the effects of drinking or taking drugs. As Richard Gelles and Claire Cornell (1985) explain:

> Because our society believes that alcohol and drugs release violent tendencies, people are given a "time out" from the normal rules of social behavior when they drink or when people believe they are drunk. Combine the time out with the desire to "hush up" instances of family violence, and you have the perfect excuse: "I didn't know what I was doing, I was drunk." (p. 19)

Social class is also frequently discussed as a possible influencer of family violence, but research has not produced a strong tie between the two. Studies show that more blue-collar or low-income battered women use community shelters, but that is probably because middle-class women have other alternatives: access to money, greater privacy, higher community status, and easier entrance to sources of help like physicians, counselors, and lawyers.

The most satisfactory explanations for why family violence occurs are those that acknowledge the existence of many contributing factors including societal influences.

SOCIAL LEGITIMIZATION OF VIOLENCE

Sociocultural Norms

Social structure and cultural practices operate in concert to legitimize, to some degree, the type and intensity of violence accepted in American society and within the family (Pagelow, 1984; Steinmetz, 1987) (see Figure 12-1).

> The United States is the most violent nation in the industrialized world. Homicide is the second most frequent cause of death among Americans between the ages of 15 and 24 (after accidents) and the most common among young black men and women. More than 2 million people are beaten, knifed, shot, or otherwise assaulted each year. (Toufexis, 1993, p. 52)

Under certain conditions American social norms condone the use of physical force. Laws define parental rights and obligations, property rights, and, to some degree, marital responsibilities. Social forces like the police and the courts see that the laws are obeyed. Socialization, in combination with life experience, tell us that these social forces are real and powerful and lead us to believe that the social rules and laws that govern our actions are fair, right, and desirable. As people go about their daily lives they frequently use force or its threat to influence others, including their children. The end result is that many of us learn that power and the use of force are useful aspects of normal life (Bersani & Chen, 1988) (see the "Diversity" box).

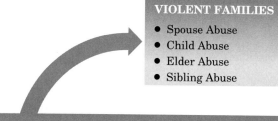

FIGURE 12-1
Sociocultural Influences on Violence
SOURCE: Adapted from S. K. Steinmetz (1987).

Cross-Cultural and Interstate Comparisons

Cross-cultural studies add credibility to the sociocultural connection between traditional norms and violent behavior. In a study of several other cultures, for example, Lester (1980) found that wife battering was more prevalent in societies where women were considered inferior to men. Also, Masumura (1979) and Steinmetz (1982), using similar comparison studies of other cultures, concluded that when higher levels of societal violence are condoned—crime, aggressive behavior, warfare, homicide, suicide—there were higher rates of marital violence as well.

Yllo (1983) examined incidents of wife battering in each state and compared data across four categories of women's status: legal, political, educational, and economic. She found that in states where a woman's overall status was either low or very high in comparison to other states, women were more likely to suffer more battering at the hands of their husbands. Wife abuse, then, was more common in states where there was a discrepancy between women's status and the prevailing cultural norms. When women's status was below or above what was generally expected, they were more likely to be subjected to physical abuse.

The Family as a Training Ground

The family is where many people receive their "basic training" in the use of aggression; they observe parents who resort to physical punishment and other forms of violence (Straus & Gelles, 1990). Custom and tradition reinforce the rightness of employing such tactics. Within certain families, even today, some partners strongly believe that the man of the family has the legitimate right to expect that his needs and wants will be attended to promptly and respectfully. Some also continue to believe that this family leader is entitled to enforce his views through "discipline" of his wife, if necessary (Margolin, Sibner, & Gleberman, 1988). In addition, they believe that parents should maintain power and authority over their children. Parents have the legal right to strike their children, and many do. As one parent observed to Suzanne Steinmetz (1977a):

> I've heard that you shouldn't spank when you're angry, but I can't agree with that, because I think that's the time you should spank; before you have a chance to completely cool off, too. I think that the spanking helps the mother or dad as well as impresses the child[ren] that they did something wrong, and when they do something bad, they are going to be physically punished for it. You don't hit them with a stick or a belt, or a hairbrush, but a good back of the hand . . . they remember it. (p. 27)

In the 1990s, as in the 1980s, a growing minority advocate that children should never be spanked or hit and physical punishment should be replaced by reason, logic, and removal of valued privileges. ("No television for you tonight"; "You're grounded for the weekend"; "Go to your room for a 'time out.'")

Many sociologists, psychologists, and other family studies professionals argue that as long as our social structure and cultural norms tolerate violent behavior in families and in other social institutions without costs to the perpetrator, violence will continue at high rates. Within families, "people hit and abuse other family members because they can" (Gelles, 1983, p. 157). Social scientist Mildred Pagelow (1984) goes so far as to describe the marriage license as "a hitting license."

Cultural Diversity and Violence: Three Examples

IMMIGRANT WOMEN

The dream of America offers freedom to immigrant women, but undocumented women married to American men can become trapped in abusive relationships by misunderstanding immigration law. The law "requires that both partners file for residency, after they've lived together for 21 months. Although the law allows for good cause exemptions, its language is so vague that an immigrant women often feels she has no choice but to live with her abuser" (Suh, 1990, p. 46).

To make matters worse, a husband often lies about having applied for residency permits or threatens to have his wife deported if she calls the police or goes to a doctor or hospital for treatment after episodes of marital violence. Cultural barriers—not knowing the language, distrust of government and community agencies, and fear of being imprisoned—also prevent women from seeking help.

NATIVE AMERICANS

Traditionally, Indian nations were family-centered, egalitarian, and nonviolent. Family violence was neither promoted nor protected in Native American culture. Child-rearing practices were founded on love and respect and discipline was based on nonphysical punishment. Rising incidents of marital battering and child abuse among Native Americans, then, are a product of modern society: alcohol abuse, poverty, unemployment, social isolation, and alienation from historical roots. In an effort to stop family violence, women from almost 300 reservations recently organized The National Coalition Against Domestic Violence to develop an abuse-prevention program that stresses the nonviolent heritage of Native Americans and condemns abuse. As one women explains, "Our children need to know

that at one time, a man could become chief only if the women in the tribe agreed that he should be" (Findlen, 1990b, p. 46). Native American women have lobbied tribal councils to take steps to discourage abuse through tougher tribal laws. They have also set up programs to inform social services and other community helping agencies of the unique tradition and special needs of Native Americans.

ASIAN-AMERICANS

Two men were given extremely lenient sentences for crimes committed against women. One beat his wife to death and was sentenced to 5 years' probation. Another abducted a 16-year-old girl and was acquitted of kidnapping and sexual assault. Both successfully employed a "cultural defense" to excuse them of their crimes. Their lawyers argued that, in their countries of origin, what these Asian-American men did was common practice and they should not be harshly punished (Findlen, 1990a).

Asian-Americans and other critics of these verdicts claim that the customs described in court are no longer practiced in the countries of origin and when they do occur, they are prosecuted as criminal behavior. In any case, critics argue that customs from the past should be given up regardless of cultural heritage if they violate basic American civil rights. Most of the criminal cases employing the cultural defense involve crimes against women and tend to involve sexual practices.

EXPLORATIONS *Can you think of other instances in which American women originally from other countries are mistreated because of native customs?*

SOURCES: B. Findlen (1990a; 1990b); and M. Suh (1990).

Only recently has the legal system given battered family members any legal protection from abuse. And only recently has physical violence been reported by large numbers of people. "Although assaults of a certain severity between strangers would automatically be classified as felonies, the same assault between in-

timates have been considered misdemeanors, if, indeed, an arrest was made at all" (Margolin et al., 1988, p. 90).

When police intervene in domestic disputes, battling spouses often protest that they have a right to hit each other, and researchers have found that even the victims of family violence commonly justify it with such explanations as "I asked for it" or "I deserved it." Many people feel that violence is justified under certain circumstances. These attitudes may have been learned in childhood, since various studies suggest a relationship between exposure to violence as a child and violent behavior as an adult (see the "Snapshots" box).

In many families the use of physical force is apparently passed down from one generation to another. Children who observe violence or who are its victims are more likely to justify violent acts and resort to them as adolescents and adults (Rosenbaum & O'Leary, 1986; Steinmetz, 1987; Stets, 1990). However, it cannot be emphasized enough that a majority of people who witness physical abuse or experience it as family members do *not* continue the violent behavior when they form new relationships or have families of their own. The cycle can be broken (Emery, 1989; Gelles & Straus, 1988).

MARITAL VIOLENCE

The most frequently used instrument for measuring marital violence is the Conflict Tactics Scales (CTS) developed by Murray Straus (1979). The CTS has 18

items that divide into three major scales. The first two scales ask how often certain power strategies were employed—rational discussion and agreement and nonverbal expressions of hostility. Most researchers who study relationship violence use only the third scale pertaining to physical force (see Figure 12-2). Items 4 through 8 are considered severe violence (Straus, 1990).

Participants are usually asked how often they engage in each of the aggressive activities on the scale (or how often their partner does). Answers fall into seven categories: never, once, twice, 3 to 5 times, 6 to 10 times, 11 to 20 times, more than 20 times (Hampton & Gelles, 1991). The scale is also used to assess violence in dating and cohabiting relationships (discussed in Chapter 4) and, with some changes in wording to assess instances of child abuse (as noted in Figure 12-2).

The CTS has been criticized for measuring only "normal" or socially acceptable types of violence like slapping, pushing, and throwing objects; ignoring gender differences in styles of aggressive behaviors—women have a tendency to overreport their own acts of violence and men to underreport theirs—and failing to ask about the severity of the injuries inflicted. Nevertheless, the scale is widely used (DeMaris, Pugh, & Harman, 1992; Walker, 1989). But, as psychologist Lenore Walker explains: "Simply counting violent acts as though they were all equal, such as occurs on the

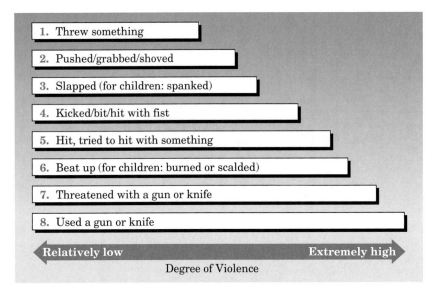

FIGURE 12-2
The Conflict Tactics Scales: Use of Physical Violence
SOURCE: S. Brehm (1992).

CTS, does not account for the cumulative impact of increasing levels of seriousness" (Walker, 1989, p. 696). Slapping and pushing are not equal to hitting with a fist or an object. Getting slapped once is not the same as getting slapped 15 to 30 times every Saturday night.

Violence against Wives

Each year, millions of women are battered by their partners. Once violence is initiated in a relationship, it almost always worsens and becomes more severe over time (Ammerman & Hersen, 1991). Plateaus and even temporary reversals may occur when police departments and the justice system temporarily intervene. But after these external barriers are removed—bail is paid, time is served—and stress recurs, violence typically continues, and quickly returns to its previous level or intensity (Walker, 1989) (see the "Point of View" box).

Research indicates that husbands who abuse their wives are frequently attempting to assert control and relieve feelings of powerlessness. Men are socialized to believe they should be self-sufficient and in charge. Many times their lives do not match these idealized images of masculinity—for example, they feel powerless when they cannot earn a good wage or their job is unsatisfying and demeaning. Their position as fam-

ily head may be additionally threatened if they are unemployed or have an employed wife with resources of her own. As socially accepted legitimate sources of power become less available, some husbands resort to displays of power and dominance through physical means (Gelles & Cornell, 1990; Walker, 1984).

The Cycle of Violence

Psychologist Lenore Walker (1979, 1984, 1989) discovered through her research with battered wives that there seems to be a *cycle of violence* consisting of three distinct stages in most battering episodes (see Figure 12-3).

Tension Building

The first stage involves *tension building*. Tension gradually escalates as the batterer behaves in ways that show his displeasure—becomes verbally abusive, does mean and intentionally hurtful things, resorts to lesser forms of physically abusive behavior: pushes, shoves, grabs, slaps. Walker (1984) writes:

The batterer expresses dissatisfaction and hostility but not in an extreme or maximally explosive form. The woman attempts to placate the batterer; doing what she thinks might please him, calm him down, or at

Domestic Violence: A Case of Love and Death

The shotgun murders last week of three members of a Clintwood family might never have happened if Virginia's legal system showed more concern about domestic violence, family members and advocates for victims say.

Lilton Estep says his sister, niece, and father needlessly died because the Dickenson County Sheriff's Department and magistrate's office didn't pay enough attention to his sister's fear for her life.

"It's a terrible situation," Estep says. "It's ridiculous. We're going to change things. It ain't going to bring anybody back, but perhaps it will stop it from happening again."

Estep says the murders would not have happened if James Sol Fox, his sister's live-in boyfriend, had been locked up 2 days earlier. Fox should have been jailed, Estep says, on charges of beating his sister and threatening to kill her with the very shotgun he used 2 days later. Instead, Fox was allowed to go free on personal recognizance bond.

About dinnertime on April 5, Fox killed his girlfriend, Jutannia Estep, 28, their 1-year-old daughter, Angela Belle Estep, and Jutannia's father, Edgar Dale Estep, 54. Fox also wounded Jutannia's mother, Freda Estep. Fox, 33, then used his shotgun to kill himself.

Elizabeth Betterley, the director of HOPE House in Norton, says legal authorities across the state often discount domestic violence. It's not uncommon, she says, for a jealous or abusive husband or boyfriend to be charged, freed with little or no bond, and then "go back and beat up or even kill his spouse or girlfriend."

Kristi VanAudenhove is administrative director of Virginians Against Domestic Violence, a statewide organization pushing for stronger domestic violence laws. She says magistrates and police need to seriously consider locking up abusive men at certain key dangerous times.

Studies indicate that the most dangerous time for a woman and her family is within 3 days of leaving the abuser, VanAudenhove says. She says special caution must come into play whenever beatings occur, guns are used, or death threats are made.

All of those warnings were there on April 3 when Jutannia Estep went to the magistrate's office in Clintwood to swear out a warrant against Fox. Family members say she called the sheriff's office begging for help because Fox had beaten her that morning and she was afraid he would carry out a threat to kill her. Instead of sending investigators, the sheriff's department told her to come in and swear out a warrant.

Sheriff's deputies picked up Fox on charges of assault and battery and using a firearm to threaten Jutannia's life. Deputies reportedly had to chase him through the woods, but Fox, 6-feet-1 and 240 pounds, cooperated after they caught him.

Deputies hauled him back before Mullins, the magistrate. She found that Fox had no criminal record and allowed him to go free on personal recognizance after he promised to stay away from Jutannia and her family.

Kyle McClanahan, the chief magistrate for the court district, says, under the state's bail reform laws people accused of crimes are entitled to reasonable bail. It must be remembered, he says, the people are only accused, not convicted.

And, he says, magistrates repeatedly see women come in to swear out warrants against husbands or boyfriends only to drop them the next day.

Nevertheless, he is sending a memorandum to all magistrates in his multicounty district. He says the memorandum will caution magistrates to "work more cautiously with this type incident."

Those accused of domestic violence—especially where injuries, guns, and death threats are involved—will find it harder to get out on bond.

EXPLORATIONS *Do you know the laws concerning domestic violence and stalking in your state? Do you think these laws are effective? What improvements would you suggest?*

SOURCE: Excerpted from D. Pardue (1993).

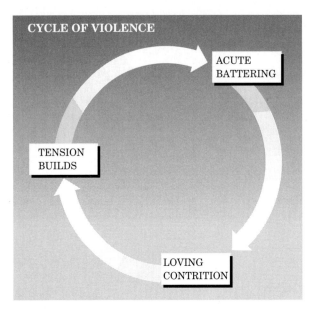

CYCLE OF VIOLENCE

ACUTE BATTERING

TENSION BUILDS

LOVING CONTRITION

INTERVENTION STRATEGIES

Step 1: Ask for help.

Step 2: Avoid violence by learning what "sets you off"; learn socially acceptable ways of gaining power and handling stress.

Step 3: Learn to talk; become comfortable not being "the authority," not being "in control."

Step 4: Learn to prevent tension buildup; accept anger; communicate clearly; develop a network of supportive friends; recognize the good things about yourself.

FIGURE 12-3
Walker's Cycle of Violence Theory and Some Intervention Strategies for Men

SOURCES: Based on L. E. Walker (1979, 1984); and E. Gondolf (1985).

least, what will not further aggravate him. She tries not to respond to his hostile actions and uses general anger reduction techniques. . . . Exhausted from the constant stress, she usually withdraws from the batterer, fearing she will inadvertently set off an explosion. He begins to move oppressively toward her as he observes her withdrawal . . . tension between the two becomes unbearable. (pp. 95, 96)

Acute Battering

Stage two is when the *acute battering incident* occurs. Typically, the wife is physically injured and emotionally shaken by the husband's verbal and physically abusive behavior: 50 percent of women must seek medical attention. Tension is reduced as the violence continues. Episodes of acute violence can last from a few minutes to several hours and include rape and other acts of sexual abuse. During this stage, at least one in four wives is forced to perform sexually, have a sexually aggressive act performed on her, or is repeatedly raped by her husband. Forced sex (marital rape) during battering episodes has more to do with power and the ability to gain control than with pleasure (Koss, 1987; Russell, 1982). As one man admits, "Yes, you could call it rape if you want to, but I did it because she got stubborn" (Gondolf, 1985, p. 71).

Loving Contrition

During stage three, *loving contrition*, the husband may express love and sorrow for his violent behavior. He may apologize repeatedly while he attempts to comfort and give first aid to his wife. As he displays feelings of remorse he may try to do things that please her and make promises to change. He may vow never to allow himself to behave in this manner again. Feeling, as many women do, that the quality of the marriage is her responsibility, confused about what role she may have had in the explosion of violence, and observing her husband's sorrow and acts of love, she may forgive him. She wants to believe that he will change; that he will never be violent again. It is important to note that stage three does not always occur. Sometimes the battering leads only to a reduction in stress and tension for the batterer. Love and an apology are not offered afterward.

Why Do Women Stay?

A woman stays in a violent relationship for many reasons. Usually, she is isolated from friends and relatives who might help her; or she has tried to leave her husband several times before and her friends and kin are no longer very supportive of her. They have lost faith in her ability or willingness to leave. Even if she goes to a crisis center for battered women, such centers give only short-term help. In most cases, a woman (most bring young children with them) can live in a crisis center for only 2 to 4 weeks at the most. This time is not sufficient to learn new behavior patterns, find a job (assuming she is not already employed), and save enough for the deposit on a new place to live. Women who have jobs and other resources are usually less financially and emotionally dependent on their spouses and are able to leave their husbands sooner.

The abused woman may stay with the batterer because she is afraid to leave. In earlier attempts, her abusive husband may have tracked her down and beaten her (or worse) and threatened her life and those of her children. She may have come to believe that she is somehow at fault for the abuse. He may tell her that if she were only a better housekeeper, mother, sexual partner—you name it—he would not be compelled to beat her. In an interview, one woman said:

> He'll say things like, "If you wouldn't run your smart mouth, I wouldn't do this." And he'll say stuff like, "I don't want to do it, you make me do it. . . ." "He always blames it on me. It's never his fault." (Wolf-Smith & LaRossa, 1993, p. 327)

She may think that if only she could improve herself in these areas, the violence would stop.

Women in violent marriages frequently describe their husbands as having a Dr. Jekyll/Mr. Hyde personality. Such women tend to believe that if only they could figure out the right approach, they could help their husbands become calmer and more loving. Many battered women believe that with the right kind of love and support the mean, destructive part of their husbands would disappear. "Obviously, this does not happen; instead, 'the good side' shrinks as the abusive behavior increases in frequency and severity" (Walker, 1989, p. 697). Many women believe their partners when they apologize and accept their excuses. As a young mother reports:

> I believe he was sorry he did it. He just can't control himself. I believe he does it before he realizes it and sometimes he doesn't even remember doing it the next morning. . . . It's just out of his memory. I think in his heart he's really sorry for doing it. He just can't help it. (Wolf-Smith & LaRossa, 1993, p. 327)

Battered women often suffer from *learned helplessness*—loss of the perceived ability to escape. Women who are regularly and repeatedly beaten become very pessimistic about their ability to function as autonomous and independent persons. They become masters at ignoring their pain and anticipating their batterer's moods and desires. Such women, in essence, learn survival techniques. At the point when these techniques or coping skills are not enough to sufficiently protect them or their children, they may finally leave. This point is usually reached after a woman has made repeated attempts to leave and when she becomes convinced that her husband is actually going to kill her or the children. In rare cases, women have killed their batterers (Browne, 1987) (see the "Dilemmas and Decisions" box). Much more often, however, he is the one who resorts to homicide.

To escape early in the relationship, a woman has to overcome her tendency to learn survival tactics that promote helplessness by, for example, "becoming angry rather than depressed and self-blaming; active rather than passive; and more realistic about the likelihood of the relationship continuing on its aversive course rather than improving" (Walker, 1984, p. 87). Once out of an abusive relationship, a battered woman will rarely connect intimately with another batterer.

Men Who Batter

Men who batter seem to repeatedly get involved with women they can abuse. As a group, they typically deny or drastically downplay the seriousness of their violent behavior. The following characteristics of male batterers have been identified across several studies (Gelles & Cornell, 1990; Mott-MacDonald, 1979; Walker, 1984, 1989). No batterer will exhibit every characteristic listed, but if several of these traits are obvious, caution is advised.

- Advocates a traditional division of family roles.
- Believes women cause their own abuse by being difficult and ignoring men's needs.
- Refuses to accept responsibility for his own problems.
- Uses violence to gain power, authority, and feelings of self-worth.
- Deals with stress through aggressive actions—punches, kicks, flies into a rage.
- Minimizes his problems by denying he has any or lying about them.
- Displays unreasonable jealousy.

DILEMMAS AND DECISIONS

When Women and Children Kill: Is It Still Murder?

"The police did all they could, but they had no control. They felt sorry for me. They told me to get a gun."—Rita.

"I didn't mean to kill him. He had hit me several times. Something inside me snapped; I grabbed the bottle and swung."—Brenda.

"They say I'm a violent person, but I'm not. I didn't want revenge. I just wanted out."—Shalanda (Gibbs, 1993, pp. 40–42).

"I walked in the door and he looked at me and started yelling, cussing me and everything, and telling me he was going to beat [me]. . . . That was the last thing I remember . . . I shot him . . . then I freaked out."—Scott (Heide, 1992, p. 62).

The stories of these women and children are typical of those convicted of murdering a parent, husband, or boyfriend. Each suffered years of countless incidents of physical and psychological abuse, sometimes followed by the man's sorrowful remorse and sometimes by silence and withdrawal. In the end, women and children who kill could see no way of escaping, and were often in fear for their lives.

Battered women find that police frequently refuse to get involved, often portraying the abusive situation as a lover's quarrel. Legal restraining orders are frequently ineffective—determined abusers simply force their way back into the house whenever they want, or stalk the women. Society offers little comfort; there is limited access to shelters or other means of support or aid.

Prosecutors, judges, and juries tend to have little or no sympathy for women who kill violent partners, de-

■ Is impulsive/defies limits.

■ Uses manipulative tactics to get what he wants; can be very charming.

■ Has low self-esteem.

■ Is often depressed.

■ Is unable to be intimate with anyone on a consistent basis.

■ Is controlling/makes unrealistic demands.

■ Cannot empathize with others.

■ Uses alcohol or drugs on a regular basis.

■ Talks about or displays his sexuality to gain power. Sex is an act of aggression.

■ Demonstrates a lack of communication and coping skills.

■ Exhibits contempt for women.

■ Has a past history of violence.

■ Has a low tolerance for stress.

Edward Gondolf, therapist and author of *Men Who Batter* (1985), believes that most men make attempts to stop their violent behavior, but admits that many drift back into a cycle of violence. Violence may be a means of regaining feelings of loss of power, control, prestige, status. Gondolf suggests several steps to break the cycle of violence (Figure 12-3). Men must learn new ways of evaluating their success and failure, gain more realistic views of male/female roles, and develop more productive means of communication, problem solving, and coping with stress.

ploring and severely punishing them for what are considered to be premeditated, revengeful acts. There is little understanding that, at the moment of the murder, although there is not always an immediate threat to the woman's life or safety, there has been a cumulative effect of years of threats and abuses. At the moment she kills, the woman perceives a real threat to her (and/or her children's) life and sees no other alternative, no way of escaping. At trial, women are held to a higher standard of behavior than their abusers, receiving longer prison terms and less sympathy than men who kill wives or girlfriends.

Similarly, adolescents who kill have most often been the victims of physical and psychological abuse by one or both parents for most of their lives. Since early childhood, they have typically taken on adult responsibilities—for example, cooking, cleaning, and caring for younger siblings. Despite great efforts to anticipate their parents' demands and try to please, they receive neither recognition nor reward from their families. The abusive parent or parents are never satisfied, accusing the adolescents of being slackers, and seem to look for any excuse to heap on additional abuse.

Violent parents of adolescent killers tend to be alcoholics and/or abusers of drugs, both legal and illegal. Because of their many family problems, the children (embarrassed by their parent's behavior and the abuse they suffer) isolate themselves from the community, friends, and relatives. They share a burden of shame from knowing their family is not like other families, or the ideal families seen on television. When, in desperation, they do seek assistance and relief from teachers, close relatives, or a nonabusing parent, they are generally unsuccessful—not believed or ignored. One young man recalls, "Just because a kid is young, don't think he's stupid. At least listen to him. Then check into it" (Heide, 1992, p. 76). Over time children become increasingly overwhelmed as the abuse worsens and they lose the ability to cope with the stress from a deteriorating situation.

Invariably the children are very uncomfortable with having killed and are sorry for what they have done. They know it was wrong, but at the same time feel relief from knowing they will not be hurt again. Many "block out" the murder. They were in what psychologists refer to as a dissociative state, aware the murder was committed, but unable to remember some or all of the events of the murder itself.

EXPLORATIONS *When a child tells a relative or friend of the violent behavior of a parent, does that person have any responsibility to act? Explain. What do you think should happen to children who kill a parent or a woman who kills a husband or boyfriend? Should they be treated the same as or differently from any other murderer?*

SOURCES: N. Gibbs (1993); and K. M. Heide (1992).

Partly as a result of the women's movement and its concern for women in violent relationships, many American cities now have shelters for battered women and their children, "hotlines" that abused women can use to seek help, and police teams especially trained for domestic intervention.

Violence against Husbands

Husband battering gets very little attention from family researchers, clinicians, or other social scientists, although several studies indicate that wives often participate in marital violence. As we might expect, women and men resort to somewhat different modes of violence. Husbands tend to use direct physical strength as they push, grab, or choke their spouses, whereas women are inclined to throw things or use objects such as kitchen knives that do not require as much physical might (Steinmetz, 1977b).

Critics who actively discourage research on husband battering point out that when a woman strikes out physically it is almost always to break out of her husband's grasp; in retaliation, or to "fight back" for what the husband is already doing to her; or in self-defense—to protect herself from being hurt more seriously (Dobash & Dobash, 1988; Walker, 1984). And when women do hit, the injuries that they inflict are much less severe than those caused by men. Violence researchers Emerson and Russell Dobash write:

There is no systematic evidence showing a pattern of . . . violence against husbands that would warrant the use of terms such as beaten or battered. . . . Indeed, our research and that of virtually everyone else who has actually studied violent events and/or their patterning in a detailed fashion reveal that when women do violence . . . it is primarily in self-defense or retaliation, often during an attack by their husbands. On occasion, women may initiate an incident after years of being attacked, but it is extraordinarily rare for women to persistently initiate severe attacks. (1988, p. 60)

There are 13 women physically abused by their partners for every one man, but "because women are usually smaller and lighter than men, they suffer a greater degree of physical injury and are more likely to have been terrorized (e.g., with a knife held to the throat for two hours), threatened, and brutalized by prolonged and repeated attacks" (Steinmetz, 1987, p. 735).

Sociologist Suzanne Steinmetz (1987) argues that, despite evidence that few men are battered by women, there is a need for more research on husband battering because *any* violence should be considered significant, especially if there are children in the family. She suggests that men are reluctant to report battering incidents because it contradicts social expectations for the male role and would stigmatize them in the community. As one battered male said: "I never took the fights outside, I didn't want anyone to know. I told the guys at work that the kids did it with a toy" (Steinmetz & Lucca, 1988, p. 239). Men also have access to more resources than women and can utilize such resources to prevent others from finding out about the abuse.

Given their greater resources, why do men stay in physically abusive relationships? Interviews provide some clues. First, such men say that their standards of living would be considerably lower if they moved out. Today, most families depend on two paychecks. Second, they are reluctant to leave comfortable and familiar homes that they may have spent hours remodeling or improving over the years. Third, because the children generally stay with the mother, some men voice a reluctance to give up their parenting role. They like being fathers and would miss the daily interaction with their children. They believe that "keeping the family together at all costs is best for the children" (Steinmetz & Lucca, 1988, p. 243). Finally, some men report that they love their wives and that the women are, in most ways, responsible mothers and marital partners. The violent attacks are an exception that causes them frustration, anxiety, pain, and bewilder-

ment. And, there are a few men who indicate that they are afraid of leaving their wives with the children, who are sometimes targets of the mother's abuse. Leaving the family home would mean that they could no longer provide protection for their children.

CHILD ABUSE

Since 1974, when Congress passed the Child Abuse Prevention Act, the National Center on Child Abuse and Neglect has operated as a resource center for people seeking information on child abuse and funding for research on its causes and treatment. The center definition of *child abuse* is:

The physical or mental injury, sexual abuse, negligent treatment, or maltreatment of a child under the age of 18 by a person who is responsible for the child's welfare under circumstances which indicate that the child's health is harmed or threatened thereby. (Gelles & Cornell, 1985, p. 20)

Sexual Abuse of Children and Young Women

Child sexual abuse—"forced, tricked, or coerced sexual behavior between a young person and an older person"—is receiving much research attention in the 1990s (Gelles & Conte, 1991, p. 332). In particular, *incest*—sex between a parent and child—is being investigated. The prevailing opinion is that incest by a father or stepfather (the most common type) is based on the adult's need to feel powerful and important. The consequences of unreported abuse are significant because, in some cases, men involved in incest have also been found to sexually abuse children from outside their immediate families and to sexually molest and rape women (Abel, Becker, Cunningham-Rathner, Mittelman, & Rouleau, 1988).

The connection between power and aggressive tendencies is evident in other relationships as well. Recent examples include several well-publicized cases of priests or clergymen who have sexually abused children, adolescents, or young adult women. These cases are examples of how the resource of authority is used to gain legitimate power, which is then used to force sexual contact. Clergymen are recognized in our society as being morally and ethically peerless. Given their standing in the community and church they have great social and personal power. When this power is employed negatively, the effects can be overwhelming (see the "Dilemmas and Decisions" box).

Physical Abuse as Discipline

Children seem to be more vulnerable to abuse at specific ages. Straus, Gelles, and Steinmetz (1980), for example, found that 3- and 4-year-old children and 15- to 17-year-old adolescents are more likely to be abused by their parents. "The 3- to 4-year-old can explore the house and the neighborhood but lacks the knowledge to do so safely. The 15- to 17-year-old is experimenting with adult autonomy and maturity. . . . The activities of both groups often represent a questioning of parental authority and control (Steinmetz, 1987). Physical punishment by a stressed-out parent can easily cross the line to abusive behavior. To regain control and assert their power and authority, parents may resort to physical force. It is estimated that between 84 and 97 percent of parents use physical means of discipline at some time during child rearing (Steinmetz, 1987).

Part of the problem for parents, as well as researchers, is to determine the point at which appropriate discipline becomes unreasonable and harmful physical abuse. Most of today's grandparents can remember the strappings and whippings they received as children, for "their own good." Parental actions of this type were once considered normal and respectable means of encouraging a "proper upbringing." These same disciplinary methods "would now be labeled as suspected child abuse if a teacher, a school nurse, a baby-sitter, or a friend saw the welts and reported them to the appropriate agency, as required by law" (Steinmetz, 1987, p. 732).

Understanding Why Child Abuse Occurs

One of the chief reasons for concern about the welfare of both parents and children is that parenting takes place in a relatively private, isolated household. American parents have more exclusive responsibility for their children than do parents in other cultures. Relatives and neighbors are not readily available to take over when a parent's patience wears thin. In the absence of other adults, the frustration of a distraught parent goes unchecked.

It sounds reasonable that the more time and effort a parent invests in child rearing, the better the results. In practice, however, things do not always work out that way. Classic research on child-rearing practices in

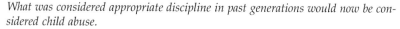

What was considered appropriate discipline in past generations would now be considered child abuse.

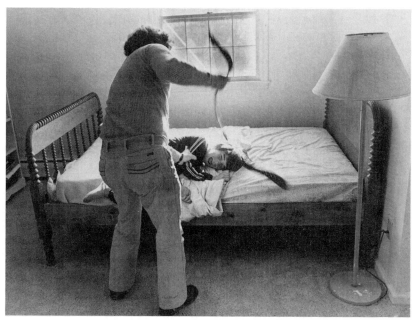

DILEMMAS AND DECISIONS

Breaking a Sacred Trust: The Clergy and Sexual Abuse

"It was so awkward. I kept thinking, it doesn't count because he's wearing a rubber. I'm still a virgin."
—Rita, a 16-year-old, sexually abused by her priest.

"I thought, if I have to give him sex, that's little in comparison to what he's giving me in return."
—Cathy, sexually abused by her minister in counseling sessions (Bonavoglia, 1992, pp. 40, 43).

This girl and the young women were each victimized by men who occupied unique positions of power and respect in their communities. When their cases became public knowledge, defenders of the clergymen frequently blamed the abused females for seducing their priests or pastors, claiming they consented to sex. Counseling experts, however, contend that consent is not an issue, that men in powerful positions can easily gain an adolescent's trust. One sexually abusive priest later said, "as a priest, I had her full trust and confidence. Yet I got sexually involved. . . . I admit my fault . . . I am truly sorry for the pain, the anxieties, and the suffering she has endured all these years" (Bonavoglia, 1992, p. 42).

Two patterns of clergy abuse have emerged. One is of young, naive, and trusting girls, who, over a period of months or years, are made to feel special because of their work for the church. Sexual advances are often swift and abrupt, with little or no explanation. If the girls protest, the clergymen tell them there is nothing immoral about what they are doing. Shouldn't he know? He is, after all, a respected minister or priest. The girls are frightened and confused by the advances, uncertain whether to tell of their ordeal or if the activity is sanctioned by God. Some feel, at first, that they have a relationship with God through their clergyman.

Another common pattern is of young women being counseled for marital and other personal crises who gradually come to depend on and trust their minister's advice and counsel. When the clergyman begins to make advances—touching inappropriately in the course of giving comfort, kissing cheeks and hands as a supportive gesture—she feels uneasy and pushes away, often telling the minister that the acts are becom-

ing too personal and inappropriate, that she feels uncomfortable. The minister often justifies the sexual activity as a means of helping her learn to accept close relationships with people or by suggesting that God wants them to have some happiness together.

Major religious denominations, as diverse as Catholic, Presbyterian, Methodist, Jewish, and Buddhist, have come under fire for how they have dealt with such sexually abusive situations. Typically, they deny responsibility for the actions of the clergymen or say that these are isolated ethical and moral lapses of individual clergy. Many do whatever is necessary to prevent publicity and rarely provide emotional or financial assistance to the girls or women, except as a means to keep them quite and avoid scandal. They rarely punish the offenders.

In many churches, guidelines are now being developed to meet problems of sexual abuse, along with training in professional ethics and sexual abuse by clergy. Girls and young women who report such abuse are increasingly being believed and supported, with their medical and counseling bills paid by the church. In addition, several states have passed laws making it a felony for therapists, including clergy, to have sex with clients, allowing no claims of consensual sex.

EXPLORATIONS *Have you read recent reports of young boys being sexually abused by clergymen? Do their personal accounts differ in any way from those of girls? Can you think of other instances in which authority figures can easily use their social positions to gain legitimate power over others for exploitive purposes, including sexual relations?*

SOURCE: A. Bonavoglia (1992).

six cultures comes to the conclusion that mothers are more stable and meet their children's needs better when parental substitutes are available. The emotional health of both mother and child is best, it appears, where others are ready to help with the tasks of parenthood (Lambert, 1971; Whiting, 1963).

The exclusive mother-child attachment made possible in middle-class communities by relatively isolated, self-sufficient households, and encouraged by the belief, expressed by child-rearing experts, that motherhood should be a continuous, full-time job, creates considerable tensions. Today, most mothers are employed and fathers are becoming increasingly involved parents. According to myth, parents are supposed to feel nothing but love and warmth for their children. In reality, the frequent demands of young children can wear down a parent's patience. If a child cries constantly despite being comforted, the parent may understandably feel rejected and angry. Without other adults to turn to, anger and rejection may build to a point where child abuse results.

It is startling to realize that small children are far more likely to be injured by their parents than by anyone else. It is not at all uncommon for physicians to be asked to treat small children suffering from unexplained fractures, severe bruises, or abrasions. The extent of the problem of child abuse is difficult to estimate accurately. The author of one study extrapolated from the data provided by interviews with more than 1,000 families that of children between the ages of 3 and 17 who live with both parents, roughly 1.4 million are physically abused by their parents in any given year (Gelles & Straus, 1988).

Child abuse poses a difficult dilemma for everyone concerned—parents, children, physicians, and social service agencies. It is not easy for some parents to determine the point at which reasonable discipline becomes unreasonable and harmful abuse. Studies of abused children and their parents have identified a number of factors associated with violence against children. In order to understand child abuse we need to look at cultural norms, the family situation, as well as parental and child characteristics (see Figure 12-4).

As you can see, "stressful life circumstances are the hallmark of the violent family. The greater stress individuals are under, the more likely they are to be violent toward their children" (Gelles & Straus, 1988, p. 85). But stress should never be used as an excuse for violent behavior. There are community-based pro-

grams and support groups in most cities and towns. Help is available for individuals or couples who want to strengthen parenting and coping skills.

Some of the suggested remedies and preventive strategies for child abuse seek to provide the kind of assistance readily available in cultures where the mother can turn to neighbors or relatives for help. For example, "crisis nurseries" have been provided in Colorado. Parents use these facilities, with no questions asked. They are safe places where children can be left for a few hours or a few days, until the parent is ready to resume responsibility for the child. Rather than look for villains, Kim Oates, member of a child protection unit, recommends:

> Look at the strengths and weaknesses in the family where abuse is suspected, and take steps to relieve some of the stresses by providing realistic support services. What is most important is the future protection and mental health of the child. Most families have the same concern for the child as the child protection worker—that is, for their child to grow up well and healthy. Many families do not have the skills to achieve this, reverting to violence in the face of stress and frustration. Supporting these families in parenting and recognizing that there must be a long-term commitment to them is for most families a more realistic approach than seeing detection and prosecution as the beginning and end of involvement with the family. (1991, p. 121)

ELDER ABUSE

Elder abuse is the latest component of family violence to be recognized and studied. Today, the elderly are one of the fastest growing segments of the population. There are currently 25 million Americans who are age 65 or older and by the turn of the century over one-half of our population will be age 50 or older. Today's elderly are a healthier group than in the past; the average life expectancy is now well over 75 years of age. Although most older Americans live independently until their deaths, a growing number of the oldest (85+ years of age) require some degree of care from someone (usually a relative) (Mancini & Blieszner, 1991).

Approximately 2.5 million old people are abused each year, about 1 of every 10 living with a family

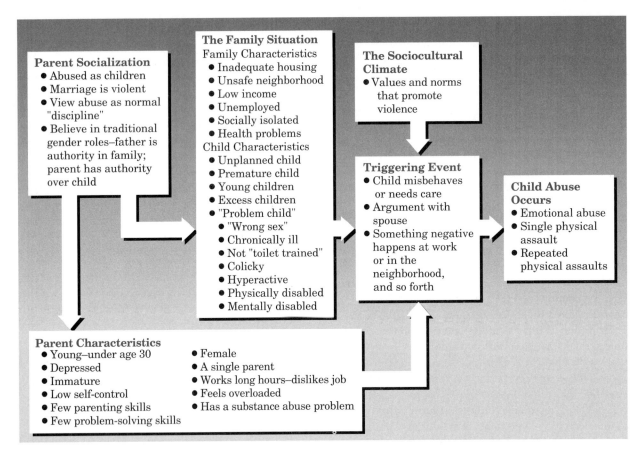

FIGURE 12-4
Factors Related to Child Abuse

SOURCES: R. J. Gelles (1973); R. J. Gelles & C. Cornell (1990); R. J. Gelles & M. A. Straus (1988); R. Hampton & R. J. Gelles (1991); S. K. Steinmetz (1987).

member (Gelles & Cornell, 1990; Giordano & Giordano, 1984). The typical profile of an abused elder is a white middle-class woman over 75 years old with a chronic physical or psychological impairment and living with a caregiver. The typical abuser is an adult middle-aged or older female relative living with the elder and experiencing a pile up of other stress in her life (Brubaker, 1991; Williams & Griffin, 1991).

The Role of Dependency

Studies have found that the elderly person who lives with his or her caregiver is at greatest risk. Dependence, after many years of independent living, is stressful to both the caregiver and the carereceiver. The more dependent the elderly person, the greater the risk

of abuse. The costs of the relationship grow more burdensome, and the benefits of companionship decrease. ''If the caregiver feels unable to escape the situation, he or she may then become abusive'' (Pillemer & Suitor, 1988, p. 255).

Recent research indicates that feelings of dependence can work both ways. If the caregiver relies on the elder for financial support, the risk of abuse rises even more dramatically. For example, in one study, 64 percent of abused elders supported their caregivers financially, while 55 percent provided housing. Very possibly the dependent adult child feels a sense of unfairness and powerlessness and a consequent loss of self-esteem. Dependence late in adulthood goes strongly against cultural expectations (Pillemer &

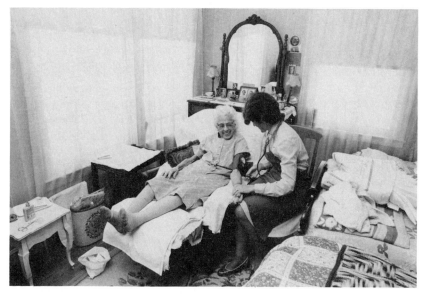

The services of a home health-care representative can reduce stress for both the caregiver and the dependent elder, resulting in higher life satisfaction for both.

Suitor, 1988). Abusive actions are tied to frustration and the false notion that power can be gained by controlling the person or the situation.

The Role of Social Isolation

Another factor related to elder abuse is *social isolation*—when an individual does not have regular contact with friends, relatives, or anyone else outside the household. Caregivers who take on all support functions without help or emotional sustenance from others often feel overloaded and "stressed out." Adding to their distress could be unemployment, low income, failing health, marital or family problems, and so forth. People who do not feel secure and satisfied in their own daily lives are more likely to feel resentful of giving care to others.

The Role of Illness

The difficulty of caregiving is also magnified if the elder is chronically ill or incapacitated physically and emotionally. Elders unable to reciprocate caregiving with a smile, a good conversation, financial help, help with household chores, or even by being responsible for some of their own physical needs are particularly at risk. If, in addition, the relationship between the caregiver and the elder was already strained by past family history—they never spent much time together;

they had dissimilar values, goals, or needs; they often fought and said hurtful things to each other—the risk of abuse is magnified.

Reducing Elder Abuse

Caregiver stress can be reduced and the risk of elder abuse diminished by the following helpful services (Pillemer & Suitor, 1988, p. 264):

- *Housing services:* short-term day-care facilities to allow relatives a break from caregiving, and permanent alternative housing if caregiving becomes impossible.

- *Health services:* home health aides, home nursing, personal-care attendants, health-care centers, and in-home occupational, speech, and physical therapy

- *Home maintenance services:* assistance with housekeeping, heavy chores, shopping, and meal preparation

- *Supportive services:* friendly visitor programs, affordable therapists and counselors, senior centers, and recreation programs

- *Guardianship and financial services:* protective services for neglected and abused elders, volunteer guardianship for elders without families, affordable financial counseling for elderly persons and their families

SUMMARY POINTS

■ There are three types of power: social power, latent power, and manifest power. Social power refers to cultural beliefs and norms that, through socialization, influence women and men to devalue women's status and assign them fewer resources and less power. Latent power is present when the less powerful partner anticipates the reaction of the more powerful partner and adjusts her or his course of action without the partner having to say a word. Manifest power relies on the use of particular tactics or strategies to bring issues forward or keep them from being raised.

■ Power strategies fall into four general categories: direct-cooperative, direct-uncooperative, indirect-cooperative, indirect-uncooperative.

■ Men more often rely on direct power strategies based on concrete resources that emphasize their individual competencies. Women more often use indirect strategies based on personal resources that exaggerate their powerlessness.

■ Employed women typically have higher self-esteem, use more direct strategies, report that marital issues are settled more fairly, and indicate that their needs are more often taken into account during marital negotiation.

■ Cooperative power strategies are the most beneficial to relationships and usually result in the greatest satisfaction of partners. When cooperative strategies (bargaining, reasoning) do not get results, competitive strategies (coercion, manipulation) may be used. Should these strategies also fail, some partners resort to threats. Finally, if verbal means of influence are not successful, physical means of asserting power may be employed.

■ The First and Second National Violence Surveys carried out by Murray Straus and his colleagues are valuable sources of information about violence in the American family.

■ These national surveys are one of the few sources of information about violence in both black and white families. Some scholars, however, caution that race is only one of the factors, and not among the most critical, to consider when trying to understand family violence.

■ Violence is not limited to any particular social class.

■ Use of alcohol or drugs is not a cause of abusive behavior in families. Rather, drinking and using drugs are socially accepted *excuses* for bad behavior.

■ Violence is influenced by sociocultural factors and the family is where people get their "basic training" in the use of violence. The marriage license is considered by some to be a "hitting license."

■ The Conflict Tactics Scales were developed by Murray Straus to assess marital violence. Although the scales have been criticized, they continue to be the instruments used most frequently in measuring violence in the family.

■ Lenore Walker proposes that most incidents of wife battering proceed through three distinct stages: tension building, acute battering, and loving contrition. She calls this three-stage sequence of events the cycle of violence.

■ Women stay in violent relationships for many reasons. Among them are social isolation from kin and friends; lack of reliable community support systems; fear that their abusive partner will find them and punish them if they leave; dependence on the partner for money, food, shelter, and love; and learned helplessness.

■ Men who batter tend to downplay and trivialize the seriousness of their violent behavior. Potential batterers share some common identifiable characteristics, including advocating traditional gender roles, externalizing problems, being unreasonably jealous, handling life problems in a physically aggressive manner, believing that battered women cause their own abuse, and being impulsive and manipulative.

■ When a woman reacts violently, it is usually to break out of her partner's grasp, to "fight back" during an abusive episode, or to protect herself from being more seriously injured by her batterer.

■ Suzanne Steinmetz argues that no matter how small the percentage of female batterers compared to male batterers, all battering should be taken seriously because of its effects on the family. Men say that they stay in battering relationships to maintain their standard of living, out of a need to be good fathers and keep the family together, and, in some cases, to protect their children from the mother's abuse.

■ Children are at greater risk of abuse between the ages of 3 and 4 years and 15 and 17 years. At these ages children tend to question parental authority and control.

■ Sociocultural factors, parental characteristics and traits, socialization experiences, and situational stress all contribute to incidents of child abuse.

■ The more dependent the elder on the caregiver or the caregiver on the elder, the greater the risk of elder abuse. Social isolation and feelings of stress from an overload of caregiving tasks are also contributing factors to elder abuse.

KEY TERMS

Power	*Indirect-cooperative strategies*
Parental power	*Indirect-uncooperative strategies*
Offspring power	*Violence*
Sibling power	*Emotional abuse*
Kinship power	*Cycle of violence*
Dyadic power	*Tension building*
Power base	*Acute battering incident*
Social power	*Loving contrition*
Latent power	*Learned helplessness*
Manifest power	*Child abuse*
Power strategies	*Child sexual abuse*
Direct-cooperative strategies	*Incest*
	Social isolation
Direct-uncooperative strategies	

REVIEW QUESTIONS

1. What is power and how can it operate as both a positive and negative force in an intimate relationship? Give examples.

2. Identify the six power resources described by French and Raven and give examples of how each resource serves as a base of power.

3. Discuss the following types of power: social, latent, and manifest. Give examples of each.

4. What are power strategies and how does gender influence their use?

5. How is power related to violent behavior in some relationships?

6. How do sociocultural norms legitimize violent behavior?

7. What is the Conflict Tactics Scales (CTS) and why is it criticized by some researchers?

8. What is the cycle of violence? Describe each stage.

9. Why do battered women tend to stay in violent relationships?

10. Why do some family scientists believe that husband battering should not be given much research attention?

11. If someone asked you why child abuse occurs, how would you explain it?

12. Why is elder abuse a recent phenomenon? Until the late 1980s and early 1990s, it was rarely mentioned as a social concern.

13

Stress: Individual and Family Perspectives

We all need a moderate amount of stress in our lives to keep us stimulated, challenged, and moving through life. Difficulties and problems entice us to remain interactive with others—looking for information, seeking advice, complaining, asserting, and so forth. To experience life's troubles and survive can be rewarding in itself. Feelings of being energized, competent, independent, and in control are aroused. There is a certain perverse pleasure in passing along personal "war stories." Tales of survival involving love affairs gone bad, neglectful marital partners, and mid-life angst are told and retold, sometimes with passion. Such personal accounts serve to remind us and others that there can be strength in the face of adversity.

More debilitating stress, however, is not always so enlightening or enabling. Perhaps that is why, when used in everyday conversation, *stress* implies a negative divergence from the normal routine of life. It encompasses the many and varied reactions of people exposed to events they find threatening or harmful to their well-being. Feelings of uneasiness, strain, tension, and pressure are associated with stress.

When something stressful occurs, people usually evaluate how much it threatens their well-being and judge their ability to deal with the consequences. They attempt to counteract the threat by identifying the cause of their discomfort, controlling the emotions it arouses, and making attempts to do something about it. In most cases, these attempts result in lower stress. The entire sequence of evaluative and protective behaviors that unfold following a stressful encounter and the outcomes of those actions are known as *the stress process* (Boss, 1987; Lazarus & Folkman, 1984; Pearlin, 1989).

This chapter facilitates a broad understanding and appreciation of the stress process by discussing it from both an individual and family perspective. Families are made up of individuals, each of whom experiences stress from a unique viewpoint. The individual reactions of family members either facilitate or hinder how the family collectively handles stress. To have a family plan of action to counter stress requires that individual members have a meeting of the minds, that they agree a problem exists and are committed to working together to solve the problem.

The chapter also focuses on the role of social support in stress resistance and identifies gender differences in the stress process. Because the stress process begins with the introduction of a stressful event or circumstance, we start our discussion there.

IDENTIFYING THE STRESSOR

Stressors are the triggers or initiators of the stress process. Although typically viewed as disruptive events causing sharp changes in patterned ways of behavior, stressors can also be predictable and planned. Stress arises out of two broad circumstances: life events and persistent hardships.

Life Events

Normative life events are the anticipated relatively common milestones that distinguish normal family life.

Such events are stressful because they require a series of changes in the routine ways people go about their daily lives. The life cycle stages we examined in Chapter 7 were organized around normative life events like marriage, the birth of a child, children maturing and leaving home, retirement, and widowhood. Through observation of those around them, media portrayals, and past experience, people basically know what to expect when normative life events occur.

The script is already developed. The sequences and patterns of change are known. It is understood, for instance, that when a first child is born the relationship between the marital partners will change as they incorporate the child into the family. It will be more difficult to find time to be alone as individuals and as a couple. The first few months are especially hectic as new family rules and relationships take shape. Employment for one or both of the partners is likely to be disrupted from several weeks to several months and the return to the workplace, after a parental leave, requires some reorientation. It is understood that accompanying the joy and excitement of parenthood are feelings of tiredness, discomfort, and role overload.

Nonnormative life events are sudden, unexpected, crisislike occurrences: the premature death of a loved one, job loss, unanticipated injury or illness, or natural disasters like floods, tornadoes, or house fires. Unlike normative life events, they do not occur uniformly

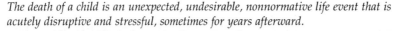

The death of a child is an unexpected, undesirable, nonnormative life event that is acutely disruptive and stressful, sometimes for years afterward.

across the population and their consequences are mostly negative.

Gauging the Impact of Events

Life events vary according to their desirability, controllability, predictability, seriousness, and whether or not they occur simultaneously with other stressors, causing an overload of problems (Thoits, 1983; Walker, 1985). Events are most stressful when undesired, unanticipated, sudden, serious, and when they occur in conjunction with other stressors. Having problems with a child, for example, may be a relatively short-lived stressor lasting only a few days or weeks, or can be an ongoing chronic concern that lasts several months or even years. Events that dash hopes for the future, bring to mind past failures, are impossible to find information about, or resist our best problem-solving attempts are especially trying.

A number of scales have been developed to help people evaluate the amount, kind, and intensity of life events. The Social Adjustment Rating Scale is one of the most popular. It assigns a number to each life event based on the amount of change or adjustment required and totals them for an overall stress score (see Table 13-1). The assumption is that the more life events that occur and the higher their numerical value, the greater the risk to mental and physical health. Life events such as the death of a marital partner, marital separation, divorce, and serving a jail term are considered the most disruptive and thus receive higher stress scores than other events.

One criticism of the Social Adjustment Rating Scale is that it does not acknowledge that many life events can be anticipated and planned for, thus reducing their stress potential. The scale also overlooks the impact of social factors like ethnicity, class, gender, and economic resources, which have been shown to affect stress outcomes. Nor does the scale take into consideration that some stressful events have both positive and negative results. In some cases, positive outcomes outweigh and temper the negative effects. Nevertheless, this scale has a wide following and enjoys extensive use.

Persistent Hardships

Unlike life events which occur, make an impact, are adjusted to, and are then usually over, *persistent hardships* are the problems that affect us on an almost daily basis over long periods of time—poverty, marital con-

flict, parental problems, ongoing illness. There is no sense of finality, only a sense of repeated assault. Chronic strain and daily hassles are two persistent hardships that have been studied throughout the 1980s and 1990s.

Chronic Strain

There are several sources of *chronic strain*. One of the most troublesome involves having too many responsibilities and not enough time to get everything done—*role overload* (Pearlin, 1989). Dual-earner couples, single parents, and caregivers of frail elders frequently complain of feeling like their work is never done; that they rarely have time to themselves.

Another source of chronic strain is *role overlap*—when key life roles are shared with others or complement the roles of others. For example, the roles of wife and husband, parent and child, worker and supervisor overlap and supplement one another. Problems occur when there are ongoing clashes over how these shared roles should be enacted—parents may disagree over how their children should be raised; a parent may struggle with an adolescent child over how to dress, whom to date, when to do homework; employees sometimes have regular conflicts with bosses over job hours, health benefits, or working conditions. These various interpersonal conflicts create strain and take a toll on well-being.

A third source of chronic strain emerges from *role conflict*—having to choose between the demands of two very important roles. Strain is especially acute when choosing to satisfy the responsibilities of one role means neglecting the other. In dual-earner and single-parent families, people often complain about how job demands consume so much time that family activities sometimes get slighted. And new parents report that child-care responsibilities consume so many hours that they are hard-pressed to find time for marital roles—talking to, listening to, and caring for each other.

Chronic strain is also created by *role captivity*—feeling trapped in a role. Although retirees, homemakers, and caregivers of elderly family members say there are many positive aspects of their lives, many also report feeling entangled in responsibilities that cause them discomfort and sometimes offer more burdens than benefits.

A final source of chronic strain is *role restructuring*—when someone has matured to the extent that she or he needs to leave a role, but others are reluctant to acknowledge the need for change (Pearlin, 1989). The

TABLE 13-1
The Social Adjustment Rating Scale

Which of these life events have you experienced in the past 6 months—or do you expect to experience in the next 6 months? After checking the appropriate boxes, go back and add up the point values. A score over 300 indicates that your health may be at risk. Perhaps you need to take measures to lower your stress level.

Life Event	Past 6 Mos.	Value	Future 6 Mos.	Life Event	Past 6 Mos.	Value	Future 6 Mos.
Death of spouse	☐	100	☐	Outstanding personal achievement	☐	28	☐
Divorce	☐	73	☐	Wife beginning or ceasing work outside the home	☐	26	☐
Marital separation from mate	☐	65	☐	Beginning or ceasing formal schooling	☐	26	☐
Detention in jail or other institution	☐	63	☐	Major change in living conditions (e.g., building a new home, remodeling, deterioration of home or neighborhood)	☐	25	☐
Death of a close family member	☐	63	☐
Major personal injury or illness	☐	53	☐	Revision of personal habits (dress, manners, association, etc.)	☐	24	☐
Marriage	☐	50	☐
Being fired at work	☐	47	☐	Troubles with the boss	☐	23	☐
Marital reconciliation with mate	☐	45	☐	Major change in working hours or conditions	☐	20	☐
Retirement from work	☐	45	☐	Change in residence	☐	20	☐
Major change in the health or behavior of a family member	☐	44	☐	Changing to a new school	☐	20	☐
Pregnancy	☐	40	☐	Major change in usual type and/or amount of recreation	☐	19	☐
Sexual difficulties	☐	39	☐	Major change in church activities (e.g., a lot more or a lot less than usual)	☐	19	☐
Gaining a new family member (e.g., through birth, adoption, oldster moving in, etc.)	☐	39	☐	Major change in social activities (e.g., clubs, dancing, movies, visiting, etc.)	☐	18	☐
Major business readjustment (e.g., merger, reorganization, bankruptcy, etc.)	☐	39	☐	Taking out a mortage or loan for a lesser purchase (e.g., for a car, TV, freezer, etc.)	☐	17	☐
Major change in financial state (e.g., a lot worse off or a lot better off then usual)	☐	38	☐	Major change in sleeping habits (a lot more or a lot less sleep, or change in part of day when asleep)	☐	16	☐
Death of a close friend	☐	37	☐
Changing to a different line of work	☐	36	☐
Major change in the number of arguments with spouse (e.g., either a lot more or a lot less than usual regarding child rearing, personal habits, etc.)	☐	35	☐	Major change in number of family get-togethers (e.g., a lot more or less than usual)	☐	15	☐
Taking out a mortgage or loan for a major purchase (e.g., for a home, business, etc.)	☐	31	☐	Major change in eating habits (a lot more or a lot less food intake, or very different meal hours or surroundings)	☐	15	☐
Foreclosure on a mortgage or loan	☐	30	☐	Vacation	☐	13	☐
Major change in responsibilities at work (e.g., promotion, demotion, lateral transfer)	☐	29	☐	Christmas	☐	12	☐
Son or daughter leaving home (e.g., marriage, attending college, etc.)	☐	29	☐	Minor violations of the law (e.g., traffic tickets, jaywalking, disturbing the peace, etc.)	☐	11	☐
In-law troubles	☐	29	☐

SOURCE: T. H. Holmes & R. H. Rahe (1967).

Poverty is a chronic strain that grinds away at the spirit as stressors accumulate and resources are limited.

young adult who keeps reminding everyone that she is being treated like a child by her family, and the apprentice who learns his job, but is refused new work responsibilities are examples of this kind of strain.

Not all persistent hardships emerge from social roles. Some constitute the overall structure of people's lives—for example, having a life-threatening illness that requires protracted care, a physical disability that severely limits movement, living in a low-income family that must constantly struggle to make ends meet, or residing in a neighborhood where crime and drug abuse are pervasive. And some hardships are only hassles that are nonthreatening but still bothersome.

Daily Hassles

Daily hassles—those "small," annoying, practical problems that are part of everyday life, like losing the car keys, having someone push ahead of you in line, sitting behind a loud, nonstop talker at the movies, getting a parking ticket, or receiving an unexpectedly large phone bill. Unlike chronic strain, hassles are not necessarily related to a particular role, but they can

nevertheless result in distress (Kanner, Coyne, Schaefer, & Lazarus, 1981) (see Table 13-2).

Stressor Pileup

Although we have presented each type of stressor as individually problematic, it is their collective pileup that leads to high stress. The effect of life events magnify the impact of chronic strains and daily hassles and vice versa. It would not be unusual in the 1990s for a mid-life couple already struggling with the chronic strains of balancing two jobs (see Chapter 7) to be faced with caring for an increasingly frail grandparent, and at the same time to have a son leaving for college, and a daughter struggling with an eating disorder. The result is stressor pileup or stress overload.

Not all people experiencing these identical stressors or even a pileup of stressors are equally troubled, however. The meaning people attach to stressful circumstances greatly affects their impact.

APPRAISAL: THREAT, HARM, OR CHALLENGE?

Appraisal—one's judgment about whether or not a particular stressor is a threat, based on past experiences as well as current options and resources—is another integral component of the stress process. Such judgments determine the variety and depth of stress reactions as well as decisions about how to handle the problem. The more accurate the appraisal, the more efficient the coping response.

Appraisal occurs in two stages—primary and secondary—and determines whether the stressor should be ignored, investigated further, or acted on immediately (Lazarus & Folkman, 1984; Folkman & Lazarus, 1988).

Primary Appraisal: What's at Stake?

Primary appraisal is the initial evaluation of the seriousness of a stressor as *irrelevant* ("Nothing to worry about; will have no effect on how I function"); *benign-positive* ("Nothing to worry about; I can handle it and the result will likely be positive"); or *stressful* ("Definitely worry; my resources may be drained"). If an event is appraised as stressful, it is usually because it

TABLE 13-2
The Daily Hassles Scale

Hassles are irritants—events that are annoying or bothersome; they often lead to upset or angry feelings. Think about how much of a hassle each item is for you today by circling the appropriate number. 0 = none or not applicable; 1 = somewhat; 2 = quite a bit; 3 = a great deal. A higher score means you are under greater stress.

0 1 2 3 . . . Misplacing or losing things	0 1 2 3 . . . Silly mistakes
0 1 2 3 . . . Troublesome neighbors	0 1 2 3 . . . Inability to express yourself
0 1 2 3 . . . Social obligations	0 1 2 3 . . . Physical illness
0 1 2 3 . . . Inconsiderate smokers	0 1 2 3 . . . Physical appearance
0 1 2 3 . . . Troubling thoughts about your future	0 1 2 3 . . . Concerns about health
0 1 2 3 . . . Thoughts about death	0 1 2 3 . . . Not seeing enough people
0 1 2 3 . . . Health of a family member	0 1 2 3 . . . Friends or relatives too far away
0 1 2 3 . . . Not enough money for clothing	0 1 2 3 . . . Preparing meals
0 1 2 3 . . . Not enough money for housing	0 1 2 3 . . . Wasting time
0 1 2 3 . . . Concerns about owing money	0 1 2 3 . . . Filling out forms
0 1 2 3 . . . Concerns about getting credit	0 1 2 3 . . . Not getting enough rest
0 1 2 3 . . . Cutting down on electricity, water, etc.	0 1 2 3 . . . Not getting enough sleep
0 1 2 3 . . . Smoking too much	0 1 2 3 . . . Problems with your lover
0 1 2 3 . . . Use of alcohol	0 1 2 3 . . . Too many things to do
0 1 2 3 . . . Use of drugs	0 1 2 3 . . . Unchallenging work
0 1 2 3 . . . Too many responsibilities	0 1 2 3 . . . Concerns about meeting high standards
0 1 2 3 . . . Care of pet(s)	0 1 2 3 . . . Gossip
0 1 2 3 . . . Planning meals	0 1 2 3 . . . Legal problems
0 1 2 3 . . . Trouble relaxing	0 1 2 3 . . . Not enough personal energy
0 1 2 3 . . . Trouble making decisions	0 1 2 3 . . . Feel conflicted over what to do
0 1 2 3 . . . Problems getting along with others	0 1 2 3 . . . Regrets over past decisions
0 1 2 3 . . . Customers or clients give you a hard time	0 1 2 3 . . . The weather
0 1 2 3 . . . Concerns about job security	0 1 2 3 . . . Difficulties with friends
0 1 2 3 . . . Don't like current work duties	0 1 2 3 . . . Not enough time for family
0 1 2 3 . . . Don't like fellow workers	0 1 2 3 . . . Prejudice and discrimination from others
0 1 2 3 . . . Not enough money for basic necessities	0 1 2 3 . . . Not enough time for recreation
0 1 2 3 . . . Too many interruptions	0 1 2 3 . . . Concerns about news events
0 1 2 3 . . . Too much time on hands	0 1 2 3 . . . Crime
0 1 2 3 . . . Having to wait	0 1 2 3 . . . Traffic
0 1 2 3 . . . Being lonely	

SOURCE: Items taken from A. Kanner et al. (1981).

is perceived as *threatening* ("I will probably be hurt by this"); *harmful* ("I will definitely be hurt by this"); or *challenging* ("This will be difficult, but I may benefit in the long run") (Lazarus & Folkman, 1984).

When a stressor is appraised as a challenge—has the potential of being uplifting, something from which esteem and satisfaction may be gained—positive emotions like excitement, even eagerness, are aroused. Under these conditions it is easier to retain a sense of control and believe that problems are solvable.

Negative emotions like fear and anxiety are triggered by appraisals of threat or harm. At stake may be losses of self-esteem, autonomy, status, prestige, economic well-being, or a long-term relationship. Other losses could include being rejected by a valued friend, separating from a parent or spouse, psychological pain, physical punishment, or even death. The more severe the anticipated loss, the more stressful the response and the less likely the person is to view the problem as something she or he can handle.

There are times when a stressor can be appraised as both a threat and a challenge. When a dual-career couple decides to move to a new location because of a terrific job offer for the husband, the employed wife may feel threatened for several reasons. At stake are prized friendships and community connections. Disgruntled children may further complicate the picture. But the move may also threaten the wife's professional

Employment is very satisfying to most women; therefore, any hint of job loss or disruption is typically appraised as potentially threatening.

goals. She is likely to feel that her entire career is at stake. Ongoing conflict between the spouses over the move and its consequences may even pose a threat to the marital relationship.

For the husband, the family move is tied to a promotion. The new job has the potential of bringing benefits like increased knowledge and skills, responsibility, recognition, and income; but it also brings the risk of alienating family members and overloading him with fresh demands. In addition, he may worry about not being able to measure up to the new work expectations.

Secondary Appraisal: What Coping Resources Are Available?

The next stage in the appraisal process, *secondary appraisal*, involves determining what options are available for dealing with the stressor ("What can I do about this?"). A stressor arouses greater distress if the demands of the situation are seen as being beyond the resources available ("I don't see how in the world I can manage this. Why must everything happen at once?"). Secondary appraisals result in coping attempts.

COPING RESOURCES

A rich system of *coping resources*—assets, skills, personal characteristics, or energies—are engaged as protective barriers when stressors are perceived as threatening (Hobfoll, 1989; Hobfoll, Freedy, & Geller, 1990). Coping resources have three main components: what we have, who we are, and what we do (Pearlin, 1989; Pearlin & Schooler, 1978). Table 13-3 summarizes the coping resources available to individuals.

What We Have: Skills, Abilities, Assets

Interpersonal skills like being competent in social situations—when meeting new people, communicating feelings and needs to others, negotiating with family members and work colleagues for needed changes—are useful coping resources. They make it possible to enlist cooperation and support and give greater control over social interaction. Financial assets such as income earned, savings accumulated, property owned, as well as job status and education level are other coping re-

TABLE 13-3
Individual Coping Resources

WHAT WE HAVE
Intellect and knowledge
Analytic and "people" skills
Ability to communicate
Ability to negotiate
Access to social support
Physical and mental health
Income and financial assets
Social status
Education

WHO WE ARE
Self-esteem
Mastery
Personality traits
Hardiness
Sense of coherence

WHAT WE DO
Coping strategies used (for example, problem solving, distancing, confronting)

SOURCES: P. Boss (1987); P. Dyk & J. Schvaneveldt (1986); L. Pearlin (1989); R. S. Lazarus & S. Folkman (1984); H. McCubbin et al. (1988).

sources. The combined effect of what we have provides some sense of independence and control—a feeling that life can be met head on and stressors can be dealt with.

Having less income, education, and job status means having fewer coping options. People who lack resources are most at risk of having additional losses. Following a divorce, for example, many women are too economically disadvantaged to upgrade their job skills or seek more education. As a result, they are likely to suffer even greater economic downturns. Feelings of malaise, powerlessness, and a sense of fatalism are activated by being less able to manage personal and family problems.

Low-income families do not fare as well as their middle-class counterparts when faced with a sudden tragedy or unexpected life event (Ulbrich, Warheit, & Zimmerman, 1989). Among low-income black families, in particular, kin and friends form a supportive network for survival (see Chapter 10). This coping resource functions as an insulator against poverty. When unexpected life events occur, however, the network, already stretched to the maximum by chronic daily stressors, is less able to provide help.

The ongoing struggle many low-income families face to pay the bills, feed and clothe the family, and provide a secure home in a safe neighborhood takes a toll. Such daily hardships are tied to "feeling run down, tired, and having no energy; feeling that everything is an effort, that the future is hopeless, that you can't shake the blues. Nagging worries make for restless sleep and there isn't much to enjoy in life" (Ross, Mirowsky, & Goldsteen, 1991, p. 353).

Who We Are: Traits and Beliefs

Besides differences in the types of coping skills and competencies possessed, psychological makeup also has a lot to do with how stress is experienced.

Psychological Resources

Over the years various psychological resources have proven to be significant barriers to stress. Two of the most prominent are *self-esteem*—a positive assessment of self-competence and worth, and *mastery*—a sense of having control over what happens in one's life. These resources represent some of the things people *are*, independent of the particular skills and abilities they possess (Bird & Harris, 1990).

Another frequently researched psychological resource is personality type. Individuals with a *type A personality* have a hurried lifestyle; push themselves to do things at work and/or at home faster and better than others, consistently set goals that are almost out of reach, and believe that their personal worth depends nearly totally on how much they can accomplish. After years of being viewed as less resistant to stress than less-driven others, researchers have discovered that type As are relatively healthy so long as they are not angry and hostile.

Hurried persons tend to react with impatience, hostility, and even anger if their goals are blocked. Built-up, unexpressed anger is linked to heart disease, stroke, and other debilitating diseases. People who are easygoing tend to be better at problem solving and less often try to avoid or distance themselves from life's difficulties (Holahan & Moos, 1987; Rodin & Salovey, 1989).

A Personal Belief System

In addition to personality traits, some personal beliefs also help people resist stress (Folkman, 1984). Personal philosophies ("I'm a survivor, I always bounce back"; "Don't let the turkeys get you down"; "Next year has to be better"; "You have to take the bad with the good"; and "Things always work out for the best") guide individuals through troubled times.

Hardiness is what Susan Kobasa and colleagues labeled the personal belief system she discovered when comparing "healthy" to "stressed-out" executives (Kobasa, 1979; Kobasa, Maddi, & Kahn, 1982; Maddi & Kobasa, 1984). Hardiness described executives displaying a strong commitment to self, a rigorous approach to life, a sense that the world has meaning, and that life can be mastered. Further studies by Kobasa have confirmed that hardiness is a coping resource used by others besides executives.

Aaron Antonovsky (1979, 1987) has also identified a personal belief system which he calls a *sense of coherence* (SOC). Sense of coherence is the "pervasive, enduring feeling of confidence that one's internal and external environments are predictable and that there is a high probability that things will work out as well as can reasonably be expected" (1979, p. 123). What both Kobasa and Antonovsky found was that personal commitments and beliefs—the generalized way people look at the world—play a central role in stress resistance. People like to believe that their world is predictable and benevolent.

Personal beliefs, goals, and commitments to a large extent influence stress reactions. Studies of rape, for example, show that rape shatters a woman's belief that the world is basically a safe place. Women tend to believe that if they follow the rules—"avoid walking in certain neighborhoods, do not walk alone at night . . . avoid hitchhiking"—and develop other protective strategies, they will be safe (Janoff-Bluman & Frieze, 1987, p. 162). Rape damages self-esteem, causes self-doubt, and brings into question the basic goodness of others. Part of the recovery from a rape experience rests on rebuilding and reestablishing a positive belief system about the self and the outside world.

What We Do: Actions Taken

The active efforts made to avoid, prevent, manage, or control stressors and prevent them from resulting in stress are collectively referred to as *coping strategies* and reliance on a particular set of strategies creates a distinct *coping style*. For example, those who cope with stressors by consistently keeping their feelings to themselves, trying not to act too hastily, and trying not to "burn their bridges" illustrate a style called self-control. Those who cope by hoping a miracle will happen, wishing the situation would go away, and fantasizing about how things might turn out display a style called escape-avoidance (see Table 13-4). Psychologists Richard Lazarus and Susan Folkman (1984) have identified seven coping styles made up of 43 separate coping strategies which they call ways of coping.

STRATEGIES AND STYLES OF COPING

Emotion-Focused Coping

When presented with a stressor, the first reaction after appraisal (irrelevant, benign-positive, stressful) is usually emotional. Stirred up emotions quickly make people aware of just how serious a particular stressor is to their well-being and affects how they ultimately cope with a problem. Some of the first coping strategies employed are ones that function to control emotional distress. Until the emotions are calmed, problem-solving strategies cannot be properly mobilized.

Emotion-focused coping, then, consists of the strategies employed to regulate the intense feelings aroused by a stressor. One way of calming the emotions is to alter the meaning of the stressor. If the stressor is viewed as less catastrophic, the person's sense of control will be heightened and his or her stress reduced. "Strategies used for this purpose include devaluing what is at stake ('Passing the exam really doesn't matter much'); focusing on the positive aspects of negative outcomes ('I'm a stronger person for having gone through this'); and engaging in positive comparisons ('It could have been much worse' or 'I'm a lot better off than the other guy')" (Folkman, 1984, p. 844). Styles of coping that are emotion-focused include: distancing, escape-avoidance, self-control, and accepting responsibility.

Problem-Focused Coping

Problem-focused coping consists of the efforts activated to alter, deflect, or in some way manage the stressor itself through direct action. Styles of problem-focused coping include: confronting and problem solving. Seeking social support can be either emotion-focused or problem-focused, depending on whether support is sought to reduce emotional distress—seeking out someone merely to listen to problems—or is sought for

TABLE 13-4
Ways of Coping

ACCEPTING RESPONSIBILITY	ESCAPE-AVOIDANCE
Criticized or lectured myself.	Wished that the situation would go away or somehow be over with.
Realized I brought the problem on myself.	Hoped a miracle would happen.
Made a promise to myself that things would be different next time.	Had fantasies about how things might turn out.
Apologized or did something to make up.	Tried to make myself feel better by eating, drinking, smoking, using drugs, or medication, and so forth.

CONFRONTING	
Stood my ground and fought for what I wanted.	Avoided being with people in general.
Tried to get the person responsible to change his or her mind.	Refused to believe that it had happened.
Expressed anger to the person(s) who caused the problem.	Took it out on other people.
Let my feelings out somehow.	Slept more than usual.
Took a big chance or did something very risky.	
Did something which I didn't think would work, but at least I was doing something.	PROBLEM SOLVING

DISTANCING	Knew what had to be done, so doubled my efforts to make things work.
Made light of the situation; refused to get too serious about it.	Made a plan of action and followed it.
Went on as if nothing had happened.	Just concentrated on what I had to do next—the next step.
Didn't let it get to me; refused to think about it too much.	Changed something so things would turn out all right.
Tried to forget the whole thing.	Drew on my past experiences; I was in a similar position before.
Looked for the silver lining, so to speak; tried to look on the bright side of things.	Came up with a couple of different solutions to the problem.
Went along with fate; sometimes I just have bad luck.	

SEEKING SOCIAL SUPPORT	SELF-CONTROL
Talked to someone to find out more about the situation.	Tried to keep my feelings to myself.
Talked to someone who could do something concrete about the problem.	Kept others from knowing how bad things were.
Asked a relative or friend I respected for advice.	Tried not to burn my bridges, but leave things open somewhat.
Talked to someone about how I was feeling.	Tried not to act too hastily or follow my first hunch.
Accepted sympathy and understanding from someone.	Tried to keep my feelings from interfering with other things too much.
Got professional help.	Went over in my mind what I would say or do.
	Thought about how a person I admire would handle the situation and used that as a model.

SOURCE: S. Folkman, R. S. Lazarus, J. Dunkel-Schetter, A. DeLongis, & R. Gruen (1986).

problem solving—advice is not only sought out but is also followed (Lazarus & Folkman, 1984; Folkman & Lazarus, 1988).

Understanding the Coping Process

The following two examples illustrate the coping process. Picture a man trapped in a car that has just been partially crushed by a concrete bridge pillar during an earthquake. Although his physical wounds are not life threatening, he is emotionally incapacitated by the emergency. Many minutes pass before he is able to

reduce his emotional distress—anxiety and fear—to the point where he can begin to think clearly. He repeats to himself, "You're not seriously hurt. Now, take control and find a way out of this thing."

As his emotions are gradually eased, the man initiates some problem-focused strategies. He decides to call out at regular intervals in the hope that someone nearby might hear him. He also tries to dig his way out through the pile of debris. After discovering that he cannot extract himself from the wreckage after multiple tries, his anxiety reemerges and he must once again rely on emotion-focused coping to combat the tension—singing favorite songs, meditating, telling himself that help will arrive soon. These coping strategies may work until help arrives or until he renews his quest for an escape route.

Under stress of a different kind is a woman who finds a lump in her breast. She repeats emotionally calming phrases to herself—"I'm going to be okay. Most lumps are benign"—and she telephones a friend. The friend drives over and her reassuring hugs and verbally calming reassurance further reduce the emotional trauma. Calmed, the woman is able to launch some problem-focused coping strategies. She calls her physician and makes an appointment for a mammogram. She will have to wait several days for an appointment. And, after the mammogram, she will have to wait several additional days for the test results. If the lump looks suspicious, she will suffer further anxiety waiting for a biopsy and its results. At each stage she will need to quiet her emotions in order to carry out her daily routine.

In both examples, the man and woman initially used emotion-focused coping to reduce their apprehension. Once their emotions were reigned in, problem-focused coping was more easily employed. The man tried to find a way out; the woman called her physician. Anxiety, fear, frustration, and anger tend to block thinking and reasoning abilities and hinder the deployment of problem-solving skills. Emotion-focused coping did not alter the fact that the man was trapped, or that the woman's health was endangered, but they did allow both to feel calmer, more comfortable, and more in control of their situations. The ability to assess alternatives and make plans were then enhanced.

Emotion-focused and problem-focused coping are used in combination during most stressful situations. The degree to which each type of coping is used depends, for the most part, on the appraised stressfulness of the situation. Situations appraised as controllable and changeable prompt the use of problem-focused coping, while situations seen as uncontrollable and unchangeable trigger the use of more emotion-focused coping. The man in the car appraised his situation as controllable and changeable and was able to think of some ways to escape. If he finds after several attempts that there is little hope and he begins to become dehydrated from lack of water and food, his appraisal may change and he may rely more heavily on emotion-focused coping.

Coping is a process that is ongoing and ever-changing. It consists of the many actions taken to deal with a stressor or series of stressors. As the demands of the situation unfold and change, so do the strategies of coping. Coping does not ensure a successful outcome because not all situations permit a just or reasonable solution.

Successful Coping

Relying on Habit or Routine

The two examples given involve people dealing with sudden life-threatening problems that require immediate attention. Other life problems appear more regularly and are less intense. When people deal with the same problems at regular intervals—for example, when a child comes down with a fever or a cold and cannot attend school and parents must find alternative care—they generally rely on their same comfortable routine or habitual ways of coping. Perhaps a grandparent lives nearby or a neighbor can be relied on in a pinch or there is a community nursing service for sick children. Whatever the choices, parents reason that if something worked in the past, it will most likely work again. Successful copers take advantage of past experiences by identifying effective coping strategies and sticking with them.

Matching the Coping Strategy to the Situation

All coping strategies do not work equally well across different stressful situations. Using a coping strategy that produces good results on the job may have no effect or a negative effect if used at home (Mattlin, Wethington, & Kessler, 1990; Pearlin & Schooler, 1978). Successful work strategies might include ignoring a supervisor's bad mood, controlling the impulse to say something negative, and distancing oneself from the problem by avoiding further personal contact. Use of these same strategies at home could lead to increased marital conflict and feelings of dissatisfaction and unhappiness (Bird & Wakat, 1993). Intimate relationships require interaction. At home, distancing and avoiding result in greater stress. Matching the coping strategy to the situation requires a period of trial and error until skill is developed.

Being Flexible

The more coping strategies known and employed, within reason, the more stress resistant the person

(Mattlin et al., 1990). Successful copers tend to have a repertoire of strategies, so when one method of dealing with a problem fails, another can quickly be substituted.

A man makes a reservation at a favorite restaurant for Wednesday evening. He knows that his wife has a hectic day planned and will be in need of some rest and relaxation. It is her dinner night, but he knows she will be tired and have a low tolerance for frustration. By helping her relax, he will gain a more attentive and rested partner. And he really needs to talk to her about something important later in the evening, so it is to his benefit as well as hers that she is fresh and alert.

Arriving home, the wife is carrying a bag of Chinese takeout food, a bottle of wine, and a new ice bag. Her head is pounding and her feet hurt. She also has a contract in her briefcase that she needs to read for a presentation the next day. At first the husband feels deflated, defeated, and tense. He quickly regroups, however, and without telling her about his plans for the evening, disappears into the bedroom and calls the restaurant to cancel the reservation. He then returns to the kitchen, insists that she sit down as he readies the food. After they eat, he suggests that she take a long bath, and he then volunteers to give her a back rub. After the back rub, he tells her about his problem and she listens and offers comfort and advice. Later, she reads the contract. The evening has been saved. Successful copers are flexible and always keep a forward flow of energy focused on the problem.

THE ROLE OF SOCIAL SUPPORT

If coping can be described as the things that people do on their own behalf to reduce stress, then *social support* may be viewed as the things others do to help friends, kin, and colleagues resist stress (Pearlin & Turner, 1987). Helpful others listen and say comforting things ("It will all work out for the best"); discourage worrying ("Let's rent the funniest videos we can find, put our feet up, and laugh ourselves unconscious"); identify ways to redefine or resolve problems ("I had the same problem once and I . . ."). Supportive others provide a place where, when hurting, people can fall back and regroup. (For additional information see Chapter 10.)

Feelings of closeness and intimacy usually lead to a reduction in stress and facilitate engagement of coping strategies (Kobasa & Puccetti, 1983). People with spouses, friends, and family members who provide psychological and material assistance are generally in better health than those with fewer social contacts.

Social Support as Process: Marriage as an Example

The spouse is the primary confidant of most married people. When a wife or husband withholds support or neglects her or his supportive function in the marriage, there seems to be no satisfying substitute. Even friends and relatives may not fill the void because the marital bond is somehow special. A qualitative study of married couples by sociologists Leonard Pearlin and Mary McCall (1990) identifies four stages in the process of giving and receiving marital support and explains why this support sometimes does not lead to a reduction in stress.

Stage 1: Revelation–Recognition (What Is the Problem?)

In stage 1 of the social support process, the distressed spouse somehow reveals that support is needed. He or she is looking for comfort, reassurance, and, perhaps, advice. The partner may be told immediately and directly, informed after some time has passed, or may make the discovery through nonverbal cues—sad looks, quiet reflective poses, deep sighs, slammed doors, banged pots and pans, and so forth.

When feelings of distress are concealed, it is usually for several reasons: to protect the spouse ("If she knew, she would be upset, too"); to take personal responsibility for the problem ("I think it's my responsibility to take care of my own problems"); or to protect privacy ("There are certain things that I could never share with anyone"). Sometimes spouses think that their partners do not really want to hear about their concerns ("My husband would be resentful if I took up his time to tell him about my problems. He thinks I spend too much time worrying about what's bothering me").

In other cases, the distressed spouse expects that the support given would be inappropriate for the situation and only add to their stress ("She's always trying to tell me how to do my job. I'm sure she would just love to give me advice that I can't use"). Finally, some fear that they would suffer a loss of self-esteem if their partner judged them as the cause of their own predicament ("Joe has told me repeatedly that I need to stand up for myself. If he knew that I was passed over for promotion again, he would say it was my own fault").

Stage 2: Appraisal (Does the Problem Deserve Support?)

In the second stage of the social support process, the partner judges whether or not the problem is a legitimate concern that deserves support. In most cases support is given, but sometimes it is withheld. Why would support be refused? Perhaps the spouse has not "been there" in the partner's own time of need ("When my mother was ill and needed around-the-clock care, he didn't lift a finger to help me"). The spouse's needs may be judged as less immediate than those of other family members ("Marla has a science project, Josh has a music recital, and Rachel needs a sponsor for a home-room field trip. I just didn't have time to listen right then"). The partner may feel overloaded with his or her own problems or have "support burnout" from having already given so much. She or he may feel drained of compassion.

Stage 3: Selection of Support Type (What Kind of Support Is Needed?)

In most cases a partner will decide to offer support. Decisions are then made about what type of support is most needed—listening, asking questions and offering advice, showing esteem and affection, or providing a distraction. The type of support must match the needs of the distressed spouse.

A supportive partner is often credited with helping to clarify what is bothering her or his spouse, to "put into words the feelings I'm having" (Pearlin & McCall, 1990, p. 52). Supportive partners also help by pointing out alternative ways of coping with a problem ("You might try talking to her in a quiet and calm way") and reminding their spouses not to self-blame ("It's not your fault the pump failed. You told them two weeks ago that the seal was weak").

By focusing on personal strengths rather than failings, the supportive partner may be able to buttress the self-esteem of their distressed husband or wife ("You're the best nurse on that shift. Haven't you received two awards for excellence in the past three years?"). Support can also distract the spouse by providing a diversion to keep her or his mind occupied with something besides the problem ("Let's go to a movie tonight"; "How about a weekend at the lake?").

Stage 4: Evaluating the Outcome (Was the Support Successful?)

Most of the time, support is successfully given and stress is reduced. Despite the well-meaning intentions of others, however, support can sometimes have negative results (Belle, 1982; Wortman & Lehman, 1985). When support attempts are unsuccessful, it is usually because the type of support given was not appropriate for the situation. The partner gave advice when the spouse just wanted someone to listen, tried to take control of the problem as if it were his or her own, or gave advice that met his or her own personal needs rather than the needs of the spouse.

Whether or not social support is evaluated positively by the receiver also depends on the timing of the help provided (Was it offered as needed or was there a troublesome delay?); the nature and manner in which help is offered (Was it extended in a kind and benevolent way?); and the personality characteristics of both the giver and receiver of the support (Nadler & Fisher, 1986). In cases where the support given is viewed as inappropriate, the support receiver may suffer a loss of self-esteem, devalue the support provided, and respond by attacking the giver as insensitive, rude, or meanspirited.

Research suggests that persons with high self-esteem more often react negatively to offered support. They seem to "reject or devalue aid because it is incongruent with their self-perceptions of competence and self-reliance" (Barrera & Baca, 1990, p. 543). Sometimes support receivers regret the help because they know that it obligates them to return the favor. "One cannot receive support without also risking the costs of rejection, betrayal, burdensome dependence, and vicarious pain" (Belle, 1982, p. 143).

The Double Standard of Social Support

In our society, there is a double standard of social support. People expect their family and friends to feel comfortable coming to them for support, but they feel uneasy about seeking help from these same people (Hobfoll et al., 1990). When asked how they would provide support for a person in crisis, people seem to know what is expected. In actual encounters, however, they frequently behave in a manner that reduces their own distress, but increases the distress of the one in need (Kessler, Price, & Wortman, 1985). People, for example, insist on visiting hospitalized relatives at times when their absence would be more appreciated.

They give advice about medications and treatment that goes against the advice of the attending physician, bring food that is prohibited, and sometimes talk incessantly when silence would be more appropriate.

And those with the most severe problems and experiencing the greatest difficulty coping are least likely to receive support. Others tend to avoid persons under the most extreme stress because it makes them feel threatened and vulnerable. Cancer patients who exude a confident and happy demeanor receive greater support than those who are downcast and depressed about their progress. Apparently, sadness and depression in others reminds people of their own frailties and triggers feelings that they, too, could become ill and vulnerable. These aroused emotions make it difficult to approach and give support to the neediest of others (Peters-Golden, 1982).

DISTRESS: THE OUTCOME OF THE STRESS PROCESS

Because psychologists and physicians were among the first scientists to study stress, and many of their patients (clients) were in unusually stressful situations, depression and anxiety have traditionally been the two most frequently studied outcomes of the stress process (see Table 13-5). This perspective suited professionals whose primary interest was in diagnosing mental and physical health disorders and dysfunctional behavior.

But, the majority of people under stress do not experience such extreme symptoms. It is only when people sustain high stress levels over long periods and lack the coping resources to solve their problems that such chronic symptoms appear—low energy, inability to think clearly, lapses in being able to take care of routine daily tasks, ruptures in friendships and family relationships, flattened emotional responsiveness, and weakened resistance to illnesses.

Beginning in the 1980s, sociologists and other social scientists began to explore in earnest how stress was experienced in nonclinical populations. They described the consequences of stress in less pathological terms, identifying how average people in everyday situations experience stress and what behaviors were tied to stress resistance.

Distress is the term used most frequently to describe the psychological (*emotional distress*) and physiological (*physical distress*) outcomes of the stress process. Emo-

TABLE 13-5

Depression and Anxiety as Symptoms of Distress

	Depression	*Anxiety*
Emotional symptoms	Blue, low spirits, sad, lonely, feel your life is a failure, feel things never turn out, bothered by things that don't usually bother you, wish you were dead	Anxious, irritable, fearful, tense, worried
Physical symptoms	No appetite, trouble concentrating, trouble remembering, trouble sleeping, everything is an effort, can't get going, talk less	Heart beats hard, shortness of breath, fainting, dizziness, cold sweats, trembling hands, feel hot all over

SOURCE: Adapted from J. Mirowsky & C. Ross (1989), p. 22.

tional distress is reflected by feelings of uneasiness, nervousness, or restlessness; feeling pressured, worried, or upset. Physical distress is manifested by a "knotted" stomach, tension headache, tight chest, or pounding heart. When coping strategies are successful, people report high life satisfaction and few emotional or physical symptoms of distress. The individual stress process is thought to unfold as depicted in Figure 13-1.

When Stress Won't Go Away, Then What?

Sometimes, despite our best coping efforts, some degree of uneasiness, worry, tension, and frustration remains with us. There may be only so much a person can do to alter or change their situation; control may be limited. For example, a man who has lost his job and cannot find a replacement because of an economic downturn, returns home after a day of searching and feels frustrated, downhearted, and sad. His mind may be consumed with negative thoughts about his value and worth as a husband and father because of his inability to provide for his family. Feeling equally distressed is a woman who cares for her elderly mother whose mind and body are debilitated by Alzheimer's disease. She understands that her mother will not recover, she will need to provide daily care without much help for a very long time. She feels alone, worried, and overwhelmed by the tasks at hand.

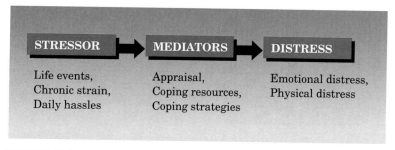

FIGURE 13-1
The Individual Stress Process

Friends and partners may offer words of encouragement and advice to this distressed pair, and each may be using many of the standard coping strategies to reduce distress, but there are only a few options available, and some of those may not be appropriate to their particular situations. The man may be limited by his education and training to certain types of jobs. The woman may not have the income to hire help with her caregiver tasks and may live far from relatives who could offer services and support.

When faced with chronic strain of this type, most people first try to persevere on their own, employing coping strategies that have served them well in the past. If these fail to reduce distress, most will then look outside of themselves for help. People generally turn to family and friends, then to their family physician or minister. These traditional sources of comfort may bring about dramatic reductions in individual distress, but sometimes more help is needed. Support or self-help groups fill this function for some. Support groups are considered "the second line of intervention" and can be divided into three types (Noshpitz, 1990).

1 *Self-Help Groups:* have a leader who teaches self-improvement and stress-reduction techniques like meditation, relaxation, or biofeedback.

2 *Mutual-Help Groups:* include organizations and associations like Alcoholics Anonymous (AA) where members support and help each other by means of shared experiences and coping skills.

3 *Peer-Help Groups:* have trained peers who work with targeted populations—at suicide hotlines, rape counseling centers, and centers for battered women.

Others turn to mental health professionals if alternative modes of intervention do not succeed in reducing their distress. Several types of individual, marital,

family, and group therapy have proven useful. Sometimes it is necessary to combine therapy with anti-anxiety medication or antidepressants prescribed by a licensed and trained professional (Kelly & Frosch, 1989).

GENDER AND STRESS

A key factor that complicates the interpretation of stress research, as well as health diagnoses and intervention practices, is gender. From the initial stressor, through appraisal, to coping, to eventual feelings of emotional and physical distress, the stress process functions differently for women and men.

Stressors

For men, employment roles provide the most potential for stress (Barnett & Baruch, 1987). Men are expected to display an unrelenting commitment to their jobs and compete for bonuses, raises, and promotions with aggressive determination. Men's work interactions are "task oriented, dominant, directive, and hierarchical" compared to women's (Aries, 1987, p. 170). Unemployment is particularly devastating to men. In the 1990s, even white-collar workers are not immune to this stressor (see the "Changing Lifestyles" box).

Since women began joining the workforce in ever-increasing numbers, the alarm has been sounded that they, like men, would soon begin to succumb to work-related stress diseases like hypertension and heart attacks. As we learned in Chapter 9, women make more job adjustments to accommodate family needs than men. They are more likely than men to experience layoffs and other career interruptions such as parental

CHANGING LIFESTYLES

White-Collar Workers: The New Unemployed

Tom Brown, 44, had been working as a regional comptroller when he got the news that he no longer had a job. "Management didn't want to talk to me after my position had been eliminated," he says. "They basically didn't want to know that I existed."

Terry Cantine, 49, was a product marketing manager when she got the ax last September. She's been brushing up on her computer skills, and she tells prospective employers she's willing to take a big pay cut, but nothing has turned up yet. Says Cantine: "My life was my job, but now I'm finding out how wrong that is."

James Kmetz was laid off last April after 4 years as a trust specialist. He received a 1-minute outplacement interview and no severance, and he has grown weary of hearing that his education and experience make him overqualified for the menial jobs he applies for.

You cannot miss the pain in these voices as a new generation of unemployed Americans describes the savage realities of today's job market. Pain compounded by shock—for these are typically the kinds of people who didn't lose jobs in past recessions. And the economy they've been thrown into is something their experience never prepared them for.

In particular, this downturn has been much tougher than past ones on older workers, who often have a harder time finding a new job, and on white-collar workers, who have long considered themselves immune to the harsh effects of business cycles.

More than 6 million people are working part time because they can't find a full-time job, and another million or so have simply given up looking for work. That means nearly 17 million people, or almost 12 percent of the labor force, are unemployed or underemployed.

One hears that being fired has lost its stigma, since most peple are beginning to recognize the change—it happens to everybody nowadays, right? Perhaps, but it still packs a wallop. Mike Meyers, 55, was a department head until he was laid off last June. He had been on the job for 11 years, since shortly after he retired from the Navy, and he's still trying to cope with the wrenching change in his life. "I'm pretty discouraged at the moment," he says. "Even the physical act of getting a résumé together has been tougher than I anticipated." I network, I call everyone I once knew as a business contact. I tell you, friendly people are not that friendly when you're out of a job."

For many of the newly unemployed, the loss of a job also means a diminished sense of self-worth and the loss of support and stimulus provided by colleagues. Ronald Spangler, 42, was laid off from a managerial job in city government just before Christmas. He recalls, with venom, feeling like an outsider when he attended holiday parties. "If you tell people you've been laid off, they start to pity you," he says. "You get treated like a nonperson, a nonentity. One of the gauges of who you are is your job."

Personal problems such as alcoholism and depression are common among the newly unemployed, and marriages are often strained. "Being unemployed is a full-time job," says Edoardo Leoncavallo, 56, a hotel architect. "There's a lot of stress to deal with, including family stress. I think my wife initially felt resentment. I think she felt, Why can't you bring home the bacon?"

EXPLORATIONS *Given that the job market changes identified here are stable trends, what advice would you give young adults about future job security? What long-term coping strategies would you recommend?*

SOURCE: Excerpted from K. Labich (1993).

leave and job mobility. Moreover, women are generally paid less and have fewer opportunities for job advancement than men. Women take more job risks, sacrifice more leisure time, and compromise career goals more often than men do. They absorb more of the pressure, frustration, and guilt caused by meshing work and family roles.

Nevertheless, results of several studies, including the federally funded Framingham Heart Study of 10,000 women and men over a 25-year period, show that the only group of employed women suffering increased heart disease are mothers with several children who work in low-paying clerical jobs. Such jobs have high demands and offer little control over working conditions (Barnett & Rivers, 1992).

For women, "paid work is actually associated with

reduced anxiety and depression" (Barnett & Rivers, 1992, p. 64). Compared to homemakers and employed men, employed women experience better physical health and lower death rates (Brenner & Levi, 1987; Verbrugge, 1983; Waldron & Jacobs, 1988). The sources of stress for women emerge primarily from taking major responsibility for marital and parental roles. This is especially true for women, who, because of poverty or other difficult social circumstances, feel like "bad mothers, bad providers, or bad spouses" (Belle, 1990, p. 886) (see the "Changing Lifestyles" box).

Appraisal

Socialization processes and life experiences combine to cause women to appraise their coping resources and ability to effect change in the family and at work as less adequate than men's. Women typically appraise life events and chronic strain as more threatening and less challenging than men do. Women are socialized to emotionally invest themselves in caring for others. Great joy can come from rearing children and providing a supportive marital environment, but there are also feelings of powerlessness that accompany caregiving. In the traditional view,

> if a woman's husband is unhappy, it is assumed to be due to her failings; if her children have problems, she is assumed to be at fault. . . . In spite of the reality that one has relatively little control over the welfare and happiness of another person, women are vulnerable to self-blame. . . . The combination of little control, relentless demands, and great responsibility exposes wives and mothers to many frustrations and failures and may account in part for the stressfulness of family roles. (Barnett & Baruch, 1987, p. 133)

Compounding the effects of normative life events like pregnancy, childbirth, menopause, and widowhood, women are also unduly threatened by some extraordinary life experiences such as sexual harassment, rape, marital violence, and incest, which can leave them feeling vulnerable and culminate in an erosion of their sense of having control over their lives.

Coping

Evidence has accumulated that women also cope differently than men. Men tend to make greater use of problem-focused coping. Women rely more often on emotion-focused strategies (crying, self-blaming,

seeking social support) and on techniques specifically directed toward reducing overall tension without directly attacking the source of the problem—meditation, relaxation exercises, jogging, aerobics, and so forth. In their book *Gender and Stress* (1987), Rosalind Barnett, Lois Biener, and Grace Baruch contend that women's reliance on emotion-focused coping is related to their appraisal of many life events and chronic strains as unchangeable and out of their immediate control.

Education seems to negate some gender differences in coping. The more education a woman has and the higher her job status, the more disposed she is to use problem-focused coping (Bird & Wakat, 1993; Schnittger & Bird, 1990). It appears that investments in education lead to enhanced employment opportunities and access to greater power and additional coping resources. Employed women regularly indicate that their work roles are an important source of satisfaction and well-being and consistently report less emotional distress than other women (Gove, 1984; Hall, Williams, & Greenberg, 1985; Kessler & McRae, 1982).

The Role of Marriage

Although we do not generally think of it that way, marriage is for both sexes a coping resource that increases stress resistance. The two primary ways that marriage improves well-being is through the supportive behavior of the marital partner and through the economic advantages provided by living in a two-income family.

Men seem to realize the biggest gains from marriage, probably because of an emotional support gap between spouses (Ross et al., 1991). Husbands are more likely than wives to say that their spouses appreciate what they do and understand them well. Wives are socialized to take good care of husbands—make sure they eat right, protect their privacy and leisure time against intrusions, cajole them into visiting the physician, and distract them from ruminating about lost opportunities, troublesome bosses, and stubborn children. (The Cathy cartoon on page 362 is about single life, but could easily be extended to cover many aspects of married life.)

Distress

Many more women than men report feeling emotionally distressed, especially being depressed (Eaton & Kessler, 1981; Fujita, Diener, & Sandvik, 1991; Landers,

CHANGING LIFESTYLES

Women in Poverty: The Stress Connection

Today, more Americans live below the poverty line than a decade ago, a phenomenon attributable to the increase in single-parent families headed by women, the concentration of most new jobs in the poorly paid service sector, the inadequacy of child support payments following divorce, unavailability of decent, affordable child care, lack of access to unemployment compensation, and the erosion of governmental economic assistance to low-income families. In addition, homelessness has also emerged in this decade as a major social problem, primarily among men, but also among significant numbers of women, typically those with young children.

The incidence of poverty is particular pronounced among minority families. Black women heading families face a risk of poverty that is more than 10 times that of white men heading families, and Puerto Rican female family heads face a poverty rate that is almost 15 times that found among white male family heads. Most people who become poor during some period of their lives only remain poor for one or two years, yet blacks and female family heads are at elevated risk of experiencing persistent poverty.

Women who live in financially strained circumstances and who have responsibility for young children are more likely than other women to experience symptoms of depression. High levels of depressive symptoms were found to be particularly common among women without confidants, child-rearing assistance, or employment and among women experiencing chronic stressful conditions, particularly those reflecting economic problems.

The association between poverty and poor mental health is not surprising when one considers that poverty imposes considerable stress on individuals and families while also attacking many potential sources of social support. Poor women experience more frequent, more threatening, and more uncontrollable life events than does the general population. Poor women are disproportionately exposed to crime and violence, to the illness and death of children, and to the imprisonment of husbands. Minority women are additionally exposed to discrimination, including discrimination-provoked violence.

Although rapid, uncontrollable change is one important source of stress, stress also results from persistent, undesirable conditions that must be endured daily. Chronic life conditions such as inadequate housing, dangerous neighborhoods, burdensome responsibilities, and financial uncertainties can be even more

1988). Women more often seek professional help for stress-related problems and are more likely than men to frequent stress clinics and receive prescribed medications for stress reduction. They are more likely to be labeled as anxious or depressed by physicians and therapists and treated for these symptoms.

When feeling distressed, women are encouraged to look within themselves for evidence of personal failures rather than examining larger societal influences on their behavior. Antidepressants are frequently prescribed to quiet women without dealing with the causes behind their problems (Biener, 1987). Approximately 70 percent of all antidepressants and tranquilizers are prescribed to women (Rodin & Ickovics, 1990). One woman refers to the obvious gender contradictions of her medication:

I take them to protect the family from my irritability because "kids are kids." I don't think it's fair for me to start yelling at them because their normal activity is bothering me. My husband says I overreact. . . . I'm an emotional person, more so than my husband who's an engineer and very calm and logical—he thinks. . . . So I take the Valium to keep me calm. . . . Frankly the kids get on his nerves, too. But he will not take anything. . . . He blows his top. . . . When I blow my top I am told to settle down. When he does it, it's perfectly alright. (Cooperstock & Lannard, 1979, p. 335)

Although society is more accepting of anger from males than females, most suffer stress in silence, as this is the masculine role expectation. Men usually withdraw from social connections and try to cope on their

potent stressors than acute crises and events. Low income women are at very high risk of experiencing just such noxious, long-term conditions.

When stressful life events and conditions occur, the woman who can share her troubles with a supportive confidant or circle of friends is less likely to be overwhelmed by them. Timely instrumental aid often can prevent a crisis from becoming a catastrophe and can prevent a stressful event from becoming a chronically stressful condition. Many poor women create mutual aid networks through which they care for and sustain each other in times of stress. Such networks are truly "strategies for survival" in a hostile world.

Yet poverty often exacts a toll on a woman's support system. The intimacy of the marital bond is often strained or broken by economic stress. Divorce is particularly common in families in which men provide very low or sporadic income. Parents living below the poverty line are less likely to be happily married than those above the poverty line, and low-income women are less likely than middle-class women to turn to their husbands as confidants, particularly during the phase of the life cycle when there are young children at home. Undermined social relationships are one of the crucial links between poverty and depression.

Poverty often enforces shared living quarters on those who would prefer to live apart, could they afford to do so. Poor women have few material resources to share with friends and relatives, and these friends and relatives are likely to experience crises and catastrophes that make material aid essential. For women with little income and little education, large social networks generally exact higher costs than they repay through the provision of supportive resources.

Women's coping strategies are constrained by poverty. To be poor generally means that one is frighteningly dependent on bureaucratic institutions such as the welfare system, public housing authority, the health-care system, and the courts. Poor women who must seek assistance from such systems often experience repeated failures that reflect no lack of imagination or effort on the woman's part, merely the fact that a powerful institution declined to respond. Repeated instances of such failure, however, may lead to the perception that one is indeed powerless to remove the major stressors from one's life. Poor women are often led by such a perception to the use of palliative coping strategies that do not attempt to change the stressful situation itself, merely to dull the pain of its persistence. Self-medication with drugs or alcohol can have such palliative intent as can overeating, sleeping during the day, and repressing thoughts of the problem.

EXPLORATIONS *What effect does poverty have on the ability of women to fulfull important societal roles? Can you think of ways to enhance the stress resistance of low-income mothers? Do you believe the effects of poverty are different for men? Explain.*

SOURCE: Excerpted from D. Belle (1990).

own. This silence is costly to men both physically and emotionally. Compared to women, men suffer more heart attacks and hypertensive diseases. They visit their physicians only when absolutely necessary, deny symptoms, delay treatment, and die at an earlier age than women (Verbrugge, 1985). They also more frequently rely on alcohol and illicit drug use to calm daily tensions (Cook, 1990).

There appears to be a widely held and incorrect belief among men that alcohol reduces stress (Sher, 1988). Biener (1987) writes:

Drinking is a prime expression of the traditional male sex role. . . . Men are more likely than women to drink with same sex friends, drinking is a predominant activity at athletic events; and male, not female, heavy drinkers increase their consumption in the presence of heavy drinking role models. . . . Alcohol provides an accepted way for men to socialize together. It is a means of symbolically demonstrating one's manliness, both to oneself and to others. Heavy drinking, in particular, exemplifies an unconventional, risk-taking style which is accepted, if not expected, in men. (p. 335)

Regardless of gender, individual stress and how it is dealt with has implications for the family. Alcoholism, substance abuse, mental illness, AIDS, and cancer are examples of stressors that happen to individuals and result in a *contagion of stress* to other family members. When a family member is ill or incapacitated in some way, there is an energy drain on the family as

1993 Cathy Guisewite. Reprinted with permission of Universal Press Syndicate. All rights reserved.

additional attention is focused on that person. There is also a financial drain from paying the medical bills and an emotional drain as family members devote increased care and concern toward the distressed person. How families function when under stress also very much affects individuals.

FAMILY STRESS: UNDERSTANDING THE PROCESS

Families serve at least three key functions in the stress process. They are *sources of stress*—what happens

Sometimes family stress is the result of a crisis, much like that experienced by these tornado victims. However, family stress is more often the result of a pile up of normative life events and chronic strains.

within the family (marital violence, an unexpected death, the birth of a child) has individual consequences. Families also serve as *conduits of stress*—what happens outside the household, at work, at school, or in the neighborhood is brought back into the family. Many of the outside events that have affected families in the 1990s have to do with economics, including increased unemployment, escalating health-care costs, and an inordinate number of natural disasters that have left many families temporarily homeless and without insurance.

In addition, families act as *mediators of stress*—shield members from stress by offering comfort, support, information, and advice. Defeats suffered on the job and in the community are easier to bear within the circle of solace and sympathy extended by family members.

Family Stress as Crisis

Most research on family stress concerns how families deal with crisis. A *crisis*, according to family stress theorist and researcher Pauline Boss (1987), is:

a change so acute, severe, and overwhelming that the family system is blocked, immobilized, and incapacitated. Stress resulting from crisis is so high that the system's resources are not maintained, customary roles and tasks are no longer performed, and individ-

uals may no longer function at optimal levels, physiologically or psychologically. (p. 700)

The Roller Coaster Model of Family Crisis

During a crisis, the normal routine of family life is disrupted and roles and responsibilities are neglected. The family enters a period of disorganization. It is not unusual for adults to temporarily lose the capacity to take care of themselves or their children. Neighbors, friends, and kin may step in and complete routine daily living tasks—prepare food, clean the house, take the children to school, and so forth. Families in crisis initially lose their ability to make decisions and solve problems (see Figure 13-2). Disorganization is followed by a period of recovery during which the family regroups and through a process of trial and error reorganizes itself. The recovery returns the family to its previous level of functioning or to a point higher or lower than previously attained. Sociologist Reuben Hill (1949) called this the *roller coaster model of family crisis*.

The ABC-X Model of Family Crisis

The *ABC-X model of family crisis* was developed by Hill (1958) to more fully explain the key factors that influence the severity of families' reactions to crisis situations. In the ABC-X model:

FIGURE 13-2
The Roller Coaster Model of Family Crisis

SOURCES: Adapted from P. Boss (1987); E. Koos (1946); D. Hansen & R. Hill (1964); and R. Hill (1949).

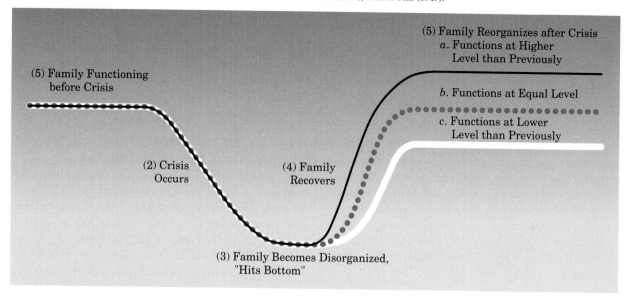

A represents the stressor event.

B represents the family's crisis-meeting resources.

C represents the definition the family makes of the event.

A, B, and C interacting together produce X, the *crisis* (Figure 13-3).

Family Stress as Adaptation

Building on Hill's theory of family crisis, family scientists Hamilton McCubbin and Joan Patterson (1983a, 1983b) proposed that family adaptation rather than crisis should be studied as the outcome of the family stress process. By changing the focus of family stress from crisis to adaptation, McCubbin and Patterson were, in effect, shifting the emphasis of the family stress process to coping. "For the first time, researchers were less concerned with why families fail and more concerned with why families succeed" (Boss, 1987, p. 702). Families were viewed less often as victims, always vulnerable to stressors, and more frequently as resilient, having the ability to cope with and recover from adversity.

Over the years, McCubbin and Patterson and their associates have continued to investigate families under stress. Their theoretical model has undergone several refinements, culminating in the *typology model of family adjustment and adaptation* (McCubbin, Thompson, Pirner, & McCubbin, 1988). They envision the family stress process as unfolding in two stages, which we present in two figures in the following section.

THE TYPOLOGY MODEL OF FAMILY ADJUSTMENT AND ADAPTATION

Stage 1: The Adjustment Phase

During stage 1 family members are faced with a stressor and attempt to adjust (the *adjustment phase*) without making any major changes in the way they normally operate. Good adjustment means that a family crisis (X) is averted because of successful coping efforts. Good adjustment depends on several factors operating in concert: (A) the stressor event, (V) family vulnerability, (T) family type, (B) family resistance resources, (C) family appraisal, and (FCB) family coping behavior (see Figure 13-4).

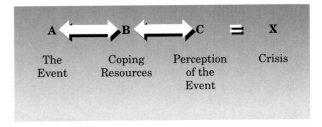

FIGURE 13-3
The ABC-X Model of Family Crisis

The Stressor Event (A)

The stressor event (A) is generally a normative or nonnormative life event or series of events that signal a need for change in family goals, roles, values, and boundaries. When parents divorce, for example, children's educational goals often need to be altered because of new economic strains on the family. Family values that formerly promoted and idealized the two-parent lifestyle may no longer seem as comfortable when the reality of living in a single-parent family hits home. A redefinition of family roles may seem in order as the custodial parent struggles with role overload. Family boundaries are strained and require broadening to incorporate two households, where there was previously one. And, in the custodial household, children and parent may feel pressured to rethink how they interact and make decisions as family power necessarily becomes more cooperative and less hierarchical (see Chapter 15).

A stressor's effect on the family depends on who is in the family and how many family members are affected. Stress is lowest if the stressor affects one member, highest when it affects all. The destruction of the family home by a hurricane would effect the entire family. All members would lose the house and its furnishings, their personal belongings, and each would feel disoriented and distressed.

On the other hand, an oldest child leaving home for college would have the most impact on that child and his or her parents. Other children in the family would probably feel only short-term effects, depending on the closeness of the sibling relationships. Any negative feelings would probably be balanced by benefits such as receiving more parental attention, having greater access to the bathroom and car, and perhaps gaining new bedroom space. The more stress the most powerful family members—usually the parents—experi-

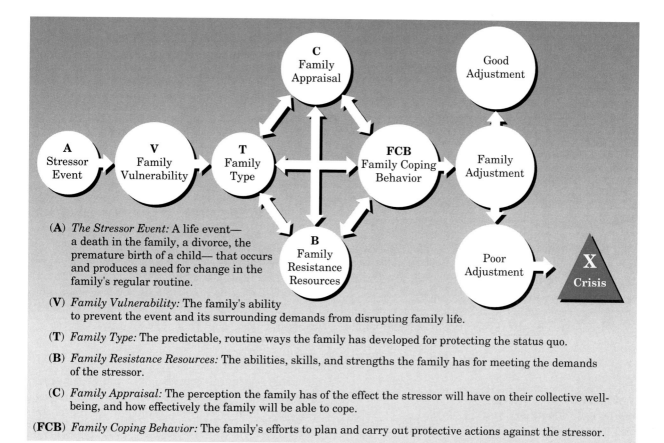

(A) *The Stressor Event:* A life event— a death in the family, a divorce, the premature birth of a child— that occurs and produces a need for change in the family's regular routine.

(V) *Family Vulnerability:* The family's ability to prevent the event and its surrounding demands from disrupting family life.

(T) *Family Type:* The predictable, routine ways the family has developed for protecting the status quo.

(B) *Family Resistance Resources:* The abilities, skills, and strengths the family has for meeting the demands of the stressor.

(C) *Family Appraisal:* The perception the family has of the effect the stressor will have on their collective well-being, and how effectively the family will be able to cope.

(FCB) *Family Coping Behavior:* The family's efforts to plan and carry out protective actions against the stressor.

FIGURE 13-4
The Typology Model of Family Adjustment and Adaptation
Stage 1: The Adjustment Phase

SOURCE: Adapted from H. McCubbin et al. (1988).

ence, the more likely there will be a contagion of stress to the rest of the family.

Family Vulnerability (V)

A family's *vulnerability* (V) to stress represents its ability to prevent the stressor from disrupting family functioning and creating a crisis. Vulnerability is heightened by the pileup of demands that surround the original stressor. In a divorce situation there is the separation of the parents and children plus additional stressors brought on by the divorce process itself, such as selling the family home and moving; economic strains from paying lawyers, child support, and spousal support; emotional strains from dealing with the loss of the family as it once was; learning to live in a single-parent family; working out visitation schedules;

and dealing with changes in the kin and friendship network (see Chapters 14 and 15).

The stage of the life cycle the family is experiencing also affects vulnerability. Families with young children or adolescent children are at greater risk of crisis because of the intensity of the demands on their time, energies, and incomes during these particular stages of life (McCubbin & Lavee, 1986; McCubbin et al., 1988).

Family Type (T)

Family type (T) represents the predictable patterns of family behavior that contribute to whether a family is *stress resistant* or *at risk* (McCubbin & McCubbin, 1989). In stress-resistant families, members have a clear idea about what they can expect from each other— whether the family typically appraises life events as threats or challenges, and what processes are in place for making rules, establishing routines, and managing problems.

A well-organized and successfully functioning family is more resistant to the effects of stress because family members are in agreement on how roles are divided within the family. In stressful times, such families are able to subordinate personal needs to family goals. In a well-organized family there is agreement on the goals toward which the family collectively moves, and mutual satisfaction with how the family meets the physical and emotional needs of its members.

Family Resistance Resources (B)

Just as personal characteristics, assets, skills, and abilities make individuals less stress prone, a similar set of coping resources protects families from stress (see Table 13-6). Two of the most often mentioned family resistance resources are family cohesion and family adaptability (Olson, Lavee, & McCubbin, 1988). *Family cohesion* refers to the close intimate feelings that family

members have for one another. *Family adaptability* describes the family's ability to alter its power structure, roles, and relationship rules as needed to facilitate change and maintain the well-being of family members.

Families with consistent policies about the use of their resources adjust more successfully to change and have a better chance of implementing their plans. These stress-resistant families bring a sense of mastery to stressful situations. When families believe that stressors are the inevitable result of outside forces or fate, they are less able to cope. Such beliefs act as barriers, blocking the family's perception of what is happening and its use of resources. A sense of mastery allows the family to more accurately appraise the threat and employ problem-solving strategies (Reiss, 1981). A family philosophy or belief system that encourages family members to pull together when trouble arises and believe that as a group they can handle most difficulties is a valuable resistance resource.

Family Appraisal (C)

Family appraisal reflects the family's judgment about how seriously a stressor will impact member well-being. It represents an estimation of the magnitude of the hardships the family must endure, as well as an evaluation of the availability of resources for dealing with the stressor. If family members are able to consider the stressor a challenge rather than a threat, they have a better chance of successfully managing any difficulties.

Family Coping Behavior (FCB)

The three coping strategies most often used by families during the adjustment phase of the stress process are avoidance, elimination, and assimilation (McCubbin & McCubbin, 1987). *Avoidance* refers to the strategy of ignoring or denying the problem, hoping that it will somehow go away. ("Those fights mom and dad have are nothing to worry about. All families have some conflict." "John says that Dad has a drinking problem, but I've never noticed him getting out of control. He says he can quit any time.")

Families who rely on *elimination* actively attempt to remove the stressor from the family or redefine it as nonthreatening. ("I know Mom has been more irritated and upset lately; it's her job. They give her more work than she can possibly handle. And she never gets a break. She even brings work home. I think she should

TABLE 13-6
Family Resistance Resources

WHAT FAMILIES HAVE
Established patterns of communication
Ability to pull together to solve a problem
Ability to draw on member knowledge and leadership
Established patterns of conflict resolution
Shared religious or spiritual orientation
Family cohesion and adaptability
Access to social support
Physical and mental health of members
Income and financial assets
Socioeconomic status

WHO FAMILIES ARE
Member esteem and morale
Shared goals
Shared values and beliefs
Shared rituals and traditions
Shared view of the world as understandable and controllable

WHAT FAMILIES DO
Coping strategies used (for example, assimilation, elimination)

SOURCES: P. Boss (1987); P. Dyk & J. Schvaneveldt (1986); L. Pearlin (1989); R. S. Lazarus & S. Folkman (1984); H. McCubbin et al. (1988).

quit.'') Avoidance and elimination are used in attempts to maintain the status quo, to keep the family operating within familiar boundaries—akin to building a protective moat around the family castle to keep intruders at bay.

Assimilation is the family's attempt to satisfy the demands of the stressor by making only minor changes in family roles and functions. When a mother returns to the work force after a long absence, the family might try to assimilate: ''Mom is working full time now so we try to help out more—Dad cooks on Tuesday evenings and Teresa and I do some of the grocery shopping.'' A couple in the third trimester of pregnancy might be overheard saying: ''The baby will take up a lot more of our time, but we're determined to protect our individual leisure hours and the time we spend together as a couple.''

Family Adjustment or Crisis (X)

Throughout the adjustment phase the family makes attempts to resist change and in many situations their resources and coping strategies prove adequate, and a crisis is averted. If the stressor is severe enough to render normal avenues of coping inadequate, however, a family crisis (X) occurs. A crisis is more probable under certain conditions:

- A family member is added to or leaves the family circle (a baby is born; a death occurs) or the family structure is changed (divorce creates two single-parent families from one two-parent family).

- The stressor is unexpected, serious, and of long duration and depletes the family's resistance resources—patience, esteem, sense of mastery, monetary savings.

- There is a pileup of previously unresolved problems that, when added to the current stressor and its aftermath, overload the family's resources.

- The family's skills, abilities, and other coping resources are inadequate to meet the stressor—insufficient income to pay for child care, no savings to take care of emergencies, inadequate knowledge of the health-care system to facilitate members receiving appropriate services.

- The family uses the stressor as an excuse to bring about needed change—marital conflict is allowed to worsen without attempts to maintain or repair the relationship, as a way of ensuring a needed separation and divorce (McCubbin et al., 1988).

At the point of crisis, family members come to realize that major changes are needed in the way they manage their daily affairs.

Stage 2: The Adaptation Phase

Attempts to implement change are initiated by the family during the *adaptation phase* of the family stress process. Adaptation is the result of a family's efforts to reorganize and recover after a family crisis (McCubbin et al., 1988; McCubbin & McCubbin, 1989).

Successful adaptation means that family members make the transition from crisis to stability; that they support the need for change and work together to solve their problems so that they do not fall back into a state of crisis (XX). Good adaptation depends on several factors operating in concert: (AA) family demands, (R) family regenerativity, (T) family type, (BB) family resistance resources, (CC) family appraisal, and (FCB) family coping behavior (see Figure 13-5). Because many of these factors coincide with those in the adjustment phase of family stress, we only explain new or significantly expanded terms.

Faced with a pileup of stressors—family demands (AA)—from trying to maintain the status quo by making as few changes as possible during the adjustment phase, the family comes to realize that its happiness and well-being depend on altering its normal ways of behaving. Family members take stock of the repairs that are needed and assess their collective ability to adapt—family appraisal (CC). The appraisal is influenced by a family's sense of regenerativity (R) and family type (T), as well as the resources (BB) available for facilitating change. Appraisal results in the family making plans and taking action—family coping behavior (FCB). Families that are able to define a crisis as a challenge or opportunity for a better life, rather than a threat, are more successful at adaptation.

Family Regenerativity (R)

Family *regenerativity* (R) represents the family's ability to make the necessary changes to recover from the disorganization and disruption of their daily life. Regenerative families are hardy. They face stressors with competence and perseverance. Regenerative families are characterized by committed and trusting relationships. They are willing to take risks and explore innovative means of recovery from family crisis.

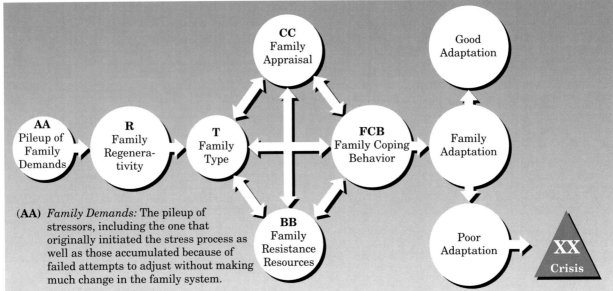

(**AA**) *Family Demands:* The pileup of stressors, including the one that originally initiated the stress process as well as those accumulated because of failed attempts to adjust without making much change in the family system.

(**R**) *Family Regenerativity:* The family's willingness and capability to make needed changes in their goals, roles, and in how they operate and interact as a group.

(**T**) *Family Type:* The predictable, routine ways the family has developed for promoting adaptation to change.

(**BB**) *Family Resistance Resources:* The abilities, skills, and strengths the family has for fostering change and adaptation within the family.

(**CC**) *Family Appraisal:* The perception the family has of the need for change and their assessment of the potential of their members to make those changes.

(**FCB**) *Family Coping Behavior:* The family's efforts to plan and carry out the changes needed.

FIGURE 13-5
The Typology Model of Family Adjustment and Adaptation
Stage 2: The Adaptation Phase

Source: Adapted from H. McCubbin et al. (1988).

Family Coping Behavior (FCB)

The three main coping strategies employed by families during the adaptation phase of the stress process are synergizing, interfacing, and compromising (McCubbin & McCubbin, 1987). *Synergizing* describes a family's cooperative efforts to pull together as a mutually supportive and interdependent group to facilitate change while minimizing family disruption. During adaptation, families rely on a shared sense of self—a "we" attitude toward problem solving.

Using *interfacing*, the family actively seeks information and support services from the community. Divorcing parents may inform their children's teachers of their separation. Some schools offer after-school peer support groups for children of divorce. Other schools provide special counseling programs and study groups for children under stress. Parents may also interface by going to the community library or bookstore to find information about the divorce process, or by joining a support organization like Parents Without Partners.

Although divorcing parents have a myriad of community resources upon which to call, families facing other stressors may not. Sometimes communities are not equipped to help families under stress or in crisis. When Hurricane Andrew struck the Florida coast in 1992, one of the main problems was the lack of support for families in crisis (see the "Point of View" box).

In other cases, there may be an organized hierarchy or bureaucracy that limits family coping. For example, during the Vietnam war, families with a captive or missing husband/father were frustrated by the lack of information provided by the military. Eventually these families formed an alliance and cooperatively worked for change.

Families sought more information, demanded access to all information, insisted on regular personal contacts with military officials, and demanded additional counseling for families in need. . . . These families also sought changes in legislation which would ensure them of benefits to their children as well as continued financial benefits and support, e.g., tax breaks, husband's continued pay and promotions. (McCubbin & Patterson, 1982, p. 41)

Even today, families of soldiers missing in Vietnam work together to obtain information and lobby the federal government for more decisive answers to their questions.

TABLE 13-7
Family Stress Resistance over the Life Course

Stress-Resistance Factors	Stages of the Family Life Cycle			
	Childfree	Childbearing and School Age	Teenage and Young Adult	Empty Nest and Retirement
Balance: Achieving an interdependence among family members that allows them to resolve conflicts and reduce chronic strain.	X	X		
Celebrations: Acknowleding birthdays, religious occasions, and other special events.	X	X	X	X
Communication: Sharing beliefs and emotions with one another. Emphasis is on how family members exchange information and caring.	X	X		X
Financial Management: Practicing sound decision-making skills for money management. Satisfaction with economic status can contribute to family well-being.	X	X	X	
Hardiness: Emphasizing family members' sense of control over their lives, commitment to the family, confidence that the family will survive no matter what, and the ability to grow, learn, and challenge each other.	X	X	X	X
Health: Promoting the physical and psychological well-being of family members.	X			X
Leisure Activities: Focusing on similarities and differences of family member preferences for ways to spend free time. Do family members prefer active or passive interests, social or personal activities?	X			
Personality: Accepting of a partner's traits, behaviors, and general outlook.	X		X	X
Support Network: Emphasizing the positive aspects of relationships with in-laws, relatives, and friends.		X	X	
Time and Routines: Creating continuity and stability in family life through family meals, chores, togetherness, and other ordinary routines.	X	X	X	X
Traditions: Honoring holidays and important family experiences carried through generations.	X	X	X	X

SOURCE: Adapted from H. McCubbin & M. McCubbin (1988).

POINT OF VIEW

Hurricane Andrew: From Crisis to Persistent Hardships

At first glance, it appears that Hurricane Andrew demolished the house just yesterday. Wooden roof beams are still exposed, windows have not been replaced and huge piles of debris clutter the driveway.

But it has been 7 months since the storm hit, and George Vargas, a 37-year-old butcher, has spent nearly every day supervising the painfully slow reconstruction of the home he shares with his wife, Amy, and their 6-year-old daughter, Isabel. He can afford the time because the storm also destroyed Homestead Meat Market, the business he and his father, now 65, operated for more than 20 years.

For Mr. Vargas and the other residents of his block on 152nd Court, these may be even worse times than the days immediately after the hurricane. Through the late summer and fall, they were buoyed by the presence of the military and by national concern about their plight.

But that interest has receded, and they say they feel isolated and tired. Having survived the winds and rain, they now find that federal and county agencies, insurance companies, and contractors often provide as many obstacles as help. What is worse, they can see no quick solutions or end to the upheaval, and no one can tell them when they might expect to resume normal lives.

"Andrew came and went in a few hours," said Margarita Rodriguez, Mr. Vargas's neighbor. "But living with the damage the storm did, and trying to recover from it, is something that just goes on and on and on."

Since last August, Mrs. Rodriguez, her husband, Ricardo, her son, Ricky, and his wife have been living in a small rented apartment 40 minutes from their home. To save money, she has acted as her own contractor.

Down the block, Lazaro Roque has already moved back into his house, after living with his family in a small trailer in his driveway through much of the fall. But his insurance settlement did not give him enough money to replace ruined furniture, and it did not cover the tools that someone stole from his house when he and his family stayed briefly with relatives in Hialeah in the days after the storm

Mr. Roque, a 31-year-old father of a 2-year-old son, John, and a daughter, Ashley, born a month after the hurricane, is also without a job. The gas station where

Families also cope by *compromising*—consider the opinions of all family members and remain open to alternatives while making decisions. Compromise is enhanced by a willingness to tolerate uncertainty, persevere through tough negotiations and sometimes uncomfortable conflict, and engage in a process of trial and error to find solutions for family problems.

Families that cope most successfully during the adaptation phase of the stress process: (1) keep the lines of communication open and make sure input is received from each family member; (2) make efforts to see that all family members' needs are taken into consideration, that each feels valued; (3) develop ways to maintain family unity and closeness; (4) seek social support from outside the family when needed; and (5) keep the demands on each family member at a reasonable level, moving slowly so change is smooth and controlled rather than rapid and distressing (McCubbin & McCubbin, 1987; McCubbin & Patterson, 1983a).

In summary, families over the life course confront many predictable as well as unanticipated stressors. How successfully they manage these demands depends to a considerable degree on the number of other stressors that pile up along the way; the perception the family have of the stressor and their capacity to manage it; and the strengths, resources, and coping abilities family members utilize to protect themselves. Table 13-7 has additional information about factors that enhance family stress resistance over the life cycle. As is indicated in the table by an "X," some stress-resistance resources are important at every stage of family life,

he worked for a dozen years was destroyed by the storm. He now spends most of his time caring for his children so his wife, who has a Dade County job with health benefits, can continue to work.

"I don't think you can ever completely come back from something like this," Mr. Roque said. "Everything has changed for all of us, even for the baby. Many of the neighbors have left, and a lot of the good jobs are gone, too."

Other hurricane-related woes have recently complicated the rebuilding effort. The worst was when the Pentagon announced this month that it intends to shut down Homestead Air Force Base, which employed 8,800 people, nearly half of them civilians, and contributed $430 million a year to the local economy.

"First my house gets torn up," said Ray Runshe, a 62-year-old military retiree, "and now they say the base is going to close. They are pulling the rug right out from underneath us."

A week after the base closing was announced, the Homestead area was struck by the same devastating winter storm that later hit the Northeast. Winds of up to 80 miles an hour overturned trailer homes, killing one woman, and blew down a tent city that had opened the first week in March to provide shelter for some of the estimated 5,000 people still homeless from the hurricane.

Dianna Ackerman and her two sons, Joseph and David, were among the people who sought shelter at the camp as soon as it opened, moving into a brown canvas tent she mockingly calls "our penthouse."

At the time of the hurricane, Ms. Ackerman was living in an apartment with her children and a friend. When the building was destroyed, the friend decided to leave town. Ms. Ackerman took her remaining belongings and moved into a trailer camp operated by the Federal Emergency Management Administration.

In some respects, Ms. Ackerman said, moving into the tent city came as a relief after the trailer camp, where she frequently heard gunfire and was robbed six times, losing a microwave oven, a coffeemaker, dishes, linen, a bicycle and her children's video games.

Ms. Ackerman said that while she hopes her lot will improve in the tent city, she still has moments of doubt.

"There are times I just have to go into the tent, close the flap and cry," she said. "It seems like this is never going to end."

EXPLORATIONS *Where do these families fit in the family stress process envisioned by Hamilton McCubbin and his colleagues? Are they in the adjustment or adaptation phase? What family resistance resources have the families employed? How have they coped? What remains to be accomplished in order to avoid another crisis?*

Source: Excerpted from L. Rohter (1993).

---

while others are more critical during the parenting years or before retirement.

Stress-resistant families are characterized by close affectional ties, predictable family routines, strong family traditions, and shared activities. They share a philosophy of loyalty, respect, and interdependence that includes a belief in the flexibility of family responsibilities, shared power, and mutual decision making.

Yet, family members in stress-resistant families are also independent. Because of the high level of trust family members have for each other, they feel secure in their right to disagree with each other and develop distinctive personalities. These characteristics enhance the family's ability to reshape rules and practices as needed to cope with stressors.

SUMMARY POINTS

■ A stressor is the event or stressful situation that triggers the stress process. There are two types of stressors, life events and persistent hardships.

■ Normative life events, compared to nonnormative ones, are predictable and scripted.

■ Appraisal is a two-stage process that individuals initiate to evaluate the impact of a stressor. Primary appraisal results in an assessment of the stressor as irrelevant, benign-positive, or stressful. Secondary appraisal represents a judgment concerning how best to cope with the stressor.

■ Coping resources consist of what we have (skills, assets, abilities); who we are (self-esteem, mastery); and what we do (coping strategies).

■ Two belief systems that appear to have a protective function in the stress process are hardiness and sense of coherence.

■ Use of a particular set of coping strategies creates a distinct coping style.

■ Emotion-focused coping (distancing, escape-avoidance) reduces stress by helping to keep the emotions under control until problem-focused coping (confronting, problem solving) can be implemented.

■ Successful copers have a large repertoire of coping strategies, match the strategy to the situation, rely on habitual forms of coping to take care of routine, repetitive kinds of problems, and remain flexible when under stress by changing strategies when necessary.

■ Social support refers to the things that friends, kin, and spouses do to help others reduce or resist stress.

■ The stress process differs by gender.

■ When under stress, people first try to handle their own problems, then look to friends and family for support and advice. If still troubled, they seek out their minister or family physician, finally turning to formal, organized support groups or a therapist as a last resort.

■ The family can be a source of stress and a conduit of stress, as well as a mediator of stress.

■ The first widely used models depicting the stress process in families were the roller coaster model of family crisis and the ABC-X model of family stress.

■ Hamilton McCubbin and his associates have revised and expanded on these models, focusing on family adaptation rather than family crisis. They propose that when confronted with a stressor, the family first tries to adjust to the event without making major changes in the way it normally operates. If the family is unsuccessful, and a crisis (X) occurs, it comes to realize that a major change is needed in the family system. If the family is successful, recovers, and adapts, a second crisis (XX) is avoided.

KEY TERMS

Stress	*Emotion-focused coping*
The stress process	*Problem-focused coping*
Stressor	*Social support*
Normative life events	*Distress*
Nonnormative life events	*Emotional distress*
Persistent hardships	*Physical distress*
Chronic strain	*Contagion of stress*
Role overload	*Crisis*
Role overlap	*Roller coaster model of family*
Role conflict	*crisis*
Role captivity	*ABC-X model of family crisis*
Role restructuring	*Typology model of family adjust-*
Daily hassles	*ment and adaptation*
Appraisal	*Adjustment phase*
Primary appraisal	*Vulnerability*
Irrelevant	*Family cohesion*
Benign-positive	*Family adaptability*
Stressful	*Avoidance*
Secondary appraisal	*Elimination*
Coping resources	*Assimilation*
Self-esteem	*Adaptation phase*
Mastery	*Regenerativity*
Type A personality	*Synergizing*
Hardiness	*Interfacing*
Sense of coherence	*Compromising*
Coping strategy	
Coping style	

REVIEW QUESTIONS

1. What is the difference between normative and nonnormative life events?

2. How do chronic strain and daily hassles differ?

3. Explain the role of appraisal in the stress process.

4. Distinguish between a coping strategy and a coping style.

5. When individuals or families are described as hardy, what does that mean relative to the stress process?

6. A woman comes home from work with a problem—her supervisor has broken a promise to promote her. She is reluctant to reveal the problem to her husband. Using the Pearlin and McCall four-stage model of marital support, discuss why the woman may wish to conceal her troubles from her husband. Provide a likely scenario for how the couple might progress through the support process once the problem is revealed.

7. Describe how women and men differ in how they experience, appraise, and cope with stress.

8. Explain how the family serves as a source of stress, a conduit of stress, and a mediator of stress. Give examples.

9. Using the typology model of family adjustment and adaptation, develop a proposal for how a family of four (mom, dad, 12-year-old daughter, 15-year-old son) might handle the stress of having the father incapacitated by a broken back (2 months in the hospital, 6 months recuperating at home). Plan on the family reaching crisis (X) in the adjustment phase of the process, but averting a crisis in the adaptation phase.

14

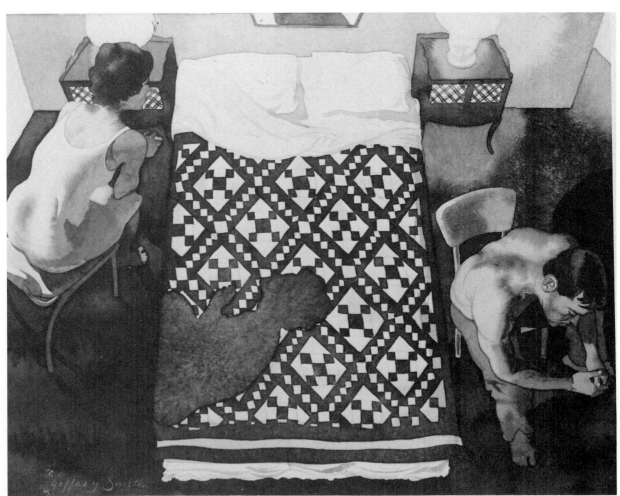

Separation and Divorce: Dissolving the Marital Bond

Very few couples anticipate when they marry that their marriages might someday be threatened by major marital problems or end in divorce. Nevertheless, at some point, almost every couple confronts potentially destructive marital issues. Some couples are able to solve such marital conflicts by themselves or with the help of friends, relatives, or professional counselors. Others eventually decide to divorce.

Divorce no longer affects just a small minority of American couples. Currently there are some 14 million divorced persons, and it is estimated that between one-half and two-thirds of all the couples who marry this year can be expected to sever their marital ties eventually (National Center for Health Statistics, 1992). Such statistics remind us how pervasive divorce has become and also underline the increasing value of understanding its impact and significance. Accordingly, in this chapter we first examine how the divorce rates have changed in recent decades, describe the process of divorce, and ask why divorce has become so much more common. Then we review some of the consequences of today's relatively high divorce rates, paying particular attention to the children of divorce.

THE HIGH RATE OF MARITAL DISSOLUTION

Only about 1 in 10 marriages begun in the year 1900 ended in divorce. The vast majority of marital dissolutions were due to death. Only since the mid-1970s have more marriages been terminated in a given year by divorce than by death (Cherlin, 1993).

There are, of course, some similarities between marriages terminated by the death of a spouse and those terminated by divorce. In both cases, family routines are interrupted and roles substantially redefined. Both are traumatic, life-changing events. But differences

America is a marrying society. Couples usually marry in their mid-twenties, for love, with half divorcing by age 31, because of unmet expectations.

also exist between them, differences that may make divorce a more difficult transition than the adjustment to a spouse's death.

One difference is that death is more common among older couples, while divorce tends to occur relatively early in people's lives. Roughly half of all divorces take place by the seventh year of marriage (U.S. Bureau of the Census, 1992). Since the average age at marriage is about 24 years, this means that approximately one-half of all spouses are no older than 31 when they divorce. For most couples of this age, the divorce is complicated by the presence of young children.

Another difference is that the situation in marriages terminated by death is less ambiguous. As traumatic as the death of one's spouse may be, it at least is a final separation. In contrast, after a divorce, and particularly when young children are involved, certain ties and obligations to the former spouse remain.

Calculating the Divorce Rate

Statistics from governmental agencies such as the Justice Department, the U.S. Bureau of the Census, and the National Office of Vital Statistics are indispensable in gauging the direction and extent of social trends like divorce. But, certain questions should be kept in mind when reading statistical information: (1) How accurate and comprehensive are the data? Do they come from a reliable source and do they represent a complete picture of the phenomenon they describe? (2) Are the data combined in categories or rates that accurately express their meaning? (3) What conclusions can properly be drawn from the data presented?

As with any display of numerical data, divorce statistics can be somewhat deceptive. One reason is that divorce statistics are incomplete. Only about half the 50 states report complete information to the federal government on the number and characteristics of divorces granted each year. Even in states that record complete data, there is no adequate information on desertion. Desertion is commonplace in many poor communities because divorce involves substantial legal fees—a luxury that many people cannot afford. Thus, in some localities a high divorce rate might better be understood as a consequence of improved legal services to low-income groups than of growing dissatisfaction with marriage.

Another reason divorce statistics can be difficult to interpret is that the rates are calculated in several ways. The *divorce/marriage ratio*—computed by comparing the number of marriage licenses granted in a certain month with the number of divorce decrees—is one of the most commonly used divorce rates. This technique is quite simple but somewhat misleading. If, for example, 400 marriage licenses were granted and 200 divorce decrees issued during a certain month, we might conclude that 50 percent of all marriages end in divorce. Yet two very different populations are being compared, the mostly young people who marry in a given year and the people who have been married from 1 to 50+ years.

Furthermore, if a substantial number of people decide to postpone or forgo marriage in a given year, the marriage rate will automatically fall, causing the divorce rate to rise, even if the number of divorces stays the same. Finally, this measure provides no way to estimate the likelihood that a first marriage will end in divorce. Among 200 divorces granted, some are issued to people who have been married at least twice before.

Such individuals are counted in the divorce statistics every time they go through the process, thus causing an inflation in the divorce rate.

There are other, less misleading ways to calculate the divorce rate. The *crude divorce rate,* for example, is defined as the number of divorces per 1,000 population. But the problem with this measure is that the 1,000 population includes many people, such as children or adults who have decided never to marry and thus are not "at risk" of divorce. A better measure is the *refined divorce rate,* the number of divorces per 1,000 married women over age 15. Because this measure compares the number of divorces granted with the number of adult women eligible for divorce, it is considered a more reliable indicator of the divorce rate.

Probably the best way to determine how many marriages eventually end in divorce would be to select a random sample of individuals marrying in a given year and follow them throughout their lives, observing when they marry and divorce. The problem with this type of longitudinal study is that it would be both expensive and time-consuming. Because the most trustworthy information currently available is the refined divorce rate, we use it to illustrate divorce trends in Figure 14-1.

A Longitudinal View of Divorce

The rising rate of divorce has probably received more public and media attention and caused more anxiety and concern than any other trend in American family life since World War II (Cherlin, 1993). Taking a longitudinal view of the refined divorce rates over the past century allows a broader perspective of this phenomenon. Essentially, the graph that appears in Figure 14-1 illustrates a trend that has three distinct stages. The first stage took place between 1880 and the mid-1960s. During this period of about 80 years, the divorce rate climbed slowly but steadily. In 1880, the rate was about 2 per 1,000 existing marriages. By 1900, the figure was up to 4; by 1920 it rose to 8.0; and by 1940 to 8.8. (The sharp rise in the divorce rate immediately after World War II indicated in Figure 14-1 is generally attributed to the breakup of spur-of-the-moment wartime marriages.) By 1960, the divorce rate was 9.2.

Then, during the second stage, in the mid-1960s—*before* the no-fault laws were put into effect—the divorce rate started to accelerate. The rate was 10.9 per 1,000 marriages in 1966; 14.9 in 1970; 20.3 in 1975; and

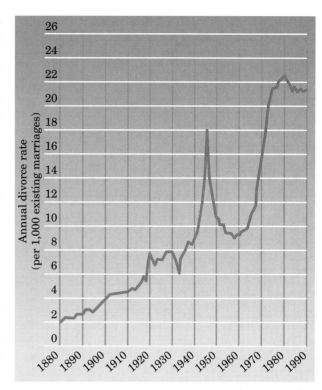

FIGURE 14-1
Divorce Rate in the United States, 1880–1990

SOURCES: P. H. Jacobson (1959); National Center for Health Statistics (1973, 1984, 1991).

22.6 in 1980. In the third stage, starting in 1986, the divorce rate had stabilized at 21.2. It is interesting to note that a marked increase in the divorce rate took place during this period in most industrial nations except Italy and Japan, suggesting that the relative instability of modern marriage is probably related to broad currents of social change and accompanying alterations in lifestyles (Sorrentino, 1990).

Interpreting the Divorce Statistics

In most discussions in which the divorce rate is mentioned, it is deplored as a sign of the times, an indication that the social fabric is unraveling. Only rarely is the high divorce rate understood as a consequence of new expectations. A high divorce rate may mean not that people's marital aptitudes are lower than they used to be, but rather that partners bring different expectations to marriage than their grandparents did. In a sense, then, the divorce rate is high not because people care less about marriage nowadays, but because they care more. They want emotional intimacy, interdependence, and trust, as well as affection and caring.

A relatively high divorce rate is a problem mainly if we assume that all marriages should remain intact until the death of a spouse. Most societies have some provision for the dissolution of marriages in which the contract between husband and wife is not being fulfilled. The statistical information telling us that nearly 2 million divorces will be granted in the United States over the next 12 months represents an enormous amount of personal suffering. Few people stop to think, however, that a great deal of personal suffering may also be *relieved* by those divorces, as they allow people to leave unsatisfying relationships.

Statistics tell us only how many couples are legally divorced, not how marriages fail, or why. What is it like personally to sever the marital bond? How does the divorce process unfold? One way to find out is to ask couples to give their personal evaluations of the events and marital interactions that occur throughout the divorce process.

THE PROCESS OF DIVORCE

How long the divorce process takes is very individual and highly variable. Sociologists Frank Furstenberg and Andrew Cherlin (1991) observe: "At one extreme are the unusual instances in which one partner discovers that the marriage is over by reading a note left on the kitchen table. . . . At the other extreme are those marriages that take 15 or 20 years to dissolve" (p. 20). Usually it is a bruising process of mutual alienation that people gradually move through over a number of years.

In most cases when a marriage begins to deteriorate, for at least one partner, little acts of thoughtlessness and minor betrayals become highly significant symptoms. Rather than the euphoric feeling of high self-esteem that accompanied the beginning of the relationship, each feels the sting of systematic, destructive criticism. Before, they had focused on each other's strengths and virtues; now the spotlight turns on frailties and shortcomings. Enthusiastic plans for a shared future are replaced by bitter recriminations over unmet promises. Where before there was deepening trust,

now the partner's loyalty can no longer be taken for granted. At some point sexual accessibility may be withdrawn, and with it go companionship and emotional support. Just as lovers cherish certain mementos of special times together, when they stray apart they find many sad reminders of love's labor lost.

Six Stations of Divorce

Anthropologist Paul Bohannan (1970) was one of the first scholars to consider divorce as a process. After extensive interviews, he concluded that divorce occurs in terms of what he identified as six "stations": (1) the emotional divorce—partners struggle with marital dissatisfaction, attempt change, confront each other, and eventually decide that the relationship must end; (2) the legal divorce—partners separate physically and consult an attorney who seeks a court order to legally end the marriage; (3) the economic divorce—partners complete the financial arrangements and divide the marital property; (4) the coparental divorce—partners negotiate and finalize the divorce, custody, and visitation arrangements; (5) the community divorce—individuals experience changes in kinship and friendship networks and explore new interests and activities; and (6) the psychic divorce—individuals try to regain a sense of identity and autonomy by becoming emotionally detached and independent from the former spouse.

Kaslow and Schwartz (1987) have developed a model identifying the actions, tasks, and feelings generated at each of Bohannan's six stations of divorce (see Table 14-1). It is good to keep in mind that people do not always progress through divorce in an orderly stagelike manner. They sometimes move back, repeating a stage, or go through several stages simultaneously.

Uncoupling

Sociologist Diane Vaughn in her book, *Uncoupling* (1986), describes relationship dissolution as a process that begins with a secret—one partner, the initiator, is unhappy and dissatisfied. The initiator begins to display discontent and attempts to communicate to his or her partner that something is wrong, hoping to provoke changes that will save the relationship. Unfortunately, in most cases, the initiator has trouble being

TABLE 14-1
Model of the Divorce Process: The Six Stages (Stations) of Divorce

Divorce Stage	Feelings	Actions and Tasks
PREDIVORCE: A TIME OF DELIBERATION AND DESPAIR		
The emotional divorce	Disillusionment Dissatisfaction Alienation Anxiety Disbelief Despair Dread Anguish Ambivalence Shock Emptiness Anger Disorganization Inadequacy Low self-esteem Loss Depression Detachment	Avoiding the issue Sulking and/or crying Confronting partner Quarreling Denial Withdrawal (physical and emotional) Pretending all is okay Attempting to win back affection Asking friends, family, or clergy for advice Bargaining
DURING DIVORCE: A TIME OF LEGAL INVOLVEMENT		
The legal divorce	Anger Hopelessness Self-pity Helplessness Confusion	Threatening Self-destructiveness Consulting an attorney or mediator Separating physically
The economic divorce	Fury Sadness	Filing for legal divorce Considering economic arrangements Considering custody arrangements
The coparental divorce and the problems of custody	Loneliness Relief Vindictiveness Indecisiveness	Grieving and mourning Telling relatives and friends Reentering workplace (unemployed women) Feeling empowered to make choices Finalizing the divorce
POSTDIVORCE: A TIME OF EXPLORATION AND REEQUILIBRIUM		
The community divorce and the problems of loneliness	Optimism Resignation Excitement Curiosity Regret Sadness	Begin reaching out to new friends Undertaking new activities Stabilizing new lifestyle and daily routine for children Exploring new interests and perhaps new job
The psychic divorce	Acceptance Self-confidence Energy Self-worth Wholeness Exhilaration Independence Autonomy	Regaining self-identity Completing psychic divorce Seeking new love and making a commitment to some permanency Becoming comfortable with new life and friends Helping children accept finality of parents' divorce and continue their relationship with both parents

SOURCE: Adapted from F. Kaslow & L. Schwartz (1987).

direct about feelings and intentions. According to Vaughn:

> Unable to articulate true feelings, thoughts, and moods easily, the initiator does not directly confront the partner in a way that allows the partner to address the basic issue ("I'm unhappy in the relationship and this is why"). Instead the initiator uses cues and hints . . . which may be difficult to interpret, or if seized on by the partner, are easily explained away. (p. 15)

At this stage, if the partner changes in a way that reduces the initiator's dissatisfaction, dissolution is postponed or forever delayed. Most couples are constantly engaged in discussing, negotiating, and problem solving. Sometimes serious problems that look unsolvable are later viewed as rough patches they somehow managed to get through.

If the unhappiness continues, however, the initiator begins to explore other options—finds ways to gain pleasure and satisfaction outside of the relationship. For example, the initiator might expand parenting or friendship roles, pursue educational goals, or start an affair. At this point, if the initiator gains renewed feelings of self-worth and affirmation from these alternative sources, the relationship may endure, but at a diminished level of involvement.

But if the dissatisfaction continues, the initiator comes to realize that the relationship must end. Vaughn explains:

> Many speak of a precise moment when they "knew the relationship was over," when "everything went dead inside," when "I realized I didn't belong there anymore." . . . The initiator's certainty results not only from the recognition that he or she no longer belongs in the relationship, but also from a sense of belonging elsewhere. (p. 81)

Now the initiator begins to use direct and indirect confrontational tactics to get the partner to admit that the relationship is over. Indirect confrontational strategies include decreasing communication to the point that the partner cannot help but notice that something is wrong, or violating a relationship rule so significant that it shocks the partner to attention. One man reveals how he used an indirect strategy to precipitate relationship dissolution:

> I wanted out of the marriage, but there was no way she would ever go for a divorce. I decided I would treat her as if we were divorced. Well, that's sort of

what I did. I slept on the couch. I never spoke to her, pretended she wasn't there. Just lived my own life. Finally, she threw me out. (p. 122)

The most frequently used direct strategy is for the initiator to simply tell the partner of his or her wish to dissolve the relationship. By this point in the uncoupling process, the initiator has decided that there is no way to save the relationship, but the partner, newly aware of the depth of the problem, may try to intervene. Sometimes the partner, awakened to the risk, makes such tremendous efforts to change that the relationship is saved.

More often, however, a physical separation occurs. Separation is an emotionally wrenching experience for both partners, but initiators tend to be better prepared because they have been planning and preparing for this inevitability for far longer than their partners. After separation, both partners seek the support of kin and friends and try to explain what happened to cause the uncoupling.

As recovery begins, each person becomes more independent, and with the passage of time, is usually able to look back and admit that there were positives as well as negatives to the relationship. As one man notes:

> I said, OK now let me evaluate the whole situation in realistic ways. I'm not going to make excuses, I don't need to make excuses anymore. Then I began to think back—What did I say; What did I do; What did she put up with; What did I put up with; How did we stifle each other. And we paid a terrible price. Nineteen years of living a substandard existence. We have a lot to make up for. What she lost, what I lost. (p. 178)

A woman says:

> I accept the fact that I'm angry with him, but . . . there'll never be another man I'll have children with. Just for the fact that we married and had children, he will always be special and because I understand his parents and his problems. I just can look at him and say, you know, the man is miserable, you know, but he is the children's father, so even though there is anger there, there's a certain amount of compassion I feel for him. (p. 184)

As part of their adjustment to divorce, all individuals develop accounts of why their marriages failed. An account serves as the divorced person's explanation of what went wrong, of why the marriage did not last.

The "Divorce Story": Why This Marriage Failed

Through their accounts, people attempt to make sense of this very painful and emotional process called divorce. The "divorce story" is used to establish understandable causes and attribute blame for the breakup. Wallerstein and Blakeslee (1989) write:

> I have yet to meet one man, woman, or child who emotionally accepts "no-fault" divorce. In their hearts, people believe in fault and in the loss associated with the decision to end a marriage. Adults almost inevitably blame each other, but rarely blame themselves. (p. 7)

Friends and kin often remark that the accounts of wives and husbands do not match. Such observations are correct. The former partner's understanding of what "really" happened varies because each valued different things in the relationship and each has different needs to attend to through his or her story. The stories or accounts become crucial coping mechanisms that help the couple get through the process of divorce and learn to function independently.

In his classic study of divorce, sociologist William Goode (1956) asked women what they believed was the main cause of their divorce. Twelve reasons were revealed. Collectively these reasons suggest two general themes: disagreements and conflict between the spouses and the husband's lack of involvement in family roles—for example, household tasks and child care.

In a later study, sociologists Gay Kitson and Marvin Sussman (1982) again asked women (and men) why they divorced. The researchers concluded that there had been a shift in accounts since Goode's study, but that marital disagreements and issues of family involvement were still primary reasons for divorce. The disagreements revolved around appropriate gender roles within marriage and the involvement issues concerned affection and sex (rather than family tasks).

In a third study, family scientists Graham Spanier and Linda Thompson (1984) reported similar results. They conclude, "Husbands and wives expressed the greatest disappointment about the mate as companion and confidant. . . . Disappointment revolved around affectional involvement and husband's failure to share roles. . . . Companionship, sex, and affection continued

Couples who share marital roles are less likely to divorce.

to be at the center of disagreement and involvement" (p. 57). The main sources of disagreement were: (1) gender role performance (for example, sharing the household work); (2) quality of the sexual relationship; (3) poor communication; and (4) changes in involvement (for example, values, time spent together).

For years, students of marriage and family life have tried to identify which marriages are most likely to end in divorce, and why. The thinking is that if we are able to recognize the causes of marital instability, preventive advice could be given, and some people might be spared the turmoil of less-than-successful marriages. Other than identifying reasons for marital dissolution from the personal accounts of the divorced, family scholars often examine larger social trends as possible contributors.

DO SOCIETAL TRENDS EXPLAIN THE DIVORCE RATE?

Although no hard evidence indicates that major shifts in cultural attitudes and values, gender roles, or the divorce laws have affected the divorce rate, many social scientists believe in a possible connection.

Changes in Cultural Attitudes and Values

We need to look particularly at what has happened to the cultural norms that formerly prevented most people from seeking a divorce. Over the past few decades, many of these widely shared attitudes that condemned divorce (particularly of couples with children) have come tumbling down. At the turn of the century, divorced persons were viewed as somewhat disreputable. Today, divorce is far more respectable. Even candidates for public office no longer view divorce as a major political liability. The disappearance of the social stigma once attached to divorce and the very prevalence of divorce today makes it an easier choice for people in unsatisfactory marriages.

Parents are less inclined to stay in an unsatisfactory marriage for the children's sake. Both parents and their children have become sensitized to divorce as a possibility, rather than an unthinkable alternative to an unhappy marriage. A substantial majority today believe that the presence of children should be no impediment to divorce. In one survey, only 19 percent of participants agreed that a couple should stay together for the sake of the children, a drop from 49 percent in 1962 (Landers, 1990). There is also an intergenerational effect, with children of divorce being more likely, in adulthood, to divorce their partners (White, 1991). Marriages in which both partners have experienced a family breakup in childhood have the highest divorce rates (Bumpass, Martin, & Sweet, 1991).

Changes in Gender Roles

If a greater societal acceptance may be one reason for the rising divorce rates of the past few decades, changes in women's educational attainment and labor-force participation are others. Divorce rates were lower several decades ago, partly because the majority of women were educationally and financially dependent on their husbands. Research studies corroborate common sense in suggesting that women—even those married to physically abusive men—are more likely to stay in a marriage when they have no economic resources of their own. It is no coincidence that as the labor-force participation of younger, more educated women began to increase rapidly in the mid-1960s, so did the divorce rate. Even today, as the wife's earnings grow, so does the likelihood that her marriage will end in divorce (Cherlin & Furstenberg, 1988; White, 1991).

Divorce rates for women with less than a high school education are 30 percent lower than for women who complete high school and 80 percent lower than for women who graduate from college (Bumpass et al., 1991). Women more frequently than men initiate separation and divorce. Women are apparently more attuned to the quality of their relationships and more often than men say that they are dissatisfied or unhappy with their marriages (Thompson & Walker, 1991).

Possibly, educated, employed women, because of their greater resources, are less disposed to remain in unsatisfactory marriages; or, possibly, men are more willing to divorce women who can provide for themselves. (Men remain longer in dependent relationships out of a sense of responsibility and guilt.) Or it may be that the additional demands experienced by both partners being employed create strains within the marital relationship. When changes in the traditional patterns of meshing employment with family roles do not occur or are slow to occur, the couple may decide to divorce rather than work through their problems. All three explanations are plausible, although none has been conclusively demonstrated. What is evident is that women who can afford to leave an unsatisfactory marriage and manage on their own more often choose divorce.

Changes in Divorce Laws

Since 1970, another significant change has taken place that reflects some of the newer ways of thinking about gender roles and the nature of the marital bond. This change is the widespread revision of the divorce laws. Few areas in marriage and family life have altered so rapidly in recent years as the legal procedure for dissolving a marriage. What sociologist Lenore Weitzman (1985) refers to as the *divorce revolution* began in 1970 when California became the first state to introduce the concept of no-fault divorce. As of 1991, all states had adopted some variation of the no-fault divorce laws.

Principles of the No-Fault Revolution

Although the new divorce laws vary substantially from one state to another, the principles of the "no-fault revolution" can be simply stated. As attorneys Doris Jonas Freed and Henry H. Foster put it, "In general, we are agreed that dead marriages should be buried, that economic circumstances should govern alimony or maintenance, and that children, when possible, should know and associate with both parents" (Freed & Foster, 1985).

Until California's ground-breaking legislation was enacted, no couple could get divorced until one of the spouses was judged guilty of some marital fault such as adultery or cruelty. The traditional premise of divorce law was that marriage is a permanent union and that it is the state's duty to preserve and protect it. In establishing grounds for divorce, the state stepped into what was formerly the church's position. It protected the marital bond by allowing its dissolution only under certain specific circumstances (see Table 14-2).

In the years before no-fault, the grounds for divorce differed from one state to another. Three legal grounds, however, had accounted for about three-quarters of all divorces: desertion, nonsupport, and cruelty. Those grounds were not necessarily the actual causes of marital breakdown. They were instead convenient categories into which attorneys could translate the complaints of their clients. Couples whose reason for divorcing did not fit the accepted categories sometimes went to great lengths to manufacture acceptable grounds.

A partner who was successful in accusing his or her spouse was rewarded with money and property. Judges in most states were required to award more than half the property to the "innocent" spouse. By making the husband and wife legal adversaries, the traditional divorce process often turned the ill will of an unsuccessful marriage into a public spectacle. No-fault was initially introduced in the hope that it would reduce the acrimony associated with divorce. Its supporters believed it would allow couples with real differences to dissolve their marriages without running a legal gauntlet that generally exacerbated tensions.

The new laws no longer require one spouse to bring charges against the other. All that is necessary is that irreconcilable differences exist and that one of the parties considers it impossible for the marriage to survive. Except where child custody is at issue, the pure no-fault states such as California expressly forbid the presentation of evidence of the spouse's wrongdoing. The record indicates that the new laws *have* reduced the acrimony of divorce by reducing the faultfinding. In Weitzman's words, "No-fault divorce laws have shifted the focus of the legal process from moral questions of fault and responsibility to economic issues of ability to pay and financial need. Today, fewer husbands and wives fight about who did what to whom.

TABLE 14-2
Comparing Traditional Divorce and No-Fault Divorce

Traditional Divorce	*No-Fault Divorce*
Restrictive law: To protect marriage	Permissive law: To facilitate divorce
Specific grounds: Adultery, cruelty, and so on	No grounds: Marital breakdown
Moral framework: Guilt vs. innocence	Administrative framework: Neither responsible
Fault: One party caused divorce	No-fault: Cause of divorce irrelevant
Consent of innocent spouse needed: Innocent spouse has power to prevent or delay the divorce	No consent needed: Unilateral divorce No consent or agreement required
Gender-based responsibilities: Husband responsible for alimony Wife responsible for custody Husband responsible for child support	Gender-neutral responsibilities: Both responsible for self-support Both eligible for custody Both responsible for child support
Financial awards linked to fault: Alimony for "innocent" spouse Greater share of property to "innocent" spouse	Financial awards based on equality and need: Alimony based on need Property divided equally
Adversarial: One party guilty, one innocent Financial gain in proving fault	Nonadversarial: No guilty or innocent party No financial gain from charges Amicable resolution encouraged

SOURCE: Excerpted from L. Weitzman (1985).

They are more likely to argue about the value of marital property, what she can earn and what he can pay" (Weitzman, 1985, p. x).

Under the new system, even the word "alimony" was dropped, in favor of *spousal support* or "maintenance." The way in which the courts decide whether to award such support has also changed. Spousal support payments are no longer used as a form of punishment for the offending spouse. The new criterion is whether one of the spouses needs temporary support while seeking gainful employment. As Weitzman notes, "While traditional alimony sought to deliver *moral* justice based on the past behavior of the parties, the new alimony was to deliver economic justice based on *financial* needs of the partners" (1985, p. 149).

Spousal support is awarded in fewer cases than before and for shorter periods of time. In short-term marriages, it is typically not awarded at all. Neither is it awarded to women who are considered immediately employable. Most spousal support awards are now transitional awards for a limited duration, usually about 2 years. The court's expectation is that during this period the spouse can find employment and achieve economic self-sufficiency.

No-fault divorce laws also ushered in new principles for making the custody decision. Under the old laws, women who wanted custody of their children were granted it almost automatically. The courts regarded the mother as a child's proper custodian. Under extraordinary circumstances, the father could gain custody, but only if he were able to prove that the mother was an unfit parent. Two changes have taken place in this respect. First, the doctrine of "maternal preference" has been replaced by statutes that emphasize the child's best interests. It is no longer a foregone conclusion that the child's interests are best served when custody is awarded to the mother. Second, unlike the old laws, which forced judges to choose one custodial parent, the new laws try to maintain the child's ties to both parents.

No-Fault Laws and the Divorce Rate

Over 20 years after California's pioneering efforts to reform the divorce laws, what has changed as a result of the "no-fault revolution"? As we have seen, these new laws reverse some traditional assumptions about matters such as whether husbands owe lifelong support to their former spouses and how custody decisions will be made. And they fundamentally change the nature of the legal proceeding from faultfinding

and blame to the division of marital property, provision of spousal support, and assignment of child custody.

One question is constantly raised about divorce laws: Have the no-fault laws inadvertently contributed to higher divorce rates? After all, the traditional requirement that a divorce could be granted only when certain conditions were satisfied created a barrier to individuals considering whether to dissolve their marriages. The no-fault rules lowered those barriers. Moreover, they allow either spouse to decide unilaterally to seek a divorce and may thus increase the likelihood of divorce. Yet, researchers who have examined no-fault divorce conclude that this has not been the case. Other social and personal factors appear to have much more influence than divorce laws on the frequency of marital dissolution (Kitson & Morgan, 1991).

EFFECT OF PERSONAL CHOICES AND BACKGROUND FACTORS

In the search for reasons for America's high rate of marital dissolution, personal choices and background characteristics may be as informative as social trends.

Deciding When to Marry

Age at marriage is still the best single predictor of divorce in the first 5 years of married life (Martin & Bumpass, 1989). People who marry early are normally less satisfied with their marriages and more frequently dissolve them, presumably because they are inadequately prepared for marital roles (Booth & Edwards, 1985). Young couples, writes sociologist Tim Heaton (1991):

> have had less time to gain social experience in dating and to form realistic expectations about adult roles; they have less time to prepare for employment; they have yet to experience the potentially disruptive experience of late adolescence; and they often violate normative expectations expressed by family, friends, or social situations by marrying young. (p. 286)

The divorce rate is about 60 percent lower for women who marry after age 25, compared to women who marry when they are still teenagers (Bumpass et al., 1991).

Having a Child before Marriage

The risk of divorce is also greater for women who have a child before marriage (Martin & Bumpass, 1989). The primary reason that premarital pregnancy is so strongly associated with divorce is that such pregnancies invariably occur when the mother is young, has not completed a high school education, and has few financial resources (Bumpass et al., 1991). These disadvantages follow her into marriage and continue to influence her life in a negative way.

Having Children within Marriage

It has been confirmed that couples who have their first child are less likely to divorce for up to a year following that birth (White & Booth, 1985). Additional children have no similar effect, however, unless the children happen to be sons, for some evidence suggests that parents of sons are less likely to divorce. Apparently, fathers are more involved with sons than with daughters. Their increased involvement seems to make parenting less stressful for mothers and results in fathers being more family-oriented. Greater family involvement by fathers, in turn, raises marital satisfaction and so lowers the likelihood of divorce (Morgan, Lye, & Condran, 1988). The risk of divorce also decreases as children grow older, reaching an all-time

The birth of a child tends to delay marital dissolution for up to one year, even longer if the child is a son. But having children within marriage is no longer a strong deterrent to divorce.

low when they leave home. Couples who remain childless have higher divorce rates than parents.

Having a Previous Marriage and Stepchildren

People in their second marriages are significantly more likely to divorce than are those in their first marriages. For women the risk is especially high if they marry a previously married childless male. Such women are twice as likely to divorce than women who wed a never-married male (Bumpass et al., 1991). But if the previously married male has a child, the marriage is much more secure.

There is a difference of opinion concerning why this trend occurs. Sociologists Teresa Martin and Larry Bumpass (1989) and Jay Teachman (1986) argue that individual characteristics are the key influencers of divorce the second time around. People who leave a second marriage typically share risk factors like early age at first marriage, less education, lower income, and so forth that carry over into the second marriage and increase the likelihood of divorce. Sociologists Andrew Cherlin (1993) and Lynn White and Alan Booth (1985), in contrast, contend that it is what happens *within* the second marriage, that is most salient. (Characteristics of remarriage are covered in Chapter 16.)

Being Racially or Ethnically Divergent

Although the divorce patterns just described are relevant for most American couples, there are some racial and ethnic differences. Black Americans have the highest divorce rate, followed by Hispanics. A major reason is that, compared to white couples, black and Hispanic couples tend to marry at young ages and are more likely to have had a premarital birth. Later marriage lowers the risk of divorce for blacks and Hispanics, but not as much as it does for whites. Having children within the marriage reduces the likelihood of divorce for Hispanic couples, but increases it for black couples (Heaton, 1991; Vega, 1991).

And What about Religion?

You may find it surprising that among the background characteristics we discuss in this section, religiosity is not one that impacts strongly on divorce. Most social scientists conclude that religion's role in reducing divorce has become less significant over the years. Although the Catholic church has a strong position against divorce, Catholic marital partners are as likely to divorce as are Protestants. It is still true, though, that in marriages in which one partner is Catholic and the other is not, the divorce rate is 40 percent higher than when both partners are Catholic (Bumpass et al., 1991).

FACTORS AFFECTING ADJUSTMENT TO DIVORCE

Regardless of why divorce happens, individuals must eventually adjust to its consequences and get on with their lives. *Adjustment* to divorce is defined as

> being relatively free of signs and symptoms of physical or mental illness; being able to function adequately in the daily role responsibilities of home, family, work, and leisure; and having developed an independent identity that is not tied to the status of being married to the ex-spouse. (Kitson & Morgan, 1991, p. 150)

Adjustment to divorce is influenced by many circumstances, including the availability of mediation services and gender differences in access to economic resources.

Mediation—An Alternative to Litigation

In this era of no-fault divorce, it is not just the laws that have changed. So, too, has the cast of characters offering professional help to people who want to dissolve their marriages. Formerly, virtually everyone who sought a divorce first hired an attorney. But under the no-fault system, the role of attorneys (as well as the roles of judges and the court system itself) have been redefined. In many states, couples are now encouraged to work out property arrangements and custody agreements by themselves or with the assistance of court-appointed mediators.

"*Mediation* is a type of negotiation in which the disputing parties are aided by a third party (or team) in making their own joint decisions" (Girdner, 1985, p. 33). The mediator or mediation team helps the separating couple negotiate an acceptable divorce agreement. The role of the mediator is to be "an advocate of the process of discussion and bargaining rather than an advocate of the particular settlement" (Trombetta, 1982, p. 69). A mediator plays a very different role from that of an attorney. Whereas lawyers serve as advocates for the spouse who hires them, mediators try to

avoid increasing the tension and hostility between divorcing spouses. If the lawyer's specialty is confrontation, the mediator's is compromise. The goal of mediators is to help their clients work out fair and suitable arrangements in a nonadversarial climate.

California was the first state, in 1981, to legislate that all parents must go through mediation before court hearings on child custody and visitation can occur (Emery & Wyer, 1987). If successfully executed, mediation makes parents more aware of the needs of their children as well as more sensitive to each other's needs. In the best of situations it sets the stage for continuing good will and collaborative decision making during the divorce process.

Gender: Who Has It Easier, Women or Men?

Women generally feel more positive about marital disruption and the divorce experience, but they also report a greater number of distress and health disorders related to divorce than men (Kitson & Holmes, 1992).

> Although men are more likely than women to experience *severe* problems of psychopathology, depression, and illness which require hospitalization, women are more likely to experience less severe but more frequent and longer-lasting physical and mental health problems, such as mild depression and anxiety about living alone, feelings of incompetence and guilt, and feelings of helplessness, unattractiveness, isolation, and loss of status. Since the severe problems that men experience affect only a small minority of divorced men, whereas the everyday adjustment problems of women are experienced by the majority of women on global indices of psychological adjustment, women as a group are likely to do more poorly than men. (Clarke-Stewart & Bailey, 1990, p. 76)

What contributes to women's typically poorer adjustment? One major contributor is women's decreased standard of living.

A Bad Economic Bargain for Women

Examining the economic impact of divorce, Weitzman (1985) concludes that, on the average, men experience a 42 percent *increase* in their standard of living in the first year following divorce, while women and their minor children expereince a 73 percent *decline* over the same period. Another study conducted over a 7-year time period finds that women's income drops 29 percent after divorce, while men's improve by 17 percent (Kitson & Holmes, 1992). And research conducted by the U.S. Census Bureau shows that women's standard of living falls 37 percent within 4 months of a divorce ("Study: Kids," 1991). Based on these results, one can only conclude that the income differential between divorced women and men is significant.

Apparently, the discrepancy in men's and women's standard of living after divorce is because men are not generally required to pay spousal support under the no-fault divorce laws—only about 15 percent of divorced women receive it (Morgan, 1991). Also, most men are not obligated to make substantial child-support payments. Moreover, even though child-support payments are not substantial, many men refuse to pay anything at all or make only partial payments. Meanwhile, women with custody must support the new household with only modest financial assistance. In general, writes Weitzman, "the courts are applying minimal and unrealistic standards of self-sufficiency. . . . The major economic result of the divorce law revolution is the systematic impoverishment of divorced women and their children. They have become the new poor" (1985, p. 323).

Recent studies of the income of households headed by divorced women suggest that the decline in their standard of living lasts longer than a year. Drawing upon data from the University of Michigan Panel Study of Income Dynamics, which shows fluctuations in household income over a period of 5 years, Weiss (1984) concluded that among families of various social classes, the income of female-headed households declines precipitously at the time of the divorce. Rather than returning to its former level over time, income remains at low levels as long as those households are headed by female single parents. Other studies evidence similar results (McLanahan & Booth, 1991).

> Women who are most at risk economically during their marriages (i.e., women of all races with little education or work experience, with large families or young children) face higher rates of poverty after divorce or separation. Those most likely to become poor are women with the smallest income or asset cushion during marriage . . . not only are these economically marginal wives less able to earn enough to support themselves, but their equally marginal husbands may be incapable of making up the short fall. (Morgan, 1991, p. 144)

Middle-class women may have some advantage over their poorer counterparts, but they too suffer great economic downturns. Morgan (1991) argues that, after divorce, middle-class women are essentially "de-

classed." They face the most dramatic financial reversals of all women, moving from "positions of income security to living much more modest and marginal lives" (p. 144).

The old divorce laws reinforced some of the obligations of the marital contract. Anyone who adhered to the marital vows could expect to be rewarded if the marriage ended in divorce, while anyone who violated them could expect to be punished. No-fault changed that. Today, marital property is divided as equally as possible between the divorcing spouses, regardless of blame or need. This more even distribution of property has been found, in the long run, to be inequitable for some women. Older middle-class women who have been in long-term marriages are particularly at risk. Their understanding of the marital contract was based on more traditional assumptions, in which the partners assumed she would never work because he would support her, while she tended to him and the children. Society no longer obeys these rules (Weitzman, 1985).

Another contributor to many women's economic downturn after divorce is their employment situation. Women's jobs are concentrated in low-level, high-stress occupational fields and almost always pay less than men's. There is a strong association between good adjustment to divorce, having higher levels of education, and working in jobs that pay more (Spanier & Thompson, 1984).

A third contributor to women's poorer adjustment to divorce is that they (90 percent of the time) have custody of the children. Although parenthood has its rewards, raising children under conditions of inadequate income and without another adult to share the daily decision making and physical and emotional tasks of child rearing is difficult.

Recent national efforts to enforce stricter standards for child support is partly a reaction by a concerned society to the economic plight of mothers and children after divorce. In 1988 the Family Support Act standardized the percentage of income that fathers should pay in child support. Fathers who fail to pay are now more routinely having their wages garnished, income tax refund checks confiscated, and property seized. Though couples may be free to negotiate the financial obligations of their divorce, children's rights to support are increasingly being protected.

The no-fault laws, which have been largely successful in reducing the emphasis on personal defects and gender-based assumptions of the traditional divorce procedure, seem to have introduced new and serious

POINT OF VIEW

No Father, and No Answers

My father was not the sort of guy who comes to mind when most people think of a deadbeat dad. He was an attorney, a judge and a respected civic leader. He was president of the local NAACP and a church deacon. Above all, he was a good father to his three daughters. As he once told me, he was not "some little boy in the ghetto who makes babies and doesn't take responsibility for his actions."

Yet for 20 years I didn't see my father or know what he looked like. And my mother never received a penny in child support. My mother and my father met in high school. After an intense relationship, she moved away with her family. A few months after she left, she told my father she was pregnant. When I was 10, my mother wanted to send me to Florida to meet my father. He demanded a blood test. Insulted and hurt, she hung up and never spoke to him again. The state of New Jersey required her to sue for child support when she applied for welfare. My mother says she got an order for a token amount, but my father was a penniless college student at the time, and the state never pursued him. My

mother often thought about "going after him," but never did. She couldn't afford a lawyer, didn't think she could win and, she says, she didn't want to hurt me.

Even though he was absent, I grew up in my father's shadow. My mother told me his name, his occupation, his alma mater, and how every time she looked at me, she saw him. But we were very different. While we were on welfare, he was climbing the corporate ladder to become a successful attorney. While we lived in a run-down house with relatives, he lived in a big house with his wife and three daughters. While I had no male role models until I went to an all-boys school on scholarship, he was president of a local NAACP chapter, a role model to boys he hardly knew. I never knew how affluent he was. And I never thought I cared. I never connected poverty and my absentee father.

I never thought I would meet him. Then my mother called one day while she was vacationing in Florida. In a joyous tone, she told me she had visited my father's mother. I was angry. All the feelings I had repressed

inequities. These laws appear to be a bad economic bargain for women.

A Bad Parental Bargain for Men

Divorce may be a better economic bargain for men, but how do they fare as parents? That most children have only limited contact with their fathers after divorce is revealed in two large national studies (Furstenberg, Nord, Peterson, & Zill, 1983; Seltzer & Bianchi, 1988). Less than 20 percent of the children had weekly visits with their fathers, and between 30 and 50 percent (depending on the study) had not seen their nonresident father for at least a year. And even when the nonresident father maintains regular contact, that parent's influence diminishes drastically because he spends far less time with his children (Furstenberg & Nord, 1985) (see the "Point of View" box).

Although it is undoubtedly true that some fathers are alienated and, in effect, pushed away from their children, most appear to voluntarily leave behind their

fathering responsibilities when they move out of the family home. Furstenberg explains:

> Men often sever ties with their children in the course of distancing themselves from their former wives. Remarriage by either partner usually hastens this process of disengagement. Geographical mobility, increased economic demands, and new family responsibilities, which often accompany remarriage, may erode the tenuous bonds between noncustodial fathers and their children. (1990, p. 388)

There are basically five reasons why fathers rarely visit their children (Loewen, 1988, p. 199):

1 The cultural expectation that women make better parents than men.

2 Conflict with or resistance from the mother to the father's visitation.

3 The fact that visitation is emotionally difficult—feel-

for 20 years came flooding back. I called my grandmother. She gave me his number. In a cold, scientific voice I told him I wanted to resolve the issue of his paternity. He asked for a test. I agreed.

Several months later we received the results. It was 99.78 percent probable that this man was my father.

Over the next 2 years, my father and I tried to establish a relationship. After the first year, it was clear that I was making most of the telephone calls. I even visited his hometown several times. When I did, I stayed with my grandmother. He never got around to visiting me.

When I first called him that summer night, I thought I had nothing to lose. But I was wrong. Once I found him I wanted to know who he was and where I came from. Most of all I wanted to know how he could stand a child of his wandering around somewhere in the world and not know if it was sick or well or starving. I realized that the gravity of the void he had left in my life had influenced my relationships and my perspectives. Knowing he knew where I was and didn't care had led me to trust friends more than family, to praise the strength and loyalty of women more than men, and to promise myself that I would be a better father. After we met, despite my anger, I still wanted his approval and his admiration. But I never felt like I had it. Our relationship is hardly more developed today than it was the day we met.

The nagging question for those of us abandoned by our fathers—however good their reasons—is "How could you?" My father has never given me a satisfactory answer. When I compared him to my brother, who will have to take financial responsibility for his illegitimate daughter or face jail under New Jersey law, he said I could not compare him to some little boy in the ghetto who rejects responsibility. The truth is I don't compare my father to my brother, or other deadbeat dads. I want to think his reasons for not supporting me are better than theirs. He called me 2 weeks in a row this month. I felt lucky, even grateful. Really. I know I have every reason to be angry and bitter for what he has not given me. But even now, and maybe forever, what I really want is a father.

EXPLORATIONS *Do you believe that this son's relationship with his father is typical of situations where the father does not acknowledge his parental responsibilities? What actions, if taken earlier in the son's life, may have resulted in a stronger bond between father and son?*

SOURCE: Excerpted from M. Mabry (1992).

ings of unfairness, anger, and rejection are pervasive.

4 The artificiality of the parent-child relationships imposed by the constraints of visitation.

5 Pressures from the father's new commitments and relationships.

Fathers who persevere and learn to deal with their negative feelings and forge a cooperative relationship with the mother are benefited in many ways. Fathers who visit feel that they are part of their children's lives; that they have some influence on how their children grow and develop. "Visitation increases the father's sense of purpose; some fathers feel a sense of exhilaration and even heroism, that they have persevered in relating to their children against legal and cultural odds" (Loewen, 1988, p. 210).

Fathers who visit also gain recognition and support from kin, friends, and colleagues for their continuing

family involvement. As one father said, "I'm treated with a lot more respect than when I was married. Most people think a guy who can help raise two kids—especially babies—is all right" (Luepnitz, 1982, p. 134). In a sense, these fathers are pioneers, behaving in ways that are contrary to gender role stereotypes and increasing the worth of fathering in a society that tends to devalue the role of fathers in child rearing. In addition, research supports the view that involved, committed fathers more often pay child support (Furstenberg & Cherlin, 1991) (see Table 14-3).

Do Race and Ethnicity Make a Difference?

Although knowledge about racial and ethnic differences in adjustment to divorce are needed in the development of educational and therapeutic programs for those specific populations, very few studies have addressed this issue. Recent research does indicate that

TABLE 14-3
How Can Noncustodial Fathers Protect Their Children?

Here are some guidelines for fathers during the first crucial months following divorce.

- Maintain a consistent pattern of frequent visits. Losing contact with a parent can be a crushing experience for a child, whose immediate response is to feel rejected and unloved. The long-term result is often a lowering of self-esteem. Consistency is as important as frequency. A visiting parent must keep promises. Don't fail to show up; try not to cancel.

- Consult your child about the visitation schedule. Many children complain that they are forced into a pattern designed only for their parents' convenience. The kids resent it and eventually begin finding excuses to avoid the visits.

- Keep up any child-support payments. Only a small percentage of women who are eligible for child support receive it. The obvious result is a greater or lesser degree of economic hardship for the children. Fathers who stop making child-support payments tend to see their children infrequently. As they fall behind, they are criticized by their ex-wives and may be denied visitation privileges.

- Subject children to as few changes as possible. In the year following separation, children experience less stress if they can remain in the same home, neighborhood, and school.

- Don't use the children as messengers or spies. Try not to ask your kids about the other parent's life. Avoid reporting to your child how angry, lonely, or economically strapped you are, in the hope that he or she will carry this information to your ex-spouse.

- Avoid using children as allies in parental battles. No child should be forced to choose one parent over another. Don't encourage a child to share your resentments toward the other parent; don't block visits.

- Avoid joining in your child's anger toward the other parent. This kind of rapport is just another way of forming alliances. Encourage your child to talk the problem over with the other parent; let them work it out.

- Keep kids out of the middle. Do *not* denigrate, malign, or badmouth the other parent. Attacking or blaming the other puts children in an untenable position. They must either lie about their feelings in order to agree with you, or bring their feelings into line with yours and basically lose a parent.

- Stay out of custody battles. The underlying motive is often to take revenge on an offending spouse, and the usual result is that the children become pawns in a shattering legal war.

- Avoid frightening the children with threats or with your worries about eventualities. At all costs, give your child the feeling that there will always be enough to eat, that he or she will always have a place to live, and that he or she will always have you.

- Stay in the role of parent. Be honest with your children and let them know when you feel bad, but don't turn them into emotional props or force them into the grown-up roles of confidant and decision maker. Reassure the children that *you know what you are doing and can take care of them.*

- If you are severely depressed (can't work, can't get out of bed) or dysfunctional (paralyzed by anxiety or bitterness) you should seek professional help. A child needs a functional mother and father.

- If children fail to resume normal development after the first year, they too should receive professional attention. Signals that help is needed are persistent anger or depression or the presence of serious behavior problems.

SOURCE: Excerpted from M. McKay, P. Rogers, J. Blades, & R. Gosse (1984).

black Americans have fewer problems with adjustment to divorce than do whites; in particular they report being less stigmatized by the divorce experience (Gove & Shin, 1989; Kitson & Holmes, 1992).

The black community of friends and kin seems to be supportive of individuals who separate and divorce, which enhances the ability to cope with negative divorce outcomes (Cherlin, 1993). The consensus is that blacks experience longer periods of marital separation before filing for divorce and consequently have an easier adjustment. But, more studies are needed before we can say with conviction that divorce outcomes and adjustment difficulties differ by race and ethnicity.

Access to Supportive Parents

Even though divorce frequently severs the ties between some friends and kin, it is through these networks of support that most individuals are able to rebound and find positive experiences that sustain them psychologically (Gerstel, 1988). Women many times are too overloaded with housework, child-care, and employment responsibilities to take advantage of the support available through clubs, churches, and friendship networks. They typically have little time for leisure and visiting.

When anthropologist Colleen Johnson interviewed divorced families over a 40-month period to investigate the supportive role of mothers during the divorce of their adult child, she found that *both* parents were essential in reducing the stress of divorce. Close to 70 percent of study participants were in contact with their parents on at least a weekly basis. Parents offered all types of support: 89 percent baby-sat or provided other personal services and 75 percent gave periodic financial help, while 22 percent offered regular financial help. Johnson remarks, "In all, we estimated that 59 percent were dependent upon their parents, in the sense that their lives would be affected without their help" (1988, p. 224).

The adults who were most closely bonded with their parents were divorced women in the greatest economic need. These women most frequently describe their relationship with their mothers as close and identify her as a friend and confidant. Johnson notes that parents of divorced children often disguise their financial help as gifts in order to maintain a more balanced and less obviously dependent relationship. One divorced mother said: "It's an emotionally fragile time in my life. It's great to know Mom is always there" (p. 225). Another woman called her mother "my security

blanket." Recalls Johnson, "In several cases the mothers' actions actually prevented children from being placed in foster homes" (p. 225).

On the down side, though divorced women appreciate the emotional and economic support provided, they chafe at giving up some control to their parents. Shared control, disagreements about how to discipline children, and loss of autonomy are frequently voiced complaints. Some divorced women prefer to keep their parents at a safe distance—far enough away to avoid entanglement but close enough to call on should something go wrong. As Cherlin and Furstenberg conclude in their book, *The New American Grandparent: A Place in the Family, A Life Apart* (1986), "grandparents in America are like volunteer firefighters: they are required to be on the scene when needed but otherwise keep their assistance in reserve" (p. 183).

Relationship with the Ex-Spouse

Divorce may mark the legal end of a marriage, but if there are children in the family, the ex-spouse's relationship continues to be a very important factor in their adjustment to divorce. Some ex-spouses have problems with continued dependency and attachment to each other. These strong attachment needs are related to difficulties in establishing a new self-identity as well as other psychological and physical health problems

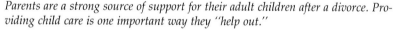

Parents are a strong source of support for their adult children after a divorce. Providing child care is one important way they "help out."

(Berman, 1988; Tschann, Johnston, & Wallerstein, 1989; White, 1991). For most ex-spouses, however, it is the conflict, acrimony, and frequent angry outbursts between spouses that cause the most pain. Turning this type of interaction around to be more cooperative is considered a major accomplishment.

Ahrons and Wallisch (1986) found in a 5-year study that about one-half of divorced parents were able to develop a satisfactory relationship. They note that of the divorced parents observed, 12 percent were "perfect pals," 38 percent "cooperative colleagues," 25 percent "angry associates," and 25 percent "fiery foes." Those with the more successful postdivorce relationships confined their discussions to child-centered issues and avoided discussion of marital issues. Couples who respected each other had the best chance of maintaining the ongoing negotiation necessary for positive functioning after divorce (Camara & Resnick, 1988; Peterson & Zill, 1986).

Capitalizing on Strengths

Sociologist Jean Veevers (1991) argues that divorce has become a "normal" event that the vast majority of families experience either directly or indirectly at some point in their history. Some divorcing persons experience extreme emotional trauma, others describe their reactions as a short-lived unpleasantness, and still others report mostly positive outcomes. A third of the women in Goode's (1956) study, for example, were categorized as having "low trauma" throughout the divorce process. Divorced mothers in another study reported that the experience had strengthened them by increasing their personal independence, giving them a new sense of competence and control, enhancing their relationships with their children, and granting them an opportunity to develop their own interests (Brown, Feldberg, Fox, & Kohen, 1976). Similar results were reported by Albrecht (1980), who found that 20 percent of men and 13 percent of women characterized their divorce as "relatively painless." And in the Kitson and Sussman (1982) study, some participants said that they felt a sense of relief or mixed feelings during the divorce process.

Admittedly, these respondents represent a small proportion of total participants in each study, but Veevers makes the point that we should look more carefully at this group of people and try to discover why they experienced divorce in a less problematic and more positive way. She identifies several factors

that are associated with a more positive divorce experience (see Table 14-4).

DIVORCE: CHILDREN'S EXPERIENCES

Today, 6 in 10 divorcing couples have children at home. Demographers predict that between 40 and 60 percent of all the children in this country will experience a parental divorce by the time they reach age 16 (Bumpass & Sweet, 1989; Norton & Glick, 1986). The odds are even greater for black children (Furstenberg, 1990). So one of the essential questions to ask about the impact of marital instability is how it affects children.

Critiquing the Research

Many researchers have examined children's reactions to divorce. Some of the most visible and often quoted studies are based on detailed longitudinal analyses of small samples of mostly white middle-class and upper-middle-class chldren of divorce (for example, Hetherington, 1989; Heatherington, Cox, & Cox, 1977; Wallerstein & Corbin, 1989; Wallerstein & Kelly, 1980). While they provide the kind of in-depth information that cannot be gleaned from one-shot surveys, they have a serious flaw. Because parents who volunteer to bring their children to a counseling center for interviews are self-selected, they and their children may be unusually troubled. If that is the case, the samples for these studies are not representative, and any generalizations from such studies are likely to be unreliable. National surveys of the impact of divorce on children (for example, Furstenberg & Nord, 1985) probably provide a more accurate portrait because they are based on nationally representative samples.

Drawing on both types of studies, we can make at least some tentative observations about the effects of divorce on children, the symptoms of distress, and the duration of the adjustment process. But, throughout this section, keep in mind that although almost all the research on children examines reactions *after* the divorce, some social scientists argue that children's distress is due more to marital conflict and other personal and family problems that are evident *before* the divorce (see the "Dilemmas and Decisions" box).

After reviewing dozens of studies on children of

TABLE 14-4
Positive Adjustment to Divorce: Identifying Strengthening Factors

Strengthening Factor	*How Factor Operates*
View of divorce	Definition of divorce as "normal" rather than as abnormal or a personal failure
Personality	Having traits that enhance the ability to cope: self-esteem, ego strength, and so on
Age	Being relatively young rather than old
Marital lifestyle	Leaving a very conflictual or abusive marriage
Length of marriage	Having a marriage of short duration
Length of termination period	Having a long period (more than 30 days) from decision to divorce to actual separation
Initiation	Being the dumper rather than the dumpee
Attachment	Having a low level of attachment to the ex-partner
Ex-partner	Having a satisfactory relationship with ex-partner
Income	Having access to adequate income and material resources
Education	Having a higher level of education
Gender roles	Having nontraditional or modern gender and/or marital roles
Networks	Having access to supportive social networks
Geographic mobility	Being geographically mobile (women only)
Peer support groups	Having access to a professionally organized group of peers
Significant other	Having a dating relationship and/or romantic attachment with a significant other

SOURCE: Adapted from J. E. Veevers (1991).

divorce, sociologists David Demo and Alan Acock (1991) argue that divorce does not have the same consequences for all children. Consequences vary along different dimensions of well-being, characteristics of children (such as age when divorce occurs) and characteristics of the families (such as parent-child relationships).

Children Are Rarely Forewarned

As common as divorce has become, few children are prepared when it happens in their own families. Most children are not warned about an impending divorce, and when it occurs they greet the separation with shock, frequently followed by denial, depression, and lowered self-esteem. These effects may persist for several years. Clearly, how children react to divorce depends partly on how parents manage the situation. Tensions can be eased if children are told about the separation in advance and are reassured that, although the parents are divorcing each other, they are not divorcing the children. But it is never easy. Wallerstein and Blakeslee explain:

> Children of all ages feel intensely rejected when their parents divorce. . . . Children get angry at their parents for violating the unwritten rules of parenthood—parents are supposed to make sacrifices for children, not the other way around. Some keep their anger hidden for years out of fear of upsetting parents or for fear of retribution and punishment; others show it. Little children may have temper tantrums; older children may explode. . . . Related to the anger is a sense of powerlessness. Children feel that they have no say, no way to influence this major event in their lives. Despite ongoing fantasies that things will magically get better, they cannot prevent divorce, fix it, rescue mom or dad, or the marriage. (1989, pp. 12, 13)

DILEMMAS AND DECISIONS

What's to Blame, Conflict or Divorce?: A New Look at Children of Divorce

Many of the problems children exhibit after their parents divorce are apparent even before the marriage ends, the first large before-and-after study of the effects has shown.

The findings, reported in the journal *Science,* suggest that staying together for the sake of the children is not necessarily helpful if the marriage is marred by conflict. The findings call into question the blame that has been attributed to divorce itself as the cause for the behavioral, emotional and academic problems commonly noted in other studies among the children of divorced parents.

The study was unusual in that it involved 17,000 British families, studied over a period of years. As a result, children whose parents ultimately divorced had been evaluated before the marriage began breaking up.

Fully half the disturbances among boys whose parents divorced and a smaller proportion of problems apparent among girls were noted by parents or teachers before the divorce. Similar effects were noted among boys in a study of 1,700 American families, the journal reported.

EFFECT ON THE CHILDREN

One of the study's authors, Dr. Lindsay Chase-Lansdale, a psychologist at the University of Chicago, said the findings suggest that "if a marriage is in trouble, there are effects on the children whether or not the parents divorce."

A coauthor, Dr. Andrew J. Cherlin, a sociologist at Johns Hopkins University, said: "More attention needs to be paid to the children when there is marital conflict. Conflict hurts children, regardless of whether it leads to divorce. If there is conflict, the children need to be sheltered from it, not caught in the middle between warring parents."

Nearly all previous studies of the effects of divorce on children focused on the period after the parents separated, and only a few compared children of divorce with those from intact families. The studies typically showed that many, if not most, children display behavioral and academic problems in the aftermath of divorce. Boys, for example, often become aggressive and disobedient and girls become anxious and depressed. And in both boys and girls, schoolwork often suffers.

The new report does not challenge these findings. Rather, it questions how much of the observed effects should be attributed to the divorce. Indeed, problems similar to those noted in the earlier studies were found among the children of divorce in the new report. Those whose parents had divorced were more likely than those from intact families to be rated by parents and teachers as having behavioral problems and to score lower on reading and mathematical achievement tests.

But since the children in the new study were rated before as well as after parental separation, the researchers could show that behavioral and academic difficulties were often apparent before the marriages dissolved. Thus, many problems in the children could be attributed more to marital discord than to the divorce itself.

"Divorce is a process that starts well before parents split and continues long afterward," Dr. Cherlin said. "Kids caught in the middle of marital conflict don't do well."

Of their current findings, the researchers said: "Overall, the evidence suggests that much of the effect of divorce on children can be predicted by conditions that existed well before the separation occurred. At least as much attention needs to be paid to the processes that occur in troubled, intact families as to the trauma that children suffer after their parents separate."

EXPLORATIONS *Does the finding that the emotional and behavioral problems of children probably originate with parental conflict prior to divorce contribute to your understanding of the divorce process? What advice would you give conflicted families with children?*

SOURCE: Excerpted from J. E. Brody (1991).

Children are rarely prepared for a parental divorce, even when they have observed severe conflict and other signs of marital problems between their parents.

The Child's Age Is Critical

Although all children are upset by divorce, the effect of the separation depends on the age of the child. Initially, young children are the hardest hit, partly because they are not able to understand what is happening. As psychologist Judith Wallerstein found, preschoolers are especially upset when their parents separate. They frequently regress in their development to a more dependent stage. Quite logically, they worry about the possibility of being abandoned by *both* parents (Wallerstein, 1980).

Slightly older children—those from 6 to 9 years of age, who are beginning to take their first steps toward independence—react somewhat differently. They often feel responsible for the breakup. The most common responses to divorce among children of this age are grief and a temporary withdrawal from schoolwork and social relationships. Children, by age 10, feel pressure to take sides, and, consequently, are often divided in their loyalties. They are very concerned about their own welfare and that of their parents. As one 10-year-old girl reveals, "Mom thinks no one worries about her. But I do" (Wallerstein & Blakeslee, 1989, p. 12).

Adolescents also experience pain and anger, and are likely to focus their anger on the parent who is perceived as the initiator of divorce. By adolescence, children can better understand why their parents divorced and are thus better able than are younger children to resolve conflicts between themselves and their parents. "Because older children have more self-confidence and

resources for fighting back, they may confront or question some aspects of family roles and functioning that younger children would not" (Hetherington, Stanley-Hagan, & Anderson, 1989, p. 305). In contrast to their younger counterparts, adolescents cope with feelings of distress by seeking support from friends, teachers, and other adults outside their immediate family. They can more easily accept the fact that they are not personally responsible for the family breakup.

Marital conflict surrounding the divorce is frequently a source of behavior problems that show up both at school and at home. School achievement is also affected (Kinard & Reinherz, 1986). In the year following divorce, children commonly become more dependent, aggressive, demanding, disobedient, and less affectionate. It is not just the children's conduct that changes. The parents' child-rearing style tends to change as well. Parents in the throes of divorce are commonly less consistent, less affectionate, and less able to control their children's behavior (Hetherington et al., 1977).

Adjustment: Is It Ever Complete?

Researchers disagree about the length of the adjustment process after divorce. Psychologist E. Mavis Hetherington and colleagues (1989) conclude that the low point is usually reached about 1 year after the separation. Subsequently, in most cases, the situation improves. Within 2 to 3 years, most children return to a normal pattern of development and experience no lasting effects. Other researchers believe that a minority of the children of divorce suffer long-term effects (Glenn & Kramer, 1985). In a longitudinal study, psychologist Judith Wallerstein and Joan Kelly (1980) found that about one-third of the children from divorced families are still emotionally bruised, unhappy, and lonely 5 years later. These children, according to the researchers, tend to be characterized by reduced self-esteem, problems in relating to others, and continued feelings of sadness or anger.

In a study based upon a nationally representative sample, Nicholas Zill noted that 14 percent of the children of divorced couples experienced distress severe enough to require psychological counseling. By comparison, less than half as many children from intact families (6 percent) had emotional or behavioral problems that warranted professional treatment. There are two ways of viewing these data. That the children of divorce are twice as likely as other children to need counseling suggests that they are experiencing more distress. Yet Zill found that six out of seven of the children of divorce do *not* seek such counseling. Presumably, this means that most children are able to cope fairly well with divorce and its aftermath (Zill, 1983).

In a 10-year follow-up study designed to chart the long-term effects of divorce, Wallerstein and Blakeslee (1989) reported that some children show the most severe symptoms of distress immediately after the separation, while others show certain lasting reactions. Ten years after divorce, the children who were very young at the time of the divorce appear to be faring better than their older brothers and sisters, presumably because the younger children are not burdened by vivid memories of the stressful events surrounding the separation. In contrast, Wallerstein and Blakeslee observe, those who were adolescents at the time of the marital dissolution remain unusually fearful of betrayal and anxious about the reliability of relationships. Although most children eventually bounce back in the wake of divorce, it is clear that marital disruption is a source of considerable stress and persistent problems for some of them.

Consequences in Adulthood

There is some evidence that adult children of divorce complete fewer years of schooling and earn less income than other adults (Amato, 1988). Some studies indicate that they are also more likely than other adults to report marital problems, marital conflict, and to divorce their spouses (Booth & Edwards, 1990; McLanahan & Bumpass, 1988). Moreover, adult children of divorce have been found in some research to score lower on measures of physical health, life satisfaction, and overall well-being compared to other adults (Amato & Keith, 1991; Glenn & Kramer, 1985; Roy, 1985).

Sociologists Paul Amato and Alan Booth (1991) conclude, after interviews with 1,243 adult children of divorce, that the differences between these adults and those from intact families is modest. Adults in their study who reported "low stress" involved with the parental divorce "were similar to those who grew up in very happily intact families" (p. 913). The key to positive adjustment is in children's secure relationships with both parents. They also emphasize that adult children of divorce are healthier if there are no subsequent divorces after the first marriage dissolves.

Protective Factors That Ward Off Stress

Three protective factors have been found to insulate children from stressful events like divorce: positive personality dispositions, an understanding family, and supportive community institutions and agencies (Garmezy, 1983). In her longitudinal study of divorced children, Hetherington notes that "temperamentally easy" children are better able to cope with the stress of divorce. She explains that for these children

> some practice in solving stressful problems under supportive conditions enhanced their later abilities to delay gratification, to persist on difficult tasks, and to be flexible and adaptive on problem-solving tasks and in social relations. In addition, if stresses did not occur simultaneously but were distributed across time, these children could cope with them more easily. (1989, p. 4)

Research findings place a heavy responsibility on parents who are ending their marriages. Parents are well-advised to remember that what they do—both in the process of separation and divorce and in its aftermath—is a major determinant of how their children will be affected by the experience (see the "Changing Lifestyles" box). As might be expected, research suggests that children who maintain a close relationship with both parents (who can control their tendency to fight with and blame each other) after divorce are less likely to have problems (Amato, 1993; Peterson & Zill, 1986). So, too, are children whose parents are well-functioning persons who can be relied on for love, emotional support, appropriate role modeling, and adequate financial support (Furstenberg & Cherlin, 1991). Children of divorce thrive under parenting styles that incorporate warmth with firm but responsive control. Offering the child a structured home environment with predictable rules and guidelines along with supportive guidance is most beneficial.

Brothers and sisters are additional sources of support. When parents, overburdened with their own adjustment problems, seem to have little emotional resources left to reach out to their children, siblings sometimes fill the gap and help each other cope (Hetherington, 1989; Wallerstein, Corbin, & Lewis, 1988). Hetherington concludes, based on her own research with children, that in the beginning stages of divorce the parent-child relationships are so unstable and upsetting and the divorce process so stressful that children receive very little relief from positive sibling relations. Later, boys more often display ambivalent or hostile reactions to siblings, competing with each other for parental and family resources (for example, affection, attention, care) that become ever more scarce during the divorce proceedings. Girls are more cohesive and supportive of each other. They are more likely to display greater caring and companionate behavior, especially toward their sisters.

Grandparents also offer support, particularly since some custodial mothers (25 to 33 percent) live with a grandparent (Hernandez, 1988). Sons who live with their mothers are observed to be better off emotionally when they can interact with a supportive grandfather (Hetherington et al., 1989). Grandmothers seem to have definite opinions about appropriate grandparent behavior after divorce (Johnson, 1988, p. 95):

What to Do	*What Not to Do*
Be there	Don't interfere
Be an advocate	Don't buy love
Provide family continuity	Don't give advice
Be loving	Don't be too protective
Be a liaison with parents	Don't discipline
Be a source of security	Don't be a fuddy-duddy
Make it easier for parents	Don't expect too much
Baby-sit	Don't nag
Just enjoy them	Don't be dull
Be fun to be with	Don't be old-fashioned

"Day care centers and schools," explains Hetherington and colleagues (1989), "that provide warm, structured, and predictable environments can offer stability to children" (p. 309). Teachers and peers at school "can validate self-worth, competence, and personal control of older children and adolescents" (p. 309). Hetherington (1989) concluded that the structure of the school environment was comforting to children under stress. For some children, school offers a place to excel as well as a place to develop close, trusting friendships. Adolescents, especially, find solace in school activities and friendship roles.

CUSTODY

Types of Custody

Sole custody is currently the most popular type of child custody after divorce, although joint custody is gaining use. There are two types of joint custody: joint legal custody and joint physical custody. Parents who have the legal responsibility to share major decisions regarding the children (for example, where they will live, educational needs, medical care) are said to have *joint legal custody*. Those who share both decision making and a residence for the children are said to have *joint physical custody*. Most commonly, parents share legal custody, but the children reside with one parent, usually the mother (Emery, 1988).

Joint custody first became available in California in 1979 and is now available in 33 states. One of the chief intentions of the new laws was to facilitate the spouses' transition to life after divorce and, particularly, to enhance their ability to cooperate in postdivorce parenting. It is certainly easier for judges to award joint custody than to choose between the parents. But, even though the new laws opened the door to fathers who want custody of their children, relatively few men have chosen to take advantage of that option.

Joint Custody: Is It Best?

Unless the parents are hostile and highly conflictual or emotionally or physically abusive toward one another, or in cases where the children are very young, joint custody is widely assumed to enhance the well-being of both children and parents. Very few studies, however, have examined the personal and family effects of joint custody (Ferreiro, 1990).

Skeptics point out that joint custody often prolongs the bitterness that caused the dissolution of the marriage in the first place. If faultfinding is no longer a prominent feature in divorce proceedings, it is still present when custody decisions are made. When divorcing spouses contest each other's abilities as primary guardian, custody disputes usually turn into bitter personal battles. Some have gone so far as to propose that the situation would be improved if the child had his or her own legal representative.

In a review article, Furstenberg (1990) describes the enthusiasm over joint custody as waning. Most research shows that only a small number of formerly married parents ask for this arrangement. It is still not known whether children benefit from dividing their time between two homes. We do not know for sure whether joint legal custody is useful for promoting parental cooperation. In *Divided Families* (1991), Furstenberg and Cherlin discuss this issue.

The rationale for joint custody is so plausible and attractive that one is tempted to disregard the disap-

CHANGING LIFESTYLES

Should We Require Classes in Divorce?

Before a very still and somber-looking audience of 80 parents, a social worker portrayed a slice of contemporary American life.

"I am a 6-year-old boy, and I live with Dad," said Aubrey Lee, the social worker, in his southern drawl. "One hour before I am supposed to visit Mom, Dad says, 'You can't see Mom. The check didn't come.'"

Mr. Lee looked hard at his audience, all mothers and fathers with pending divorce cases in this Atlanta suburb, and asked, "How do I feel?"

How a child feels in the turmoil of divorce—before, during and after the breakup of the family—was the subject of a 4-hour seminar that brought these parents one morning last week to the Cobb County Juvenile Court. They were not there voluntarily: They were ordered by the court to attend.

"If you don't go, you don't get a divorce," said Judge Watson L. White, chief judge of the Cobb County Superior Court.

Here and in some other parts of the country, judges in divorce proceedings are sending warring parents to court-required seminars to open their eyes to the trauma of divorce for children. Their aim, they say, is to force parents to cease battle long enough to consider the repercussions.

"The purpose," Judge White said, "is to make parents listen to experts who say, 'This is what is happening to your children, this is what they are feeling, and here are some things you can do to lessen the trauma.' Children don't want to take sides, but they are pushed and pulled and torn. We want to lessen the bitterness and help parents communicate with each other for the benefit of the children."

Judge White said he believed the program was having an effect. "Some couples are compromising and are settling their caes without a bitter court fight because they realize it would hurt their child and isn't worth it," he said.

Cobb County's program, which is called "Children Cope With Divorce: Seminar for Divorcing Parents," began in October 1988 and has served as the model for similar programs that began recently in Atlanta, Savannah, and Decatur, Ga. It has also been duplicated in Marion, Ohio, St. Petersburg, Fla., and Indianapolis.

pointing evidence and support it anyway. But based on what is known now, we think custody and visitation matter less for children than two [other] factors . . . how much conflict there is between the parents and how effectively the parent the child lives with functions. It is likely that a child who alternates between the homes of a distraught mother and an angry father will be more troubled than a child who lives with a mother who is coping well and who once a month sees a father who has disengaged from his family. (p. 75)

There is also some evidence that children living with a parent of the opposite sex are at greater risk of problem behavior (Peterson & Zill, 1986). This may help to explain why, as a number of studies show, boys experience more turmoil than girls in the aftermath of divorce. Some family scholars maintain that children of school age, especially, are better off in the custody of their same-sex parent (Camara & Resnick, 1988; Zill, 1988). According to Hetherington and associates (1989):

> Boys in the custody of their fathers are more mature, social, and independent; are less demanding; and have higher self-esteem than do girls in their father's custody. Sons, however, are also less communicative and less overtly affectionate, perhaps as a result of less exposure to women's expressiveness. Girls in the custody of their fathers show higher levels of aggression and behavioral problems and fewer incidences of prosocial behavior than do girls in the custody of their mothers. (p. 306)

Nevertheless, these authors conclude that so few studies have examined this issue that we must be cautious in making assumptions. It may, after all, be the quality

The fast-paced curriculum touches on emotional, psychological, social, and economic implications for children in a divorce. It also deals with how and what parents should tell children about a divorce, and how they can help them deal with separation and visitation.

The program addresses the needs of children according to their age and developmental level. It is a mixture of lectures, films, and role playing by a pair of seminar leaders, who dramatize common conflicts that arise in families as a result of divorce. The audience is encouraged to comment on the behavior of parents and children in these scenarios, and how they affect and often manipulate each other.

"Parents see themselves in our role playing, and they begin to recognize things they typically do out of anger toward each other," said Bev Bradburn-Stern, the social worker who designed the seminar for Families First, an Atlanta social service and counseling agency that runs the program.

Judges say there have been complaints from lawyers about the program, especially at the beginning. "Lawyers thought we were intervening with their clients and were creating another bureaucratic step in the divorce process," said Judge Ayers of Indianapolis.

After the seminar, many parents said they had not wanted to attend, and in some cases were angry about being forced to do so. But they also said that in the end, they had found the seminar useful.

"I thought, 'I don't need it, they won't tell me anything,' " said Patrick Brownlee, a restaurant manager who has two sons, 4 years and 19 months old. "But I learned I need to listen more to my kids, and not be so strict when they first come back after visiting their mother."

Jim Brown, a drafting engineer who has a 3-year-old son, said: "I don't advocate mandated programs, but this has a lot of value. I was aware that my son needs to be comforted by both his parents, but now I will make an extra effort."

Carla Kirby, a Juvenile Court clerical worker who has two sons, 1 and 2, said she had not looked forward to the program.

"I was apprehensive and didn't know what to expect," she recalled. ""I did get something out of it. There is so much uncertainty when you get a divorce. This helps you know what to expect."

EXPLORATIONS *If you were asked to help plan a short course for divorced parents, what information would you include? Would you ever ask parents to bring their children to class? At what point in the course would you do this and under what circumstances?*

SOURCE: Excerpted from C. Lawson (1992).

---

of the parent-child relationship and whether custody was actively sought or a forced choice rather than gender that most influences the parent-child relationship and the subsequent development of the child within that relationship. In any case, deciding on custody—and on what is in the best interests of the child—is likely to remain one of the thorniest questions that has to be answered when a marriage is dissolved.

In conclusion, for every marriage that breaks up there are undoubtedly several in which the partners remain unhappily married. Indeed, many people remain in destructive or physically abusive relationships for years (Strube & Barbour, 1983). The marriage stays intact out of habit more than anything else. The quality of the relationship is painfully bad, but more painful still is the prospect of facing life alone. Sometimes neither spouse has the strength or the vision to see what their lives might be like without the other. Sometimes

either or both spouses know that they could not survive economically or emotionally without the other.

We might view today's more liberal grounds for divorce as a reflection of newer assumptions about the satisfactions that marriage is supposed to offer. In the past, as indicated, companionship was not an important or widely shared expectation in marriage, and so it made sense that the only allowable grounds for divorce were those that clearly specified a breach of contract, such as adultery, desertion, drunkenness, or neglect of support.

Laws that allow divorce because of irretrievable breakdown or incompatibility reflect the increasingly widespread quest for love and emotional intimacy in marriage. How one balances the desire for mutual satisfaction and happiness with the need for long-term commitment and marital stability is, of course, a matter of personal judgment.

SUMMARY POINTS

■ Since 1880 the American divorce rate has climbed steadily, reaching a plateau in the late 1980s. A similar trend, though less dramatic, exists in most industrialized countries.

■ Between one-half and two-thirds of all couples who marry today are eventually expected to divorce.

■ According to Paul Bohannan and Diane Vaughn, divorce is a process that involves several "stations" or stages of uncoupling.

■ Divorced individuals usually develop personal accounts of why their marriages failed. This "divorce story" serves as a way of coping with emotional trauma and pain, facilitates the development of understandable causes for the divorce, and establishes blame.

■ Over time the reasons for divorce have remained fairly consistent: disagreements over marital roles and dissatisfaction with the partner's involvement in family life. Today, issues of disagreement more often focus on sharing family roles and issues of involvement center on companionship, affection, and sex.

■ Collectively, individuals' evaluations of their marriages, societal trends, and personal choices and background characteristics explain today's high divorce rates.

■ Persons who are said to have successfully adjusted to divorce are relatively free of mental or physical symptoms of distress, able to attend in a competent manner to family and work responsibilities, and are acting in an autonomous and independent manner, free of emotional dependence on the ex-spouse.

■ In divorce mediation, the married couple meet together with an impartial third party or mediation team to identify, discuss, and ultimately resolve any issues they have over the divorce settlement or child-custody arrangements.

■ Women, in contrast to men, typically experience a drop in their standards of living after divorce that is so dramatic and long lasting that sociologist Lenore Weitzman refers to divorced women and their children as the "new poor."

■ Compared to men, the majority of divorced women experience a greater number of longer-lasting stress and health disorders. Their poorer adjustment to divorce is complicated by the sharp decrease in income they experience, the nature and status of their jobs, and the fact that they typically have custody of the children.

■ Noncustodial fathers often voluntarily drop out of their children's lives because of cultural expectations that fathers are less competent parents, conflict with the custodial mother, uneasiness and emotional distress during visits with the child, feelings that the rules of visitation make the parent-child relationship artificial or shallow, and pressure from a new relationship or second marriage and family.

■ Black couples, because they generally have a lengthier period of time between separation and divorce and receive greater support from kin and community for their decision to divorce, are less stigmatized by divorce and usually have an easier adjustment than other couples.

■ Parents offer many different kinds of support to their adult children during the divorce process.

■ Maintaining a positive, or at least a civil, relationship with the ex-spouse is very important for good adjustment after divorce.

■ Jean Veevers identifies 16 factors that are related to defining divorce as a strengthening rather than a traumatic event.

■ According to E. Mavis Hetherington, children of divorce typically reach the lowest point of their distress within 1 year of the separation and recover to a normal pattern of development within a 2- to 3-year period.

■ How children react to divorce depends on many factors, including age of the child; level of conflict between the parents; income, education, and stress level of the parent with custody; and the child's relationship with each parent.

■ Sole custody is the most common type of child-custody arrangement, although joint custody is becoming a strong alternative. The type of custody is probably less important to a child's adjustment to divorce than is the quality of the parent-child relationship and whether custody was a forced choice or actively sought.

■ Having an easy temperament, an understanding family, and a supportive network of community institutions and agencies helps insulate children from divorce.

■ As our expectations for emotionally intimate and interdependent relationships have increased, so, too, has divorce.

KEY TERMS

Divorce/marriage ratio
Crude divorce rate
Refined divorce rate
Divorce revolution
Spousal support

Adjustment
Mediation
Sole custody
Joint legal custody
Joint physical custody

REVIEW QUESTIONS

1. What are the six stations of divorce and the actions, tasks, and feelings that accompany them?

2. Describe the process of uncoupling identified by Diane Vaughn.

3. What is a "divorce story" and how does the development of one assist in the divorce process?

4. What factors contribute to today's high divorce rate?

5. What major changes have taken place in the divorce laws since 1970?

6. What factors influence adult adjustment to divorce?

7. Why is no-fault divorce called a bad economic bargain for women?

8. Under what conditions is divorce a positive or strengthening experience?

9. What are the consequences of divorce for children?

15

Illustration by Adam Niklewicz

Single-Parent Families

For the first time in several years, in the 1992 presidential election year, the "plight" of the *single-parent family*—one parent with the primary responsibility for raising biological or adopted children—was brought to the attention of the general public. Vice President Dan Quayle briefly made headlines because of some disparaging remarks about the TV character Murphy Brown, a highly paid professional woman who gave birth to a child without benefit of marriage. Quayle argued that, by excluding the father, Murphy was not setting a good example for today's generation of young adults; that it was behavior like Murphy's that was leading to the moral decay and decline of family values. Controversy reigned for a few days as both the famous and the not so famous took sides on the issue of unwed parenthood and the state of the modern American family. Both political parties jostled for the position of "defender of the family" and the press, which brought the incident to light, pointed out the hypocrisy of the whole business. What surprised many people was that single-parent families are the fastest growing family type in the United States today.

In this chapter we devote most of our discussion to single-parenting after divorce, having already examined birth rates and parenting styles of unwed mothers in previous chapters. We begin by identifying demographic trends and stereotypical assumptions and follow up by investigating the real-life experiences of single-parent families. We will pay particular attention to the common concerns as well as the life satisfactions reported by the adults and children in single-parent families.

TRENDS AND ASSUMPTIONS ABOUT SINGLE PARENTS

How Many Single-Parent Families?

A rapid increase in single-parent families is one of the chief reasons that the typical American household is smaller today than in past generations. Until 1970, 10 percent of American families were single-parent families; by 1980 the figure had more than doubled to 21 percent. Single-parent families now represent 25 percent of all American families. Almost 16 million or 26 percent of the children under 18 now live in a single-parent family. Of those children, 39 percent live with a divorced parent and 31 percent live with a parent who has never married (see Figure 15-1) (Barringer, 1991).

If current trends continue, it is estimated that between 60 and 70 percent of American children will live in a single-parent family by age 18 (Demo & Acock, 1991). For black children the percentage is estimated to be even higher because 60 percent of black children under 18 already live in a single-parent home, up from 36 percent in 1970. Among Hispanics, 35 percent of families are single-parent families (U.S. Bureau of the Census, 1990a).

FIGURE 15-1

Changes in Single-Parent Families: 1970–1991

SOURCE: R. Suro (1992).

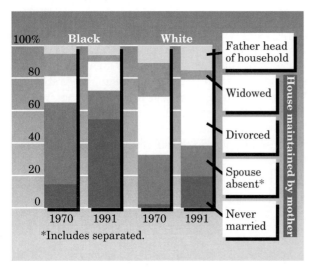

Why They Are Overlooked by Researchers

Single-parent families are often overlooked or ignored by social scientists in favor of studying the process of divorce or remarried families after divorce because of two false assumptions. Although these assumptions rang true throughout much of our history, recent demographic and social changes have rendered them unreliable.

The first assumption is that most single-parent families result from marital dissolution. Although it is correct that among white families higher divorce rates are the chief reason for the increase of single-parent families, among black families much of the rise is due to the rapid escalation in births to unwed mothers. Other avenues to single parenthood are long-term separation, desertion, death, and adoption. For many individuals the single-parent family is a deliberate choice, for others it is a reality with which they must learn to cope (see the "Dilemmas and Decisions" box).

The second assumption is that because most divorced women and men remarry relatively soon after marital dissolution, the single-parent family is but a brief transitional stage between divorce and remarriage—not a "real" family. The facts belie this assumption, too. There is a growing trend toward delaying remarriage. In the 1980s, the average interval between divorce and remarriage was 3 years. By 1990, the interval had increased to about 6 years when there were children in the family (U.S. Bureau of the Census, 1990a). Most children in a single-parent home will, in fact, never experience a second family. Most will grow to adulthood with their single-parent mom or dad (Demo, 1992). Some single parents prefer the single life to remarriage; others want very much to marry again.

Current thinking, buttressed by several major studies of families after divorce, is that both children and parents need time to adjust to divorce and acclimate to single parenthood before considering another marriage. In effect, the family that quickly remarries must progress through three normally very stressful periods of adjustment, one right after the other. First comes the divorce with all its attendant stressors, followed by living in a single-parent family (or for some children, dividing their time between two single-parent families—mom's and dad's). Finally, in many cases, there is remarriage—yet another major life transition (or for some children, two remarriages, one for *each* parent). Swift passage through these jarring experiences typi-

DILEMMAS AND DECISIONS

Varied Reasons for Single Motherhood

Interviews conducted around the country with single mothers of varying races and economic conditions suggested that the decision to bear a child involves a mixture of practical, emotional, and spiritual considerations and is usually not a straightforward choice.

For Jean Pollard it was not a matter of choice at all. "He wasn't a planned child," Ms. Pollard, 34 years old, said of her 3-month-old son who lives with her in a shelter for homeless families in Houston. She was laid off from work, she said, and then the child's father reneged on a promise to marry her.

"I wanted kids, but I always figured when I had a child I would be married, the typical American dream," she said. "Sometimes it doesn't work out like that."

Like many single mothers, Ms. Pollard sees the value of marriage. But she went on, "Marriage doesn't guarantee anything anymore because it's not like it used to be with our parents."

For Debbie Spain, staying married was not an option. A 32-year-old medical secretary in Boston, Ms. Spain was beaten by the father of her first child and ended a brief marriage to her second child's father, who was an alcoholic. "Just because you have someone's last name doesn't mean that's going to solve any problems," she said.

Both of her children remain in close contact with their fathers, but Ms. Spain finds they are happier now that she is raising them alone. "I just decided I'm going to do it right as much as I can," she said.

For Patty Friedmann, having a child was more important than having a husband. Ms. Friedmann, a 45-year-old writer in New Orleans, deliberately became pregnant when she was single and 28 because she wanted a child. Ms. Friedmann, who is now married, described how women can assert their identities by making such choices.

The many different reasons that women give for being single mothers suggest that their lives reflect a variety of trends in American life.

"You can't isolate single parenting by women as a discrete phenomenon," said Barrie Thorne, a professor of sociology at the University of Southern California. "You have to see it in the context of an overall change in attitudes toward many sexual and family issues including the status of women, divorce and premarital sex."

Single mothers argued that although their families may not be considered conventional they are nonetheless valid.

Grace Cox, a 35-year-old typographer in Houston, has one child from an early marriage that ended in divorce and another born to her as a single mother.

"When you have kids by yourself, you have to work harder at making sure they have what they need and at keeping the family together," she said, adding, "This is a family too."

Like several other women, Fran Ramer, a 42-year-old Chicago businesswoman who is a single mother, said she was deeply committed to the family as a social ideal and saw herself adapting that ideal to reality.

She said, "I don't disagree with Quayle about family values, but I think he is a little behind the times about what a family is."

EXPLORATIONS   *What changes have occurred in cultural attitudes and behaviors regarding sexual and family issues that make single-parent families more socially acceptable in the 1990s?*

SOURCE: Excerpted from R. Suro (1992).

cally creates a pileup of stressors that can affect physical and emotional well-being.

FACING A RESEARCH BIAS

You might think that, given the number of single-parent families and the amount of research in this area of study, most of the questions about the nature of the single-parent family and its effect on parents and their children would have definitively been answered. Such is not the case. There is still much to learn. Even today, researchers in family studies, sociology, psychology, and related fields continue to conclude chapters, books, and articles on this topic by saying that additional studies are needed for a clearer understanding of single-parent families.

Clinical Impressions May Be Unreliable

One problem is that much of the research on single-parent families comes from clinical sources. Families who are troubled and seek help from professionals are more often studied because they are an easily available group. This type of research typically

> assumes that living in a single-parent household is at best problematic and at worst the source of major social problems, and thus seeks to identify what negative effects the single-parent condition has on family members. The single-parent condition is assumed to be the cause of a family member's inappropriate sex-role behavior, achievement problems, low self-esteem, depression, immaturity, and sexual precocity. Few studies control for other causal explanations, such as the family's socioeconomic status and degree of access to social supports, the custodial parent's sex and employment opportunities, the child's age, sex, and involvement with the noncustodial parent, or the relationship between the parents before and after the single-parent family's formation. (Thompson & Gongla, 1983, p. 109)

Knowledge from clinical studies is sorely needed because a number of parents and children in single-parent families do rely on therapists and other similarly trained professionals for help with adjustment problems. Such studies, nevertheless, may not reflect the typical responses of *most* single-parent family members—those who do not receive professional help.

To apply the information gleaned from these studies to the more normal population of single-parent families results in generalizations that can promote pathological interpretations and increase social stigma.

False Interpretations, Missing Information

A related problem is that when studies of single-parent families are carried out, important details about how such households differ from intact families are sometimes interpreted as flaws in the family. The thinking among some social critics is that because this family is different, it must be problem-laden. Difference does not, of course, equal a pathological or deeply troubled existence. Distressed parents and children are found in all types of families.

Another problem is that because many studies of single-parent families fail to reveal whether the family results from divorce, death, adoption, or other circumstances, there is no way to discern whether the differences discovered through research are due to a particular family variation or to other factors. Other related concerns include the use of mostly white respondents and the failure to consider family socioeconomic status.

THE PROCESS OF BECOMING A SINGLE-PARENT FAMILY AFTER DIVORCE

Single-parent families are not all alike and should not be generalized into one homogenous group, but they share some characteristics because of their common experience of bringing up their children without benefit of a partner. Sociologist Robert Weiss, author of *Going It Alone* (1979), was one of the first researchers to conduct a thorough investigation of the single-parent family after divorce. His findings and those of other researchers point to two very distinct changes that occur in most families as they move from intact family status to single-parent family status.

A New Family Partnership Is Forged

First, the authority structure of the family changes. What had previously been a coalition of two parents who functioned as a decision-making team to deal with family responsibilities and provide love, support, and discipline disintegrates. Second, a new partnership emerges between the single parent and the children. "The children are promoted: the custodial parent relinquishes some decision-making control and then begins to engage the children as if they were junior partners" in the family enterprise (Thompson & Gongla, 1983, p. 107).

Together this new partnership begins to evolve and operate differently from the intact two-parent model as the children assume additional responsibility for the daily functioning of the family. A single mother with four children aged 11 to 16 remarks:

> As soon as I was on my own, I sat down with the children—I always had a good rapport with the children—and I told them, "Now things are different. Instead of, more or less, it being a family of mother and four children, we're all one family with all equal responsibility, and we all have a say, and we're all very important. And if it is going to work right, we all have to be able to cooperate with each other." (Weiss, 1985, p. 67)

Another adds:

> Before the divorce, I just did it all. . . . After the divorce, and I was working, the kids had to do a lot. I don't get home till after 5:30, so they have to start dinner. They put in loads of clothes, and really do a lot of the cleaning. Since I'm not here, I have to trust them to do it,

Single-parent families rely on a working partnership of parent and children cooperating to accomplish the daily tasks of running a household: shopping, doing laundry, preparing meals, taking care of younger children.

and the more clearly it's laid out, the more likely it gets done. . . . The little ones can't do as much, and I want to be fair, so there's a lot of working in pairs, and trading off every week, things like that. (Stinson, 1991, p. 58)

Greater Equity, Shared Power, A Closer Bond

Social scientists Edward Thompson and Patricia Gongla describe the single-parent family as "characterized by greater equity, more frequent interaction, more discussion, and heightened cohesiveness (i.e., greater intimacy and companionship)" (1983, p. 107). Together, family members establish new family rules, share the household work, solve problems, make decisions, share power, and spend more leisure and recreational time together.

Single-parent families generally evidence close parent-child bonds. Family closeness varies, of course, depending on the number and ages of the children and the individual personalities of family members. Larger families and families with adolescent children, for example, are not as cohesive as are small families or families with school-age or younger children. Families with more children have more complex time schedules and encounter greater difficulty planning and organizing shared activities. Adolescent children have a need to develop some independence from their families, which may temporarily increase the distance between themselves and their custodial parents.

Degree of family closeness is also influenced by parenting style. Adults who use an authoritative style of parenting based on reasoning and joint decision making form a closer bond with their children than parents who rely on very strict, rigidly enforced rules, or parents who prefer an uninvolved and distant, "anything goes" parenting style (Macklin, 1987).

COMMON CONCERNS AND MISUNDERSTANDINGS

Regardless of how a single-parent family is formed, by divorce or in some other way, most share some common concerns: social stigma, a lower family income compared to two-parent families, and an overload of daily responsibilities. And based on the few reliable studies available, these effects of single parenthood appear to be similar across racial and ethnic groups. Each problem is to some extent defined and exacerbated by cultural expectations that encourage certain patterns of feeling and behaving in families, regardless of family type.

Would the "Real" American Family Please Stand Up?

The cornerstone of the "problem of the single-parent family" is that we as a society idealize the two-parent family. We consistently act as though the two-parent family has no problems, that it is a perfect union of two partners who interact in continually positive and supportive ways, raising happy, successful children to adulthood. Some fantasize that, if somehow we could bring back the 1950s or even earlier eras, family life would again be perfect, or nearly so. Sociologist William Goode said that this kind of thinking is a distortion of American family history based on a reverence and nostalgia for fictional families of past generations (1963). Family historians through their research and scholarly writings have attempted in the last two decades to correct this biased notion.

We sometimes forget that even two-parent families seem to manage successfully when only one of the parents has the primary responsibility for running the family and rearing the children. Military families and families in which one parent is in prison, for example, may face lengthy parental absences. During one parent's absence, such families operate much like single-parent families. And when the absent parent returns, one of the most stress-producing adjustments for family members is reemergence of the other adult and the inevitable changes in daily activities and family interaction that results. Other examples are families in which one parent's scheduled activities make it difficult for children to spend time with him or her—travels frequently for business purposes, leaves early for work and returns late, or is overly involved in community and volunteer activities.

Physical separations are not the sole catalyst for family reorganization in two-parent families. Intact families also act much like single-parent families when there is a psychological separation between parent and children. Family members may become emotionally distant to escape an unhappy or abusive parent, or a parent addicted to substances like alcohol or drugs. Frequent absences and minimal communication may mean that the role responsibilities for both parents are performed by one (Gongla & Thompson, 1987). The point is that two-parent families vary. Not all are the idealized perfect environment for adults or children, yet we do not label them as dysfunctional or problem-laden simply because a significant minority have serious difficulties or do not operate as culturally expected.

In some single-parent families both parents con-

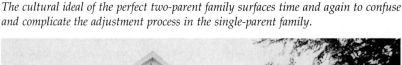

The cultural ideal of the perfect two-parent family surfaces time and again to confuse and complicate the adjustment process in the single-parent family.

tinue to maintain a high level of involvement with the children despite their physical separation. The children may stay with the noncustodial parent every other week or on weekends; the parents may have a friendly relationship and regularly communicate about the children; both parents may think of themselves as a primary custodial parent and take major responsibility for parenting tasks; or both may interact with the children daily (Gongla & Thompson, 1987). This *binuclear family*—a mother and a father living in separate households who continue to remain active parents to their children—is in many ways behaving as a two-parent family. The point is that the way family members interact and how they view their connections and responsibilities to each other vary substantially, regardless of family type.

Dealing with Social Stigma

Another related concern is dealing with the social stigma of being in a single-parent family. Because, as a society, we have a tendency to dichotomize, then label and treat single parents and their children differently from two-parent or intact families, members of such families come to understand and believe that they are somehow different from the "normal" American family. This cultural misconception leads to thoughtless remarks that take a toll, contributing to feelings of being deprived and inadequate. One single parent recounts the story of her son coming home from a boy scout meeting in a very distressed state:

> The scoutmaster indicated that the family was like the tepee, with three poles holding it up, the father pole, the mother pole, and the child pole. Without each member of the family, the tepee could not stand! What a message to give a child from a single-parent family. "You are flawed" or "There is something unnatural about your family." (Hodges, 1986, p. 194)

Single parents and their children often hear stories and other negative comments like this one. Social rejections add up, one on top of another, to become negative influences for children and their parents.

Recognition of such slights have resulted in some recent attempts to reduce stigma. A recent "Sesame Street" rerun, for example, featured a young bird explaining to Kermit the Frog, "Mom's tree is over there; back there is Daddy's tree. They live in different places, but they both love me." The same episode showcased

children's drawings of their families, some of which were single-parent families. And since 1987, the National Education Association has attempted to direct more programs toward children who do not fit the two-parent model of family life. "Banana Splits," a support group for children after divorce, is used in more than 100 schools. In this program, children, with parental permission, are guided by an informed counselor or teacher through free-ranging discussions of their feelings and experiences (National Education Association, 1988). "Kids Turn," a program used by attorneys in San Francisco, consists of a series of six 90-minute programs directed toward single parents and their children. It receives good reviews by participants: the children are particularly responsive to seeing their feelings expressed through puppets ("Helping children," 1988).

Coming to Terms with Role Overload and Role Conflict

Acting Alone: Learning the Role

A third concern shared by single parents of separation and divorce is the difficulty of assuming the role of sole adult in the family, with all the attendant responsibilities and demands. Not surprisingly, researchers who compare the self-reported happiness of those who are married with single parents find that sole parents are not as happy. Many feel overworked and anxious. Single mothers spend more time worrying than other mothers and say they are less satisfied with their lives (McLanahan & Adams, 1987). A greater number of single mothers with young children seek help for depression than any other population group (Macklin, 1987). They generally earn less income than single fathers, have less education, and have fewer opportunities to date and otherwise spend time on personal needs (De Frain & Eirick, 1981).

Whatever tasks were delegated to the partner—washing the dishes, fixing the toilet, making social arrangements—are now the responsibility of one parent. Facing life alone after the routines of married life, divorced men and women frequently feel adrift and directionless. Studies of female-headed families indicate that, to a remarkable extent, marital disruption and unwed pregnancy effectively sever the relationship with the parent (generally the father) who lives outside the home. The National Survey of Children shows that nearly one-half of all children in single-parent families have not seen their nonresident fathers for at least 1 year. Even when the nonresident parent maintains frequent contact, it is rarely the case that the children spend substantial time with that parent, or have bedrooms in his or her residence (Furstenberg & Nord, 1985). Other research corroborates this finding (Lewin, 1990).

Making Time for Parenting Roles

Parents without the emotional or economic support of a coparent are the most overloaded of all parents. As a result of having so many responsibilities, single parents have been found to monitor their older children's activities less closely than parents in intact families. Many admit that they know less about their children's friends and their specific activities at any given moment than they would like (Hetherington, 1989). This does not imply that single parents care less about their children than other parents. Sole-custodial parents simply have less time available for parental supervision. Like other parents, most make diligent efforts to teach their children to be self-reliant, independent problem solvers and to make good judgments based on parental guidance and instruction.

School-age and adolescent children in single-parent families, compared to children in two-parent families, are expected to take on more household work and assume greater responsibility for the care of younger siblings. "For many children, the increased practical and emotional responsibilities accelerate the development of self-sufficiency and maturity" (Hetherington, Stanley-Hagan, & Anderson, 1989, p. 308). Only if the single parent makes excessive demands that are beyond the developmental abilities of the children, do they experience negative feelings about their greater level of participation. Children pushed to perform such tasks and make such decisions will then display feelings of incompetence and low self-esteem. Children given an overload of responsibilities, on the other hand, will generally express resentment and dissatisfaction.

Relaxing Standards

Single parents, like parents in intact families, are pulled in two different directions as family and employment roles conflict and compete for their time and energy. Single parents of divorce soon learn that it is almost impossible to maintain the household in the manner they achieved as a two-parent family. Faced with the reality of letting some tasks remain undone

or experiencing further overload, most parents opt for relaxing some of their standards.

The alternative is to stay up later at night or arise even earlier in the morning, with the result being increased feelings of tiredness, irritability, and disorientation, or having to ask the children to take on more family work. Neglecting housework seems a better option to most single parents than spending less time with their children, increasing the children's already heavier chore assignment, or further neglecting their own personal needs. It is a common and persistent worry of single parents that they expect too much of their children. Some go to great lengths to shield their children from as many new expectations as possible, often increasing their own work load as a consequence (Weiss, 1979).

Maintaining Grandparent Relationships

A potential source of role conflict concerns sorting out and maintaining complex kin relationships. Grandparent relationships are especially important to children, and single parents usually try to maintain those strong connections. On the positive side, grandparents play a crucial mediating role in keeping kin networks vital and functioning. They are among the first to offer support to the single-parent family. Not only are they primary transmitters of cultural, personal, and family values, but they are sources of unconditional love and conveyers of special favors and prized activities (for example, movie tickets, shopping excursions, vacation trips, weekend sleepovers, and those forbidden but cherished junk foods). Grandparents tend to idealize their grandchildren and this positive relationship enhances children's well-being (Furstenberg & Cherlin, 1991).

On the negative side, grandparents sometimes focus too much on their own needs, leading them to display demanding, controlling behaviors that can theaten the autonomy of the single-parent family. Overprotective, indulgent, interfering, and power-hungry are terms used by some single parents to describe grandparents who demonstrate traits that impede family relationships (Wilks, 1990). When grandparents are viewed as troublesome rather than supportive, single parents may cut back on visits with them, and sometimes even ask grandparents to stay completely away. This unfortunate family circumstance may then escalate into a legal battle as grandparents seek visitation rights through the court system (see the "Snapshots" box).

SNAPSHOTS

Grandparents Battle for Visitation Rights

Since 1965, a crazy quilt of statutes has given grandparents the right to petition for some visitation rights, but legislation varies widely from state to state. And if grandparents win their case in, for instance, Connecticut, they have to start over again if their grandchildren move to New York.

William and Nadine Perrydore won visitation rights to their twin granddaughters, who moved with their mother to another state after their parents split up. The 8-year-olds now spend some holidays and five weeks in summer with their grandparents.

Despite the emotional and financial costs, grandparents should go to court if it's the only way to resolve the conflict, says Dr. Arthur Kornhaber, a Lake Placid, N.Y., psychiatrist and president of the Foundation for Grandparenting. "Many times grandparents have been legislated out of existence because of temporary problems," he says. In almost every case, Kornhaber says, it is in the best interest of the child to visit with grandparents. "It's a deep spiritual bond."

EXPLORATIONS *What other steps might grandparents take before suing for visitation rights? Under what conditions should visitation rights of grandparents be considered in the child's best interest? Under what circumstances should visitation be restricted?*

SOURCES: Excerpted from K. Ames, D. Rosenberg, & N. Christian (1991).

Nurturing and advising their children, keeping workplace demands within bounds, dealing with societal barriers—cultural norms that define their families as problem-laden, lack of social programs and policies to support them—and reacting to the needs of kin and friends leave single parents feeling, at times, like there is no one looking out for *them.* They typically have little time to take care of their own emotional and intimacy needs. Such overload is complicated by lean economic circumstances that make the daily existence of many families precarious.

Managing Lean Economic Resources

Probably the concern that is most responsible for influencing the standard of well-being in single-parent families is the economic context within which they operate. Their most pressing dilemma, the one that characteristically leads to chronic stress, is having economic resources stretched to their limit (McLanahan, 1983; McLanahan & Booth, 1991). For women in particular, as noted in Chapter 14, divorce amounts to a financial setback. One-half of the women awarded child support either receive no support, or the fathers are delinquent

or behind in their child-support payments (see Figure 15-2).

As was explained in Chapter 14, single mothers typically earn lower than average incomes, and state and local governments provide only meager benefits (U.S. Bureau of the Census, 1990b). Even for middle-class single mothers, the issue of family finance is fraught with bitterness and anxiety. As one mother recalls:

> I remember one week, living with my son soon after the divorce, when we had one package of hot dogs for the whole week for both of us. The whole financial aspect of the divorce knocked me for a loop. I was really unprepared for it. I was confident that I could earn enough money, but the change in lifestyle was really radical. Suddenly, all those ways of letting off steam weren't there and that was a shock. I couldn't even afford to go to the movies. (Baruch, Barnett, & Rivers, 1983, p. 230)

A study of 2,800 children sponsored by the Census Bureau and carried out by social scientists Suzanne Bianchi and Edith McArthur over a 3-year period, shows that after their parents separated the family incomes of children dropped 37 percent within 4 months

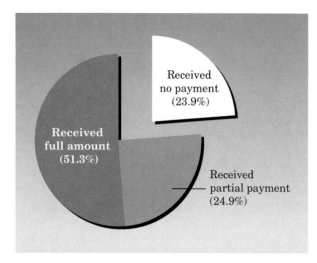

FIGURE 15-2
Child-Support Payments Received

SOURCE: U.S. Bureau of the Census (1990b).

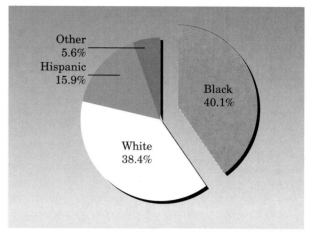

FIGURE 15-3
Makeup of Families Receiving AFDC Benefits

SOURCE: House Ways and Means Committee (1991).

and remained at about that level for the next 16 months. The study, published in 1991 under the title *Family Disruption and Economic Hardship: The Short-Run Picture for Children,* also concludes that within 4 months of the parental separation the percentage of children living in conditions of poverty increased from 19 to 36 percent. And during the same time period, the percentage of children's families that received food stamps increased from 10 to 27 percent.

The majority of the children studied (90 percent) lived with their mothers, who tried to make up for the drop in family income by finding a job, taking on a second or third job, or applying for social services benefits such as Aid to Families with Dependent Children (AFDC) and the food stamp program. (Figures 15-3 and 15-4 have additional information on AFDC benefits.) Child support also helped close the family income deficit, as did practical assistance from kin and friends.

Only 44 percent of the children in the Census Bureau study received child support from their nonresident parent, most usually the father. Figure 15-5 illustrates the effect of marital dissolution on family income over the first 16 months the children and their families were tracked by Bianchi and McArthur. Beginning in 1994, in an attempt to help children like the ones in this study, Congress has mandated that each state require the automatic withholding of child-support payments from the noncustodial parent's paycheck.

Sociologists Sara McLanahan and Karen Booth

(1991), of the Institute for Research on Poverty, conclude that the two choices open to most poor single mothers are unattractive: apply for social services assistance or find a full-time job that will improve living standards only marginally, while putting the family at risk of losing other needed benefits such as Medicaid and public housing (see Figure 15-6).

Aid to Families with Dependent Children (AFDC) is one of the few government programs available to single parents, but it falls short in several ways. Because it is available only to poor families, AFDC has little impact on the economic hardship of low- and

FIGURE 15-4
Family Size of AFDC Recipients

SOURCE: House Ways and Means Committee (1991).

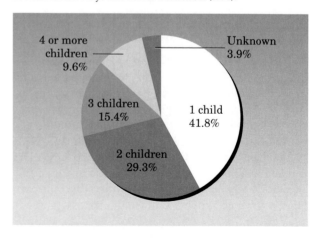

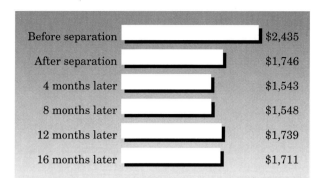

FIGURE 15-5
Decline in Children's Monthly Family Income
SOURCE: U.S. Bureau of the Census (1991).

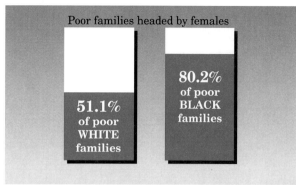

FIGURE 15-7
Women Bear the Brunt
SOURCE: R. I. Kirkland (1992).

middle-income families. And AFDC benefits do not normally keep up with inflation because state governments regularly fail to enact increases. Social policies and family programs, according to some family studies professionals, are consistently misdirected because their aim is toward the idealized family, rather than the more needy "real" family (McLanahan & Booth, 1991).

Black single-parent families, in particular, are stretched to the economic breaking point. The low AFDC allowance for single mothers leaves many children living in these families below the poverty level (see Figure 15-7). The percentage of black families in

FIGURE 15-6
Coming Up Short
SOURCE: R. I. Kirkland (1992).

ANNUAL INCOME Example: Mother with two children, Pennsylvania, 1992	WELFARE MOTHER	WORKING MOTHER
Welfare	$5,052	NONE
Food stamps	$2,427	$2,503
Earnings	NONE	$8,000
Earned income tax credit	NONE	$1,384
GROSS INCOME	$7,479	$11,887
Work-related expenses	NONE	$1,900
Social Security tax	NONE	$612
Paid child care	NONE	$2,700
DISPOSABLE INCOME	$7,479	$6,675
POVERTY THRESHOLD FOR FAMILY OF THREE	$10,857	$10,857

poverty (28 percent) is almost double their representation in the American population. In black female-headed families, only 34 percent of children have a full-time employed mother (U.S. Bureau of the Census, 1990a). For Hispanic children the same trend is true; 29 percent have mothers who are employed full time.

> Although many of these single parents may live in areas where jobs are scarce, their lack of work skills and experience, along with their limited education, compounds the employment difficulties.... Problems securing adequate child care may further complicate the single parent's ability to seek a job. All working parents face obstacles in finding acceptable child care arrangements, but the single parent has no spouse or second parent present at home who can help out or fill in on a regular, or even occasional basis. (U.S. Bureau of the Census, 1990a, p. 22)

One of the greatest risks to poor single-parent families, especially mother-headed families, is homelessness. Such families make up approximately 75 percent of the homeless in some urban areas (Axelson & Dail, 1988).

It is sometimes assumed that most single-parent families are recipients of a fair number of assets from a previous marriage, but a survey of some 1,800 such families in Wisconsin finds that at the time of divorce the average value of the property divided was $7,800 (women got about 50 percent of this figure), not a substantial amount (Seltzer & Garfinkel, 1990). Children growing up in a single-parent family that must struggle daily for economic survival have been found to suffer the consequences: having fewer educational op-

POINT OF VIEW

It's Not Like Mr. Mom

José Díaz, 33, was thrilled when his daughter Jennie was born 3 years ago. While his wife continued working as a legal secretary for a Boston firm, he was happy to quit his job as a graphic designer and stay home with the baby. "I always wanted her," he says. "When she was born, I took care of her. I cut her nails. I cut her hair." Last January, after less than 5 years of marriage, the child's mother served Díaz with divorce papers—and sought custody of Jennie. He was both stunned and angry. So far he has won a string of difficult court battles over his daughter's placement. But going it alone hasn't been easy. Though he now works as a technical illustrator and gets $248 monthly in child support from his wife, Díaz is struggling to afford health insurance. If he tries to leave her with a baby-sitter, Jennie grabs him by the trousers and cries, "Daddy, don't go!" Yet he can't imagine living apart from her.

Díaz is part of a rapidly growing segment of the U.S. population: single fathers. Last year they accounted for 1.2 million U.S. households. According to a recent study, about two-thirds of single fathers are divorced—but 25 percent have never tied the marital knot—and only 7.5 percent are widowers.

Many men who have come to take an active role in bringing up their children simply aren't willing to give them up when a marriage or relationship dissolves. Traditionally, mothers were almost automatically awarded custody of a couple's children, especially very young ones. But now judges place more emphasis on the best interests of the child—and with fewer moms staying home full time these days, those interests aren't nearly so clear-cut as they once were. Men now are more likely to ask for custody and judges are more likely to give it.

Children living with single dads get one important benefit that those with single mothers often don't: noncustodial mothers are far more likely to stay in touch with kids than noncustodial fathers are.

Women—just like men—can abandon their parental role for a variety of troubling reasons. According to Eric Rogers, the mother of his three daughters never showed up at the custody hearing over their placement 6 years ago. The Berkeley, Calif., tile layer and his children—Brianna, 11, and her twin sisters, Erica and Monique, 12—don't even know where she is.

Rogers runs his household—a three-bedroom du-

portunities leads to having fewer adult employment opportunities, which results in lower lifetime earnings than more advantaged children (Macklin, 1987; McLanahan & Booth, 1991).

The United States, unlike other industrialized countries, does not provide subsidized day care, national health insurance, or a guaranteed minimum child-support benefit. Such provisions would undoubtedly smooth the economic life of a single parent (Holden & Smock, 1991). Family scientist Arlene Skolnick (1991) points out that Europeans view the family as an institution that needs the support of the wider society. Family policy is part of the general economic plan of most European countries. Such plans provide a range of support services for families and children regardless of income, with no stigma attached. In America, economic policy has been based on the myth that families are self-sufficient and consequently should take care of their own needs.

Another common misconception is that, because most single-parent families are headed by mothers, it is acceptable to leave fathers out of research and policy decisions.

SINGLE FATHERS: A GROWING MINORITY

There is little information available on single fathers because they have been relatively rare compared to single mothers. Mothers have custody in 85 percent and fathers in 15 percent of single-parent families.

We do know that in the beginning months of parenting, custodial fathers express feelings of confusion, apprehension, and resentment about their parenting abilities (Hetherington & Stanley-Hagan, 1986). Additionally, many feel uneasy about community reaction

plex on a quiet, tree-lined street—with a firm hand and a structured schedule. "In the beginning, people thought I wouldn't be able to handle it," he says. "I had to teach them to take some of the pressure off me." At 5, Brianna became an expert at braiding her sisters' hair, while Monique learned to do ponytails. Today the girls each take weekly kitchen duty, which includes cooking and washing dishes. They also take turns sleeping in the coveted single bedroom—a privilege they can lose if they don't clean it up or their schoolwork doesn't measure up. "He's nice, but sometimes he has to be strict," says Brianna of her father. "Are we hard on him? Sometimes, yes," adds Erica.

Single fatherhood imposes big changes on a man's life. Richard Tangherlini, 33, of Quincy, Mass., worked staggered shifts as a truck loader for Budweiser, but he says that when his wife left him in 1991 with two young sons, he couldn't afford day care that would be available round the clock. So he quit work and went on welfare to take care of Christopher, now 3, and Richard Matthew, 4. At first, he says, "I was devastated. I didn't know how to play with the kids." He had always cooked but didn't know much about bedtimes or laundry. "The underwear turned out blue," he recalls. "I didn't even know what sizes the kids were." With some advice from his ex-mother-in-law and a friendly female neighbor, Tangherlini is less daunted by domesticity. He has even drawn on his past experience sewing generator covers for a hazardous-waste management company, and has turned his needle to reupholstering the living-room sofa and making curtains.

Greg Dawson, 38, an airplane inspector, had his children thrust upon him suddenly when his divorced wife—who had custody of them—died unexpectedly last year. Now he is bringing up Courtney, 8, and Matthew, 10, in the remote wilderness of Quilcene, Wash. They live in a tiny one-room cabin with a trailer attached; the bathroom is an outhouse and their lights are battery powered. Every weekday Dawson, who is planning to build a modern house, gets the kids up at 5 A.M. and delivers them to the baby-sitter by 6; she later takes them to the school-bus stop. He shaves in the car on his way to work in Port Angeles, an hour away. "I really wasn't prepared for this, and I could use some help," he says. "I think I'm a better father now, but I'm still not a very good cook—and I really don't know what it's like not to feel tired anymore."

EXPLORATIONS *Do you think* similar *or* different *is the best word to describe the overall experiences of single fathers compared to those of single mothers?*

SOURCE: Excerpted from J. Seligmann, D. Rosenberg, P. Wingert, D. Hannah, & P. Annin (1992). ✺

---

to their unique circumstances—they do not fit the usual pattern of family life (see the "Point of View" box). These feelings subside within about 2 years.

Compared to single mothers, single fathers, 2 years into parenthood, report better adjustment and fewer child-care problems. This is probably because, in contrast to mothers, fathers tend to be older, have higher levels of education, access to greater financial resources, and care for smaller families with school-age and adolescent children (Hetherington et al., 1989; Meyer & Garasky, 1993).

Nevertheless, fathers report some of the same concerns as single mothers. Parenting responsibilities, for example, limit job performance. Single fathers, as a general rule, do not accept work assignments that require frequent travel or long-distance moves. They are, much more than other men, conscious of the length of their workdays. Many find that coworkers and colleagues are not very understanding of meetings that are postponed, cut short, or rescheduled because of child-related demands. Just as for mothers, giving family roles priority over work roles remains a questionable and unsupported decision for fathers (Greif, 1990).

Many divorced single fathers feel that the courts are biased against them. "I was having to prove I could be a mother," one father says (Seligmann, Rosenberg, Wingert, Hannah, & Annin, 1992, p. 71). Most believe that parental standards for fathers, particularly when young children are involved, are much stricter than for mothers. A father complains, "You have to prove yourself to be not only an equal parent, but a substantially better one, and you are not allowed to make any mistakes" (p. 71). Regardless of these slights, most single fathers, particularly those who elect to have custody, view themselves as competent parents, are comfortable with their family roles, and report satisfying relationships with their children (Macklin, 1987).

Single fathers contend that their rights and concerns are often overlooked and trivialized when single parenthood is discussed and public policy changes are proposed.

As single fathers and mothers work out the kinks inherent in their new family structures and evolving parent-child relationships, two questions that inevitably arise for the unattached are: Am I ready to date again? How will my dating affect the children?

DOES DATING CHANGE FAMILY RELATIONSHIPS?

Beginning to date again creates some anxious moments. The rituals of dating can seem strangely inappropriate, especially for middle-aged people looking for new partners. There is a feeling that the entire process—the waiting for phone calls, the sexual tension, the awkwardness associated with new people in unfamiliar situations—should have been left behind in adolescence. Despite these objections, dating is an important part of a return to a normal, socially active life.

Custodial parents' serious dating relationships can mean changes in the operation of the newly forged parent-child partnership. Dating parents spend less time with their children and more time with their new love interest. Family communication and closeness may suffer. Many children feel jealous and quietly attempt to regain the close connection with their parent; other children openly compete with this "outsider" for parental attention, affection, and intimacy.

One woman, upon seeing that her children were becoming jealous of her strong attachment to a new dating partner, realized that she was indeed spending much less time with them. She then made a concerted effort to include the children when it seemed appropriate.

> It's reasonable to assume that any man I'd be interested in would have the capacity to take an interest in my children as I would his. If he objects to including my kids in our plans, it's time to start wondering if *I* want to include *him* in my life. Why must one choose between one's kids and dating? (Atlas, 1984, p. 49)

Another woman used a different approach when her 5-year-old daughter was consistently making rude, insensitive, and disapproving remarks in front of her dating partner. She finally said to her daughter:

> "Look, it's not your fault that your father and I are not together anymore. I know you want your father and me to be together again, but it's not going to happen, and nothing you can do will change that." The daughter accepted this explanation and became nicer to her mother's friends. (p. 50)

These represent the accounts of two divorced single mothers to children's reactions to their dating. There are other responses that would be as effective, depending on the situation. The thing to remember is that children should not have so much power in the family that they can veto all dates or make the parent and his or her date miserable out of jealousy or for other reasons.

On the other hand, parents owe it to their children to make specific arrangements for shared time and special activities and to listen to their children and respond to any concerns they may have about specific dating partners or dating arrangements—for example, sleeping over, spending weekends with a date, and so forth. Moreover, children may need an extra share of reassurance and nurturing if a parent's serious dating relationship breaks up (see the "Dilemmas and Decisions" box).

What should operate in parental dating situations is the *principle of responsible selfishness*—being a responsible parent *and* also giving oneself permission to meet a basic personal need. "Single parents who martyr themselves, sacrificing everything for their children, usually end up feeling resentful and unfulfilled" (McKay, Rogers, Blades, & Gosse, 1984, p. 150).

Because of emphasis on the costs of single parenthood, negative aspects receive the vast majority of attention from all sides. What is often ignored is that despite the many and varied stressors of single parents and their children, most, when interviewed, point out positive aspects as well.

SIGNS OF POSITIVE ADJUSTMENT

Developing Independence and Self-Confidence

As we have noted throughout this chapter, being the sole adult caregiver in a family is usually accompanied by an overload of responsibilities, and complicated by limited access to economic resources. It is also true that survivers of single parenting often have feelings of having more power and control over their lives as well

Although Murphy Brown in the popular sitcom is an economically secure upper-middle-class television reporter, single mothers across the nation have identified with the uncertainty, pride, overload, and sense of accomplishment brought to the role.

as enhanced feelings of independence, pride, self-esteem, and self-confidence (Kaslow & Schwartz, 1987; Shaw, 1991). In one study of single-parent mothers, some of the women interviewed reflected on these newfound feelings:

> Wendy, age 40. . . . "I like my independence. I wouldn't like to go back. It's hard. I think you take a lot of knocks, and some of them take a hell of a lot of getting over, and you think you're not gonna get over them but somehow you do." Barbara at 36. . . . "I think it's just a sense of achievement, you know. I mean you feel like a phoenix rising from the ashes—your marriage being in ashes—to suddenly rise again." Jane, 31. . . . "It's made me a lot stronger, because I was determined that I wasn't going to give in to it." Finally, Rachel [32]. . . . "At the end of it all, you can turn round and think, I've brought those children up on my own, and you can look and you think, I've done it!'" (Shaw, 1991)

Because they are familiar with the daily running of a household and the needs of children, mothers (as well as fathers, if their past participation in these aspects of family life was active) do not have to learn everything from scratch. This history of competence makes the transition to single parenthood somewhat easier.

Gaining the Support of Others

Earlier, in another context, we described the role of grandparents in the single-parent family. There is also evidence that support from other kin and friends make some difficulties easier to bear. Family and friends who have weathered divorces and single-parent living are valuable sources of advice and comfort. In many ways, they have much to offer as role models. (For additional information on the role of supportive kin and friend networks, see Chapters 10 and 14.)

In addition, many parents obtain help from organized support groups for single parents, such as Parents Without Partners, where they can talk to other adults in similar situations and share information on how to deal with specific problems. Large numbers of single parents participate in these social organizations (McLanahan, 1983). As one parent commented, "I needed new friends—someone to talk to about important decisions—someone who shares the feelings of a single parent" (Hogan, Buehler, & Robinson, 1983, p. 130).

DILEMMAS AND DECISIONS

Parental Dating and Breaking Up: Helping Children Cope

According to Lawrence Kutner (1992), psychologist and journalist, some children may need help after the breakup of a single parent's serious dating relationship. In a recent column in *The New York Times*, Kutner writes:

> Soon after her mother broke up with the man she had been dating, 9-year-old Jane asked to sleep in her mother's bed.
>
> "She wanted to comfort me," said Barbara, a recently divorced psychologist who spoke on the condition that her full name not be used. "She told me, 'He wasn't good for us, Mom. Besides, you have me.' "
>
> Children of single parents have a tremendous emotional investment in the parent's dating.
>
> Yet their feelings can be ambivalent or even contradictory. The person their parent is involved with can be both a potential savior and a threat, a provider of love and a rival for it.
>
> It's not surprising that many children react dramatically when their single parents end a relationship. For some, the breakup is as traumatic as the earlier divorce, and it may bring about the same emotions.
>
> Preschoolers and children in early elementary school in particular tend to form attachments to these dating partners quickly.
>
> When the relationship ends, these young children often blame themselves and wonder what it was about them that caused the breakup. They sometimes conclude that their behavior or even the way they look makes them unlovable.
>
> "To the child, this adult may have represented hope, a replacement for the loss triggered by the parent's death or divorce," said Dr. JoAnne Pedro-Carroll, the director of the Children of Divorce Intervention Program at the University of Rochester. "Children who go through this several times are likely to have a more intense sense of loss."
>
> Young children also identify very strongly with the parent's emotions. When they see their parent in pain, they worry that they will lose that parent's love.
>
> Jane's reassurances to her mother that the man wasn't right "for us" and that "you have me" reflect this intense identification and fear of loss.
>
> Adolescents, whose lives no longer revolve solely around what happens at home, may handle the breakup more easily.
>
> "The older the children, the more resources and the more of an outside life they have," said Dr. Neil Kalter of the Center for the Child and the Family at the University of Michigan at Ann Arbor, and the author of *Growing Up With Divorce* (Ballantine Books, 1991).
>
> He has found that these other involvements help them handle the stress better than younger children.
>
> Still, some older adolescents may become extremely upset over the breakup because they are protective of their parent. This is especially likely if they are living with a parent, usually a mother, whom they think of as vulnerable and dependent on them.
>
> These adolescents may have seen the other adult as someone who could take care of their parent, so that

Watching Out for the Children

Many children in single-parent families dream about their mothers and fathers getting back together and working through their problems. When the Gallup organization last surveyed adolescents aged 13 to 17 they asked two questions about divorce. The first question was: Do you think it is too easy or not easy enough for people in this country to get divorced? Of those interviewed, 76 percent said "too easy"; 24 percent replied

"too hard." The second question was: Do you think that most people who get divorced have tried hard enough to save their marriages? Of the adolescents sampled, 75 percent responded "didn't try hard enough" and 25 percent replied "tried hard enough" (Gallup Organization, 1989). Over time, during the process of adjustment, children gradually realize that their parents will not reunite.

Single parents fret and worry over how their chil-

they could leave home. If the parent's relationship ends, they feel an obligation to stay home and care for their parent.

There also appear to be differences in how boys and girls handle these breakups, and in how they influence future relationships. "Girls who lose their fathers early and whose fathers don't remain involved with them may, throughout their adolescence and adulthood, view men as unreliable," said Dr. Sandra Loucks, a psychologist at the University of Tennessee Medical Center in Knoxville.

Barbara, who spent several years as a single mother before marrying and divorcing again, worries that she is already seeing signs of that attitude in Jane's behavior.

"My daughter sees men as people who go in and out of our life," she said. "It gives her a sense that she can't count on them. She tells me that she's never going to marry. I don't remember feeling that way when I was her age."

Psychologists caution that although many children have strong emotional reactions when a parent ends a dating relationship, "Some children don't seem to be bothered by it," Kalter said. "If they're doing well in other areas like school and friendships, that's a sign that they're probably just very emotionally resilient."

Kutner concludes by giving the following advice to parents who wish to date:

One of the simplest ways to prevent your children from becoming upset if you end a dating relationship is to have waited a while before getting those children involved. That stops them from becoming emotionally invested in an adult who, from their perspective, abandons them.

Once your dating relationship is more serious and your child becomes a part of it, don't try to do everything together as if you were a family.

"Spend time alone with your child while you're dating," advises Dr. Neil Kalter of the Center for the Child and the Family at the University of Michigan. "That provides more continuity, no matter what happens to your relationship with the other adult."

If you do break up with the other person, here are some things to bear in mind:

■ Remember that your child's fundamental needs are to feel loved and protected.

In times of crisis a child may not be able to express those needs directly. Reassure her that you won't be abandoning her, even though your relationship with this other person didn't work out. Children can weather these losses when their parents give them a sense that they'll still be cared for and loved.

■ Try not to terminate your child's relationship with the other adult abruptly—this increases his feeling of abandonment.

"It's enormously helpful if both the parent and the person who's leaving explain to the children that it's not their fault," Kalter said. If both adults do this, the children are less likely to feel that they are being lied to.

If possible, have the other adult gradually reduce his or her contact with the child instead of breaking off abruptly.

EXPLORATIONS *What are some ways to counter a child's belief, after the breakup of her single-parent mother's dating relationship, that men are people who cannot be counted on, that they display a lack of commitment to others?*

SOURCE: Excerpted from L. Kutner (1992).

dren will fare. They experience a sense of urgency to reorganize and restructure their lives, moving quickly to achieve family unity and provide income, discipline, and nurturance to children. In the process, they invariably cross over the invisible cultural boundaries that define masculine and feminine behavior. Mothers in single-parent families, for example, "acquire and demonstrate a greater degree of dominance, assertiveness, and independence while custodial fathers find them-selves in situations eliciting high degrees of warmth, nurturance, and tenderness" (Kurdek & Siesky, 1980, p. 250). Children model these behaviors and tend to approach life in a more androgynous, less gender-role stereotypical fashion.

Children in single-parent families regularly assume a variety of household responsibilities and forge a more egalitarian relationship with their parents, thereby broadening their competencies and skills as

Parental Support Given Adolescents: The "Weekend Father," the "Everyday Mother"

Clearly, fathers and mothers play different roles in the support networks of their adolescent children. While overall the mother-adolescent relationship is closer than the father-adolescent relationship, fathers are more likely than mothers to spend time with their teens specifically engaging in fun activities. Most of the time mothers spend with their children consists of dealing with their everyday needs and problems, or of being with them while taking care of other responsibilities, such as preparing a meal.

The lower involvement of fathers in the daily lives of their children may help to explain why there is less overt conflict between fathers and teens than between mothers and teens. Much of the conflict that occurs in these families concerns relatively minor, common problems, such as needing or wanting something, whether it be clothes, money, or use of the car, or such things as talking on the telephone or doing homework, matters that are almost always handled by mothers. Furthermore, even though fathers commonly serve as authority figures, mothers are the enforcers. Mothers have the responsibility of relaying, explaining, and often justifying rules and decisions to their children, who are not always happy with the outcomes. Thus, mothers hear much of the complaining and have to deal with the resistance. Also, disciplining children for rule infractions is almost always the mother's chore, with the father serving in a backup capacity, and almost always more symbolically than in actions.

Even though fathers spend less time with their children than do mothers, the time spent with them tends to be more enjoyable for both parties, focusing on "fun activities" or outings. This may be a continuation of early patterns in the division of labor between mothers and fathers. It appears that fathers devote more of their time to play than do mothers when their children are infants.

This is not to imply that the father-teen relationship is all good while the mother-teen relationship is all bad. In fact, considering the likelihood of being listed as a support, the likelihood of being seen as a confidante, and the teens' self-reports of their closeness to each parent, clearly the mother-adolescent relationship, on average, is closer than the father-adolescent relationship. While teenagers recognize and appreciate the shared time with their fathers, when they define support they suggest that other things are equally, and probably more, important. The role of the mother as a confidante and the fact that she is the one who deals directly with their everyday, ongoing needs and concerns, means that despite the increased conflict that can result, teenagers see their mothers as more supportive and their relationship as being closer.

One way in which noncustodial fathers can make up for their decreased significance as authority figure or provider, and prevent declining attachment on the part of their children, is to provide them with gifts, shopping trips, and other tangible signs of their continued concern and involvement. Whether or not this is the father's motivation, this kind of interaction is very common:

> I used to like going there [to father's house] because it was a chance to get away, and he'd buy us things and take us to the beach and stuff. (F, 15)

well as their definitions of gender-appropriate behavior. Being told that their work is valued and that their families really need them, results in many children realizing a highly developed sense of responsibility and feeling like part of a cooperative, productive team. From these experiences, they gain self-esteem and self-confidence.

Adolescents in single-parent families are evaluated as being more mature; they also report feelings of being in control of their lives and exhibit more autonomous actions. This greater maturity seems to stem from the higher status acquired from being in supportive, confidant relationships with their custodial mothers (Demo & Acock, 1991). The give-and-take of the parent-child relationship is highly valued by adolescents. In her book, *Adolescents, Family, and*

They [mother and father] have it worked out where he always buys our shoes and winter coats and stuff. But he's all the time giving us stuff—something we say we need or something he knows I'd really like but mom can't get it. (M, 14)

Whether the father-child relationship is affected by or dependent upon his gift buying is debatable. Clearly it is an aspect of the noncustodial father role that the teens take for granted.

Besides gift-giving, the "weekend father" phenomenon involves entertaining the children with outings and excursions, and letting them do things they do not ordinarily do. Common activities include shopping trips, eating at restaurants, seeing movies, attending sporting events, and, especially with younger teens, going to a zoo or amusement park. As the adolescents get older, they lose interest in these sorts of activities. Finding a suitable alternative is not easy; indeed, in many cases contact drops in frequency as the children get too old for outings.

When divorced fathers are compared with divorced mothers, a striking difference emerges in the area of parent-child confiding. About half the teens talk to their noncustodial fathers about matters of interest to them, but are less likely to talk to them about problems or more personal matters. This is especially clear when they compare their relationships with their fathers and their relationships with their mothers:

Oh, they're pretty different. I don't talk to my dad like I talk to my mom, you know, about problems and things that are really important to me. I don't know why, really. Well, I guess because he doesn't live here and he doesn't know about a lot of the things I do and the people I know and stuff. But even then, if he did, I'm not sure I'd talk to him like I do my mom. He's a different kind of person. He doesn't really open up a

lot, and he's real busy with work and stuff, so we never really do sit around and just talk about stuff. (F, 16)

I don't see him all that much, so when I do go, we like to talk and catch up on things . . . but it's more like how I'm doing in school, and if I'm playing basketball, or stuff that's going on with people I know. (M, 14)

The adolescents frequently suggest that since their fathers are not around, it is especially difficult to fill them in on personal matters. Furthermore, several doubt that they would do so even if they shared a residence, citing the father's personality or the relatively greater ease with which they can talk to and confide in their mothers.

The most significant difference between divorced mothers and fathers is that none of the teens feel that their fathers confide in them. Certainly this is due in part to the convenience of sharing a residence and the ready availability of mothers for providing personal support. Divorced fathers, on the other hand, see their children only intermittently, making personal interaction more problematic. Most of the teens, however, explain it as some facet of the father's personality:

He's not much of a talker. I don't think he even talked to my mom all that much when they were married. (F, 15)

I guess he's kind of a quiet person, like shy or something. I guess I'm kind of like that, too. (M, 13)

EXPLORATIONS *Do you think father-child relationships are different when the father is the custodial parent? How so?*

SOURCE: Excerpted from K. M. Stinson (1991).

Friends (1991), which examines, in part, the adolescent response to single life, social scientist Kandi Stinson concludes:

In a way, the adolescents in these situations are getting a fuller, more complex, and perhaps more realistic perspective on family living and relationships. They not only receive from the family, they give to it, thus being

exposed to the burdens as well as the benefits of living in a family. They see their mothers as strong and capable in some situations and as in need of support in others, as being good listeners at the same time that they need someone to listen to them. (p. 62)

Based on in-depth interviews with 30 adolescents and their custodial parents, she summarizes differences in the kind of support provided by mothers and fathers as revealed by their adolescent children (see the "Point of View" box).

When children's adjustment to single-parent family life is rated, one question often left unanswered is, What was the family situation like for the children *before* living in a single-parent family? Often, it is automatically assumed that children move from a healthy, well-adjusted, intact family where the parents just could not quite see eye to eye on certain family matters, into a new and more troublesome single-parent situation. But the truth is that single-parent life may insulate some children from health-threatening family conflict (Gottman & Katz, 1989; Mechanic & Hansell, 1989).

As we observed in Chapter 14, the reality is that before the divorce, children in many families are exposed to parents who frequently fight, remain angry at each other for days, and are in many ways emotionally or physically abusive toward each other. Given these circumstances, parents may be so intent on their own marital problems that they ignore children's needs. This is one of the primary reasons some children report that single parenthood, though problematic, is an improvement over two-parent family life. Having one parent leave may actually reduce the anxiety and stress in family relationships, permit an increase in the frequency and intimacy of communication among family members, and enhance the child's sense of self-worth (Gongla & Thompson, 1987).

Over the past three decades, the single-parent family has emerged as a major family form. As this family type has increased in numbers so, too, have concerns about its economic and social consequences. These concerns have led to extended discussions and debates over what should be done to help single parents and their children. Laws and public policies have been crafted and legislation passed for the purpose of improving their lives. There has also been a cultural awakening pertaining to the responsibility of neighborhoods and communities to look out for the collective well-being of families. The process of national soul searching and public response to it is expected to continue throughout the 1990s.

SUMMARY POINTS

■ The single-parent family is the fastest growing family type.

■ Twenty-six percent of all American children under age 18 currently live in a single-parent family. The figure is highest among black children (60 percent) and Hispanic children (35 percent).

■ Divorce accounts for most of the increase in single-parent households among white families, while for black families births to unwed mothers is the main cause.

■ The single-parent family has been largely ignored due to the false assumption that single parenthood is merely a transitional stage between divorce and remarriage. Most children, however, who experience single parenthood through divorce or because their custodial parent never married, grow to adulthood within a single-parent home.

■ Family members who experience divorce, then live in a single-parent household, and finally experience remarriage are essentially passing through three typically very stressful life events, one right after the other. Swift passage through these life-altering events can result in a pileup of stressors that negatively affect well-being.

■ Robert Weiss has found that most families of divorce experience two distinct changes in family functioning as they adjust to being a single-parent family. First, the old authority structure dissolves. Next, a more egalitarian coalition of custodial parent and children emerges.

■ Research on single-parent families is often biased by portrayals of such families as overly troubled compared to other family types.

■ Single-parent families share some common problems, including idealization of the two-parent family, social stigma, role overload and role conflict, and economic stress.

■ Economic stress is the most pressing problem of the single-parent family. A recent longitudinal study sponsored by the Census Bureau found that children's family incomes dropped 37 percent within the first 4 months after a parental separation and remained low for months after. Less than half the children received support payments from the nonresident parent.

■ Current social services programs like AFDC are inadequate to meet the needs of most children and their families and seem to penalize the single parent who is employed.

■ Single fathers, compared to mothers, have access to greater economic resources, are more highly educated, have more time for personal pursuits like dating, and usually have custody of older children.

■ Over time, single mothers and fathers come to view themselves as competent parents who, on the whole, have rewarding relationships with their children.

■ Single mothers, in contrast to other mothers, spend more time worrying about their families, are less satisfied with their lives, and, when their children are young, more often seek help for depression.

■ When a single parent begins to date, the children may feel abandoned and jealous of the dating partner. Attempts are made to regain family closeness, sometimes through less than positive means.

■ Although single parenthood is accompanied by some problems, over time, most mothers and fathers report benefiting from the experience.

■ Children in single-parent families typically grow up to be more androgynous than their counterparts, modeling the behavior of their less traditional parents. Their skills, competencies, and self-esteem are broadened by their greater involvement in family matters.

KEY TERMS

Single-parent families
Binuclear family
Principle of responsible selfishness

REVIEW QUESTIONS

1. What false assumptions about single-parent families have resulted in their being overlooked by social scientists?

2. What characteristics do single parents have in common?

3. Discuss the causes and consequences of economic stress in single-parent families.

4. Compile a list of 10 questions you would like to ask single-parent families. Talk to two single parents in their thirties, one male and one female, each with at least one child under age 7. Compare and contrast their experiences. What conclusions do you draw from your interviews? Are there any obvious gender differences? Explain.

5. Ask an adolescent or young adult who grew up in a single-parent family (for at least 5 years) to discuss common concerns as well as benefits gained from the experience. Write a one-page summary of your findings and compare your results to those of other class members.

6. What are the typical reactions of children to a single parent's serious dating relationship? What tips would you give parents on how to handle this situation?

16

Illustration by Cary Austin

Remarriage After Divorce: The Second Time Around

The growing recognition of the prevalence of remarriage after divorce and the increasing awareness of the distinctive concerns of stepfamilies are reflected in book titles such as *What Am I Doing in a Stepfamily*, *Stepkids: A Survival Guide for Teenagers in Stepfamilies*, and *Growing Up with Divorce*. Many shops now stock greeting cards to recognize divorce, as well as occasional cards for stepparents and their children. There are newsletters concerned with remarriage as well as a periodical called the *Stepfamily Bulletin*. And, recently, the *Journal of Divorce* changed its title to the *Journal of Divorce and Remarriage*. Despite these changes and an increased societal willingness to accept families of remarriage, some stigma persists even among the socially prominent:

> When George Bush's only daughter was married last June, it was a simple affair. The private ceremony took place at Camp David, not the White House. There were only 133 guests, and the media were not invited. Why the lack of formality for a president's daughter? It was Dorothy Bush Koch's second marriage. (DeWitt, 1992, p. 61)

Until as recently as the 1920s, remarriage normally followed the death of a spouse. Today, 84 percent of women and 86 percent of men who remarry are divorced rather than widowed. Widowhood occurs later in life than divorce and more frequently happens to women (U.S. Bureau of the Census, 1991). More than 10 million households in the United States consist of at least one spouse who has remarried and over 5 million remarried couples have at least one stepchild living with them. Of all the weddings in a given year, 45 percent include a previously married bride or groom, up from 32 percent in 1970 (Coleman & Ganong, 1991; DeWitt, 1992) (see Figure 16-1). So it is a matter of some concern to understand how marriage and family relationships differ the second time around.

425

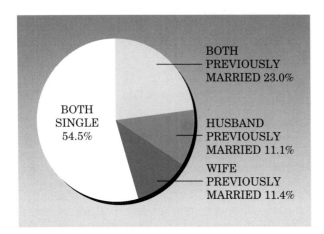

FIGURE 16-1
Almost One-Half of All Marriages Are Actually Remarriages

SOURCE: P. M. DeWitt (1992).

Social scientists are becoming increasingly interested in remarriage and stepfamilies, topics that until a few years ago attracted little scholarly attention. This is still new territory for many researchers, and key questions remain unexplored. But we can sketch some of the characteristics of the process of starting over after divorce, identify who remarries and how quickly, and explore the question of whether second marriages are different. We can also look at the complexities of child rearing in stepfamilies, describe the various challenges stepfamilies face, and examine some of the benefits of life in a stepfamily.

REMARRIAGE RATES: TRENDS AND BARRIERS

As noted in Chapter 5, ours is still a marriage-oriented society. A high percentage of people who divorce, particularly those in their twenties and thirties, eventually remarry, which is an impressive reminder not only of the appeal of marriage but also of the obstacles still associated with the divorced status. Personal needs for intimacy, companionship, and sex are more easily satisfied in marriage. Moreover, there are economic incentives to remarry, particularly for people who are struggling financially in the wake of a divorce. And there is a desire for help with child rearing.

Nevertheless, most people are not in a hurry to re-marry. Only about one in six people who divorce have already found someone they want as a new partner and remarry within a year. And even these individuals are not necessarily rushing into new marriages as quickly as this statistic seems to indicate, since couples are commonly separated for some time before their divorce is granted. Some 65 percent of women and 70 percent of men eventually remarry, about half within 7 years of their divorce (Bumpass, Sweet, & Martin, 1990; Glick & Lin, 1986). Of those, about two-thirds cohabit before deciding to marry (Bumpass & Sweet, 1989).

Ethnic Differences

Rates of remarriage differ by race, with blacks remarrying at a slower rate than whites: 75 percent of white women remarry, but fewer than one-half of black women do so. "One-quarter remarry in about 3 years among white women, whereas it is about 8 years before one-quarter of black women have remarried" (Bumpass et al., 1990, p. 753).

One reason for this discrepancy is that black women face a more pronounced marriage squeeze than white women, as indicated in Chapter 5: the number of black males to females decreases at a much faster pace over the life course (Tucker & Taylor, 1989). Health-related illnesses, life-threatening living conditions, incarceration, and other effects of racial discrimination reduce the pool of eligible black male marital partners. Discrimination also results in lower educational and economic attainment among black men, making it difficult for them to provide economic support for their families.

Black women cope with this situation by remaining single longer after a divorce. They learn to rely more on their own personal and emotional resources. When they need additional help, black women count on extended kin and friend networks (Kitson & Holmes, 1992; Taylor, Chatters, Tucker, & Lewis, 1990). It is not unusual for extended kin to assist a single mother by relieving her of some household chores and child-care responsibilities. Because of this help, some mothers are able to seek full-time jobs or further their education (Wilson, 1989).

Hispanic women and men take more time to remarry than either whites or blacks. This trend is mostly because of religious proscriptions. The majority of Hispanics are of the Catholic faith, which has severe restrictions on divorce and remarriage.

Differences by Age and Gender

The average age at the time of remarriage is 35 for women and 39 for men (National Center for Health Statistics, 1992). The decision to remarry hinges, to a large extent, on the availability of potential partners and the ability to successfully attract an eligible mate—each of which is influenced by age and gender.

Men's pool of eligible partners is larger than women's. It is socially acceptable for men to marry younger females, which gives them a wider range of marital choices in first and subsequent marriages. And, with age, increasing numbers of women become single because of widowhood, further increasing the pool of eligibles for men.

Men's value as potential partners generally does not decrease with age. Men's wages, status, and power tend to increase as they grow older, and, upon retirement, many have access to benefits and pensions that allow them to consider another marriage. They continue to be viewed as possible marital partners despite graying hair, wrinkles, and sagging pectorals.

Women do not have this social advantage. Among women under age 25, about 90 percent remarry. "This proportion declines sharply with age to about 60 percent for women in their 30s, and to less than a third for women over age 40" (Bumpass et al., 1990, p. 753). Loss of physical attractiveness is considered a major social drawback for women. Graying hair and wrinkles may be marks of a distinguished older man, but, for a woman, these normal biological signs of aging typically bring on ageist stereotypes (Wolfe, 1991). In addition, women usually have custody of children, which further reduces their appeal as romantic partners. Parenting responsibilities leave them little time and fewer resources to pursue new relationships.

Children as Barriers

Children tend to have a depressing effect on remarriage. Of women with one or two children, 25 percent will *never* remarry, while 40 percent of women with three or more children will not remarry. Sociologist Larry Bumpass and his colleagues (1990) write, "It is 7 years before half of the mothers with one or two children have remarried, and it is almost 14 years for those with three or more children" (p. 753).

There are at least three reasons why children increase the emotional and economic costs of remarriage. First, potential marital partners may be cautious about taking on a ready-made family. Second, the custodial parent may be equally reluctant to interrupt children's lives for a second time—in this case, to form a stepfamily with all its complex relationships. And third, as we learned in Chapter 15, children may purposely inter-

Children complicate the dating and remarriage process for women. The older a woman is when she divorces and the more children she has, the longer the delay in remarriage.

cede in the courtship process to prevent the formation of a new marital relationship.

Effects of Motivation, Income, and Education

Motivation, income, and education also influence the remarriage rate. Men's motivation to remarry may be higher than women's, because, compared to women, men experience greater satisfaction and say they are happier within marital relationships. Divorced men report being lonelier and undergo more physical and mental health problems than remarried men (Ross, Mi-

Successful women with high earnings are not in any particular hurry to remarry. Even though their pool of eligibles is smaller, they tend to set high standards and take their time selecting a new marital partner.

rowsky, & Goldsteen, 1991). Remarriage offers two major health benefits: social support and economic security. Although both women and men gain these benefits from remarriage, women tend to accrue greater economic rewards and men receive more emotional support.

The higher the income of the divorced male, the more likely he is to remarry. As we stated previously, the pool of potential partners for most men seeking to remarry is large, and income is a key resource in the ability to find and attract a new mate. Unlike men, women with higher incomes are less likely to marry again (Coleman & Ganong, 1991). When they earn more, women report using their added resources to delay remarriage as they take time to experience their newly autonomous lifestyles and explore the numerous social options open to them.

Marriage does not enhance women's physical and emotional well-being to the extent it does men's (Ross et al., 1991). Thus, when women can support themselves financially, they tend to establish higher expectations for relationship quality and are more selective in their choice of romantic partners (Vaughn, 1986). For economically secure women, marital rewards may decline as alternative ways of meeting emotional and intimacy needs expand—for example, through friendships and cohabitation. Marital opportunities may be fewer because of norms specifying that women should marry men whose earnings are equal to or higher than their own.

For white women, education is strongly linked to income—the more education a woman has, the greater her annual earnings—but education alone has little direct influence on her decision to remarry. But, among black women, remarriage is strongly and directly tied to education level. Black women with less education tend to remarry sooner than other women (Smock, 1990). Less-educated black women have fewer resources than most other population groups and, consequently, may be more highly motivated to remarry as a way of gaining a more financially secure life.

On the whole, we might regard remarriage as evidence that most people choose not to do without marriage for long because it meets so many of their needs. But regardless of motivation and intentions, for most couples, marriage is definitely *not* the same the second time around. The literature on remarriage offers some clues about the somewhat different expectations remarried adults bring to the experience.

WHY SECOND MARRIAGES ARE DIFFERENT

We might well conclude that remarried people have a relatively low marital aptitude; that they marry again and again, repeating the same experience—and presumably the same mistakes. But interviews with twice-married people reveal a different story.

First Marriage, a Training Ground

The first marriage, which most regret, is viewed as being undertaken for the wrong reasons and perhaps at the wrong time. The majority see it as their apprenticeship for a more successful second marriage. After interviewing dozens of people about their second marriages, one writer commented:

> Many of the couples saw their first marriage as a kind of training school, like the college they had left with academic degrees but little knowledge of themselves. Divorce was their diploma. All agreed that the second marriage was the real thing at last. They had entered it with much clearer ideas about the things that really mattered to them, whether those things were love, friendship, understanding, sex, or money. (Westoff, 1975, p. 11)

Here, for example, is what one man had to say about his first marriage:

> My first marriage was an almost completely automatic act, the thing I was supposed to do after graduation from college, something expected of me at that point in my life. Nobody made me aware of the preparation or skills I would need in relating to women, or sex, or child rearing. I had to face most of those important things just winging it, by trial and error. (p. 11)

First-person accounts of the differences between first and subsequent marriages are subjective and therefore somewhat unreliable. Statements such as these could be regarded as the justifications people offer for their personal choices. For most people, admitting that a second marriage had worked out no better than the first would amount to an acknowledgment of failure, perhaps evidence of an inability to sustain any intimate relationship. Yet there is reason to conclude that second marriages are different in certain ways.

Realistic Expectations

Research suggests that divorced individuals approach second marriages with somewhat different expectations and apply a different set of standards to these marriages. As one woman tells it:

> When I was young, I was looking for someone exotic, different from anyone I'd known. I wanted a man who wouldn't remind me of my family. He had to be special, maybe even a little weird. The second time around I wanted someone more like me, someone I could live with. I've had the excitement and passion of being with a man who would always be foreign and untouchable. Now I want someone I'll recognize and fit with. (McKay, Rogers, Blades, & Gosse, 1984, p. 253)

People who marry a second time describe themselves as more realistic, more flexible, and wiser about relationships than when they first married.

Second-timers are much more pragmatic and less likely to allow romantic notions to influence their marital choices. A 48-year-old graphic artist says:

> When I meet a man, I have a tendency to fill in the blanks with my own projections. With the slightest bit of help from him I can quickly sculpt a beautiful person from the few things I know. I fight that temptation all the time, and I do it by asking questions. Lots of questions. I pay attention to how he reacts to things, I listen to his stories, I ask him who his heroes are. (McKay et al., 1984, p. 252)

Most people who have gone through marriage, disillusionment, and then divorce approach love and romance from a different perspective, one of cautious examination. They do not wish to make another mistake. Commenting on remarriage, one woman explains the difference using these words:

> I think second marriages are less idealistic and a little more realistic. You realize that it's going to be tough at times but you also know that you have to work things out. Coming to a second marriage is like coming into a ballgame with the bases loaded. You've got to come through with a hit. What you realize after you've been divorced is that you've got to make it work. You just have to keep working out the rules of the game. (Furstenberg, 1980, p. 448)

Older and Wiser

Those who remarry have a certain advantage because they are typically older and more mature than people who marry for the first time. Interviews with remarried people suggest that many do apply lessons learned in a previous marriage. For example, one researcher found that remarried people are more likely than their once-married counterparts to take a critical look at their own behavior as a contributor to dissatisfaction in the relationship. From one man's perspective:

> I am discovering new ways of reacting. In the other marriage, there was a lot of sarcasm and a lot of reacting rather than acting. I have learned a lot of things, and I know now when I am being defensive. When there is something about the situation that makes me uncomfortable, I say so, whereas in the other marriage I wasn't able to. (Furstenberg, 1980, p. 450)

There is no way of knowing for sure whether certain traits of second marriages should be attributed mainly to what people learned from a previous marriage or to their greater maturity. Nevertheless, the end result seems to be positive for the second relationship.

Flexible Roles

Another characteristic of remarried people is their more open approach to marital and family roles. In second marriages, couples tend to exhibit greater flexibility in the performance of household chores, more shared decision making, and increased emotional exchange (Furstenberg & Spanier, 1984). At the end of the first year of a 3-year longitudinal study, remarried women expressed higher satisfaction with their marriages if their husbands were more involved in caring for the children. By the third year, the most satisfied wives were in marriages in which husbands shared household and child-care responsibilities about equally and decision making in the family was more egalitarian (Guisinger, Cowan, & Schuldberg, 1989).

More Susceptible to Divorce

Just as with first marriages, most couples in second marriages report being happy and satisfied. And, just as with first marriages, reports of overall marital satisfaction have little to do with the rate of divorce. Knowledge of individuals' evaluations of their marital satisfaction does not tell us much about the process of how they arrive at that assessment, nor does it mean that satisfying marriages require little adjustment and have few problems.

Slightly more second marriages than first marriages end in divorce for two main reasons. First, most second marriages are entered into by people who have already experienced a divorce. Divorced persons have demonstrated their willingness to dissolve a less than satisfying relationship and are knowledgeable of the divorce process—how to file for divorce, how to negotiate custody, and so forth. Second, remarriages are more complex structures than first marriages. Norms and rules of appropriate behavior are not clearly defined, making it easier to take missteps that cause marital and family conflict and dissatisfaction (Cherlin, 1993).

Past research informs us of how adults go about selecting a partner for remarriage. It also helps us understand that remarriage can be satisfying for adults if they pay attention to why their first marriages were unsuccessful, choose more carefully the second time around, and display a willingness to change some of their own negative behaviors. Another way to examine remarriage is to look at it from the perspective of meeting new challenges.

MEETING THE CHALLENGES OF STEPFAMILY LIFE

There are many challenges for remarried family members to overcome or learn to live with as they become accustomed to each other in a new family situation. The most problematic challenges include dealing with negative stereotypes, living with the ambiguity of having few clear-cut norms or other customs to guide behavior, combating feelings of instant closeness as well as expectations for divided loyalties, and meshing the financial needs of multiple households. We begin by identifying the impact of negative stereotypes on stepfamilies.

Negative Stereotypes

Cultural stereotypes of children and adults in stepfamilies are significantly less positive than stereotypes of intact two-parent families (Ganong, Coleman, & Mapes, 1990). Although perceptions are shifting, even today, stepfamilies face negative stereotypes about their personal and family lives. These collective cultural views encourage the acceptance of many "basic truths" about families that do not necessarily ring true. Images of the "wicked" stepmother, the "abusive" stepfather, and the "neglected" stepchild continue to be part of our societal belief system (Bryan, Coleman, & Ganong, 1986; Dainton, 1993). Family therapists Emily and John Visher in their book on stepfamiles, *Old Loyalties, New Ties* (1988) write:

> "Confusion," "complexity," "resentment," "jealousy," "guilt," "chaos"—these are a few of the [words associated with] "stepfamily." . . . There are also phrases like "hidden agendas," "alienation," "walking on eggs," "never enough time," "not as good." Once in a while a timid voice mentions "love," "challenge," "humor," "exciting," and a phrase such as

"parental happiness," but usually the word "stepfamily" conjures up a negative image. While the word "family" may denote hearth and home, pictures of Cinderella shivering by the ashes of the fire tend to accompany "stepfamily." (p. 3)

The first step in combating negative stereotypes and inappropriate cultural expectations is to discard preconceived notions of what a family *should* be like and acknowledge stepfamily differences. It is useful for stepfamilies to recognize that remarriage does not recreate a once-married family situation. Usually, learning to understand and accept life's realities in a stepfamily has positive results, as is illustrated by this adolescent's comments:

> I hate to admit this, but since my stepfamily's new lifestyle is so different than what I was used to, I've learned that there is more than one way to live. There are parts of that lifestyle that I'm going to copy when I marry and have a family some day. (Visher & Visher, 1988, p. 241)

Some authors even suggest changing the name stepfamily to a term that has a less negative connotation—*blended, reconstituted,* or *binuclear* family, for example. Others believe that altering terminology would only bring on more confusion, ambiguity, and stigma (Lofas & Sova, 1985; Hughes, 1991).

Lack of Rituals and Clear-Cut Guidelines

A second challenge for stepfamilies is dealing with what sociologist Andrew Cherlin (1981, 1993) refers to as *remarriage as an incomplete institution,* because many of the norms, rituals, and institutional solutions available to people in first marriages are not clearly defined in second marriages. Stepparents and children are expected to build intimate relationships with few firm guidelines (Fine & Schwebel, 1991). This uncertainty about how family roles should be enacted is referred to as *role ambiguity.* In remarried families, role ambiguity is caused by four factors (Dainton, 1993):

- Being unsure about which family responsibilities belong to whom. (Who takes the children to school, attends parent-teacher conferences, takes out the trash?)

POINT OF VIEW

My Wife-in-Law and Me: A Mother-Stepmother Relationship

Every two weeks my 15-year-old son loads his collection of 300 comic books into two long cardboard boxes constructed for this purpose. These two boxes, together with his own and his 18-year-old sister's duffel bags and stereo boxes, get brought down to the car, and I take this cargo over to their father's house, about a half mile away. Two weeks later, they and their belongings come back to me. My husband and I separated 7 years ago, after almost a year of intense and painful discussion. In retrospect, those discussions seemed to have paved the way for a fundamental renegotiation of our relationship, from husband and wife to coparents. Even then we realized dimly that because of our children, our relationship would always be around in some form. Thus, we were able to construct an amicable divorce based on a basic agreement over two major points: money and custody. Two years later, he remarried, and he and Ann subsequently became the parents of Sam, a 2-year-old from El Salvador, who is now 4.

The major and often crippling difficult issues raised by disagreements over money and custody have not happened to us. There are three reasons for this, I think. For one thing, we were able to leave behind us, at least operationally, the mutual emotional entanglements that often persist after the relationship is officially "over." We were able to put aside issues of blame, guilt, recrimination, and the like. Second, Jeff has always had the view that he is, and should be, an equally involved and responsible parent—until recently, a relatively unusual stance for males in our society. The importance of this equality cannot be overestimated, because it has given us a grounding of common involvement and trust. Third, he, through his family, has the financial resources to provide generously for our children, without anyone having to sacrifice.

I am mainly going to write about my relationship with Ann, my "wife-in-law." Much of what goes on is negotiated by the two of us. It is Ann and I, rather than Jeff and I, who have tended to arrange schedules, doctors' appointments, and so on, although over the years those roles have declined as the children have begun to make their own plans. It is we who have the overlap-

■ Being undecided about exactly which behaviors are appropriate in each new stepfamily role. (Is it okay for a stepparent to discipline, hug, counsel, and protect stepchildren?)

■ Being uncertain about which family member's expectations are the most important to meet. (Dad wants me to study after school, but Donny needs a ride to soccer practice, and my stepmom asked me to start dinner. What should I do?)

■ Being unsure about how making certain decisions will affect other family members. (If I go to Florida with my dad over the holidays, I will miss the family celebrations with my mom and stepbrothers. How will they feel about that? How will dad feel if I turn him down?)

Initially, many stepparents expect that the parenting role in the stepfamily will be very similar to the parenting role in a once-married family. Frustration typically accumulates as the stepparent meets with resistance and even open hostility when attempting to apply parenting skills and family rules from the first family to the second family. Failure to institute more suitable guidelines based on the new stepfamily structure generally leads to dissatisfaction and distress (Visher & Visher, 1988).

Consider the situation of a typical stepfamily. Mary has custody of two children from her former marriage. John wants to remain in close contact with his son, who is living nearby with his mother, John's ex-wife. Now Mary has not only two children of her own, but a stepson. John has to balance his responsibilities to his son (who no longer lives with him) with those of his stepchildren, with whom he now shares a household. Both Mary and John have to deal with their ex-spouses. And the entire family consists of a variety of "steps"—stepbrothers and stepsisters, stepfathers and stepmothers, stepgrandparents. The family structure of this newly created unit bears a certain resemblance to the organization chart of a multinational corporation.

Obviously, the potential strains multiply in this new,

ping roles of mother—two people on one base, as it were—and we who sometimes get in each other's way.

Thinking about specific issues that have come up for me, I find that several themes keep emerging.

- The issue of a third person sharing the intimate daily life of your children.

- The construction of a required intimate relationship with someone you don't know at all, a woman who is "just like" your friends in many ways but who situationally cannot be your friend.

- The mutual invasion of familial boundaries of time and space, so that decisions that have been intrafamilial become contingent on two families.

- The necessary interplay between rules (such as two weeks here and two weeks there) and relationships (how the exceptions get constructed and allowed), and the complex interactions that take place in the journey back and forth between rights and responsibilities.

I have had trouble with many aspects of my situation of bringing up my children in joint custody with their father and stepmother. I have not liked being told about appropriate extracurricular activities for them, although I have liked help and support about rule setting. I have not liked being personally involved with someone whose concerns, feeling, and interests I cannot

share. I have not liked sharing my children's time, the decoration of my vacation living room, my own vacation schedule, although I have often been grateful for my times of solitude, built as they are on the basic assumption that my children were always all right. I have not liked needing "permission" before making some of my own plans.

I think, however, that all these negative experiences are relatively trivial. When one family becomes two families, the questions of rules, boundaries, arrangements, and the differing goals and purposes of individuals become more formal and explicit, more institutional in a way, even as the relationships between and among the players become more complex. Divorces, when there are children, are ongoing relationships that survive, even beyond the children's growing up. We need to think of divorce, therefore, not only as a severing of connection, but as a reconnection on different terms.

EXPLORATIONS   *Is wife-in-law a good term for the relationship that has developed between the two women described here? Can you think of a better term? What are the benefits of having terms to describe ongoing and important relationships in stepfamilies?*

SOURCE: Excerpted from S. Turner (1989).

more complex family. John's son, who visits frequently, may feel jealous of his father's attention to the new stepchildren. Mary would prefer to be friendlier with John's ex-wife than he would like her to be. For his part, John is obliged to remain on good terms with his "ex" because he wants to remain in close contact with his son. Meanwhile, his ex-wife feels that he is being more generous with his stepchildren than with his own son.

Remarried adults and their children face problems for which there are no conventional solutions, no clear-cut guidelines (see the "Point of View" box). Some—such as the matter of how children should address a parent's new spouse—are problems of etiquette as well as a source of awkwardness. But they also reflect the failure of our language to incorporate terms for stepfamily relationships. If a child has a "dad" already, what does she or he call a stepfather? How is a step-

grandmother to be addressed? Which people are considered family?

Other situations that arise for remarried people can be even more troubling. Imagine the dilemma faced by a couple whose teenage stepchildren want to date each other. Another potentially explosive area is where to draw the line as close and intimate relationships develop between stepparents and stepchildren. The Mia Farrow–Woody Allen–Soon Yi triangle illustrates this concern. What exactly are the rights and responsibilities of stepparents to stepchildren (see the "Snapshots" box)? Should there be some culturally imposed guidelines?

As you can see, "styles, habits, customs, and modes of interaction that were part of the old family (especially in the single-parent stage) do not necessarily work in the new remarried family" (Rosenberg & Hajal, 1985, p. 289). In the absence of time-honored or

SNAPSHOTS

Romance in Stepfamilies: When Is It Incestuous?

What is a stepfamily? And what are appropriate and socially acceptable relationships between parents and children who are not related biologically but through marriage or other long-term commitments?

Mental health professionals who counsel stepfamilies tend to see the Allen-Farrow situation as an aberration—a sensationalized issue—rather than one of the problems stepparents commonly face, such as conflicts over discipline and favoritism.

Sexual relationships between stepfathers and young adult stepdaughters are hardly commonplace, said Constance Ahrons, a professor of sociology at the University of Southern California, but "it happens—and it happens primarily because boundaries are very unclear in stepfamilies."

Is the Woody-Soon-Yi affair incest? "I cannot comment . . . because he claims he wasn't a parent figure," Ahrons said. But, "in general, I would say, yes, if someone has been in the role of mother's lover and the child was 9 when he came into her life [as Soon-Yi was], I would say yes, there's a power relationship."

Said Doris Jacobson, a professor in the School of Social Welfare at the University of California, Los Angeles: "The first issue here, it seems to me, is what's the family?

"In my view, even when consenting adults live together, there's a different commitment to family than if they're married and have made a public commitment to each other. [The Allen-Farrow] situation is confused, or obfuscated, in a way, by the fact that Woody Allen never lived in the household. He came in every day."

In cases such as Allen's and Farrow's, "There are no guidelines from society about appropriate behavior."

Because of this, Jacobon said, "The barriers to what is usually considered incest are weaker and more confusing."

And, if there is sex between a stepparent and a consenting young adult stepchild, what do we call that?

"It's not incest under the law," said Jeannette Lofas, founder and president of the New York–based Step Family Foundation. But, "We consider it emotional incest and spiritual incest because of the devastation it causes."

Psychotherapist Karen Savage, writing in *The Good Stepmother: A Practical Guide*, said, "Incest between father, or father figure, and daughter is the most frequently broken of the incest taboos."

Teenage rebellion may fuel the relationship. "Most often, they don't really want sexual contact. It may be one of their weapons for playing one parent against another."

Lofas, a marriage and family therapist who has been both a stepchild and a stepparent, suggested that there may be more than an attraction to Allen involved: "Soon-Yi is having an age-appropriate competition with her adopted mom. What's the best way to get after Mom?"

EXPLORATIONS *Do you think we need to better define what is appropriate behavior between stepparents and stepchildren? What are two guidelines you would propose to combat role ambiguity in stepfamilies?*

SOURCE: Excerpted from B. Beyette (1992).

socially recognized guidelines, couples are left to work out their own arrangements. These arrangements are further complicated by the need to feel close to new family members without feeling, at the same time, that doing so jeopardizes loyalty to family members from the first marriage.

Instant Closeness

Because of our cultural expectation that all families should be close, the pull to become an instant family is intense. Parents, especially, are conscious of this need and strive to facilitate family togetherness. As one woman remarks:

> The hardest part for me is that I wanted an "instant" family. I felt that these kids would be mine. My position was that you didn't vote for me and I didn't vote for you. But . . . we are stuck with each other. With that simple philosophy, we should all love each other and be one big happy family. But it doesn't work that way. (Fishman & Hamel, 1981, p. 186)

Parents may have been dating for several months or even years and have gotten to know each other fairly well. Children do not necessarily have this advantage. One young man recalls meeting his stepbrother for the first time: "One day he was just there with his suitcase in my room. All of a sudden he was supposed to be my brother and I didn't even know what cereal he liked" (Rosenberg & Hajal, 1985, p. 289). Changes in status also accompany these seemingly sudden changes in family structure. Almost overnight, a child can go from being the oldest in a family of two siblings to being a middle child in a family of five siblings. Such shifts in roles can mean a loss of privileges as well as an obligation to take on additional family responsibilities. Both children and adults need time to adjust to change.

Divided Loyalties

Divided loyalties are another serious challenge. Because of the unique configuration of stepfamilies, each family member struggles with the accommodation of new and old families and the determination of primary loyalties. Children, as well as parents, feel this tug. In the words of a 12-year-old California boy, "If I go to Disneyland or something like that with my real dad, I don't tell my stepfather, because I don't want him to feel bad for not taking me to places like that" ("Marriage," 1984, p. 136).

Sometimes divided loyalties of stepchildren lead them to look for faults in the new stepparent in order to maintain the belief that their parent is always first or best. Withdrawal from the stepparent is another form of self-protection—it keeps the stepparent at a distance and, thus, further ensures against loyalty conflicts. An adolescent's words convey how this tactic works:

> We never see eye-to-eye. She's so different from my mother. Just the constant comparison—that she doesn't cook as well as my mother, that she lays down more rules. Different kinds of things are expected, and we never really developed much of a relationship. I feel she tries to become more involved in my affairs than she's welcome to. That particularly causes me to draw away from her. (Fishman & Hamel, 1981, p. 186)

Intense loyalty to a parent can also result in a child's jealousy of a parent's new spouse. In one study, for example, girls whose mothers had remarried tended to have more behavioral problems than girls who lived with mothers who had divorced and not remarried. This was true despite the advantages of remarriage—such as higher family income and a more stable living arrangement (Peterson & Zill, 1986). While any explanation must be regarded as speculative, such problems may be manifested in the tensions daughters feel when the special bond they have with their mothers is threatened by the arrival of a stepparent.

Handling the Family Money

How a stepfamily handles money can be a challenge to their becoming a close, smoothly operating family unit (Giles-Sims & Crosbie-Burnett, 1989b; Lown & Dolan, 1988). Research shows that there are basically two ways that stepfamilies handle money. In the "two-pot" method, each parent controls the money designated for that parent's child and the general household expenses are paid by assigning specific bills to each marital partner. In the "one-pot" method, all family money is pooled and then considered a common resource. The "one-pot" method has been found to enhance positive regard among family members as well as contribute to feelings of satisfaction with family life (Ganong & Coleman, 1989a). Overall, couples in second marriages are more egalitarian than those in first marriages when making decisions about how the family money should be spent (Ganong & Coleman, 1989b).

For some, the division of money is an extremely touchy issue. Suggestions that money be pooled can raise feelings of anxiety and resistance because of past events in a previous marriage. Money may have been used as a source of power within an earlier marriage to the extent that one partner felt too dependent on or controlled by the other. In other cases, how money was spent or divided during and after the divorce produces bad memories as well as a resolve to always be financially autonomous in future relationships. When one partner or the other has been victimized in an earlier relationship, it is best to listen carefully to their protests and remain flexible and open to their feelings in this matter.

The juggling of financial obligations to biological children and stepchildren, and to the former and current spouse, can also be a challenge. "In families where there is money to fight over, it is likely to cause more disputes than do the children" (Franks, 1988, p. 163) (see the "Snapshots" box).

SNAPSHOTS

Meeting the Financial Challenge

A remarried couple has a child of their own as well as children from their previous marriages. The wife's ex-husband has not paid any child support for several months. Her new husband makes up the difference in the family budget, but then is unable to pay the full amount he is legally obligated to pay in child support to his former wife and children. He feels a pressing responsibility to help support the new wife and child of his remarriage and his stepchildren, but is depressed and feels guilty over how meeting this responsibility causes financial hardship for his first family.

EXPLORATIONS *How should the father balance his financial obligations? Does he owe more loyalty to his first or second family? Do you see a solution to his problem? Explain.*

✱

CHILDREN OF REMARRIAGE: VICTIMS OR RASCALS?

Two major themes dominate articles on children in stepfamilies. One theme is that stepchildren are beset with numerous problems that are directly attributable to being in a stepfamily and, as a result, are disadvantaged compared to children in intact families. The second theme centers on the often-reported finding that children are the key to successful adaptation in stepfamilies; that their behavior can make or break the new marital bond. Given the importance of these themes in shaping what we currently know about stepfamilies, it seems appropriate to examine each more closely.

Children as Victims

Demographer Paul Glick (1989) estimates that of children born in the early 1980s, 35 percent will eventually live in a stepfamily. By the year 2000, he further predicts, over 50 percent of these children will be stepdaughters and stepsons. These statistics and similar others are the cause of much alarm and worry. Many view children of remarriage as victims of yet another set of circumstances that require long-term adjustment.

The Deficit-Comparison Perspective

After reviewing 305 studies of the effects of remarriage on children, 114 of which were selected for further analysis, family scientists Larry Ganong and Marilyn Coleman (1986) concluded that much of the research in the area proceeds from a problem-oriented framework or *deficit-comparison perspective*. From this perspective, children in stepfamilies are seen as victims of a stepfamily lifestyle that "produces undesirable effects on children" (1986, p. 310).

Ganong and Coleman divided studies into two general categories, "clinical," or applied, studies and "empirical" studies. Clinical studies most often relied on the impressions gained from clients who came in for counseling. Sometimes authors described educational or self-help programs they had developed for stepfamilies. Other times, they used case studies or interviews conducted in their offices as a data source. Clinical studies more frequently portrayed children in stepfamilies as plagued by problems. By comparison, empirical studies were usually based on surveys or interviews unconnected with any counseling or therapy services. Collectively, the empirical investigations found few differences between stepchildren and other children on such factors as thinking and reasoning ability, emotional and physical distress, personality characteristics, attitudes and behaviors toward others, or quality of family relationships.

Ganong and Coleman concluded that, because clinicians wrote many more of the books and articles about stepfamilies, the deficit-comparison approach had greater visibility in both professional and lay publications, reinforcing cultural stereotypes about stepfamilies as deviant and stepchildren as victims. But, clinical researchers were also credited with more often viewing stepfamilies as complex family systems and studying remarriage as a process that requires some adjustment on the part of individual family members.

The Normative-Adaptive Perspectives

Many of the scholars currently studying stepfamilies have discarded the deficit-comparison perspective in favor of considering divorce and remarriage as a normal life event. From this *normative-adaptive perspective*, stepfamilies are viewed as normally occurring family types in which children and parents learn to adapt to a new lifestyle. Evidence from various studies indicates that younger children, compared to adolescents, seem able to adjust faster and more successfully to remarriage and more easily become attached to a stepparent (Hetherington & Clingempeel, 1988). Adolescents, because they are accustomed to having greater power in the single-parent family and have developed greater interaction skills, more frequently confront and question parents about new family rules and roles (Hetherington, Stanley-Hagan, & Anderson, 1989).

But adolescent reactions are also a factor of age. Young adolescents (12- and 13-year-olds), because of the jarring physical and emotional changes that accompany puberty, are more vulnerable to the adjustments that remarriage implies. Older adolescents (17- and 18-year-olds), on the other hand, seem more accepting of the remarriage, since they "are anticipating their departure from the home and new young adult roles and relationships. The introduction of a stepparent may even relieve responsibilities for emotional and economic support of their divorced parents" (Hetherington et al., 1989, p. 305).

Children in remarried families are usually better off financially, with most moving from mother-headed families to two-parent families in which both parents are earners. They are less likely to live in poverty and more likely to complete their education and, in turn, to have access to better jobs as adults. Children of remarriage also fare better when household responsibilities are considered, because there is another adult in the household to share family chores as well as parenting responsibilities. And, even though contact between noncustodial parents and their children decreases following remarriage, most family scientists conclude that children are not adversely affected by this arrangement because, in most cases, children's visits with noncustodial parents have already dropped off considerably over the course of time (Clingempeel & Segal, 1986; Kurdek & Sinclair, 1986).

Children will perceive some events relative to remarriage as positive; others will be emotionally difficult for them. Certainly, existing family routines will be upset. And, as indicated, remarriage changes the child's status in established kin networks, introducing new brothers and sisters, grandparents, and aunts and uncles to the family (Santrock & Sitterle, 1987; Zill, 1988).

Children as Rascals

The children-as-rascals theme supports the theory that children tend to have a negative effect on the marital satisfaction of most couples. Since some 60 percent of divorcing couples have children under age 18, the formation of satisfactory relationships in stepfamilies is difficult to attain (Ihinger-Tallman, 1988; White & Booth, 1985). When asked to speculate on reasons for the higher marital dissolution rate among remarried couples—approximately 60 percent as compared to about 50 percent of first marriages—some family scholars, like sociologist Marilyn Ihinger-Tallman (1988), maintain that, of the factors that can serve as catalysts, "the presence of stepchildren is more likely to be the critical factor that tips a remarriage toward divorce" (p. 30).

When children are young, opportunities for private and intimate moments may be limited by child-care responsibilities; a remarried couple may not think they have a right to take time for themselves. The consequence is that the development of the couple's own relationship is neglected. When children are older, conflict instead of neglect becomes the primary concern. Remarriages that include adolescent stepchildren experience the highest divorce rates. The increase in acrimony and distress attributed to parent-child disagreements over family roles and rules is cited as one of the key reasons that adolescents in step relationships leave home sooner than adolescents in other family types (White & Booth, 1985).

Many children feel powerless when their parents split and powerless again when one or more of their parents remarry. How they behave has a lot to do with the stability of the marriage. In a stepmother's words:

> Basically, I'm a mother at heart. But it's turned out to be an extremely disappointing situation for me. The whole experience of being a stepparent has just beaten down my self-confidence about being a parent myself. . . . I've done all the things that I am supposed to do,

the right things, and the kids don't love me. . . . I love my husband dearly and wish that things could have been easier for us . . . I would say that 95 percent of our fights are over the kid's situation. One-on-one, we're very well matched, we're very compatible, we have a good time together, but when they're around, the fur flies. I could have a much better marriage if it weren't for the kids. (Francke, 1983, pp. 203–205)

Remarried couples, as one researcher observes, often feel uncomfortable as parents and marital partners (Weingarten, 1985). Differences over child rearing represent one of the greatest sources of conflict for these couples.

"The attachments children build to new stepparents and to the strangers who become their brothers and sisters become critical factors in the successful functioning and longevity of the new marriage" (Ihinger-Tallman, 1987, p. 178). Family researchers Margaret Crosbie-Burnett (1984) and Constance Ahrons and Lynn Wallisch (1987) in their extensive research on stepfamilies conclude that a satisfactory stepparent-stepchild relationship is one of the key predictors of family well-being and marital happiness in remarried families. When stepparent and stepchild do not get along, tremendous pressure is placed on the new marital relationship.

STEPMOMS AND STEPDADS: CULTURAL NORMS THAT BIND

What tends to be ignored about stepfamilies is that, despite the inevitable parent-child conflicts that arise, most manage to create vital and satisfying family relationships. And, in some cases, when the noncustodial biological parent is physically or psychologically distant, the stepparent is able to be very effective as a substitute parent and positive role model (Seltzer & Bianchi, 1988). Of all the barriers that stepparents must overcome, cultural expectations and the aftermath of socialization are perhaps the most powerful.

Stepmothers: Socialization for Failure

Stepmothers, compared to stepfathers, report greater dissatisfaction with their family roles and exhibit higher levels of distress related to carrying out family responsibilities (Ahrons & Wallisch, 1987). This is most likely because they assume more responsibility than fathers for the daily management and rituals of the household. Face-to-face daily contacts with the children place stepmothers in the position of being there when unpopular decisions must be made at a moment's notice ("No, you can't go to Jo's after school, you promised your father you would clean out the garage"; "Yes, you can spend the night at Ken's, but only after you straighten your room and do your homework").

Socialized to believe that they should be the loving, attentive, caring centers of the family, stepmothers almost immediately try too hard to achieve emotional closeness. "Many stepmoms—especially those with no children of their own—have a strong need to prove themselves as parents" (Ahrons, personal communication). These urgent attempts are nearly universally rejected by children, who typically object to anyone who tries to take the place of their biological mother.

This rejection, in combination with strong feelings of being outside the family system, drives some stepmothers to push even harder to assume a traditional maternal role. They want to evidence that they are not "wicked stepmothers" (Guisinger et al., 1989). The more strenuously they press for closeness, the more determined the children seem to resist. Eventually, most stepmothers realize that, despite their resolve to develop good relationships with their stepchildren, it is a process that benefits from time, communication, and trust. Intimacy is the consequence of cooperative efforts by all concerned.

The biological father's reluctance to take responsibility for parenting his own children also serves as a major obstacle for stepmothers. When a father's children from his first marriage visit, the father may hang back and expect the stepmother to take on the traditional tasks of mothering, often seeing these responsibilities as "women's work." The husband who neglects to increase his involvement with his children usually finds that his new marriage is becoming more and more strained as his wife resists taking on what she views as his parenting roles. His relationship with his children also suffers because they want him to care for them, play with them, and in as many ways as possible show them *his* love.

Stepfathers: Expectations Meet Reality

Stepfathers indicate that they receive contradictory messages concerning their rights and obligations to children and stepchildren (see the "Changing Lifestyles" box). According to traditional cultural prescriptions, fathers are the family advisors and disciplinarians. In remarried families, stepfathers frequently begin with unrealistic notions of being an "advisor-healer"—someone who can blend two sets of children together seamlessly so that they act and react as an integrated family team (Papernow, 1988). Typically, children actively resist this blending process, much as they foil the stepmother's instant love approach. After several attempts, stepfathers generally come to realize that they need to retreat and put less pressure on children to become a "new" family.

Discipline of stepchildren is another bothersome issue facing stepfathers. A common complaint of stepfathers is that they receive little respect for their adult status in the family. For example, one stepfather complained that his stepson showed a "complete lack of any acknowledgement of my right to correct him or have him obey when asked (told) to do something—like clean up his room or be home at a certain time" (Giles-Sims & Crosbie-Burnett, 1989a, p. 1071).

The mother's attitudes complicate the issue of discipline. Mothers, too, struggle with the dilemma of how much authority a stepfather should have, with many concluding that they, not the stepfather, should have major responsibility. The following two remarks were made by interviewed mothers:

Decide in your own mind who is in charge of your children. If the natural father is around and involved, try to work out children's problems with him, with you taking most charge. Involve the stepfather only if you feel out of control or overwhelmed.

I have never counted on their stepdad to provide discipline, not even to put them to bed. That is not his responsibility. Those children are *my* responsibility and it is one that I choose to have. He married *me*, he only has to live with them, not discipline them. (Giles-Sims & Crosbie-Burnett, 1989b, p. 1071)

In a study of 44 young adolescent children who lived in stepfamilies, 70 percent reported that their families had successfully or very successfully adapted to remarried life (Knaub & Hanna, 1984). Discipline was viewed as one of the major issues in their families. The children recommended that, when faced with this problem, a stepparent should proceed gradually and carefully. It seems that the stepfather who can acknowledge the children's reluctance and his wife's ambivalence about his parental role, and is able to step back for awhile, allow some time to pass, and then

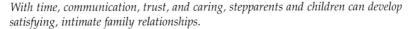

With time, communication, trust, and caring, stepparents and children can develop satisfying, intimate family relationships.

Being a Stepfather: Why Isn't There a Script?

More feared than loved in family fable, the stepfather in the American home of the 1990s is winning new respect for performing a role for which there is no script and the moments of applause and limelight are few.

"Being a stepfather, especially if there are teen-agers in the house, is probably one of the most humiliating and difficult tasks a man can take on," said Thomas Seibt, a marriage and family therapist in Los Angeles. He is also one of 13 million stepfathers in the country.

"It is starting to sink in that the flexible guy who approaches stepfamily life without the intention of re-creating a nuclear family, but a functional group whatever form it takes, is some kind of hero," said Dr. Larry Ganong, a stepfather. He is a professor at the University of Missouri who, with his wife, Dr. Marilyn Coleman, has extensively studied stepfamilies.

From their studies, Dr. Ganong concludes that "the stepfather-child relationship is perhaps the best predictor of a stepfamily's success and can make or break a second marriage."

Because women usually win custody of children in divorce cases, their new husbands must adapt to living with someone else's children. If they are adolescents—in a rebellious time of life that can unnerve natural parents—the challenge can be overwhelming and quickly sour the new marriage.

Conflicts over territoriality and discipline, especially with teenagers, are part of the reason that second marriages fail at an even greater rate than first marriages;

that children in stepfamilies drop out of school more than children in single-parent households do; and that many experts worry what kind of parents the angry, hurt children will become.

Stepfathers who overcome anger, frustration, and loss of face in these confrontations are often those whose new marriages succeed. It takes precise navigation in largely unchartered waters. Advice books are usually not read until a crisis develops and egos are already raw, researchers report.

"Everyone who gets married and starts a family has a general idea of how mothers and fathers are supposed to behave, but when you ask them about stepparents, all you get is shrugged shoulders," said Dr. Lawrence Kurdek, a professor of psychology at Wright State University in Dayton, Ohio, who studies stepfamilies.

The stepparent has few role models on television and in movies. Stepfathers are infrequently portrayed and when they are, as in the 1970 series "The Brady Bunch," little distinction is made between them and biological fathers. Or the script imbues them with the characteristics of storybook stepmothers: cold, emotionally distant, malevolent.

Dr. Benjamin Spock was humbled by the stepparenting quagmire after marrying a woman with a 10-year-old daughter. "Being a stepfather was the most painful experience in my life, and it was obviously even more painful for my stepdaughter," he said in a talk last year. He said he had rewritten a section on step-

proceed with caution to establish some kind of consensus, has a better chance of providing the level of love, support, and guidance needed by the children. The best strategy seems to be for stepparents to first gain the support of their partners and then wait for opportunities to gain the acceptance of their stepchildren. Stepfathers who take a secondary, monitoring role as parents instead of a take charge, disciplinary role have better relationships with the stepchildren (Fine & Kurdek, 1992).

Stepfathers may also find that the mother-child relationship is especially close, facilitated by years of single-parent living. This special bond may make it

difficult for the mother and child to separate emotionally and create a place for the stepfather. In other cases, the stepparent may be ignored or pushed aside by the remarried mother because of feelings of guilt over having focused attention and love on someone besides the children. Or the mother may be trying to compensate for the disruptions in her children's lives caused by the divorce and remarriage by demoting the stepfather to a less prominent position in the family (Visher & Visher, 1989).

For stepmothers, then, the challenge is not to push too hard for close, intimate relationships with stepchildren. For stepfathers, the challenge is to stifle the

parenting on the basis of his experience chronicled in his book *Baby and Child Care.*

Some live-in stepfathers feel like distant, unwanted relations overstaying their visits.

Researchers and clinicians generally agree that young children, with greater physical and emotional dependence on adults, may quickly accept a stepfather's help and discipline. Teenagers are preoccupied with changing sexuality, schoolwork, friends, and sports and are straining to break free of adult authority. They choose to adhere to parental discipline only out of fear, or love and respect, to which the stepfather initially has no claim. He may never have.

"In the beginning of a remarriage, stepdads should be like polite strangers in their new wife's home and talk to the teen-age kids, but not intervene or exercise too much control over their lives," said E. Mavis Hetherington, a University of Virginia psychologist who has tracked stepfamilies over years. "There's too much hostility in the kids who at that age want independence, not control."

Faced with conflict, some stepfathers overreact and disengage from the children. " 'I married you, not your kid,' they tell their wives, and leave all the problems to her," Dr. Hetherington said. She recommends being "the authoritative parent," a person high in warmth, responsiveness, and communication, who monitors children's activities without demanding unquestioning obedience.

Compounding the stepfather's problems are the mixed messages he receives from the legal system and from society in general. Many stepfathers provide full financial support for their new wives' children but have few legal rights unless they adopt them, but adoption is impossible in most states unless the natural father consents. A natural father, in fact, retains greater legal rights to minors even if he disappears and leaves their rearing and education to the stepfather.

David Chambers, a law professor at the University of Michigan, cites the case of a Michigan man whose wife died after 3 years of marriage. The widower petitioned the courts for custody of his three stepchildren, then age 4, 6, and 11; the court awarded custody to the biological father, who had provided no child support and had little contact with the children for most of their lives.

Social conditioning can lead both partners in a second marriage into the trap of believing men are providers who set and enforce family rules—an antique proposition even for a first marriage; for stepfamilies, it is a prescription for disaster.

Whatever role a stepfather takes, issues with the children must be resolved or the marriage will quickly falter, said Constance Ahrons, a professor at the University of Southern California who is a family therapist and author of *Divorced Families* (W. W. Norton, 1989). "If the relationship with the kids doesn't work," Dr. Ahrons said, "the marriage isn't going to work."

She told of a Wisconsin couple who began life together with five adolescents from their previous marriages: "After a year they couldn't handle it. They separated but didn't divorce, planning to live together again after the last of the teen-agers leaves home."

EXPLORATIONS *What would you say are the three most pressing challenges for stepfathers? How might we as a society ease these challenges? What can stepfathers do in their own behalf?*

SOURCE: Excerpted from J. Nordheimer (1990).

desire to be the family advisor-healer and disciplinarian. In each case, the underlying issue appears to be that the remarried individual is basing his or her expectations on traditional gender roles—women are to nurture and promote loving relationships within the family while men are to provide guidance and discipline. These role expectations do not necessarily mesh well with the realities of how life progresses in a stepfamily.

Stepfamily needs are very much based on the past histories and present concerns of family members who have already experienced life-shaping events in their families of origin, gone through a divorce, spent a period of time in a single-parent family, and, finally, are experiencing a remarriage. It takes time to become a family. Experiences in earlier family situations mold and modify responses to the new family situation. Showing up with boxes and a suitcase, or even going through a ritual wedding ceremony, does not confer family status. Time needs to pass, conversations need to occur, trust needs to be built, and love must be earned for a family to exist. Children's positive adjustment to stepfamily life is enhanced by adequate parental supervision and guidance, parental displays of warmth and affection, and consistent role modeling (Astone & McLanahan, 1991; Hetherington & Clingempeel, 1992). Satisfying relationships can and do develop, as we point out next.

CREATING SATISFYING NEW RELATIONSHIPS

As we have noted throughout this chapter, it is the complexity of the families created by remarriage, as well as the special need to negotiate new relationships in the absence of clear-cut rules, that make stepfamilies different from other families—and, in many ways, more demanding. The primary task of the stepfamily, according to Emily and John Visher, founders of The Stepfamily Association of America, "is that of moving from an absence of emotional connections between people, now living under one roof, to a sense of belonging to a group of individuals who feel connected to one another" (1990, p. 4). In order to accomplish these feelings of connectedness and belonging, the following tasks are essential (p. 5):

1 The remarried couple must accomplish solidification and maturation of their new relationship.

2 The previously existing bonds between parent and child must be maintained or improved.

3 New relationships between stepparents and stepchildren and between stepsiblings must be developed.

TABLE 16-1
What Are the Characteristics of a Successfully Remarried Family?

Emily and John Visher (1990) identify six characteristics of adults in stepfamilies that they believe are critical to individual and family well-being.

1. LOSSES HAVE BEEN MOURNED

The individual stepfamily adults have mourned their losses and are ready to proceed to a new pattern of life. In most stepfamilies there have been important losses for everyone, some of which tend to go unrecognized. For example, people who have sought a divorce in a previous relationship have experienced the loss of their dream of a successful marriage. A person who has never been previously married must give up expectations and hopes for a different kind of marriage, which did not involve dealing with stepchildren and a former spouse.

Accepting losses and letting go of the past is necessary if one is to make a satisfactory adjustment to the present and look forward to the future. Frequently, both adults and children find that group contacts with others who are dealing with similar changes are helpful in enabling them to move ahead.

2. EXPECTATIONS ARE REALISTIC

A second characteristic of adults in successful stepfamilies is that they have the realistic expectation that their family will be different from a first marriage family. Reasons why stepfamilies are different from nuclear families include:

- Adults and children are coming together at very different places in their individual, marital, and family life cycles.
- All members of the new family unit bring ways of doing things that are different because of their previous family patterns.
- Parent/child bonds precede rather than follow the formation of the couple relationship.
- There is a biological parent in another household or in memory.
- Fifty percent of children in stepfamilies move back and forth between parental households.
- Stepparents have little or no legal relationship with their stepchildren.

3. THERE IS A STRONG, UNIFIED COUPLE

Another important characteristic of successful remarried families is that they have strong and unified couples to lead them. With the parent/child bonds preceding the new-couple relationship and the couple trying to "have a honeymoon in the midst of a crowd," stepfamily adults need to plan for time alone to nourish their relationship. Often remarried parents have difficulty trusting in an intimate relationship again, or they feel guilty for shifting some of their attention away from their children in order to form a solid bond with their new spouse. In well-functioning stepfamilies, remarried parents realize that, while their children continue to need them, they also need the sense of security that comes from a stable couple and the assurance that the stepfamily unit will continue. The children also benefit from experiencing the model of a couple that is happy and working well together as a pattern for their own future couple relationships.

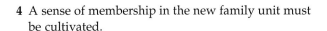

4 A sense of membership in the new family unit must be cultivated.

The characteristics of adults who have successfully adapted to stepfamily life are described in Table 16-1.

When 232 remarried couples were asked what advice they would give to other couples thinking of remarrying after a divorce, their counsel centered on seven different topics, including "communication, family relationships, spouse compatibility, dealing with children, the person him/herself, the previous marriage, and counseling or outside help" (Hobart, 1990, p. 140). Specific advice offered by the couples is in Table 16-2.

Even though it takes time and patience to build new family relationships, the end result appears to be positive. In one investigation, 91 percent of parents and 81 percent of children reported being members of stepfamilies that exhibited a large amount of sharing behavior; 78 percent of parents and 66 percent of children said that they felt close to other family members; and 67 percent of both parents and children indicated feeling comfortable and relaxed in their new families. Moreover, when their responses were compared, children in stepfamilies and intact families gave very similar descriptions of daily family life pertaining to "how much they did things with their parents, the rules around the home, how much say they had in decision-making, and how much they argued over family rules" (Furstenberg & Cherlin, 1991, p. 82).

TABLE 16-1 *(continued)*
What Are the Characteristics of a Successfully Remarried Family?

4. CONSTRUCTIVE RITUALS ARE ESTABLISHED

Good relationships grow from positive shared memories, and feelings of belonging develop from familiar ways of doing things. The establishment of rituals and traditions is an important characteristic of successful stepfamilies. As a rule, members have shared their past history concerning ceremonies, special events, and ways of doing things that are important to them. When possible, former important traditions are retained or combined in new ways as new rituals are established. In fact, one remarried mother remarked, "I think the adults in successful stepfamilies are flexible and resourceful, and their sense of humor is incredible." On the day they were married, one couple, each of whom had children, gave their children a silver cup with the date engraved on it. Later, these cups were used on special occasions and their significance helped to create a sense of belonging to a family unit.

5. SATISFACTORY STEP-RELATIONSHIPS HAVE FORMED

Step-relationships do not develop and fall into place when the couple forms a solid bond. Members of well-functioning remarried families perceive that these relationships need to be developed and that the time this takes depends on a number of factors: The age of the children; the number and ages of stepsiblings; and whether they are "resident" or "nonresident" family members who come and go with less time to relate to the new household.

Stepparents enter the picture with little power or authority as far as the children are concerned. From the first, successful couples work together and support one another in their household decisions. The fact that there are many satisfactory roles for stepparents other than that of "parent" often opens the way for numerous rewarding stepparent/stepchild interactions, even within the same household.

6. THE SEPARATE HOUSEHOLDS COOPERATE

The final characteristic we feel is of major significance in successful stepfamilies is that of developing a "parenting coalition," which includes the adults from both of the child's households who are involved in raising the children. For many adults, unfortunately, it is not possible to work out a cooperative rather than a competitive relationship with an ex-spouse, even on such an important topic as sharing in the care of their mutual children. Nevertheless there are an increasing number of remarried families in which the adults have recognized the value of such cooperation, both for themselves as well as for their children.

Parents may coparent after a divorce, but when there is a remarriage, whether stepparents are involved in a direct or a tangential way with their stepchildren, they become part of the parenting coalition. When the adults in the children's households cooperate, children go between households more easily. They are not caught up in crossfire between hostile and competitive parents and stepparents, and the adults as well as the children experience greater satisfaction. There is a sharing of parenting responsibility by the adults, and the children have fewer loyalty conflicts.

SOURCE: Excerpted from E. Visher & J. Visher (1990).

TABLE 16-2
Advice for Couples Contemplating Remarriage

Over 200 couples in second marriages gave the following advice to others thinking of remarrying. Notice that, overall, women and men gave similar responses, but there are also some interesting differences.

Advice Given	Percent of Men Advising	Percent of Women Advising
See importance of open, honest communication	23	30
Clarify expectations, reasons for remarriage	15	18
Ensure compatibility re values and philosophies	13	18
Be patient, supportive, compromising with new family	15	17
Work hard for meaningful harmonious relationships	8	12
Seek counseling, outside help if needed	6	13
Try to learn from prior marriage experiences	9	9
Try to ensure all can get along together in remarriage	6	8
Do live together before remarriage	8	6
Forget/forgive negative aspects of prior marriage	7	7
Relocate in a totally new home environment	5	8
Have respect for complexity of remarriage family situation	4	8
Be open and equitable in treatment of all children	4	8
Realize personalities, relationships of children are already formed	4	7
Be happy, honest, and true with/to yourself	3	7
Beware of children's attempts to undermine the marriage	3	4
Make time alone for the two spouses	2	4
See importance of total family involvement in activities	2	3
Don't remarry, especially when there are children	0.4	3.9

SOURCE: C. Hobart (1990).

Successful adaptation to married life was also evidenced in a national survey. The remarried were found to be just as likely as the once-married to report feeling "very happy" and to describe the present as the happiest time of their lives. Like most of their once-married counterparts, the majority of those who remarried reported that marriage complements many of their basic values. There were no appreciable differences between these two groups in level of irritability toward their spouses for what they did or did not do. Neither were there differences in the frequency of disagreements or fights (Weingarten, 1985). The conclusion of many family scientists is that, with the passage of time,

many couples cope successfully with the challenges of remarriage and are as likely as once-married couples to report high marital satisfaction and good emotional well-being (Bray, Berger, & Silverblatt, 1987; Kurdek, 1989; Whyte, 1990).

Over the past decade, remarriage following a divorce has come to be regarded as less problem-laden and more normative in that the family situation creates some initial stress as members learn to handle the special challenges of a stepfamily. Reflecting this change in perspective, research more often focuses on describing and understanding relationships in stepfamilies.

SUMMARY POINTS

■ Between 65 and 70 percent of women and men who divorce eventually remarry.

■ Incentives to remarry include personal needs for companionship, sex, and intimacy, as well as concerns about having another adult in the family to facilitate child rearing and to ensure family financial security.

■ Well over one-half of couples in their second marriages have cohabited prior to remarriage.

■ Of individuals who divorce, about half remarry within 7 years, with black and Hispanic couples remarrying at a slower rate than whites.

■ Women are less likely than men to remarry, especially if they are over age 40. While about 90 percent of women under age 25 remarry, only 60 percent of women in their thirties and less than one-third of women over age 40 remarry.

■ The higher the income of a divorced man, the more likely he is to remarry. But, income and education function as deterrents to remarriage for most women.

■ People seem to be less romantic and more cautious when establishing a marital partnership for the second time. Second-timers also appear to be more flexible about marital roles and responsibilities and share more of the household tasks and family decisions.

■ Major challenges to stepfamily life include dealing with negative stereotypes, living with ambiguous norms and guidelines, expecting instant closeness among family members, striving to remain loyal to both first and second families, and meeting financial responsibilities.

■ Remarriage does not recreate a first-marriage situation. The only "basic truth" about stepfamilies is that differences in family history, role expectations, and behavior will distinguish family interaction. Maintaining a slow and steady pace toward the goal of family unity and keeping an open mind about marital roles are critical to a satisfying stepfamily life.

■ There are two major themes that appear repeatedly in professional and lay publications when the topic is children in stepfamilies. One theme portrays children of remarriage as victims, the other pictures them as rascals.

■ Children-as-victims advocates believe that remarriage complicates and changes children's lives so dramatically that they are severely disadvantaged.

■ Children-as-rascals advocates believe that the anxieties and conflicts aroused by stepchildren in remarried families often lead to marital dissatisfaction and a second divorce.

■ In comparison to stepfathers, stepmothers feel the most dissatisfaction with family roles and report higher levels of distress. For both stepmoms and stepdads the challenge is to put traditional gender roles aside and take time to build trust and establish whatever parent-child ties are best for their particular families.

■ Emily and John Visher, founders of the Stepfamily Association of America, describe six characteristics

that identify adults who have successfully adapted to stepfamily life: losses have been mourned, expectations are realistic, a strong unified couple exists, constructive rituals are established, satisfactory step-relationships have formed, and the separate households cooperate.

■ Remarried couples in one study gave the following advice to other couples who were thinking of remarriage: see the importance of open, honest communication; clarify expectations and reasons for remarriage; be patient, supportive, and compromising with new family members; and work hard for meaningful, harmonious relationships.

KEY TERMS

Blended family
Reconstituted family
Binuclear family
Remarriage as an incomplete institution

Role ambiguity
Deficit-comparison perspective
Normative-adaptive perspective

REVIEW QUESTIONS

1. Discuss why marriages are different the second time around.

2. What two major themes are most frequently voiced in articles on children in stepfamilies? Do either of the two themes represent your beliefs? Explain.

3. Describe the primary challenges of stepfamily life. Which two challenges do you think have the most influence on adaptation in stepfamilies? Given these challenges, why is it that there is little difference between remarried and once-married couples on reports of marital satisfaction and emotional well-being?

4. Explain how cultural norms become formidable obstacles for stepparents trying to carry out parenting responsibilities in stepfamilies.

5. Interview a couple with stepchildren who have been married for at least 5 years. Ask them what advice they would give other couples thinking of remarrying. Develop a list of their suggestions and ask each to rank the items listed, beginning with number 1 as most important. Compare the lists generated by your informants to the list compiled by Hobart in Table 16-2. Write a summary of your findings.

Appendix
Managing Personal and Family Finances

Ignorance about money management is a luxury no one can afford. Today, it is essential that *both* partners in cohabiting or marital relationships be knowledgeable about money and involved in financial management. It is assumed that both partners will be employed before and after marriage for an indeterminate period of time. No longer is there the assumption that the woman is working solely for "extra money." Women, typically, are working for the same reasons as men—to enjoy the challenges of a satisfying position, put their education and training to use, and, of course, earn money to support the family.

Regardless of which partner earns the higher income, it is important that they work together to make financial decisions. Discussions will not lead to binding decisions that are made once and forever, with no allowance for change. Discussions are continuous throughout a relationship. There are always new situations that arise, requiring new decisions to reinforce already established goals, or that alter the direction of goals.

Several surveys over the past decade indicate that most men feel that the family income should be considered as belonging equally to both partners, but are reluctant to admit that the partner should have the same rights over actually spending it. While the use of joint checking accounts has increased, along with more egalitarian attitudes toward marriage, this has not led to the sharing of income in actual practice. As a consequence, many women do "not have access to money that they can regard as being rightfully their own, and some may spend a significant part of their married lives in a (perhaps unacknowledged) state of dependency" (Burgoyne, 1990, p. 635).

Married and cohabiting couples have more arguments about the management of money than about the amount of money they have to manage! Conflicts about money are often an expression of something else, a conflict in goals and lifestyles. Each partner

brings to the relationship a highly individual sense of what money means, and it may take time to resolve differences and forge a new "couple" sense of managing their finances.

Although conflicts over money issues are one of the foremost causes of divorce, learning to listen to each other's concerns about money and search out mutually satisfying alternatives to problems may help to preserve the relationship. Cooperation and compromise may help resolve difficulties when there is a clash of attitudes. For example, in unions made up of a "saver" and a "spendthrift," each partner needs to help prepare the family budget. Each should also take a turn at paying the bills. As the realities of family income and expenses are realized, compromise may be more easily achieved and spending brought into line with available income. The potential for conflict is reduced when partners discuss and resolve financial issues before they become a protracted source of disagreement.

THE ROLE OF FINANCIAL PLANNING

Financial planning is a lifelong process and the earlier it begins, the more successful the process will be. The purpose of this appendix is to introduce you to some of the major topics in financial planning. Like so many fields of study, personal finance is a rapidly changing discipline. If you learn to plan your finances while your present situation is less complex, you will be better able to cope with personal and economic changes as they occur throughout your life.

It is important to realize that most people do not smoothly progress through the life course from singleness to marriage, to parenthood, and then to retirement, a time when they are supposed to enjoy their grandchildren and travel across the country. Some people never marry, others choose not to have children, and an increasing number divorce and remarry. Some life transitions, such as marriage or the birth of a child, are positive and satisfying. Other family changes are sudden, unexpected, and occasionally devastating. Lingering illness or accidents can take a toll on emotions and finances. Whatever their origin, whether the consequences are joy or sorrow, the ultimate effect of change is inevitably financial! And the best means of dealing with life changes and their financial consequences is to have a continuing awareness of your personal finances so that adaptation to life's changing events is less traumatic.

Financial planning enables people to use their money more effectively. In learning to understand the role of money in financial planning, there are some crucial questions to consider: "How much money will it take to achieve my individual and family goals? Will I be able to reach my goals if I have less money, but learn how to better manage the money that I have?" No one can answer these questions for you as the answer is very personal. When you begin to answer these questions in very specific and personal terms, the practical result is action which only *you* can take.

This appendix first explores the practical matter of preparing a family budget. Every dollar spent is a decision made. A carefully constructed budget is one way to make sure that spending decisions express not just immediate preferences, but also long-term goals. Then we examine what is probably the largest single expense over a lifetime—taxes. While everyone is legally obligated to pay taxes, many people are unwittingly overpaying because they are unaware of many allowable deductions and don't keep up with changes in the tax laws.

Another area of financial management that we explore is the use of credit. Depending on how and when you use it, and what credit sources you draw upon, it can be either a flexible tool in financial management or a dangerous and expensive trap. In the final sections of this appendix, we look at two elements in any long-range financial planning, insurance programs that serve as a base for financial security and saving and investment plans that allow individuals and families to work toward long-term financial security.

Short-Term Needs, Long-Term Goals

Many single people indulge themselves financially. Long-term financial planning does not seem necessary.

Money is viewed mainly as a source of pleasure and enjoyment in the present—something to use for clothes, cars, entertainment, vacations. Marriage means redefining goals and priorities, particularly for young couples with children. Concerned now with long-term objectives, they give greater importance to savings, investment plans, and insurance.

The transition from short-term pleasures to long-term goals is typically a difficult one. Sometimes the very expenditures couples most enjoyed before marriage now have to be deferred to meet their long-term objectives, such as the purchase of a house.

All the important decisions about the financial partnership are dependent on carefully defined goals. Do both partners agree whether or not to have children, and about how to meet such expenses as the children's education? How important is it to have a house? Will both spouses be employed continuously, even after children are born? Just as every expenditure is a decision, every major decision implies a commitment to pay for it. For couples in every income bracket, the most basic financial fact is that there is never enough money to meet every need or preference. Therefore, pursuing any goal means deferring certain other goals or desires.

Thus, financial planning begins when an individual or couple differentiates between necessities and luxuries, what they *have* to have and what they *want* to have. It is often true that what one spouse regards as a luxury, the other defines as a necessity. This is one reason for beginning financial planning. If the family expenditures are not to become a constant source of irritation and arguments, the needs and desires of every member of the family must be recognized. Even for those on the most modest budget, there are many different ways to spend family money. Each family's budget is highly individual, different in many ways from the budget of any other family, reflecting their values and goals.

Another reason for designing a budget is to identify the spending leaks that exist for most couples. Leaks are the unintended spending decisions that account for a substantial percentage of the expenditures. Eating out several times each week, for example, can become an expensive habit. By adding up the unanticipated expenses that do not really offer long-term satisfactions, couples often see how they might more efficiently meet important long-term goals. (See Worksheet 1, "Financial Goals Identification Worksheet" for an exercise to help in identifying your financial goals.)

Budgeting

A budget is a basic tool in money management. It helps individuals and couples see how income is actually spent so they can work realistically toward their goals. It is helpful in deciding what expenses might be reduced in order to save money for more important things. For those who have trouble living within their means, a well-designed budget can help to avert financial disaster. If properly designed, a budget allocates enough money for the necessities of food, clothing, and shelter. It anticipates occasional crises, such as medical problems and car repairs, allows for vacations and still sets some money aside for the future.

Since no two families, even those at the same income level, allocate money in the same proportion, budgeting cannot consist of applying a predetermined percentage for each category of a family's expenditures. Budgeting begins with the important job of record keeping. Family members need to keep track of their actual expenditures for at least 2 months. Careful records of how money is spent generally demonstrate at least two things: first, what the actual spending priorities are, and second, what everyone spends. Most individuals typically spend more than he or she is aware of spending. Keeping careful records of actual expenses for a couple of months will generally help in constructing a more realistic budget and identifying the spending leaks.

The second step in budgeting is to list anticipated income on a monthly basis. Include salary, interest from savings, tax refunds, and other income you are sure to have. If you do this for a whole year in advance, remember to anticipate those months when you will have extra income from seasonal bonuses or when interest or dividends from investments or savings will be paid. You are inviting problems if your budget is based on future income that is uncertain. Enter all income in the income column of Worksheet 2, "Income and Expenditures Worksheet."

The next step is to list your fixed, or basic, lifestyle expenses, the ones you are already committed to, such as rent or mortgage payments, utilities, transportation, and credit payments. These fixed expenses are the result of past choices. If interest or dividends on investments are reinvested, or left in the account, that money is not available for other purchases. Enter the reinvested interest and dividends in the savings category of the worksheet.

It is a common mistake to make so many purchases

with credit that future earnings are almost entirely committed to meeting monthly payments. When buying on credit, people too often ignore the total cost of items purchased and count only the monthly payment. Especially with major purchases such as household appliances, furniture, and electronics, credit purchases not only reduce a family's financial flexibility until the payments are completed, but cost a lot in interest charges too.

The last step is to assign the remaining income to discretionary lifestyle, or variable expenses—clothing, recreation, gifts, travel and vacations, personal allowances, and miscellaneous items, such as magazines and newspapers. It may seem natural to save only what is left over at the end of the month, but by then any money that has not been set aside for a special purpose will have been spent. A realistic savings plan requires setting aside a fixed amount at the beginning of the month. Most people find that savings plans work best if they are followed systematically and if the money is set aside to meet specific short- and long-term goals.

Once a budget is constructed, you should ask these questions about it: Is too much money committed in advance? Do both spouses have a personal allowance large enough to keep them from feeling so constrained by the budget that they can't enjoy the money being earned? Any budget should allow for some impulse buying. Although it is useful to follow the budget as a guide for family spending, no budget should be inflexible. It is not a rigid plan, but is designed to achieve your long-term goals.

In most families, the budget has to change drastically with the birth of the first child. It changes again from time to time as additional children are born, parents's earnings increase/decrease, children leave home for college or other reasons, and retirement.

A difficult point for a young couple to remember is that not everything can be done at once. It is foolish to try within the first few years to attain the lifestyle that one's parents may have taken 20 years to achieve. And it may be difficult to maintain that lifestyle if a parent stays at home for several years in order to raise the children. Many couples are not able to set aside money for long-term security until they have been married 10 years or more, partly because inflation can cause prices to rise at least as rapidly as income, especially in the early years of one's career.

A well-designed budget should help to distinguish short-term capabilities from long-term goals. It should also provide a guide for moving toward those goals.

MAJOR EXPENDITURES—CHILDREN'S NEEDS, CARS, HOUSING

Having a Child

We can see how hard it is to put a price tag on long-term goals when we consider the costs associated with rearing a child. The decision to have a child is different from any other financial decision. Cost is probably not a factor in the decision to have the first child. The fact that birth rates are relatively low among affluent, well-educated couples suggests that they, at least in part, think of additional children in terms of cost. They tend to have fewer children, so they can provide the best opportunities for their children. And indeed, when all the hidden costs of bearing and rearing a child are added up, children may turn out to be nearly as expensive as the family home. No young couple can afford to overlook such costs as they plan for the future.

How much do children cost today? The expenses begin with medical care during pregnancy and include hospital facilities for the delivery. Then the newborn needs medicine, layette, crib, baby clothes, and diapers. For most children there will be an additional room in the house and visits to a pediatrician. Over the next few years, in addition to the obvious costs—clothing, food, medical care—a family with young children will also pay for baby-sitters, toys and birthday parties, and nursery school. Throughout childhood and adolescence there will be expenses for entertainment, hobbies and sports, family pets, and perhaps summer camp. Later on, of course, the expenses may include such items as a car (along with the costs of maintaining and insuring it) and college.

Buying a Car

Buying a car also requires long-range planning. To assess the costs accurately, they should be amortized—that is, spread out over every year of the car's useful life. The expense of gas, oil, regular maintenance, tires, repairs, and insurance should also be taken into account. Depreciation is an important cost factor too, for one of the differences between a house and a car is that the market value of a house often increases over time, whereas the value of a car depreciates, or decreases. Cars lose much of their value in the first year or two of ownership. Thus, a low-mileage, well-maintained, used car may be a lower cost alternative to buying a new car. And a reliable mechanic who can make a well-informed judgment about the condition of a used car is a valuable consultant before you make the purchase.

Many of us are discouraged with the process involved with buying a car. Traditionally, the process involves a great deal of haggling, in order to arrive at

INSTRUCTIONS FOR WORKSHEET 1
FINANCIAL GOALS IDENTIFICATION WORKSHEET

Now that you have decided to identify what is important to you, pick a quiet time to either sit down and think by yourself or with your spouse or partner. This is a shared activity by family members. Only if each has an opportunity for an input into the process and feels that the needs and concerns of each person are incorporated into the financial planning, will the plan have any chance to succeed.

Worksheet 1 lists many of the most common financial goals. Short-term (ST) goals are what you wish to achieve within the next few weeks, the next month, in 6 months or a year, up to 5 years from now. Goals must be reasonable, measurable, and reachable within a given time period.

Financial security is not achieved through a series of short-term goals. Much of what we want to achieve in life requires planning over time periods longer than the 5 years of short-term goals. Long-term (LT) goals tend to fall into several general areas that usually require some effort to narrow and define in terms that are specific, measurable, and achievable within a given time period.

Those who rent an apartment may be able to make saving for a down payment on a home a short-term goal, if they can achieve the goal in less than 5 years. If it takes more than 5 years, it is a long-term goal. For parents of young children, college education for their children is a common long-term goal. The longest term goal of all is retirement, which may come 30 to 40 years after taking that first job after graduation.

WORKSHEET 1
Financial Goals Identification Worksheet

Priority of Goal High Med. Low N/A	Short- or Long-Term	Achieve Goal by (Date)	$ to Achieve Goal	Goal
5 4 3 2 1 0	ST LT	___/___/___	$ _____	1. Establish emergency fund.
5 4 3 2 1 0	ST LT	___/___/___	$ _____	2. Adequate auto insurance.
5 4 3 2 1 0	ST LT	___/___/___	$ _____	3. Adequate home insurance.
5 4 3 2 1 0	ST LT	___/___/___	$ _____	4. Adequate health insurance.
5 4 3 2 1 0	ST LT	___/___/___	$ _____	5. Adequate life insurance.
5 4 3 2 1 0	ST LT	___/___/___	$ _____	6. Pay off credit card balance.
5 4 3 2 1 0	ST LT	___/___/___	$ _____	7. New/used car/truck.
5 4 3 2 1 0	ST LT	___/___/___	$ _____	8. Furniture.
5 4 3 2 1 0	ST LT	___/___/___	$ _____	9. Save for home down payment.
5 4 3 2 1 0	ST LT	___/___/___	$ _____	10. Stereo system.
5 4 3 2 1 0	ST LT	___/___/___	$ _____	11. Television set.
5 4 3 2 1 0	ST LT	___/___/___	$ _____	12. Children's education.
5 4 3 2 1 0	ST LT	___/___/___	$ _____	13. Comfortable retirement.
5 4 3 2 1 0	ST LT	___/___/___	$ _____	14. Invest to reduce taxes.
5 4 3 2 1 0	ST LT	___/___/___	$ _____	15. Reduce income taxes.
5 4 3 2 1 0	ST LT	___/___/___	$ _____	16. Buy home.
5 4 3 2 1 0	ST LT	___/___/___	$ _____	17. Leisure-time activities (specific activity).
5 4 3 2 1 0	ST LT	___/___/___	$ _____	18. Start own business.
5 4 3 2 1 0	ST LT	___/___/___	$ _____	19. Vacation.
5 4 3 2 1 0	ST LT	___/___/___	$ _____	20. Prepare will(s).
5 4 3 2 1 0	ST LT	___/___/___	$ _____	21. Financial support of parents.
5 4 3 2 1 0	ST LT	___/___/___	$ _____	22. Wedding.
5 4 3 2 1 0	ST LT	___/___/___	$ _____	23. Honeymoon.
5 4 3 2 1 0	ST LT	___/___/___	$ _____	24. Home furnishings.
5 4 3 2 1 0	ST LT	___/___/___	$ _____	25. Roof/siding for home.
5 4 3 2 1 0	ST LT	___/___/___	$ _____	26. Second home (vacation home).
5 4 3 2 1 0	ST LT	___/___/___	$ _____	27. Ski/fishing boat.
5 4 3 2 1 0	ST LT	___/___/___	$ _____	28. Jet ski.
5 4 3 2 1 0	ST LT	___/___/___	$ _____	29. Travel trailer/motorhome.
5 4 3 2 1 0	ST LT	___/___/___	$ _____	30. Second car/truck/motorcycle.
5 4 3 2 1 0	ST LT	___/___/___	$ _____	31. Charitable contribution to _____.

Other goals:

Priority of Goal High Med. Low N/A	Short- or Long-Term	Achieve Goal by (Date)	$ to Achieve Goal	Goal
5 4 3 2 1 0	ST LT	___/___/___	$ _____	32. _____.
5 4 3 2 1 0	ST LT	___/___/___	$ _____	33. _____.
5 4 3 2 1 0	ST LT	___/___/___	$ _____	34. _____.
5 4 3 2 1 0	ST LT	___/___/___	$ _____	35. _____.

WORKSHEET 2
Income and Expenditures Worksheet

Income		Expenditures	
Employment		**Basic lifestyle**	
Wages	$ _____	Mortage/rent	$ _____
Wages	$ _____	Other housing	$ _____
Self-employment	$ _____	Electricity	$ _____
Total employment income	$ _____	Gas	$ _____
		Telephone	$ _____
Investment income		Cable TV	$ _____
Interest	$ _____	Real estate tax	$ _____
Dividends	$ _____	Vehicle loan payments	$ _____
Int./Div. (nontaxable)	$ _____	Other transportation	
Rental income	$ _____	Gas/oil	$ _____
Capital gains (sale of securities)	$ _____	Repairs	$ _____
Partnerships	$ _____	State/local registration	$ _____
Total investment income	$ _____	Inspection fees	$ _____
		Personal property tax	$ _____
Other income		Food	
Pensions	$ _____	Food eaten at home	$ _____
Social Security	$ _____	Food eaten out	$ _____
Other	$ _____	Clothing	$ _____
Total other income	$ _____	Medical/dental expense	$ _____
		Insurance	
Total income	$ _____	Auto	$ _____
		Life/health	$ _____
Total income	$ _____	Homeowner's/renter's	$ _____
Total expenditures	− $ _____	Retirement	$ _____
		Other	$ _____
Cash surplus (deficit)	$ _____	Savings	$ _____
		Total basic lifestyle expenses	$ _____

The surplus is available for achieving other goals, additional purchases, or more credit.

A deficit indicates a need to reduce expenses, to bring expenditures in line with income.

Expenditures	
Discretionary lifestyle	
Gifts	$ _____
Recreation/entertainment	$ _____
Vacation/other travel	$ _____
Professional expenses	$ _____
Contributions	$ _____
Total discretionary lifestyle expenses	$ _____
Income and employment taxes	
Federal income tax	$ _____
State/local income tax	$ _____
FICA/FICA Medicare	$ _____
Total income and employment taxes	$ _____
Total expenditures	$ _____

a better price. For those uneasy with such tactics, there is also the feeling they are the loser in the transaction if they paid the full sticker price. The good news is that a new trend among car manufacturers and dealers is the offering of cars at the same fixed price to all buyers. They offer no haggle, no hassle, and lower prices, with sales people on salary rather than on commission, making the process much more friendly. It is worth your while to search out these car companies and dealers. They offer a refreshing change from the past where the car dealer and consumer were essentially in an adversarial relationship.

In purchasing and maintaining a car, as in any other major investment, good information and sound advice are indispensable. Automotive magazines and *Consumer Reports,* with its annual *Buying Guide,* are useful references.

Buying a House

The choice of housing is even more complex than that of transportation. For most couples, the purchase of a house is the family's largest single investment. Living in an apartment, however, is often a convenient alternative, involving fewer responsibilities and less maintenance. How should you decide what type of housing best suits your needs?

Before deciding to buy a house, it is beneficial to figure out and compare the long-range housing costs of renting versus buying. The cost of renting over a period of years can easily be calculated by adding up the annual rental, plus an increase of several percent each year, plus the cost of renter's insurance. The cost of home ownership is more difficult to determine, for maintenance, repair, and taxes must be added to the mortgage payments.

The traditional rules of thumb on how much a family can afford for housing no longer seem to apply because of variations in the economy, including recession, inflation, changing interest rates, and the uncertainty of steady employment. Perhaps the most meaningful measures of how much a family can spend on a house today are the amount of cash they have saved or can borrow for a down payment and the amount they can afford for the monthly mortgage payment. Family members, particularly parents of young couples, are increasingly providing money for the down payment that allows for purchase of the first home.

A mortgage amounts to a long-term purchase on the installment plan. Examine a mortgage carefully and you may be dismayed to find that the interest over the typical 30-year repayment period may be double the amount of the mortgage. This may seem unreasonable, but actually it may not be as expensive as renting a house. First, property taxes and interest charges on the mortgage are all allowable tax deductions. Those who choose to rent are allowed to take the standard deduction, which is usually less than the itemized deductions allowed to homeowners. The standard deduction for single persons is slightly more than half that allowed for couples. Thus, singles may achieve even more benefit from buying a home. And second, real estate generally increases in value, enabling home buyers to increase their net worth over time. Despite interest charges on a mortgage, most individuals and couples find that it is cheaper in the long run to buy a house than to rent one. A third factor, not directly related to economics, is the feeling one gains from home ownership, including pride of ownership, an enhanced sense of financial and personal security and privacy, and the development of a sense of community.

As with any other purchase, it pays to shop around before signing a mortgage agreement. The availability of mortgages depends on general economic conditions and on the availability of money from lending institutions. Interest rates on mortgages vary considerably from one source to another, so it does pay to shop around for the best rates and other contract terms. Monthly payments, which usually include real estate taxes and homeowner's insurance, repay a portion of the loan principal each month, as well as the interest, so that at the end of the mortgage, the entire loan—both principal and interest—is paid off.

TAXES

The total of all types of taxes are the biggest single expense for most of us, though of course we have no choice about paying them. Federal income and Social Security taxes make the main difference between gross income and take-home pay, and most states and some localities have also levied additional income taxes. Most states and an increasing number of cities and counties also levy sales taxes, and along with taxes on real estate and personal property (which vary from state to state), the total tax paid is a staggering amount. It is no wonder that people frequently complain about their taxes and support initiatives to lower state and local taxes. The surprising thing is that millions of people every year pay *more* taxes than they are legally required to pay. Overpayment is usually the result of overlooking allowable deductions—all too easy to do if you file federal tax forms 1040A or 1040EZ (for single persons only), which require taking the standard deduction, rather than itemizing deductions. But there are actions you can take to reduce the level of taxes.

There is a long list of allowable deductions, some of which people are unaware. Once a home is purchased with its attendant mortgage interest and real estate tax deductions, many other deductions become available, such as charitable contributions (both cash contributions as well as clothing or household goods donated to various organizations). Other deductions include moving expenses (if the move is job-related) and unreimbursed business expenses (subject to limitations based on your level of income). Tax laws change from year to year. It is important to be well informed about the newest allowable deductions before filling out the annual tax forms, as even seemingly minor changes may affect the amount of tax paid.

Once they list all allowable deductions and fill out the other forms, most people can generally compute their own taxes and not overpay, although complex forms, tables, and regulations contribute to many errors. Some common errors at this point include using the wrong filing status in the tables to find the tax due and using the wrong standard deduction, which varies according to filing status, and which is based in part on marital status and age. Those over 65 and/or blind are entitled to an additional deduction. Errors are also commonly made in figuring the earned income credit for lower-income families and the child-care credit for parents who are both employed, in school, or looking for work, and in calculating depreciation on business equipment by those who are self-employed. When the financial situation is particularly complex, it may be advisable and less expensive to consult an accountant or tax preparation service, than to do it yourself and overpay your taxes.

One of the most costly alternatives is filing the federal tax return electronically through a tax preparer to receive the refund more quickly. For paper returns mailed to the IRS, the refund is often received in 6 to 8 weeks. The least expensive electronic filing option, with the refund deposited to a checking or savings account in about 2 weeks, may cost as little as $20 or as much as $40. For a total fee of $70 to as much as $100, a tax preparer can often deliver a check for the refund in 2 or 3 days. This is known as a RAL (refund anticipation loan), which is essentially a loan to the taxpayer for 2 weeks until the federal tax refund is paid to the lender. (Some states have also begun electronic filing programs.) The convenience of receiving the refund in 2 days is very expensive. There is a standard finance charge regardless of the size of the refund. The APR (annual percentage rate) varies according to the amount of the refund. One lender has been levying a $34 finance charge as the cost of the credit. For a $3,000 refund, the APR is 23 percent, higher than any credit card rate, up to a truly staggering 259 percent for a $300 refund, a rate worthy of any loan shark! College students, in particular, tend to favor RALs, especially just before spring break. Earlier preparation and filing of their tax returns by mail would make an additional $70 to $100 available, whether it is to pay for necessities or to enjoy spring break.

Accountants and tax preparers often make these additional suggestions to their clients who want to avoid overpayment of taxes. Your records should include paid bills and canceled checks, an account of money spent for the support of dependents not living with you, and expenditures that relate to business, such as the business use of your home or car. It is especially important to keep permanent records of all expenses related to owning a house. If you buy a house and then sell it a few years later at a profit, the profits are taxable, unless you buy a replacement home of equal or higher value. Many expenses—capital improvements on the house, closing costs, broker's fees—are recognized by the IRS as factors in reducing the tax on profits. And most important, determine the tax consequences of your actions *before* you make major decisions and before the end of the year. After you make the decisions or if you wait until after December 31 to seek tax advice, all you can do then is pay the tax and suffer the consequences of bad decisions.

CREDIT

Using Credit

Credit is the mainstay of the business world. Without it, few companies could grow. Businesses borrow money in order to increase their productivity and earnings; properly managed, money is used to make more money.

There are some instances in which individuals

might use money as businesses do. A low-cost student loan, for example, might reasonably be considered a type of borrowing that will pay for itself by increasing future earning power. But generally, credit has a much different use by consumers. For the consumer, credit is a means of deferring payment or breaking down the cost of a purchase into manageable installments. Those "small monthly payments" have a remarkable way of looking inconsequential at the time a purchase is made, but appearing much larger when added to the payments for several other installment purchases. For a business, credit can be used to increase income. For a family, credit amounts to a mortgage on future income, without in any way increasing it.

Most people find credit easy to get. When you first apply you will be judged by your job, your income, your other assets, the way you have managed a checking account, and your record in paying routine bills. Credit records are compiled by the three national credit bureaus, Equifax, Trans Union Corp., and TRW. The information stored in their files serves as a credit history for more than 100 million Americans. The files are confidential; only stores, banks, and other businesses offering credit, employment, or insurance, as well as the individual concerned, have the legal right to examine them.

A credit rating is based on several indications of your ability to make payments. Before extending credit, a lending institution will ask:

1 How capable are you of repaying a debt? The answer is based on your estimated monthly income minus your fixed expenses, including other debts.

2 What is your net worth? What assets—savings, life insurance, stocks, vehicles, or real estate—do you own? The creditor wants to know whether your assets will cover the loan if you cannot repay it.

3 What is your past credit experience? Have you paid bills consistently and promptly? Be prepared to list all current debt. You may also be asked how long you have lived at the same address, or at least in the same community. People who move often from place to place are relatively bad credit risks because they may be hard to trace if they default on a loan.

4 Two other common factors upon which you are rated are home ownership and occupation. Home owners are considered better risks than renters. Professional occupations score higher than retirees, who generally score higher than blue-collar workers.

Maintaining a good credit rating is important, if for no other reason than to have it available for emergencies. Some people believe they will be regarded as a good credit risk if they pay cash for all their purchases and maintain a good employment record. But this is not necessarily true. Potential creditors are interested in proof that you have already repaid borrowed money. Thus, it may be a good idea to apply for a bank or store credit card—which will establish your credit rating—even if you never intend to use it. Then charge a couple of purchases and pay the account in full. Ironically, the best time to apply for credit is well before you need it.

Anyone who is turned down on a credit application is entitled by law to know why. Credit bureaus sometimes make mistakes. Stores or banks sometimes deny credit, illegally, on the basis of sex or race. The legal right to review one's own credit rating means that anyone can protect that rating against mistakes or discriminatory practices. In response to numerous complaints, the national credit bureaus are generally making it easier to review your own credit report (see Box 1).

Credit Cards

Credit cards can be a great convenience. They serve as security when renting cars and guaranteeing a hotel room for late arrival, two transactions virtually impossible to do with cash. Some cards offer the added convenience of borrowing cash quickly and easily in automated teller machines, by writing checks, or with a cash advance at any bank. For emergencies, the cards are invaluable, and allow travel without carrying large amounts of cash. But it is precisely the convenience of credit cards that leads to their misuse. They allow impulse purchases on items too expensive to buy with cash. For people who have trouble living within their means, credit cards are a passport to disaster because they make spending so much easier. Banks and other institutions offering cards encourage their use because they are highly profitable. People begin using cards as a convenience and assume they will avoid interest charges by paying the account in full each month. But many soon get in the habit of making minimum payments toward a fairly large balance—while the institutions offering the cards profit immensely from the interest charges and other fees (see Box 2).

There are three different types of credit cards. The first is the travel and entertainment card, with Amer-

BOX 1

Credit Bureaus and Your Rights

The industry's standard practice has been to provide a free copy of a credit report to anyone who has been denied credit within the past 60 days, provided the person can furnish the bureau with a copy of the rejection letter. Federal law requires that when lenders deny credit based on information in a credit report, they must inform applicants of this and provide them with the name and address of the credit bureau.

Write and obtain a copy of your credit report. If a mistake has been made by the credit bureau by one of your creditors (which could include former landlords), federal law requires that the report be corrected. Unfortunately, that has not been an easy process for many consumers. All too many people in recent years have complained of errors in their credit reports and have had little success in getting corrections made. In the past, at least, when credit information on persons with the same name, but different Social Security numbers, was mixed together, the credit bureaus resisted all but the most insistent efforts to correct the errors. As a result, changes are proposed to the federal law to make the credit bureaus more responsive to complaints.

To forestall more severe legislation, credit bureaus have generally worked to respond more quickly to complaints and make corrections. Only Trans Union has been less responsive, making the report available free of charge *only* if the person provided Trans Union with the rejection letter. Equifax provides a free copy of the report to consumers requesting one. TRW is now furnishing one free copy of a credit report yearly to each person.

These changes are due in part to the efforts of the attorneys general of 18 states. Agreements with Equifax and TRW were reached in 1992, and go a long way in reforming serious problems. These agreements are even more important as attempts at more restrictive federal legislation face stiff opposition in Congress because of heavy lobbying by the credit bureaus.

Some credit card providers have arranged to give the holders of their cards regular credit reports and notify them automatically whenever anyone asks for and receives a copy of their credit file. For example, Chemical Bank recently offered this service free for a 3-month trial period. After that, $20 would be charged on the cardholder's Visa or MasterCard for a year's subscription to TRW's Credit Report Monitor. This may not be a good use of $20, as much of this information is available free of charge. On the other hand, there would be no need to request these reports.

People with busy lifestyles are generally not going to make regular requests for this information, so this may be an inexpensive method of being more aware of one's credit report and credit rating. One part of the service, though, is of particular interest. On the regular quarterly reports, reports of negative information are also included. Early notification of erroneous, negative information may decrease the time and effort required for corrections, rather than years after the error was made.

You may obtain credit reports from these credit bureaus:

Equifax Information Service Center
P.O. Box 4081
Atlanta, GA 30302

TRW National Consumer Assistance Center
P.O. Box 749029
Dallas, TX 75234-9029

Trans Union Corp.
P.O. Box 7000
North Olmsted, OH 44070

SOURCES: Schwartz, E. I., Schiller, Z., Konrad, W., & Forest, S. A. (1991); Schwartz, E. I., & Konrad, W. (1991); "How to make the most of your monitor service membership" (1992).

ican Express as the best known. A yearly membership fee of $55 is charged for the basic American Express "green" cards, but no interest if you pay on time. Most people need no more than one card of this type, for it enables you to cash checks, obtain travelers checks,

and pay for restaurants, hotel bills, airline tickets, and other purchases. If you are in the habit of paying on time, the membership fee may be a reasonable price to pay for the convenience it offers.

A second type of card is the single-use card. Oil

BOX 2

Hidden Costs of Using Credit Cards

If you think that the interest paid on the balance of your credit card is the only cost to using the card, you couldn't be more wrong. There are several more "hidden" costs, generally tucked away in the fine print, according to the Bankcard Holders of America, a consumer group in Herdon, VA. These costs can increase the effective interest rate to 30 percent or more. Some of these costs are:

- Charging $10, or more, if you exceed the credit line of the card.

- Charging $6 to $8 for making a payment more than 15 days late.

- Charging $15 for missing a payment.

- Requiring average fees of $2.50 for cash advances, on top of the interest charge.

- Requiring smaller minimum payments on accounts, which encourages stretching out the repayment and results in higher total interest costs.

- Offering to allow "good" customers to occasionally skip payments while the outstanding balance continues to incur interest charges.

Bankcard Holders of America offers the following tips to reduce the cost of using credit cards:

- If you pay your balance in full each month, find and use a card with no annual fee that offers at least a 25-day grace period before interest is charged.

- If you don't pay your balance in full each month, find a card with a lower interest rate and make your payment as soon as you receive the bill. This reduces the average daily balance used to calculate finance charges.

- Pay more than the minimum payment. Over time, this substantially reduces the total interest paid.

- Avoid going over the credit limit or paying late.

- Avoid cash advances on cards that charge fees for the privilege.

- You don't necessarily benefit if your credit card announces a lower interest rate. The lower rate may apply only to present cardholders, not new ones. The outstanding balance may still be subject to the old, higher interest rates.

SOURCES: "Do 'secret fees' help credit cards rob you?" (1992); Pae, P. (1992).

companies, hotel chains, car rental firms, and department stores offer these cards as an incentive to use their products and services. Most of them cost nothing to obtain, and no interest is charged if you pay on time—generally within about 30 days of the billing date. Overall usage is much less than the other types of credit cards.

The most familiar type of credit card is the so-called "bank" card, MasterCard or Visa. Although some cards do not charge an annual usage fee, others have fees ranging from $15 to $30, and such cards can be more expensive to use than travel and entertainment cards for several reasons. The period of time allowed to pay bills is generally less than that allowed with travel and entertainment cards, which means you are more likely to run up interest charges. If you use the

borrowing privilege that most bank cards offer, the interest starts immediately and the rates are high. This is a convenient but expensive form of credit and should be used only when necessary.

Visa and MasterCard credit cards are no longer issued just by banks or even by other traditional financial institutions. Today, some of America's largest corporations offer their own versions of Visa and MasterCard. In 1990, AT&T introduced its Universal Card, with no annual fee and a variable interest rate, features which are increasingly being offered by competing cards. The card offers discounts on long-distance calling. In September 1992, General Electric (GE) and General Motors (GM) upped the ante with the introduction of their own cards. GE's card has somewhat higher rates and annual fee, but offers $10 discounts for every $500 charged that can be used for products and services offered by two dozen companies, including GE.

GM, hoping to increase sales of its cars, offers up to $500 in rebates each year, which can be accumulated for up to 7 years and used to purchase and lease GM vehicles. GM's card has no annual fee and has lower rates than GE's card and is less flexible in how the discounts are used.

Should you carry and use one of these corporation-issued cards or one from your local bank? The primary consideration in choosing any card should be the interest rate charged and the annual fee. If you pay the balance in full each month, a lower annual fee is more important. However, a lower interest rate is of greater concern if the balance is not paid off each month. Then consider the level of other fees. Finally, consider cards like those of AT&T, GE, and GM *only* if you stand to substantially benefit from the rebates and discounts offered. A dedicated Ford or Honda owner would perceive no value in the GM card. Due to increased competition, bank cards may offer similar programs, or changing economic conditions may result in decreased rebates and discounts in the future. Remember, incentive programs like this do not necessarily last forever.

Credit Cards and College Students

Even though college students may have little or no current income, they are the targets of extensive campaigns to sign students up for credit cards. Issuers of credit cards even rent space on campus in order to hand out credit card applications. It is as if the regular criteria of a job, income, stable residence, and other criteria are suspended for students, except for the fact that in a few years, as college graduates, they are a growing market and will become very desirable customers. It is estimated that half of the nation's full-time college students head back to campus each fall with credit cards.

Once students have their credit card, perhaps one in which the parents are included as coapplicants (and are liable for paying all charges), it is relatively easy to get a second, third, and fourth card. One sophomore student recently got his first Visa with his mother as the coapplicant. After showing responsibility by making his payments in a timely manner, a second and third card were obtained. He didn't really want the cards, but applied to obtain a 2-liter bottle of cola or other small incentive items. After only 2 years, he was

even offered a preapproved American Express card. His responsibility in the use of credit prevailed—the student turned down the last two cards.

Not all students are this wise in the use of credit. The ease of making purchases is very seductive, leading many to feel a sense of financial empowerment. Most who fall victim do not intentionally set out to charge so many purchases. Occasionally, students acquire $6,000 to $10,000 in charges, have no way to repay them, and of course, end up with *no* credit cards. They also end up with a damaged credit rating which will make it difficult to obtain needed auto and home mortgage loans later on. Credit cards can be very useful to students when it comes to buying textbooks and supplies, or even paying for gas when they travel home. But unfortunately, just being in college does not bestow upon them good financial sense or knowledge of money management. Abuse of cards has left many students deeply in debt before they ever reach graduation and the job market.

Loans

"Buy now, owe nothing for 60 days, then pay a small monthly charge." Or "Buy in October, but make no payments until next year." Such offers persuade people to buy things for which they cannot afford to pay cash, especially items such as household appliances, electronics, and home furnishings. Without realizing it, many people end up paying a great deal for this convenience. Installment purchases often involve interest rates much higher than credit cards. For the consumer, it turns out to be more expensive to buy credit from the dealer selling the item than from almost any other source. The important thing to remember about installment buying, as with any other type of credit, is to read the contract carefully and understand the interest charges clearly. In general, consumers are well advised to borrow money elsewhere, preferably from the low-interest credit sources discussed below, and use the cash to pay for such purchases.

It takes a well-informed consumer to shop wisely for a loan. There are a wide range of lending institutions to choose from and a sometimes confusing vocabulary of credit terms. And as you might expect, the cost of credit varies widely from one lender to another. There are several types of lending situations that are best avoided because of the high interest rates they charge. Small loan companies, for example, are among the most costly. Using the cash advance privilege that most bank credit cards offer is, as noted previously, quite convenient, but often is a very expensive source of credit.

Having a good credit rating allows you to qualify for a personal bank loan. After dealing with one bank long enough to have an established account, you may be able to borrow on a personal note. This source of credit is almost always less expensive than others. The interest rates charged by different banks for the same type of loan vary, so make sure to shop at several banks before signing an agreement.

Credit unions are another good source of money. These organizations consist of members belonging to a particular profession or employed by the same employer or industry, and generally offer their members higher interest (than banks) on savings. Credit unions also lend money to their members, usually with more favorable interest rates than banks can offer because the banks have higher costs of doing business.

CRISIS PLANNING

A financial crisis can strike any individual or family. After working and saving for years in order to afford a home and furnishings, a family may lose everything from a natural disaster such as earthquake, hurricane, or fire. Sickness and accidents bring medical expenses that add financial woes to physical ones. Unexpected death leaves in its wake not only heartache but may also be accompanied by nearly overwhelming financial problems. Thus, one of the main goals of any family's long-range financial plans should be to provide for basic financial security against such crises.

A first step in designing a family protection package is to conduct an inventory of the benefits you are already entitled to, such as Social Security benefits for death, disability, and retirement. Social Security benefits tend to be minimal, depending upon the person's average earnings that were subject to Social Security taxes. Even at that, it is extremely difficult to qualify for disability benefits.

In addition, some small and most medium and large businesses extend this protection by offering health insurance, life insurance, and a pension plan for their employees. When looking for a job, few young people pay much attention to these fringe benefits, but they vary widely from one firm to another, so they should be examined closely. In choosing among several job

offers, you might do better to take a job at a slightly lower salary if the firm offers a superior benefits package. What the company pays in benefits will not seem as tangible as salary, but can add up to a substantial amount.

Assume that it would cost the employer $1,500 to provide certain benefits for each employee. If employees had to buy the same benefits themselves, the cost would be nearly $2,100 in taxable income. The difference between the employee's cost of $2,100 and the employer's cost of $1,500 is the amount of state and federal income tax and Social Security tax paid on the $2,100. Thus, employer-provided benefits are received tax free by the employee.

When interviewing for a job, find out what kind of health insurance is provided, how much life insurance is included, and what type of pension plan is offered to employees. In some companies, employees have to contribute to the pension plan; in others the employer pays the full amount. Is there a plan allowing employees to contribute their own money to increase retirement benefits? Two unfortunate trends of the 1990s are that fewer benefits are being provided by employers and employees are being required to pay an ever-increasing share of the cost of the benefits they do receive.

Once you have completed an inventory of benefits to which you are already entitled, you can figure out what additional coverage is needed to anticipate possible crises. An adequate protection plan for most families consists of at least five types of insurance: disability, health, renters or homeowners, automobile, and life insurance.

Protecting Yourself against Death, Disability, and Disaster

Property insurance for homes and household goods covers losses due to such causes as fire, theft, or damage because of accidents. Where there is a property loss, the owner must prove ownership before losses will be covered. An inventory of personal belongings, along with copies of the bills for them, is invaluable in settling property loss claims. Photographs of furnishings and personal property also help prove the amount of loss. Such records should be kept in a bank safety deposit box or other safe location away from the home and updated regularly. Remember, too, that as the value of a house increases over time, your policy should reflect the cost to repair or rebuild the home.

College students, as well as those recently entering employment, often fail to purchase renter's insurance to cover their belongings. The cost is generally quite reasonable and provides much needed protection. Unmarried students living in a college dorm or even an off-campus apartment may actually be covered under their parent's policy. Young married couples comprise a new family and household and need their own policy.

Many young, unmarried people see no reason to be concerned about property or life insurance. But even a single person with little property and no dependents has to be concerned about medical and disability coverage. If you are unable to support yourself because of sickness or injury, disability insurance provides benefits. Disability is a more likely possibility than death and presents a greater threat to financial security to singles and young, childless couples.

And no one should drive without auto insurance. In fact, it is required by law in most states. Part of the coverage pays for repairs or replacement of your vehicle if it is damaged. An even more important aspect is the liability coverage, which protects *your* financial resources in the event that an accident is your fault. The insurance provides for your legal defense and pays the injured party. Even if you have few financial resources today, your future earnings or even an inheritance could be used to satisfy a judgment against you.

Compared with other types of coverage, the purchase of life insurance may seem rather complicated. But if you approach it as you would any other purchase, two essential facts become clear: first, the purpose of life insurance is to provide a continuing source of income for dependents if a family wage earner dies; and second, one should shop around for the lowest premium, or cost, of the insurance one needs.

Why does it often seem so complicated? Most people don't buy insurance; it is sold to them. They sign up without first determining what they really need or whether they could get it elsewhere at a lower price. Thus, little or no buyer resistance allows insurance companies to turn simple plans into complex programs to make them seem more attractive. The insurance business is highly competitive, and salespeople promote policies that bring them the highest commission, whether or not they are the best policies for the insured, in coverage or cost. As a general rule, college students and young singles need little or no life insur-

ance because usually no one is dependent upon them for income or services.

Basically, there are two kinds of life insurance, term and ordinary life. Term insurance is the simplest and the least expensive. For a certain period of time—the term of the policy—the insurance company receives a specified premium and promises to pay the face value of the policy if the insured dies. The term is generally 5 years, after which the policy has to be renewed with a somewhat higher premium to account for the greater probability of death as the insured gets older. Term insurance has no savings or lending provisions and gives no refund if the policy is canceled or expires, but it is the best buy because it is considerably cheaper than other kinds of insurance and does exactly what it is designed to do. The commission for term insurance is lower than for other kinds of policies, so sales agents have a great incentive to sell you something else.

The second type of life insurance, ordinary life, has many variations, some developed in the 1980s to compete with high-yielding, noninsurance investments. What they all have in common is that the premium generally remains unchanged throughout the life of the insured because it is an average of the lifetime premium. At the beginning, therefore, it is higher than needed to pay for the protection. The excess is invested by the company and returns more than enough money to cover the higher cost of protection in later years. At the same time, this reserve is available to the policyholder as cash value that can be borrowed. If the policy is canceled at any point, the cash value is returned to the policyholder.

In order to buy what you need and nothing more, remember what life insurance should do: provide an income for dependents if the wage earner dies. How much insurance do you need? The answer depends on a number of factors. Like other aspects of financial planning, life insurance has to be tailored to family income and budget, but must also take into account such factors as whether the surviving spouse can support the family. Generally, it is not possible for the average wage earner to buy enough insurance to provide income for a nonemployed spouse for the rest of her or his lifetime and also provide for the needs of raising and educating the children. Increasingly, the wife, as well as the husband, must be prepared to support the family on her or his income, with some assistance from life insurance proceeds if a spouse dies. Another point to consider is that the surviving spouse

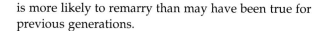

is more likely to remarry than may have been true for previous generations.

Buying Insurance

Keep these points in mind when buying insurance:

1 The cost of similar coverage may vary as much as 100 percent from one insurance company to another, so compare prices before you buy. Companies with higher costs of doing business and higher premiums are often the most aggressive in their sales tactics.

2 The basic purpose of life insurance is to provide protection for dependents if the primary wage earner dies. Policies that include a savings program or the privilege of borrowing the cash value may sound more attractive, but invariably cost more than basic term insurance. Families with young children need the most insurance that they can buy for their premium dollar.

3 There are ways of buying less expensive coverage than that offered by traditional insurance companies. Some employers provide group policies that allow employees to buy additional insurance at low cost. Professional associations and several reputable companies selling only by mail also provide low-cost term policies. Be forewarned that some mail-order companies offer some of the most expensive coverage available.

4 It is cheaper to pay premiums annually than quarterly or monthly.

5 Should both husband and wife be insured? If both are employed and the earnings of both are essential to family well-being, both should be insured. For the spouse who is not employed, but contributes to family well-being through care of the children and other services, insurance may also be needed to purchase replacement services in the event of her or his death.

6 Although premiums are low on policies for young children, the money is better spent on insuring the parent(s). Consider that children would likely suffer more financially from the death of a parent, than the other way around. Remember, this is a financial decision, first, last, and always. Insurance for children is often sold on the emotional appeal of insuring your child's future insurability. The agent may say, "Wouldn't you feel bad if your child is unable to qualify for insurance upon reaching adulthood?"

The fact is that only a very small percentage of adults cannot qualify for life insurance.

ESTATE PLANNING

Many couples who have arranged insurance coverage for their family fail to take another important step in managing family finances—preparing a will. Some think wills are unnecessary because they assume the surviving spouse will automatically get everything the other owned. Others, especially in the early years of marriage, do not believe they have enough assets to make it worthwhile. They might change their minds if they added up the value of their personal possessions, their house, car, furnishings, retirement plans, and life insurance. And finally, no one likes to contemplate the possibility of premature death.

However, if you don't have a will, state law determines how your property is divided among heirs. Unless you specify with a will that all property goes to your spouse, who you would naturally expect to care for your children, state law may divide the estate between the surviving spouse and the children. This gives the spouse fewer options in how the funds are used.

Another concern is who will be the guardians of young children should both parents die in an accident. Should it be your 62-year-old parents who are looking forward to retirement? They love their grandchildren dearly, but when they are in their 70s, will they be capable of dealing with teenagers? Or should it be your sister (a mother of two) who is willing and capable of caring for two more? Or your spouse's brother, who has difficulty holding a job and managing money and moves often? A will allows you to make your best choice (with the assent of the potential guardian), rather than leaving the decision to the courts, even to choosing a nonrelative if that is the best alternative.

To be valid, a will must adhere to state law, so it should be drawn up with the assistance of an attorney. The process involves, first, listing all your beneficiaries, including family, friends, and charitable organizations, and then listing all the assets to be distributed. The will names an executor of the estate and designates a guardian for the children, in the event of both parents' death. An executor can be the surviving spouse, relative, friend, attorney, or other financial advisor. In drawing up a will, consult an attorney about the advisability of arranging family assets so as to avoid excessive estate taxes. Finally, any will should be reviewed regularly. Relationships change, and the nature and value of the estate change. Likewise, moving from one state to another may necessitate changes. Periodic review will help to ensure that property and money will be distributed as you want them to be.

A will is not necessary, however, to pass some property to heirs. Life insurance and pension plans can easily pass to a named beneficiary, generally a spouse, parent, or child, whichever is most appropriate at the time. You may change beneficiaries later as needed. For example, single persons might first name their parent(s) as the beneficiary of their employer-provided life insurance. After marriage, the spouse can be designated as the beneficiary.

Joint checking and savings accounts give the surviving spouse immediate access to those accounts, if they own the accounts as joint tenants with right of survivorship (JTWROS). Such ownership can be used by husbands and wives, an elderly parent and an adult child who is helping manage the finances, or by unrelated persons living together. The potential danger is that either party has the right to write checks and spend the money in the account. So be sure that you fully trust the other party, especially in the case of joint tenants who are not related.

SAVINGS AND INVESTMENTS— WORKING TOWARD FINANCIAL SECURITY

Emergency Fund

Attitudes toward regular savings are quite different from what they were a generation or two ago. Even though most people still think some money should be saved, there is a greater emphasis today on immediate enjoyment, even if it means going into debt temporarily. It used to be customary for financial advisors to recommend that couples build up an emergency fund equivalent to at least 3 to 6 months' income. This was supposed to provide enough cash to cover emergencies, most illnesses, the loss of a job, or unexpected major bills. Today, because government programs and employee benefit plans cover some of these emergen-

cies, and with easy access to credit, fewer families feel it is necessary to keep that much money in savings. But savings amounting to at least a few months' income can still prove to be very helpful. In the event of an emergency, nothing beats having cash, or assets that can be quickly converted to cash.

The total assets of many families grow even without specific saving or investment plans. For example, over time, the market value of most homes increases and pension plans accumulate considerable value, virtually out of sight of the employee who owns the plan. The disadvantage of such assets is that they are not liquid: they cannot be converted easily into cash for emergencies. That is one of the main reasons to maintain savings as an emergency fund.

The simple advice that a family should save regularly is easy to give and hard to follow. However, here are some savings strategies that have been used successfully:

1 Have your bank automatically transfer funds from your checking account to a savings account at the beginning of the month before the bills are paid. You are much more likely to save regularly if it is both automatic and not delayed until all the bills are paid.

2 After the payments are completed to repay a loan for a car, appliance, or other major purchase, or to pay off the balance on a credit card, make the same payments to yourself and deposit them in a savings account.

3 If you have difficulty saving anything from your ordinary income, you might plan to save money from such unusual sources as tax refunds, expense account reimbursements, raises, and bonuses.

Where to Keep Savings and Investments

There are many possibilities today for depositing your savings. With the extremely low interest rates being paid in the early 1990s, banks are no longer the automatic choice for savings and investments, although it would be hard to argue with the bank as one of the top choices for the emergency fund or other basic savings. Increasingly, consumers who are either more sophisticated or more desperate for higher yields on their savings are choosing money market or similar accounts with stock brokerage firms or mutual fund companies. Others are choosing investments of varying risk in stocks, bonds, U.S. government securities, as well as commodities and real estate. While some investors achieve enviable long-term profits, novices nearly universally incur losses exceeding their profits.

Once basic financial security is secured through a combination of savings, insurance, and employment benefits, it is important to consider investment in some of the above mentioned investments. But it must be done intelligently. In recent years, too many people have invested in unfamiliar investments, often relying on inexperienced or unscrupulous brokers or advisors. It is exceedingly important to understand the risk involved in an investment and know exactly what it is you are buying. No one should ever invest in something one does not understand from a salesperson who brushes aside one's concerns or just tells the investor not to worry, nothing can go wrong. In fact, that is a clue that you should worry and find another advisor. And never put more in a risky investment than you can afford to lose.

Nothing is certain in investments. The price of stocks variously go up and down with the economy or are influenced by other factors. Likewise, interest rates may go up or down pretty much according to the state of the economy, but have been known to go against traditional wisdom due to special or unexpected conditions. Knowing how to invest in an uncertain economy is generally a job for an experienced, professional, financial advisor. The inexperienced investor with relatively little to invest is generally advised to invest in good quality mutual funds which purchase shares in a large number of stocks and/or bonds to diversify or spread the risk among many investments. The emphasis here is on *good quality* mutual funds. Several consumer- and business-oriented magazines such as *Business Week, Forbes, Money,* and *Kiplinger's Personal Finance Magazine* have regular features on mutual funds as well as periodic listings of funds, giving their yields and return.

This is not to say that all investors should be advised by professionals. For those willing to spend the time studying the market, successful investing that beats the performance of the pros is possible. One of the most beneficial college courses over your lifetime may be one on personal financial planning. If any one generalization may be made that would apply to managing individual and family financial matters in the 1990s, it is that change is going to be the rule, rather than the exception. The nature of basic financial institutions such as banks is undergoing continuous change, adjusting to changing regulations and economic conditions. We are seeing the evolution of our economy into one that is increasingly responsive to worldwide events. For individuals and families to achieve financial security and success, they must either acquire the necessary skills and knowledge or seek the assistance of trusted and reliable advisors.

The absolute amount of income is *not* necessarily directly related to individual or couple happiness. Of course, those with more income can consume more goods and services, thus making certain aspects of life more comfortable and enjoyable. But in terms of feeling contented with their financial situation, those who manage a modest income well are more contented than those who mismanage larger incomes.

References

Chapter 1

ALLEN, J. P., & TURNER, E. (1990). Diversity. *American Demographics, 12*, 34–38.

BANNER, L. (1983). *American beauty.* New York: Knopf.

BEAN, F. D., & TIENDA, M. (1987). *The hispanic population of the United States.* New York: Russell Sage Foundation.

BECK, R., & BECK, S. (1989). The incidence of extended households among middle-aged black and white women. *Journal of Family Issues, 10*, 147–168.

BERRY, M., & BLASSINGAME, J. (1982). *The black extended family.* Chicago: University of Chicago Press.

BILLER, H. (1971). *Father, child, and sex role.* Lexington, MA: Heath.

BOWMAN, P., & HOWARD, C. (1985). Race-related socialization, motivation, and academic achievement: A study of black youth in three-generation families. *Journal of the American Academy of Child Psychiatry, 24*, 134–141.

BOYDSTON, J. (1991). The pastoralization of housework. In L. Kerber & J. De Hart (Eds.), *Women's America: Refocusing the past* (pp. 148–161). New York: Free Press.

BROWN, B. (1976, September). How women see their roles: A change in attitudes. *New Dimensions of Mental Health.* Washington, DC: U.S. Department of Health, Education, and Welfare, Public Health Service.

BROWN, D. (1970). *Bury my heart at wounded knee: An Indian history of the American west.* New York: Holt.

CANCIAN, F. (1987). *Love in America.* New York: Cambridge University Press.

CANCIAN, F., & GORDON, S. (1988). Changing emotional norms in marriage: Love and anger in U.S. women's magazines since 1900. *Gender and Society, 2*, 308–342.

CHAFE, W. (1986). *The unfinished journey: America since World War II.* New York: Oxford University Press.

CHAN, S. (1986). Parents of exceptional Asian children. In M. K. Kitano & P. C. Chinn (Eds.), *Exceptional Asian children and youth* (pp. 36–53). Reston, VA: Council for Exceptional Children.

CHEN, J. (1980). *The Chinese of America.* San Francisco: Harper & Row.

CONER-EDWARDS, A., & EDWARDS, H. (1988). The black middle class: Definition and demographics. In A. Coner-Edwards & J. Spurlock (Eds.), *Black families in crisis: The middle class.* New York: Brunner/Mazel.

COUGHLIN, E. K., (1991, April 10). Burgeoning Asian population in America proves a challenge and a boon to scholars. *The Chronicle of Higher Education,* p. A5.

DANIELS, R. (1990). *Coming to America.* New York: HarperCollins.

DEGLER, C. (1980). *At odds: Women and the family in America from the Revolution to the present.* New York: Oxford University Press.

DELGADO-GAITAN, C. (1987). Tradition and transitions in the learning process of Mexican children. In G. Spindler & L. Spindler (Eds.), *Interpretive ethnography of education: At home and abroad* (pp. 333–359). Hillsdale, NJ: Erlbaum.

DEMO, D. H., & ACOCK, A. (1991). The impact of divorce on children. In A. Booth (Ed.), *Contemporary families* (pp. 162–191). Minneapolis, MN: National Council on Family Relations.

DEMOS, J. (1982). The changing faces of fatherhood: A new exploration of American family history. In S. Cath, A. Gurwitt, & J. Ross (Eds.), *Father and child: Developmental and clinical perspectives* (pp. 425–450). Boston: Little, Brown.

DEMOS, J. (1986). *Past, present, and personal: Family life and the life course in American history.* New York: Oxford University Press.

DIZARD, J. E., & GADLIN, H. (1990). *The minimal family.* Amherst, MA: University of Massachusetts Press.

DRESSLER, W. W. (1985). Extended family relationships, social support, and mental health in a southern black community. *Journal of Health and Social Behavior, 26*, 39–48.

EVANS, S. (1989). *Born for liberty: A history of women in America.* New York: Free Press.

EXTER, T. (1990). Demographic forecasts. *American Demographics, 12*, 55.

FILENE, P. (1986). *Him/her/self: Sex roles in modern America.* Baltimore: Johns Hopkins University Press.

GADLIN, H. (1977). Private lives and public order: A critical view of the history of intimate relations in the United States. In G. Levinger & H.. L. Raush (Eds.), *Close relationships* (pp. 33–72). Amherst, MA: University of Massachusetts Press.

GOLDING, J. M. (1990). Division of household labor, strain, and depressive symptoms among Mexican Americans and non-Hispanics. *Psychology of Women Quarterly, 14*, 103–117.

GOODE, W. (1963). *World revolution and family patterns.* New York: Free Press.

GRANGER, J. M. (1989). African American family policy or national family policy: Are they different? *Urban League Review, 13*, 43–51.

GREEN, B., SACK, W., & PAMBURN, A. (1981). A review of child psychiatric epidemiology with specific reference to American Indian and Alaska Native children. *White Cloud Journal, 2*, 22–36.

GUTMAN, H. (1975). *Slavery and the numbers game.* Urbana, IL: University of Illinois Press.

GUTMAN, H. (1983). Persistent myths about the Afro-American Family. In M. Gordon (Ed.), *The American family in socio-historical perspective* (pp. 459–481). New York: St. Martin's.

HAMPSON, R. B., BEAVERS, W. R., & HULGUS, Y. (1990). Cross-ethnic family differences: Interactional assessment of white, black, and Mexican-American families. *Journal of Marital and Family Therapy, 16*, 307–319.

HARDWICK, E. (1978, Winter). Domestic manners. *Daedalus,* 1–11.

HARRISON, A., WILSON, M., PINE, C., CHAN, S., & BURIEL, R. (1990). Family ecologies of ethnic minority children. *Child Development, 61,* 347–362.

HARTMANN, S. (1982). *The homefront and beyond: American women in the 1940s.* Boston, MA: Twayne.

HINES, P. M., & BOYD-FRANKLIN, N. (1982). Black families. In M. McGoldrick, J. K. Pearce, & J. Giordano (Eds.), *Ethnicity and family therapy* (pp. 87–110). New York: Guilford.

An interview with Daniel Yankelovich. (1992). *Family Affairs, 5,* 1–2, 13–15.

JONES, J. (1985). *Labor of love, labor of sorrow.* New York: Basic Books.

KITANO, H., & DANIELS, R. (1988). *Asian Americans: Emerging minorities.* Englewood Cliffs, NJ: Prentice-Hall.

LONDON, H., & DEVORE, W. (1988). Layers of understanding: Counseling ethnic minority families. *Family Relations, 37,* 310–314.

LYND, R. S., & LYND, H. (1929). *Middletown: A study of modern American culture.* New York: Harcourt, Brace.

MALSON, M. R., MUDIMBE-BOYI, E., O'BARR, J. F., & WYER, M. (1990). *Black women in America.* Chicago: University of Chicago Press.

MICHAELSEN, R. (1983). We also have a religion: The free exercise of religion among Native Americans. *American Indian Quarterly, 7,* 111–142.

MINTZ, S., & KELLOGG, S. (1988). *Domestic revolutions: A social history of American family life.* New York: Free Press.

NEELY, S. (1991). *Snowbird Cherokees: People of persistence.* Athens, GA: University of Georgia Press.

NIETHAMMER, C. (1977). *Daughters of the earth.* New York: Collier Books.

O'HARE, W. (1990a). A new look at Asian Americans. *American Demographics, 12,* 26–31.

O'HARE, W. (1990b). The rise of Hispanic households. *American Demographics, 12,* 40–43.

O'NEILL, N., & O'NEILL, G. (1972). *Open marriage.* New York: Evans.

ORTIZ, R. D. (1984). *Indians of the Americas: Human rights and self-determination.* London: Zed Books.

PLECK, J. H. (1987). American fathering in historical perspective. In M. S. Kimmel (Ed.), *New directions in research on men and masculinity.* Newbury Park, CA: Sage Publications.

PONZETTA, G. E. (1991). *Assimilation, acculturation, and social mobility.* New York: Garland.

RUBIN, L. (1976). *Worlds of pain.* New York: Basic Books.

RUSHFORTH, S., & UPHAM, S. (1992). *A Hopi social history.* Austin, TX: University of Texas Press.

SCHAEFER, R. (1990). *Racial and ethnic groups* (4th ed.). Glenview: Scott, Foresman/Little, Brown.

SKOLNICK, A. (1973). *The intimate environment* (1st ed.). Boston: Little, Brown.

SKOLNICK, A. (1978). *The intimate environment* (2nd ed.). Boston: Little, Brown.

SKOLNICK, A. (1991). *Embattled paradise. The American family in an age of uncertainty.* New York: Basic Books.

STACEY, J. (1990). *Brave new families.* New York: Basic Books.

STAPLES, R. (1988). The emerging majority: Resources for nonwhite families in the United States. *Family Relations, 37,* 348–354.

STOVALL, M. E. (1989). Myths of the American family: An historical perspective. *Family Perspectives, 23,* 133–148.

SURO, R. (1992, January 5). A family matter. *Roanoke Times and World-News,* pp. E1, E3.

SWAP, S., & KRASNOW, J. (1992). *A saga of Irish-American achievement: Constructing a positive identification* (Rep. No. 11). Baltimore, MD: Johns Hopkins University, Center on Families, Communities, Schools, and Children's Learning.

TAYLOR, R. J., CHATTERS, L. M., TUCKER, M. D., & LEWIS, E. (1990). Developments in research on black families: A decade review. *Journal of Marriage and the Family, 52,* 993–1014.

TEACHMAN, J. D., POLONKO, K. A., & SCANZONI, J. (1987). Demography of the family. In M. B. Sussmann & S. K. Steinmetz (Eds.), *Handbook of marriage and the family* (pp. 3–36). New York: Plenum.

THORNTON, R. (1987). *American Indian holocaust and survival: A population history since 1492.* Norman, OK: University of Oklahoma Press.

TSAI, S. (1986). *The Chinese experience in America.* Bloomington, IN: Indiana University Press.

U.S. BUREAU OF THE CENSUS. (1991). *Population Profile of the United States: 1991.* (Current Population Reports, Series P-23, No. 173). Washington, DC: U.S. Government Printing Office.

U.S. BUREAU OF THE CENSUS. (1992, February). *How we're changing.* (Current Population Reports, Series P-23, No. 177). Washington, DC: U.S. Government Printing Office.

U.S. BUREAU OF LABOR STATISTICS. (1992, March). *Women and work.* Washington, DC: U.S. Department of Labor.

VEGA, W. A. (1990). Hispanic families in the 1980s. *Journal of Marriage and the Family, 52,* 1015–1024.

VEROFF, J., DOUVAN, E., & KULKA, R. A. (1981). *The inner American.* New York: Basic Books.

WALDROP, J. (1990). Shades of diversity. *American Demographics, 12,* 30–34.

WARE, S. (1989). *Modern American women: A documentary history.* Chicago, IL: Dorsey.

WELLS, R. (1982). *Revolutions in America's lives.* Westport, CT: Greenwood.

WETZEL, J. R. (1990). American families: 75 years of change. *Monthly Labor Review, 113*(3), 4–13.

WHITELEY, P. M. (1988). *Deliberate acts: Changing Hopi culture through the Oraibi split.* Tucson, AZ: University of Arizona Press.

WILSON, M. (1989). Child development in the context of the black extended family. *American Psychologist, 22,* 246–258.

WORSNOP, R. (1991). Asian Americans. *Editorial Research Reports, 1*(30), 945–968.

ZOGLIN, R. (1992, June 1). Where fathers and mothers know best. *Time,* p. 33.

Chapter 2

The AAUW report: How schools shortchange girls. (1992). A joint publication of the American Association of University Women Educational Foundation and the National Education Association. Wellesley, MA: Center for Research on Women.

ADLER, J., SPRINGEN, K., GLICK, D., & GORDON, J. (1991, June 24). Drums, sweat, and tears. *Newsweek,* pp. 46–51.

ANDERSON, M. L. (1988). *Thinking about women: Sociological perspectives on sex and gender.* New York: Macmillan.

Bad year for girls? (1990, April 16). *Newsweek,* p. 81.

BARNETT, R. C., & BARUCH, G. K. (1987). Social roles, gender, and psychological distress. In R. C. Barnett, L. Biener, & G. K. Baruch (Eds.), *Gender and stress* (pp. 122–143). New York: Free Press.

BASLOW, S. (1986). *Gender stereotypes: Traditions and alternatives.* Pacific Grove, CA: Brooks-Cole.

BEM, S. (1975). Sex role adaptability: One consequence of psychological androgeny. *Journal of Personality and Social Psychology, 31,* 634–643.

BERK, S. (1985). *The gender factory: The apportionment of work in American households.* New York: Plenum.

BERNARD, J. (1982). *The future of marriage.* New Haven, CT: Yale University Press.

BIRD, G. W., & RATCLIFF, B. B. (1990). Children's participation in family tasks: Determinants of mothers' and fathers' reports. *Human Relations, 43,* 865–884.

BLEIER, R. (1988). *Science and gender: A critique of biology and its theories on women.* New York: Pergamon.

BRIDENTHAL, R. (1981). The family tree: Contemporary patterns in the United States. In A. Swerdlow, J. Kelly, & P. Vine (Eds.), *Household and kin* (pp. 121–134). Old Westbury, NY: Feminist Press.

BUSH, D. M., & SIMMONS, R. G. (1987). Gender and coping with the entry into early adolescence. In R. C. Barnett, L. Biener, & G. K. Baruch (Eds.), *Gender and stress* (pp. 185–217). New York: Free Press.

BUTLER, M., & PAISLEY, W. (1980). *Women and the mass media: Sourcebook for research and action.* New York: Human Sciences Press.

CANCIAN, F. (1987). *Love in America.* New York: Cambridge University Press.

CANTER, R. J., & AGETON, S. S. (1984). The epidemiology of adolescent sex-role attitudes. *Sex Roles, 11,* 657–676.

CATH, S. H., GURWITT, A., & GUNSBERG, L. (Eds.). (1989). *Fathers and their families.* Hillsdale, NJ: Analytic Press.

CAZENAVE, N. A. (1984). Race, socioeconomic status, and age: The social context of American masculinity. *Sex Roles, 11,* 639–656.

CHODOROW, N. (1978). *The reproduction of mothering.* Berkeley, CA: University of California Press.

CHUSMIR, L. H., & KOBERG, C. S. (1990). Gender identity and sex role conflict among working women and men. *Journal of Psychology, 6,* 567–575.

CLEARY, P., & MECHANIC, D. (1983). Sex differences in psychological distress among married people. *Journal of Health and Social Behavior, 24,* 111–121.

COOK, E. P. (1985). *Psychological androgyny.* New York: Pergamon.

CORDES, C. (1985, January). At risk in America. *APA Monitor,* pp. 9–11, 25.

DAVIS, A. (1981). *Women, race, and class.* New York: Random House.

DEAUX, K. (1984). From individual differences to social categories: An analysis of a decade's research on gender. *American Psychologist, 39,* 105–116.

DEAUX, K., & KITE, M. (1987). Thinking about gender. In B. Hess & M. Ferree (Eds.), *Analyzing gender.* Beverly Hills, CA: Sage.

DEL BOCA, F. K., & ASHMORE, R. D. (1980). Sex stereotypes through the life cycle. In L. Wheeler (Ed.), *Review of personal and social psychology* (pp. 163–192). Beverly Hills, CA: Sage.

DESTEFANO, L., & COLASANTO, D. (1990, February). Unlike 1975, today most Americans think men have it better. *The Gallup Poll Monthly,* pp. 25–36.

DOYLE, J. (1985). *Sex and gender: The human experience.* Dubuque, IA: William C. Brown.

DURKIN, K. (1985). *Television, sex-roles, and children.* London: Open University Press.

EPSTEIN, C. F. (1987). Multiple demands and multiple roles: The conditions of successful management. In F. J. Crosby (Ed.), *Spouse, parent, worker: On gender and multiple roles* (pp. 23–35). New Haven, CT: Yale University Press.

EPSTEIN, C. F. (1988). *Deceptive distinctions: Sex, gender and the social order.* New Haven, CT: Yale University Press.

FAGOT, B. I. (1984). Teacher and peer reactions to boys' and girls' play styles. *Sex Roles, 11,* 691–702.

FAGOT, B. I., HAGAN, R., LEINBACH, M. D., & KRONSBERG, S. (1985). Differential reaction to assertive and communicative acts of toddler boys and girls. *Child Development, 56,* 1499–1505.

FEINMAN, S. (1981). Why is cross-sex-role behavior more approved for girls than for boys? *Sex Roles, 7,* 289–300.

FEINMAN, S. (1984). A status theory of the evaluation of sex-role and age-role behavior. *Sex Roles, 10,* 445–456.

FERREE, M. (1991). Beyond separate spheres: Feminism and family research. In A. Booth (Ed.), *Contemporary families* (pp. 103–121). Minneapolis, MN: National Council on Family Relations.

FRANKLIN, C. W. (1988). *Men and society.* Chicago: Nelson-Hall.

GEWERTZ, D. (1976). Personal communication.

GIELE, J. Z. (1988). Gender and sex roles. In N. J. Smelser (Ed.), *Handbook of sociology* (pp. 291–323). Newbury Park, CA: Sage.

GILBERT, L. A. (1985). *Men in dual-career families.* Hillsdale, NJ: Erlbaum.

GILLIGAN, C. (1988). Adolescent development reconsidered. In C. Gilligan, J. Ward, & J. Taylor (Eds.), *Mapping the moral domain* (pp. ix–xxxix). Cambridge, MA: Harvard University Press.

GOODE, W. J. (1963). *World revolution and family patterns.* New York: Free Press.

GOODMAN, E. (1992, May 5). Women shorted in news coverage. *Roanoke Times and World-News,* p. A9.

GUMP, J. (1980). Reality and myth: Employment and sex role ideology in black women. In F. Denmark & J. Sherman (Eds.), *The psychology of women* (pp. 223–245). New York: Psychological Dimensions.

HARNETT, O., & BRADLEY, J. (1986). Sex-roles and work. In D. J. Hargreaves & A. M. Colley (Eds.), *The psychology of sex-roles* (pp. 215–232). New York: Harper & Row.

HOFFMAN, L. (1984). Work, family, and the socialization of the child. In R. D. Parke, R. N. Emede, H. P. McAdoo, & G. P. Sackett (Eds.), *Review of child development research: Vol. 7, The family* (pp. 223–282). Chicago: University of Chicago Press.

HOFFMAN, L. (1987). The effects of children on maternal and paternal employment. In N. Gerstel & H. E. Gross (Eds.), *Families and work* (pp. 362–394). Philadelphia: Temple University Press.

HOFFMAN, L. (1989). Effects of maternal employment in the two-parent family. *American Psychologist, 44,* 283–292.

HYDE, J. S. (1986). Gender differences in aggression. In J. S. Hyde & M. C. Linn (Eds.), *The psychology of gender* (pp. 51–66). Baltimore: Johns Hopkins University Press.

IOANILLI, S. (1990, January/February). Changing perspectives on a man's world. *The Humanist,* pp. 21–23.

KOHLBERG, L. A. (1966). A cognitive-developmental analysis of children's sex role concepts and attitudes. In E. Maccoby

(Ed.), *The development of sex differences*. Palo Alto, CA: Stanford University Press.

LAMB, M. E. (1987). *The fathers' role: Cross-cultural perspectives*. Hillsdale, NJ: Erlbaum.

LANGMAN, L. (1987). Social stratification. In M. B. Sussman & S. K. Steinmetz (Eds.), *Handbook of marriage and the family* (pp. 211–249). New York: Plenum.

LA ROSSA, R. (1988). Fatherhood and social change. *Family Relations, 37*, 451–457.

LEWIS, C. (1986). Early sex-role socialization. In D. J. Hargreaves & A. M. Colley (Eds.), *The psychology of sex-roles* (pp. 95–117). New York: Harper & Row.

LEWIS, L. L., & DEAUX, K. (1983, August). *Gender stereotyping: Subcategories and their contents*. Paper presented at the annual meeting of the American Psychological Association. Anaheim, CA.

LEWIS, R. A., & SALT, R. E. (Eds.). (1986). *Men in families*. Beverly Hills, CA: Sage.

LICHTER, R., LICHTER, L., & ROTHMAN, S. (1986). From Lucy to Lacey: TV's dream girls. *Public Opinion, 9*, 16–19.

LINDSEY, L. L. (1990). *Gender roles: A sociological perspective*. Englewood Cliffs, NJ: Prentice-Hall.

LLOYD, B. (1989). Rules of the gender game. *New Scientist, 2*, 60–64.

LOSH-HESSELBART, S. (1987). Development of gender roles. In M. B. Sussman & S. K. Steinmetz (Eds.), *Handbook of marriage and the family* (pp. 535–563). New York: Plenum.

LYONS, N. (1988). Two perspectives: On self, relationships, and morality. In C. Gilligan, J. Ward, & J. Taylor (Eds.), *Mapping the moral domain* (pp. 21–45). Cambridge, MA: Harvard University Press.

MACCOBY, E. E., & JACKLIN, C. N. (1974). *The psychology of sex differences*. London: Oxford University Press.

MACHUNG, A. (1989). Talking career, thinking job: Gender differences in career and family expectations of Berkeley seniors. *Feminist Studies, 15*, 35–38.

MALSON, M. R. (1983). Black women's sex roles: The social context for a new ideology. *Journal of Social Issues, 39*, 101–113.

MARKMAN, H. (1984). The longitudinal study of couples' interactions: Implications for understanding and predicting the development of marital distress. In K. Hahlweg & N. Jacobson (Eds.), *Marital interaction: Analysis and modifications* (pp. 253–281). New York: Guilford.

MEAD, M. (1935). *Sex and temperament in three primitive societies*. New York: Morrow.

MEAD, M. (1949). *Male and female*. New York: Morrow.

MONEY, J., & EHRHARDT, A. (1974). *Man and woman, boy and girl*. New York: Mentor.

NICHOLSON, J. (1984). *Men and women: How different are they?* Oxford, England: Oxford University Press.

OSTLING, R. N. (1992). Is school unfair to girls? *Time, 139*(8), 62.

PEPLAU, L. (1983). Roles and gender. In H. Kelley, E. Berscheid, A. Christensen, J. Harvey, T. Huston, G. Levinger, E. McClintock, L. Peplau, & D. Peterson (Eds.), *Close relationships* (pp. 220–264). New York: Freeman.

PLECK, J. (1987). The contemporary man. In M. Scher, M. Stevens, G. Good, & G. Eichenfield (Eds.), *Handbook on counseling and psychotherapy with men* (pp. 16–27). Beverly Hills, CA: Sage.

POWER, T. (1981). Sex typing in infancy: The role of the father. *Infant Mental Health Journal, 2*, 226–240.

REINHOLD, R. (1983, May 6). An overwhelming violence-TV tie. *The New York Times*, p. C27.

ROSEN, E. (1987). *Bitter choices: Blue-collar women in and out of work*. Chicago: University of Chicago Press.

RUBIN, L. B. (1984). *Intimate strangers: Men and women together*. New York: Harper & Row.

SADKER, M., & SADKER, D. (1985, March). Sex roles and achievement conflicts. *Personality and Social Psychology Bulletin, 5*, 352–355.

SAPIRO, V. (1986). *Women in American society*. Palo Alto, CA: Mayfield.

SCHUSTER, S. (1992, September 29). Schools shortchange girls. *Roanoke Times and World-News*, p. A9.

SHAPIRO, L., MURR, A., & SPRINGEN, K. (1991, June 17). Women who kill too much. *Newsweek*, p. 63.

SINGLETON, C. H. (1986). Biological and social explanation of sex-role stereotyping. In D. J. Hargreaves & A. M. Colley (Eds.), *The psychology of sex-roles*, (pp. 3–26). New York: Harper & Row.

STANWORTH, M. (1983). *Gender and schooling*. London: Hutchinson.

STEPHENS, W. (1963). *The family in cross-cultural perspective*. New York: Holt.

THOMPSON, L., & WALKER, A. (1991). Gender in families: Women and men in marriage, work, and parenthood. In A. Booth (Ed.), *Contemporary families* (pp. 76–102). Minneapolis, MN: National Council on Family Relations.

TOWNSEND, B., & O'NEIL, K. (1990). Women get mad. *American Demographics, 12*(8), 26–32.

VEGA, W. (1991). Hispanic families in the 1980s. In A. Booth (Ed.), *Contemporary families* (pp. 297–306). Minneapolis, MN: National Council on Family Relations.

Virginia Slims Opinion Poll: A 20-year perspective of women's issues. (1990). New York: The Roper Organization.

WEISS, R. S. (1985). Men and the family. *Family Process, 24*, 49–58.

WEITZMAN, L. (1984). Sex-role socialization: A focus on women. In J. Freeman (Ed.), *Women: A feminist perspective* (pp. 122–154). Palo Alto, CA: Mayfield.

WEST, C., & ZIMMERMAN, D. H. (1987). Doing gender. *Gender and Society, 1*, 125–151.

WILLIAMS, D. G. (1988). Gender, marriage, and psychosocial well-being. *Journal of Family Issues, 9*, 452–468.

ZAVELLA, P. (1987). *Women's work and Chicano families*. Ithaca, NY: Cornell University Press.

ZINN, M. B. (1993). Family, feminism, and race in America. In L. Richardson & V. Taylor (Eds.), *Feminist frontiers III* (pp. 406–420). New York: McGraw-Hill.

Chapter 3

AINSWORTH, M., BLEHAR, M., WATERS, E., & WALL, S. (1978). *Patterns of attachment: A psychological study of the strange situation*. Hillsdale, NJ: Erlbaum.

ALLEN, K. (1989). *Single women/family ties*. Beverly Hills, CA: Sage.

AUGUSTINE, J. S. (Ed.). (1982). *The Indian family in transition*. New Delhi: Vikas.

BELLAH, R., MADSEN, R., SULLIVAN, W., SWIDLER, A., & TIPTON, S. (1985). *Habits of the heart: Individualism and commitment in American life*. Berkeley, CA: University of California Press.

BERSCHEID, E., SNYDER, M., & OMOTO, A. (1989). Issues in studying close relationships. In C. Hendrick (Ed.), *Close relationships* (pp. 63–91). Newbury Park, CA: Sage.

BOWLBY, J. (1969, 1973, 1980). *Attachment and loss.* New York: Basic Books.

BRADBURY, T. N., & FINCHAM, F. D. (1990). Attributions in marriage: Review and critique. *Psychological Bulletin, 107,* 3–33.

BRANDEN, N. (1980). *The psychology of romantic love.* Los Angeles: J. P. Tarcher.

BREHM, S. S. (1985). *Intimate relationships.* New York: Random House.

BREHM, S. S. (1992). *Intimate relationships* (2nd ed). New York: McGraw-Hill.

BRICKMAN, P., DUNKEL-SCHETTER, C., & ABBEY, A. (1987). The development of commitment. In P. Brickman, C. Wortman, & R. Sorrentino (Eds.), *Commitment, conflict, and caring* (pp. 145–220). Englewood Cliffs, NJ: Prentice-Hall.

BUUNK, B., & BRINGLE, R. (1987). Jealousy in love relationships. In D. Perlman & S. Duck (Eds.), *Intimate relationships: Development, dynamics, and deterioration* (pp. 123–148). Beverly Hills, CA: Sage.

CANCIAN, F. (1986). The feminization of love. *Signs, 11,* 692–709.

CANCIAN, F. (1987). *Love in America.* New York: Cambridge University Press.

CAPELLANUS, A. (1959). *Art of courtly love* (J. J. Perry, Trans.). New York: Ungar.

CHELUNE, G., ROBINSON, J., & KOMMOR, M. (1988). A cognitive interactional model of intimate relationships. In V. J. Derlega (Ed.), *Communication, intimacy, and close relationships* (pp. 11–41). New York: Academic Press.

CLARK, M. S., & REIS, H. T. (1988). Interpersonal processes in close relationships. *Annual Review of Psychology, 39,* 609–672.

DAVIS, M. H., & OATHOUT, H. A. (1987). Maintenance of satisfaction in romantic relationships: Empathy and relational competence. *Journal of Personality and Social Psychology, 53,* 397–410.

DERLEGA, V. J. (1984). Self-disclosure and intimate relationships. In V. J. Derlega (Ed.), *Communication, intimacy, and close relationships* (pp. 1–9). New York: Academic Press.

DION, K. L., & DION, K. K. (1988). Romantic love: Individual and cultural perspectives. In R. J. Sternberg & M. L. Barner (Eds.), *The psychology of love* (pp. 264–289). New Haven, CT: Yale University Press.

DUTTON, D., & ARON, A. (1974). Some evidence for heightened sexual attraction under conditions of high anxiety. *Journal of Personality and Social Psychology, 4,* 510–517.

FISH, R., & FISH, L. (1986). Quid pro quo revisited: The basis of marital therapy. *American Journal of Orthopsychiatry, 56,* 371–384.

FRAZIER, P. A., & ESTERLY, E. (1990). Correlates of relationship beliefs: Gender, relationship experience and relationship satisfaction. *Journal of Social and Personal Relationships, 7,* 331–352.

GOLEMAN, D. (1992, November 24). After kinship and marriage, anthropology discovers love. *The New York Times,* pp. C1, C12.

GOTTMAN, J. M., & KROKOFF, L. J. (1989). Marital interaction and satisfaction: A longitudinal view. *Journal of Consulting and Clinical Psychology, 57,* 47–52.

HAAS, A., & HAAS, K. (1990). *Understanding sexuality.* Boston: Times Mirror/Mosby.

HATFIELD, E. (1984). The dangers of intimacy. In V. J. Derlega (Ed.), *Communication, intimacy, and close relationships.* New York: Academic Press.

HATFIELD, E. (1988). Passionate and companionate love. In R. J. Sternberg & M. L. Barnes (Eds.), *The psychology of love* (pp. 191–217). New Haven, CT: Yale University Press.

HATFIELD, E., & WALSTER, G. W. (1978). *A new look at love.* Lantham, MA: University Press of America.

HAZAN, C., & SHAVER, P. (1987). Romantic love conceptualized as an attachment process. *Journal of Personality and Social Psychology, 52,* 511–524.

HILL, C. T., PEPLAU, L. A., & ZICK, R. (1976). Breakups before marriage: The end of 103 affairs. *Journal of Social Issues, 32,* 147–168.

HOCHSCHILD, A. (1989). *Second shift.* New York: Viking.

HOLMES, J. G., & REMPEL, J. K. (1989). Trust in close relationships. In C. Hendrick (Ed.), *Close relationships* (pp. 187–220). Newbury Park, CA: Sage.

HSU, F. L. K. (1981). *Americans and Chinese: Passage to difference* (3rd ed.). Honolulu: University Press of Hawaii.

HUSTON, T. L., MCHALE, S. M., & CROUTER, A. C. (1986). When the honeymoon's over: Changes in the marriage relationship over the first year. In S. Duck & R. Gilmour (Eds.), *The emerging field of personal relationships* (pp. 109–132). Hillsdale, NJ: Erlbaum.

LEE, J. A. (1973). *The colors of love.* Ontario: New Press.

LEE, J. A. (1977). A typology of styles of loving. *Personality and Social Psychology Bulletin, 3,* 173–182.

LEE, J. A. (1988). Love styles. In R. J. Sternberg & M. L. Barnes (Eds.), *The psychology of love* (pp. 38–67). New Haven, CT: Yale University Press.

LEVINGER, G. (1983). Development and change. In H. H. Kelley et al. (Eds.), *Close relationships* (pp. 315–358). New York: Freeman.

LIEBOWITZ, M. R. (1983). *The chemistry of love.* Boston: Little, Brown.

MILLER, G. R., & PARKS, M. (1982). Communication in dissolving relationships. In S. Duck (Ed.), *Personal relationships: Vol. 4, Dissolving personal relationships* (pp. 127–154). London: Academic Press.

MILLER, L. C., & READ, S. J. (1987). Why am I telling you this? Self-disclosure in a goal-based model of personality. In V. J. Derlega & J. H. Berg (Eds.), *Self-disclosure* (pp. 35–58). New York: Plenum.

MONTGOMERY, B. M. (1988). Quality communication in personal relationships. In S. Duck (Ed.), *Handbook of personal relationships* (pp. 343–366). New York: Wiley.

MYERS, D. T. (1987). The socialized individual and individual autonomy. In E. F. Kittay & D. T. Myers (Eds.), *Women and moral theory* (pp. 139–153). Totowa, NJ: Rowman & Littlefield.

NODDINGS, N. (1984). *Caring.* Berkeley, CA: University of California Press.

PARROTT, W. G., & SMITH, R. H. (1987, August). *Differentiating the experiences of envy and jealousy.* Paper presented at the annual meeting of the Western Psychological Association. San Francisco, CA.

PFEIFFER, S. M., & WONG, P. (1989). Multidimensional jealousy. *Journal of Social and Personal Relationships, 6,* 181–196.

REISS, I. L. (1971). *The family system in America.* New York: Holt.

ROGERS, L. E., & MILLAR, F. E. (1988). Relational communication.

In S. Duck (Ed.), *Handbook of personal relationships* (pp. 289–305). New York: Wiley.

RUBIN, Z., PEPLAU, L., & HILL, C. (1981). Loving and leaving: Sex differences in romantic attachments. *Sex Roles, 7,* 821–835.

SALOVEY, P., & RODIN, J. (1989). Envy and jealousy in close relationship. In C. Hendrick (Ed.), *Close relationships* (pp. 221–245). Newbury Park, CA: Sage.

SATTEL, J. W. (1989). Men, inexpressiveness, and power. In L. Richardson & V. Taylor (Eds.), *Feminist frontiers II* (pp. 270–274). New York: Random House.

SHAVER, P. R., & HAZAN, C. (1988). A biased overview of the study of love. *Journal of Social and Personal Relationships, 5,* 473–501.

SHAVER, P. R., SCHWARTZ, J., KIRSON, D., & O'CONNOR, C. (1987). Emotion knowledge: Further exploration of a prototype approach. *Journal of Personality and Social Psychology, 52,* 1061–1087.

SMITH-ROSENBERG, C. (1989). The female world of love and ritual: Relations between women in nineteenth-century America. In L. Richardson & V. Taylor (Eds.), *Feminist frontiers II* (pp. 229–249). New York: Random House.

SPRECHER, S. (1987). The effects of self-disclosure given and received on affection for an intimate partner and stability in the relationship. *Journal of Social and Personal Relationships, 4,* 115–128.

STERNBERG, R. J. (1986). A triangular theory of love. *Psychological Review, 93,* 119–135.

STOKES, J. P. (1987). The relation of loneliness and self-disclosure. In V. J. Derlega & J. H. Berg (Eds.), *Self-disclosure* (pp. 175–201). New York: Plenum.

THOMPSON, L. (1989, November). *Marital responsibility: Contextual and relational morality.* Paper presented at the annual meeting of the National Council on Family Relations, New Orleans, LA.

WEINRAUB, J. (1973, June 3). India's traditional arranged marriages take a modern turn. p. 68.

WHITE, G. K. (1981). Physical attractiveness and courtship progress. *Journal of Personality and Social Psychology, 39,* 360–368.

Chapter 4

BAILEY, B. L. (1988). *From front porch to back seat: The history of courtship in America.* Baltimore: Johns Hopkins University Press.

BAXTER, L. A. (1986). Gender differences in heterosexual relationship rules embedded in break-up accounts. *Journal of Social and Personal Relationships, 3,* 289–306.

BAXTER, L. A., & WILMOT, W. W. (1985). Taboo topics in close relationships. *Journal of Social and Personal Relationships, 2,* 253–269.

BERG, J. H., & MCQUINN, R. D. (1986). Attraction and exchange in continuing and noncontinuing dating relationships. *Journal of Personality and Social Psychology, 50,* 942–952.

BERNARD, J. (1982). *The future of marriage* (2nd ed.). New York: Bantam.

BIRD, G. W., STITH, S. M., & SCHLADALE, J. (1991). Psychological resources, coping strategies, and negotiation styles as discriminators of violence in dating relationships. *Family Relations, 40,* 45–50.

BOERINGER, S. B., SHEHAN, C. L., & AKERS, R. (1991). Social contexts and social learning in sexual coercion and aggression: Assessing the contribution of fraternity membership. *Family Relations, 40,* 58–64.

BRADSHER, K. (1990, January 7). For every five young women, six young men. *The New York Times,* p. 10.

BURKE, P. J., STETS, J. E., & PIROG-GOOD, M. A. (1988). Gender identify, self-esteem, and physical and sexual abuse in dating relationships. *Social Psychology Quarterly, 51,* 272–285.

CATE, R., & LLOYD, S. (1988). Courtship. In S. Duck (Ed.), *Handbook of personal relationships* (pp. 409–427). Newbury Park, CA: Sage.

CATE, R., & LLOYD, S. (1992). *Courtship.* Newbury Park, CA: Sage.

CHRISTOPHER, F. S., & CATE, R. M. (1982). *Factors involved in premarital sexual decision-making.* Paper presented at the International Conference on Personal Relations. Madison, WI.

CHRISTOPHER, F. S., & FRANDSEN, M. M. (1990). Strategies of influence in sex and dating. *Journal of Social and Personal Relationships, 7,* 89–106.

DEKESEREDY, W. (1988). *Woman abuse in dating relationships: The role of male peer support.* Toronto: Canadian Scholar's Press.

DILORIO, J. (1989). Being and becoming coupled: The emergence of female subordination in heterosexual relationships. In B. J. Risman & P. Schwartz (Eds.), *Gender in intimate relationships* (pp. 94–104). Belmont, CA: Wadsworth.

Don't! Stop! or Don't Stop! (1989). *Psychology Today, 23*(3), 62.

DUCK, S. (1988). *Relating to others.* Chicago, IL: Dorsey.

EMERY, B., LLOYD, S., & CASTLETON, A. (1989, November). *Why women hit back.* Paper presented at the annual meeting of the National Council on Family Relations. New Orleans, LA.

FISH, R., & FISH, L. (1986). Quid pro quo revisited: The basis of marital therapy. *American Journal of Orthopsychiatry, 56,* 371–384.

FOA, E. B., & FOA, U. G. (1980). Resource theory: Interpersonal behavior in exchange. In K. Gergen, M. Greenberg, & R. Willis (Eds.), *Social exchange: Advances in theory and research* (pp. 77–102). New York: Plenum.

FOWLES, J. (1988, June 5). Coming soon: More men than women. *The New York Times.*

GARRETT-GOODING, J., & SENTER, R. (1987). Attitudes and acts of sexual aggression on a university campus. *Sociological Inquiry, 57,* 348–371.

GIBBS, N. (1991, June 3). When is it rape? *Time,* 48–54.

GREENE, G. (1964). *Sex and the college girl.* New York: Dial.

GUTTENTAG, M., & SECORD, P. (1983). *Too many women? The sex ratio question.* Beverly Hill, CA: Sage.

HATFIELD, E., TRAUPMANN, J., & SPRECHER, S. (1985). Equity and intimate relations: Recent research. In W. Ickes (Ed.), *Compatible and incompatible relationships* (pp. 91–140). New York: Springer-Verlag.

HUSTON, T., SURRA, C. A., FITZGERALD, N. M., & CATE R. M. (1981). From courtship to marriage: Mate selection as an interpersonal process. In S. Duck & R. Gilmour (Eds.), *Personal relationships: Vol. 2, Developing personal relationships* (pp. 53–87). New York: Academic.

ITOLI, K., & POWELL, B. (1992, August 10). Take a hike, Hiroshi. *Newsweek,* pp. 38–39.

JOHNSON, M., & MILARDO, R. (1984). Network interference in pair relationships: A social psychological recasting of Slater's theory of social regression. *Journal of Marriage and the Family, 46,* 893–899.

KILPATRICK, D., BEST, C., SAUNDERS, B., & VERONEN, L. J. (1988). Rape in marriage and dating relationships: How bad is it for mental health? *Annals of the New York Academy of Sciences, 528,* 335–344.

KNOX, D., & WILSON, K. (1983). Dating problems of university students. *College Student Journal, 17,* 225–228.

KOMAROVSKY, M. (1985). *Women in college.* New York: Basic Books.

KOSS, M., DINERO, T., SEIBEL, C., & COX, S. (1988). Stranger and acquaintance rape: Are there differences in the victim's experience? *Psychology of Women Quarterly, 12,* 1–24.

KOSS, M., & OROS, C. (1982). Sexual experiences survey: A research instrument investigating sexual aggression and victimization. *Journal of Consulting and Clinical Psychology, 50,* 445–457.

LANE, K. E., & GWARTNEY-GIBBS, P. A. (1985). Violence in the context of dating and sex. *Journal of Family Issues, 6,* 45–59.

LEE, L. (1984). Sequences in separation: A framework for investigating endings of the personal (romantic) relationship. *Journal of Social and Personal Relationships, 1,* 49–73.

LEMASTERS, E. E. (1957). *Modern courtship and marriage.* New York: Macmillan.

LESLIE, L., HUSTON, T., & JOHNSON, M. (1986). Parental reactions to dating relationships: Do they make a difference? *Journal of Marriage and the Family, 48,* 57–66.

LLOYD, S. A. (1991). The darkside of courtship: Violence and sexual exploitation. *Family Relations, 40,* 14–20.

LUNDBERG-LOVE, P., & GEFFNER, R. (1989). Date rape: Prevalence, risk factors, and a proposed model. In M. A. Pirog-Good & J. E. Stets (Eds.), *Violence in dating relationships* (pp. 169–184). New York: Praeger.

MUEHLENHARD, C. L., & LINTON, M. (1987). Date rape and sexual aggression in dating situations: Incidence and risk factors. *Journal of Counseling Psychology, 34,* 186–196.

MULLER, K. Q. (1992, November 24). Teen survey: "No" on a date could mean "yes." *Roanoke Times and World-News,* p. E3.

MURSTEIN, B. I. (1980). Mate selection in the 1970s. *Journal of Marriage and the Family, 42,* 777–792.

MURSTEIN, B. I. (1987). A clarification and extension of the SVR theory of dyadic pairing. *Journal of Marriage and the Family, 49,* 929–933.

New social struggle in Japan: Finding marrying women. (1992, August 9). *Baltimore Sun,* p. A1.

PERLMAN, D., & FEHR, B. (1987). The development of intimate relationships. In D. Perlman & S. Duck (Eds.), *Intimate relationships: Development, dynamics, and deterioration* (pp. 13–42). Beverly Hills, CA: Sage.

REISS, I. (1980). *Family systems in America* (3rd ed.). New York: Holt.

Romance. (1990). *Life, 13,* 42–44.

RUSBULT, C. E. (1987). Responses to dissatisfaction in close relationships. In D. Perlman & S. Duck (Eds.), *Intimate relationships: Development, dynamics, and deterioration* (pp. 209–237). Beverly Hills, CA: Sage.

STETS, J. E., & PIROG-GOOD, M. A. (1987). Violence in dating relationships. *Social Psychology Quarterly, 50,* 237–246.

SURRA, C. A. (1985). Courtship types: Variations in interdependence between partners and social networks. *Journal of Personality and Social Psychology, 56,* 357–375.

SURRA, C. A. (1987). Reasons for changes in commitment: Variations by courtship type. *Journal of Social and Personal Relationships, 4,* 17–33.

SURRA, C. A. (1988). The influence of the interactive network on developing relationships. In R. M. Milardo (Ed.), *Families and social networks* (pp. 48–81). Newbury Park, CA: Sage.

SURRA, C. A. (1990). Research and theory of mate selection and premarital relationships. *Journal of Marriage and the Family, 52,* 844–865.

SURRA, C. A. (1991). Mate selection and premarital relationships. In A. Booth (Ed.), *Contemporary families* (pp. 54–75). Minneapolis, MN: National Council on Family Relations.

SURRA, C. A., & MILARDO, R. (1991). The social psychological context of developing relationships: Interactive and psychological networks. In W. H. Jones & D. Perlman (Eds.), *Advances in personal relationships:* Vol. 3. London: Jessica Kingsley Publishers.

TAYLOR, R. J., CHATTERS, L. M., TUCKER, M., & LEWIS, E. (1991). Developments in research on black families. In A. Booth (Ed.), *Contempoary families.* Minneapolis, MN: National Council on Family Relations.

WARD, S. K., CHAPMAN, K., COHN, E., WHITE, S., & WILLIAMS, K. (1991). Acquaintance rape and the college social scene. *Family Relations, 40,* 65–77.

WILKERSON, I. (1991, December 2). Black-white marriages rise, but couples still face scorn. *The New York Times,* p. B6.

WINSTON, D. (1991, January 11). Towson state survey on date rape. *Baltimore Sun,* pp. D1, 4.

Chapter 5

ALLEN, K. (1989). *Single women/family ties.* Beverly Hills, CA: Sage.

BARUCH, G., BARNETT, R., & RIVERS, C. (1983). *Lifeprints: New patterns of love and work for today's women.* New York: McGraw-Hill.

BELL, A., & WEINBERG, M. S. (1978). *Homosexualities: A study of diversity among men and women.* New York: Simon and Schuster.

BERNARD, J. (1973). *The future of marriage.* New York: Bantam.

BIRD, C. (1972). Women should stay single. In H. Hart (Ed.), *Marriage: For and against.* New York: Hart.

BLASBAND, D., & PEPLAU, L. (1985). Sexual exclusivity versus openness in gay male couples. *Archives of Sexual Behavior, 14,* 395–412.

BLUMSTEIN, P., & SCHWARTZ, P. (1989). *American couples: Money, work, sex.* New York: Morrow.

BLUMSTEIN, P., & SCHWARTZ, P. (1989). American couples. In A. S. Skolnick & J. A. Skolnick (Eds.), *Family in transition* (pp. 267–278). Boston: Foresman.

BLUMSTEIN, P., & SCHWARTZ, P. (1990). Intimate relationships and the creation of sexuality. In D. P. McWhirter, S. A. Sanders, & J. M. Reinisch (Eds.), *Homosexuality/heterosexuality: Concepts of sexual orientation* (pp. 307–320). New York: Oxford University Press.

BUMPASS, L. L., & SWEET, J. A. (1989). National estimates of cohabitation. *Demography 26*(4), 617–618.

BUMPASS, L. L., & SWEET, J. A. (1991). The role of cohabitation in declining rates of marriage. *Journal of Marriage and the Family, 53,* 913–927.

BUUNK, B. P., & VAN DRIEL, B. (1989). *Variant lifestyles and relationships.* Newbury Park, CA: Sage.

CALDWELL, M., & PEPLAU, L. (1984). The balance of power in lesbian relationships. *Sex Roles, 10*, 587–600.

CLARKE, C. V. (1989). Financial strategies for unmarrieds. *Black Enterprise. 20*(3), 95–96, 98.

DEMARIS, A., & LESLIE, G. (1984). Cohabitation with the future spouse: Its influence upon marital satisfaction and communication. *Journal of Marriage and the Family, 46*, 77–84.

DEMARIS, A., & RAO, K. (1992). Premarital cohabitation and subsequent marital stability in the United States. *Journal of Marriage and the Family, 54*, 178–190.

DEWITT, P. M. (1992). All the lonely people. *American Demographics, 14*(4), 44–46, 48.

EXTER, T. (1990). Alone at home. *American Demographics, 12*, 55.

FARBER, N. (1990). The significance of race and class in marital decisions among unmarried adolescent mothers. *Social Problems. 37*(1), 51–63.

40-and-older bachelors don't want marriage. (1991, November 2). *Roanoke Times and World News*, pp. E1, 4.

FOST, D. (1992). Cruising at 60 is no fun alone. *American Demographics, 14*(4), 47.

GALLUP ORGANIZATION. (1989). Gallup Report. Princeton, NJ: Gallup Organization.

GROSS, J. (1991, June 16). More young single men hang on to apron strings. *The New York Times*, pp. A1, 18.

GWARTNEY-GIBBS, P. (1986). The institutionalization of premarital cohabitation. *Journal of Marriage and the Family, 48*, 423–434.

HARRY, J. (1983). Gay male and lesbian relationships. In E. D. Macklin & R. H. Rubin (Eds.), *Contemporary families and alternative lifestyles*. Beverly Hills, CA: Sage.

KURDEK, L. A., & SCHMITT, J. P. (1986). Relationship quality of partners in heterosexual married, heterosexual cohabiting, gay, and lesbian relationships. *Journal of Personality and Social Psychology, 51*, 711–720.

LANDERS, R. K. (1990). Are Americans still in love with marriage? *Editorial Research Reports, 1*, 382–394.

LANER, M. (1977). Permanent partner priorities: Gay and straight. *Journal of Homosexuality, 3*, 21–39.

LARSON, J., & EDMONDSON, B. (1991). Should unmarried partners get married benefits? *American Demographics, 13*(3), 47.

MACKLIN, E. D. (1974). *Unmarried heterosexual cohabitation*. Unpublished memo.

MACKLIN, E. D. (1987). Nontraditional family forms. In M. B. Sussman & S. K. Steinmetz (Eds.), *Handbook of marriage and the family* (pp. 317–353). New York: Plenum.

MINTZ, S., & KELLOGG, S. (1988). *Domestic revolutions: A social history of American family life*. New York: Free Press.

MORGAN, E. (1966). *The Puritan family*. New York: Harper & Row.

NEWCOMB, M., & BENTLER, P. (1981). Marital stability and satisfaction among cohabitors. *Journal of Personality Assessment, 44*, 147–154.

O'HARE, W., POLLARD, K., MANN, T., & KENT, M. (1991). African Americans in the 1990s. *Population Bulletin, 46*, 2–39.

PEPLAU, L. A., & COCHRAN, S. D. (1980, September). *Sex differences in values concerning love relationships*. Paper presented at the annual meeting of the American Psychological Association. Montreal, Canada.

PEPLAU, L. A., & COCHRAN, S. D. (1990). A relationship perspective on homosexuality. In D. P. McWhirter, S. A. Sanders, J. M. Reinisch (Eds.), *Homosexuality/heterosexuality: Concepts of sexual orientation* (pp. 321–349). New York: Oxford University Press.

PEPLAU, L. A., & GORDON, S. L. (1991). The intimate relationships of lesbians and gay men. In J. N. Edwards & D. H. Demo (Eds.), *Marriage and family in transition* (pp. 479–496). Boston: Allyn and Bacon.

RAMSEY, J., LATHAM, J. D., & LINDQUIST, C. (1978, August). *Long-term same-sex relationships: Correlates of adjustment*. Paper presented at the annual meeting of the American Psychological Association. Toronto, Canada.

RICHE, M. F. (1991). The future of the family. *American Demographics, 13*(3), 44–45.

RISMAN, B., HILL, C., RUBIN, Z., & PEPLAU, L. (1981). Living together in college: Implication for courtship. *Journal of Marriage and the Family, 43*, 77–84.

ROHA, R. R. (1990). Legal side of living together. *Changing Times, 44*(10), 73–75.

SORRENTINO, C. (1990). The changing family in international perspective. *Monthly Labor Review, 113*, 41–55.

STAPLES, R. (1981). Black singles in America. In P. Stein (Ed.), *Single life* (pp. 40–51). New York: St. Martin's.

STEIN, P. (1975). Singlehood. *The Family Coordinator, 24*, 489–503.

STEIN, P. (1981). Single life: *Unmarried adults in social context*. New York: St. Martin's.

SURRA, C. A. (1991). Research and theory on mate selection and premarital relationships in the 1980s. In A. Booth (Ed.), *Contemporary families* (pp. 54–75). Minneapolis, MN: National Council on Family Relations.

TAYLOR, R., CHATTERS, L., TUCKER, M., & LEWIS, E. (1991). Developments in research on black families. In A. Booth (Ed.), *Contemporary families.* (pp. 275–296). Minneapolis, MN: National Council on Family Relations.

TEACHMAN, J., & POLONKO, K. (1990). Cohabitation and marital stability in the United States. *Social Forces, 69*, 207–220.

THOMSON, E., & COLELLA, U. (1992). Cohabitation and marital stability: Quality of commitment? *Journal of Marriage and the Family, 54*, 259–267.

THORNTON, A. (1988). Cohabitation and marriage in the 1980s. *Demography, 25*, 497–508.

U.S. BUREAU OF THE CENSUS. (1988, March). *Marital status and living arrangements* (Current Population Reports Series P-20, No. 433). Washington, DC: U.S. Government Printing Office.

URBANSKA, W. (1986). *The singular generation*. New York: Doubleday.

USDANSKY, M. L. (1992, July 17). Wedded to the single life: Attitudes, economy delaying marriages. *USA Today*, p. A8.

VOBEJDA, B. (1991, November 17). Why more and more black women will never marry. *Roanoke Times and World News.* pp. F1, 6.

WALDROP, J., & EXTER, T. (1991). Living in sin. *American Demographics, 13*, 12–15.

WATKINS, S. C. (1984). Spinster. *Journal of Family History, 9*, 310–325.

WETZEL, J. R. (1990). American families: 75 years of change. *Monthly Labor Review, 113*, 4–14.

Chapter 6

ADLER, J., WRIGHT, L., MCCORMICK, J., ANNIN, P., COHEN, A., TALBOT, M., HAGER, M., & YOFFE, E. (1991, December 9). Safer sex. *Newsweek*, pp. 52–56.

ALLEGEIER, E. R., & ALLEGEIER, A. R. (1991). *Sexual interactions*. Lexington, MA: Heath.

ATWATER, L. (1982). *The extramarital connection: Sex, intimacy, and identity.* New York: Irvington.

BACHRACH, C., & HORN, M. (1987). *Married and unmarried couples in the U.S.* Hyattsville, MD: Department of Health and Human Services.

BARRON, D., & YANKELOVICH, D. (1980). *Today's American woman: How the public sees her.* New York: Public Agenda Foundation.

BELL, A. P., & WEINBERG, M. S. (1978). *Homosexualities: A study of diversity among men and women.* New York: Simon & Schuster.

BILLY, J. O., & UDRY, J. R. (1985). The influence of male and female best friends on adolescent behavior. *Adolescence, 20,* 21–32.

BLUMSTEIN, P., & SCHWARTZ, P. (1983). *American couples.* New York: Morrow.

BLUMSTEIN, P., & SCHWARTZ, P. (1990). Intimate relationships and the creation of sexuality. In D. P. McWhirter, S. A. Sanders, & J. M. Reinisch (Eds.), *Homosexuality/heterosexuality: Concepts of sexual orientation* (pp. 307–320). New York: Oxford University Press.

CASS, V. C. (1990). The implications of homosexual identity formation for the Kinsey Model and Scale of Sexual Preference. In D. P. McWhirter, S. A. Sanders, & J. M. Reinisch (Eds.), *Homosexuality/heterosexuality: Concepts of sexual orientation* (pp. 239–266). New York: Oxford University Press.

CHILMAN, C. (1990). Promoting healthy adolescent sexuality. *Family Relations, 39,* 123–131.

CHRISTOPHER, F. S., & ROOSA, M. W. (1990). An evaluation of an adolescent prevention program: Is "just say no" enough? *Family Relations, 39,* 68–72.

CROOKS, R., & BAUR, K. (1990). *Our sexuality.* Redwood City, CA: Benjamin/Cummings.

DeLAMATER, J., & MacQUORDALE, P. (1980). *Premarital sexuality.* Madison, WI: University of Wisconsin Press.

DENNIS, W. (1992). *Hot and bothered: Sex and love in the nineties.* New York: Viking.

ELLIS, B. J., & SYMONS, D. (1990). Sex differences in sexual fantasy: An evolutionary psychological approach. *Journal of Sex Research, 27,* 527–555.

Facing grim data on young males: Blacks grope for ways to end blight. (1990, July 17). *The New York Times,* p. A14.

FAY, R. F., TURNER, C. F., KLASSEN, A. D., & GAGNON, J. H. (1989). Prevalence and patterns of same-gender sexual contact among men. *Science, 243,* 338–348.

FOOTE, N. (1954). Sex as play. *Social Problems, 1,* 159–163.

FORD, C. S., & BEACH, F. A. (1951). *Patterns of sexual behavior.* New York: Harper.

FORSTE, R. T., & HEATON, T. B. (1988). Initiation of sexual activity among female adolescents. *Youth and Society, 19,* 250–268.

FRANCOEUR, R. T. (1987). Human sexuality. In M. B. Sussman & S. K. Steinmetz (Eds.), *Handbook of marriage and the family* (pp. 509–534). New York: Plenum.

FRANK, E., & ANDERSON, C. (1991). The sexual stages of marriage. In J. N. Edwards & D. H. Demo (Eds.), *Marriage and family in transition* (pp. 186–190). Boston: Allyn and Bacon.

GALLUP ORGANIZATION. (1989, February). Knowledge of AIDS is widespread. Many taking preventive measures. *Gallup Report, 281,* 24–27.

GLAZER, S. (1989). Sex education: How well does it work? *Editorial Research Reports, 1,* 338–350.

GREELEY, A. M., MICHAEL, R. T., & SMITH, T. W. (1990). Americans and their sexual partners. *Society, 27,* 36–42.

GREENBLAT, C. S. (1991). Sexuality in the early years of marriage. In J. N. Edwards & D. H. Demo (Eds.), *Marriage and family in transition* (pp. 175–185). Boston: Allyn and Bacon.

HARRIS, L., & ASSOCIATES. (1986). *American teens speak: Sex, myths, TV, and birth control.* New York: Louis Harris and Associates.

HARRIS, L., & ASSOCIATES. (1988). *Sex education and AIDS education in the schools.* New York: Louis Harris and Associates.

HAYES, C. (1987). *Risking the future: Adolescent sexuality, pregnancy and childbearing, Vol. 1,* Washington, DC: National Academy Press.

HERDT, G. (1990). Developmental discontinuities and sexual orientation across cultures. In D. P. McWhirter, S. A. Sanders, & J. M. Reinisch (Eds.), *Homosexuality/heterosexuality: Concepts of sexual orientation* (pp. 208–236). New York: Oxford University Press.

HEREK, G. M. (1988). Heterosexuals' attitudes toward lesbians and gay men: Correlates and gender differences. *The Journal of Sex Research, 25,* 451–477.

HITE, S. (1987). *The Hite Report: Women and love.* New York: Knopf.

HOFFERTH, S. L. (1987). Contraceptive decision-making among adolescents. In S. L. Hofferth & C. D. Hayes (Eds.), *Risking the future: Adolescent sexuality, pregnancy, and childbearing: Vol. 2,* Washington, DC: National Academy Press.

HUNT, M. (1974). *Sexual behavior in the 1970s.* New York: Dell.

JACOBY, A. P., & WILLIAMS, J. D. (1985). Effects of premarital sexual standards and behavior on dating and marriage desirability. *Journal of Marriage and the Family, 47,* 1059–1065.

KAGAY, M. R. (1991, June 18). Poll finds AIDS causes single people to alter behavior. *The New York Times,* p. A1.

KANTROWITZ, B. (1990). Breaking the poverty cycle. *Newsweek, 115*(22), 78.

KINSEY, A., & GEBHARD, P. (1953). *Sexual behavior in the human female.* Philadelphia, PA: Saunders.

KINSEY, A., POMEROY, W., & MARTIN, C. (1948). *Sexual behavior in the human male.* Philadelphia, PA: Saunders.

KLASSEN, A., WILLIAMS, C., & LEVITT, E. (1989). *Sex and morality in the U.S.* Middletown, CT: Wesleyan University Press.

KOTTAK, C. (1991). *Anthropology: The exploration of human diversity.* New York: McGraw-Hill.

KURDEK, L. A. (1988). Correlates of negative attitudes toward homosexuals in heterosexual college students. *Sex Roles, 18,* 727–738.

MACKLIN, E. D. (1987). Nontraditional family forms. In M. B. Sussman & S. K. Steinmetz (Eds.), *Handbook of marriage and the family* (pp. 317–354). New York: Plenum.

MASTERS, V., & JOHNSON, W. H. (1976). *The pleasure bond.* New York: Bantam.

MASTERS, V., & JOHNSON, W. H. (1986). *Sex and human loving.* Boston: Little, Brown.

McCARTHY, P. (1989). Ageless sex. *Psychology Today, 22*(3), 62.

McWHIRTER, D. P., SANDERS, S. A., & REINISCH, J. M. (Eds.). (1990). *Homosexuality/heterosexuality: Concepts of sexual orientation.* New York: Oxford University Press.

MILLER, B. C., McCOY, J. K., & OLSON, T. D. (1986). Dating age and stage as correlates of adolescent sexual behavior. *Journal of Adolescent Research, 1,* 361–371.

MILLER, B. C., & MOORE, K. (1991). Adolescent sexual behavior, pregnancy, and parenting: Research through the 1980s. In A. Booth (Ed.), *Contemporary families: Looking forward, looking back* (pp. 307–326). Minneapolis, MN: National Council on Family Relations.

MOORE, K., & PETERSON, J. (1989). *The consequences of teenage pregnancy: Final report.* Washington, DC: Child Trends.

MOORE, K. M., SIMMS, M. C., & BETSEY, C. L. (1986). *Choice and circumstance.* New Brunswick, NJ: Transaction Books.

New teen-age codes amid old anxiety. (1989, February 22). *The New York Times,* p. B11.

NEWCOMER, S. F., & UDRY, J. R. (1987). Parental marital status effects on adolescent sexual behavior. *Journal of Marriage and the Family, 49,* 235–240.

PAINTER, K. (1991, March 5). Fewer kids save sex for adulthood. *USA Today,* pp. D1, D8.

PRATT, W. F. (1990). *Premarital sexual behavior, multiple sexual partners, and marital experience.* Paper presented at the annual meeting of the Population Association of America. Toronto, Canada.

RANDOLPH, L. B. (1990, August). Sex and young blacks. *Ebony,* pp. 46–50.

REISS, I. L. (1986). *Journey into sexuality: An exploratory voyage.* Englewood Cliffs, NJ: Prentice-Hall.

REISS, I. L. (1991). *An end to shame: Shaping our next sexual revolution.* New York: Prometheus.

RICHARDSON, L. (1986). Another world. *Psychology Today, 19,* 22–27.

ROBINSON, I., ZISS, K., GANZA, B., & KATZ, S. (1991). Twenty years of the sexual revolution, 1965–1985: An update. *Journal of Marriage and the Family, 53,* 216–220.

ROPER ORGANIZATION. (1985). *The Virginia Slims American women's opinion poll.* New York: Roper Organization.

SALHOLZ, E. (1990, March 12). The future of gay America. *Newsweek, 115,* 20–27.

SANDERS, S. A., REINISCH, J. M., & McWHIRTER, D. P. (1990). Homosexuality/heterosexuality: An overview. In D. P. McWhirter, S. A. Sanders, & J. M. Reinisch (Eds.), *Homosexuality/heterosexuality: Concepts of sexual orientation* (pp. XIX–XXVII). New York: Oxford University Press.

SARREL, L., & SARREL, P. (1990). *Sexual unfolding.* Boston: Little, Brown.

SAVIN-WILLIAMS, R. C. (1990). *Gay and lesbian youth: Expressions of identity.* New York: Hemisphere.

SELIGMANN, J. (1990, September 17). A new survey on sex. *Newsweek, 172,* 174.

SMITH, E., & UDRY, J. R. (1985). Coital and noncoital sexual behaviors of white and black adolescents. *American Journal of Public Health, 75,* 1200–1203.

SMITH, T. W. (1990, February). *Adult sexual behavior in 1989: Number of partners, frequency, and risk.* Paper presented at the American Association for the Advancement of Science. New Orleans, LA.

SMITH, T. W. (1991). Adult sexual behavior in 1989: Number of partners, frequency of intercourse, and risk of AIDS. *Family Planning Perspectives, 23*(3), 102–107.

SONENSTEIN, F. L., PLECK, J. H., & KU, L. C. (1989). Sexual activity, condom use, and AIDS awareness among adolescent males. *Family Planning Perspectives, 21*(3), 152–158.

SPRECHER, S. (1988). A revision of the Reiss premarital sexual permissiveness scale. *Journal of Marriage and the Family, 50,* 821–828.

STARK, E. (1989). Teen sex: Not for love. *Psychology Today, 22,* 10–11.

STOLLER, R. J., & HERDT, G. (1985). Theories of origins of male homosexuality: A cross-cultural look. *Archives of General Psychiatry, 42*(4), 399–404.

TAYLOR, R., CHATTERS, L., TUCKER, M., & LEWIS, E. (1991). Developments in research on black families. In A. Booth (Ed.), *Contemporary families* (pp. 275–296). Minneapolis, MN: National Council on Family Relations.

THORNTON, A. D. (1990). The courtship process and adolescent sexuality. *Journal of Family Issues, 11,* 239–273.

TOUFEXIS, A. (1992, August 17). Bisexuality: What Is It? *Time,* pp. 49–51.

VANCE, C. (1984). *Pleasure and danger: Exploring female sexuality.* London: Routledge.

VERMEULEN, K. (1990, June 30). Growing up in the shadow of AIDS. *The New York Times,* p. E1.

VISHER, E., & VISHER, J. (1988). *Old loyalties, new ties.* New York: Brunner/Mazel.

WALDROP, J. (1991). First love. *American Demographics, 13*(7), 4.

WALES, L. H., & KLUCKHOHN, R. (1974). *The Navaho.* Cambridge: Harvard University Press.

WILLIAMS, J. D., & JACOBY, A. P. (1989). The effects of premarital heterosexual and homosexual experience on dating and marriage desirability. *Journal of Marriage and the Family, 51,* 489–497.

WILSON, M. (1987, April 16). Frontlines: Coming out to new perspective. *Windy City Times,* p. 8.

WINTER, L. (1988). The role of sexual self-concept in the use of contraceptives. *Family Planning Perspectives, 20,* 123–127.

Chapter 7

ALDOUS, J. (1978). *Family careers: Developmental change in families.* New York: Wiley.

ALDOUS, J. (1990). Family development and the life course: Two perspectives on family change. *Journal of Marriage and the Family, 52,* 571–583.

AQUILINO, W. S. (1990). The likelihood of parent and child coresidence: Effects of family structure and parental characteristics. *Journal of Marriage and the Family, 52,* 405–419.

AQUILINO, W. S., & SUPPLE, K. R. (1991). Parent-child relations and parents' satisfaction with living arrangements when adult children live at home. *Journal of Marriage and the Family, 53,* 13–27.

BARBER, C. E. (1989). Transition to the empty nest. In S. J. Bahr & E. T. Peterson (Ed.), *Aging in the family* (pp. 15–33). Lexington, MA: Lexington Books.

BECK, R. W., & BECK, S. W. (1989). The incidence of extended households among middle-aged black and white women. *Journal of Family Issues, 10,* 147–168.

BECKMAN, L. J., & GIORDANO, J. A. (1986). Illness and impairment in elderly couples. *Family Relations, 34,* 257–264.

BENGTSON, V., & ROBERTSON, J. (Eds.). (1985). *Grandparenthood.* Beverly Hills, CA: Sage Publications.

BLUMSTEIN, P., & SCHWARTZ, P. (1983). *American couples.* New York: Morrow.

BOUVIER, L. F., & DE VITA, C. J. (1991). The baby boom: Entering midlife. *Population Bulletin, 46*(3), 1–34.

BRIM, O., & KAGAN, J. (1980). *Constancy and change in human development.* Boston, MA: Harvard University Press.

BRUBAKER, T. (Ed.). (1990). *Family relationships in later life.* Beverly Hills, CA: Sage Publications.

BRUBAKER, T. (1991). Families in later life. In A. Booth (Ed.), *Contemporary families* (pp. 226–248). Minneapolis, MN: National Council on Family Relations.

BURTON, L., & BENGTSON, V. (1985). Black grandmothers. In V. Bengtson & J. Robertson (Eds.), *Grandparenthood* (pp. 61–77). Beverly Hills, CA: Sage Publications.

CARTER, B., & McGOLDRICK, M. (Eds.). (1989). *The changing family life cycle: A framework for family therapy.* Boston: Allyn and Bacon.

CHERLIN, A., & FURSTENBERG, F. (1986). *The new American grandparent.* New York: Basic Books.

COHEN, R. (1987). Suddenly I'm the adult. *Psychology Today, 21*(5), 70–71.

COLARUSSO, C. A., & NEMIROFF, R. A. (1981). *Adult development: A new dimension in psychodynamic theory and practice.* New York: Plenum.

COWAN, C. P., & COWAN, P. A. (1992). *When partners become parents.* New York: J. Wiley.

COWAN, C. P., & COWAN, P. A. (1992). Why the passage to parenthood rocks even the best couples today. *Psychology Today, 25*(4), 59–63, 78–79.

CUBER, J. F., & HARROFF, P. (1968). *Sex and the significant Americans.* Baltimore, MD: Penguin.

DEAN, A., KOLODY, B., WOOD, P., & ENSEL, W. (1989). Measuring the communication of social support from adult children. *Journal of Marriage and the Family, 44,* 71–79.

DELLMAN-JENKINS, M., PAPALIA, D., & LOPEZ, M. (1987). Teenagers' reported interaction with grandparents. *Lifestyles, 8,* 35–46.

DUVALL, E. (1988). Family development's first forty years. *Family Relations, 37,* 127–134.

ERIKSON, E. (1963). *Childhood and society.* New York: Norton.

FITZPATRICK, M. A. (1988). *Between husbands and wives: Communication in marriage.* Newbury Park, CA: Sage Publications.

FLAHERTY, M., FACTEAU, L., & GARVER, P. (1987). Grandmother functions in multigenerational families: An exploratory study of black adolescent mothers and their infants. *Maternal Child Nursing Journal, 16,* 61–73.

GILFORD, R. (1986). Marriages in later life. *Generations, 10,* 16–20.

GILLIGAN, C. (1982). *In a different voice: Psychological theory and women's development.* Cambridge, MA: Harvard University Press.

GILLIGAN, C. (1988). *Mapping the moral domain: A contribution of women's thinking to psychological theory and education.* Cambridge, MA: Harvard University Press.

GLENN, N. (1990). Quantitative research on marital quality in the 1980s: A critical review. *Journal of Marriage and the Family, 52,* 818–831.

GLENN, N. (1991). The recent trend in marital success in the United States. *Journal of Marriage and the Family, 53,* 261–270.

GLENN, N., & McLANAHAN, S. (1981). The contribution of marital happiness to global happiness. *Journal of Marriage and the Family, 43,* 409–421.

GOODMAN, E. (1991, June 4). The "two-someness' of marriage is not what it used to be. *Roanoke Times and World-News,* p. A7.

GROSS, J. (1991, June 16). More young single men hang on to apron strings. *The New York Times,* pp. A1, 18.

HAREVEN, T. (1987). Historical analysis of the family. In M. B. Sussman & S. K. Steinmetz (Eds.), *Handbook of marriage and the family* (pp. 37–58). New York: Plenum.

HEINEMANN, G. D. (1982). Why study widowed women: A rationale. *Women and Health, 7,* 17–29.

HEINEMANN, G. D., & EVANS, P. L. (1990). Widowhood: Loss, change, and adaptation. In T. H. Brubaker (Ed.), *Family relationships in later life* (pp. 142–168). Newbury Park, CA: Sage Publications.

KIVETT, V. (1985). Grandfathers and grandchildren: Patterns of association, helping, and psychological closeness. *Family Relations, 34,* 565–571.

KLEBAN, M., BRODY, E., SHOONOVER, C., & HOFFMAN, C. (1989). Family help to the elderly: Perceptions of sons-in-law regarding parent care. *Journal of Marriage and the Family, 51,* 303–312.

LAUER, R. H., & LAUER, J. C. (1986). Factors in long-term marriages. *Journal of Family Issues, 7,* 382–390.

LEVINSON, D. (1978). *The seasons of a man's life.* New York: Knopf.

LEWIS, R., FRENEAU, P., & ROBERTS, C. (1979). Fathers and the postparental transition. *Family Coordinator, 28,* 514–520.

LYND, R. S., & LYND, H. M. (1929). *Middletown.* New York: Harcourt, Brace.

MALATESTA, V. J. (1989). On making love last in a marriage: Reflections of 60 widows. *Clinical Gerontologist, 9,* 64–67.

MANCINI, J. A., & BLIESZNER, R. (1991). Aging parents and adult children. In A. Booth (Ed.), *Contemporary families* (pp. 249–264). Minneapolis, MN: National Council on Family Relations.

MATTESSICH, P., & HILL, R. (1987). Life cycle and family development. In M. B. Sussman & S. K. Steinmetz (Eds.), *Handbook of marriage and the family* (pp. 437–469). New York: Plenum.

MATTHEWS, S. H., & ROSNER, T. (1988). Shared filial responsibility: The family as the primary caregiver. *Journal of Marriage and the Family, 50,* 185–195.

McCULLOUGH, P., & RUTENBERG, S. (1989). Launching children and moving on. In B. Carter & M. McGoldrick (Eds.), *The changing family life cycle* (pp. 285–309). Boston: Allyn and Bacon.

NEUGARTEN, B., & NEUGARTEN, D. (1987). The changing meaning of age. *Psychology Today, 21*(5), 29–33.

O'REILLY, B. (1992). How to take care of aging parents. *Fortune, 125*(10), 108–112.

OSTROFF, J. (1991). Targeting the prime-life consumer. *American Demographics, 13,* 30–34, 52–53.

PAUKER, S., & AROND, M. (1989). *The first year of marriage: What to expect, what to accept and what you can change.* New York: Warner Books.

PRETO, N. G. (1989). Transformation of the family system in adolescence. In B. Carter & M. McGoldrick (Eds.), *The changing family life cycle* (pp. 255–286). Boston: Allyn and Bacon.

A profile of older Americans. (1990). American Association of Retired Persons: Washington, DC.

RAUP, J., & MYERS, J. (1989). The empty nest syndrome: Myth or reality? *Journal of Counseling and Development, 68,* 180–183.

REMONDET, J. H., & HANSSON, R. O. (1987). Assessing a widow's grief: A short index. *Journal of Gerontological Nursing, 13,* 30–34.

ROBINSON, J. (1991). Quitting time. *American Demographics, 13,* 34–36.

ROLLINS, B. C., & CANNON, K. L. (1974). Marital satisfaction over the family life cycle: A reevaluation. *Journal of Marriage and the Family, 36,* 271–282.

ROSENFELD, A., & STARK, E. (1987). The prime of our lives. *Psychology Today, 21*(5), 62–72.

ROSS, C. E., MIROWSKY, J., & GOLDSTEEN, K. (1991). The impact of the family on health. In A. Booth (Ed.), *Contemporary families* (pp. 341–360). Minneapolis, MN: National Council on Family Relations.

RYFF, C. (1986). The subjective construction of self and society: An agenda for life-span research. In V. W. Marshall (Ed.), *Later life: The social psychology of aging.* Beverly Hills, CA: Sage Publications.

SCHMIDT, A., & PADILLA, A. (1983). Grandparent-grandchild interaction in Mexican-American groups. *Hispanic Journal of Behavioral Sciences, 5,* 181–198.

SCHNAIBERG, A., & GOLDENBERG, S. (1989). From empty nest to crowded nest: The dynamics of incompletely launched young adults. *Social Problems, 36,* 251–269.

SELIGSON, M. (1974). *The eternal bliss machine: America's way of wedding.* New York: Bantam.

SHEEHY, G. (1976). *Passages: Predictable crisis in adult life.* New York: Bantam.

SMEEDLING, T. M. (1990). Economic status of the elderly. In R. H. Binstock & L. K. Geoge (Eds.), *Handbook on Aging and the Social Sciences* (pp. 362–381). New York: Academic Press.

SOLDO, B. J., & AGREE, E. M. (1988). America's elderly. *Population Bulletin, 43*(3), 1–35.

SPANIER, G. (1976). Measuring dyadic adjustment. *Journal of Marriage and the Family, 41,* 15–28.

STEPHENS, W. (1963). *The family in cross-cultural perspective.* New York: Holt.

STONE, R., CAFFERATA, G., & SANGL, J. (1987). Caregivers of the frail elderly: A national profile. *The Gerontologist, 27,* 622–632.

TAYLOR, R. J., CHATTERS, L. M., TUCKER, M. B., & LEWIS, E. (1991). Developments in research on black families. In A. Booth (Ed.), *Contemporary families* (pp. 275–296). Minneapolis, MN: National Council on Family Relations.

THOMAS, J. (1986). Gender differences in satisfaction with grandparenting. *Psychology and Aging, 1,* 215–219.

TREAS, J., BENGTSON, V. L. (1987). The family in later years. In M. B. Sussman & S. K. Steinmetz (Eds.), *Handbook of marriage and the family* (pp. 625–648). New York: Plenum.

WALKER, A. J., & PRATT, C. C. (1991). Daughters' help to mothers: Intergenerational aid versus caregiving. *Journal of Marriage and the Family, 53,* 3–12.

WALKER, A. J., THOMPSON, L., & MORGAN, C. S. (1987). Two generations of mothers and daughters: Role position and interdependence. *Psychology of Women Quarterly, 11,* 195–208.

WEITZMAN, L. J. (1985). *The divorce revolution.* New York: Free Press.

WILCOX, M. D. (1992). Boomerang kids. *Kiplinger's Personal Finance Magazine, 46*(10), 83–86.

WILSON, M. (1984). Mothers' and grandmothers' perceptions of parental behavior in three-generation black families. *Child Development, 55,* 1333–1339.

WILSON, W. J. (1989). The ghetto underclass: Social science perspectives. *Annals of the American Academy of Political and Social Science, 501,* 8–192.

ZINN, L., POWER, C., YANG, D. J., CUNEO, A. Z., & ROSS, D. (1992). Move over, boomers: The busters are here—and they're angry. *Business Week,* (3297), pp. 74–79, 82.

ZUBE, M. (1982). Changing behavior and outlook of aging men and women. *Family Relations, 31,* 147–156.

Chapter 8

ABBEY, A., ANDREWS, F., & HALMAN, L. (1991). Gender's role in responses to infertility. *Psychology of Women Quarterly, 15,* 295–316.

ADAMS, G., ADAMS-TAYLOR, S., & PITTMAN, K. (1989). Adolescent pregnancy and parenthood: A review of the problem, solutions, and resources. *Family Relations, 38,* 223–229.

American Demographics. (1990, January). p. 37.

BACHRACH, C. (1984). Contraceptive practice among American women. *Family Planning Perspectives, 16*(6), 253–258.

BACHRACH, C., & HORN, M.(1987). *Married and unmarried couples in the U.S.* Hyattsville, MD: U.S. Department of Health and Human Services.

BACKRACH, C., ADAMS, P., SAMBRANO, S., & LONDON, K. (1990). *Adoption in the 1980s* (Advance Data No. 181, from Vital and Health Statistics). Hyattsville, MD: National Center for Health Statistics.

BARNETT, R. C., & BARUCH, G. K. (1987). Social roles, gender, and psychological distress. In *Gender and stress* (pp. 122–143). New York: Free Press.

BARUCH, G. K., BARNETT, R. C., & RIVERS, C. (1983). *Lifeprints: New patterns of love and work for today's women.* New York: McGraw-Hill.

BELKIN, L. (1985, May 23). Parents weigh costs of children. *The New York Times.*

BIANCHI, S. M. (1990). America's children's mixed prospects. *Population Bulletin, 45,* 1–43.

BIGNER, J. J., & BOZETT, F. W. (1990). Parenting by gay fathers. In K. Boh, G. Sgritti, & M. B. Sussman (Eds.), *Homosexuality and family relations* (pp. 155–173). New York: Haworth.

BIGNER, J. J., & JACOBSEN, R. B. (1989). The value of children to gay and heterosexual fathers. In F. W. Bozett (Ed.), *Homosexuality and the family* (pp. 163–171). New York: Harrington Park.

BLOOM, D. E., & TRUSSELL, J. W. (1984). What are the determinants of delayed childbearing and permanent childlessness in the U.S.? *Family Relations, 29,* 181–183.

BOWLBY, J. (1953). *Child care and the growth of love.* Baltimore, MD: Penguin.

BOYD, C. J. (1989). Mothers and daughters: A discussion of theory and research. *Journal of Marriage and the Family, 51,* 291–301.

BOZETT, F. W. (1987). Gay fathers. In F. W. Bozett (Ed.), *Gay and lesbian parents* (pp. 3–22). New York: Praeger.

BOZETT, F. W. (1988). Gay fatherhood. In P. Bronstein, & C. P. Cowan (Eds.), *Fatherhood today: Men's changing role in the family* (pp. 214–235). New York: Wiley.

BROBERG, G. C. (1988). Fatherhood: Rediscovered in empirical research. *Family Relations, 22,* 75–85.

CHRISTOPHER, F. S., & ROOSA, M. W. (1990). An evaluation of an adolescent pregnancy prevention program: Is "just say no" enough? *Family Relations, 39,* 68–72.

CUTLER, B. (1990). Rock-a-buy Baby. *American Demographics, 12*(1), 35–39.

DEMO, D. (1992). Parent-child relations: Assessing recent changes. *Journal of Marriage and the Family, 54,* 104–117.

Despite troubles, members say families stay close. (1991, November 22). *Roanoke Times and World-News*, p. A3.

DiLapi, E. M. (1989). Lesbian mothers and the motherhood hierarchy. In F. W. Bozett (Ed.), *Homosexuality and the family* (pp. 101–121). New York: Harrington Park.

Dreyfous, L. (1991, October 15). One is enough: A look at the pros and cons of having, and being, an only child. *Roanoke Times and World-News*, pp. E1, 3.

Dubow, E., & Luster, T. (1990). Adjustment of children born to teenage mothers: The contribution of risk and protective factors. *Journal of Marriage and the Family, 52*, 393–404.

Ethnic babies come to toyland (1991, June). *American Demographics, 13*, 10.

Exter, T. (1990). Married with kids. *American Demographics, 12*, 55.

Farber, N. (1990). The significance of race and class in marital decisions among unmarried adolescent mothers. *Social Problems, 37*, 51–63.

Fischer, L. R. (1986). *Linked lives: Adult daughters and their mothers.* New York: Harper & Row.

Fischer, L. R. (1991). Between mothers and daughters. *Marriage and Family Review, 16*, 237–248.

Forrest, J., & Singh, S. (1990). The impact of public-sector expenditures for contraceptive services in California. *Family Planning Perspectives, 22*(4), 161–172.

Furstenberg, F. (1991). As the pendulum swings: Teenage childbearing and social concern. *Family Relations, 40*, 127–138.

Furstenberg, F., Levine, J., & Brooks-Gunn, J. (1990). The daughters of teenage mothers: Patterns of early childbearing in two generations. *Family Planning Perspectives, 22*(2), 54–61.

Gallup, G. H., & Newport, F. (1990). Virtually all adults want children, but many of the reasons are intangible. *The Gallup Poll Monthly, 297*, 8–22.

Gelder, L. V. (1991, March/April). A lesbian family. *Ms.*, pp. 44–47.

Gilbert, L., Hanson, G., & Davis, B. (1982). Perceptions of parental role responsibilities: Differences between mothers and fathers. *Family Relations, 31*, 261–269.

Goldsteen, K., & Ross, C. E. (1989). The perceived burden of children. *Journal of Family Issues, 10*, 504–526.

Gregory, S. C. (1992, August 10). Teaching young fathers the ropes. *Time, 140*, 49.

Greil, A. L., Leitko, T. A., & Porter, K. L. (1988). Infertility: His and hers. *Gender and Society, 2*, 172–199.

Hammonds, K. H., & Symonds, W. C. (1991, April 15). *Business Week, 3209*, pp. 90–92.

Higgins, B. S. (1990). Couple infertility: From the perspective of the close-relationship model. *Family Relations, 39*, 81–86.

Hoeffer, B. (1985). Children's acquisition of sex-role behavior in lesbian mother families. *American Journal of Orthopsychiatry, 51*, 536–544.

Houseknecht, S. K. (1987). Voluntary childlessness. In M. B. Sussman and S. K. Steinmetz (Eds.), *Handbook of marriage and the family* (pp. 369–395). New York: Plenum.

Jones, L. (1980). *Great expectations.* New York: Coward, McCann, and Geoghegan.

Kantrowitz, B. (1986, June 16). Only but not lonely. *Newsweek*, pp. 66–67.

Kantrowitz, B. (1990). Breaking the poverty cycle. *Newsweek, 115*(22), 78.

Kenkel, W. F. (1985). The desire for voluntary childlessness among low-income youth. *Journal of Marriage and the Family, 47*, 509–512.

Kisker, E. (1985). Teenagers talk about sex, pregnancy, and contraception. *Family Planning Perspectives, 17*(3), 83–89.

Kolata, G. (1987, September 22). Tests of fetuses rise sharply amid doubts. *The New York Times*, p. D6.

Kolata, G. (1989). *The baby doctors.* New York: Delacorte.

LaRossa, R. (1988). Fatherhood and social change. *Family Relations, 37*, 451–457.

LaRossa, R., Gordon, B. A., Wilson, R., Bairan, A., & Jaret, C. (1991). The fluctuating image of the 20th century American father. *Journal of Marriage and the Family, 53*, 987–997.

LeMasters, E. E., & DeFrain, J. (1989). *Parents in contemporary America.* New York: Wadsworth.

Lewin, E., & Lyons, T. (1982). Everything in its place: The coexistence of lesbianism and motherhood. In W. Paul, J. C. Gonsiorek, & M. E. Hotvedt (Eds.), *Homosexuality: Social, psychological, and biological issues* (pp. 249–273). Beverly Hills, CA: Sage Publications.

Lidz, T. (1968). *The person: His development through the life cycle.* New York: Basic Books.

Los Angeles Times. (1990, October 23). p. A6.

Magnet, M. (1992, August 10). The American family, 1992. *Fortune*, pp. 43–49.

McAdoo, H. P. (Ed.). (1988). *Black families.* Newbury Park, CA: Sage Publications.

McAdoo, H. P. & McAdoo, J. L. (Eds.). (1985). *Black Children.* Beverly Hills, CA: Sage Publications.

McAdoo, J. L. (1986). Black fathers' relationships with their children. In R. Lewis, & R. Salt (Eds.), *Men in families* (pp. 169–180). Beverly Hills, CA: Sage Publications.

McBride, B. A. (1990). The effects of parent education/play group programs on father involvement in child rearing. *Family Relations, 39*, 250–256.

McLanahan, S., & Adams, J. (1987). Parenthood and psychological well-being. In W. R. Scott & J. Blake (Eds.), *Ananual review of sociology* (pp. 237–257). Palo Alto, CA: Annual Review.

McLanahan, S., & Booth, K. (1991). Mother-only families: Problems, prospects, and politics. In A. Booth (Ed.), *Contemporary families* (pp. 405–428). Minneapolis, MN: National Council on Family Relations.

Menaghan, E. G. (1989). Psychological well-being among parents and nonparents. *Journal of Family Issues, 10*, 547–565.

Miall, C. E. (1989). The stigma of involuntary childlessness. In A. Skolnick & J. Skolnick (Eds.), *Family in transition* (pp. 387–404). Boston: Scott, Foresman.

Mindel, C. H., Habenstein, R. W., & Wright, R. (Eds.). (1988). *Ethnic families in America: Patterns and variations* (3rd ed.). New York: Elsevier.

Mintz, S., & Kellogg, S. (1988). *Domestic revolutions: A social history of American family life.* New York: Free Press.

Mosher, W. D. (1990). *Fecundity and infertility in the United States* (Advance Data, 192). Washington, DC: U.S. Department of Health and Human Services.

National Center for Health Statistics. (1992, July). Annual summary of births, marriages, divorces, and deaths. *Vital Sta-*

tistics (No. 40). Washington, DC: U.S. Department of Health and Human Services.

NATIONAL COMMITTEE FOR ADOPTION. (1989). *Adoption Factbook II*. Washington, DC: National Committee for Adoption.

O'HARE, V. P., POLLARD, K. U., MANN, T. L., & KENT, M. M. (1990). African Americans in the 1990s. *Population Bulletin, 46*(1), 11.

PARKE, R. D., & SAWIN, D. B. (1977). Fathering: It's a major role. *Psychology Today*, pp. 28–32.

PEAR, R. (1991, December 3). Bigger number of new mothers are unmarried. *The New York Times*, p. E7

PENNINGTON, S. (1987). Children of lesbian mothers. In F. W. Bozett (Ed.), *Gay and lesbian parents* (pp. 58–74). New York: Praeger.

PIES, C. A. (1990). Lesbians and the choice to parent. In K. Boh, G. Sgritta, & M. B. Sussman (Eds.), *Homosexuality and family relations*. New York: Haworth.

PITTMAN, J. F., WRIGHT, C. A., & LLOYD, S. A. (1989). Predicting parenting difficulty. *Journal of Family Issues, 10,* 267–286.

PRATT, W. F., MOSHER, W. D., BACHRACH, C., & HORN, M. (1984). *Understanding U.S. fertility: Findings from the National Survey of Family Growth*. Washington, DC: Population Reference Bureau.

RAUCH, J. (1989). Kids as capital. *Atlantic Monthly, 264,* 56–61.

RAWLINGS, S. W. (1989). Single parents and their children. In Current Population Reports, *Studies in Marriage and the Family* (Series P-23, No. 162). Washington, DC: Bureau of the Census.

ROSSI, A. S. (1977, Spring). A biosocial perspective on parenting. *Daedalus*, pp. 1–3.

SECCOMBE, K. (1991). Assessing the costs and benefits of children: Gender comparisons among childfree husbands and wives. *Journal of Marriage and the Family, 53,* 191–202.

SPOCK, B. (1945). *Baby and child care*. New York: Duell, Sloan & Pearce.

SPOCK, B., & ROTHENBERG, M. (1985). *Baby and child care*. New York: Dutton.

STECKEL, A. (1987). Psychosocial development of children of lesbian mothers. In F. W. Bozett (Ed.), *Gay and lesbian parents* (pp. 75–85). New York: Praeger.

STRONG, C., & SCHINFELD, J. S. (1984). The single woman and artificial insemination by donor. *Journal of Reproductive Medicine, 29,* 293–299.

Taking baby steps toward a daddy track. (1991, April 15). *Business Week, 3209,* pp. 90–92.

TAYLOR, R. CHATTERS, L., TUCKER, M., & LEWIS, E. (1991). Developments in research on black families. In A. Booth (Ed.), *Contemporary families* (pp. 275–296). Minneapolis, MN: National Council on Family Relations.

TIMBERLAKE, C. A., & CARPENTER, W. D. (1990). Sexuality attitudes of black adults. *Family Relations, 39,* 87–91.

UMBERSON, D., & GOVE, W. R. (1989). Parenthood and psychological well-being. *Journal of Family Issues, 10,* 440–462.

U.S. BUREAU OF THE CENSUS. (1991). *Population Profile of the United States: 1991* (Current Population Reports, Series P-23, No. 173). Washington, DC: U.S. Government Printing Office.

USDANSKY, M. L., & PUENTE, M. (1991, December 4). A baby doesn't mean marriage anymore. *USA Today*, p. A8.

VEEVERS, J. (1979). Voluntary childlessness: A review of issues and evidence. *Marriage and Family Review, 2,* 3–26.

VEEVERS, J. (1990). *Childless by choice*. Toronto: Butterworth.

VEGA, W. (1991). Hispanic families. In A. Booth (Ed.), *Contemporary families* (pp. 297–306). Minneapolis, MN: National Council on Family Relations.

WEITZ, R. (1984). What price independence? Social reactions to lesbians, spinsters, widows, and nuns. In J. Freeman (Ed.), *Women: A feminist perspective* (pp. 454–464). Berkeley, CA: Mayfield.

WILSON, W. (1987). *The truly disadvantaged: The inner city, the underclass, and public policy*. Chicago: University of Chicago Press.

Chapter 9

AHLBURG, D. A., & DE VITA, C. J. (1992, August). New realities of the American family. *Population Bulletin*. Washington, DC: Population Reference Bureau.

ANDERSON, K. (1988). A history of women's work in the United States. In A. H. Stromberg & S. Harkness (Eds.), *Women working* (pp. 25–41). Mountain View, CA: Mayfield.

ASTRACHAN, A. (1986). *How men feel*. New York: Doubleday.

BARNETT, R. C., & BARUCH, G. K. (1987). Social roles, gender, and psychological distress. In R. C. Barnett, L. Biener, & G. K. Baruch (Eds.), *Gender and stress* (pp. 122–143). New York: Free Press.

BARNETT, R. C., MARSHALL, N., & PLECK, J. (1992). Men's multiple roles and their relationship to men's psychological distress. *Journal of Marriage and the Family, 54,* 358–367.

BARNETT, R. C., & RIVERS, C. (1992). The myth of the miserable working woman. *Working Woman, 2,* 62–65, 83–85.

BARUCH, G. K., BARNETT, R., & RIVERS, C. (1983). *Lifeprints: New patterns of love and work for today's women*. New York: McGraw-Hill.

BERHEIDE, C. W. (1984). Women's work in the home. *Marriage and Family Review, 7,* 37–55.

BIRD, C., & FREMONT, A. (1989). *Gender, social roles, and health*. Paper presented at the annual meeting of the American Sociological Association. San Francisco.

BIRD, G. A., & BIRD, G. W. (1985). Determinants of mobility in dual-career families. *Journal of Marriage and the Family, 47,* 753–758.

BIRD, G. A., GOSS, R., & BIRD, G. W. (1990). Effects of home computer use on father's lives. *Family Relations, 39,* 438–442.

BIRD, G. W., & BIRD, G. A. (1984). Determinants of family task sharing: A study of husbands and wives. *Journal of Marriage and the Family, 46,* 345–355.

BIRD, G. W., & BIRD, G. A. (1986). Strategies for reducing role strain in dual-career families. *International Journal of Sociology of the Family, 16,* 83–94.

BIRD, G. W., & BIRD, G. A. (1987). In pursuit of academic careers: Observations and reflections of a dual-career couple. *Family Relations, 36,* 97–100.

CAMINITI, S. (1992, August 10). Who's minding America's kids? *Fortune*, pp. 50–53.

CROSBY, F. (1991). *Juggling*. New York: Free Press.

EPSTEIN, C. (1987). Multiple demands and multiple roles: The conditions of successful management. In F. Crosby (Ed.), *Spouse, parent, worker: On gender and multiple roles* (pp. 23–43). New Haven, CT: Yale University Press.

EHRLICH, E. (1989, March 20). The mommy track. *Business Week*, pp. 126–129, 132, 134.

FALUDI, S. (1991). *Backlash: The undeclared war against American women*. New York: Crown.

FARBER, E., ALEJANDRO-WRIGHT, M., & MUENCHOW, S. (1988). Managing work and family: Hopes and realities. In E. Zigler & M. Frank (Eds.), *The parental leave crisis* (pp. 161–176). New Haven, CT: Yale University Press.

FERREE, M. M. (1987). Family and job for working-class women: Gender and class systems seen from below. In N. Gerstel & H. Gross (Eds.), *Families and work* (pp. 289–301). Philadelphia: Temple University Press.

FERREE, M. M. (1991). Feminism and family research. In A. Booth (Ed.), *Contemporary families* (pp. 103–121). Minneapolis: National Council on Family Relations.

FORD FOUNDATION. (1989). *Work and family responsibilities: Achieving a balance*. New York: Author.

FOX, M. F., & HESSE-BIBER, S. (1984). *Women at work*. Palo Alto, CA: Mayfield.

GALEN, M., SCHILLER, Z., HAMILTON, J., & HAMMONDS, K. H. (1991, March 18). Ending sexual harassment: Business is getting the message. *Business Week*, pp. 98, 100.

GARLAND, S. B., & SEGAL, T. (1991, October 21). Thomas vs. Hill: The lessons for corporate America. *Business Week*, p. 32.

GERSTEL, N., & GROSS, H. (1985). *Commuter marriage*. New York: Guilford.

GILBERT, L. A. (1985). *Men in dual-career families*. Hillsdale, NJ: Erlbaum.

GILBERT, L. A. (1987). Women and men together but equal: Issues for men in dual-career marriages. In M. Scher, M. Stevens, G. Good, & G. Eichenfield (Eds.), *Handbook of counseling and psychotherapy with men* (pp. 278–293). Newbury Park, CA: Sage Publications.

GILBERT, L. A. (1988). *Sharing it all*. New York: Plenum.

GILBERT, L. A. (1993). *Two careers, one family: Facing personal and cultural changes in America*. Newbury Park, CA: Sage Publications.

GORE, S., & MANGIONE, T. (1983). Social roles, sex roles and psychological distress. *Journal of Health and Social Behavior, 24*, 300–312.

GREENHAUS, J. H. (1988). The intersection of work and family roles. In E. Goldsmith (Ed.), *Work and family: Theory, research and applications* (pp. 23–44). Corte Madera, CA: Select Press.

GUELZOW, M., BIRD, G. W., & KOBALL, B. (1991). An exploratory path analysis of the stress process for dual-career men and women. *Journal of Marriage and the Family, 53*, 151–164.

GUPTA, N., & JENKINS, G. (1985). Dual-career couples. In T. Beehr & R. Bhagat (Eds.), *Human stress and cognition in organizations* (pp. 141–175). New York: Wiley.

GUTEK, B., REPETTI, R., & SILVER, D. (1988). Nonwork roles and stress at work. In C. L. Cooper & R. Payne (Eds.), *Causes, coping, and consequences of stress at work* (pp. 141–174). New York: Wiley.

HEWLETT, S. (1991). *When the bough breaks*. New York: Basic Books.

HILLER, D., & PHILLIBER, W. (1986). The division of labor in contemporary marriage: Expectations, perceptions and performance. *Social Problems, 33*, 191–201.

HOCHSCHILD, A. (1989). *The second shift*. New York: Viking.

HOFFMAN, L. W. (1979). Maternal employment: 1979. *American Psychologist, 34*, 859–865.

HOFFMAN, L. W. (1984). Work, family, and the socialization of the child. In R. D. Parke (Ed.), *The family: Vol. 7, Review of child development research* (pp. 223–282). Chicago: University of Chicago Press.

HOFFMAN, L. W. (1989). Effects of maternal employment in the two-parent family. *American Psychologist, 44*, 283–292.

HOLDEN, T., & WIENER, J. (1992, July 13). Revenge of the "office ladies." *Business Week*, pp. 42–43.

HOLDER, D. P., & ANDERSON, C. M. (1989). Women, work, and the family. In M. McGoldrick, C. M. Anderson, & F. Walsh (Eds.), *Women in families* (pp. 357–379). New York: Norton.

KAMERMAN, S., & HAYES, C. (1982). *Families that work: Children in a changing world*. Washington, DC: National Academy Press.

KANG, G. (1991, August 18). Women told families work better as a team. *Roanoke Times and World News*, p. E4.

KANTROWITZ, B., & WINGERT, P. (1993, February). Being smart about the mommy track. *Working Woman*, pp. 48–51, 80–81.

KELLY, R. M. (1991). *The gendered economy: Work, careers, and success*. Newbury Park, CA: Sage Publications.

KNAUB, P. (1986). Growing up in a dual-career family: The children's perceptions. *Family Relations, 35*, 431–437.

KOMTER, A. (1989). Hidden power in marriage. *Gender and Society, 3*, 187–216.

LA CROIX, A. Z., & HAYNES, S. G. (1987). Gender differences in the health effects of workplace roles. In R. C. Barnett, L. Biener, & G. K. Baruch (Eds.), *Gender and stress* (pp. 96–121). New York: Free Press.

LAWSON, C. (1992, April 30). A man's child-care crusade. *The New York Times*, pp. C1, C6.

LEIN, L. (1979). *Families without villains*. Lexington, MA: Lexington Books.

LEWIS, S., & COOPER, C. (1988). Stress in dual-earner families. In B. Gutek & A. Larwood (Eds.), *Women and work: Vol. 3* (pp. 139–168). Newbury Park, CA: Sage Publications.

LUBIN, A. (1987). *Managing success: High-echelon careers and motherhood*. New York: Columbia University Press.

MARSHALL, R., & PAULIN, B. (1987). Employment and earnings of women: Historical perspectives. In K. Koziara, M. Moskow, & L. Tanner (Eds.), *Working women: Past, present, future* (pp. 1–36). Washington, DC: Bureau of National Affairs.

MENAGHAN, E. G., & PARCELL, T. L. (1991). Parental employment and family life: Research in the 1980s. In A. Booth (Ed.), *Contemporary families* (pp. 361–380). Minneapolis: National Council on Family Relations.

MINTZ, S., & KELLOGG, S. (1988). *Domestic revolutions: A social history of American family life*. New York: Free Press.

MORTIMER, J. T., & SORENSEN, G. (1987). Men, women, work, and family. In N. Gerstel & H. Gross (Eds.), *Families and work* (pp. 139–167). Philadelphia: Temple University Press.

NIEVA, V., & GUTEK, B. (1980). Sex effects in evaluation. *Academy of Management Review, 5*, 267–276.

PAINTON, P., SACHS, A., & REID, J. (1991). Office crimes. *Time, 138*(15), pp. 52–54, 63, 64.

PETERSON, K. S. (1992, November 12). The sexes work toward a new era of understanding. *USA Today*, p. 14D.

PIOTRKOWSKI, C. S. (1978). *Work and the family system*. New York: Free Press.

PIOTRKOWSKI, C. S., RAPOPORT, R. N., & RAPOPORT, R. (1987). Families and work. In M. B. Sussman & S. K. Steinmetz (Eds.), *Handbook of marriage and the family* (pp. 251–284). New York: Plenum.

PIOTRKOWSKI, C. S., & REPETTI, R. (1984). Dual-earner families. *Marriage and Family Review, 7,* 99–124.

PLECK, J. (1985). *Working wives, working husbands.* Newbury Park, CA: Sage Publications.

PLECK, J. (1987). The contemporary man. In M. Scher, M. Stevens, G. Good, & G. Eichenfield (Eds.), *Handbook of counseling and psychotherapy with men* (pp. 16–27). Beverly Hills, CA: Sage Publications.

PLECK, J., & RUSTAD, M. (1980). *Husbands' and wives' time in family work and paid work in the 1975–76 study of time use.* Wellesley, MA: Wellesley College Center for Research on Women.

REXROAT, C., & SHEHAN, C. (1987). The family life cycle and spouses' time in housework. *Journal of Marriage and the Family, 49,* 737–750.

RICHARDSON, L. (1992, September 2). No cookie cutter answers in "mommy wars." *The New York Times,* pp. B1, B5.

ROPER ORGANIZATION. (1990). A 20-year perspective on women's issues. The 1990 Virginia Slims opinion poll. New York: Roper Organization.

ROSS, C. E., & MIROWSKY, J. (1988). Child care and emotional adjustment to wives' employment. *Journal of Health and Social Behavior, 29,* 127–138.

ROSS, C. E., MIROWSKY, J., & GOLDSTEEN, K. (1991). The impact of the family on health. In A. Booth (Ed.), *Contemporary families* (pp. 341–360). Minneapolis, MN: National Council on Family Relations.

SALTZMAN, A. (1991). Trouble at the top. *U.S. News and World Report, 110,* (23), pp. 40–42, 44, 46–48.

SCARR, S., PHILLIPS, D., & McCARTNEY, K. (1989). Working mothers and their families. *American Psychologist, 44,* 1402–1409.

SCHNITTGER, M., & BIRD, G. W. (1990). Coping among dual-career men and women across the family life cycle. *Family Relations, 39,* 199–205.

SCHROEDER, P. (1989). Toward a national family policy. *American Psychologist, 44,* 1410–1413.

SEGAL, A. T., & ZELLNER, W. (1992, June 8). Corporate women. *Business Week,* pp. 74–76, 78.

SEKARAN, U. (1986). *Dual-career families.* San Francisco: Josey-Bass.

SKINNER, D. (1982). The stressors and coping patterns of dual-career families. In H. I. McCubbin, A. Cauble, & J. Patterson (Eds.), *Family stress, coping, and social support.* Springfield, IL: Charles C Thomas.

SKOW, J. (1989, August). The myth of male housework. *Time,* p. 62.

STAINES, G. L., POTTICK, K. J., & FUDGE, D. A. (1986). Wives' employment attitudes and husbands' attitudes towards work and life. *Journal of Applied Psychology, 71,* 118–128.

STRIPLING, M. A., & BIRD, G. W. (1990, November). *Antecedents and mediators of well-being among employed women.* Paper presented at the meeting of the National Council on Family Relations. Seattle, WA.

THOMPSON, L. (1991). Family work. *Journal of Family Issues, 12,* 181–196.

TOWNSEND, B., & O'NEILL, K. (1990). American women get mad. *American Demographics, 12*(8), 26–32.

U.S. BUREAU OF THE CENSUS. (1992, August). Money income of households, families, and persons in the United States. *Current Population Reports* (Report No. 174, p. 60). Washington, DC.

U.S. BUREAU OF LABOR STATISTICS. (1990, March). *Women and work.* Washington, DC: U.S. Department of Labor.

U.S. BUREAU OF NATIONAL AFFAIRS. (1986). *Work and family: A changing dynamic.* Washington, DC.

U.S. DEPARTMENT OF LABOR. (1992, March). News release from the Women's Bureau.

VAMOS, M. N. (1992, June 8). The gains are slow, say many women. *Business Week,* p. 77.

VERBRUGGE, L. M., & MADANS, J. H. (1985). Social roles and health trends of American women. *Milbank Memorial Fund Quarterly/Health and Society, 63,* 691–735.

VOYDANOFF, P. (1987a). Women's work, family, and health. In K. S. Kaziara, M. H. Moskow, L. D. Tanner (Eds.), *Working women* (pp. 64–96). Washington, DC: Bureau of National Affairs.

VOYDANOFF, P. (1987b). *Work and family life.* Newbury Park, CA: Sage Publications.

WAKAT, P., & BIRD, G. W. (1990). *Well-being in dual-career marriages.* Paper presented at the annual meeting of the Southeastern Council on Family Relations. Charleston, SC.

WAMPLER, K., & KINGERY, D. (1985, November). *Emphasizing the wife's career: Predictors and consequences.* Paper presented at the meeting of the National Council on Family Relations. Dallas, TX.

WETHINGTON, E., & KESSLER, R. C. (1989). Employment, parental responsibility, and psychological distress: A longitudinal study of married women. *Journal of Family Issues, 10,* 527–546.

What to do if you're a victim of sexual harrassment. (1992, January). *Ladies Home Journal,* p. 46.

Chapter 10

ARGYLE, M., & HENDERSON, M. (1985). *The anatomy of relationships.* London: Heinemann.

ARIÈS, P. (1975, August). The family, prison of love: A conversation with Philippe Ariès. *Psychology Today.*

BANE, M. J. (1976). *Here to stay: American families in the twentieth century.* New York: Basic Books.

BELL, R. (1981). *Worlds of friendship.* Beverly Hills, CA: Sage Publications.

BELLAH, R. N., MADSEN, R., SULLIVAN, W. M., SWIDLER, A., & TIPTON, S. M. (1985). *Habits of the heart.* New York: Harper & Row.

BERGER, J. (1991, October 7). For 200 in the Tenzer family, grandpa's circle is unbroken. *The New York Times,* pp. A1, B5.

BLANKENHORN, D. (1989). Ozzie and Harriet: Have reports of their death been greatly exaggerated? *Family Affair, 2*(2–3), 10.

BLIESZNER, R., & ADAMS, R. (1992). *Adult friendship.* Newbury Park, CA: Sage Publications.

BLOCK, J. (1980). *Friendship: How to give it and how to get it.* New York: Macmillan.

BOTT, E. (1957). *Family and social network.* London: Tavistock.

BREHM, S. S. (1992). *Intimate relationships.* New York: McGraw-Hill.

BURTON, L. M., & DILWORTH-ANDERSON, P. (1991). The intergenerational family roles of aged black Americans. *Marriage and Family Review, 16,* 311–329.

CALDWELL, M., & PEPLAU, L. A. (1982). Sex differences in same-sex friendship. *Sex Roles, 8,* 721–731.

CANCIAN, F. (1987). *Love in America*. New York: Cambridge University Press.

CANTOR, M. H. (1979). The informal support system of New York's inner city elderly: Is ethnicity a factor? In D. Gelfand & A. Kutzik (Eds.), *Ethnicity and aging: Theory, research, and policy* (pp. 67–73). New York: Springer.

CAPLOW, T., BAHR, H., CHADWICK, B., HILL, R., & WILLIAMSON, M. H. (1982). *Middletown families: Fifty years of change and continuity*. Toronto: Bantam.

CELLIS, W. (1993, February 24). Colleges battle culture and poverty to swell Hispanic enrollments. *The New York Times*.

COCHRAN, M., LARNER, M., RILEY, D., GUNNARSSON, L., & HENDERSON, C. R. (1990). *Extending families: The social networks of parents and their children*. Cambridge, MA: Cambridge University Press.

DAVIS, K. E. (1985). Near and dear: Friendships and love compared. *Psychology Today, 52*, 22–30.

DAVID, K. E., & TODD, M. J. (1982). Friendship and love relationships. *Advances in descriptive psychology: Vol. 2*. Greenwich, CT: JAI.

DAVIS, K. E., & TODD, M. J. (1985). Assessing friendship: Prototypes, paradigm cases and relationship description. In S. Duck & D. Perlman (Eds.), *Understanding personal relationships* (pp. 17–37). Beverly Hills, CA: Sage Publications.

DEMOS, J. (1970). *A little commonwealth*. New York: Oxford University Press.

DERLEGA, V. J., WINSTEAD, B. A., WONG, P., & HUNTER, S. (1985). Gender effects in an initial encounter. *Journal of Social and Personal Relationships, 2*, 25–44.

DESTEFANO, L. (1989). Most Americans enjoy preparing for the hectic holidays. *Gallup Poll Monthly, 291*, 25–39.

DESTEFANO, L. (1990). Pressures of modern life bring increased importance to friendship. *Gallup Poll Monthly, 294*, 24–33.

ELLISON, C. G. (1990). Family ties, friendship, and subjective well-being among black Americans. *Journal of Marriage and the Family, 52*, 298–310.

FINCH, J. (1989). *Family obligations and social change*. Cambridge, MA: Polity.

FIRTH, R. (1964, October). Family and kinship in industrial society. *Sociological Review Monograph No. 8: The Development of Industrial Societies*.

FISCHER, C. S. (1982). *To dwell among friends: Social networks in town and city*. Chicago: University of Chicago Press.

FISCHER, L. R. (1991). Between mothers and daughters. *Marriage and Family Review, 16*, 237–248.

FOX, M. F., GIBBS, M., & AUERBACH, D. (1985). Age and gender dimensions of friendship. *Psychology of Women Quarterly, 9*, 489–502.

GOETTING, A. (1990). Patterns of support among in-laws in the United States. *Journal of Family Issues, 11*, 67–90.

GRAHAM, H. (1983). Caring: A labour of love. In J. Finch & D. Groves (Eds.), *A labour of love: Women, work, and caring*. London: Routledge.

HAREVEN, T. K. (1987). Historical analysis of the family. In M. B. Sussman & S. K. Steinmetz (Eds.), *Handbook of Marriage and the family* (pp. 37–57). New York: Plenum.

HAYS, R. B. (1985). A longitudinal study of friendship development. *Journal of Personality and Social Psychology, 48*, 909–924.

HAYS, R. B. (1988). Friendship. In S. Duck (Ed.), *Handbook of personal relationships* (pp. 391–407). New York: Wiley.

HENDRIX, L. (1975). Kinship ties. Movers and stayers in the Ozarks. In N. Glazer-Malbin (Ed.), *Old family/new family*. New York: Van Nostrand.

JOHNSON, F. L., & ARIES, E. J. (1983). The talk of women friends. *Women's Studies International Forum, 6*, 353–361.

KLEIMAN, D. (1990, December 5). Even in the frenzy of the 90s, dinner time is still family time. *The New York Times*, pp. A1, C6.

LASCH, C. (1977). *Haven in a heartless world*. New York: Basic Books.

LASCH, C. (1979). *The culture of narcissism*. New York: Norton.

LASLETT, P. (1965). *The world we have lost: England before the industrial age*. New York: Scribner.

LASSWELL, M., & LOBSENZ, N. M. (1983). *Equal time*. Garden City, NY: Doubleday.

LEE, G. (1980, November). Kinship in the seventies. *Journal of Marriage and the Family*, pp. 923–934.

LEE, H. (1962). *To kill a mockingbird*. New York: Popular Library.

LOCKE, M. (1992, November 29). Families deserting elderly at emergency room. *Roanoke Times and World-News*, p. 83.

MCADAMS, D. P. (1985). Motivation and friendship. In S. Duck & D. Perlman (Eds.), *Understanding personal relationships* (pp. 85–105). Beverly Hills, CA: Sage Publications.

MCADOO, H. P. (1988). *Black families*. Newbury Park, CA: Sage Publications.

MIELL, D., & DUCK, S. (1986). Strategies in developing friendships. In V. J. Derlega & B. A. Winstead (Eds.), *Friendship and social interaction* (pp. 129–143). New York: Springer-Verlag.

MINTZ, S., & KELLOGG, S. (1988). *Domestic revolutions*. New York: Free Press.

MUTRAN, E. (1985). Intergenerational family support among blacks and whites. *Journal of Gerontology, 40*, 382–389.

PARLEE, M. B. (1979). The friendship bond. *Psychology Today, 46*, 42–54.

REIS, H. T. (1986). Gender effects in social participation: Intimacy, loneliness, and the conduct of social interaction. In R. Gilmour & S. Duck (Eds.), *The emerging field of personal relationships* (pp. 91–105). New York: Erlbaum.

RITCHEY, M., & RITCHEY H. (1980). The significance of best-friend relationships in adolescence. *Psychology in Schools, 17*, 536–540.

ROSE, S. M. (1985). Same and cross-sex friendships and the psychology of homosociality. *Sex Roles, 12*, 63–74.

ROSENTHAL, C. (1985). Kinkeeping in the familial division of labor. *Journal of Marriage and the Family, 47*, 965–974.

ROSS, C. E., MIROWSKY, J., & GOLDSTEEN, K. (1991). The impact of the family on health. In A. Booth (Ed.), *Contemporary families* (pp. 341–360). Minneapolis, MN: National Council on Family Relations.

RUBIN, L. (1985). *Just friends*. New York: Harper & Row.

SHERROD, D. (1989). The influence of gender on same-sex friendships. In C. Hendrick (Ed.), *Close relationships* (pp. 164–185). Newbury Park, CA: Sage Publications.

SKOLNICK, A. (1992). *Embattled paradise: The American family in an age of uncertainty*. New York: Basic Books.

SPREY, J. (1991). Studying adult children and their parents. *Marriage and Family Review, 16*, 221–235.

STACK, C. B. (1974). *All our kin: Strategies for survival in a black community*. New York: Harper & Row.

STERNBERG, R. J. (1986). A triangular theory of love. *Psychological Review, 93*, 119–135.

VEROFF, J., DOUVAN, G., & KULKA, R. A. (1981). *The inner American: A self-portrait from 1957–1976*. New York: Basic Books.

WINSTEAD, B. (1986). Sex differences in same-sex friendships. In V. J. Derlega & B. A. Winstead (Eds.), *Friendship and social interaction* (pp. 81–108). New York: Springer-Verlag.

WRIGHT, P. H. (1985). The acquaintance description form. In S. Duck & D. Perlman (Eds.), *Understanding personal relationships* (pp. 39–62). London: Sage Publications.

WRIGHT, P. H. (1989). Gender differences in adult's same- and cross-gender friendships. In R. Adams & R. Blieszner (Eds.), *Older adult friendship: Structure and process* (pp. 197–221). Newbury Park, CA: Sage Publications.

Chapter 11

ARGYLE, M., & HENDERSON, M. (1985). *The anatomy of relationships*. London: Heinemann.

ARNOLD, T., & ARNOLD R. (1992, April). Tom and Roseanne's marriage guide. *Ladies Home Journal*, p. 134.

BACH, G. R., & DEUTSCH, R. M. (1974). *Pairing*. New York: Wm. C. Brown.

BACH, G. R., & WYDEN, P. (1968). *The intimate enemy*. New York: Morrow.

BAUCOM, D. H. (1987). Attributions in distressed relations. In D. Perlman & S. Duck (Eds.), *Intimate relationships* (pp. 177–205). Newbury Park, CA: Sage Publications.

BAXTER, L. A., & DINDIA, K. (1990). Marital partner perceptions of marital maintenance strategies. *Journal of Social and Personal Relationships, 7*, 187–208.

BURGOON, M., & MILLER, G. R. (1985). An expectancy interpretation of language and persuasion. In H. Giles & R. St. Clair (Eds.), *Recent advances in language, communication, and social psychology* (pp. 199–229). Hillsdale, NJ: Erlbaum.

CANCIAN, F. (1987). *Love in America*. New York: Cambridge University Press.

CANCIAN, F., & GORDON, S. (1986, September). *The expressive self: Social construction of marital anger and love since 1900*. Paper presented at the annual meeting of the American Sociological Association. New York.

CANCIAN, F., & GORDON, S. (1988). Changing emotional norms in marriage: Love and anger in U. S. women's magazines since 1900. *Gender and Society, 2*, 308–342.

CUBER, J. F., & HARROFF, P. B. (1968). *Sex and the significant Americans*. Baltimore: Penguin.

DINDIA, K., & BAXTER, L. A. (1987). Strategies for maintaining and repairing marital relationships. *Journal of Social and Personal Relationships, 4*, 143–158.

DINKMEYER, D., & CARLSON, J. (1984). *Time for a better marriage*. Circle Pines, MN: American Guidance Service.

DUCK, S. (1988). *Relating to others*. Chicago: Dorsey.

DUNCAN, B., & ROCK, J. (1993). Saving relationships: The power of the unpredictable. *Psychology Today, 26*(1), 46–52.

FITZPATRICK, M. A. (1988). *Between husbands and wives: Communication in marriage*. Newbury Park, CA: Sage Publications.

HALL, J. (1984). *Nonverbal sex differences: Communication accuracy and expressive style*. Baltimore: Johns Hopkins University Press.

HOCHSCHILD, A. (1989). *The second shift*. New York: Viking.

HOLTZWORTH-MUNROE, A., & JACOBSON, N. S. (1985). Causal attributions of married couples: When do they search for causes? What do they conclude when they do? *Journal of Personality and Social Psychology, 48*, 1398–1412.

KNUDSON, R. M., SOMMERS, A. A., & GOLDING, S. L. (1980). Interpersonal perception and mode of resolution in marital conflict. *Journal of Personality and Social Psychology, 38*, 751–763.

KOMAROVSKY, M. (1967). *Blue-collar marriage*. New York: Vintage Books.

MALTZ, D., & BORKER, R. (1982). A cultural approach to male-female miscommunication. In J. J. Gumperz (Ed.), *Language and social identity* (pp. 156–172). Cambridge: Cambridge University Press.

McCROSKEY, J., LARSON, C. E., & KNAPP, M. L. (1971). *An introduction to interpersonal communication*. Englewood Cliffs, NJ: Prentice-Hall.

McKAY, M., DAVIS, M., & FANNING, P. (1983). *Messages: The communication book*. Oakland, CA: New Harbinger.

MONTGOMERY, B. M. (1988). Quality communication in personal relationships. In S. Duck (Ed.), *Handbook of personal relationships* (pp. 343–359). New York: Wiley.

NOLLER, P. (1984). *Nonverbal communication and marital interaction*. New York: Pergamon.

NOLLER, P. (1987). Nonverbal communication in marriage. In D. Perlman & S. Duck (Eds.), *Intimate relationships* (pp. 149–175). Newbury Park, CA: Sage Publications.

NOLLER, P., & FITZPATRICK, M. A. (1991). Marital communication in the eighties. In A. Booth (Ed.), *Contemporary families* (pp. 42–53). Minneapolis: National Council on Family Relations.

NORTON, R. W. (1988). Communicator style theory in marital interaction: Persistent challenges. In S. Duck (Ed.), *Handbook of personal relationships* (pp. 307–324). New York: Wiley.

PEPLAU, L. A., & GORDON, S. (1985). Women and men in love: Gender differences in close heterosexual relationships. In V. O'Leary, R. Unger, & B. Wallston (Eds.), *Women, gender, and social psychology* (pp. 257–291). Hillsdale, NJ: Erlbaum.

PETERSON, D. R. (1983). Conflict. In H. Kelley, E. Berscheid, A. Christensen, J. Harvey, T. Huston, G. Levinger, L. Peplau, & D. Peterson (Eds.), *Close relationships* (pp. 360–396). New York: Freeman.

RAUSH, H., BARRY, W., HERTEL, R., & SWAIN, M. (1974). *Communication, conflict and marriage*. San Francisco: Jossey-Bass.

RETZINGER, S. M. (1991). *Violent emotions: Shame and rage in marital quarrels*. Newbury Park, CA: Sage Publications.

RUBIN, L. B. (1984). *Intimate strangers: Men and women together*. Harper & Row.

RUSBULT, C. E., VERETTE, J., WHITNEY, G., SLOVIK, L., & LIPKUS, I. (1991). Accommodation processes in close relationships: Theory and preliminary empirical evidence. *Journal of Personality and Social Psychology, 60*, 53–78.

SCHAAP, C. (1984). A comparison of the interaction of distressed and nondistressed married couples in a laboratory situation: Literature survey, methodological issues, and an empirical investigation. In K. Hahlweg & N. S. Jacobson (Eds.), *Marital interaction* (pp. 133–158). New York: Guilford.

TANNEN, D. (1986). *That's not what I meant: How conversational style makes or breaks relationships*. New York: Ballantine Books.

TANNEN, D. (1990a). *You just don't understand: Women and men in conversation*. New York: Ballantine Books.

TANNEN, D. (1990b, July 17). Can we talk here? *Roanoke Times and World News.* pp. A1, 4.

TANNEN, D. (1992, March 31). "She said/he said." Television special on PBS.

THOMPSON, L., & WALKER, A. (1991). Gender in families. In A. Booth (Ed.), *Contemporary families* (pp. 76–102). Minneapolis: National Council on Family Relations.

VEROFF, J., DOUVAN, E., & KULKA, R. A. (1981). *The inner Americans.* New York: Basic Books.

Chapter 12

ABEL, G., BECKER, J., CUNNINGHAM-RATHNER, J., MITTLEMAN, M., & ROULEAU, J. (1988). Multiple paraphiliac diagnoses among sex offenders. *Bulletin of the American Academy of Psychiatry and the Law, 16,* 153–168.

AMMERMAN, R. T., & HERSEN, M. (1991). Family violence. In R. T. Ammerman & M. Hersen (Eds.), *Case studies in family violence* (pp. 3–13). New York: Plenum.

BERNARD, J. (1972). *The future of marriage.* New York: Bantam.

BERSANI, C. A., & CHEN, H. (1988). Sociological perspectives in family violence. In V. Van Hasselt, R. Morrison, & A. Bellack (Eds.), *Handbook of family violence* (pp. 57–86). New York: Plenum.

BIRD, G. W., & FREEMAN, G. (1993). *Power strategies: Antecedents and consequences.* Manuscript submitted for publication.

BIRD, G. W., STITH, S. M., & SCHLADALE, J. (1991). Psychological resources, coping strategies, and negotiation styles as discriminators of violence in dating relationships. *Family Relations, 40,* 45–50.

BONAVOGLIA, A. (1992). The sacred secret. *Ms, II*(5), 40–45.

BREHM, S. (1992). *Intimate relationships.* New York: McGraw-Hill.

BROWNE, A. (1987). *When battered women kill.* New York: Free Press.

BRUBAKER, T. (1991). Families in later life: A burgeoning research area. In A. Booth (Ed.), *Contemporary families* (pp. 226–248). Minneapolis, MN: National Council on Family Relations.

CANCIAN, F. (1987). *Love in America: Gender and self-development.* New York: Cambridge University Press.

DeMARIS, A., PUGH, M., & HARMAN, E. (1992). Sex differences in the accuracy of recall of witnesses of portrayed dyadic violence. *Journal of Marriage and the Family, 54,* 335–345.

DOBASH, E., & DOBASH, R. (1988). Research as social action: The struggle for battered women. In K. Yllo & Bograd (Eds.), *Feminist perspectives on wife abuse* (pp. 51–74). Newbury Park, CA: Sage Publications.

EMERY, R. E. (1989). Family violence. *American Psychologist, 44,* 321–328.

FALBO, T., & PEPLAU, L. (1980). Power strategies in intimate relationships. *Journal of Personality and Social Psychology, 38,* 618–628.

FINDLEN, B. (1990a). Culture: A refuge for murder. *Ms, 1*(2), 47.

FINDLEN, B. (1990b). In search of a nonviolent past. *Ms, 1*(2), 46.

FOA, E. B., & FOA, U. G. (1980). Resource theory: Interpersonal behavior as exchange. In K. J. Gergen, U. S. Greenber, & R. H. Willis (Eds.), *Social exchange: Advances in theory and research* (pp. 77–94). New York: Plenum.

FRENCH, J. T., & RAVEN, B. (1959). The bases of social power. In D. Cartwright (Ed.), *Studies in social power* (pp. 150–167). Ann Arbor: University of Michigan Press.

GELLES, R. J. (1973). Child abuse as psychopathology: A sociological critique and reformulation. *American Journal of Orthopsychiatry, 43,* 611–621.

GELLES, R. J. (1983). An exchange/social control theory of intrafamily violence. In D. Finkelhor, R. Gelles, G. Hotaling, & M. Straus (Eds.), *The dark side of families* (pp. 151–164). Beverly Hills, CA: Sage Publications.

GELLES, R. J., & CONTE, J. (1991). Domestic violence and sexual abuse of children. In A. Booth (Ed.), *Contemporary families* (pp. 327–340). Minneapolis, MN: National Council on Family Relations.

GELLES, R. J., & CORNELL, C. (1985). *Intimate violence in families.* Beverly Hills, CA: Sage Publications.

GELLES, R. J., & CORNELL, C. (1990). *Intimate violence in families* (2nd ed.). Beverly Hills, CA: Sage Publications.

GELLES, R. J., & STRAUS, M. A. (1988). *Intimate violence.* New York: Simon and Schuster.

GIBBS, N. (1993, January 18). Till death do us part. *Time, 141,* pp. 38–45.

GIORDANO, N., & GIORDANO, J. (1984). Elder abuse: A review of the literature. *Social Work, 29,* 232–236.

GONDOLF, E. (1985). *Men who batter.* Holmes Beach, FL: Learning Publications.

GRYL, F., STITH, S. M., & BIRD, G. W. (1991). Close dating relationships among college students: Differences by use of violence and by gender. *Journal of Social and Personal Relationships, 8,* 243–264.

HAMPTON, R., & GELLES, R. J. (1991). A profile of violence toward black children. In R. L. Hampton (Ed.), *Black family violence* (pp. 21–34). Lexington, MA: Lexington Books.

HAMPTON, R., GELLES, R. J., & HARROP, J. (1989). Is violence in black families increasing? A comparison of 1975 and 1985 national survey rates. *Journal of Marriage and the Family, 51,* 969–980.

HEIDE, K. M. (1992). Why kids kill parents. *Psychology Today. 25*(5), 62–66, 76–77.

JOHNSON, P. (1976). Women and power: Towards a theory of effectiveness. *Journal of Social Issues, 32,* 99–110.

KOMTER, A. (1989). Hidden power in marriage. *Gender & Society, 3,* 187–216.

KOMTER, A. (1991). Gender, power and feminist theory. In K. Davis, M. Leijenaar, & J. Oldersma (Eds.), *The gender of power* (pp. 42–62). Newbury Park, CA: Sage Publications.

KOSS, M. P. (1987, October). *The women's health research agenda: Violence against women.* Paper presented at the National Institutes of Mental Health, American Psychological Association, and National Coalition for Women's Mental Health conference on the Women's Mental Health Research Agenda, Washington, DC.

LAMBERT, W. W. (1971). Cross-cultural backgrounds to personality development and the socialization of aggression: Findings from the six-culture study. In W. W. Lambert & R. Weisbrod (Eds.), *Comparative perspectives on social psychology.* Boston: Little, Brown.

LESTER, D. A. (1980). A cross-cultural study of wife abuse. *Aggressive Behavior, 6,* 361–364.

LLOYD, S., KOVAL, J., & CATE, R. (1989). Conflict and violence in dating relationships. In M. Pirog-Good & J. Stets (Eds.), *Violence in dating relationships* (pp. 126–142). New York: Praeger.

LOCKHART, L. L. (1991). Spousal violence: A cross-racial perspective. In R. L. Hampton (Ed.), *Black family violence* (pp. 85–101). Lexington, MA: Lexington Books.

Mancini, J. A., & Blieszner, R. (1991). Aging parents and adult children: Research themes in intergenerational relations. In A. Booth (Ed.), *Contemporary families* (pp. 249–264). Minneapolis, MN: National Council on Family Relations.

Margolin, G., Sibner, L., & Gleberman, L. (1988). Wife battering. In V. Van Hasselt, R. Morrison, & A. Bellach (Eds.), *Handbook of family violence* (pp. 87–117). New York: Plenum.

Masumura, W. T. (1979). Wife abuse and other forms of aggression. *Victimology, 4*, 46–59.

McDonald, G. W. (1980). Family power. In F. M. Berardo (Ed.), *Decade review: Family research 1970–1979* (pp. 111–124). Minneapolis, MN: National Council on Family Relations.

Meyer, J. (1991). Power and love: Conflicting conceptual schemata. In K. Davis, M. Leijenaar, & J. Oldersma (Eds.), *The gender of power* (pp. 21–41). Newbury Park, CA: Sage Publications.

Mott-MacDonald, F. (1979). *Report on Belmont Conference on Spouse Abusers.* Available from the Center for Women Policy Studies, Washington, DC.

Oates, R. K. (1991). Child physical abuse. In R. T. Ammerman & M. Hersen (Eds.), *Case studies in family violence* (pp. 113–134). New York: Plenum.

O'Brien, J. E. (1971). Violence in divorce-prone families. *Journal of Marriage and the Family, 33*, 692–698.

Pagelow, M. D. (1981). *Woman-battering: Victims and their experiences.* Beverly Hills, CA: Sage Publications.

Pagelow, M. D. (1984). *Family violence.* New York: Praeger.

Pardue, D. (1993, April 17). Of love and death: Is domestic violence disregarded? *Roanoke Times & World-News.* pp. A1, A8.

Peplau, L., & Gordon, S. (1985). Women and men in love: Gender differences in close heterosexual relationships. In V. O'Leary, R. Unger, & B. Wallston (Eds.), *Women, gender, and social psychology* (pp. 257–291). Hillsdale, NJ: Erlbaum.

Pillemer, K., & Suitor, J. (1988). Elder abuse. In V. Van Hasselt, R. Morrison, A. Bellack, & M. Hersen (Eds.), *Handbook of family violence* (pp. 247–270). New York: Plenum.

Rosenbaum, C., & O'Leary, V. (1986). The treatment of marital violence. In N. S. Jacobson & A. S. Gurman (Eds.), *Clinical handbook of marital therapy* (pp. 385–405). New York: Guilford.

Russell, D. (1982). *Rape in marriage.* New York: Macmillan.

Scanzoni, J., & Polonko, K. (1980). A conceptual approach to explicit marital negotiation. *Journal of Marriage and the Family, 42*, 31–44.

Steinmetz, S. K. (1977a). *The cycle of violence: Assertive, aggressive, and abusive family interaction.* New York: Praeger.

Steinmetz, S. K. (1977b). Wife beating, husband beating: A comparison of the use of physical violence between spouses to resolve marital fights. In M. Roy (Ed.), *Battered women: A psychosociological study of domestic violence.* New York: Van Nostrand Reinhold Company.

Steinmetz, S. K. (1982). A cross-cultural comparison of violence. *International Journal of Family Psychiatry, 2*, 337–351.

Steinmetz, S. K. (1987). Family violence. In S. K. Steinmetz & M. Sussman (Eds.), *Handbook of marriage and the family* (pp. 725–765). New York: Plenum.

Steinmetz, S. K., & Lucca, J. (1988). Husband battering. In V. Van Hasselt, R. Morrison, A. Bellack, & M. Hersen (Eds.), *Handbook of family violence* (pp. 233–246). New York: Plenum.

Stets, J. E. (1990). Verbal and physical aggression in marriage. *Journal of Marriage and the Family, 52*, 501–514.

Straus, M. A. (1979). Measuring intrafamily conflict and violence: The Conflict Tactics (CT) Scales. *Journal of Marriage and the Family, 41*, 75–88.

Straus, M. A. (1990). The Conflict Tactics Scale and its critics: An evaluation and new data on validity and reliability. In M. A. Straus & R. J. Gelles (Eds.), *Physical violence in American families.* New Brunswick, NJ: Transaction Books.

Straus, M. A., & Gelles, R. J. (1986). Societal change and change in family violence from 1975 to 1985 as revealed in two national surveys. *Journal of Marriage and the Family, 48*, 465–479.

Straus, M. A., & Gelles, R. J. (1990). *Physical violence in American families.* New Brunswick, NJ: Transaction Books.

Straus, M. A., Gelles, R. J., & Steinmetz, S. K. (1980). *Behind closed doors: Violence in the American family.* New York: Doubleday.

Straus, M. A., & Sweet, S. (1992). Verbal/symbol aggression in couples: Incidence rates and relationships to personal characteristics. *Journal of Marriage and the Family, 54*, 346–357.

Suh, M. (1990). Braving a new world. *Ms. 1*(2), 46.

Szinovacz, M. E. (1987). Family power. In M. B. Sussman & S. K. Steinmetz (Eds.), *Handbook of marriage and the family* (pp. 651–693). New York: Plenum.

Thompson, L. (1991). Family work: Women's sense of fairness. *Journal of Family Issues, 12*, 181–196.

Thompson, L., & Walker, A. (1991). Gender in families: Women and men in marriage, work, and parenthood. In A. Booth (Ed.), *Contemporary families* (pp. 76–102). Minneapolis, MN: National Council on Family Relations.

Toufexis, A. (1993, April 19). Seeking the roots of violence. *Time, 141*, 52–53.

Violent homes create out-of-control children. (1993, January 17). *Roanoke Times & World-News,* p. A12.

Walker, L. E. (1979). *The battered woman.* New York: Harper & Row.

Walker, L. E. (1984). *The battered woman syndrome.* New York: Springer.

Walker, L. E. (1989). Psychology and violence against women. *American Psychologist, 44*, 695–702.

Whiting, B. (1963). *Six cultures: Studies of child rearing.* New York: Wiley.

Williams, D., & Griffin, L. (1991). Elder abuse in the black family. In R. Hampton (Ed.), *Black family violence: Current research and theory* (pp. 117–126). Lexington, MA: Lexington Books.

Winter, D. G. (1988). The power motive in women and men. *Journal of Personality and Social Psychology, 54*, 510–519.

Wolf-Smith, J., & LaRossa, R. (1993). After he hits her. *Family Relations, 41*, 324–329.

Yllo, K. (1983). Using a feminist approach in quantitative research: A case study. In D. Finkelhor, R. J. Gelles, G. Hotaling, & M. A. Straus (Eds.), *The dark side of families* (pp. 277–288). Beverly Hills, CA: Sage Publications.

Chapter 13

Antonovsky, A. (1979). *Health, stress, and coping.* San Francisco: Jossey-Bass.

Antonovsky, A. (1987). *Unraveling the mystery of health.* San Francisco: Jossey-Bass.

ARIES, E. (1987). Gender and communication. In P. Hendrick (Ed.), *Sex and gender* (pp. 149–176). Newbury Park, CA: Sage Publications.

BARNETT, R. C., & BARUCH, G. K. (1987). Social roles, gender, and psychological distress. In R. C. Barnett, L. Biener, & G. K. Baruch (Eds.), *Gender and stress* (pp. 122–143). New York: Free Press.

BARNETT, R. C., BIENER, L., & BARUCH G. K. (1987). *Gender and stress.* New York: Free Press.

BARNETT, R. C., & RIVERS, C. (1992). The myth of the miserable working woman. *Working Woman, 17*(2), 62, 64, 88–90.

BARRERA, M., & BACA, L. (1990). Recipient reactions to social support: Contributions of enacted support, conflicted support, and network orientation. *Journal of Social and Personal Relations, 7,* 541–551.

BELLE, D. (1982). Social ties and social support. In D. Belle (Ed.), *Lives in stress: Women and depression* (pp. 133–144). Beverly Hills, CA: Sage Publications.

BELLE, D. (1990). Poverty and women's mental health. *American Psychologist, 45,* 385–389.

BIENER, L. (1987). Gender differences in use of substances. In R. C. Barnett, L. Biener, & G. K. Baruch (Eds.), *Gender and stress* (pp. 330–349). New York: Free Press.

BIRD, G. W., & HARRIS, R. (1990). A comparison of role strain and coping strategies by gender and family structure among early adolescents. *Journal of Early Adolescence, 10,* 141–158.

BIRD, G. W., & WAKAT, P. (1993). *Women and men in dual-career marriages: Sense of coherence, coping, and well-being.* Manuscript submitted for publication.

BOSS, P. (1987). Family stress. In M. B. Sussman & S. K. Steinmetz (Eds.), *Handbook of marriage and the family* (pp. 695–723). New York: Plenum.

BRENNER, S., & LEVI, L. (1987). Long-term unemployment among women. *Social Science and Medicine, 25,* 153–161.

COOK, E. (1990). Gender and psychological distress. *Journal of Counseling and Development, 68,* 371–375.

COOPERSTOCK, R., & LENNARD, H. (1979). Some social meanings of tranquilizer use. *Sociology of Health and Illness, 1,* 331–346.

DYK, P., & SCHVANEVELDT, J. (1986, November). *Coping as a concept in family theory.* Paper presented at the annual meeting of the National Council on Family Relations, Dearborn, Michigan.

EATON, W., & KESSLER, L. (1981). Rates of symptoms of depression in a national sample. *American Journal of Epidemiology, 114,* 528–538.

FOLKMAN, S. (1984). Personal control and stress and coping processes: A theoretical analysis. *Journal of Personality and Social Psychology, 46,* 839–852.

FOLKMAN, S., & LAZARUS, R. (1988). Coping as a mediator of emotion. *Journal of Personality and Social Psychology, 54,* 466–475.

FOLKMAN, S., LAZARUS, R. S., DUNKEL-SCHETTER, J., DELONGIS, A., & GRUEN, R. (1986). The dynamics of a stressful encounter. *Journal of Personality and Social Psychology, 50,* 992–1003.

FUJITA, F., DIENER, E., & SANDVIK, E. (1991). Gender differences in negative affect and well-being: The case for emotional intensity. *Journal of Personality and Social Psychology, 61,* 427–434.

GOVE, W. (1984). Gender differences in mental and physical illness: The effects of fixed roles and nurturant roles. *Social Science and Medicine, 19,* 77–84.

HALL, L., WILLIAMS, C., & GREENBERG, S. (1985). Supports, stressors, and depressive symptoms in low income mothers. *American Journal of Public Health, 75,* 518–522.

HANSEN, D., & HILL, R. (1964). Families under stress. In H. Christensen (Ed.), *Handbook of marriage and the family* (pp. 782–819). Chicago: Rand McNally.

HILL, R. (1949). *Families under stress.* New York: Harper & Row.

HILL, R. (1958). Generic features of families under stress. *Social Casework, 49,* 139–150.

HOBFOLL, S. (1989). Conservation of resources: A new attempt at conceptualizing stress. *American Psychologist, 44,* 513–524.

HOBFOLL, S., FREEDY, C., & GELLER, P. (1990). Conservation of social resources: Social support resource theory. *Journal of Social and Personal Relationships, 7,* 465–478.

HOLAHAN, C., & MOOS, R. (1987). Personal and contextual determinants of coping strategies. *Journal of Personality and Social Psychology, 52,* 946–955.

HOLMES, T. H., & RAHE, R. H. (1967). The social readjustment ratings scale. *Journal of Psychosomatic Research, 11,* 213–218.

JANOFF-BLUMAN, R., & FRIEZE, I. (1987). The role of gender in reactions to criminal victimization. In R. Barnett, L. Biener, & G. Baruch (Eds.), *Gender and stress* (pp. 159–184). New York: Free Press.

KANNER, A., COYNE, J., SCHAEFER, C., & LAZARUS, R. S. (1981). Comparison of two modes of stress measurement: Daily hassles and uplifts vs. major life events. *Journal of Behavioral Medicine, 4,* 1–39.

KELLY, K. V., & FROSCH, W. (1989). Parmaco therapy. In *Treatment of psychiatric disorders: A task force report of the American Psychiatric Association* (Vol. 3, pp. 2585–2589). Washington, DC: American Psychiatric Association.

KESSLER, R., & MCRAE, J. (1982). The effect of wive's employment on the mental health of married men and women. *American Sociological Review, 47,* 216–227.

KESSLER, U., PRICE, R., & WORTMAN, C. (1985). Social factors in psychopathology: Stress, social support, and coping processes. *Annual Review of Psychology, 36,* 531–572.

KOBASA, S. (1979). Stressful life events, personality, and health: An inquiry into hardiness. *Journal of Personality and Social Psychology, 37,* 1–11.

KOBASA, S., MADDI, S., & KAHN, S. (1982). Hardiness and health: A prospective study. *Journal of Personality and Social Psychology, 52,* 244–252.

KOBASA, S., & PUCCETTI, M. (1983). Personality and social resources in stress resistance. *Journal of Personality and Social Psychology, 45,* 839–850.

KOOS, E. (1946). *Families in trouble.* New York: King's Crown Press.

LABICH, K. (1993). The new unemployed. *Fortune, 127*(5), 40–49.

LANDERS, S. (1988, October). Facts confound myths of women, depression. *APA Monitor,* p. 5.

LAZARUS, R. S., & FOLKMAN, S. (1984). *Stress, appraisal, and coping.* New York: Springer.

MADDI, S., & KOBASA, S. (1984). *The hardy executive: Health under stress.* Homewood, IL: Dow Jones-Irwin.

MATTLIN, J., WETHINGTON, E., & KESSLER, R. (1990). Situational determinants of coping and coping effectiveness. *Journal of Health and Social Behavior, 31,* 103–122.

MCCUBBIN, H., & LAVEE, Y. (1986). Critical targets in military family life programs. In G. Brown & M. Scheirer (Eds.), *The *development and evaluation of human service programs in the military.* New York: Pergamon.

McCubbin, H., & McCubbin, M. (1988). Typologies of resilient families. *Family Relations, 37,* 247–254.

McCubbin, H., & Patterson, J. (1982). Family adaptation to crises. In H. McCubbin, A. Cauble, & J. Patterson (Eds.), *Family stress, coping, and social support* (pp. 26–47). Springfield, IL: Charles C Thomas.

McCubbin, H., & Patterson, J. (1983a). Family transitions: Adaptation to stress. In H. McCubbin & C. Figley (Eds.), *Stress and the family: Vol. 1, Coping with normative and nonnormative transitions* (pp. 5–25). New York: Brunner/Mazel.

McCubbin, H., & Patterson, J. (1983b). The family stress process: The double ABCX model of adjustment and adaptation. In H. McCubbin, M. Sussman, & J. Patterson (Eds.), *Social stress and the family* (pp. 7–38). New York: Haworth.

McCubbin, H., Thomson, A., Pirner, P., & McCubbin, M. (1988). *Family types and strengths.* Edina, MN: Bellwether Press.

McCubbin, M., & McCubbin, H. (1987). Family stress theory and assessment. In H. McCubbin & A. Thompson (Eds.), *Family assessment inventories for research and practice* (pp. 3–32). Madison: University of Wisconsin Press.

McCubbin, M., & McCubbin, H. (1989). Theoretical orientations to family stress and coping. In C. Figley (Ed.), *Treating families under stress* (pp. 3–43). New York: Brunner/Mazel.

Mirowsky, J., & Ross, C. (1989). *Social causes of psychological distress.* New York: Aldine de Gruyter.

Nadler, A., & Fisher, J. (1986). The role of threat to self-esteem and perceived control in recipient reaction to help. In L. Berkowitz (Ed.), *Advances in experimental and social psychology* (pp. 81–122). Orlando, FL: Academic Press.

Noshpitz, J. D. (1990). Treatment for stress-related disorders. In J. D. Noshpitz & R. D. Coddington (Eds.), *Stressors and the adjustment disorders* (pp. 630–650). New York: Wiley.

Olson, D. H., Lavee, Y., & McCubbin, H. I. (1988). Types of families and family responses to stress across the family life cycle. In D. Klein & J. Aldous (Eds.), *Social stress and family development* (pp. 16–43). New York: Guilford.

Pearlin, L. (1989). The sociological study of stress. *Journal of Health and Social Behavior, 30,* 241–256.

Pearlin, L., & McCall, M. (1990). Occupational stress and marital support. In J. Eckenrode & S. Gore (Eds.), *Stress between work and family* (pp. 39–60). New York: Plenum.

Pearlin, L., & Schooler, C. (1978). The structure of coping. *Journal of Health and Social Behavior, 19,* 2–21.

Pearlin, L., & Turner, H. A. (1987). The family as a context of the stress process. In L. Pearlin & H. A. Turner (Eds.), *Stress and health: Issues in research methodology* (pp. 143–165). New York: Wiley.

Peters-Golden, M. (1982). Breast cancer: Varied perceptions of social support in the illness experience. *Social Science Medicine, 16,* 483–491.

Reiss, D. (1981). *The family's construction of reality.* Cambridge: Harvard University Press.

Rodin, J., & Ickovics, J. (1990). Women's health. *American Psychologist, 45,* 1018–1034.

Rodin, J., & Salovey, P. (1989). Health psychology. *Annual Review of Psychology, 40,* 533–579.

Rohter, L. (1993, March 29). Clinging to thin hope in debris of hurricane. *The New York Times,* p. A9.

Ross, C., Mirowsky, J., & Goldsteen, K. (1991). The impact of the family on health: The decade review. In A. Booth (Ed.), *Contemporary families* (pp. 341–360). Minneapolis, MN: National Council on Family Relations.

Schnittger, M., & Bird, G. W. (1990). Coping among dual-career men and women across the family life cycle. *Family Relations, 39,* 199–205.

Sher, K. (1988). Stress response dampening. In H. Blane & K. Leonard (Eds.), *Theories of drinking and alcoholism.* New York: Guilford.

Thoits, P. (1983). Dimensions of life events that influence psychological distress: An evaluation and synthesis of the literature. In H. Kaplan (Ed.), *Psychosocial stress: Trends in theory and research* (pp. 33–103). New York: Academic.

Ulbrich, P., Warheit, G., & Zimmerman, R. (1989). Race, socioeconomic status, and psychological distress: An examination of differential vulnerability. *Journal of Health and Social Behavior, 30,* 131–146.

Verbrugge, L. (1983). Multiple roles and physical health of women and men. *Journal of Health and Social Behavior, 24,* 16–30.

Verbrugge, L. (1985). Gender and health. *Journal of Health and Social Behavior, 26,* 156–182.

Waldron, I., & Jacobs, J. (1988). Effects of labor force participation on women's health: New evidence from a longitudinal study. *Journal of Occupational Medicine, 30,* 977–983.

Walker, A. (1985). Reconceptualizing family stress. *Journal of Marriage and the Family, 47,* 827–837.

Wortman, C., & Lehman, D. (1985). Reactions of victims of life crisis: Support attempts that fail. In I. G. Sarason & B. Sarason (Eds.), *Social support: Theory, research and application* (pp. 463–490). Dordrecht, The Netherlands: Martinus Nijhoff.

Chapter 14

Ahrons, C., & Wallisch, L. (1986). The relationship between former spouses. In S. Duck & D. Perlman (Eds.), *Close relationships: Development, dynamics, and deterioration* (pp. 269–296). Beverly Hills, CA: Sage Publications.

Albrecht, S. L. (1980). Reactions and adjustments to divorce: Differences in experiences of males and females. *Family Relations, 29,* 59–68.

Amato, P. (1988). Long-term implications of parental divorce for adult self-concept. *Journal of Family Issues, 9,* 201–213.

Amato, P. (1993). Children's adjustment to divorce: Theories, hypotheses, and empirical support. *Journal of Marriage and the Family, 55,* 23–38.

Amato, P., & Booth, A. (1991). Consequences of parental divorce and marital unhappiness for adult well-being. *Social Forces, 69,* 895–914.

Amato, P., & Keith, B. (1991). Parental divorce and adult well-being. *Journal of Marriage and the Family, 53,* 43–58.

Berman, W. (1988). The role of attachment in the post-divorce experience. *Journal of Personality and Social Psychology, 54,* 496–503.

Bohannan, P. (1970). The six stations of divorce. In P. Bohannan (Ed.), *Divorced and after* (pp. 29–55). New York: Doubleday.

Booth, A., & Edwards, J. N. (1985). Age at marriage and marital instability. *Journal of Marriage and the Family, 47,* 67–75.

Booth, A., & Edwards, J. N. (1990). Transmission of marital and family quality over the generations: The effects of parental divorce and unhappiness. *Journal of Divorce, 13,* 41–58.

BRODY, J. E. (1991, June 7). A new look at children and divorce. *The New York Times,* p. A18.

BROWN, C., FELDBERG, R., FOX, E., & KOHEN, J. (1976). Chance of a new lifetime. *Journal of Social Issues, 32,* 119–133.

BUMPASS, L., MARTIN, T., & SWEET, J. (1991). The impact of family background and early marital factors on marital disruption. *Journal of Family Issues, 12,* 22–42.

BUMPASS, L., & SWEET, J. (1989). Children's experience in single-parent families. *Family Planning Perspectives, 6,* 256–260.

CAMARA, K. A., & RESNICK, G. (1988). Interparental conflict and cooperation: Factors moderating children's post-divorce adjustment. In E. M. Hetherington & J. D. Arasteh (Eds.), *Impact of divorce, single parenting, and stepparenting on children* (pp. 169–195). Hillsdale, NJ: Erlbaum.

CHERLIN, A. (1993). *Marriage, divorce, remarriage.* Cambridge, MA: Harvard University Press.

CHERLIN, A., & FURSTENBERG, F. (1986). *The new American grandparent: A place in the family, a life apart.* New York: Basic Books.

CHERLIN, A., & FURSTENBERG, F. (1988). The changing European family. *Journal of Family Issues, 9,* 291–297.

CLARKE-STEWART, K. A., & BAILEY, B. (1990). Adjusting to divorce: Why do men have it easier? *Journal of Divorce, 13,* 75–94.

DEMO, D., & ACOCK, A. (1991). The impact of divorce on children. In A. Booth (Ed.), *Contemporary families* (pp. 162–191). Minneapolis, MN: National Council on Family Relations.

EMERY, R. (1988). *Marriage, divorce, and children's adjustment.* Newbury Park, CA: Sage Publications.

EMERY, R., & WYER, M. (1987). Divorce mediation. *American Psychologist, 42,* 472–480.

FERREIRO, B. W. (1990). Presumption of joint custody: A family policy dilemma. *Family Relations, 39,* 420–426.

FREED, D., & FOSTER, H. (1985). *Family law in the fifty states.* Chicago: American Bar Association.

FURSTENBERG, F. (1990). Divorce and the American family. *Annual Review of Sociology, 16,* 379–403.

FURSTENBERG, F., & CHERLIN, A. (1991). *Divided families: What happens to children when parents part.* Cambridge, MA: Harvard University Press.

FURSTENBERG, F., & NORD, C. (1985). Parenting apart: Patterns of childrearing after marital disruption. *Journal of Marriage and the Family, 47,* 905–912.

FURSTENBERG, F., NORD, C., PETERSON, J., & ZILL, N. (1983). The life course of children of divorce: Marital disruption and parental contact. *American Sociological Review, 48,* 656–668.

GARMEZY, N. (1983). Stressors in childhood. In N. Garmezy & M. Rutter (Eds.), *Stress, coping, and development in children* (pp. 43–84). New York: McGraw-Hill.

GERSTEL, N. (1988). Divorce and kin ties: The importance of gender. *Journal of Marriage and the Family, 50,* 209–219.

GIRDNER, L. K. (1985). Adjudication and mediation: A comparison of custody decision-making processes involving third parties. In C. A. Everett (Ed.), *Divorce mediation: Perspectives on the field* (pp. 33–47). New York: Haworth.

GLENN, N. D., & KRAMER, K. B. (1985). The psychological well-being of adult children of divorce. *Journal of Marriage and the Family, 48,* 905–912.

GOODE, W. (1956). *Women after divorce.* Glencoe: Free Press.

GOVE, W. R., & SHIN, H. (1989). The psychological well-being of divorced and widowed men and women: An empirical analysis. *Journal of Family Issues, 10,* 122–144.

HEATON, T. B. (1991). Time-related determinants of marital dissolution. *Journal of Marriage and the Family, 53,* 285–295.

HERNANDEZ, D. J. (1988). Demographic trends and living arrangements of children. In E. M. Hetherington & J. D. Arasteh (Eds.), *Impact of divorce, single-parenting, and stepparenting on children.* Hillsdale, NJ: Erlbaum.

HETHERINGTON, E. M. (1989). Coping with family transitions: Winners, losers, and survivors. *Child Development, 60,* 1–14.

HETHERINGTON, E. M., COX, M., & COX, R. (1977). The aftermath of divorce. In J. H. Stevens & M. Matthews (Eds.), *Mother-child, father-child relations.* Washington, DC: National Association for the Education of Young Children.

HETHERINGTON, E. M., STANLEY-HAGAN, M., & ANDERSON, E. (1989). Marital transitions: A child's perspective. *American Psychologist,* 303–312.

JACOBSON, P. H. (1959). *American marriages and divorce.* New York: Rinehart.

JOHNSON, C. L. (1988). *Ex familia: Grandparents, parents, and children adjust to divorce.* New Brunswick, NJ: Rutgers University Press.

KASLOW, F., & SCHWARTZ, L. (1987). *The dynamics of divorce.* New York: Brunner/Mazel.

KINARD, E. M., & REINHERZ, H. (1986). Effects of marital dissolution on children's school aptitude and achievement. *Journal of Marriage and the Family, 48,* 285–294.

KITSON, G. C., & HOLMES, W. (1992). *Portrait of divorce.* New York: Guilford.

KITSON, G. C., & MORGAN, L. A. (1991). The multiple consequences of divorce: A decade review. In A. Booth (Ed.), *Contemporary families* (pp. 150–161). Minneapolis, MN: National Council on Family Relations.

KITSON, G. C., & SUSSMAN, M. B. (1982). Marital complaints, demographic characteristics, and symptoms of mental distress in divorce. *Journal of Marriage and the Family, 44,* 87–101.

LANDERS, R. K. (1990, July 6). Are Americans still in love with marriage? *Editorial Research Reports,* pp. 382–394.

LAWSON, C. (1992, January 23). Requiring classes in divorce. *The New York Times,* pp. C1, C8.

LOEWEN, J. W. (1988). Visitation fatherhood. In P. Bronstein & C. P. Cowan (Eds.), *Fatherhood today: Men's changing role in the family* (pp. 195–213). New York: Wiley.

LUEPNITZ, D. (1982). *Child custody: A study of families after divorce.* Lexington, MA: Lexington Books.

MABRY, M. (1992). No father, and no answers. *Newsweek, 119*(18), 50.

MARTIN, T. C., & BUMPASS, L. (1989). Recent trends in marital dissolution. *Demography, 26,* 37–51.

MCKAY, M., ROGERS, P., BLADES, J., & GOSSE, R. (1984). *The divorce book.* Oakland, CA: New Harbinger.

MCLANAHAN, S., & BOOTH, K. (1991). Mother-only families. In A. Booth (Ed.), *Contemporary families* (pp. 405–428). Minneapolis, MN: National Council on Family Relations.

MCLANAHAN, S., & BUMPASS, L. (1988). Intergenerational consequences of family disruption. *American Journal of Sociology, 94,* 130–152.

MORGAN, L. (1991). *After marriage ends.* Newbury Park, CA: Sage Publications.

MORGAN, S., LYE, D., & CONDRAN, G. (1988). Sons, daughters, and the risk of marital disruption. *American Journal of Sociology, 94*, 110–129.

NATIONAL CENTER FOR HEALTH STATISTICS. (1973). *100 years of marriage and divorce statistics* (Vital and Health Statistics, Series 21, No. 24). Washington, DC: U.S. Government Printing Office.

NATIONAL CENTER FOR HEALTH STATISTICS. (1984). *Final divorce statistics 1984* (Vital Statistics Report, Advance Report). Washington, DC: U.S. Government Printing Office.

NATIONAL CENTER FOR HEALTH STATISTICS. (1991). *Final divorce statistics 1991* (Vital Statistics Report, Advance Report). Washington, DC: U.S. Government Printing Office.

NATIONAL CENTER FOR HEALTH STATISTICS. (1992). *Divorce, child custody, and child support* (Series P-23). Washington, DC: U.S. Government Printing Office.

NORTON, A., & GLICK, P. (1986). One-parent families: a social and economic profile. *Family Relations, 35*, 9–17.

PETERSON, J., & ZILL, N. (1986). Marital disruption, parent-child relationships, and behavior problems in children. *Journal of Marriage and the Family, 48*, 295–307.

ROY A. (1985). Early parental separation and adult depression. *Archives of General Psychiatry, 42*, 987–991.

SELTZER, J. A., & BIANCHI, S. M. (1988). Children's contact with absent parents. *Journal of Marriage and the Family, 50*, 663–677.

SORRENTINO, C. (1990). The changing family in international perspective. *Monthly Labor Review, 113*, 41–58.

SPANIER, G., & THOMPSON, L. (1984). *Parting: The aftermath of separation and divorce.* Beverly Hills, CA: Sage Publications.

STRUBE, M., & BARBOUR, L. (1983). The decision to leave an abusive relationship. *Journal of Marriage and the Family, 45*, 785–793.

Study: Kids get poorer after divorce. (1991, March 1). *Los Angeles Times*, p. A3.

TEACHMAN, J. (1986). First and second marital dissolution: A decomposition exercise for whites and blacks. *Sociological Quarterly, 27*, 571–590.

THOMPSON, L., & WALKER, A. (1991). Gender in families. In A. Booth (Ed.), *Contemporary families* (pp. 76–102). Minneapolis, MN: National Council on Family Relations.

TROMBETTA, D. (1982). Custody evaluation and custody mediation: A comparison of two dispute interventions. *Journal of Divorce, 6*, 65–77.

TSCHANN, J., JOHNSTON, J., & WALLERSTEIN, J. (1989). Resources, stresses, and attachment as predictors of adult adjustment after divorce. *Journal of Marriage and the Family, 51*, 1033–1046.

U.S. BUREAU OF THE CENSUS. (1992). *Statistical abstract of the United States.* Washington, DC: U.S. Government Printing Office.

VAUGHN, D. (1986). *Uncoupling: Turning points in intimate relationships.* New York: Oxford University Press.

VEEVERS, J. E. (1991). Traumas versus strengths: A paradigm of positive versus negative divorce outcomes. *Journal of Divorce and Remarriage, 15*, 99–126.

VEGA, W. (1991). Hispanic families in the 1980s. In A. Booth (Ed.), *Contemporary families* (pp. 297–306). Minneapolis, MN: National Council on Family Relations.

WALLERSTEIN, J. S. (1980). California's children of divorce. *Psychology Today*, 67–75.

WALLERSTEIN, J. S., & BLAKESLEE, S. (1989). *Second chances: Men, women, and children a decade after divorce.* New York: Ticknor & Fields.

WALLERSTEIN, J. S., & CORBIN, S. (1989). Daughters of divorce: Report of a ten-year follow-up. *American Journal of Orthopsychiatry, 59*, 593–604.

WALLERSTEIN, J. S., CORBIN, S., & LEWIS, J. (1988). Children of divorce: A ten-year study. In E. M. Hetherington & J. Arasteh (Eds.), *Impact of divorce, single-parenting, and stepparenting on children* (pp. 198–214). Hillsdale, NJ: Erlbaum.

WALLERSTEIN, J. S., & KELLY, J. B. (1980). *Surviving the breakup: How children actually cope with divorce.* New York: Basic Books.

WALLERSTEIN, J. S., & KELLY, J. B. (1989). *Second chances: Men, women, and children a decade after divorce.* New York: Ticknor & Fields.

WEISS, R. S. (1984). The impact of marital dissolution on income in single-parent households. *Journal of Marriage and the Family, 46*, 115–119.

WEITZMAN, L. (1985). *The divorce revolution: The unexplored consequences.* New York: Free Press.

WHITE, L. (1991). Determinants of divorce. In A. Booth (Ed.), *Contemporary families* (pp. 141–149). Minneapolis, MN: National Council on Family Relations.

WHITE, L., & BOOTH, A. (1985). The transition of parenthood and marital quality. *Journal of Family Issues, 6*, 435–449.

ZILL, N. (1983). *Marital disruption and the child's need for psychological help.* Washington, DC: National Institute for Mental Health.

ZILL, N. (1988). Behavior, achievement, and health problems among children in stepfamilies. In E. M. Hetherington & J. D. Arasteh (Eds.), *Impact of divorce, single-parenting, and stepparenting on children* (pp. 325–368). Hillsdale, NJ: Erlbaum.

Chapter 15

AMES, K., ROSENBERG, D., & CHRISTIAN, N. (1991, December 2). Grandma goes to court. *Newsweek*, pp. 67, 69.

ATLAS, S. L. (1984). *Parents without partners sourcebook.* Philadelphia: Running Press.

AXELSON, L., & DAIL, P. (1988). The changing character of homelessness in the United States. *Family Relations, 37*, 463–469.

BARRINGER, F. (1991, June 7). Changes in U.S. households: Single parents amid solitude. *The New York Times*, pp. A1, A18.

BARUCH, G., BARNETT, R., & RIVERS, C. (1983). *Lifeprints: New patterns of love and work for today's women.* New York: McGraw-Hill.

BERNSTEIN, A. (1992, November 23). When the only parent is daddy. *Business Week*, (3294), 122, 127.

BIANCHI, S., & McARTHUR, E. (1991). *Family disruption and economic hardship; The short-run picture for children.* (U.S. Bureau of the Census. Current Population Reports, Series P-70, No. 23). Washington, DC: U.S. Government Printing Office.

DE FRAIN, J., & EIRICK, R. (1981). Coping as divorced single parents: A comparative study of fathers and mothers. *Family Relations, 30*, 265–274.

DEMO, D. H. (1992). Parent-child relations: Assessing recent changes. *Journal of Marriage and the Family, 54*, 104–117.

DEMO, D. H., & ACOCK, A. (1991). The impact of divorce on children. In A. Booth (Ed.), *Contemporary families* (pp. 162–191). Minneapolis, MN: National Council on Family Relations.

FURSTENBERG, F., & CHERLIN, A. (1991). *Divided families: What happens to children when parents part?* Cambridge, MA: Harvard University Press.

FURSTENBERG, F., & NORD, C. (1985). Parenting apart: Patterns of childrearing after marital disruption. *Journal of Marriage and the Family, 47,* 893–904.

GALLUP ORGANIZATION. (1989). Gallup youth survey. Princeton, NJ: Gallup Organization.

GONGLA, P., & THOMPSON, E. H. (1987). Single-parent families. In M. B. Sussman & S. K. Steinmetz (Eds.), *Handbook of marriage and the family* (pp. 397–418). New York: Plenum.

GOODE, W. J. (1963). *World revolution and family patterns.* New York: Free Press.

GOTTMAN, J. M., & KATZ, L. F. (1989). Effects of marital discord on young children's peer interaction and health. *Developmental Psychology, 25,* 373–381.

GREIF, G. (1990). *The daddy track and single fathers.* Lexington, MA: Lexington Books.

Helping children cope with divorce. (1988, August 26). *Los Angeles Times,* p. A1.

HETHERINGTON, E. M. (1989). Coping with family transitions: Winners, losers, and survivors. *Child Development, 60,* 1–14.

HETHERINGTON, E. M., & STANLEY-HAGAN, M. (1986). Divorced fathers: Stress, coping, and adjustment. In M. Lamb (Ed.), *The father's role: Applied perspectives* (pp. 103–134). New York: Wiley.

HETHERINGTON, E. M., STANLEY-HAGAN, M., & ANDERSON, E. R. (1989). Marital transitions: A child's perspective. *American Psychologist, 44,* 303–312.

HODGES, W. F. (1986). *Interventions for children of divorce.* New York: Wiley.

HOGAN, M. J., BUEHLER, C., & ROBINSON, B. (1983). Single parenting: Transitioning alone. In H. I. McCubbin & C. R. Figley (Eds.), *Stress and the family: Vol. 1, Coping with normative transitions* (pp. 116–132). New York: Brunner/Mazel.

HOLDEN, K. C., & SMOCK, P. J. (1991). The economic costs of marital dissolution: Why do women bear a disproportionate cost? *Annual Review of Sociology, 17,* 51–78.

HOUSE WAYS AND MEANS COMMITTEE. (1991). *Overview of Entitlement Programs.* Washington, DC: Government Printing Office.

JOST, K. (1992, April). Welfare reform. *CQ Researcher,* pp. 315–335.

KASLOW, F., & SCHWARTZ, L. (1987). *The dynamics of divorce.* New York: Brunner/Mazel.

KIRKLAND, R. I. (1992). What we can do now. *Fortune, 125*(11), 41–48.

KURDEK, L., & SIESKY, A. (1980). Sex role self-concepts of single divorced parents and their children. *Journal of Divorce, 3,* 249–261.

KUTNER, L. (1992, January 23). Children need help after a breakup, too. *Roanoke Times and World News,* Extra.

LEWIN, T. (1990, June 4). Father's vanishing act called common drama. *The New York Times,* p. A18.

MACKLIN, E. D. (1987). Nontraditional family forms. In M. B. Sussman & S. K. Steinmetz (Eds.), *Handbook of marriage and the family* (pp. 317–353). New York: Plenum.

MCKAY, M., ROGERS, P., BLADES, J., & GOSSE, R. (1984). *The divorce book.* Oakland, CA: New Harbinger.

MCLANAHAN, S. (1983). Family structure and stress: A longitu-

dinal comparison of two-parent and female-headed families. *Journal of Marriage and the Family, 45,* 347–357.

MCLANAHAN, S., & ADAMS, S. (1987). Parenthood and psychological well-being. *Annual Review of Sociology, 13,* 237–257.

MCLANAHAN, S., & BOOTH, K. (1991). Mother-only families: Problems, prospects, and politics. In A. Booth (Ed.), *Contemporary families* (pp. 405–428). Minneapolis, MN: National Council on Family Relations.

MECHANIC, D., & HANSELL, S. (1989). Divorce, family conflict, and adolescents' well-being. *Journal of Health and Social Behavior 30,* 105–116.

MEYER, D., & GARASKY, S. (1993). Custodial fathers: Myths, realities, and child support policy. *Journal of Marriage and the Family, 55,* 73–89.

NATIONAL EDUCATION ASSOCIATION. (1988). *Educating students from divorced and single-parent homes.* Washington, DC: National Education Association.

SELIGMANN, J., ROSENBERG, D., WINGERT, P., HANNAH, D., & ANNIN, P. (1992, December 14). It's not like Mr. Mom. *Newsweek,* pp. 70–72.

SELTZER, J., & GARFINKEL, I. (1990). Inequity in divorce settlements: An investigation of property settlements and child support awards. *Social Science Research, 19,* 82–111.

SHAW, S. (1991). The conflicting experiences of lone parenthood. In M. Hardey & G. Crow (Eds.), *Lone parenthood* (pp. 143–155). Toronto: University of Toronto Press.

SKOLNICK, A. (1991). *Embattled paradise: The American family in an age of uncertainty.* New York: Basic Books.

STINSON, K. M. (1991). *Adolescents, family, and friends: Social support after parents' divorce or remarriage.* New York: Praeger.

SURO, R. (1992, May 26). For women, varied reasons for single motherhood. *The New York Times,* p. A12.

THOMPSON, E. H., & GONGLA, P. A. (1983). Single-parent families: In the mainstream of American society. In E. D. Macklin & R. H. Rubin (Eds.), *Contemporary families and alternative lifestyles* (pp. 97–124). Beverly Hills, CA: Sage Publications.

U.S. BUREAU OF THE CENSUS. (1990a). *Studies in marriage and the family: Single parents and their children.* (Current Population Reports, Series P-23, No. 162). Washington, DC: U.S. Government Printing Office.

U.S. BUREAU OF THE CENSUS. (1990b). *Child support and alimony: 1987.* (Current Population Reports, Series P-23, No. 167). Washington, DC: U.S. Government Printing Office.

U.S. BUREAU OF THE CENSUS. (1991). *Family disruption and economic hardship: The short-run picture for children.* (Current Population Reports, Series P-70, No. 23). Washington, DC: U.S. Government Printing Office.

WEISS, R. (1979). *Going it alone: The family life and social situation of the single parent.* New York: Basic Books.

WEISS, R. (1985). Growing up a little faster: The experiences of growing up in a single-parent structure. In R. H. Moos & J. A. Schaefer (Eds.), *Coping with life crises.* New York: Plenum.

WILKS, C. (1990). Grandparents in custody and access disputes. *Journal of Divorce, 13*(3), 1–13.

Chapter 16

AHRONS, C. R. Professor of Social Work, University of Southern California, Los Angeles, personal communication.

AHRONS, C. R., & WALLISCH, L. (1987). Parenting in the binuclear family: Relationships between biological and stepparents. In K. Pasley & M. Ihinger-Tallman (Eds.), *Remarriage and stepparenting* (pp. 225–256). New York: Guilford.

ASTONE, N., & MCLANAHAN, S. (1991). Family structure, parental practices, and high school completion. *American Sociological Review, 56*, 309–320.

BEYETTE, B. (1992, September 7). Romance within stepfamilies result of unclear boundaries. *Roanoke Times and World News,* p. E6.

BRAY, J., BERGER, S., & SILVERBLATT, A. (1987). Family process and organization during early remarriage. In J. P. Vincent (Ed.), *Advances in family intervention, assessment, and theory: Vol. 4* (pp. 253–280). Greenwich, CT: JAI.

BRYAN, L., COLEMAN, M., & GANONG, L. (1986). Person perception: Family structure as a cure for stereotyping. *Journal of Marriage and the Family, 48*, 169–174.

BUMPASS, L., & SWEET, J. (1989). *National estimates of cohabitation: Cohort levels and union stability* (NSFH Working Paper No. 2). Madison: University of Wisconsin, Center for Demography and Ecology.

BUMPASS, L., SWEET, J., & MARTIN, T. (1990). Changing patterns of remarriage. *Journal of Marriage and the Family, 52*, 747–756.

CHERLIN, A. (1981). *Marriage, divorce, and remarriage.* Cambridge, MA: Harvard University Press.

CHERLIN, A. (1993). *Marriage, divorce, and remarriage.* Cambridge, MA: Harvard University Press.

CHERLIN, A., & MCCARTHY, J. (1985). Remarried couple households. *Journal of Marriage and the Family, 47*, 23–30.

CLINGEMPEEL, G., & SEGAL, S. (1986). Stepparent-stepchild relationships and the psychological adjustment of children in stepmother and stepfather families. *Child Development, 57*, 474–484.

COLEMAN, M., & GANONG, L. (1991). Remarriage and stepfamily research in the 1980s: Increased interest in an old family form. In A. Booth (Ed.), *Contemporary families* (pp. 192–207). Minneapolis, MN: National Council on Family Relations.

CROSBIE-BURNETT, M. (1984). The centrality of the step relationship: A challenge to family theory and practice. *Family Relations, 33*, 459–464.

DAINTON, M. (1993). The myths and misconceptions of the stepmother identity. *Family Relations, 42*, 93–98.

DEWITT, P. M. (1992). The second time around. *American Demographics, 14*(11), 60–63.

FINE, M., & KURDEK, L. (1992). The adjustment of adolescents in stepfather and stepmother families. *Journal of Marriage and the Family, 54*, 725–736.

FINE, M., & SCHWEBEL, A. (1991). Stepparent stress: A cognitive perspective. *Journal of Divorce and Remarriage, 17*, 1–15.

FISHMAN, B., & HAMEL, B. (1981). From nuclear to stepfamily ideology: A stressful change. *Alternative Lifestyles, 4*, 181–204.

FRANCKE, L. (1983). *Growing up divorced.* New York: Simon & Schuster.

FRANKS, H. (1988). *Remarriage.* London: Bodley Head.

FURSTENBERG, F. (1980). Reflections on remarriage. *Journal of Family Issues, 1*(4), 443–453.

FURSTENBERG, F., & CHERLIN, A. (1991). *Divided families: What happens to children when parents part.* Cambridge, MA: Harvard University Press.

FURSTENBERG, F., & SPANIER, G. (1984). *Recycling the family: Remarriage after divorce.* Beverly Hills, CA: Sage Publications.

GANONG, L., & COLEMAN, M. (1986). A comparison of clinical and empirical literature on children in stepfamilies. *Journal of Marriage and the Family, 48*, 309–318.

GANONG, L., & COLEMAN, M. (1989a). Financial decisions shared in remarriages. *Stepfamily Bulletin, 11*, 16–18.

GANONG, L., & COLEMAN, M. (1989b). Preparing for remarriage: Anticipating the issues, seeking solutions. *Family Relations, 38*, 28–33.

GANONG, L., COLEMAN, M., & MAPES, D. (1990). A meta-analytic review of family structure stereotypes. *Journal of Marriage and the Family, 52*, 287–297.

GILES-SIMS, J., & CROSBIE-BURNETT, M. (1989a). Adolescent power in stepfather families: A test of normative-resource theory. *Journal of Marriage and the Family, 51*, 1065–1078.

GILES-SIMS, J., & CROSBIE-BURNETT, M. (1989b). Stepfamily research: Implications for policy, clinical interventions, and further research. *Family Relations, 38*, 19–23.

GLICK, P. (1989). Remarried families, stepfamilies, and stepchildren: A brief demographic analysis. *Family Relations, 38*, 24–27.

GLICK, P., & LIN, S. L. (1986). Recent changes in divorce and remarriage. *Journal of Marriage and the Family, 48*, 737–741.

GUISINGER, S., COWAN, P., & SCHULDBERG, D. (1989). Changing parent and spouse relations in the first year of remarriage of divorced fathers. *Journal of Marriage and the Family, 51*, 445–456.

HETHERINGTON, E. M., & CLINGEMPEEL, W. (1988, March), *Coping with remarriage: The first two years.* Symposium presented at the Southeastern Conference on Human Development, Charleston, SC.

HETHERINGTON, E. M., & CLINGEMPEEL, W. (1992). Coping with marital transitions: A family systems perspective. *Monographs of the Society for Research in Child Development, 57* (2–3, Serial No. 227).

HETHERINGTON, E. M., STANLEY-HAGAN, M., & ANDERSON, E. (1989). Marital transitions: A child's perspective. *American Psychologist, 44*, 303–312.

HOBART, C. (1990). Relationships between the formerly married. *Journal of Divorce and Remarriage, 14*(2), 1–23.

HUGHES, C. (1991). Stepparents: Wicked or wonderful? Brookfield, VT: Gower.

IHINGER-TALLMAN, M. (1987). Sibling and stepsibling bonding in stepfamilies. In K. Pasley & M. Ihinger-Tallman (Eds.), *Remarriage and stepparenting* (pp. 164–182). New York: Guilford.

IHINGER-TALLMAN, M. (1988). Research on stepfamilies. *Annual Review of Sociology, 14*, 25–48.

KITSON, G., & HOLMES, W. (1992). *Portrait of divorce.* New York: Guilford.

KNAUB, P., & HANNA, S. (1984). Strengths of remarried families. *Journal of Divorce, 8*(3), 41–54.

KURDEK, L. (1989). Relationship quality for newly married husbands and wives: Marital history, stepchildren, and individual-difference predictors. *Journal of Marriage and the Family, 51*, 1053–1064.

KURDEK, L., & SINCLAIR, R. (1986). Adolescent's views on issues related to divorce. *Journal of Adolescent Research, 1*, 373–387.

LOFAS, J., & SOVA, D. (1985). *Stepparenting.* New York: Zebra Books.

LOWN, J. M., & DOLAN, E. M. (1988). Financial challenges in remarriage. *Lifestyles, 9*, 73–88.

Marriage, divorce, remarriage. (1984, October). *Harper's Bazaar,* pp. 134–138.

MARTIN, T., & BUMPASS, L. (1989). Recent trends and differentials in marital disruption. *Demography, 26,* 37–51.

MCKAY, M., ROGERS, P., BLADES, J., & GOSSE, R. (1984). *The divorce book.* Oakland, CA: New Harbinger.

NATIONAL CENTER FOR HEALTH STATISTICS. (1992, August). Monthly Vital Statistics Report. Hyattsville, MD: National Center for Health Statistics.

NORDHEIMER, J. (1990, October 18). Stepfathers: The shoes rarely fit. *The New York Times,* pp. C1, C6.

PAPERNOW, P. (1988). Stepparent role development: From outsider to intimate. In W. R. Beer (Ed.), *Relative strangers* (pp. 54–82). Totowa, NJ: Rowman & Littlefield.

PETERSON, J., & ZILL, N. (1986). Marital disruption, parent-child relationships and behavior problems in children. *Journal of Marriage and the Family, 48,* 295–308.

ROSENBERG, E., & HAJAL, F. (1985). Stepsibling relationships in remarried families. *Social Casework, 66,* 287–292.

ROSS, C. E., MIROWSKY, J., & GOLDSTEEN, K. (1991). The impact of the family on health. In A. Booth (Ed.), *Contemporary Families* (pp. 341–360). Minneapolis, MN: National Council on Family Relations.

SANTROCK, J., & SITTERLE, K. (1987). Parent-children relationships in stepmother families. In K. Pasley & M. Ihinger-Tallman (Eds.), *Remarriage and stepparenting* (pp. 135–154). New York: Guilford.

SELTZER, J., & BIANCHI, S. (1988). Children's contact with absent parents. *Journal of Marriage and the Family, 50,* 663–677.

SMOCK, P. (1990). Remarriage patterns of black and white women: Reassessing the role of educational attainment. *Demography, 27,* 467–473.

TAYLOR, R., CHATTERS, L. TUCKER, M., & LEWIS, E. (1990). Developments in research on black families. *Journal of Marriage and the Family, 52,* 993–1014.

TUCKER, M., & TAYLOR, R. (1989). Demographic correlates of relationship status among black Americans. *Journal of Marriage and the Family, 51,* 655–665.

TURNER, S. (1989). My wife-in-law and me: Reflections on a joint-custody stepparenting relationship. In N. B. Maglin & N. Schniedewind (Eds), *Women and stepfamilies: Voices of anger and love* (pp. 310–320). Philadelphia, PA: Temple University Press.

U.S. BUREAU OF THE CENSUS. (1991). *Studies in household formation: Remarriage among women in the United States* (Current Population Reports, Series P-23, No. 169). Washington, DC: U.S. Government Printing Office.

VAUGHN, D. (1986). *Uncoupling: Turning points in intimate relationships.* New York: Oxford University Press.

VISHER, E., & VISHER, J. (1988). *Old loyalties, new ties.* New York: Brunner/Mazel.

VISHER, E., & VISHER, J. (1989). Parenting coalitions after remarriage. *Family Relations, 38,* 65–70.

VISHER, E., & VISHER, J. (1990). Dynamics of successful stepfamilies. *Journal of Divorce and Remarriage, 14,* 3–12.

WEINGARTEN, H. R. (1985). Marital status and well-being: A national study comparing first-marrieds, currently divorced, and remarried adults. *Journal of Marriage and the Family, 47,* 655–659.

WESTOFF, L. A. (1975, August 10). Two-time winners. *The New York Times Magazine,* pp. 10–12, 15.

WHITE, L. K., & BOOTH, A. (1985). The quality and stability of remarriages: The role of stepchildren. *American Sociological Review, 50,* 689–698.

WHYTE, M. K. (1990). *Dating, mating, and marriage.* New York: Aldine de Gruyter.

WILSON, M. (1989). Child development in the context of the black extended family. *American Psychologist, 44,* 380–385.

WOLFE, N. (1991). *The beauty myth: How images of beauty are used against women.* New York: Morrow.

ZILL, N. (1988). Behavior, achievement, and health problems among children in stepfamilies. In E. M. Hetherington & J. D. Arasteh (Eds.), *Impact of divorce, single parenting, and stepparenting on children.* Hillsdale, NJ: Erlbaum.

Appendix

BURGOYNE, C. B. (1990). Money in marriage: How patterns of allocation both reflect and conceal power. *The Sociological Review, 38,* 634–665.

Do "secret fees" help credit cards rob you? (1992, June 19). *Roanoke Times and World News,* p. A9.

How to make the most of your monitor service membership. (1992, March). Dallas: TRW.

PAE, P. (1992). Avoiding credit-card costs. *Smart Money, 1*(2), 63.

SCHWARTZ, E. I., & KONRAD, W. (1991, August 26). Equifax' exit may not tame the consumer backlash. *Business Week,* (3228), 30.

SCHWARTZ, E. I., SCHILLER, Z., KONRAD, W., & FOREST, S. A. (1991, July 29). Credit bureaus: Consumers are stewing—and suing. *Business Week,* (3224), pp. 69–70.

Permissions Acknowledgments

CHAPTER 1 Figure 1-3: From W. O'Hare, "A New Look at Asian Americans," reprinted with permission © *American Demographics*, Vol. 12, 1990. For subscription information, please call (800) 828-1133. **Box (Changing Lifestyles):** Excerpts from Richard Zoglin, "Where Fathers and Mothers Know Best," *Time*, June 1, 1992. Copyright 1992 Time Inc. Reprinted by permission.

CHAPTER 2 Figure 2-1: Adapted from *Gender: Stereotypes and Roles*, Third Edition by Susan A. Baslow. Copyright © 1992 Wadsworth, Inc. Adapted by permission of Brooks/Cole Publishing Company, Pacific Grove, California 93950. **Table 2-1:** From *Psychological Androgyny* by E. P. Cook. Copyright © 1985. Reprinted by permission of Allyn & Bacon. **Box (Diversity):** "Bad Year for Girls?" from *Newsweek*, April 16, 1990. © 1990 Newsweek, Inc. All rights reserved. Reprinted by permission. **Box (Changing Lifestyles):** From J. Adler et al., "Drums, Sweat and Tears," from *Newsweek*, June 24, 1991. © 1991 Newsweek, Inc. All rights reserved. Reprinted by permission.

CHAPTER 3 Figure 3-1: From *The Psychology of Love*, edited by R. J. Sternberg and M. L. Barnes. Copyright © 1988. Reprinted by permission of Yale University Press. **Table 3-1:** From J. A. Lee, "Love Styles" in *The Psychology of Love*, edited by R. J. Sternberg and M. L. Barnes. Copyright © 1988. Reprinted by permission of Yale University Press. **Box (Diversity):** From Daniel Goleman, "After Kinship and Marriage, Anthropology Discovers Love," *The New York Times*, November 24, 1992. Copyright © 1992 by The New York Times Company. Reprinted by permission.

CHAPTER 4 Figure 4-1: From J. Fowles, "Coming Soon: More Men Than Women," *The New York Times*, June 5, 1988. Copyright © 1988 by The New York Times Company. Reprinted by permission. **Figure 4-2:** From *Family Systems in America*, Third Edition by Ira L. Reiss, copyright © 1980 by Holt, Rinehart and Winston, Inc., reprinted by permission of the publisher. **Figure 4-3:** From *Relating to Others* by S. Duck. Copyright © 1988. Reprinted by permission of Open University Press. **Figure 4-4:** From D. Winston, "Towson State Survey on Date Rape," *The Baltimore Sun*, January 11, 1991. Reprinted with permission of *The Baltimore Sun*, copyright © 1991 The Baltimore Sun Co. **Table 4-1:** Reprinted with permission from L. A. Baxter, "Gender Differences in Heterosexual Relationship Rules Embedded in Break-up Accounts," *Journal of Social and Personal Relationships*, Vol. 3, No. 3, September 1986, by permission of Sage Publications Ltd. **Table 4-2:** From P. Lundberg-Love and R. Geffner, "Date Rape," in *Violence in Dating Relationships*, edited by M. A. Pirog-Good and J. E. Stets. Copyright © 1989, Praeger Publishers, an imprint of Greenwood Publishing Group, Inc., Westport, CT. Reprinted with permission. **Table 4-3:** Reprinted with permission from L. Lee, "Sequences in Separation," *Journal of Social and Personal Relationships*, Vol. 1, No. 1, March 1984, by permission

of Sage Publications Ltd. **Box (Changing Lifestyles):** From Isabel Wilkerson, "Black-White Marriages Rise, But Couples Still Face Scorn," *The New York Times*, December 2, 1991. Copyright © 1991 by The New York Times Company. Reprinted by permission.

CHAPTER 5 Figure 5-1: From *Marriage and the Family Today*, Fourth Edition by Keith Melville. Copyright © 1988. Reprinted by permission of McGraw-Hill, Inc. **Figure 5-2:** From R. K. Landers, "Are Americans Still in Love with Marriage?" *Editorial Research Reports*, Vol. 1, 1990. Reprinted by permission of Congressional Quarterly, Inc. **Figure 5-3:** From M. L. Usdansky, "Wedded to the Single Life: Attitudes, Economy Delaying Marriage," *USA Today*, July 17, 1992. Copyright 1992, USA Today. Reprinted with permission. **Table 5-1:** Adapted from *Single Life: Unmarried Adults in Social Context*, by Peter J. Stein, St. Martin's Press, 1981. © 1981 Peter J. Stein, Ph.D. **Box (Changing Lifestyles):** From D. Fost, "Cruising at 60 is No Fun Alone," reprinted with permission © *American Demographics*, Vol. 14, No. 4, 1992. For subscription information, please call (800) 828-1133. **Box (Diversity):** From V. Vobejda, "Why More and More Black Women Will Never Marry," *The Washington Post*, November 17, 1991. © 1991 The Washington Post. Reprinted with permission. And from N. Farber, "The Significance of Race and Class in Marital Decisions among Unmarried Adolescent Mothers," © 1990 by The Society for the Study of Social Problems. Reprinted from *Social Problems*, Vol. 37, 1990, by permission. **Box (Snapshots):** From L. A. Peplau and S. L. Gordon, "The Intimate Relationships of Lesbians and Gay Men," in *Marriage and Family in Transition*, edited by J. N. Edwards and D. H. Demo, Allyn & Bacon, 1991.

CHAPTER 6 Figure 6-1: From M. R. Kagay, "Poll Finds AIDS Causes Single People to Alter Behavior," *The New York Times*, June 18, 1991. Copyright © 1991 by The New York Times Company. Reprinted by permission. **Figure 6-2:** Adaptation of Kinsey Scale from *Sexual Behavior in the Human Male*, by A. Kinsey, W. Pomeroy, and C. Martin. Copyright 1948. Reprinted by permission of The Kinsey Institute for Research in Sex, Gender, and Reproduction, Inc. **Table 6-1:** From Catherine S. Chilman, "Promoting Healthy Adolescent Sexuality," *Family Relations*, Vol. 39, No. 2, 1990. Copyrighted 1990 by the National Council on Family Relations, 3989 Central Ave., NE, Suite 550, Minneapolis, MN 44521. Reprinted by permission. **Table 6-2:** Reproduced with the permission of The Alan Guttmacher Institute from Tom W. Smith, "Adult Sexual Behavior in 1989: Number of Partners, Frequency of Intercourse and Risk of AIDS," *Family Planning Perspectives*, Vol. 23, No. 3, May/June 1991. **Table 6-3:** From *Homosexuality/Heterosexuality: Concepts of Sexual Orientation*, edited by David P. McWirter, Stephanie A. Sanders, and June Machover Reinisch. Copyright © 1990 by The Kinsey Institute for Research in Sex, Gender, and Reproduction. Reprinted by permission of Oxford University Press,

Inc. **Table in Box (Dilemmas and Decisions):** From "Safer Sex," from *Newsweek,* December 9, 1991. © 1991, Newsweek, Inc. All rights reserved. Reprinted by permission. **Box (Point of View):** From Karla Vermeulen, "Growing Up in the Shadow of AIDS," *The New York Times,* June 30, 1990. Copyright © 1990 by The New York Times Company. Reprinted by permission. **Box (Changing Lifestyles):** From Anastasia Toufexis, "Bisexuality—What Is It?" *Time,* August 17, 1992. Copyright 1992 Time Inc. Reprinted by permission. **Box (Snapshots):** From P. McCarthy, "Ageless Sex," *Psychology Today,* Vol. 22, No. 3, 1989. Reprinted with permission from *Psychology Today* Magazine. Copyright © 1989 (Sussex Publishers, Inc.).

CHAPTER 7 Figure 7-1: From "A Profile of Older Americans," AARP, 1990. **Figure 7-2:** From Andrus Gerontology Center, University of Southern California, in B. O'Reilly, "How to Take Care of Aging Parents," *Fortune,* May 18, 1992. © 1992 Time Inc. All rights reserved. **Figure 7-3:** From G. D. Heinemann and P. L. Evans, "Widowhood: Loss, Change, and Adaptation," in *Family Relationships in Later Life,* edited by P. H. Brubaker. Copyright © 1990. Reprinted by permission of Sage Publications Inc. **Figure 7-4:** From Boyd C. Rollins and Kenneth L. Cannon, "Marital Satisfaction over the Family Life Cycle: A Reevaluation," *Journal of Marriage and the Family,* Vol. 36, No. 2, 1974. Copyrighted 1974 by the National Council on Family Relations, 3989 Central Ave., NE, Suite 550, Minneapolis, MN 55421. Reprinted by permission. **Figure 7-5:** Adapted from *Between Husbands and Wives: Communication in Marriage,* by M. A. Fitzpatrick. Copyright © 1988. Reprinted by permission of Sage Publications, Inc. **Table 7-1:** From *Adult Development: A New Dimension in Psychodynamic Theory and Practice,* by C. A. Colarusso and R. A. Nemiroff. Copyright © 1981. Reprinted by permission of Plenum Publishing Corp. **Table 7-2:** From L. F. Bouvier and C. J. De Vita, "The Baby Boom: Entering Midlife," *Population Bulletin,* Vol. 46, No. 3, November 1991. Reprinted by permission of the Population Reference Bureau Inc. **Box (Point of View):** From Richard Cohen, "Suddenly I'm the Adult?" *Psychology Today,* May 1987. © 1993, The Washington Post Writer's Group. Reprinted with permission. **Box (Point of View):** From Ellen Goodman, "The 'Two-someness' of Marriage is Not What It Used to Be," *Roanoke Times & World News,* June 4, 1991. © 1991, The Boston Globe Newspaper Company. Reprinted with permission. **Box (Dilemmas and Decisions):** M. D. Wilcox, "Boomerang Kids," excerpted with permission from the October 1992 issue of *Kiplinger's Personal Finance Magazine.* Copyright © 1992 The Kiplinger Washington Editors, Inc. Figure from J. Gross, "More Young Single Men Hang on to Apron Strings," *The New York Times,* June 16, 1991. Copyright © 1991 by The New York Times Company. Reprinted by permission. **Box (Snapshots):** From V. J. Malatesta, "On Making Love Last in a Marriage: Reflections of 60 Widows," *Clinical Gerontologist,* Vol. 9, 1989, The Haworth Press, Inc., 10 Alice Street, Binghamton, New York 13904. Copyright © 1989.

CHAPTER 8 Figure 8-1: From G. H. Gallup and F. Newport, "Virtually All Adults Want Children, But Many of the Reasons Are Intangible," *The Gallup Poll Monthly,* Vol. 297, 1990. Reprinted by permission of The Gallup Organization. **Figure 8-2:** From M. L. Usdansky and M. Puente, "A Baby Doesn't Mean Marriage Anymore," *USA Today,* December 4, 1991. Copyright 1991, USA Today. Reprinted with permission. **Figure 8-3:** From "Ethnic Babies Come to Toyland," reprinted with permission © *American Demographics,* Vol. 13, June 1991. For subscription information, please call (800) 828-1133. **Figure 8-4:** From B. Cutler, "Rock-a-Buy Baby," reprinted with permission © *American Demographics,* Vol. 12, No. 1, 1990. For subscription information, please call (800) 828-1133. **Figure 8-5:** From R. Pear, "Bigger Number of New Mothers are Unmarried," *The New York Times,* December 3, 1991. Copyright © 1991 by The New York Times Company.

Reprinted by permission. **Table 8-1:** From T. Exter, "Married with Kids," reprinted with permission © *American Demographics,* Vol. 12, 1990. For subscription information, please call (800) 828-1133. **Box (Snapshots):** From H. K. Hammonds and W. C. Symonds, "Where Paternity Leave is Catching On," reprinted from April 15, 1991 issue of *Business Week* by special permission, copyright © 1991 by McGraw-Hill, Inc. **Box (Snapshots):** From "Surrogate Mothers," *Los Angeles Times,* October 23, 1990. Copyright 1990, Los Angeles Times. Reprinted by permission. **Box (Point of View):** From Sara McLanahan and Karen Booth, "Mother-Only Families: Problems, Prospects, and Politics," *Contemporary Families,* 1991. Copyrighted 1991 by the National Council on Family Relations, 3989 Central Avenue, NE, Suite 550, Minneapolis, MN 55421. Reprinted by permission. **Box (Changing Lifestyles):** From Sophfronia Scott Gregory, "Teaching Young Fathers the Ropes," *Time,* August 10, 1992. Copyright 1992 Time Inc. Reprinted by permission. **Box (Changing Lifestyles):** From L. V. Gelder, "A Lesbian Family," *Ms.,* March/April, 1991.

CHAPTER 9 Figure 9-1: From Dennis A. Ahlburg and Carol J. DeVita, "New Realities of the American Family," *Population Bulletin,* Vol. 47, No. 2, August 1992. Reprinted by permission of Population Reference Bureau Inc. **Figure 9-3:** From S. Caminiti, "Who's Minding America's Kids?" *Fortune,* August 10, 1992. Courtesy of *Fortune* magazine. **Table 9-2:** From *When the Bough Breaks: The Cost of Neglecting our Children* by Sylvia Ann Hewlett. Copyright © 1991 by Sylvia Ann Hewlett. Reprinted by permission of Basic Books, a division of HarperCollins, Publishers, Inc. **Table 9-3:** From S. Caminiti, "Who's Minding America's Kids?" *Fortune,* August 10, 1991. Courtesy of *Fortune* magazine. **Table 9-4:** From *The Gendered Economy: Work, Careers, and Success* by R. M. Kelly. Copyright © 1991. Reprinted by permission of Sage Publications, Inc. **Box (Changing Lifestyles):** From Lynda Richardson, "No Cookie-Cutter Answers in 'Mommy Wars,'" *The New York Times,* September 2, 1992. Copyright © 1992 by The New York Times Company. Reprinted by permission. **Box (Diversity):** From T. Holden and J. Wiener, "Revenge of the Japanese 'Office Ladies,'" reprinted from July 13, 1992 issue of *Business Week* by special permission, copyright © 1992 by McGraw-Hill, Inc.

CHAPTER 10 Figure 10-1: Adapted from D. Miell and S. Duck, "Strategies in Developing Friendships," in *Friendship and Social Interaction,* edited by V. D. Derlega and B. A. Winstead, 1986. Reprinted by permission of Springer-Verlag. **Table 10-1:** From *Extending Families: The Social Network of Parents and Their Children,* M. Cochran, M. Larner, D. Riley, L. Gunnarsson, and C. R. Henderson, 1990. Reprinted by permission of Cambridge University Press. **Table 10-2:** From *The Anatomy of Relationships,* Michael Argyle and Monika Henderson, 1985. Reprinted by permission of the Peters Fraser & Dunlop Group Ltd. **Table 10-3:** From *Adult Friendship* by R. Blieszner and R. Adams. Copyright © 1992. Reprinted by permission of Sage Publications, Inc. **Box (Point of View):** From Joseph Berger, "For 200 in the Tenzer Family, Grandpa's Circle Is Broken," *The New York Times,* October 7, 1991. Copyright © 1991 by The New York Times Company. Reprinted by permission. **Box (Diversity):** From William Celis, "Colleges Battle Culture and Poverty to Swell Hispanic Enrollments," *The New York Times,* February 24, 1993. Copyright © 1993 by The New York Times Company. Reprinted by permission. **Box (Snapshots):** From M. Locke, "Families Deserting Elderly at Emergency Room Door," *The Roanoke Times & World News,* November 29, 1991. Reprinted by permission of The Associated Press. **Box (Snapshots):** From L. DeStefano, "Most Americans Enjoy Preparing for the Hectic Holidays," *Gallup Poll Monthly,* Vol. 291, 1989. Reprinted by permission of The Gallup Organization. **Box (Changing Lifestyles):** From Dena Kleiman, "Even in the Frenzy of the '90s, Dinner Time Is Still Family Time," *The New York Times,* December 5, 1990.

Copyright © 1990 by The New York Times Company. Reprinted by permission.

CHAPTER 11 Box (Snapshots): From Tom Arnold and Roseanne Arnold, "Tom and Roseanne's Marriage Guide," *Ladies' Home Journal*, April 1992. Copyright © 1992, Meredith Corporation. Used with the permission of *Ladies' Home Journal* magazine. **Box (Diversity):** From *That's Not What I Meant: How Controversial Style Makes or Breaks Relationships* by D. Tannen, 1986, William Morrow & Co. **Box (Dilemmas and Decisions):** From *Pairing* by G. R. Bach and R. M. Deutsch, 1974, David McKay Co.

CHAPTER 12 Figure 12-1: From S. K. Steinmetz, "Family Violence," in *Handbook of Marriage and the Family* edited by S. K. Steinmetz and M. Sussman, 1987. Reprinted by permission of Plenum Publishing Corporation. **Figure 12-2:** From *Intimate Relationships,* Second Edition, by S. Brehm. Copyright © 1992. Reprinted by permission of McGraw-Hill, Inc. **Table 12-1:** From J. T. French and B. Raven, "The Bases of Social Power," in *Studies in Social Power,* edited by D. Cartwright, University of Michigan Press, 1959. Reprinted with permission. **Table 12-2:** Reprinted with permission from G. Gryl, S. M. Stith, and G. W. Bird, "Close Dating Relationships Among College Students: Differences by Use of Violence and by Gender," *Journal of Social and Personal Relationships*, Vol. 8, 1991. Copyright 1991, by permission of Sage Publications Ltd. And from Gloria W. Bird, Sandra M. Stith, and Joann Schladale, "Psychological Resources, Coping Strategies, and Negotiation Styles as Discriminators of Violence in Dating Relationships," *Family Relations*, Vol. 40, No. 1, 1991. Copyrighted 1991 by the National Council on Family Relations, 3989 Central Ave. NE, Suite 550, Minneapolis, MN 55421. Reprinted by permission. **Box (Snapshots):** From "Violent Homes Create Out-of-Control Children," *Roanoke Times & World-News,* January 17, 1993. Reprinted by permission: Tribune Media Services. **Box (Point of View):** From D. Pardue, "Of Love and Death: Is Domestic Violence Disregarded?" *Roanoke Times & World-News*, April 17, 1993. Reprinted by permission of the Roanoke Times & World-News.

CHAPTER 13 Figures 13-4 and 13-5: From *Family Types and Strengths* by H. McCubbin, A. Thomson, P. Pirner, and M. McCubbin, Bellwether Press, 1988. **Table 13-1:** From T. H. Holmes and R. H. Rahe, "The Social Readjustment Ratings Scale," *Journal of Psychosomatic Research*, Vol. II, 1967. Reprinted by permission of Pergamon Press Ltd., Oxford, England. **Table 13-2:** From A. Kanner et al., "Comparison of Two Modes of Stress Measurement: Daily Hassles and Uplifts vs. Major Life Events," *Journal of Behavioral Medicine*, Vol. 4, 1981. Reprinted by permission of Plenum Publishing Corporation. **Table 13-4:** From S. Folkman, R. S. Lazarus, J. Dunkel-Schetter, A. DeLongis, and R. Gruen, "The Dynamics of a Stressful Encounter," *Journal of Personality and Social Psychology*, Vol. 50, 1986. Copyright 1986 by the American Psychological Association. Reprinted by permission. **Table 13-5:** Adapted from *Social Causes of Psychological Distress* by J. Mirowsky and C. Ross, New York: Aldine de Gruyter. Copyright © 1989 John Mirowsky and Catherine Ross. **Table 13-7:** From Hamilton I. McCubbin and Marilyn A. McCubbin, "Typologies of Resilient Families: Emerging Roles of Social Class and Ethnicity," *Family Relations,* Vol. 37, No. 3, 1988. Copyrighted 1988 by the National Council on Family Relations, 3989 Central Ave. NE, Suite 550, Minneapolis, MN 55421. Reprinted by permission. **Box (Changing Lifestyles):** From Kenneth Labich, "Unemployed," *Fortune*, March 8, 1993. © 1993 Time Inc. All rights reserved. **Box (Changing Lifestyles):** From Deborah Belle, "Poverty and Women's Mental Health," *American Psychologist*, March 1990. Copyright 1990 by the American Psychological Association. Reprinted by permission. **Box (Point of View):** From Larry Rohter, "Clinging to Thin Hope in Debris of Hurricane," *The New York Times*, March 29, 1993. Copyright © 1993 by The New York Times Company. Reprinted by permission.

CHAPTER 14 Figure 14-1: From *American Marriages and Divorce,* by Paul H. Jacobson, Holt, Rinehart and Winston, 1959. **Table 14-1:** Reprinted with permission from *The Dynamics of Divorce* by F. Kaslow and L. Schwartz, Brunner/Mazel, copyright © 1987. **Table 14-2:** Reprinted with the permission of The Free Press, a Division of Macmillan, Inc. from *The Divorce Revolution: The Unexpected Social and Economic Consequences For Women and Children in America* by Lenore J. Weitzman. Copyright © 1985 by Dr. Lenore J. Weitzman. **Table 14-3:** From *The Divorce Book* by M. McKay, P. Rogers, J. Blades and R. Gosse. Reprinted with permission by New Harbinger Publications, Oakland, CA. **Table 14-4:** Adapted from J. E. Veevers, "Traumas vs. Stress: A Paradigm of Positive versus Negative Divorce Outcomes," © Haworth Press, originally published in *Journal of Divorce and Remarriage*, Vol. 15(1/2), 1991. **Box (Point of View):** From M. Mabry, "No Father, and No Answers," from *Newsweek,* May 4, 1992. © 1992 Newsweek, Inc. All rights reserved. Reprinted by permission. **Box (Dilemmas and Decisions):** From Jane E. Brody, "A New Look at Children and Divorce," *The New York Times,* June 7, 1991. Copyright © 1991 by The New York Times Company. Reprinted by permission. **Box (Changing Lifestyles):** From Carol Lawson, "Requiring Classes in Divorce," *The New York Times*, January 23, 1992. Copyright © 1992 by The New York Times Company. Reprinted by permission.

CHAPTER 15 Figure 15-1: From Roberto Suro, "Changes in Single-Parent Families: 1970-1991," *The New York Times,* May 26, 1992. Copyright © 1992 by The New York Times Company. Reprinted by permission. **Figures 15-6 and 15-7:** From R. I. Kirkland, "What We Can Do Now," *Fortune* June 1, 1992. © 1992 Time Inc. All rights reserved. **Box (Dilemmas and Decisions):** From Roberto Suro, "For Women, Varied Reasons for Single Motherhood," *The New York Times,* May 26, 1992. Copyright © 1992 by The New York Times Company. Reprinted by permission. **Box (Snapshots):** From K. Ames, D. Rosenberg, and N. Christian, "Grandma Goes to Court," from *Newsweek,* December 2, 1991. © 1991 Newsweek, Inc. All rights reserved. Reprinted by permission. **Box (Point of View):** From J. Seligmann, D. Rosenberg, P. Wingert, D. Hannah, and P. Annin, "It's Not Like Mr. Mom," from *Newsweek,* December 14, 1992. © 1992, Newsweek, Inc. All rights reserved. Reprinted by permission. **Box (Dilemmas and Decisions):** From Lawrence Kutner, "Children Need Help After a Breakup, Too," *The New York Times*, January 23, 1992. Copyright © 1992 by The New York Times Company. Reprinted by permission. **Box (Point of View):** From *Adolescents, Family, and Friends: Social Support After Parent's Divorce or Remarriage,* by K. M. Stinson. © 1991, Greenwood Publishing Group, Inc., 1991. Reprinted with permission.

CHAPTER 16 Figure 16-1: From P. M. DeWitt, "The Second Time Around," reprinted with permission © *American Demographics*, Vol. 14, No. 11, 1992. For subscription information, please call (800) 828-1133. **Table 16-1:** From E. Visher and J. Visher, "Parenting Coalitions after Remarriage," © Haworth Press, Inc. Table was originally published in *Journal of Divorce and Remarriage*, Vol. 14, No. 2, 1990. **Table 16-2:** From C. Hobart, "Relationships between the Formerly Married," © 1990 Haworth Press, Inc. Table was originally published in the *Journal of Divorce and Remarriage*, Vol. 14, No. 2, 1990. **Box (Point of View):** From S. Turner, "My Wife-in-Law and Me: Reflections on a Joint-Custody Step-Parenting Relationship," in *Women and Step-Families: Voices of Anger and Love,* edited by N. B. Maglin and N. Schniedewind. © 1989 by Nan Bauer Maglin and Nancy Schniedewind. Reprinted by permission of Temple University Press. **Box (Snapshots):** From Beverly Beyette, "Romance Within Stepfamilies Result of Unclear Boundaries," *Roanoke Times & World-News,* September 7, 1992. Copyright 1992, Los Angeles Times. Reprinted by permission. **Box (Changing Lifestyles):** From J. Nordheimer, "Stepfathers: The Shoes Rarely Fit," *The New York Times,* October 18, 1990. Copyright © 1990 by The New York Times Company. Reprinted by permission.

PHOTO CREDITS

Page 2: Bill Barrett, *SF59,* bronze, 11″ high × 10″ wide × 6″ deep. Courtesy Bill Barrett, photo by Diane Padys; page 7: J. S. King/The Bettmann Archive; page 11: Lewis W. Hine/George Eastman House Collection; page 12: Culver Pictures; page 15: Jean-Claude Lejeune/Stock, Boston; page 21: Randy Matusow/Monkmeyer; page 24: Ernest H. Robl; page 29: Joel Gordon; page 32: Sandra Filippucci/The Image Bank; page 40: Barbara Rios/Photo Researchers; page 44: Photofest; page 48: Elizabeth Crews/Image Works; page 51: P. Conklin/Monkmeyer; page 53: Joel Gordon; page 60: John H. Howard/The Newborn Group; page 62: Joel Gordon; page 68: Bettmann; page 74: Joel Gordon; page 80: Rhoda Sidney/Monkmeyer; page 82: Jim Whitmer/FPG; page 86: Jacob Lawrence, *The Lovers,* 1946. Collection of Harpo Marx, photo by Geoffrey Clements; page 88: Nancy D'Antonio/Photo Researchers; page 91: Spencer Grant/FPG; page 102: Barbara Rios/Photo Researchers; page 104: Bob Mahoney, Liverpool, Syracuse, New York; page 112: Fernand Léger, *Three Women,* 1921. Oil on canvas, $6'\frac{1}{4}'' \times 8'3''$. The Museum of Modern Art, New York. Mrs. Simon Guggenheim Fund; page 115: Michael Weisbrot; page 121: Gatewood/Image Works; page 125: Reuters/Bettmann; page 128: Michael Weisbrot; page 129: Joel Gordon; page 136: Gaston Lachaise, *Couple (Dans la Nuit),* 1935, Nelson A. Rockefeller Collection, National Trust for Historic Preservation; page 139: Everett Collection; page 145: Paul Conklin/Monkmeyer; page 150: Hugh Rogers/Monkmeyer; page 152: By courtesy of the Ashmolean Museum, Oxford; page 158: Joel Gordon; page 161: Barbara Alper/Stock, Boston; page 168: David George Marshall, *Old Couple,* 1980. Collection of Lenny Kislin; page 178: Harriet Gans/Image Works; page 182: Elizabeth Crews/Image Works; page 184: Beringer/Dratch/Image Works; page 187: Susan Lapides/Design Conceptions; page 189: Joel Gordon; page 198: David Shultz/Mary Holland & Company, Artists Representatives; page 201: Michael Weisbrot; page 205: Elizabeth Crews/Stock, Boston; page 207: Michael Dwyer/Stock, Boston; page 212: Richard Hutch-ings/Photo Researchers; page 219: Griffin/Image Works; page 236: Jacob Lawrence, *Images of Labor,* 1980. Gouache, $25'' \times 18\frac{1}{2}''$. Courtesy Francine Seders Gallery, photo by Chris Eden; page 238: Bettmann; page 240: Rhoda Sidney/Monkmeyer; page 244: M. Richards/Photo Edit; page 249: Robert Llewellyn; page 253: Harvey Stein/Photo Researchers; page 266: Jacob Lawrence, *Builders—Family,* 1974. Collection of Gwendolyn and Jacob Lawrence; page 274: Shumsky/Image Works; page 275: Mike Rizza/Picture Cube; page 278: Peter Russell Clemens/International Stock; page 279: John Olson/Life Magazine © 1969 Time Warner Inc.; page 287: Joel Gordon; page 292: Susan Walp, *The Couple,* 1980. Oil on canvas, 30″ × 42″. Courtesy of the artist; page 296: Everett Collection; page 300: Michael Weisbrot; page 303: H. Armstrong Roberts; page 309: David Dobbs, Dobbs Photography, Decatur, Georgia; page 310: Herbert L. Stormont/Unicorn Stock Photos; page 314: Ted Wolter, Gilbert, Arizona; page 318: Rhoda Sidney/Monkmeyer; page 323: James L. Shaffer/Photo Edit; page 335: Bob Kalman/Image Works; page 339: Wm Thompson/Picture Cube; page 342: Paul Klee, *Actor's Mask,* 1924/252. Oil on canvas mounted on board, $14\frac{1}{2}'' \times 13\frac{3}{8}''$. The Museum of Modern Art, New York. The Sidney and Harriet Janis Collection; page 344: David Wells/Image Works; page 347: Gale Zucker/Stock, Boston; page 349: Joel Gordon; page 362: UPI/Bettmann; page 374: Jeffrey J. Smith, New York City; page 376: Michael Siluk/Image Works; page 381: OneWorld Photographic, Gainesville, Florida; page 385: Robert Llewellyn; page 391: Nancy Durrell McKenna/Photo Researchers; page 395: Frances M. Fox/Omni-Photo Communications; page 402: Adam Niklewicz/Bruch and Moss; page 407: McGlynn/Image Works; page 408: Jack Spratt/Image Works; page 416: Mark Antman/Image Works; page 417: © 1992 CBS Inc.; page 424: Cary Austin/Creative Freelancers; page 427: Peter Byron/Monkmeyer; page 428: H. Armstrong Roberts; page 429: Daemmrich/Image Works; page 439: Michael Weisbrot/Stock, Boston

Name Index

Subject Index